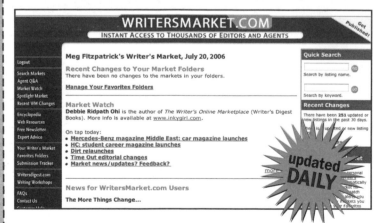

2007 Guide to Literary Agents

Joanna Masterson, Editor

WRITER'S DIGEST BOOKS
CINCINNATI, OH

Editorial Director, Writer's Digest Books: Jane Friedman
Managing Editor, Writer's Digest Market Books: Alice Pope

Guide to Literary Agents Web site: www.guidetoliteraryagents.com
Writer's Market Web site: www.writersmarket.com
Writer's Digest Web site: www.writersdigest.com

Distributed in Canada by Fraser Direct
100 Armstrong Avenue
Georgetown, ON, Canada L7G 5S4
Tel: (905) 877-4411

Distributed in the U.K. and Europe by David & Charles
Brunel House, Newton Abbot, Devon, TQ12 4PU, England
Tel: (+44) 1626 323200, Fax: (+44) 1626 323319
E-mail: postmaster@davidandcharles.co.uk

Distributed in Australia by Capricorn Link
P.O. Box 704, Windsor, NSW 2756 Australia
Tel: (02) 4577-3555

ISSN: 1078-6945
ISBN-13: 978-1-58297-432-3
ISBN-10: 1-58297-432-2

Cover design by Kelly Kofron/Claudean Wheeler
Interior design by Clare Finney
Production coordinated by Robin Richie
Illustrations © Dominique Bruneton/PaintoAlto

Attention Booksellers: This is an annual directory of F+W Publications.
Return deadline for this edition is December 31, 2007.

Contents

Look at agency's website 1ˢᵗ for guidelines for query submission.
BJish

SEALING THE DEAL

PERSPECTIVES

MARKETS

RESOURCES

INDEXES

From the Editor

I believe your home says a lot about who you are. Unfortunately, I'm a newlywed living in a tiny one-bedroom apartment. Don't get me wrong, being married is great, but I don't think our white plaster walls have anything positive to say about us. Thanks to a small budget, we're currently doomed to mismatched plaid furniture, curtains made by an utterly inexperienced seamstress (yours truly) and a bathroom slathered in pink tile.

I'm dreaming of the day we can move into a house and start fresh. We're talking comfortable (non-plaid) furniture, a well-equipped kitchen so we can cook together and a nice-sized yard so we can get a dog.

As a writer, you have the luxury of starting fresh every time you put pen to paper. You have complete control over the way a story unfolds and can make your book truly unique through expertise, plot twists, character traits, etc. But none of these is as important as voice—at least that's what agent Joseph Regal says in his interview on page 61. He believes voice inspires the most passion, and as an editor and reader, I tend to agree.

Voice is an author's distinctive style. It's what makes an agent think: No one but this author can write this book in this way. Just like a house, though, your writing needs both a solid foundation and detailed craftsmanship. An agent will never get to the heart of your book if you don't first learn to follow all the rules for editing and submitting your work.

That's where *Guide to Literary Agents* comes into play. Its step-by-step articles and interviews with industry experts will help you secure quality representation by explaining query letters, contract lingo, how to research agents and more. Plus it provides hundreds of listings for agents who might be interested in your book! With all of these technical details in line, it's your voice that will really shine through to the agent.

As you work toward your goal of getting published, please visit www.guidetoliteraryagents. com and sign up for my new monthly newsletter. Also, feel free to e-mail me your success stories, as well as suggestions for improving the book. I'd love to read them while sitting on my new couch with my new dog, with something cooking in my new oven. Hey, a girl can dream, can't she?

Joanna Masterson

Joanna Masterson
literaryagent@fwpubs.com

Editor's Note: Listings for production companies and script contests are no longer included in this book. Updated versions of these listings can be found online at WritersMarket.com.

How to Use This Book

Searching for a literary agent can be overwhelming, whether you've just finished your first book or you have several publishing credits on your résumé. You are more than likely eager to start pursuing agents and anxious to see your name on the spine of a book. But before you go directly to the listings of agencies in this book, take a few minutes to familiarize yourself with the way agents work and how you should approach them. By doing so, you will be more prepared for your search and ultimately save yourself time and unnecessary grief.

Read the articles

This book begins with feature articles that explain how to prepare for representation, offer strategies for contacting agents, and provide perspectives on the author/agent relationship. The articles are organized into three sections appropriate for each stage of the search process: **Getting Started**, **Contacting Agents**, and **Sealing the Deal**. You may want to start by reading through each article, and then refer back to relevant articles during each stage of your search.

Since there are many ways to make that initial contact with an agent, we've also provided a section called **Perspectives**. These personal accounts from agents and published authors offer information and inspiration for any writer hoping to find representation.

Decide what you're looking for

A literary or script agent will present your work directly to editors or producers. It's the agent's job to get her client's work published or sold and to negotiate a fair contract. In the **Literary Agents** and **Script Agents** sections, we list each agent's contact information and explain what type of work the agency represents and how to submit your work for consideration.

Publicists can promote your work before or after an agent or publisher has taken an interest in it. Often publicists can drum up media time for their clients and help them get the exposure they need to make a sale or increase the number of books they sell.

For face-to-face contact, many writers prefer to meet agents at **Conferences**. By doing so, writers can assess an agent's personality, attend workshops and have the chance to get more feedback on their work than they get by mailing submissions and waiting for a response. The section of conferences is divided into regions, and lists only those conferences agents and/or editors attend. In many cases, private consultations are available, and agents attend with the hope of finding new clients to represent.

Utilize the extras

Aside from the articles and listings, the book offers a section of **Resources**. If you come across a Web site, organization or publishing term with which you aren't familiar, check out

Frequently Asked Questions

1 **Why do you include agents who are not seeking new clients?** Some agents ask that their listings indicate they are currently closed to new clients. We include them so writers know the agents exist and know not to contact them at this time.

2 **Why do you exclude fee-charging agents?** There is a great debate in the publishing industry about whether literary agents should charge writers a reading or critiquing fee. There are fee-charging agents who make sales to prominent publishers. However, we have received a number of complaints in the past regarding fees, and therefore have chosen to list only those agents who do not charge fees.

3 **Why are some agents not listed in *Guide to Literary Agents*?** Some agents may not have responded to our requests for information. We have taken others out of the book after receiving very serious complaints about them. Refer to the General Index in the back of the book to see why a previously listed agency isn't listed in this edition.

4 **Do I need more than one agent if I write in different genres?** More than likely, no. If you have written in one genre and want to switch to a new style of writing, ask your agent if she is willing to represent you in your new endeavor. Most agents will continue to represent clients no matter what genre they choose to write. Occasionally, an agent may feel she has no knowledge of a certain genre and will recommend an appropriate agent to her client. Regardless, you should always talk to your agent about any potential career move.

5 **Why don't you list more foreign agents?** Most American agents have relationships with foreign co-agents in other countries. It is more common for an American agent to work with a co-agent to sell a client's book abroad than for a writer to work directly with a foreign agent. We do, however, list agents in the United Kingdom, Australia and Canada who sell to publishers both internationally and in the United States.

6 **Do agents ever contact a writer who is self-published?** If a self-published author attracts the attention of the media or if his book sells extremely well, an agent might approach the author in hopes of representing him.

7 **Why won't the agent I queried return my material?** An agent may not answer your query or return your manuscript for several reasons. Perhaps you did not include a self-addressed, stamped envelope (SASE). Many agents will discard a submission without a SASE. Or, the agent may have moved. To avoid using expired addresses, use the most current edition of *Guide to Literary Agents* or access the information online at www.writersmarket.com. Another possibility is that the agent is swamped with submissions. Agents can be overwhelmed with queries, especially if the agent has recently spoken at a conference or has been featured in an article or book.

the Resources section for a quick explanation. Also, note the gray tabs along the edge of each page. The tabs block off each section so they are easier to flip to as you conduct your search.

Finally—and perhaps most importantly—are the **Indexes** in the back of the book. These can serve as an incredibly helpful way to start your search because they categorize the listings according to different criteria. For example, you can look for literary agents by name or according to their specialties (fiction/nonfiction genres), openness to submissions and geographic location. Similarly, you can search for script agents by name or according to format (e.g., plays/sitcoms), specialties, openness to submissions and geographic location. Plus, there is a General Index that lists every agent, publicist and conference in the book.

Listing Policy and Complaint Procedure

For More Info

Listings in *Guide to Literary Agents* are compiled from detailed questionnaires, phone interviews, and information provided by agents. The industry is volatile, and agencies change frequently. We rely on our readers for information on their dealings with agents and changes in policies or fees that differ from what has been reported to the editor of this book. Write to us (*Guide to Literary Agents*, 4700 E. Galbraith Rd., Cincinnati, OH 45236) or e-mail us (literaryagent@fwpubs.com) if you have new information, questions or problems dealing with the agencies listed.

Listings are published free of charge and are not advertisements. Although the information is as accurate as possible, the listings are not endorsed or guaranteed by the editor or publisher of *Guide to Literary Agents*. If you feel you have not been treated fairly by an agent or representative listed in *Guide to Literary Agents*, we advise you to take the following steps:

- First try to contact the agency. Sometimes one phone call, letter or e-mail can clear up the matter.

- Document all your correspondence with the agency. When you write to us with a complaint, provide the name of your manuscript, the date of your first contact with the agency and the nature of your subsequent correspondence.

We will keep your letter on file and attempt to contact the agency. The number, frequency and severity of complaints will be considered when deciding whether or not to delete an agency's listing from the next edition. *Guide to Literary Agents* reserves the right to exclude any agency for any reason.

Agent Basics

Preparing for Representation

A writer's job is to write. A literary agent's job is to find publishers for her clients' books. Because publishing houses receive more unsolicited manuscripts each year, securing an agent is becoming increasingly necessary. Finding an eager and reputable agent is a difficult task. Even the most patient writer can become frustrated or disillusioned. As a writer seeking agent representation, you should prepare yourself before starting your search. Learn when to approach agents, as well as what to expect from an author/agent relationship. Beyond selling manuscripts, an agent must keep track of the ever-changing industry, writers' royalty statements, fluctuating reading habits—and the list goes on.

WHAT CAN AN AGENT DO FOR YOU?

An agent will believe in your writing and know an audience interested in what you write. As the representative for your work, your agent will tell editors your manuscript is the best thing to land on her desk this year. But beyond being enthusiastic about your manuscript, there are a lot of benefits to using an agent.

For starters, today's competitive marketplace can be difficult to break into, especially for unpublished writers. Many larger publishing houses will only look at manuscripts from agents. In fact, approximately 80 percent of books published by the major houses are acquired through agents.

But an agent's job isn't just getting your book through a publisher's door. The following describes the various jobs agents do for their clients, many of which would be difficult for a writer to do without outside help.

Agents know editors' tastes and needs

An agent possesses information on a complex web of publishing houses and a multitude of editors to make sure her clients' manuscripts are placed in the right hands. This knowledge is gathered through relationships she cultivates with acquisition editors—the people who decide which books to present to their publisher for possible publication. Through her industry connections, an agent becomes aware of the specializations of publishing houses and their imprints, knowing that one publisher only wants contemporary romances while another is interested solely in nonfiction books about the military. By networking with editors over lunch, an agent also learns more specialized information—which editor is looking for a crafty Agatha Christie-style mystery for the fall catalog, for example.

Agents track changes in publishing

Being attentive to constant market changes and shifting trends is another major requirement of an agent. An agent understands what it may mean for clients when publisher A merges

Getting Started

To-Do List for Fiction Writers

1 **Finish your novel** or short story collection. An agent can do nothing for fiction without a finished product.

2 **Revise your novel.** Have other writers offer criticism to ensure your manuscript is as polished as you believe possible.

3 **Proofread.** Don't ruin a potential relationship with an agent by submitting work that contains typos or poor grammar.

4 **Publish** short stories or novel excerpts in literary journals, proving to potential agents that editors see quality in your writing.

5 **Research** to find the agents of writers whose works you admire or are similar to yours.

6 **Use the indexes in the back of this book** to construct a list of agents who are open to new writers and looking for your type of fiction (e.g., literary, romance, mystery).

7 **Rank your list.** Use the listings in this book to determine the agents most suitable for you and your work and to eliminate inappropriate agencies.

8 **Write your synopsis.** Completing this step will help you write your query letter and be prepared for when agents contact you.

9 **Write your query letter.** As an agent's first impression of you, this brief letter should be polished and to the point.

10 **Read about the business** of agents so you are knowledgeable and prepared to act on any offer.

with publisher B and when an editor from house C moves to house D. Or what it means when readers—and therefore editors—are no longer interested in westerns, but instead can't get their hands on enough Stephen King-style suspense novels.

Agents get your manuscript read faster

Although it may seem like an extra step to send your manuscript to an agent instead of directly to a publishing house, the truth is an agent can prevent writers from wasting months sending manuscripts that end up in the wrong place or buried in someone's slush pile. Editors rely on agents to save them time as well. With little time to sift through the hundreds of unsolicited submissions arriving weekly in the mail, an editor is naturally going to prefer a work that has already been approved by a qualified reader (i.e., the agent) that knows the editor's preferences. For this reason, many of the larger publishers accept agented submissions only.

Agents understand contracts

When publishers write contracts, they are primarily interested in their own bottom line rather than the best interests of the author. Writers unfamiliar with contractual language may find themselves bound to a publisher with whom they no longer want to work. Or, they may find

To-Do List for Nonfiction Writers

1. **Formulate a concrete idea** for your book. Sketch a brief outline making sure you have enough material for an entire book-length manuscript.

2. **Research** works on similar topics to understand the competition and determine how your book is unique.

3. **Write sample chapters.** This step should indicate how much time you will need to finish and if your writing needs editorial help.

4. **Publish** completed chapters in journals. This validates your work to agents and provides writing samples for later in the process.

5. **Polish your outline** so you can refer to it while drafting a query letter and so you are prepared when agents contact you.

6. **Brainstorm** three to four subject categories that best describe your material.

7. **Use the indexes in this book** to find agents interested in at least two of your subject areas and who are looking for new clients.

8. **Rank your list.** Narrow your list further by reading the listings of agencies you found in the indexes, and organize the list according to your preferences.

9. **Write your query.** Give an agent an excellent first impression by professionally and succinctly describing your premise and your experience.

10. **Read about the business** of agents so you are knowledgeable and prepared to act on any offer.

themselves tied to a publisher who prevents them from getting royalties on their first book until subsequent books are written. Agents use their experiences to negotiate a contract that benefits the writer while still respecting the publisher's needs.

Agents negotiate—and exploit—subsidiary rights

Beyond publication, a savvy agent keeps in mind other opportunities for your manuscript. If your agent believes your book will also be successful as an audio book, a Book-of-the-Month Club selection, or even a blockbuster movie, she will take these options into consideration when shopping your manuscript. These additional opportunities for writers are called subsidiary rights. Part of an agent's job is to keep track of the strengths and weaknesses of different publishers' subsidiary rights offices to determine the deposition of these rights regarding your work. After the contract is negotiated, the agent will seek additional money-making opportunities for the rights she kept for her client.

Agents get escalators

An escalator is a bonus that an agent can negotiate as part of the book contract. It is commonly given when a book appears on a best-seller list or if a client appears on a popular television show. For example, a publisher might give a writer a $50,000 bonus if he is picked for a book club. Both the agent and the editor know such media attention will sell more books, and the agent negotiates an escalator to ensure the writer benefits from this increase in sales.

Agents track payments

Since an agent only receives payment when the publisher pays the writer, it is in the agent's best interest to make sure the writer is paid on schedule. Some publishing houses are notorious for late payments. Having an agent distances you from any conflict over payment and allows you to spend your time writing instead of making phone calls.

Agents are strong advocates

Besides standing up for your right to be paid on time, agents can ensure your book gets a better cover design, more attention from the publisher's marketing department, or other benefits you may not know to ask for during the publishing process. An agent can also provide advice during each step of the process, as well as guidance about your long-term writing career.

See Also

ARE YOU READY FOR AN AGENT?

Now that you know what an agent is capable of, ask yourself if you and your work are at a stage where you need an agent. Look at the To-Do List for Fiction and Nonfiction writers on pages 6 and 7, and judge how prepared you are for contacting an agent. Have you spent enough time researching or polishing your manuscript? Sending an agent an incomplete project not only wastes your time, but also may turn off the agent in the process. Literary agents are not magicians, and they cannot solve your personal problems. An agent will not be your banker, CPA, social secretary or therapist. Instead, agents will endeavor to sell your book because that is how they earn their living.

Moreover, your material may not be appropriate for an agent. Most agents do not represent poetry, magazine articles, short stories, or material suitable for academic or small presses; the agents' commission does not justify spending time submitting these types of works. Those agents who do take on such material generally represent authors on larger projects first, and then adopt the smaller items as a favor to the client.

If you strongly believe your work is ready to be placed with an agent, make sure you are personally ready to be represented. In other words, consider the direction in which your writing career is headed. Besides skillful writers, agencies want clients with the ability to produce more than one book. Most agents will say they represent careers, not books. So as you compose your query letter—your initial contact with an agent—briefly mention your potential. Let an agent know if you've already started drafting your second novel and that your writing is more than a half-hearted hobby.

WHEN DON'T YOU NEED AN AGENT?

Although there are many reasons to work with an agent, an author can benefit from submitting his own work. For example, if your writing focuses on a very specific area, you may want to work with a small or specialized publisher. These houses are usually open to receiving material directly from writers. Small presses can often give more attention to a writer than a large house can, providing editorial help, marketing expertise, and other advice directly to the writer.

Some writers use a lawyer or entertainment attorney instead of an agent. If a lawyer specializes in intellectual property, he can help a writer with contract negotiations. Instead of giving the lawyer a commission, the lawyer is paid for his time only.

And, of course, some people prefer working independently instead of relying on others to do their work. If you are one of these people, it is probably better to shop your own work instead of constantly butting heads with an agent. And despite the benefits of working with an agent, it is possible to sell your work directly to a publisher—people do it all the time.

Assessing Credibility

What to Look for When Researching Agents

Many people would not buy a used car without at least checking the odometer, and savvy shoppers would consult the blue books, take a test drive and even ask for a mechanic's opinion. Much like the savvy car shopper, you want to obtain the best possible agent for your writing, so you should do some research on the business of agents before sending out query letters. Understanding how agents operate will help you find an agent appropriate for your work, as well as alert you about the types of agents to avoid.

Many writers take for granted that any agent who expresses interest in their work is trustworthy. They'll sign a contract before asking any questions and simply hope everything will turn out all right. We often receive complaints from writers regarding agents *after* they have lost money or have work bound by contract to an ineffective agent. If writers put the same amount of effort into researching agents as they did writing their manuscripts, they would save themselves unnecessary grief.

The best way to educate yourself is to read all you can about agents and other authors. Organizations such as the Association of Authors' Representatives (AAR), the National Writers Union (NWU), American Society of Journalists and Authors (ASJA) and Poets & Writers, Inc., all have informational material on finding and working with an agent. (These, along with other helpful organizations, are listed on page 262.)

See Also

Publishers Weekly (www.publishersweekly.com) covers publishing news affecting agents and others in the publishing industry; discusses specific events in the "Hot Deals" and "Behind the Bestsellers" columns; and occasionally lists individual author's agents in the "Forecasts" section. The Publishers Lunch newsletter (www.publishersmarketplace.com) comes free via e-mail every workday and offers news on agents and editors, job postings, recent book sales and more.

Useful Web sites

Even the Internet has a wide range of sites where you can learn basic information about preparing for your initial contact and specific details on individual agents. You can also find online forums and listservs, which keep authors connected and allow them to share experiences they've had with different editors and agents. Keep in mind, however, that not everything printed on the Web is a solid fact; you may come across the site of a writer who is bitter because an agent rejected his manuscript. Your best bet is to use the Internet to supplement your other research. (For particularly valuable Web sites, refer to Online Tools on page 266.)

See Also

Once you've established what your resources are, it's time to see which agents meet your criteria. Below are some of the key items to pay attention to when researching agents.

LEVEL OF EXPERIENCE

Through your research, you will discover the need to be wary of some agents. Anybody can go to the neighborhood copy center and order business cards that say she is a literary agent, but that title does not mean she can sell your book. She may lack the proper connections with others in the publishing industry, and an agent's reputation with editors can be a major strength or weakness.

Agents who have been in the business awhile have a large number of contacts and have the most clout with editors. They know the ins and the outs of the industry and are often able to take more calculated risks. However, veteran agents can be too busy to take on new clients or might not have the time to help develop the author. Newer agents, on the other hand, may be hungrier, as well as more open to unpublished writers. They probably have a smaller client list and are able to invest the extra effort to make your book a success.

If it's a new agent without a track record, be aware that you're taking more of a risk signing with her than with a more established agent. However, even a new agent should not be new to publishing. Many agents were editors before they were agents, or they worked at an agency as an assistant. This experience in publishing is crucial for making contacts in the publishing industry and learning about rights and contracts. The majority of listings in this book explain how long the agent has been in business, as well as what she did before becoming an agent. You could also ask the agent to name a few editors off the top of her head who she thinks may be interested in your work and why they sprang to mind. Has she sold to them before? Do they publish books in your genre?

If an agent has no contacts in the business, she has no more clout than you do. Without publishing prowess, she's just an expensive mailing service. Anyone can make photocopies, slide them into an envelope and address them to "Editor." Unfortunately, without a contact name and a familiar return address on the envelope, or a phone call from a trusted colleague letting an editor know a wonderful submission is on its way, your work will land in the slush pile with all the other submissions that don't have representation. You can do your own mailings with higher priority than such an agent could.

PAST SALES

Agents should be willing to discuss their recent sales with you: how many, what type of books, and to what publishers. Keep in mind, though, that some agents consider this information confidential. If an agent does give you a list of recent sales, you can call the publishers' contracts department to ensure the sale was actually made by that agent. While it's true that even top agents are not able to sell every book they represent, an inexperienced agent who proposes too many inappropriate submissions will quickly lose her standing with editors.

You can also find out details of recent sales on your own. Nearly all of the listings in this book offer the titles and authors of books with which the agent has worked. Some of them also note to which publishing house the book was sold. Again, you can call the publisher and affirm the sale. If you don't have the publisher's information, simply go to your local library or bookstore to see if they carry the book. Consider checking to see if it's available on Web sites like Amazon.com, too. You may want to be wary of the agent if her books are nowhere to be found or are only available through the publisher's Web site. Distribution is a crucial component to getting published, and you want to make sure the agent has worked with competent publishers.

TYPES OF FEES

Becoming knowledgeable about the different types of fees agents may charge is crucial to conducting effective research. Most agents make their living from the commissions they receive after selling their clients' books, and these are the agents we've listed. Be sure to ask about any expenses you don't understand so you have a clear grasp of what you're paying for. Described below are some types of fees you may encounter in your research.

Office fees

Occasionally, an agent will charge for the cost of photocopies, postage and long-distance phone calls made on your behalf. This is acceptable, so long as she keeps an itemized account of the expenses and you've agreed on a ceiling cost. The agent should only ask for office expenses after agreeing to represent the writer. These expenses should be discussed up front, and the writer should receive a statement accounting for them. This money is sometimes returned to the author upon sale of the manuscript. Be wary if there is an up-front fee amounting to hundreds of dollars, which is excessive.

Reading fees

Agencies that charge reading fees often do so to cover the cost of additional readers or the time spent reading that could have been spent selling. Agents also claim that charging reading fees cuts down on the number of submissions they receive. This practice can save the agent time and may allow her to consider each manuscript more extensively. Whether such promises are kept depends upon the honesty of the agency. You may pay a fee and never receive

Warning Signs! Beware of . . .

Important

- Excessive typos or poor grammar in an agent's correspondence.

- A form letter accepting you as a client and praising generic things about your book that could apply to any book. A good agent doesn't take on a new client very often, so when she does, it's a special occasion that warrants a personal note or phone call.

- Unprofessional contracts that ask you for money up front, contain clauses you haven't discussed or are covered with amateur clip-art or silly borders.

- Rudeness when you inquire about any points you're unsure of. Don't employ any business partner who doesn't treat you with respect.

- Pressure, by way of threats, bullying or bribes. A good agent is not desperate to represent more clients. She invites worthy authors but leaves the final decision up to them.

- Promises of publication. No agent can guarantee you a sale. Not even the top agents sell everything they choose to represent. They can only send your work to the most appropriate places, have it read with priority and negotiate you a better contract if a sale does happen.

- A print-on-demand book contract or any contract offering you no advance. You can sell your own book to an e-publisher any time you wish without an agent's help. An agent should pursue traditional publishing routes with respectable advances.

a response from the agent, or you may pay someone who never submits your manuscript to publishers.

Officially, the Association of Authors' Representatives' (AAR) Canon of Ethics prohibits members from directly or indirectly charging a reading fee, and the Writers Guild of America (WGA) does not allow WGA signatory agencies to charge a reading fee to WGA members, as stated in the WGA's Artists' Manager Basic Agreement. A signatory may charge you a fee if you are not a member, but most signatory agencies do not charge a reading fee as an across-the-board policy.

Reading fees vary from $25 to $500 or more. The fee is usually nonrefundable, but sometimes agents agree to refund the money if they take on a writer as a client, or if they sell the writer's manuscript. Keep in mind, however, that payment of a reading fee does not ensure representation.

No literary agents who charge reading fees are listed in this book. It's too risky of an option for writers, plus nonfee-charging agents have a stronger incentive to sell your work. After all, they don't make a dime until they make a sale. If you find that a literary agent listed in this book charges a reading fee, please contact the editor.

Critique fees

Sometimes a manuscript will interest an agent, but the agent will point out areas requiring further development and offer to critique it for an additional fee. Like reading fees, payment of a critique fee does not ensure representation. When deciding if you will benefit from having someone critique your manuscript, keep in mind that the quality and quantity of comments varies from agent to agent. The critique's usefulness will depend on the agent's knowledge of the market. Also be aware that agents who spend a significant portion of their time commenting on manuscripts will have less time to actively market work they already represent.

In other cases, the agent may suggest an editor who understands your subject matter or genre and has some experience getting manuscripts into shape. Occasionally, if your story is exceptional or your ideas and credentials are marketable but your writing needs help, you will work with a ghostwriter or co-author who will share a percentage of your commission, or work with you at an agreed upon cost per hour.

An agent may refer you to editors she knows, or you may choose an editor in your area. Many editors do freelance work and would be happy to help you with your writing project. Of course, before entering into an agreement, make sure you know what you'll be getting for your money. Ask the editor for writing samples, references or critiques he's done in the past. Make sure you feel comfortable working with him before you give him your business.

An honest agent will not make any money for referring you to an editor. We strongly advise writers not to use critiquing services offered through an agency. Instead, try hiring a freelance editor or joining a writer's group until your work is ready to be submitted to agents who do not charge fees.

Author FAQs

Expert Answers to Common Questions

There are some questions writers ask time and time again. A handful of the most common ones are answered below by several professional literary agents. You can find these, and other frequently asked questions, on WritersMarket.com.

A few months ago, I received a nice rejection letter from an agent at a large agency. Now, someone else has recommended I try a certain other agent at the same agency who would be more appropriate for my type of material. Would this be all right?

When trying to find an agent, I think it's best to be as aggressive as possible. So yes, you should contact the other agent. However, you should definitely let the agent know about your previous dealings with the agency. Agents don't like surprises.

Greg Dinkin

—**Greg Dinkin** *handles general nonfiction, business and gambling titles at Venture Literary in San Diego, California.*

How long after requesting a proposal (in response to a query) does an agent expect to receive the proposal for a nonfiction book? Should the proposal be largely complete prior to querying prospective agents?

It's smart to have a complete proposal before beginning the query process. It should include an overview, author bio, comparative and competitive works section, marketing information, proposed format details, table of contents and narrative chapter outline. You should also have one or more complete sample chapters. These chapters are critical for a previously unpublished author, perhaps less so for those already successfully published. Consider also whether supplementary materials, such as sample illustrations or tear sheets of articles published in prestigious publications, might strengthen your case. An author may have a great idea, but a sketchy proposal will make an agent doubt that the author can actually produce the book.

Allowing more than a few weeks to pass between the request for a proposal and its delivery isn't such a great idea either. You run the risk of losing the agent's initial enthusiasm, or (worst case scenario) another author may approach her with a strong proposal for a similar project, which she accepts. In the latter case, the agent will be reluctant to take on a competitive work and will almost certainly turn you down.

—**Anne Hawkins** *is an agent at John Hawkins & Associates in New York City.*

I will be attending a small-town book and writer's conference next month. Do such affairs generate good leads and/or publicity? Is it possible to find a top-notch agent at one of these events?

Wherever two or three authors and an agent are gathered, go. Here's a secret: Even when an agency's directory info and Web site says they don't accept unpublished authors (ours included), we're always prowling for the next big book from an unknown writer. It's what we live for. Though we've landed with many titles atop *The New York Times* Best Seller list, our agents still attend four or five of these regional gigs annually. Other agencies do the same. There's only one reason we all do the Indiana Jones thing, going to the ends of the earth and enduring the brain-numbing torture of nonstop pitches: to find the unclaimed gem. And so, get thee to a conference and corner an agent in a hallway, after a session, during a meal or after hours.

Rick Christian

Photo by Tyler Christian.

> —**Rick Christian** *is president of Alive Communications, Inc., located in Colorado Springs, Colorado. The agency handles fiction, Christian living, how-to and commercial nonfiction.*

What does it mean when agents say they accept simultaneous submissions, or that they prefer exclusive reads?

When agents say they accept simultaneous submissions, it means we will look at something that has been sent to other agents at the same time. When I read a submission and like it, I'll ask for the entire manuscript on an exclusive basis, meaning that I will be the only agent reading it. I usually ask for a three-week exclusive. Once those three weeks are over, the author is free to submit elsewhere.

> —**B.J. Robbins** *established her Los Angeles-based agency in 1992. The agency represents literary and commercial fiction, memoir, biography, narrative history, pop culture, sports, travel/adventure and health/medicine.*

I'm getting ready to try to publish my latest novel. Though I got a good response to my first one, I didn't even try submitting it because I thought the material was too personal. Will having a shelved novel hurt my chances at publication?

Writing experience doesn't hurt. I like to see previous novels mentioned in a query letter, even if those novels were never published. Because writing is a craft that takes time and dedication to improve, there's usually a learning curve between a first novel and a second. So I do expect a second novel to be more advanced. Also, it shows more focus, dedication and productivity when a writer can produce more than one manuscript. Remember that agents are hoping to find writers who are aiming for long-term careers, not just one-book wonders.

> —**Rachel Vater** *is an agent at Lowenstein-Yost Associates in New York City.*

Do I have to get the rights to use trademarked or copyrighted material in my manuscript, or will my agent do it for me?

Copyright is such a complicated area of law with so many grey areas that a scholar could scour dozens of volumes of literature on the subject and still not have an answer to this seemingly simple question. Some important basic concepts to keep in mind are: One owns the copyright to what one writes, whether the copyright is registered or not; anyone can sue anyone; and ideas are not copyrightable.

When you use other people's copyrighted words in your work, it is important to obtain a formal written and signed permission form from each person whom you quote. Authors are responsible for determining whether permissions are necessary and they must procure them, not agents. Publishers will often assist authors in this endeavor by providing the permission forms and guidelines, but most publisher/author contracts will put the entire onus on the author to find out whether permissions are necessary to obtain for extracts and quotes, and then procure them. Even when publishers do help, the contracts will usually require the authors to indemnify the publisher against all claims (even frivolous claims), suits and judgments related to this aspect of the publishing agreement. Persistent agents are sometimes successful at getting some publishers to take responsibility for frivolous claims, but it's rare that they'll take the responsibility for obtaining permissions. When in doubt about questions of copyright, it's always advisable to consult an attorney.

> —**Sheree Bykofsky**'s *New York agency represents over 100 book authors in all areas of adult nonfiction, as well as literary and commercial fiction. She teaches publishing at NYU and is the co-author of the best-selling* The Complete Idiot's Guide to Getting Published *(Pearson).*

In general, how do agents charge?

The majority of legitimate agents charge a 15 percent commission on domestic rights licenses and 20 percent on foreign rights licenses. Often the agent splits her commission on subsidiary rights sales with a specialist subagent, most frequently in connection with the placement of foreign or movie/TV rights. It is common for legitimate agents to be reimbursed out of client income for extraordinary expenses. A writer should ask the agent about these costs before agreeing to work with her. Typically, they include extraordinary mailing costs, photocopying and book orders for use in the exploitation of subsidiary rights. Generally speaking, authors should never send money to an agent for any reason.

Richard Henshaw

> —**Rich Henshaw** *opened his New York City agency in 1995. The firm represents an eclectic mix of nonfiction and commercial fiction with an emphasis on thrillers, mysteries, science fiction, fantasy and women's fiction.*

I recently parted ways with my agent after a few years of representation. As I move forward, do I tell a prospective agent that I previously worked with another agent? If I am fortunate to find another agent, do I send copies of the publishers' rejection letters so there won't be a duplication of effort?

Absolutely, and you should be able to speak to what did and did not work in the relationship with your former agent. Candor is the best policy; it prevents most misunderstandings and can even lead to a more creative and productive agent/client relationship. Most agents will want to see where the work has been submitted. It is possible, depending on the

William Clark

agent's clout and access, that previous submissions won't matter to him or her.

> —**William Clark** *founded Wm Clark Associates in 1997 in New York City.*

Is it ethical to continue to send queries to publishers when I already have an agent who agrees to take on my manuscript?

Don't do it. The reason you have an agent is to do the business of placing your work while you proceed with your writing. If you think your agent is not working hard to place your work, you need to terminate the relationship before you begin submitting anything yourself. If you get an agent after you've sent work out to a publisher and before you've heard back, make sure you tell your agent. That's not a problem at all and is in fact pretty common with genre writers. Your agent may be able to help you get your manuscript out of the heaping pile of slush, too, since a good agent will know most of the editors to whom you're sending material.

> —**Janet Reid** *opened JetReid Literary Agency after spending 15 years in book publicity. Her agency is actively seeking narrative fiction and nonfiction.*

Does it prove troublesome in the long run to use a pseudonym? Is there a lot of legal or financial paperwork that goes along with using a pen name?

There is not a lot of legal or financial paperwork involved in using a pen name, although you do need to be careful when signing publishing contracts to make sure the publisher doesn't acquire ownership of the name. Ideally, the author will want to be free to use the pen name with respect to whatever type of writing she chooses. You will use your real legal name to sign any contracts and to receive payments (and, thus, pay taxes), although the contract will commit the publisher to using only the pseudonym in connection with the marketing of the book. Copyright registrations can be made in pseudonyms so the "public" record is kept consistent.

> —**Elaine P. English** *represents novelists at her Washington, D.C. literary agency. She is also an attorney specializing in media and publishing law.*

Editing Options

Perfecting Your Manuscript

by Susan Titus Osborn

Mark Twain once wisely said: "You don't get a second opportunity to make a good first impression." Writers should keep this mantra in mind when preparing to contact an agent. Certainly the best impression you can make is with a sensational story, but agents will never spend a moment getting to know your characters or zipping through your plot twists if the manuscript is littered with grammatical mistakes. Your chances of getting published can be reduced dramatically the instant an editor sees a typo, misused word or inappropriate punctuation mark. Bad transitions, unrealistic dialogue and mundane opening chapters bring about even more doom. Avoid these publishing pitfalls by thoroughly editing your work—either on your own or with the help of other professionals.

EDITING YOU CAN DO

The first step is to make sure your story is grammatically sound. Line-by-line editing may seem like a boring, elementary task, but words are the building blocks of your manuscript and they must be constantly refined.

Be specific

People tend to think in the abstract, but you need to use more concrete words when writing. Start by eliminating weak verbs such as "was, were, is, had, have," and any form of "to be." *He skipped down the road, humming his favorite tune* paints a much clearer picture than simply writing *He is happy*. Often when you eliminate a "to be" verb, you also get rid of an "ing." Instead of writing *The man was ambling down the road*, use *The man ambled down the road*. Simple past tense flows smoothly and is usually more effective. Dynamic verbs in the past tense can rid your story of many unnecessary adverbs as well. Instead of writing *He walked slowly*, use *He ambled*. It evokes a more precise mental image and displays tight writing—a trait nearly every editor adores.

When it comes to nouns, you may look at a tree and think of it as a tree, but you should be more specific in your writing. Consider naming the type of tree—eucalyptus, magnolia, aspen—you want the reader to visualize. Be careful not to get too specific, though. Using

SUSAN TITUS OSBORN is the director of the Christian Communicator Manuscript Critique Service. She has authored 28 books, as well as numerous articles, and has taught at more than 140 writers' conferences. Her latest book is *A Special Kind of Love*, published by Broadman & Holman and Focus on the Family. Susan can be reached at susanosb@aol.com.

Getting Started

legalese, medical terms or jargon only understood by a small segment of the population can interrupt your flow and alienate the reader.

Another important task is to eliminate any words, sentences, or paragraphs that don't further your storyline. Go through your manuscript word by word and ask yourself: What will happen if I leave that out? If the answer is nothing, then cut it. This especially applies to adjectives, which should only be used sparingly. Rather than writing *The thin, narrow black ribbon of highway wound through the velvety, emerald-green dense jungle that lurked on either side of the black ribbon of highway,* use *The narrow ribbon of highway wound through the dense jungle that lurked on either side.* Leaving out negative words can also make your writing clearer. Instead of writing *He was very often not on time,* say *He usually came late.*

You should eliminate irrelevant material on a larger scale, too. Ask yourself if a scene is necessary. If not, delete it. Use judgment in deciding which characters should be described and in how much detail, what facts are relevant and what can be left out. Steve Laube of the Steve Laube Agency points out that many writers try to say too much in one manuscript. "It appears the writer wants to cover every possible angle and ends up wearing out the reader. Today's nonfiction readers want their books to be snappy and memorable, not long and laborious." Amidst all your nitpicky revisions, don't forget to take a look at your manuscript as a whole. Reel yourself back in if you start to stray from the book's central plot or outline. If you feel really frustrated at the idea of leaving stuff out, consider whether or not your idea could work well as a series.

Be active

Whether you're writing a novel or a nonfiction book, you should always try to keep your reader involved in the story. You can accomplish this by keeping your sentences in the active voice, with the subject doing the acting, rather than being acted upon as in passive voice. *The car slammed into the man* is more powerful than *The man was hit by the car.* Also, using descriptive verbs filled with action moves the reader along. For instance, look at these dynamic verbs for movement: strut, skip, stomp, slither, stumble, stagger, sashay, swagger, sneak and stride. Aren't they more exciting than walk?

Readers are always interested in learning about other people, so using anecdotes and other fiction techniques can really make your nonfiction come alive. On first rough drafts, writers often tell the story either from an observer's viewpoint or from the main character's mind. Both of these locations are boring. Readers want to participate in the action. They want to join in the excitement and experience the events as they are happening. Thus, the adage: show, don't tell.

Dialogue is another key to engaging your reader. "Frequently the novelist gives too much backstory in the form of a narrative or an interior monologue," says Laube. "It stops the story dead in its tracks." Nothing moves a story along better than dialogue, but Laube cautions that one of the biggest problems he sees is weak dialogue. "The dialogue needs to be crisp and distinct. The reader needs to be able to put the scene into a 'movie of the mind.'"

Be natural

Have you ever gone to a boring lecture where the speaker droned on in a monotone voice? Although your readers can't hear you, it's critical to change your tone by varying the length and structure of your sentences. Writing in a simple style won't diminish your content, but it will make the story sound more natural. Plus, when a sentence is shorter, it usually becomes stronger.

Agent Etta Wilson of March Media, Inc. warns against getting too informal. "I think the paragraph as the basic organizational form of thought is becoming obsolete. I find it becoming more common not to write in complete sentences. This is probably a result of computer

Minding the Details

1 **Always place a comma before a conjunction introducing an independent clause.** In other words, place a comma between two independent clauses separated by a conjunction. Independent clauses have a subject and a verb, and they can stand alone.

The situation looked hopeless, but there was one remaining chance for success. Or, *The situation looked hopeless, but I didn't believe it.*

2 **Do not join independent clauses with a comma if they lack a conjunction.** They need to be joined with a semi-colon, or they can be cut into two separate sentences.

The situation looked hopeless; there was one remaining chance for success. Or, *The situation looked hopeless. There was one remaining chance for success.*

3 **You do not need a comma to separate a dependent clause from an independent clause when they are joined with a conjunction.** Each clause must have a subject in order to need a comma before the conjunction.

I was told the situation looked hopeless but didn't believe it.

4 **Be careful not to overuse punctuation.** Fewer commas are used today than in the past. Also avoid the overuse of dashes, exclamation points, semi-colons, ellipses and colons. A good reference for proper punctuation is Strunk and White's *Elements of Style*.

5 **Form the possessive singular of nouns by adding apostrophe "s" ('s).**

Mary's house and *Charles's farm.*

Exceptions are the possessives of ancient proper names ending in "s." *Moses'* and *Jesus'.*

6 **Possessives such as "hers," "yours" and "its" have no apostrophe.** "It's" is the contraction for "it is."

The shade stunted its growth. It's now growing in the sun.

7 **The number of the subject determines the number of the verb.** If the subject is singular, the verb must also be singular. Use a singular verb form after "each, either, everyone, everybody, neither, nobody and someone."

Surely someone here knows how to use this computer program.

8 **A participial phrase at the beginning of the sentence must refer to the grammatical subject.** Be careful not to leave your participles dangling.

On arriving in Atlanta, I discovered my luggage was missing.

Arriving refers to me and not to my luggage. Since the luggage never arrived, it would be wrong to say: *Upon arriving in Atlanta, my luggage was missing.*

communication, and it's often effective, but if overdone and not true to the voice of the character, it can turn off the agent.''

It's all about balance and keeping your writing on a parallel level with your reader. You don't want to talk down to them, but you also don't want to be obscure. By using 10-cent words rather than ones not commonly used in conversation, you can express profound thoughts and still write in a clear manner.

It also helps to read your dialogue out loud to make sure it doesn't sound contrived. Your words should flow in a conversational manner as if you were sitting at your kitchen table having a cup of tea with a friend. Try to keep your dialogue tags simple, too. Sometimes they can be eliminated altogether if it is obvious who is speaking. ''He said'' is a perfectly good tag and is usually better than ''he uttered, he articulated or he expressed.'' You can use an occasional word like whispered, shouted or asked, but what really matters is what he said (i.e., the words within the quotation marks).

Your paragraphs need to flow into each other as well. If the transition seems rough, add an introductory clause or phrase to smooth it out. *After several hours of traveling, we arrived.* Or, *When we reached Phoenix, we were greeted by our host.*

Be original

Opening paragraphs and chapters need to be both original and captivating. If you can't draw the agent in, you won't be able to interest either editors or readers.

''The biggest editing mistake I see in manuscripts is that the writer doesn't work hard enough on the project's opening,'' says Janet Kobobel Grant of Books & Such. ''Take for example a fiction submission I just looked at—and rejected. It starts out with a 35-word ad for a bed and breakfast. I was snoozing by the time I finished reading the ad. Nothing invited me into the novel; nothing gave a sense of conflict or an issue to be concerned about.

''Here's a winning nonfiction lead: 'It was midnight in Last Chance, Colorado.' Yup, that's a lead for a nonfiction book. Now, I think it could have been improved on. Starting a book with 'It was' is seldom a good idea. But this lead tells me the author is going to pull me into his book by spinning a yarn, and it sounds like it might be a good one.

''Try a variety of ways to enter into your first chapter; don't settle for the first idea that comes to you. And when you decide on an idea, hone it again and again, going after it with the editing side of your brain until you can't imagine how to improve one word. That's when you know you've done your best to draw the reader into the rest of the book.''

Wilson, who specializes in representing children's authors, agrees that originality shines through in a well-edited manuscript. ''Most writers I hear from are doing a super job with the mechanics of preparing their manuscripts, and I've noted significant progress in developing the marketing portion of proposals. What is tougher to find is truly original and captivating writing in the manuscripts themselves. While it's true that all children go through basic developmental stages, today's highly competitive market calls for unusual combinations and unique approaches in writing about concepts and situations. Too many of us are writing from our memories of childhood, and the world is changing too fast for that! The solution: Get to know several children well and read what's currently selling.''

SEEKING OUTSIDE HELP

Most people have trouble editing their own work. Once your manuscript is as polished as you can get it, it's time to seek the opinions of other writers and professionals.

Writers' conferences

One of the best ways to meet agents, editors and professional writers who can help you polish your work is to attend a writers' conference. You can find these listed in market guides, such as this one, and on the Internet. Choose one that has hands-on critique sessions where a professional writer will actually work with you on your manuscript. Often there is a fee for this, but the results are well worth it. Also, choose a conference that offers one-on-one time with agents. In choosing an agent, it is best to meet in person to see if you are a good fit for the working relationship.

If you have a book proposal ready before the conference, take it with you. However, with all you learn there, you will probably want to revise it afterward. If you don't have a proposal ready, take a one-sheet summary of your book. It should include information on your bio, target audience and the marketability of your book. Also, before you go, create a 30-second pitch for your book and describe it in a salable way.

Writing groups

Another way to get feedback on your work is to join a local writing group and get together weekly or monthly to talk shop and critique manuscripts. Other writers can see where something is missing, unclear or unnecessary. Plus, it helps to maintain your writing schedule if you need to have another chapter finished to take to the group. Often times your writing becomes real to you when you share it with others, and writers going through the same process as you can provide valuable feedback. You may not always agree with their advice, but if several people are commenting on a certain passage of your work, you probably need to revise it.

You can find out about writing groups in your area from local bookstores, writers' organizations, conferences or newspapers. If your schedule makes it difficult to attend an actual meeting, consider joining an online writing group. They often provide the same perks as in-person meetings, and allow you to connect with writers all over the world. You can find a slew of online writing groups by doing a simple Internet keyword search.

Books doctors

If you don't feel comfortable in a group setting, you might consider having a book doctor or editor at a critique service professionally edit your work. Again, these can be found in market guides and online. When choosing one, make sure the critiquers are actively publishing. Also, ask the critiquer for three references of people who will recommend his services. It might also help to ask for the names of published books that were critiqued by the service. Fees vary, but make sure you get a quote for your entire proposal or book rather than an hourly fee. That way you will know the exact cost.

Also keep an eye out for agents who recommend a specific book doctor. There could be some sort of scam involved where the agent receives a kickback for sending the author to that particular book doctor. Certainly agents can recommend professional editors, but they should always give you a list to choose from, and it should always ultimately be your choice on who to use.

Building a Reputation

How New Authors Get Noticed

by Janice M. Pieroni

Writers tend to focus all of their energy on the act of writing. While great manuscripts make wonderful calling cards, the format and content of the book is only part of the picture. Authors can also lay the groundwork for success by increasing the public's awareness of their names and ideas and showing agents they have the personal characteristics necessary to achieve and sustain success. These elements, coupled with extraordinary writing, help persuade agents to represent new writers.

Writers should begin to build strong reputations even before they approach agents for representation. Most industry insiders look favorably on writers who have invested not only in their writing, but also in themselves. Many authors are surprised to discover that there are so many things—aside from developing writing skills—that they can do to stand out from the crowd. Some of the most common opportunities are listed below.

Enter contests

One way you can build your reputation is by entering—and hopefully winning—reputable contests. Contests exist for all types of writing, but they can be especially beneficial for fiction writers, who typically have fewer opportunities than nonfiction writers to build their platform in other ways. Contests allow writers to snag the attention of judges, who are often well-known, established writers or other industry professionals. The benefits of winning can include valuable editorial feedback, validation and recognition, establishing credentials, publication, monetary awards, teaching posts, and more.

Be careful not to enter too many contests haphazardly. Three to eight well-chosen contests in a calendar year provide ample opportunity to make a name for yourself. Well-known contests include Pulitzer Prizes and PEN/Faulkner Awards for Fiction, but the best contests for writers to enter are ones suited to your skill level. Many contests charge entry fees, ranging from $5-75. Make sure before entering contests that the prizes offered are ones you would like to receive, and that they outweigh the cost to enter. For example, some contests sponsored by publishers offer the prize of publication to the winner. Writers should only enter such contests if they would be delighted to have their book taken on by the sponsoring publisher.

Prior to entering, writers should also try to determine if the contest is legitimate. Questions

JANICE PIERONI, an entertainment/publishing attorney and founder of Story Arts Management (www.storyartsmanagement.com), helps writers develop, edit and market screenplays, fiction and nonfiction manuscripts/book proposals and television movies/pilots. She has worked as a writer and executive for Universal Studios, led seminars at various academic institutions and has been an adjunct faculty member at Tufts University and Emerson College.

to ask or research include: Who are the panel of readers who will judge manuscripts and choose winners? Are they established authors and other industry professionals, or are they interns and other unpublished writers? Which writers have won in the past? Did winning advance their careers? How many winners will be selected? Be wary of contests with an overabundance of winners. Such contests could have the secondary purposes of generating income through events such as award ceremonies that require plane travel and accommodations, or sales of framed award ceremony plaques and other memorabilia.

Establish expertise

When evaluating manuscripts—particularly those for nonfiction—publishers are extremely interested in whether authors can make significant contributions to boosting book sales. They often look for evidence that authors can and will aggressively assist in selling books by supplementing bookselling events and media appearances publishers might set up with other events and appearances—preferably in a string of cities.

Nonfiction writers can begin to build audiences for their work by establishing themselves as experts even before approaching agents with manuscripts. Some writers already have credentials and careers in the fields about which they have written. Such writers can build from this solid base by creating professional, informative Web sites and/or newsletters and speaking at seminars and conferences. Membership in relevant professional or charitable organizations also can be helpful, particularly since most provide built-in audiences and frequently will sponsor events promoting members' books. Such writers also would be wise to make appearances in the media and try to get listed on expert journalists' call lists for when they need quotes.

Writers who have not yet established themselves as experts on the topics about which they have written typically have to work even harder to garner a book-buying audience. Some of the ways in which they can begin to accomplish this include earning degrees or certificates, taking continuing education courses, attending workshops and gaining work experience. If you cannot get hired in the fields in which you hope to become an expert, try volunteering or participating in internships or apprenticeships. In addition, you should look into whether you are eligible to join relevant professional organizations.

Another way to gain recognition is by joining or heading committees that set up seminars and conferences in specific fields. You may start out introducing the speakers or moderating panels, but as your skills develop, you can begin to command speaking engagements and media opportunities of your own. Often the first such engagement occurs when a scheduled speaker or panel member cancels or is unable to get to the seminar or conference, and a last-minute replacement is needed.

Teaching is another route many writers take. Fiction writers often can land opportunities to teach composition at the college, graduate or continuing education level even if they have not had books published, provided they have been published in literary journals, magazines or other significant media. Often a terminal degree, such as a Master of Fine Arts, is required. Teaching at colleges known for their writing programs can give you the opportunity to work with more established writers on the faculty, who might help you land an agent.

Publish articles

A third way in which you can build name recognition among a specific audience is by publishing articles in newspapers, magazines, trade journals, literary journals and other types of media. It also demonstrates to agents that you have worked with editors and are presumably able to meet deadlines. Writers often are paid for articles and columns, so they frequently can earn money while working on their book on the side. Although writing columns can be time-consuming, they are particularly helpful toward establishing writers as authorities in their fields.

Writers who fear writing to editors' specifications or having to meet deadlines could ease themselves into the newspaper and magazine world by first writing editorials. After a few editorials, it would be wise to gain experience working with editors, handling specific assignments and meeting deadlines by writing articles for newspapers and magazines.

Fiction writers can similarly collect published clips by submitting their short stories and poetry to literary journals or consumer magazines that accept fiction submissions.

Behave professionally

Personal conduct certainly plays a role in how good of a reputation an author conveys. Writers can up their credibility by consistently exhibiting the personal characteristic agents look for most: professionalism in all its many dimensions, including focus, commitment and good judgment.

Another part of building a professional relationship is the art of being a class act. Sometimes writers seeking representation introduce themselves by blaming other agents for their manuscript not selling. While undoubtedly circumstances or individuals can sometimes limit or even ruin an author's chances for success, it's probably not a good idea to launch a new relationship by blaming others who aren't there to explain or defend themselves. Doing so makes most people uncomfortable and generally raises doubts about the author's character and judgment. Publishing and affiliated industries are highly competitive industries mostly staffed by conscientious, caring and skillful individuals. Sometimes their efforts pay off, and sometimes they don't. If you feel you must provide an explanation, more generous statements such as "it wasn't a good match" will probably suffice. Save the drama for the page.

In addition, you should avoid getting sidetracked or sidetracking your agent. Authors should respect and cherish their writing time. The sooner you master the art of gracefully saying "no" to invitations and requests, the more you will be at your best as a writer. Due to the nature of agents' roles as gatekeepers, there is a tendency by some writers to take advantage of their services. Consequently, agents tend to get more than their fair share of requests to mentor writers' friends and relatives, get manuscripts or screenplays into the hands of actors who are often not right for the projects, and appear at charity events with big admission ticket prices. Unless agents have conveyed that they enjoy such opportunities and do not feel burdened by them, it's best to not put them in the position of having to gracefully decline.

Finally, it makes agents' jobs so much easier when they can wholeheartedly recommend not only their clients' work, but also their clients as people. Agents who find authors who are delightful to work with, meet deadlines and handle rewrites well can be reasonably confident they will behave similarly when working with editors or publishers. This professional reputation, coupled with creating work that shows immense talent in its writing and its presentation, can put authors in an ideal position to attract an agent.

Effective Communication

Getting Your Foot in the Door

O nce your work is prepared and you have a solid understanding of how literary agents work, the time is right to contact an agent. Your initial contact determines the agent's first impression of you, so you want to be professional and brief.

Again, research plays an important role in getting an agent's attention. You want to show the agent you've done your homework. Read the listings in this book to learn agents' areas of interest, check out agents' Web sites to learn more details on how they do business, and find out the names of some of their clients. If there is an author whose book is similar to yours, call the author's publisher. Someone in the contracts department can tell you the name of the agent who sold the title, provided an agent was used. Contact that agent, and impress her with your knowledge of the agency.

Finding an agent can often be as difficult as finding a publisher. Nevertheless, there are four ways to maximize your chances of finding the right agent: submit a query letter or proposal; obtain a referral from someone who knows the agent; meet the agent in person at a writers' conference; or attract the agent's attention with your own published writing.

SUBMISSIONS

The most common way to contact an agent is through a query letter or a proposal package. Most agents will accept unsolicited queries. Some will also look at outlines and sample chapters. Almost none want unsolicited complete manuscripts. Check the How to Contact subhead in each listing to learn exactly how an agent prefers to be solicited.

Agents agree to be listed in directories such as *Guide to Literary Agents* to indicate what they want to see and how they wish to receive submissions from writers. As you start to query agents, make sure you follow their individual submission directions. This, too, shows an agent you've done your research.

Like publishers, agencies have specialties. Some are only interested in novel-length works. Others are open to a variety of subjects and may actually have member agents within the company who specialize in only a handful of the topics covered by the entire agency.

Before querying any agent, first consult the Agent Specialties Indexes in the back of this book for your manuscript's subject, and identify those agents who handle what you write. Then, read the agents' listings to see which are appropriate for you and your work.

REFERRALS

The best way to get your foot in an agent's door is to be referred by one of her clients or by an editor or another agent she has worked with in the past. Since agents trust their clients, they will usually read referred work before over-the-transom submissions. If you are friends

Contacting Agents

Lessons in Etiquette

Via Mail
- Address the agent formally and make sure her name is spelled correctly.
- Double-check the agency's address.
- Include a SASE.
- Use a clear font and standard paragraph formatting.
- A short handwritten thank-you note can be appropriate if the agent helped you at a conference or if she provided editorial feedback along with your rejection.
- Don't include any extraneous materials.
- Don't try to set yourself apart by using fancy stationary. Standard paper and envelopes are preferable.

Via E-mail
- Address the agent as you would in a paper letter—be formal.
- If it's not listed on the Web site, call the company to get the appropriate agent's e-mail address.
- Include a meaningful subject line.
- Keep your emotions in check: Resist the temptation to send an angry response after being rejected, or to send a long, mushy note after being accepted. Keep your e-mails businesslike.
- Don't type in all caps or all lower case. Use proper punctuation and pay attention to grammar and spelling.
- Don't overuse humor—it can be easily misinterpreted.
- Don't e-mail about trivial things.

On the Phone
- Be polite: Ask if she has time to talk, or set up a time to call in advance.
- Get over your "phone phobia." Practice your conversation beforehand if necessary.
- Resist the urge to follow up with an agent too quickly. Give her time to review your material.
- Never make your first contact over the phone unless the agent calls you first or requests you do so in her submission guidelines.
- Don't demand information from her immediately. Your phone call is interrupting her busy day and she should be given time to respond to your needs.
- Don't call to get information you could otherwise obtain from the Internet or other resources.
- Don't have your spouse, secretary, best friend or parent call for you.

In Person
- Be clear and concise.
- Shake the agent's hand and greet her with your name.
- Be yourself, but be professional.
- Maintain eye contact.
- Don't monopolize her time. Either ask a brief question or ask if you can contact her later (via phone/mail/e-mail) with a more in-depth question.
- Don't get too nervous—agents are human!

with anyone in the publishing business who has connections with agents, ask politely for a referral. However, don't be offended if another writer will not share the name of his agent.

CONFERENCES

Going to a conference is your best bet for meeting an agent in person. Many conferences invite agents to give a speech or simply be available for meetings with authors, and agents view conferences as a way to find writers. Often agents set aside time for one-on-one discussions with writers, and occasionally they may even look at material writers bring to the conference. Often these critiques cost an extra fee, but if an agent is impressed with you and your work, she may ask to see writing samples after the conference. When you send your query, be sure to mention the specific conference where you met and that she asked to see your work.

Because this is an effective way to connect with agents, we've asked agents to indicate in their listings which conferences they regularly attend. We've also included a section of Conferences, starting on page 230, where you can find more information about a particular event.

See Also

PUBLISHING CREDITS

Some agents read magazines or journals to find writers to represent. If you have had an outstanding piece published in a periodical, an agent wanting to represent you may make contact. In such cases, make sure the agent has read your work. Some agents send form letters to writers, and such agents often make their living entirely from charging reading fees and not from commissions on sales.

However, many reputable and respected agents do contact potential clients in this way. For them, you already possess attributes of a good client: You have publishing credits and an editor has validated your work. To receive a letter from a reputable agent who has read your material and wants to represent you is an honor.

Occasionally, writers who have self-published or who have had their work published electronically may attract an agent's attention, especially if the self-published book has sold well or received a lot of positive reviews.

Recently, writers have been posting their work on the Internet with the hope of attracting an agent's eye. With all the submissions most agents receive, they probably have little time to peruse writers' Web sites. Nevertheless, there are agents who do consider the Internet a resource for finding fresh voices.

Contacting Agents

Crafting a Query

Writing the Best Possible Letter

The query letter is the catalyst in the chemical reaction of publishing. Overall, writing a query letter is a fairly simple process that serves one purpose—getting an agent or editor to read your manuscript. A query letter is the tool that sells you and your book using brief, attention-getting words. Fiction and nonfiction query letters share the same basic elements, but there are differences you should consider for each category.

FICTION QUERIES

Here's a general rule of thumb when querying an agent for a fiction manuscript: Do not contact the agent regarding your novel until the entire manuscript is written and ready to be sent. A query letter for a work of fiction generally contains the following elements.

Step By Step

• **The hook.** Your first paragraph should be written to hook the agent and get her to request a few chapters or the whole manuscript. The hook is usually a special plot detail or a unique element that's going to grab the agent's attention.

• **About the book.** It is important to provide the agent with the technical statistics of your book: title, genre and word count. An easy way to estimate your manuscript's word count is to multiply the number of manuscript pages by 250 and then round that number to the nearest ten thousand.

• **The story.** This is the part of your letter where you provide a summary of your plot, introduce your main characters and hint at the main conflict that drives the story. Be careful not to go overboard here, either in content or in length. Only provide the agent with the basic elements she needs to make a decision about your manuscript.

• **The audience.** You must be able to tell the agent who the intended audience is for your novel. Many writers find it helpful to tell the agent the theme of their novel, which then signifies the intended audience and to whom the novel will appeal.

• **About you.** Tell the agent who you are and how you came to write your novel. In this paragraph, you should only provide those qualifications that are relevant to your novel. List any special qualities you have for writing a novel in your genre. Also, list any writing groups to which you belong, publishing credentials, awards won, etc. Remember, though, if you don't have any of the above, don't stress your inexperience or dwell on what you haven't accomplished.

• **The closing.** Make sure you end your query on a positive note. You should thank the agent for her time and offer to send more information (a synopsis, sample chapters or the complete manuscript), upon request. Be sure to also mention that you've enclosed a self-addressed, stamped envelope (SASE) for the agent's convenience.

NONFICTION QUERIES

Unlike fiction manuscripts, it is acceptable to query an agent about a nonfiction book before the manuscript is complete. The following seven elements should be included in a nonfiction query.

Step By Step

• **The hook.** The hook is usually a special detail or a unique element that's going to grab the agent's attention and pull her in. Oftentimes, nonfiction writers use statistics or survey results, especially if the results are astounding or unique, to reel in the agent.

• **The referral.** Why are you contacting this particular agent? A recommendation from an author she currently represents, an acknowledgment in a book they have represented, or because the agent has a strong track record of selling books on the subject about which you're writing? No matter the answer, knowing what type of work the agent represents shows her that you're a professional.

• **About the book.** It is important to provide the agent with the technical statistics of your book, including the title and sales handle—a short, one-line statement explaining the primary goal of your book. In his book *How to Write a Book Proposal,* 3rd Edition (Writer's Digest Books), agent Michael Larsen says that a book's handle "may be its thematic or stylistic resemblance to one or two successful books or authors." One example Larsen uses to further explain a sales handle is *"Fast Food Nation* meets fashion." Essentially, the handle helps the agent decide whether your book is a project she can sell.

• **Markets.** Tell the agent who will buy your book (i.e., the audience) and where people will buy it. Research potential markets according to various demographics (including age, gender, income, profession, etc.), and then use the information to find solid figures that verify your book's audience is significant enough to warrant publication. The more you know about the potential markets for your book (usually the top three or four markets), the more professional you appear to the agent.

• **About you.** Tell the agent who you are and why you are the best person to write this book. In this paragraph, you should only provide qualifications that are relevant to your book, including career and academic background and publication credentials (as they relate to the subject of your book).

• **The closing.** Make sure you end your query on a positive note. Thank the agent for her

Contacting Agents

Mistakes to Avoid

Tips

• Don't use any cute attention-getting devices like colored stationery or odd fonts.

• Don't send any unnecessary enclosures, such as a picture of you or your family pet.

• Don't waste time telling the agent you're writing to her in the hopes that she will represent your book. Get immediately to the heart of the matter—your book.

• Don't try to "sell" the agent by telling her how great your book is or comparing it to those written by best-selling authors.

• Don't mention that your family, friends or "readers" love it.

• Don't send sample chapters that are not consecutive chapters.

time and tell her what items you have ready to submit (proposal, sample chapters, complete manuscript, etc.) upon request. Also mention that you've enclosed a self-addressed, stamped envelope (SASE) for the agent's convenience.

FORMATTING YOUR QUERY

There are no hard-and-fast rules when it comes to formatting your query letter, but there are some widely accepted guidelines like those listed below, adapted from *Formatting & Submitting Your Manuscript*, by Jack and Glenda Neff, and Don Prues (Writer's Digest Books).

- Use a standard font or typeface (avoid bold, script or italics, except for publication titles), like 12-point Times Roman.
- Your name, address and phone number (plus e-mail and fax, if possible) should appear in the top right corner or on your letterhead. If you would like, you can create your own letterhead so you appear professional. Simply type the same information mentioned above, center it at the top of the page and photocopy it on quality paper.
- Use a 1-inch margin on all sides.
- Address the query to a specific agent, preferably the one who handles the type of work you're writing.
- Keep it to one page.
- Include a SASE or postcard for reply, and state in the letter you have done so (preferably in your closing paragraph).
- Use block format (no indentations or extra space between paragraphs).
- Single-space the body of the letter and double-space between paragraphs.
- Thank the agent for considering your query letter.

Bad Fiction Query

The author's phone number and e-mail address are missing—include all pertinent contact information.

Always address your query to a specific agent.

Do not query an agent if your fiction manuscript is not finished and fully revised.

Don't ask an agent for advice or criticism—that's not the agent's job nor the purpose of the query.

Never mention that this is the first book you've written—it singles you out as an amateur. While it's good to have publishing credits or professional expertise, they're only worth mentioning if they are relevant to the book being proposed.

This is vague and has no "hook" to capture the agent's attention. What will make it different from other romance novels?

Vincent Barnes
1302 Amateur Rd.
Sheboygan, WI 53081

April 25, 2006

General Agents, Inc.
10 Anywhere Dr.
Detroit, MI 48215

Dear Sir/Madam,

I'm about to finish my novel and wanted to give you a heads up because I know I'll need an agent to help sell it. Please take a look at the enclosed sample chapters and let me know if you think publishers will like my book.

This is my first time writing a romance novel, but I've had a couple science articles published in online magazines. I worked in a hospital laboratory for 15 years and thought it would be fun to trade in all those cold hard facts for a good old-fashioned love story.

My novel—titled *Many Miles of Love*—is about a shy midwestern girl named Lauren who falls in love with Ray, a boisterous salesman from Baltimore. The couple goes through many highs and lows together, including being separated from one another several times due to circumstances beyond their control. In the end, of course, they are able to come together and make a happy life for themselves.

The book will probably end up around 70,000 words and will be read mostly by women. I've already had a variety of family members look over the beginning chapters, and all of them are curious to know what happens next.

I put in an application with the U.S. Copyright Office last week. I've also been doing some research on how much authors get paid for novels these days. When you respond, please include any information on possible advances and royalties for my book.

Many thanks,

Vincent Barnes

You should describe your potential audience more specifically than just men or women. Also, mentioning that your family likes the book will get you nowhere. You would be better served to point out if it has been read/critiqued by a few local writing groups.

Don't mention copyright information or payment expectations. This is simply a query to assess an agent's interest in your novel.

Good Fiction Query

Brent Thompson
62 Fiction Dr.
Naples, FL 34104
(630)555-6009
brent.thompson@email.com

January 11, 2006

Mr. Alexander Diaz
The Best Literary Agency
546 Representative Blvd.
New York, NY 10001

Address your
query to a specific
agent.

Dear Mr. Diaz,

Say why you have
chosen to query
this particular
agent.

I heard you speak at the Southwestern Florida Writer's Conference last month, where you mentioned an interest in seeing more young adult fiction submissions filled with both adventure and heart. I have just the story for you—a 60,000-word novel geared toward preteen and teenage boys entitled *The Mysterious Map*.

Always state
your novel's
genre, title and
word count.

The book opens in the North Carolina countryside, where 15-year-old Rowan Hampton has discovered a secret map. He's certain it will lead to treasure, but he and his best friend Karl soon realize the clues are of a more personal nature. As they move from town to town, Rowan begins to question details of his childhood that now seem unclear. What really happened to his younger sister? Can he trust everything his parents say? Who left him this map, and where will it lead?

Briefly tell what
the novel is
about.

I'm a native of the Carolinas, where I taught middle-school English for 35 years. While I was teaching, a few chapters of Rowan's journey were published in the *Lowland's Literary Journal*. After retiring last year, I dedicated myself to completing the novel.

Provide relevant
background
information about
yourself, including
professional
experience,
publishing
credentials, etc.

My manuscript is ready to be sent at your request.

I look forward to hearing from you.

Sincerely,

Brent Thompson

Bad Nonfiction Query

The author's address and phone number are missing—include all pertinent contact information.

Juanita Nielson
Kansas City, MO
badwriter@email.com

December 9, 2006

Always address your query to the agent's full name, even if you've seen it shortened elsewhere. It's professional to make a formal first impression.

Charles Mortenson
Agent & Agent Representatives
39 W. Main St.
Boston, MA 02209

Dear Chuck,

Questions can prove to be an interesting way to "hook" an agent, but don't be too vague. Ask a question nobody is asking—one that shows why your book is unique.

Did you know there are actually six branches—or types—of yoga that people can practice? Did you know that chanting the word "Om" stems from the scientific theory that the universe is constantly in motion?

Only send these materials if requested in the agent's submission guidelines. Also, don't bother telling an agent what your friends think; show the agent why the book must be published and must be written by you.

For more enlightening information on yoga, please look over my outline and sample chapters and let me know if you think this book will interest publishers. I have already shared my idea with a few friends and they all agree I would be great at writing this book.

I've been taking yoga classes on and off for several years now, and they have really helped me get through some tough times. I want to write a book about yoga so other people can see the benefits of it. I have never attempted to write a book before, but I've been taking some local college courses and even attended a writer's conference last year.

Yoga has been such a big trend lately that there are probably lots of interested readers out there. I know other books about yoga have already been published, but mine will be more personal and geared toward people who don't know much about the physical and spiritual practice.

Try to include a few main points that differentiate your book from others on the market. Also, make sure you are enough of an expert to provide this information to potentially thousands of readers.

I've been a stay-at-home mom for the past 8 years, and think this book can signify a new direction for my life. Hopefully with your help selling and an editor's help revising, this book can land on the bestseller list.

Thanks for your time,

Juanita Nielson

Don't pitch an idea based on a trend because trends eventually fade. Make sure you have a deep grasp on who your target readers will be, and make sure you will actually be able to reach them if they aren't already reading books on your topic.

Don't point out your (or the book's) shortcomings. If it needs editorial help, get some before you send it to an agent.

Good Nonfiction Query

Gayle Matthews
1999 Published Way
Durham, CA 95938
(773)555-6868
gmatthews@email.com

July 30, 2005

Lynn Kobayashi
Kobayashi & Brown, Inc.
55 Acceptance St. NW
Seattle, WA 98101

Always address a specific agent.

Dear Ms. Kobayashi,

The hook: Provide concrete information and indisputable reasoning for why your book fills a void in the market. Explain how your target audience fits into the proposal.

California, Washington and Oregon have long been the wine centers of the United States, but they are far from being the only places people can learn about and enjoy the vineyard culture. Nearly every state in the country—including Alaska—has a winery, and many of them are producing quality, affordable products. Recent research shows that wine is the favored alcoholic drink among Americans, and that almost all who drink it regularly are purchasing American wines. However, many do not have the time or money to travel all the way to the West Coast to do tours and tastings.

Explain a few details about the book, as well as why you are querying this particular agent.

Your Web site states you specialize in travel writing, so I'd like to propose a series of guidebooks that take people on tours of local vineyards. The books would be categorized by region (Northeast, Mid-Atlantic, Southeast, Midwestern, etc.) and would focus on the best wineries to visit in each neighboring state. Not only would each entry provide specific travel details, but information on the vineyard's history, specialties and overall atmosphere would also be included. There would also be a tremendous opportunity for beautiful photography and detailed maps.

If possible, talk about your book from a sales perspective.

Since no other travel books about wine have been broken down in this manner, there are multiple sales opportunities. Aside from national bookstores, the guidebooks could be marketed in vineyards, wine shops, tourism bureaus and local specialty stores in each region.

Provide professional background information relevant to the writing of this book.

I have been a professor of Viticulture and Enology for the past 12 years and help organize an annual conference with other wine professionals to discuss industry trends. I have a deep love for both wine and travel, and have already visited more than 100 wineries across the country. I also write a syndicated newspaper column about wine and have contributed to both consumer and trade magazines on the topics of travel and vineyards.

Show you've followed the agent's submission guidelines and make a polite offer.

Enclosed are a detailed outline, professional bio and three sample chapters. I would be glad to go over more specifics of my proposal at your convenience.

Sincerely,

Gayle Matthews

The Art of the Synopsis

Summing Up Your Novel

by Evan Marshall

Many new writers think that when their manuscripts are finished, their work is done. Wrong! Nowadays agents and editors are likely to ask to see a synopsis as well as your manuscript. As a marketing tool, the synopsis is even more important than the query letter—though if your query letter isn't just right, you won't reach the synopsis stage at all.

Too often at my agency I hear something to the effect of, "Why should I have to write a synopsis of my novel? I've already written the novel!" Or, "By the time I finish the synopsis, I could have half the novel written!"

Unfortunately, the synopsis is a necessary tool you're going to have to learn to master if you want to make it as a novelist. It's something agents need. Very often, in response to a query letter, they will ask to see a synopsis and the first three chapters of your novel, or they may ask to see the synopsis alone. Everyone works differently.

Editors, too, need a synopsis. They often request that a writer or agent include one with the manuscript. Why? Editors are extremely overworked and must plow through mountains of material. A simple way to find out whether a novel is worth spending a lot of time on is to read the sample chapters, and if the writing is appealing, read the synopsis to see if the writer also knows how to plot a good story. Those are the two factors agents and editors look for in their hunt for new talent: good writing and good storytelling.

SYNOPSIS BASICS

So what, exactly, is a synopsis? It's a summary of your novel, written in a way that conveys the excitement of the novel itself. Before we get into how to do that, here are some basic things you should know about setting up your synopsis.

The synopsis is always written in the present tense. In the synopsis, you tell your whole story. You do not—even in the case of a mystery—leave out the solution in an attempt to induce an agent or editor to request the manuscript. Nor do you pick up where your sample chapters leave off. As mentioned above, your synopsis is your novel—your entire novel—in miniature.

There's no hard-and-fast rule about how long a synopsis should be, but most agents and editors agree that a too-long synopsis defeats its own purpose. Some agents and editors

EVAN MARSHALL is a literary agent and author with nearly 30 years of publishing experience. Excerpted from *The Marshall Plan for Getting Your Novel Published* © 2003 by Evan Marshall. Used with permission of Writer's Digest Books, an imprint of F+W Publications, Inc. Visit your local bookseller or call (800)448-0915 to obtain your copy.

request extremely short synopses (see The Short Synopsis on page 38), which aren't really synopses at all, but more like jacket or cover copy, or what Hollywood calls "coverage." As a rule, I like to aim for one page of synopsis for every 25 pages of manuscript. This would mean a 400-page manuscript gets a synopsis of about 16 pages. But this rule is often broken, depending on the novel itself. A mystery, for example, may require a longer synopsis because of the level of detail that must be presented. Eventually you'll find yourself allowing your synopses to seek their own length, and that they'll almost always come out about right.

To achieve such conciseness, you must write as clean and tight as you know how. Don't do what many writers do and try to keep boiling down your actual novel until it's short enough. Instead, learn to write in a synoptic style—read a section or chapter of your novel and simply retell it, as you might describe a great book or movie to a friend.

Leaving out unnecessary adverbs and adjectives, focus on your story's essential points. Much must be left out, such as inconsequential specifics of a particular incident.

Actual dialogue from your novel is rarely needed, though a few chosen lines can be effective. Remember, whereas in a novel you should show rather than tell, in a synopsis you should tell. Here, it's okay simply to write: Yvette is furious, though you would not write that in your novel. You would show us how Yvette's anger manifests itself.

Write your synopsis as one unified narrative. Don't divide it into sections or chapters. Use paragraphing and short transitions to signify these breaks.

Professional novelists know how to put together a synopsis that makes agents and editors sit up and take notice—and ask for the manuscript.

SYNOPSIS SPECIFICS

The hook

To create an arresting hook for your synopsis, start with your story's lead character and the crisis that has befallen him—the crisis that begins the story. Then explain what your lead must do in order to remedy the crisis; in other words, what is his story goal? For example:

> RHONDA STERN has always considered herself immune to the danger and unpleasantness of the outside world, quietly creating tapestries in the house she occupies alone on lush, secluded Bainbridge Island, Washington. But the world intrudes in a horrible way when one morning a desperate criminal breaks into Rhonda's home and takes her hostage, threatening to kill her if she doesn't help him get off the island. Now Rhonda must fight to save her life while at the same time trying not to help a man she knows is guilty of murder.

The back-up

Right after your hook paragraph, back up a little to give some further background that makes the situation clearer. This is where you should also make sure you've covered the basics: your lead's age, occupation, marital status (if you haven't already given us this information in the hook); the time (past—if so, when?—present, or future); and the place.

The meat

Now move on to the action of your story. Give us not only the things that happen to make up your plot, but also how your lead character feels about them or is affected by them.

So many synopses are dull because the author has left out the emotional component. Remember that people read novels primarily to be moved emotionally; they want to live the story through the lead. The only way they can do that is to know how the lead feels. In other words, emotions and feelings are plot; they are as important as the things that happen.

Words are precious in the synopsis, so pick the best ones you can! Use strong action words and keep the action crisp, clean and clear.

Formatting Your Synopsis

Type your real name (not a pseudonym if you are using one). ——

Your novel's genre. ——

Double space twice. ——

Type your name (or pseudonym if you are using one). ——

Indent first paragraph and start text of synopsis.

Use headers as shown. ——

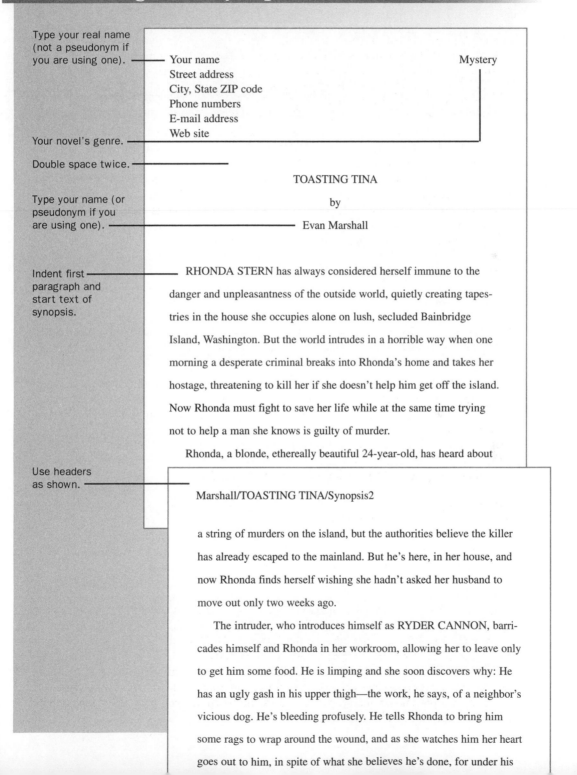

Your name   Mystery
Street address
City, State ZIP code
Phone numbers
E-mail address
Web site

TOASTING TINA

by

Evan Marshall

RHONDA STERN has always considered herself immune to the danger and unpleasantness of the outside world, quietly creating tapestries in the house she occupies alone on lush, secluded Bainbridge Island, Washington. But the world intrudes in a horrible way when one morning a desperate criminal breaks into Rhonda's home and takes her hostage, threatening to kill her if she doesn't help him get off the island. Now Rhonda must fight to save her life while at the same time trying not to help a man she knows is guilty of murder.

Rhonda, a blonde, ethereally beautiful 24-year-old, has heard about

Marshall/TOASTING TINA/Synopsis2

a string of murders on the island, but the authorities believe the killer has already escaped to the mainland. But he's here, in her house, and now Rhonda finds herself wishing she hadn't asked her husband to move out only two weeks ago.

The intruder, who introduces himself as RYDER CANNON, barricades himself and Rhonda in her workroom, allowing her to leave only to get him some food. He is limping and she soon discovers why: He has an ugly gash in his upper thigh—the work, he says, of a neighbor's vicious dog. He's bleeding profusely. He tells Rhonda to bring him some rags to wrap around the wound, and as she watches him her heart goes out to him, in spite of what she believes he's done, for under his

Think miniature

Very often in a novel, there are secrets and other information that must at some point be revealed. For some reason, many writers believe that in a synopsis they must reveal all of this information right up front. Not so. In your synopsis, reveal secrets and other surprising information in exactly the same spots where you have done so (or intend to do so) in the novel itself.

Stay out of it

Don't let your scaffolding show. By this I mean don't use devices that suggest the mechanical aspects of your story. This is another reason you shouldn't run character sketches at the beginning of the synopsis, or use headings within the synopsis such as Background or Setting. Work these elements smoothly into the story; give us background when it's necessary for the reader to understand something.

Pace it right

As you near the end of your story, indicate its quickened pace by using shorter paragraphs that give a speeded-up, staccato effect. For example:

> Rhonda stands at the edge of the bridge, her gaze locked on Ryder as he slips deeper into the water. At the other end of the bridge, Denis cries out to her, begging her to believe he's not the killer.

Tips for Writing the Short Synopsis

Tips

- Use the present tense.
- Lead off with a strong hook sentence—anything that will grab the attention of your reader.
- Only start a new paragraph for broad transitions in your story.
- Do not use dialogue.
- Quickly introduce your lead, the opposition, the romantic interest and any other important characters while setting up the story in terms of place and time.
- Quickly state the conflict between your lead and the opposition; then state the lead's story goal.
- Stick to the high points of your lead's main story line.
- Do not include any subplots.
- Move smoothly from one event to another; avoid the choppiness often seen in beginners' short synopses—a result of having whittled down a longer synopsis without regard for smoothness of reading.
- Use powerful verbs and few, if any, adverbs and adjectives.
- Tell the entire story.

Maximum drama

This is your novel in miniature, and you want to leave the reader of your synopsis with the same great feeling he'll have after reading your book. The way to do that is to slow down a little at the novel's end, after the story has resolved itself and you're in the Wrap-Up, and really bear down on the emotional elements. These are what produce that goose-bumps-at-the-back-of-the-neck feeling when we finish a wonderful novel. Go into more detail here; give us a line of dialogue if that's appropriate.

Polish it

The editing of your synopsis is, in a way, more important than the editing of your book—though I would never tell you it's okay to do less than your best work on either.

Because a synopsis is briefer than a novel, errors stand out more clearly. Make yours as close to perfect as you can, even if that means several rounds of editing. Check for misspelled words, awkward sentence structure, confusing writing and grammatical and typographical errors. Be consistent in referring to your characters: Don't write Ryder in one place and Gannon in another. Stick with one name for each character to avoid confusion.

Make it your business to master the synopsis. Don't be one of those writers who says, "I just can't write a synopsis." They're usually the writers who get the poorer deals or no deal at all.

The synopsis is a necessary tool for a novelist, as, say, the preliminary study is for many painters. Once you get the technique down, you'll probably even find writing the synopsis fun.

Professional Proposals

Packaging Your Nonfiction Submission

by Michael Larsen

Some writers find it easier to write a book than a proposal. For others, writing the proposal is the most creative part of producing a book. Why? Because you have the freedom to plan the book in the way that excites you most without bearing the responsibility for writing it, changing your vision to suit your publisher's needs, or being pressured by the deadline that comes with a contract.

Even one of the following 10 hot buttons can excite editors enough to buy your book:

- Your idea
- Your title
- Your writing
- Your credentials
- Your book's timing
- Your ability to promote your book
- The size of the markets for your book
- Your book's subsidiary rights potential
- Your book's potential for bulk sales to businesses
- Your book's potential as a series of books that sell each other

Your job: Push as many hot buttons as you can.

As competitive books prove, there is not just one way to write a proposal any more than there is just one way to write a book. My approach has evolved over the last three decades, and it continues to evolve as what editors need to see changes. I don't want to waste a second of your time, my time or the time of the writers we work for, so I've outlined the fastest, easiest way I know for you to produce a rejection-proof proposal and obtain the best editor, publisher and deal for your book.

Most proposals range from 30 to 50 pages. Your proposal will have three parts (the introduction, the outline and the sample chapter) in a logical sequence, each of which has a goal. Your goal is to impress agents and editors enough with each part of your proposal to convince them to go on to the next.

MICHAEL LARSEN runs a literary agency with his wife Elizabeth Pomada in San Francisco. Excerpted from *How to Write a Book Proposal*, 3rd Edition © 2003 by Michael Larsen. Used with permission of Writer's Digest Books, an imprint of F+W Publications, Inc. Visit your local bookseller or call (800)448-0915 to obtain your copy.

Preparing Your Proposal

Contacting Agents

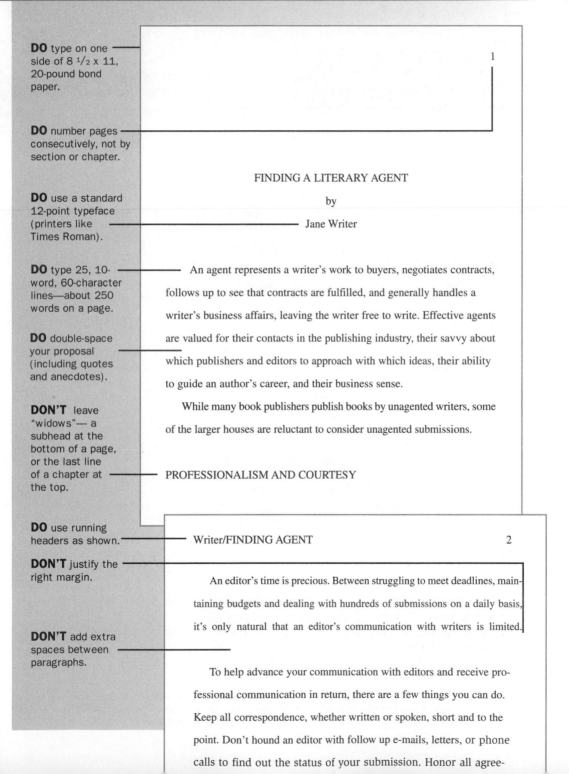

DO type on one side of 8 ½ x 11, 20-pound bond paper.

DO number pages consecutively, not by section or chapter.

DO use a standard 12-point typeface (printers like Times Roman).

DO type 25, 10-word, 60-character lines—about 250 words on a page.

DO double-space your proposal (including quotes and anecdotes).

DON'T leave "widows"— a subhead at the bottom of a page, or the last line of a chapter at the top.

DO use running headers as shown.

DON'T justify the right margin.

DON'T add extra spaces between paragraphs.

1

FINDING A LITERARY AGENT

by

Jane Writer

An agent represents a writer's work to buyers, negotiates contracts, follows up to see that contracts are fulfilled, and generally handles a writer's business affairs, leaving the writer free to write. Effective agents are valued for their contacts in the publishing industry, their savvy about which publishers and editors to approach with which ideas, their ability to guide an author's career, and their business sense.

While many book publishers publish books by unagented writers, some of the larger houses are reluctant to consider unagented submissions.

PROFESSIONALISM AND COURTESY

Writer/FINDING AGENT   2

An editor's time is precious. Between struggling to meet deadlines, maintaining budgets and dealing with hundreds of submissions on a daily basis, it's only natural that an editor's communication with writers is limited.

To help advance your communication with editors and receive professional communication in return, there are a few things you can do. Keep all correspondence, whether written or spoken, short and to the point. Don't hound an editor with follow up e-mails, letters, or phone calls to find out the status of your submission. Honor all agree-

THE INTRODUCTION

Your introduction should prove that you have a marketable, practical idea and that you are the right person to write about it and promote it. The introduction has three parts: the overview, resources needed to complete the book, and about the author. They give you the opportunity to provide as much ammunition about you and your book as you can muster.

The overview

The overview consists of 12 parts, nine of which are optional:

Your subject hook: This is the most exciting, compelling thing that you can write in as few words as possible that justifies the existence of your book. Use a quote, event, fact, trend, anecdote, statistic, idea or joke. For example, your subject hook could be an anecdote about someone using your advice to solve a problem followed by a statistic about the number of people with the problem.

Your book hook: This includes your title, your selling handle and the length of your book.

- Your title: The titles for most books have to tell and sell. Make sure yours says what your book is and gives browsers an irresistible reason to buy it.
- Your selling handle: This is a sentence that ideally says, "[Your book's title] will be the first book to . . . " You can also use Hollywood shorthand by comparing your book to one or two successful books: "[Your book's title] is *Seabiscuit* meets *What to Expect When You're Expecting.*"
- The length of your book (and number of illustrations, if it will have them): Provide a page or word count for your manuscript that you determine by outlining your book and estimating the length of your chapters and back matter.

Step By Step

Markets for your book: List the groups of people who will buy your book and the channels through which it can be sold, starting with the largest ones.

Your book's special features (Optional): This includes humor, structure, anecdotes, checklists, exercises, sidebars, the tone and style of your book and anything you will do to give the text visual appeal. Use competitive books as models.

A foreword by a well-known authority (Optional): Find someone who will give your book credibility and salability to write a foreword. If getting a foreword isn't possible, write: "The author will contact [names of three potential authorities] for a foreword."

Answers to technical or legal questions (Optional): If your book is on a specialized subject, name the expert who has reviewed it. If your book may present legal problems, name the intellectual property attorney who has reviewed it.

Your back matter (Optional): Check competitive books to see if your book needs an appendix, glossary, resource directory, bibliography or footnotes.

Your book's subsidiary rights possibilities (Optional): Start with the most commercial category, whether it's movie rights, foreign rights, book club rights or even merchandising rights (for products like T-shirts), which usually require a book to be a best seller before manufacturers will be interested.

Spin-offs (Optional): If your book can be a series or lend itself to sequels, mention up to five of them in descending order of their commercial appeal.

A mission statement (Optional): If you feel a sense of mission about writing and promoting your book, describe it in one first-person paragraph.

Your platform (Optional): In descending order of impressiveness, list what you have done and are doing to promote your work and yourself.

Your promotion plan (Optional): List in descending order of importance what you will do to promote your book after it's published. If you're writing a reference book or a gift book, you may not need a promotion plan. Also, small and medium-sized houses outside of New

A Professional Presentation

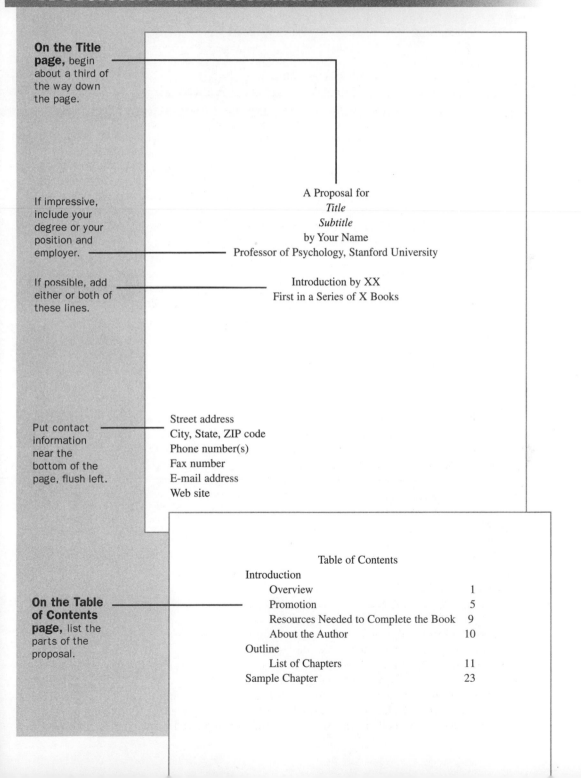

On the Title page, begin about a third of the way down the page.

If impressive, include your degree or your position and employer.

If possible, add either or both of these lines.

Put contact information near the bottom of the page, flush left.

A Proposal for
Title
Subtitle
by Your Name
Professor of Psychology, Stanford University

Introduction by XX
First in a Series of X Books

Street address
City, State, ZIP code
Phone number(s)
Fax number
E-mail address
Web site

On the Table of Contents page, list the parts of the proposal.

Table of Contents

Contacting Agents

York don't need the promotional ammunition big publishers do. At the beginning of your career, or if your idea or your ability to promote your book isn't as strong as it needs to be to excite Big Apple publishers, you may find small and medium-sized publishers more receptive to your work.

Also list books that will compete with and complement yours. Provide basic information on the half-dozen most important titles.

Resources needed to complete the book

Starting with the largest expense, list out-of-pocket expenses of $500 or more for a foreword, permissions, travel or illustrations (not for office expenses). Use a round figure for how much each will cost and give the total. (You or your agent may decide not to include the dollar amounts when submitting your proposal, but you do have to know what they are because they affect the money you need to write your book, as well as the negotiation of your contract.)

About the author

Include everything you want editors to know about you—that isn't already in your platform—in descending order of relevance.

THE OUTLINE

Your outline is a paragraph to a page of prose outlining your chapters to prove that there's a book's worth of information in your idea and that you have devised the best structure for organizing it. Aim for about one line of outline for every page of text you guesstimate; for example, 19 lines of outline for a 19-page chapter. To help make your outlines enjoyable to read, start each one with the strongest anecdote or slice of copy from each chapter, then outline it.

SAMPLE CHAPTER

Include the one sample chapter that best shows how you will make your book as enjoyable to read as it is informative.

Tips for Proofreading and Submitting

Tips

- **Read aloud** and follow along with your index finger under each word.

- **Proofread back to front** so you can concentrate on the words and not be seduced into reading the proposal.

- **Submit without staples** or any other form of binding. Paper clips are acceptable, but they leave indentations.

- **Use paper portfolios.** Insert your proposal in the right side of a double-pocket folder. You can use the left pocket for writing samples, illustrations, supporting documents and your business card if the left flap is scored. Put a self-adhesive label on the front of the folder with your book's title and your name.

- **Make everything 8½ × 11.** This makes it easy to reproduce and submit via mail or e-mail.

Formatting Your Script

Ten Ways to Make Peace With the Process

by Candy Davis

Conscientious screenwriters like you wake up at 3 a.m. fretting about the thousands of small technical goofs that might make an agent think you are an idiot. What about the weird margins? How do I make the actors do what I want? Should I put in the camera angles? The truth is that you don't need to worry about any of this stuff.

A screenwriter's sole job is to conjure up an irresistible, glistening soap bubble of an idea and set it adrift in the imagination of someone who is willing to pay to own it. Here are 10 ways to forget those annoying details and get from FADE IN to FADE OUT without fading away from stress.

1. Forget about control

When it comes to filmmaking, as a screenwriter you're pretty much at the bottom of the heap. Once a screenplay leaves your hands, thousands of creative, rich, egotistical and high-handed people are going to have their way with it no matter what you do. As long as the check clears, who cares? Nothing sells like a bulletproof story, and no amount of cute decoration will give a weak script the legs it needs to attract a big audience.

2. Forget about length

Ninety minutes is all you get. At one page per minute, that's 90 pages. It's true that the absolute limit for a script is 130 pages, but that's a fat script. It leaves no time for the talent to run, bleed or quiver in pain. A fat script will immediately become a lean script to make room for the quivering, so aim to write tight.

3. Forget about the credit sequence

No way are you going to get control of what happens while the opening credits roll. Are you trying to put the director out of a job? He will eat you for breakfast. Just begin with FADE IN—the first words of every screenplay. Sneak in your brilliant credit sequence with a brief hint, cramming as powerful an image as possible into a few words:

CANDY DAVIS, freelance editor and founder of Ink Dance Literary Services (www.InkDance.biz), writes award-winning novels, short stories and screenplays, two of which have been sold and one produced. She is best known for her edgy fiction dealing with complex and sensitive themes.

FADE IN:
A vast desert dawn rolls out under a tipsy, SPUTTERING plane.

The director will take it from there.

4. Forget about camera directions

The writer sends out a script on speculation to sell an illusion that any director can mold into a reflection of himself. This is called a spec script, and it should be fun to read. That means no camera directions, no technical advice and no editorial suggestions.

The shooting script is not your problem. Let the director worry about the technical details, such as which camera to use and how to position it. Menial jobs like numbering the scenes will be assigned to some poor, tortured underling. Writers who can't keep their hands off the technical directions are easily carried away:

We CRAB RIGHT for a LONG TAKE. TRACK IN for WORM'S EYE TWO-
SHOT to catch Jack's double-take past Mary's left ankle.

The shooting script is about as much fun to read as a wiring diagram, so don't go there. Instead, relax and write:

Jack double-takes.

5. Forget about covering the page with words

Every page of a script should look clean, with as few words as possible. Think of a script as a skeleton of images, each bone surrounded by lots of white space in which the director directs and the actor acts.

Hold your script upside down at arm's length. Do you see a feathery drift of words like seeds scattered on snow? That's perfect. If you are looking at a page crammed with so much text that it looks like the skid marks at a 12-car pile up, it's time to cut.

Keep action open-ended and dialogue simple without destroying the dazzle factor. Cut action lines to a single sentence if possible.

Insert a line space between distinct actions to give the actors a BEAT (a Hollywood ''moment'') to develop the emotional impact:

INT. BAR—NIGHT

Jack and Mary dance.

Closer.

A tentative kiss.

JACK

Come back to the ship with me.

MARY

What about Lance?

6. Forget about casting, directing and SFX

At a character's first entrance in the script, use full caps for her name and add a brief, general thumbnail that could fit any actress Central Casting can corral:

MARY, tanned and trim, enters the bar like it's alien territory.

Dump that big chunk of text describing every shrug, eye gleam and moustache twitch. The actors are going to do it their way, so let it go. You may suggest the general action, but let the actors handle the accompanying performance (gasps, head nods, etc.)

While you're at it, throw out all those parentheticals—also called wrylies—just under the character caption that are supposed to cue the actor on how to deliver the speech:

> JACK
> (wryly)
>
> You never said you were married.

Jack (the actor) may want to say this in any of a thousand ways.

And don't mess with the special effects, the forbidden province of the inferno artist. If you want an alien, just say so. Mr. Inferno Artist will whip up one that speaks Japanese, wears a tuxedo and burps on cue.

7. Forget about fancy sluglines

Good sluglines, which serve as master scene headings, describe where and when the scene takes place, but they leave the details to the imagination. The set designer is an artiste, and he will flick his cigarette ashes on you if you ramble. So you can forget about describing Scene 2 as taking place at star-spangled midnight on Pawtuxet Bay.

You only get two choices on the first word: interior (INT.) or exterior (EXT.). And you get two choices on timeframe: day (DAY) or night (NIGHT). Between those two ends of the slugline comes the briefest description you can squeeze out:

> EXT. BEACH—DAY

A beach is a beach as far as you are concerned. Call it a beach, and let the set designer dress the scene with his own brand of sun, sand and surf.

8. Forget about new and clever ways to start a scene

Action comes first after the slugline. Not dialogue. Not setting. Not a history lesson—just brief and interesting action:

> Mary sinks her teeth into a cockroach.

Don't get tangled up in exactly how Mary's lips wrinkle or how the roach squirms.

9. Forget about dialogue

Contrary to popular myth, a screenplay is not about the dialogue. Listen to a short sound byte from a film played on the radio, and you hear mostly silence punctuated by heavy breathing, some shuffling and a few words you can't quite make out. That's how a movie is supposed to sound. It's a visual medium. If the audience can't see it, you don't need it. A screenplay is about the subtext that happens between the words:

> JACK
>
> You, uh . . .

They kiss.

> JACK
>
> . . . want a drink?

Cut each speech to no more than three BEATS (one beat equals one idea/sentence):

Contacting Agents

MARY

I know where you are trying to take this.
I'm not your party girl—nor Lance's.

10. Forget about font, margins and tabs

The formatting rules for scripts would send anybody into anaphylactic shock:

- 12-point Courier font only.
- Plain, white, 20 lb. paper.
- Action lines begin at the left margin, 15 spaces (1.5 inches) from the edge.
- Right margin is ragged at half an inch.
- Character cues begin at 37 spaces (3.1 inches).
- Dialogue begins at 25 spaces (2.5 inches).
- Wrylies are not recommended, but if you feel suicidal, they begin at 31 spaces (3.1 inches).
- Use full caps for scene headings, character cues and dubbed sounds.

Want to hear another 300 pages of this? Read *The Screenwriter's Bible*, by David Trottier. Fortunately, you don't need to reach for the Excedrin just yet. A little over a hundred bucks buys you peace of mind in the form of a computer program that does everything for you except sit in the chair and type. Choose among Movie Magic Screenwriter, Final Draft, Hollywood Screenplay, Scriptware and Sophocles Screenwriting Software. Each program offers free trial downloads, too. You write. It formats. Bliss.

Blow that soap bubble, but deliver it in a form Hollywood can love you for—a good-looking script in professional format. No need to stress about it.

Things to Remember

1. Buy two pieces of 80 lb. card stock in some innocuous color for the covers, and don't write anything on them. Save outrageous for Saturday night.

2. Put three 1¼ inch all-brass brads (Acco #5 fasteners only) into the three holes you are going to punch in the left side of the script. Use the expensive brads so the script doesn't fall apart. Bash them flat so they don't stab the agent you are trying to impress. One-inch Chicago screws are also acceptable.

3. Run spell check before you print the script. Nothing makes you look like an amateur more than a typo.

Making a Commitment

What to Do Before and After You Sign

O nce you've received an offer of representation, you must determine if the agent is right for you. As flattering as any offer may be, you need to be confident that you are going to work well with the agent and that she is going to work hard to sell your manuscript.

Evaluate the offer

You need to know what to expect once you enter into a business relationship. You should know how much editorial input to expect from your agent, how often she gives updates about where your manuscript has been and who has seen it, and what subsidiary rights the agent represents.

More importantly, you should know when you will be paid. The publisher will send your advance and any subsequent royalty checks directly to the agent. After deducting her commission—usually 10 to 15 percent—your agent will send you the remaining balance. Most agents charge a higher commission of 20 to 25 percent when using a co-agent for foreign, dramatic or other specialized rights. As you enter into a relationship with an agent, have her explain her specific commission rates and payment policy.

Some agents offer written contracts and some do not. If your prospective agent does not, at least ask for a "memorandum of understanding" that details the basic relationship of expenses and commissions. If your agent does offer a contract, be sure to read it carefully, and keep a copy for yourself. Since contracts can be confusing, you may want to have a lawyer or knowledgeable writer friend check it out before signing anything.

The National Writers Union (NWU) has drafted a Preferred Literary Agent Agreement and a pamphlet, *Understand the Author-Agent Relationship*, which is available to members. The union suggests clauses that delineate such issues as:

- the scope of representation (One work? One work with the right of refusal on the next? All work completed in the coming year? All work completed until the agreement is terminated?)
- the extension of authority to the agent to negotiate on behalf of the author
- compensation for the agent and any co-agent, if used
- manner and time frame for forwarding monies received by the agent on behalf of the client
- termination clause, allowing client to give about 30 days to terminate the agreement
- the effect of termination on concluded agreements as well as ongoing negotiations
- arbitration in the event of a dispute between agent and client.

What Should I Ask?

The following is a list of topics the Association of Authors' Representatives suggests authors discuss with literary agents who have offered to represent them. Please bear in mind that most agents are not going to be willing to spend time answering these questions unless they have already read your material and wish to represent you.

1. Are you a member of the Association of Authors' Representatives?

2. How long have you been in business as an agent?

3. Do you have specialists at your agency who handle movie and television rights? Foreign rights?

4. Do you have subagents or corresponding agents in Hollywood and overseas?

5. Who in your agency will actually be handling my work? Will the other staff members be familiar with my work and the status of my business at your agency?

6. Will you oversee or at least keep me apprised of the work that your agency is doing on my behalf?

7. Do you issue an agent/author agreement? May I review the language of the agency clause that appears in contracts you negotiate for your clients?

8. How do you keep your clients informed of your activities on their behalf?

9. Do you consult with your clients on any and all offers?

10. What are your commission rates? What are your procedures and time frames for processing and disbursing client funds? Do you keep different bank accounts separating author funds from agency revenue? What are your policies about charging clients for expenses incurred by your agency?

11. When you issue 1099 tax forms at the end of each year, do you also furnish clients—upon request—with a detailed account of their financial activity, such as gross income, commissions and other deductions and net income for the past year?

12. In the event of your death or disability, what provisions exist for my continued representation?

13. If we should part company, what is your policy about handling any unsold subsidiary rights to my work?

Reprinted with the permission of the Association of Authors' Representatives (www.aar-online.org).

Sealing the Deal

If you have any concerns about the agency's practices, ask the agent about them before you sign. Once an agent is interested in representing you, she should be willing to address any questions or concerns that you have. If the agent is rude or unresponsive, or tries to tell you that the information is confidential or classified, the agent is uncommunicative at best and, at worst, is already trying to hide something from you.

The waiting game

Once you've signed and dated the contract, you can take a deep breath and get back to what you really want to do: writing that next book. Let your agent do her job while you continue to do yours. Periodically, though, you should ask your agent for a full report of where your manuscript has been sent, including the names of publishing houses and editors. Then, contact a few of the editors/publishers on the list to see if they know your agent and have a strong working relationship with her.

If the agent has ever successfully sold anything to the editor before (or at least sent the editor some promising work), an editor should remember her name. It's a small world in publishing, and news of an agent's reputation spreads very fast. You should trust your agent, but it's ultimately your responsibility to make sure she's following through on her end of the agreement.

Keep in mind there is no limit on how long it should take an agent to sell a book; sometimes it's 10 days and sometimes it's a year and a half. Be patient, but also have an idea of how many submissions are going out and how many responses are coming in. Agents should return their clients' phone calls or e-mails quickly and keep them informed about prospects. An agent should also consult her clients about any offers before accepting or rejecting them.

If things don't work out

Since this is a business relationship, a time may come when it is beneficial for you and your agent to part ways. Unlike a marriage, you don't need to go through counseling to keep the relationship together. Instead, you end it professionally on terms upon which you both agree.

First, check to see if your written agreement spells out any specific procedures. If not, write a brief, businesslike letter, stating that you no longer think the relationship is advantageous and you wish to terminate it. Instruct the agent not to make any new submissions and give her a 30- to 60-day limit to continue as representative on submissions already under consideration. You can ask for a list of all publishers who have rejected your unsold work, as well as a list of those who are currently considering it.

If your agent charges for office expenses, you will have to reimburse her upon terminating the contract. For this reason, you may want to ask for a cap on expenses when you initially enter into an agency agreement. If your agent has made sales for you, she will continue to receive those monies from the publisher, deduct her commission and remit the balance to you. A statement and your share of the money should be sent to you within 30 days. You can also ask that all manuscripts in your agent's possession be returned to you.

If you've been scammed

If you have trouble with your agent and you've already tried to resolve it to no avail, it may be time to call for help. Please alert the writing community to protect others. If you find agents online, in directories or in this book that aren't living up to their promises or are charging you money when they're listed as nonfee-charging agents, please let the Web master or editor of the publication know. Sometimes they can intervene for an author, and if no solution can be found, they can at the very least remove a listing from their directory so that no other authors will be scammed in the future. All efforts are made to keep scam artists out, but in a world where agencies are frequently bought and sold, a reputation can change overnight.

If you have complaints about any business, consider contacting The Federal Trade Commission, The Council of Better Business Bureaus or your state's attorney general. (For full details, see Reporting a Complaint below). Legal action may seem like a drastic step, but sometimes people do it. You can file a suit with the attorney general and try to find other writers who want to sue for fraud with you. The Science Fiction & Fantasy Writers of America's Web site offers sound advice on recourse you can take in these situations. For more details, visit www.sfwa.org/beware/overview.html.

If you live in the same state as your agent, it may be possible to settle the case in small claims court. This is a viable option for collecting smaller damages and a way to avoid lawyer fees. The jurisdiction of the small claims court includes cases in which the claim is $5,000 or less. (This varies from state to state, but should still cover the amount for which you're suing.) Keep in mind that suing takes a lot of effort and time. You'll have to research all the necessary legal steps. If you have lawyers in the family, that could be a huge benefit if they agree to help you organize the case, but legal assistance is not necessary.

Above all, if you've been scammed, don't waste time blaming yourself. It's not your fault if someone lies to you. Respect in the literary world is built on reputation, and word gets around about agents who scam, cheat, lie and steal. Editors ignore their submissions and writers avoid them. Without clients or buyers, a swindling agent will find her business collapsing.

Meanwhile, you'll keep writing and believing in yourself. One day, you'll see your work in print, and you'll tell everyone what a rough road it was to get there, but how you wouldn't trade it for anything in the world.

Reporting a Complaint

If you feel you've been cheated or misrepresented, or you're trying to prevent a scam, the following resources should be of help.

- The Federal Trade Commission, Bureau of Consumer Protection (CRC-240, Washington DC 20580). While the FTC won't resolve individual consumer problems, it does depend on your complaints to help them investigate fraud, and your speaking up may even lead to law enforcement action. Contact the FTC by mail, call (877)382-4357 or visit www.ftc.gov.

- Volunteer Lawyers for the Arts (1 E. 53rd St., 6th Floor, New York NY 10022) is a group of volunteers from the legal profession who assist with questions of law pertaining to the arts. You can phone the group's hotline at (212)319-2787, ext. 1, and have your questions answered for the price of the call. For more information, visit www.vlany.org.

- The Council of Better Business Bureaus (4200 Wilson Blvd., Suite 800, Arlington VA 22203-1838) is the organization to contact if you have a complaint or if you want to investigate a publisher, literary agent or other business related to writing and writers. Contact your local BBB or visit www.bbb.org.

- Your state's attorney general. Don't know your attorney general's name? Go to www.attorneygeneral.gov. This site provides a wealth of contact information, including a complete list of links to each state's attorney general Web site.

Know Your Rights

Breaking Down Industry Lingo

Most writers who want to be published envision their book in storefronts and on their friends' coffee tables. They imagine book signings and maybe even an interview on "Oprah." Usually the dream ends there; after all, having a book published seems exciting enough. In actuality, a whole world of opportunities exists for published writers beyond seeing their books in print. These opportunities are called subsidiary rights.

Subsidiary rights, or subrights, are the additional ways that a book can be presented. Any time a book is made into a movie or excerpted in a magazine, a subsidiary right has been sold. If these additional rights to your book are properly exploited, you'll not only see your book in a variety of forms, but you'll also make a lot more money than is possible on book sales alone.

Unfortunately, the terminology of subsidiary rights can be confusing. Phrases such as secondary rights, traditional splits or advance against royalty could perplex any writer. And the thought of negotiating the terms of these rights with a publisher can be daunting.

Although there are many advantages to working with agents, the ability to negotiate subrights is one of their best qualities. If the agent knows a house can make money with a right, she will grant that right to the publisher when the contract is negotiated. Otherwise, the agent will keep, or retain, certain rights for her clients, which she will try to exploit by selling them to her own connections.

If you want to work with an agent, there are two reasons why you should have a basic understanding of subrights. First, you'll want to be able to intelligently discuss these rights with your agent. (Although, you should feel comfortable asking your agent any question you have about subrights.) Second, different agents have more expertise in some subright areas than others. If you think your book would make a great movie, you should research the agents who have strong film connections. A knowledge of subrights can help you find the agent best suited to help you achieve your dreams.

An agent negotiates subrights with the publishing house at the same time a book is sold. In fact, the sale of certain subrights can even determine how much money the publisher offers for the book. But the author doesn't get paid immediately for these rights. Instead, the author is paid an advance against royalties. An advance is a loan to the author that is paid back when the book starts earning money. Once the advance is paid, the author starts earning royalties, which are a predetermined percentage of the book's profit.

The agent always keeps certain rights, the publisher always buys certain rights and the others are negotiated. When an agent keeps a right, she is then free to sell it at will. If the agent does sell it, the money she receives from the purchasing company goes immediately to the author, minus the agent's commission. Usually the companies who purchase rights pay royalties instead of a one-time payment.

If the publisher keeps the right, any money that is made from it goes toward paying off the advance. Because the publisher kept the right, they will keep part of the money it makes. For most rights, half the money goes to the publisher and half goes to the writer, although for some rights the percentages are different. This separation of payment is called a traditional split because it has become standard over the years. And, of course, the agent takes her commission from the author's half.

Most agents have dealt with certain publishers so many times that they have preset, or boilerplate, contracts. This means they've already agreed to the terms of certain rights, leaving only a few rights to negotiate. The following describes the main subrights and discusses what factors an agent takes into account when deciding whether or not to keep a right. As you read through this piece, carefully consider the many opportunities for your book, and encourage your agent and publisher to exploit these rights every chance they get.

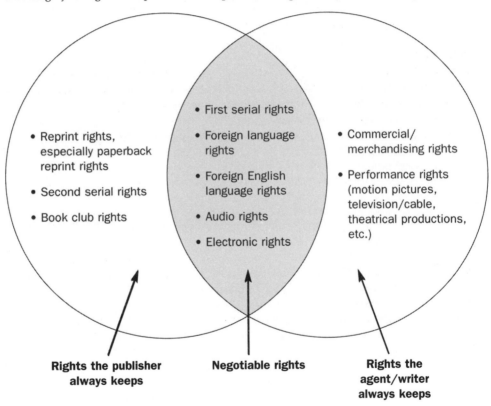

- Reprint rights, especially paperback reprint rights
- Second serial rights
- Book club rights

- First serial rights
- Foreign language rights
- Foreign English language rights
- Audio rights
- Electronic rights

- Commercial/ merchandising rights
- Performance rights (motion pictures, television/cable, theatrical productions, etc.)

Rights the publisher always keeps   **Negotiable rights**   **Rights the agent/writer always keeps**

RIGHTS THE PUBLISHER ALWAYS KEEPS

The following subrights are always kept by the publisher and are often called nonnegotiable rights. Money earned from these rights is split between the publisher and the author, and the author's share goes toward paying back the advance. Selling these rights helps repay the advance faster, which hopefully means the writer will receive royalty checks sooner.

Reprint rights

In publishing, a reprint right refers to the paperback edition of the book. When a hardcover book is reprinted in paperback, the reprint right has been used. According to Donald Maass of the Donald Maass Literary Agency, "In deals with major trade publishers, it's a long-standing practice to grant them control of reprint rights. However, in some cases—a small-press deal, for instance—we withhold these rights.'' Traditionally, if a hardcover book sold really well, paperback houses bought the rights to reprint the book in a more affordable version. Any money earned from the paperback was then split 50/50 between the publisher and writer. Paperback houses often paid substantial amounts of money for these reprint rights.

But the recent consolidation of publishing houses has changed the value of reprint rights. ''In the old days, most books were hardcover, and paperbacks were cheap versions of the book,'' explains Maass. ''Today, so many paperback publishers have either merged with a hardcover publisher or begun their own hardcover publisher that the business of selling reprint rights has diminished.'' Now, many publishers make what is called a hard/soft deal, meaning the house will first print the book in hardcover and, if the book sells well, it will then reprint the book in paperback. This type of deal can still benefit writers because they no longer have to split the money earned from reprint with the publisher. Instead, they earn royalties from both the hardcover and paperback versions.

Book club rights

These days, it seems that a book club exists for every possible interest. There are the traditional book clubs, like Book-of-the-Month and its paperback counterpart, the Quality Paperback Book Club. But there are also mystery book clubs, New Age book clubs, book clubs for writers and artists and even online book clubs. Most book clubs are very selective, and you should be flattered if your book is chosen. Like reprint rights, any money made from book club rights is split 50/50 between the publisher and the writer. If an agent believes a book will appeal to a certain book club's audience, she will target the manuscript to publishers who have a good relationship with—or who own—that book club.

Serial rights

A serial is an excerpt of the book that appears in a magazine or in another book. To have your book serialized is wonderful because excerpts make additional money for you and provide great publicity for your book. There are actually two types of serial rights: first serial and second serial. First serial means the excerpt of the book is available before the book is printed. A second serial is an excerpt that appears after the book is in bookstores. First serial rights are actually negotiable; sometimes the right to use them is kept by the agent. Usually an agent's decision is based upon her knowledge of the publications available in the book's subject. If she doesn't know the various magazines, she will let the publisher have this right. Second serial rights, however, are almost always granted to the publisher.

Nonfiction books are more commonly excerpted than fiction. Nonfiction usually stands alone well, and magazines are eager to use these excerpts because they usually cost less than hiring a freelancer to write original material. While rare, serialized fiction still pops up every now and then. For example, a portion of Haruki Murakami's *Kafka on the Shore* (Knopf 2005) appeared in the Winter 2005 edition of *The Paris Review*.

NEGOTIABLE RIGHTS

The owner of these subrights is always determined when the book is sold. Often an agent and editor must compromise for these rights. In other words, an agent may agree to sell foreign rights if she can keep electronic rights. Or, an editor will offer more money if he can obtain the audio rights to a book.

Foreign language rights

If your book might appeal to audiences in countries where English isn't spoken, then you'll want an agent who has good connections with foreign co-agents. According to James Vines of The Vines Agency, Inc., foreign co-agents work on behalf of U.S. agencies and approach foreign publishers with manuscripts and proposals. They typically have appointments booked at big trade shows like Frankfurt Book Fair, London Book Fair and BookExpo America, where a lot of foreign deals happen. Usually an agent charges a 20 percent commission when a foreign co-agent is used, and the two split the earnings.

"All of my clients have benefited from the sale of foreign rights," continues Vines. For example, *Kokology* (Fireside 2003), by Tadahiko Nagao and Isamu Saito, started as a big phenomenon in Japan, selling more than 4 million copies. A game you play about psychology, it's one of those ideas that crosses all languages and cultural boundaries because it's uniquely human. We all want to know more about ourselves." Vines sold the book to Simon & Schuster, and then worked with a co-agent to sell it all over the world.

When agents are considering how a book will do abroad, they must be aware of trends in other countries. "Most agents try to stay on top of the foreign markets as much as possible and listen to what foreign co-agents have to say," says Vines. He also points out that writers can benefit from different subrights over a period of time depending on how well a subright is selling.

Many publishing houses have foreign counterparts, and often an agent will grant the publisher these rights if she knows the book can be printed by one of these foreign houses. If the publisher has foreign language rights, the author receives an average of 75 percent of any money made when the book is sold to a foreign publisher.

British rights

Like foreign language rights, the owner of a book's British rights can sell the book to publishers in England. Australia was once included in these rights, but Australian publishers are becoming more independent. If an agent keeps these rights, she will use a co-agent in England and the two will likely split a 20 percent commission. If a publisher has these rights, the traditional split is 80/20, with the author receiving the larger share.

Electronic rights

Several years ago, Stephen King caused a big commotion in the publishing world first by using an electronic publisher for his book, *Riding the Bullet*, and then by self-publishing his serialized novel, *The Plant*. Many publishing professionals worried that King would start a trend drawing writers away from publishers, while others claimed only high-profile writers could ever compete successfully with the vast amount of information on the Web. Regardless, King's achievement showed that readers are paying attention to the Internet.

Basically, electronic rights refer to the hand-held electronic, Internet and print-on-demand versions of a book. This right is currently one of the hottest points of contention between agents and publishers because the potential for these rights is unknown—it is quite possible that electronic versions of a book will make a lot of money one day.

This area of publishing is changing so rapidly that both agents and editors struggle with how to handle electronic rights. Many publishers believe any version of a book is the same material as the printed book, and, therefore, they should own the rights. Agents worry, however, that if the publisher lets the book go out of print, the rights to the book will never be returned to the author.

Audio rights

Before people feared that the Internet would cause the end of traditional book publishing, people worried about audio versions of books. In actuality, audio books have complemented their printed counterparts and have proved to be a fantastic source of additional income for the person who owns the rights to produce the book in audio form—whether through cassette tape, compact disc or uploading onto an iPod.

Many publishers own audio imprints and even audio book clubs, and if they are successful with these ventures, an agent will likely grant the audio rights to the publisher. The traditional split is 50/50. Otherwise, the agent will try to save this right and sell it to a company that can turn it into a profit.

RIGHTS THE AGENT/WRITER ALWAYS KEEPS

When a book is sold, an agent always reserves two rights for her authors: performance and merchandising. Some books are naturally more conducive to being made into films or products, and when they do, there is usually a lot of money to be made. A smart agent can quickly identify when a book will be successful in these areas.

Performance rights

Many writers fantasize about seeing their book on the big screen. And a lot of times, agents share this dream—especially for best-selling titles. If your agent feels your book will work well as a movie, or even as a television show or video game, she will sell these rights to someone in the entertainment industry. This industry works fairly differently than the publishing industry. Usually a producer options the right to make your book into a movie. An option means the producer can only make the movie during a specific amount of time, such as one year. If the movie isn't made during that time period, the rights revert back to the writer. You can actually option these rights over and over—making money for every option—without the book ever being made into a movie.

As with foreign rights, agents usually work with another agent to sell performance rights. Usually these agents live in Los Angeles and have the connections to producers that agents outside California just don't have. Agents normally take a 20 percent commission from any money made from performance rights. That 20 percent will be split if two agents partnered to sell the rights.

Merchandising rights

Merchandising rights create products—calendars, cards, action figures, stickers, dolls—that are based on characters or other elements of your book. Few books transfer well into such products, but they can be successful when they do. If a producer options the performance rights to your book, the merchandising rights are usually included in the deal.

For example, agent Steven Malk of Writers House made wonderful use of these two rights for his client Elise Primavera and her book, *Auntie Claus* (Silver Whistle/Harcourt 1999). According to Malk, "When I first read the manuscript of *Auntie Claus* and saw a couple of Primavera's sample illustrations, I immediately knew the book had a lot of possibilities in the subrights realm. First of all, the character of *Auntie Claus* is extremely memorable and unique, and from a visual standpoint, she's stunning. Also, the basic concept of the book is completely fresh and original, which is very hard to accomplish with a Christmas book.

"The first thing I did was to approach Saks Fifth Avenue with the idea of featuring *Auntie Claus* in their Christmas windows. In addition to using the book as the theme for their window displays, they created some merchandise that was sold through Saks. It's a perfect project for them; the character of Auntie Claus is so sophisticated and refined, and it seemed ideal for their windows."

Like Malk did for Primavera, many agents successfully exploit subsidiary rights every day. If you want the most for your book, look for an agent who has the know-how and connections to achieve your publishing potential.

Improve Your Book Contract

Nine Negotiating Tips

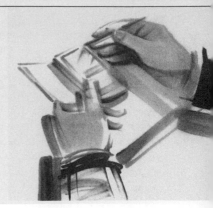

by The Authors Guild

Even if you're working with an agent, it's crucial to understand the legal provisions associated with book contracts. After all, you're the one ultimately responsible for signing off on the terms set forth by the deal. Below are nine clauses found in typical book contracts. Reading the explanation of each clause, along with the negotiating tips, will help clarify what you are agreeing to as the book's author.

1. Grant of Rights

The Grant of Rights clause transfers ownership rights in, and therefore control over, certain parts of the work from the author to the publisher. Although it's necessary and appropriate to grant some exclusive rights (e.g., the right to print, publish and sell print-book editions), don't assign or transfer your copyright and use discretion when granting rights in languages other than English and territories other than the United States, its territories and Canada. Also, limit the publication formats granted to those that your publisher is capable of exploiting adequately.

- Never transfer or assign your copyright or ''all rights'' in the work to your publisher.
- Limit the languages, territories and formats in which your publisher is granted rights.

2. Subsidiary Rights

Subsidiary rights are uses that your publisher may make of your manuscript other than issuing its own hardcover or paperback print book editions. Print-related subsidiary rights include book club and paperback reprint editions, publication of selections, condensations or abridgments in anthologies and textbooks and first and second serial rights (i.e., publication in newspapers or magazines either before or after publication of the hardcover book). Subsidiary rights not related to print include motion picture, television, stage, audio, animation, merchandising and electronic rights.

Subsidiary rights may be directly exploited by your publisher or licensed to third parties. Your publisher will share licensing fees with you in proportion to the ratios set forth in your contract. You should receive at least 50 percent of the licensing proceeds.

- Consider reserving rights outside the traditional grant of primary print book publishing rights, especially if you have an agent.

- Beware of any overly inclusive language, such as "in any format now known or hereafter developed," used to describe the scope of the subsidiary rights granted.
- Make sure you are fairly compensated for any subsidiary rights granted. Reputable publishers will pay you at least 50 percent of the proceeds earned from licensing certain categories of rights, much higher for others.

3. Delivery and Acceptance

Most contracts stipulate that the publisher is only obligated to accept, pay for and publish a manuscript that is "satisfactory to the publisher in form and content." It may be difficult to negotiate a more favorable, objective provision, but you should try. Otherwise, the decision as to whether your manuscript is satisfactory, and therefore publishable, will be left to the subjective discretion of your publisher.

- If you cannot do better, indicate that an acceptable manuscript is one which your publisher deems editorially satisfactory.
- Obligate your publisher to assist you in editing a second corrected draft before ultimately rejecting your manuscript.
- Negotiate a nonrefundable advance or insert a clause that would allow you to repay the advance on a rejected book from re-sale proceeds paid by a second publisher.

4. Publication

Including a publication deadline in your contract will obligate your publisher to actually publish your book in a timely fashion. Be sure that the amount of time between the delivery of the manuscript and the publication of the book isn't longer than industry standard.

- Make sure you're entitled to terminate the contract, regain all rights granted and keep the advance if your publisher fails to publish on or before the deadline.
- Carefully limit the conditions under which your publisher is allowed to delay publication.

5. Copyright

Current copyright law doesn't require authors to formally register their copyright in order to secure copyright protection. Copyright automatically arises in written works created in or after 1978. However, registration with the Copyright Office is a prerequisite to infringement lawsuits and important benefits accrue when a work is registered within three months of initial publication.

- Require your publisher to register your book's copyright within three months of initial publication.
- As previously discussed in Grant of Rights, don't allow your publisher to register copyright in its own name.

6. Advance

An advance against royalties is money that your publisher will pay you prior to publication and subsequently deduct from your share of royalty earnings. Most publishers will pay, but might not initially offer, an advance based on a formula which projects the first year's income.

- Bargain for as large an advance as possible. A larger advance gives your publisher greater incentive to publicize and promote your work.
- Research past advances paid by your publisher in industry publications such as *Publishers Weekly*.

Sealing the Deal

7. Royalties

You should earn royalties for sales of your book that are in line with industry standards. For example, many authors are paid 10 percent of the retail price of the book on the first 5,000 copies sold, 12.5 percent of the retail price on the next 5,000 copies sold, and 15 percent of the retail price on all copies sold thereafter.

- Base your royalties on the suggested retail list price of the book, not on net sales income earned by your publisher. Net-based royalties are lower than list-based royalties of the same percentage, and they allow your publisher room to offer special deals or write off bad debt without paying you money on the books sold.
- Limit your publisher's ability to sell copies of your book at deep discounts—quantity discount sales of more than 50 percent—or as remainders.
- Limit your publisher's ability to reduce the percentage of royalties paid for export, book club, mail order and other special sales.

8. Accounting and Payments

Your accounting clause should establish the frequency with which you should expect to receive statements accounting for your royalty earnings and subsidiary rights licensing proceeds. If you are owed money in any given accounting period, the statement should be accompanied by a check.

- Insist on at least a bi-annual accounting.
- Limit your publisher's ability to withhold a reserve against returns of your book from earnings that are otherwise owed to you.
- Include an audit clause in your contract which gives you or your representative the right to examine the sales records kept by the publisher in connection with your work.

9. Out of Print

Your publisher should only have the exclusive rights to your work while it is actively marketing and selling your book (i.e., while your book is "in print"). An out-of-print clause will allow you to terminate the contract and regain all rights granted to your publisher after the book stops earning money.

It is crucial to actually define the print status of your book in the contract. Stipulate that your work is in print only when copies are available for sale in the United States in an English language hardcover or paperback edition issued by the publisher and listed in its catalog. Otherwise, your book should be considered out of print and all rights should revert to you.

- Don't allow the existence of electronic and print-on-demand editions to render your book in print. Alternatively, establish a floor above which a certain amount of royalties must be earned or copies must be sold during each accounting period for your book to be considered in print. Once sales or earnings fall below this floor, your book should be deemed out of print and rights should revert to you.
- Stipulate that as soon as your book is out of print, all rights will automatically revert to you regardless of whether or not your book has earned out the advance.

Joseph Regal

An Agent in Search of Voice

by Joanna Masterson

J oseph Regal's first dream was to be a painter. That artistic passion later translated into playing classical piano at Juilliard, and then studying poetry with Kenneth Koch at Columbia University. By the time he graduated, Regal was singing with a rock band. Realizing that it would be good to commit to something for more than a few years, he decided to stick with the band and see if they could make it in the music industry. Despite some success with an album and tour, Regal took on a day job as an assistant at the literary agency Russell & Volkening to help pay the rent. That's when Regal realized he loved, to put it in his words, "being a midwife more than a mother."

"Creating music was rewarding," he says, "but being part of so many people's creative endeavors as an agent was in a way more fun. A bad gig was a calamity; a rejection at my day job meant I'd just try submitting to someone else tomorrow. It worked for me, and I left music for the joys of being a professional dilettante."

Regal—who started his own New York-based literary agency in 2002—found his artistic past to be ideal training for his career as an agent. "I believe I have a certain empathy to the plight of the writer," he says. "I know what it's like to struggle with the blank page, with the pain of seeing a year's work dismissed in a paragraph in a review.

"I feel I can make a difference as an advocate for people I admire. That's profoundly satisfying. And even on bad days (and there are many), I still feel that I am doing something worthwhile with my life. I feel like a proud parent some of the time, an admiring acolyte other times, and all of the time grateful that I can make a living helping wonderful artists reach an audience."

Regal's agency reaches those audiences by selling about 25 books a year, several of which have made it to the best-seller list. But Regal cautions writers against paying too much attention to huge successes like *The Da Vinci Code* or *The Devil Wears Prada*, insisting writers have a better chance at success if they spend their time finding a great story to tell in a unique voice.

Your agency represents best-selling authors Audrey Niffenegger and Daniel Wallace, whose breakout novels, *The Time Traveler's Wife* and *Big Fish*, impressed both readers and reviewers. What is it about an unknown author's work that makes you want to take a chance on him/her?

The answer is simple: I love original new voices. Nothing is more exciting to me than picking something up and falling in love, finding that unanticipated jewel where everything works— story, characters and writing. Both of those books were unsolicited slush pile submissions,

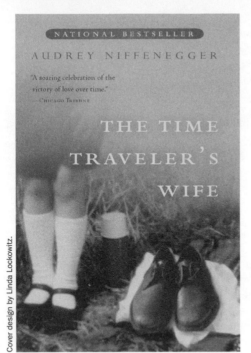

Cover design by Linda Lockowitz.

Author Audrey Niffenegger's ''voice'' in *The Time Traveler's Wife* (Harvest Books 2004) encouraged Joseph Regal to pluck her manuscript from the slush pile. It went on to be a *New York Times* bestseller.

and each had that special something right from the first pages. The writers were interested in telling emotionally affecting stories about people in familiar situations (losing a loved one, dealing with a difficult parent), but the voices were completely new and fresh. And aside from the crisp writing, the point of view—the way the authors came at creating these very real characters and getting the reader involved in their lives—was different from that of any other writer, but appropriate in each story.

Selling both [books] was a bit challenging. Most editors felt they wouldn't find audiences, since they weren't like other books. *Big Fish* was deemed too small, and *The Time Traveler's Wife* was greeted with some confusion (and derision) as science fiction. But each seemed special to me—a unique instant classic—and it was obvious both writers had thought hard about how to tell their stories. They had also each honed their prose to something absolutely distinctive; I could probably guess each writer's work from just one paragraph. It's more than just the writing and storytelling, though; both writers had worked through a very specific and personal way of seeing the world.

All of these things together create what's called ''voice,'' and if there's any single element that needs to be there for me as a reader, that's it. And obviously not every distinctive voice is going to work for every reader, agent or editor (including me), but it's that one essential thing that inspires the most passion.

For many authors, the idea of finding an agent can lead to overwhelming feelings of doubt—or even false hope. What steps do you recommend they take to get the ball rolling on a successful writing career?

There's no better step than writing a fantastic book. This is a trick very difficult to pull off, so try to enjoy the process as much as possible. It is entirely possible that you may never be published, and even if you're certain you will be, shouldn't you at least enjoy the ride? Just focus on writing the purest possible expression of the world as you know it. If something in it doesn't quite feel right, or if anything doesn't seem the best you can possibly make it, then go back to work. Keep working until you know in your gut and your heart that you have something unassailable—that you have created the best thing you possibly can. Often this takes many years, especially with first books. But it's sort of like working out: Once all that muscle is in place, it takes much less work to maintain it.

You encountered a slew of best-selling and award-winning authors while working as an assistant at Russell & Volkening: Anne Tyler, Annie Dillard, Howell Raines and Jim Lehrer to name a few. What was that like? How did they help shape the type of agent you are today?

If I hadn't been lucky enough for my first job to be working with those writers, I wouldn't be an agent today, period. I assisted at the agency just as a day job . . . but working with such talented writers, most of whom were wonderful people as well, I gradually found myself attracted to the idea of doing for others what I hoped someone would do for me as a musician.

I also learned the best possible lesson: Good writers can pay the bills. Most of those writers were literary writers with tiny audiences for the first decade of their careers. But each had a distinctive voice, a very personal worldview, and each honed their craft and improved book by book until they found their audience. It was enormously instructive for me to see that someone like Anne Tyler didn't start in that place; she grew into it, both artistically and commercially. She found her audience over time. That let me be confident that if I found a bunch of talented writers and nourished them, eventually enough of them would become commercially viable that my agency could survive. Of course it's always nice when it happens with the first book!

I think in some ways they also shaped the kind of agent I became in personality as well. They are all generally so grounded, respectful and professional that I came to expect that as part of the relationship. When the genius Eudora Welty takes the time to be considerate and sweet with you—a new young assistant—it leaves an indelible impression.

The Regal Literary Agency listing in this book states: "We are more like managers than agents." What do you mean by that?

The publishing world has changed drastically even in my brief 15 years in it. Agents weren't involved then in the same way they need to be today. They got a book from their writer, perhaps made some editorial suggestions, and submitted it. If they sold it, they negotiated a contract, and then they would engage various co-agents to handle ancillary rights such as film, foreign, serial, etc. While that is all still true, the stakes are higher, the margin for error smaller, and the time editors have to devote to a book harder to come by.

Agents have had to step into that gap, which has been to our benefit in many ways, but has also added a great deal of stress. One of the benefits is a closer relationship with the writer. We do much of the real editing, often working through several drafts, while the publisher usually only goes through it once. And when the author has a crisis, he/she calls us, not the editor.

In addition, the concept of a "house author" is largely superannuated, not only because the editor might be fired or move on, but also because the house itself could be bought and restructured. One ramification of this is blindness to the long-term progress of the author. It would be rare today for a publisher to stick by a literary author like Anne Tyler the way Knopf did for the 15 years it took her to reach more than 5,000 readers with a novel. Obviously Knopf is very happy they had faith in her work, but that lesson is largely lost on the big houses today.

The implication is that we agents had better be looking a decade down the line, because the house won't be—thus we end up making decisions about careers that are more like managing than agenting. It's far beyond selling a book. Some specific results of this are that we hired an in-house publicist to think about possibilities for our writers year-round, not only when a new book is coming out. We have also forged a special relationship with a speaking agency to get some of our writers out in front of college audiences and at other events in order to increase their visibility.

One of your best-selling authors—John Twelve Hawks—combines the fantasy and thriller genres in his book *The Traveler*. Since this is becoming common practice, how should writers narrow down potential agents if their work falls in a couple different markets?

I represent John precisely because his work falls between several stools. He approached me because of a book I sold called *Across the Nightingale Floor*, which was a mix of fantasy, history and literary fiction. He said I would understand that, despite appearances, he wasn't writing genre fiction. Indeed, I did understand, because to me his book wasn't fantasy at all. He describes the world in which we live, with recognizable events, people, places and technology.

I can say that mixing genres does create some problems. Most people want books that are easy to put in one box or another . . . until those hybrids succeed, at which point people are much more open to something like the next *Time Traveler's Wife*. Needless to say, there's a bit of irony here: Those same people weren't open to that book originally because it didn't fit in any category, and then when it's published, people flock to it precisely because it doesn't fit into the same mold as everything else. So it can be tough being original, but don't be afraid of that. Once you break through, the thing that made it difficult to break through becomes the thing that draws a faithful audience to your work.

Another of your agency's clients—Mitch Cullin—recently had his best seller *Tideland* adapted to the big screen. How often does this happen for authors and what is the process like?

We've had an extraordinary success rate with books to film, in part because we handle unusual writers, such as Alicia Erian and Gregory David Roberts, whose books *Towelhead* and *Shantaram* are being made into films. Their books don't typically fit in a prescribed category, which can make them very difficult to sell, but once they're in the world, they tend to attract more attention than many other books.

The process can be many things, but one thing it tends not to be is satisfying. Mitch Cullin has a great relationship with [filmmaker] Terry Gilliam and is happy with the film *Tideland*, but often, especially with bigger budget projects, the studio wants the author cut from the picture. They'd rather pretend there is no author since there are already so many competing voices in the mix. Some authors add to this problem by being unrealistic about how much of the book will actually show up on the screen, demonstrating an ignorance of the process that makes it easier for the producers to dismiss their ideas.

Even if the screenwriter and studio are good enough to recognize the primacy of the original creator of the story, it can be a bumpy ride. My general advice to authors is to take the money and buy a house or put it away for their kid's college fund and pretend it never happened. If there is eventually a film—a 1 in 40 chance at best—it is still possible that it won't please the author (or the author's fans), so it's just better to look at it as money, not any kind of artistic endeavor.

Many agents say they take their careers very personally because they are passionate about the books they represent, but at the same time have to take on the serious role of salesperson and negotiator. Authors often encounter this same dilemma: How do you balance the business side of publishing with the pleasure of creating/selling a book?

I am not sure it is ever completely possible to balance such divergent emotional and financial needs. There are days when you lose yourself in the creative process, but there are also days when all you can think about is whether there is an audience for what you are doing. As agents, we do need to think about whether there is that audience for something we care about, and we need to come up with strategies to reach that audience. But at the same time, it has to start in the same pure place it should start with the writer: simple pleasure in the thing itself, for no gain and no purpose other than pleasure. I've learned enough to know that a book has a chance to be big when I get completely lost in the reading of it. If it's a Saturday and I'm sitting at the kitchen table flipping pages three hours after I sat down, that's a good book.

Script Agent Secrets

The Inside Scoop From Film, TV and Stage Reps

by Joanna Masterson

I t's no secret—Hollywood is a tough place to make a name for yourself. The same can be said of New York City, where hundreds of struggling screenwriters and playwrights vie for the attention of what seems like a handful of agents and producers. So, what can launch your script to the top? The following four agents offer their professional opinions, along with some advice, on how to navigate the often intimidating worlds of television, theatre and film.

Jason Dravis is a partner at the Monteiro Rose Dravis Agency, where he has been an agent for the past six years. He specializes in family entertainment and is heavily involved in the animation industry.

Joyce Ketay opened her agency in 1978. The company has steadily gained a reputation for representing an eclectic mix of theatrical projects, including Michael Cristofer's *The Shadow Box* and Tony Kushner's *Angels in America*.

Paul S. Levine opened his literary agency in 1996, but has been representing authors as a lawyer since 1981. He has more than 100 clients and works with television scripts, movie scripts, nonfiction books and novels on a variety of subjects.

Wendi Niad started her career as a talent coordinator and writer at the Comedy Store. She was also assistant to motion picture literary agent Dave Wirtschafter, who is now president of the William Morris Agency. Preferring to work closely with clients in a less corporate environment, she opened her own management company in 1997.

What qualities in a script most grab your attention?

Dravis: I want an engaging script with well-rounded characters and a story that is unique. I have read many scripts that were well written, but with a story that we all have seen many times. A fresh voice is what grabs my attention the most, and it's one of the hardest things to capture.

Ketay: I need to hear the poetry of the language and feel the relevance of the subject.

Levine: You know it when you see it. I look for stuff in screenplays that I can sell, that are marketable and that are what the networks and cable channels are looking for.

Niad: I look for character development. There's nothing like opening a script and immediately being hooked into a character, getting invested in him/her and following what you hope to be a beautiful arc.

JOANNA MASTERSON is editor of *Guide to Literary Agents*. She can be reached via e-mail at literaryagent@fwpubs.com.

What personality traits or habits help writers break into the business?

Dravis: Talent is obviously the big trait that comes to mind, but I really like to see writers who simply love to write and who play with characters. It's about storytelling and having the talent to put the story on paper.

Jason Dravis

Ketay: Theatre is a different business than film or television. Personality traits are not that important. What does help, though, are connections. Assisting a well-established writer is a very good idea. If you are brand new to the business and haven't graduated NYU, Julliard or Yale, it could help to intern at a theatre, producing office or even at an agency. Be nice to all assistants—they are the directors, producers and artistic directors of the future and they have long memories.

Levine: Writers need to have a thick skin and not fall apart when somebody rejects them. They also need patience when waiting on production companies and networks to whom I've sent material. It takes them a long time to get back to me. Don't bug me. I'll call you as soon as I know something.

Niad: A writer who is successful in this business is, first and foremost, a writer—someone who writes and writes and rewrites and writes some more. If you've got the material and the ideas, then you also need to be someone who is outgoing, personable, eager to please and who has a thick skin and knows how to read people. You need to be able to give the executives what they want even when they themselves have no clue what they want—which is quite often! The executives need to know that you're fun and easy to work with and that you get it and can deliver the goods. They need to know you don't have any problem writing and rewriting and then being rewritten by someone else. Someone who is going to spend a development meeting arguing about why you disagree with the executive's notes is not going to be working with that executive for long.

What is the most nitpicky thing you care about when reviewing submissions?

Dravis: I would like to say paper stock, but really what drives me crazy is a script that simply has no direction.

Ketay: Blind submissions to an agent are useless. Inquiry letters are almost as useless. I have only asked for one play from a blind inquiry letter and that was because I was already fascinated by the subject matter. One play in 25 years—this is why connections are important. If someone I respect calls me and says you must read this play, I will read it.

Levine: I care that it's typo-free and grammatically correct. I hate finding errors that can't be corrected by spell check (e.g., *your* versus *you're*). People rely too much on spell check.

Niad: Granted everyone makes mistakes, but when I'm given a query letter that has obvious misspellings and grammatical errors, and spells my name wrong, why would I request a script from that person? More often than you'd like to hear about, we get scripts that have the name of a character that's been changed from a previous draft sprinkled throughout, confusing us as to who the "new" character is. It becomes tedious to read. You become so focused and angry about the lack of professionalism that it colors your reading.

How long should authors give agents to sell their script?

Dravis: Until the agent no longer believes in it. I have witnessed scripts sold in two days or eight years. It's always about finding the right filmmaker in which to entrust a story.

Ketay: Legend has it that it took Audrey Wood eight years to sell *Glass Menagerie*. My feeling is if your agent is working for you and is still convinced that you are the greatest thing since sliced bread, why change.

Levine: Sometimes I'm successful in the first round of submissions. Sometimes it takes three or four or more rounds before I'm successful, and I usually submit 10 at a time. We're talking 40 or 50 submissions before something happens.

Niad: I think it depends on how much your agent believes in it and what the script calls for. If it's not a high concept, easily saleable script, then it may need an attachment, such as a director or an actor, to get it sold. That could take years. You could also be a victim of bad timing—as all terrorist scripts were immediately following 9/11—and therefore may have to wait until a more appropriate time.

What is the most unique thing about the TV/film/theatre industry that scriptwriters should keep in mind while writing?

Dravis: In any situation, you always need to keep the audience in mind.

Levine: The thing about Hollywood is there are no rules, and if there are rules, they are made to be broken. This is very unlike the book business, which is much more traditional and structured.

Niad: Film is a visual medium. So much can be said without dialogue. New writers tend to overwrite. This tends to make the reader feel like the writer is being condescending and therefore the reader often becomes resentful of obvious and superfluous dialogue. Professional writers know how to trust their audience and their ability as writers to communicate emotions and realizations without dialogue.

What themes/genres are popular in the market right now? Will it remain that way for a while?

Ketay: You write what you need to write. It never works (except in television) to write something because you think it might be commercial.

Levine: Do not write to whatever the current trend is. By the time that screenplay is sold, that trend will have long passed and a new trend will have started up. Write what you know and write from your heart. For example, right now horror movies are pretty popular. By the time I sell the next horror script that trend will have moved on to something else. Right now it's impossible to sell a sci-fi script. Six months from now that certainly could change.

Paul S. Levine

Niad: Horror that can be made cheaply is popular, and quality thrillers and high-concept comedies will always be viable genres. You will always find trends depending on what is doing well at the box office. The mistake is attempting to chase the trends. The key is to try to be ahead of the curve.

Adaptations seem to be popping up all over the place. Talk a little about the pros and cons of writing and selling them versus original material.

Dravis: I have sold many books recently and the pros of this appear to be the built-in audience. The story has been taken for a test drive, and it's easier to buy a car once you've sat behind the wheel.

Ketay: Musical adaptations of films are very popular right now, as are musicals using rock group songs. If this is what you want to do, get the rights first.

Levine: Probably 60-70 percent of the movies you've seen in the past three or four Academy Award seasons are based on either books, graphic novels or comic books. My dream client can write both a good manuscript for a book and a good screenplay for the same project. If the client is not versatile enough to write both ways (book and screenplay), then the fallback is to write a screenplay based on a published or an about-to-be published book. Hollywood takes comfort in the fact that somebody else said yes first—mainly the publisher. I rarely sell an original spec screenplay anymore. I mostly sell adaptations.

Niad: First and foremost, I would never recommend writing an adaptation unless you have optioned the rights. If you have the rights to previously published material that has been successful, it will be easier to sell than unproven original material. However, it usually costs significant money for an individual to option the rights to something, and more likely than not, if it's proven material, someone within the industry has already optioned them. The major production companies and studios have people that track soon-to-be-published novels, as well as seek out other works such as plays and foreign films. Your best bet as an unproven writer might be to seek out an obscure piece of material that adapts well to today's market if you're set on writing adaptations. This will prove your ability as a writer to update material and literally adapt it to current times.

Wendi Niad

What's a common novice mistake?

Dravis: Only having one or two scripts. I want to see several things.

Niad: Not researching and learning the correct structure of a screenplay. Structure is a technical thing that anyone can learn if they have the inclination. Everyone who writes and submits screenplays believes he/she has the ability to write concept, characters and dialogue. I don't know whether it's because they think it's easy or that it doesn't matter, but less than 1 percent of the unsolicited material we receive is written with the proper format and structure of a movie. Every movie you see has the same structure—from *Memento* to *Mission: Impossible*. Certain things must happen by page 30, page 45, page 60, 75, 90, etc. You need to remember that a screenplay is a written movie with each page being one minute of screen time.

Getting the Word Out

Professional Advice From Publicists

by Joanna Masterson

I f there's one thing writers know, it's that their work is never finished. You write a book, find an agent, attract a publisher, make revisions, and all the while you've got a million other ideas swarming around in your head for the next book. Just as agents can relieve an author's workload by dealing with contracts and business meetings, hiring an independent publicist can take some of the weight of promoting your book off your shoulders. You'll still be part of the process (and success), but the detailed work will be left to a professional. Below, three experts explain what you can expect from the publicist/author relationship.

Alice B. Acheson has been an independent publicist since 1981. She provides marketing, publicity and subsidiary rights campaigns (national and/or local) for publishers and authors of fiction and nonfiction.

Rod Mitchell has been a freelance literary publicist for more than 20 years. His boutique agency and full-service company, Adventures in Media, Inc., is located in Houston, Texas, and represents both self-published and trade published authors of nonfiction books.

Sherri Rosen opened her New York agency in 1997. She works with eclectic clients whose writing focuses on self-help, sex, spirituality, personal inspiration, etc.

At what stage in the publishing process should an author contact a publicist? Is it ever too late?

Acheson: The earlier the better, so that marketing opportunities are not lost because of missed deadlines. However, the author should try to get the publishing house to commit to as much marketing as possible before contacting a freelance publicist. If the author and freelance publicist are solely responsible for the marketing, the publisher will have little vested interest. That said, six months prior to publication date would be a good benchmark. It is too late when the book is due next week.

Mitchell: We prefer to launch campaigns 30 days in advance of release so we can send out galleys to reviewers, morning network shows and syndicated radio shows. Is it ever too late? This depends on a number of factors: Was a professional publicist on the scene previously? How well did the book sell in the first six months? Does the book have longevity, regardless of how long it has been released? We typically do not represent books that are over one year old unless the author is an expert in a field that would allow us to pitch him/her to news and talk programs.

Rosen: The author needs to contact the publicist at least six months in advance, mainly

JOANNA MASTERSON is editor of *Guide to Literary Agents*. She can be reached via e-mail at literaryagent@fwpubs.com.

if the author is interested in having galleys sent out for book reviews to places that require the galleys three months before the publishing date of the book. Our philosophy is that it is never too late to contact a publicist to do publicity.

What personality traits and/or habits do you look for in potential clients?

Acheson: I look at how their philosophy, enthusiasm and personality compare with mine. Are they available to consult during my nine-to-five day and from a site where they can read and write notes? Do they work in a business-like manner? Are they willing to proceed according to a timeline, providing material in a timely fashion so that I don't have to burn the midnight oil to comply with a deadline? Are they willing to listen, learn and work together? They may not take my suggestion, but it should be a partnership (i.e., telling me why a suggestion is not appropriate, which might lead to another suggestion).

Photo by Tom Graves.

Alice B. Acheson

Mitchell: We migrate toward authors who have a friendly, positive and confident personality. We also like authors who are not afraid to express themselves with a commanding voice and presence. Talk and news shows prefer authors who have fascinating and thought-provoking points of views. We feign away from those who are arrogant or inflexible in their thought process.

Rosen: I look for someone who is easy to get along with and who is personable—in many cases an author who is a great self-promoter. This is a two-way street and both the author and I must work together to get the book out there.

What is the most critical thing an author should look for when hiring a publicist?

Acheson: Authors should look at the publicist's reputation and how long he/she has been in book publicity. Authors should also try to determine the publicist's dedication to their project. Will the book be handled routinely, or passed to someone in the firm with little experience? Contacts are not absolutely necessary, but the ability to find the appropriate contact is. For example, a publicist may never have worked on a bowling book and therefore has no contact with those magazines, but she should quickly be able to ferret out those who will make an impact.

Mitchell: Nothing beats experience, and a publicist with experience promoting books similar to the author's book is an added bonus. An author should want a publicist who has a well-rounded background in pitching print and electronic media all over the country (not just locally or regionally), with an expansive contact list of major market and syndicated radio and television stations. (Ask the publicist how many contacts are in his/her database.) A publicist should be willing to provide references of both authors they've represented and those in the media who are willing to vouch for the publicist.

Rosen: Authors need to look at a publicist's experience and see whom the publicist has worked with. Has the publicist worked on the particular genre in the past? What were the results? Does the author like the publicist? Does the author feel as though the publicist takes personal interest in the author and the book? Is the publicist respectful to the author? Is the publicist good at following up with contacts?

What do publicists do that authors can't do on their own?

Acheson: Authors can't talk to book review editors because they haven't built up trust of judgment or a working relationship over the years, and don't know the rules under which they operate. The same is generally true about interviewers. The media, in general, doesn't want to talk to authors for three basic reasons: It is very difficult to say no to someone who has labored for years on a project; most authors don't understand how to pitch their book; and many don't know when to say thank you and hang up. By nature, most are writers, not marketers.

Rosen: Publicists can see a much bigger picture and view of how to proceed because they are coming into the project fresh, open and perhaps with ideas of thinking outside of the box.

Does it matter where a publicist is located?

Acheson: Since I live on an island far west of Seattle, my answer is pretty obvious. If the publicist has experience and contacts, location is not an issue. On the other hand, if it is truly a regional book, or one that will at least begin regionally, then the first choice should be someone whose prime experience is that region. And, if the author lives on the East Coast and is unavailable after 5 p.m., it doesn't make sense to hire a publicist on the West Coast, no matter how qualified he/she is. It would limit constructive conversation to hours between noon and 5 p.m., with lunch interrupting that time.

Mitchell: I live in Houston, Texas, and I can count on one hand the number of authors I have personally met over the past 20 years. It doesn't matter where you live; what matters is experience and a long working history with media contacts that are located across the country.

Rosen: I have lived out of town and in New York City, and I feel it is best to live in New York City. I am living in the center of one of the biggest arenas of publishing, and I have the opportunity to connect with people in the publishing world, as well as radio and television producers. I am also able to meet my clients, and personal touch is a very powerful tool in book publishing.

Rod Mitchell

What are some things an author should expect a publicist to ask of them?

Acheson: One practical chore I always require of authors is filling out an extensive author questionnaire, which includes a request for a headshot. That form provides a wealth of marketing possibilities for future action.

Mitchell: Publicists should gather a biography (they should be able to assist in the writing of this bio), recent photographs and a copy of the book (for both reading and scanning for the press kit). They should also assist the author in preparing interview questions and talk points for interviews, and provide suggestions for appearances that are outside media (churches, schools, civic organizations, etc.).

Rosen: Publicists will often have the author contemplate on any contacts they may have and manifest a list. Authors may also have to stop by their local bookstores to introduce themselves.

What is the most important marketing tool these days?

Acheson: The Internet, and by that I mean e-mail and the ability to transfer information quickly, be it a promotion sheet, news that can be used to revitalize a pitch (e.g., inclusion on a best-seller list) or reiteration of something sent by mail and not received (saving the cost of sending a second book).

Mitchell: Bar none, the first and most important marketing tool is the Internet. Authors should ask the publicist if he can provide this service. Also, if the author is an expert on a

Perspectives

particular topic, or has a particularly newsworthy story or idea disclosed in the book, the publicist should pitch national news desks with the author as a news contributor. Nothing grabs the public's attention more then an author who has a breakthrough piece of information or comments that will enhance a timely news story.

Most authors hear about book tours, radio interviews and book reviews. What are some of the more creative marketing options out there?

Acheson: Naturally, the options are driven by the book. For a book I worked on named *Old Turtle*, we painted a Volkswagen Beetle to look like Old Turtle, transported it in a trailer across the country, painted the trailer appropriately so that it became a traveling billboard, and two employees spoke to children about the themes of the book. Along the way, we collected "a million messages of peace" from the children for delivery to the United Nations—which later became another book.

Mitchell: In some cases publicists will contract with other freelancers who specialize in providing book tours, like BookTours.com in Boston.

Rosen: Perhaps a creative way to market a book would be through branding—connecting the author and/or the book with a particular store or product that is well known. Or, running a contest on the author's Web site, depending upon the type of book, and at the same time getting press on the contest.

Sherri Rosen

What is the biggest misconception about publicists?

Acheson: That we are wealthy. Authors think publicists' fees are expensive, but they do not realize how labor intensive the work is. Every day we spend hours updating our databases so that our contacts' information is current. A book sent to the wrong person becomes a holiday gift from someone in the mailroom. Publicity, versus advertising, is free. Publicists are asking the media to donate time or space. When weighed against those costs, publicity is not expensive.

Mitchell: Authors think they can pay for their publicists with the royalties they receive from a publisher or distributor. Even if the author is self-published, the dollars they will see back are long in coming. Also, first-time authors have no idea how much a publicist charges—retainer fees run from $1,000-10,000 per month. Some publicists also charge on a per-venue basis, which means they only pay for the actual bookings (interviews and appearances) that the publicist delivers. This is often misleading, and the ultimate price an author will pay, especially if the publicist is well connected, could be $5,000-$10,000 per month. Most authors cannot afford services that run this high.

Rosen: That they take no for an answer. If one pitch doesn't work, then we try other ways to get the author in the door.

Perspectives

Dealing With Denial

Learning From Rejection Letters

by Barbara DeMarco-Barrett

Rejection is a fact of life for all writers. Yet, you hear this so much that you may begin to develop a laissez-faire attitude about it. "Yeah, yeah, I can handle rejection," you say—at least until those rejection letters start pouring in. That's when the self-doubts and recriminations start stacking up, when you contemplate an avocation that's more enjoyable and less ego-harming than trying to get published.

Believe me, I know. I went through three agents, more than two dozen rejections and a ton of revision before my first book was published. It was eight years from when I began writing to when it sold. I watched my son transform from a chunky toddler to a lanky 10-year-old. And that wasn't even the first book I wrote. I have two unpublished novels and one book proposal buried beneath the Christmas decorations in the garage that I can promise you will never see the light of day.

"But don't you feel like all that work was a big waste of time?" my students ask, fearful that they may encounter the same obstacles I did.

"No," I tell them. "Those projects taught me how to write a novel and how to craft a book proposal and for that I am ever thankful."

Similarly, rejections can teach you what you need to do if you let them. Those early rejections of my book had messages embedded in them. "The writing bookshelf is a crowded shelf," I read over and over again. That led me to slant my book for busy people who want to write, which was something I hadn't seen done.

Finding an agent and getting your book published rarely happens right away. And rarely is the path smooth and straightforward. Usually it's rutted and serpentine, which is one reason you hear that patience, perseverance and a thick skin are three necessary qualities for writers. Not to mention the years of reading and writing before your craft is such that a publisher will pay you for your book. It's true: You have to write so many words before any of them stick.

But at a certain point, you feel certain that your work is good enough to garner an agent's attention. So you craft a query letter to the best of your ability, you send it to a list of 10 agents and you hold your breath, hoping for the best.

WELCOME TO THE WORLD OF REJECTION

It happens to the best writers. In Catherine Wald's *The Resilient Writer: Tales of Rejection and Triumph from 23 Top Authors*, author Chris Bohjalian talks about how he collected 250

BARBARA DEMARCO-BARRETT is author of *Pen on Fire: A Busy Woman's Guide to Igniting the Writer Within* (Harcourt 2004) and host of "Writers on Writing," which airs weekly and is archived at www.penonfire.com/writersonwriting.

rejection slips before he finally sold a short story. (A short story!) Many writers would never continue to write and submit after 25 rejections, but most writers who are successful today underwent a ton of rejection. It's part of the writing life.

You also need to realize that getting rejected doesn't mean your writing is bad or that you're untalented—only that it's not for that particular agent. A rejection could mean that there are already too many books on the subject, that the agent recently took on a similar project or that the agent simply has no personal interest in the subject matter. Or, maybe the agent is simply having a bad day.

Agents face rejection, too, and the best agents are persistent and believe in you. New York City literary agent John Ware, who represents Jon Krakauer (*Into Thin Air*), says, "I once sold a book after 17 rejections, on the 18th round, for $150,000."

TYPES OF REJECTION LETTERS

There are three basic types of rejection letters: the form rejection (the most demoralizing of all), the form with a note (hopeful) and a personalized letter (yay!). But what does each one mean?

Form rejection

Most of us are all too familiar with the form rejection letter. In it, the agent politely states the manuscript was not for her. The subtext here: "It's way off track for us," says literary agent Nancy Love, based in New York. "There are shades of meaning in the way proposals and manuscripts are rejected."

And yet, agents continually say, "Don't take it personally." As a writer, you want to respond, "Uh-huh, sure. Don't take it personally . . . right."

"The fact is, rejection hurts," says Julie Barer, president of Barer Literary in New York. "And it takes super human strength (or a lot of therapy) not to take it personally. You've been slaving over your novel or your nonfiction project for possibly years, putting all your spare time, creative energy and hopes and dreams into it. How can it not feel bad when someone says they're not interested? But the cold hard truth of the matter is that if you want to have a career as a writer, you're going to have to learn to deal with rejection, because it's an enormous part of the publishing process."

And it does help a little if you look at it from the agent's point of view.

"Writers need to understand that agents and editors are inundated with submissions, so if they took the time to personalize every rejection they make, then they would have less time to spend on clients that they do take on," says Matthew Carnicelli, president of Carnicelli Literary Management in New York City.

Hardly a soothing balm, but a true one.

Form rejection with a note

When you receive a form rejection with a note jotted somewhere on the page, the day suddenly seems sunnier, the air sweeter. There's hope! In fact, a note scribbled on the page is usually intended to give you hope.

"A note means 'this didn't work here, but don't give up hope,'" says Love.

Adds California literary agent Kimberly Cameron of Reece Halsey North: "We try to write a note when we feel the material was close. I suggest to all writers that when they receive a form rejection letter, they should just say, 'It wasn't the right fit. Next!' They must keep going in this business—perseverance pays off."

But for New York City agent Linda Konner, also an author, personal notes mean little. "Who cares? A rejection is a rejection in my book. I'm a Jerry McGuire kind of agent: If you like the book, show me the money. You can keep your kind words. Tough? Sure, but if you haven't developed a thick skin after a few years in the publishing business, you're going to suffer. Unfortunately, some of my clients do suffer, but I feel they usually bring needless suffering upon themselves."

Julie Castiglia, founder of the Castiglia Literary Agency in California, concurs: "In some cases, a form rejection without a note is not that much different from a personalized rejection. For whatever reason, it means it isn't right for us. There are so many reasons for a rejection. A lot of times agents are just too busy to answer personally. Plus, we've found if we do go into a few details about why it was rejected, the writer inevitably writes back and wants more."

Personalized rejection letter

This is the most palatable type of rejection. Agents are busy, so if you receive a personally-written letter, you can be sure to take it as a sign—a very good sign.

"Sometimes, if I'm interested in a project but have reservations, I'll write the author a letter explaining my concerns and invite them to resubmit, if they revise the manuscript," says Barer. "Don't take this kind of invitation lightly. Agents receive so much unsolicited mail, that if we take the time to reach out to you and give you encouragement or feedback, pay attention."

Of course there's also the best thing of all: the phone call or e-mail. Most, if not all, agents will call or e-mail you if they want to either see more of your work or represent you. Be assured: If you are getting a phone call, it's good news.

LOOK FOR CONSENSUS

The way in which your work is rejected can be informative. For instance, if you've received a dozen form letters with no notes whatsoever, you may want to take a close look at your project and what may be wrong with it. Jeff Kleinman of Folio Literary Management says work is generally rejected because the writing is not strong enough (especially for fiction), the writer's platform isn't large enough (especially for nonfiction) or the project's concept isn't big enough.

Barer agrees: "If a number of agents are all citing the same reason that they are passing on the project—no one likes the main character, the central plot just isn't believable or there are already too many books out there on this subject matter—then you should take this feedback into serious consideration."

Consensus speaks loudly and informs. Konner advises authors to either rethink and re-write, or move on. "Don't get bent out of shape," she says. "Just move ahead to the next project. Who knows, your agent might be able to sell that first book second."

WHEN AN AGENT SUGGESTS REVISION

What about when you receive a personal letter from an agent who suggests ways you might consider improving your work? Should you resubmit to that agent once you've revised?

"An author can always re-approach an agent if they've rewritten their material," says Castiglia. "To go back to an agent without any rewriting would be a mistake."

Konner agrees: "If the agent suggests you get back to her and offers ideas for revising the proposal, then by all means do so, and as quickly as possible. If she's not terribly encouraging to begin with, why would you re-approach her at all? There are some 300 literary agents in AAR (Association of Authors' Representatives) alone, with probably hundreds of others not in the group. It's best to go with someone who recognizes your greatness right off the bat! If one agent—no matter how much you might want her—doesn't share your vision for your book and your publishing career, there are plenty of others who will."

Be judicious in re-approaching agents, though. Make sure you've rewritten your work significantly before returning the material to them; otherwise, it will be a waste of your time and theirs.

Bonnie Nadell, vice president of Frederick Hill Bonnie Nadell in Los Angeles, says, "It depends on how they approach me again. If it is done in a good polite way, I often will read it again just to see if there are such large differences that it would sway me to take it on. But if I remember why it was not for me the first time or if they come back and want an immediate response, I do say it is time to try someone new."

TURN REJECTION INTO A POSITIVE

Remember that in writing, as in life, it's more about the journey than the destination. If you continue to write and learn your craft, the likelihood is that one day your work will see publication. It may not be on your timeline, but few things in the arts (and life) are.

"Don't give up on yourself, your efforts and your work," says Cameron. "My advice is to keep working on your craft, think positively and write from your heart. If you do that, there's a good chance you'll succeed in publishing."

Conference Etiquette

Agents Share Good and Bad Experiences

by Will Allison

Writers' conferences offer a rare opportunity for writers to meet literary agents and have all the makings of, well, a train wreck. Imagine eager authors buttonholing agents in bathrooms and elevators, or cutthroat agents backstabbing one another over cocktails as they angle to land promising authors. It's a dangerous intersection of ambition, art and commerce.

Fortunately, conferences usually provide a more genteel mingling of agents and prospective clients than one might imagine. For would-be authors, the key is to understand the agents' perspective. In the following roundtable, four seasoned agents share their success stories, bad experiences and advice regarding writers seeking representation at conferences.

Regina Brooks is founder and president of Serendipity Literary Agency LLC. She has participated in the Washington Independent Writers Conference, Writers Retreat Workshop, SEAK Medical & Legal Fiction Writing Conference and Society of Children's Book Writers & Illustrators (SCBWI) conferences.

Marlene Connor heads the Connor Literary Agency in Minneapolis, Minnesota. Over the years, she has attended the Kansas City Writers' Conference, Oklahoma Romance Writers' Conference, Detroit Black Writers' Conference and a number of others.

Mike Farris handles both fiction and nonfiction books at the Farris Literary Agency, Inc. Conferences he has attended include the Oklahoma Writers' Federation Conference, Rocky Mountain Fiction Writers Colorado Gold, Pikes Peak Writers Conference, Black Hills Writers Conference, Screenwriting Conference in Santa Fe, Women Writing the West, Ozark Writers League Conference, Bay Area Writers League Conference and Sleuthfest.

Dr. James Schiavone established his Florida literary agency in 1996. He regularly attends The Key West Literary Seminar and the South Florida Writer's Conference held in the Miami area, and recently attended the Million Dollar Writer's Program held for the first time in Atlanta.

What do you do at conferences?

Brooks: Doing workshops at a conference helps me get a better sense of the writers in attendance. The questions are much more pointed, and we can often get beyond the general questions (e.g., What do you want to see in a query?) and focus on the nitty-gritty stuff (e.g., Am I interested in their idea? How should their concept be shaped so that it will sell?). The

---

WILL ALLISON's (www.willallison.com) short stories have appeared in *Zoetrope: All Story*, *Glimmer Train*, *One Story*, *The Kenyon Review*, *Shenandoah*, *American Short Fiction*, *Atlanta* and other magazines.

writer and agent get the most out of a conference when the writers have sent materials beforehand. This gives the agent a chance to more fully review the materials prior to the one-on-ones.

Connor: I've spoken on panels, conducted workshops and met with authors. I've also attended conferences as an author.

Farris: We do anything they ask of us—we've been involved in one-on-one pitch meetings, panels, workshops and formal presentations. My wife [who is also an agent] was even auctioned off for a lunch with the winning writer.

Schiavone: I have been asked to conduct group sessions (a welcome challenge for a former academic) dealing with the essential elements of searching out and getting agency representation. I have also been asked to critique proposals and sample writings of several participants. Another valuable activity is the scheduling of one-on-one meetings with agents. This is about the only way an aspiring author can become involved in a personal way with a number of agents. I also enjoy discussions dealing with book contract negotiations, which writers should become involved in.

Talk about your best experience with a prospective client at a conference.

Connor: The one that sticks out the most is meeting a mystery writer. The meeting at the conference made it easier to work with this writer later on. At least we felt we knew one another—what we looked like—rather than it being just a voice over the phone.

Farris: A very unassuming gentlemen lingered outside in the hallway following a presentation. He took no more than a minute or so to politely introduce himself, briefly pitch his novel and ask if I'd take a look. He was very pleasant and his pitch was intriguing, so we asked for a submission. His novel was published in the spring of 2006, and we have received considerable film interest from Hollywood regarding both that novel and his next.

Schiavone: My best experience was running into an author with several publications. Although his publishers were all small presses, we were able to work together in getting a major publisher for his latest work within only a few months. While the author could have sent a query letter to me, which may well have led to representation, the face-to-face contact proved to be most fortunate.

. . . And your worst?

Brooks: Don't be a stalker! I know you've heard of the standoffish, intimidating-type agent, but that's not my style. I'm very approachable, and I try to make time for everyone who's interested in meeting with me. There was this one author who simply would not go away. She had presented her idea to me three times. She sat at my table to try to "soak in as much as she could," but she wouldn't leave and she wouldn't shut up. Every time I made a comment to another author, she'd chime in with something like, "So, should I try that same approach with my book?" She went on and on until I had to ask her to rotate to another table.

Regina Brooks

Photo by Marirosa M. Garcia.

Connor: My worst experience is not about a specific writer, but more about being exhausted—the travel, the hustle and bustle of luggage, being picked up at the airport, checking in, changing clothes, then jumping into the fray of a conference—it's often a bit much.

Farris: A writer was disappointed when we told him that we didn't handle the genre in which he wrote. For the next three days, every time I saw him, he buttonholed me to urge me to start handling that genre and to look at his novel. I found myself on the lookout for him so I could duck away, but he had remarkable radar. He just didn't seem to grasp the concept that we weren't interested in what he had to sell. At this point, even if he wrote in a genre we handled, I wouldn't want to represent him no matter how talented he might be because I think he'd be way too high maintenance.

How, when and where do you prefer to be approached by prospective clients at conferences?

Brooks: There's often time set aside for writers to meet with agents, such as one-on-ones or at evening cocktails where agents can mix it up over drinks. Writers can also catch me after a panel or presentation, unless I'm running to do another one. Writers should keep in mind that agents are pretty much "on" as soon as we reach the conference, so they shouldn't feel put off if an agent wants a few minutes to herself now and then to recuperate.

Connor: That's a tough call. I always try to tell writers that agents are just human beings with families, faults, hunger issues, etc. Some of us like to keep to the schedule, while others are chatty and informal. It's hit or miss.

Farris: We don't really care where we're approached—pitch meetings are fine, but so are encounters in the hallways or just about anywhere else (except the restrooms). That's why we go to conferences—to meet writers.

Schiavone: I'm very informal and will talk with participants who approach me during a break. My preference, however, is for scheduled meetings with individuals and/or small group meetings prearranged by the conference coordinators. Lunch and dinner are good times to sit and converse with participants. I always have a supply of business cards available to facilitate further contact after the conference is over.

Cover design by David Timmons.

Agent Mike Farris met author Mike Nichols in 2002 at a tiny writers' conference in Texas. He arranged a deal for Nichols' novel, *Balaam Gimble's Gumption*, to be published by John M. Hardy Publishing in Houston. The book went on to win the Texas Institute of Letters John Bloom Humor Award as the funniest Texas book of 2004.

What are some common faux pas writers make with agents at conferences?

Brooks: Sometimes writers get overly excited and make promises they can't keep. A common one I hear is "I'll get the manuscript out to you next week." This from an author who hasn't had the manuscript peer-reviewed, hasn't edited it and in some cases hasn't even finished writing it.

Connor: Wanting us to take material with us.

Farris: The most common faux pas is to assume that the agent wants to read their work. On more than one occasion, we've had writers tell us they were going to send us their manuscripts; not ask us, mind you—tell us. Another faux pas is for writers to argue with the agent when the agent declines to accept a submission. The argument is usually punctuated

Photo by Finley Stewart.

Mike Farris

by such statements as, "It's a surefire best seller," or "You'll be sorry if you don't; it's going to make some agent a lot of money."

Do you prefer to receive manuscripts at conferences, or have them sent to your office afterward?

Brooks: I absolutely hate having to take manuscripts back home with me. It's not that I'm not interested; it's a function of not having the strength to carry them all. Writers must keep in mind that many agents live in New York, and that involves cabs, trains and other forms of public transportation from the airport. It can be very cumbersome trying to carry manuscripts back to the office. I remember once telling an author I'd take her materials with me because I was eager to read them on my three-hour flight home. Unfortunately, other authors overheard me, and about five of them wanted me to do the same for them. I decided not to take any and have continued to practice that rule.

Connor: Sent to my office afterward.

Schiavone: My preference is for authors to send their materials to me at my office.

Dr. James Schiavone

What's your best advice for a writer seeking an agent at a conference?

Brooks: Be sure the agent remembers your project and your name, and if you think it will be a while before you send the project to the agent's office, be sure the agent recognizes your work. At each conference, I give attendees a secret code to put on packages they send me. This secret code helps me and my assistants recognize solicited material.

Connor: Whatever you tell the agent that gets the agent excited needs to be in the proposal or manuscript.

Farris: Be prepared to pitch your work in a minute or less. You never know when you might share an elevator with an agent and you have no more than one or two floors to hook them with your pitch. That means you have to know your own work inside and out and be able to boil it down to its essence. Remember, the writer's goal in a pitch is not to tell the agent, beat-by-beat, every detail of the book; rather, it's to intrigue the agent enough to want to read the book.

Schiavone: Find out from the agent just what it is he would like to see from you. If the agent requests a query only, you should remind him that you met him at the conference. If the agent will accept proposals or manuscripts, you should follow through accordingly. Visit with as many agents as possible. Some conferences have only one or two available. Give him your business card and let him know you intend to follow through seeking representation. And good luck—attending a conference may be the answer to fulfilling your dreams.

Leaping Into the Fray

My First Adventure With an Agent

by Sean Murphy

first spoke with my agent, Peter Rubie, in the summer of 1999 under pleasant and unusual circumstances: I'd just discovered that I'd won the Hemingway Award for a First Novel, a manuscript award administered by Hilary Hemingway of the Sanibel Island Hemingway Festival. Peter had judged that competition and was impressed enough with my entry, *The Hope Valley Hubcap King*, to award it the grand prize. He was now phoning to see, as he put it in his particularly British-American way, whether it might be possible to work with me. I would later realize he wasn't just being polite. He really was calling to get a feel for my personality and ability to take guidance, because, as he put it, "some writers are impossible to work with!"

Our conversation soon moved onto other areas of mutual interest—jazz, writers such as John Dufresne and Herman Hesse (I left that conversation with a mile-long list of suggested readings) and inevitably, given my novel's subject, Zen and the contemplative life. I should point out that most of our subsequent phone conversations have been more brief and to-the-point, although we've often met when I've visited New York to discuss ideas at greater length. Agents—at least the successful ones—tend to be busy, and I try not to intrude too much on Peter's time with unscheduled or lengthy phone calls. But these first conversations were very much getting-to-know-you exchanges and had a more leisurely quality to them.

Sean Murphy

I had a positive feeling about the encounter, and I must have passed inspection on his side too, because he phoned back the following week to say he'd decided to take me on. Although Peter felt strongly about the prospects for *The Hope Valley Hubcap King*, he thought it needed more work before it was ready to be shopped around. Luckily, I felt the same way. The manuscript was 95 percent there, but my "everyman" hero, Bibi Brown, was as Peter politely put it, "still a bit blank." These first conversations were exciting ones for me—not only was I speaking with an actual New York agent about the novel I'd worked on in obscurity for the last 12 years, but Peter seemed as excited as I was about getting it into print.

SEAN MURPHY has published *The Finished Man* (Bantam/Dell 2004), a comic tale of writers and the writing life, and the satiric comedy *The Time of New Weather* (Bantam/Dell 2005) since releasing *The Hope Valley Hubcap King* (Bantam/Dell) in 2002. Sean appears at many workshops and leads his own Big Sky Writing Workshops. See his Web site at www.murphyzen.com.

Cover art by Tom Hallman; cover design by Marietta Anastassatos.

Author Sean Murphy attracted the attention of agent Peter Rubie by winning the Hemingway Award for a First Novel. After countless submissions—and a hiatus while he wrote a nonfiction book of American Zen stores—his novel, *The Hope Valley Hubcap King*, was published by Bantam/Dell.

I went on to explain—somewhat naively, in retrospect—that I hoped to make my living entirely as a writer. Peter immediately asked whether I had any areas of expertise that might be appropriate for nonfiction books, which tend to sell more easily than fiction. Most people read at least some nonfiction in their areas of work, hobbies or other interests, while not everyone reads fiction. As an added bonus, nonfiction books can often be sold on the strength of a good proposal and a few sample chapters. This means nonfiction authors have the possibility of receiving money up front to subsidize them during the writing, whereas fiction writers generally have to complete a work before it can sold.

I responded to Peter's question with an idea I'd been nursing for some time. As a practitioner of Zen meditation for the past 12 years, I'd read numerous popular books that presented enlightening encounters between ancient Zen masters and their students. I wanted to assemble a similar volume composed entirely of contemporary encounters between American Zen teachers and their students.

Peter was enthusiastic enough to suggest I set aside revisions on *Hubcap King* and write up a 25- 30-page proposal on the Zen book that we could shop around to publishers. Since fiction is often difficult to place, Peter thought he would be in a stronger position to sell *Hubcap King* if I was already a published author. Plus, there was the possibility of receiving an advance that might fund me during revisions of *Hubcap King*. This proved to be a wise strategy, and one I have often recommended to my own writing students in the years since.

I spent the next months researching and writing the proposal for what would become *One Bird, One Stone: 108 American Zen Stories*. After several rounds of revision and suggestions from Peter, who insisted the proposal be as strong as possible, we were ready by February 2000 to submit to publishers.

Let's make a deal

Although Peter assured me we'd place the book, I was entirely unprepared for what followed. We received an offer within the first two weeks, but the figure was too low to fund the travel required. (I would later spend months interviewing Zen teachers across the United States.) With mixed feelings, I turned it down. Then, one Friday afternoon, Peter phoned just before I was scheduled to fly to London to visit my fiancée. A second publisher was very interested and could improve on the earlier offer, but they'd have to see more material. Could I e-mail them some more Zen stories before 5 p.m. New York time?

At the time, my computer was an ancient Macintosh with a failing black-and-white monitor, and it possessed only the most tenuous concept of what the Internet actually was. Sensing my stress at trying to send the new material through cyberspace in the next couple of hours, it completely refused to cooperate. There followed a flurry of calls to Peter, to one of his assistants who was a computer expert but didn't know Macintoshes, to one of his friends who understood Macintoshes, back to the editor at the new house and to their technical department, who transferred me over to someone who understood old Macintoshes, then back to the now nearly frantic editor, who finally suggested, "Have you tried emptying the cache?"

"What's that?" I asked.

I managed to get the material over just after 5 p.m.—early enough to meet their deadline but too late to hear anything before Monday. I was having drinks with my fiancée and her friend at the OXO Tower in London the following week when the rest of the story played out. A rush of cell phone calls to and from Peter confirmed that the two publishers were now making counteroffers, and we'd reached a zone where the figures were good enough that I could afford to do the book. I kept having to run into the hallway to escape the noisy bar and hear what Peter was saying, then run back to report to my companions before the cell phone rang again.

By 5 p.m. the decision was clear: Renaissance Books, a small house that specialized in spiritual titles, had outbid a division of one of the "big eight" publishers. After talking to their editor, Joe McNeely, Peter and I felt they were in the best position to produce and promote *One Bird, One Stone* effectively. Having received the final news while standing in the hall beside the men's bathroom with one finger pressed in my ear to keep out the noise, I went back and ordered champagne. I couldn't help but laugh at my introduction to the publishing world: I'd sold a book I hadn't yet written, and had not yet sold the novel I had written!

However, the drama was not yet over. Joe McNeely, a karate black belt, knew the Zen world and had strong ideas about the book's content and presentation—ideas that would make the book twice as long and infinitely more complicated than the book I thought I'd proposed. Peter was mostly hands-off by this point. Having negotiated the contract, which went back and forth several times before being approved, he left it up to me and Joe to hash out the details of content and layout. Peter stepped back in when it became apparent that the book Joe thought he was getting would take twice as long to write as the one I'd planned. With Peter's help, we reached a satisfactory compromise—and the final book, I must admit, was much stronger than my original concept.

A return to fiction

Meanwhile, Peter began shopping my revised version of *The Hope Valley Hubcap King* to the large publishing houses. But despite the Hemingway Award and my nonfiction title-in-process, it proved much slower to sell. A number of editors expressed interest, but as Peter explained, publishers like to be able to tell their distributors and sales reps on which shelf a title is expected to sit, and *Hubcap King* didn't fit any of the traditional categories. While there have been many successful novels that fall between genres, like *A Confederacy of Dunces* or *Hitchhikers Guide to the Galaxy*, they tend to be the types of books that keep publishing executives awake at night, and their tendency is to shy away.

After some months, however, we received an offer from Bantam Dell's Liz Scheier, who said she became so absorbed while reading the manuscript on an airplane that she finally had to be tapped on the shoulder by a flight attendant, who politely informed her that the plane had landed and was now empty of passengers.

One Bird, One Stone came out at last in April 2002 and *The Hope Valley Hubcap King* in October of the same year. *Hubcap King* made the Book Sense 76 list of recommended titles and sold out its first printing in a month, far exceeding our expectations. Oddly enough—bearing in mind the novel's rejections on grounds that it was difficult to classify—it turned out uniqueness was exactly what sales reps and reviewers most appreciated. They tended, however, to frame it in terms like "fresh, daring and quirky," while *Publishers Weekly* wrote:

"This book has 'future cult classic' written all over it." On the strength of this success, Peter made a deal with Bantam Dell for my next two novels, *The Finished Man* and *The Time of New Weather*, which were issued in 2004 along with a new trade paperback edition of *The Hope Valley Hubcap King*.

Lessons learned

Over the years my relationship with my agent has become more solid and more matter-of-fact. I don't expect Peter to provide close feedback on current manuscripts, though I do talk over ideas and presentation with him. He makes suggestions for new directions and sometimes discourages me from ideas that he doesn't feel have strong potential, or that aren't right for the current publishing trends. Fortunately, I'm one of those authors with far more ideas than I can ever get to in a lifetime, so it's good to have some guidance on which to choose. He's proven to be a strong negotiator, consistently improving the quality of my contracts with publishers, selling several foreign editions of my novels and connecting me with a Hollywood film agent.

I've learned that there are some things I can expect from an agent, and some things I can't. An agent isn't there to hold your hand, to support you emotionally (though they may definitely encourage and provide reassurance at times), or to make career decisions for you. They are there to guide you in making appropriate choices in preparing a manuscript, as well as in promotion and overall career direction. An agent's job is to place your manuscript with the right publisher for the best money possible, to negotiate a contract, sell subsidiary rights and provide advice in the next stage in your career. It's a partnership.

"The best author/agent relationships exist as a result of trust," says Peter. "An author's priority, once they're sure they've found the right agent, is to do all they can to help build that trust. An agent's suggestions don't have to be obeyed implicitly, but they provide an objective point of view, and an author has to exhibit a willingness to re-examine his direction and to be guided appropriately. Most people want to be led, or they want to be in charge—but it's a difficult trick to go arm in arm together down the unfamiliar and sometimes difficult road that exists in today's tough publishing market. An author has to make his or her own decisions, but you're not operating in isolation. As an agent, I'm there to give as much help as you need."

Literary Agents

A gents listed in this section generate 98-100 percent of their income from commission on sales. They do not charge for reading, critiquing or editing your manuscript or book proposal. It's the goal of an agent to find salable manuscripts: Her income depends on finding the best publisher for your manuscript.

Since an agent's time is better spent meeting with editors, she will have little or no time to critique your writing. Agents who don't charge fees must be selective and often prefer to work with established authors, celebrities or those with professional credentials in a particular field.

Some agents in this section may charge clients for office expenses such as photocopying, foreign postage, long-distance phone calls or express mail services. Make sure you have a clear understanding of what these expenses are before signing any agency agreement. While most agents deduct expenses from the advance or royalties a book earns, a few agents included in this section charge their clients a one-time up-front "marketing" or "handling" fee.

SUBHEADS

Each agency listing is broken down into subheads to make locating specific information easier. In the first section, you'll find contact information for each agency. You'll also learn if the agents within the agency belong to any professional organizations; membership in these organizations can tell you a lot about an agency. For example, members of the Association of Authors' Representatives (AAR) are prohibited from charging reading or evaluating fees. Additional information in this section includes the size of each agency, its willingness to work with new or unpublished writers, and its general areas of interest.

Member Agents: Agencies comprised of more than one agent list member agents and their individual specialties. This information will help you determine the appropriate person to whom you should send your query letter.

Represents: This section allows agencies to specify what nonfiction and fiction subjects they represent. Make sure you query only those agents who represent the type of material you write.

O—¬ Look for the key icon to quickly learn an agent's areas of specialization. In this portion of the listing, agents mention the subject areas they're currently seeking, as well as those subject areas they do not consider.

How to Contact: Most agents open to submissions prefer an initial query letter that briefly describes your work. While some agents may ask for an outline and a specific number of sample chapters, most don't. You should send these items only if the agent requests them. In this section, agents also mention if they accept queries by fax or e-mail, if they consider simultaneous submissions, and how they prefer to obtain new clients.

Recent Sales: To give you a sense of the types of material they represent, the agents list specific titles they've sold, as well as a sampling of clients' names. Note that some agents consider their client list confidential and may only share client names once they agree to represent you.

Terms: Provided here are details of an agent's commission, whether a contract is offered and for how long, and what additional office expenses you might have to pay if the agent agrees to represent you. Standard commissions range from 10-15 percent for domestic sales and 15-20 percent for foreign or dramatic sales (with the difference going to the co-agent who places the work).

Writers' Conferences: A great way to meet an agent is at a writers' conference. Here agents list the conferences they usually attend. For more information about a specific conference, check the Conferences section starting on page 230.

Tips: In this section, agents offer advice and additional instructions for writers.

SPECIAL INDEXES

Literary Agents Specialties Index: This index (page 276) organizes agencies according to the subjects they are interested in receiving. This index should help you compose a list of agents specializing in your areas. Cross-referencing categories and concentrating on agents interested in two or more aspects of your manuscript might increase your chances of success.

Openness to Submissions Index: This index (page 331) lists agencies according to how receptive they are to new clients.

Geographic Index: For writers seeking an agent close to home, this index (page 336) lists agents by state.

Agents Index: This index (page 342) provides a list of agents' names in alphabetical order, along with the name of the agency for which they work. Find the name of the person you would like to contact, and then check the agency listing.

General Index: This index (page 354) lists all agencies, publicists and conferences appearing in the book.

Quick Reference Icons

At the beginning of some listings, you will find one or more of the following symbols:

N Agency new to this edition

Canadian agency

International agency

Agency actively seeking clients

Agency seeking both new and established writers

Agency seeking mostly established writers through referrals

Agency specializing in certain types of work

Agency not currently seeking new clients

Find a pull-out bookmark with a key to symbols on the inside cover of this book.

Literary Agents

◨ DOMINICK ABEL LITERARY AGENCY, INC.

146 W. 82nd St., #1B, New York NY 10024. Fax: (212)595-3133. E-mail: agency@dalainc.com. Estab. 1975. Member of AAR. Represents 100 clients. Currently handles: adult nonfiction books; adult novels.
How to Contact Query with SASE.
Terms Agent receives 15% commission on domestic sales; 20% commission on foreign sales.

◨ CAROLE ABEL LITERARY AGENT

160 W. 87th St., #7D, New York NY 10024. Fax: (212)724-1384. E-mail: caroleabel@aol.com. 50% of clients are new/unpublished writers. Currently handles: nonfiction books.
How to Contact Query with SASE or via e-mail or fax.
Recent Sales *Instant Self Hypnosis*, by Forbes Blair (Sourcebooks); *Wordplay*, by L. Myers and L. Goodman (McGraw Hill).

◨◨ ◨ ACACIA HOUSE PUBLISHING SERVICES, LTD.

51 Acacia Rd., Toronto ON M4S 2K6 Canada. Phone/Fax: (416)484-8356. **Contact:** (Ms.) Frances Hanna. Estab. 1985. Represents 100 clients. Currently handles: 30% nonfiction books; 70% novels.
- Ms. Hanna has been in the publishing business for 30 years, first in London as a fiction editor with Barrie & Jenkins and Pan Books, and as a senior editor with a packager of mainly illustrated books. She was condensed books editor for 6 years for *Reader's Digest* in Montreal and senior editor and foreign rights manager for William Collins & Sons (now HarperCollins) in Toronto. Mr. Hanna has over 40 years of experience in the publishing business.
Member Agents Bill Hanna, vice president (business, self-help, modern history).
Represents Nonfiction books, novels. **Considers these nonfiction areas:** Animals; biography/autobiography; language/literature/criticism; memoirs; military/war; music/dance; nature/environment; theater/film; travel. **Considers these fiction areas:** Action/adventure; detective/police/crime; literary; mainstream/contemporary; mystery/suspense; thriller.
- ⦿ This agency specializes in contemporary fiction—literary or commercial. Actively seeking outstanding first novels with literary merit. Does not want to receive horror, occult, or science fiction.
How to Contact Query with outline, SASE. *No unsolicited mss.* No e-mail or fax queries. Responds in 6 weeks to queries. Returns materials only with SASE.
Recent Sales Sold over 75 titles in the last year. Also made numerous international rights sales. This agency prefers not to share information on specific sales or clients.
Terms Agent receives 15% commission on English language sales; 20% commission on dramatic sales; 25% commission on foreign sales. Charges clients for photocopying, postage, courier.
Tips "We prefer that writers be previously published, with at least a few short stories or articles to their credit. Strongest consideration will be given to those with 3 or more published books. However, we would take on an unpublished writer of outstanding talent."

◨ ADAMS LITERARY

7845 Colony Rd., C4, #215, Charlotte NC 28226. (212)786-9140. Fax: (212)786-9170. E-mail: info@adamsliterary .com. Web site: www.adamsliterary.com. **Contact:** Tracey Adams. Estab. 2004. Member of AAR.
- Prior to becoming an agent, Ms. Adams worked in the marketing and editorial departments of Greenwillow Books and Margaret K. McElderry Books.
- ⦿ Adams Literary is a full-service literary agency exclusively representing children's book authors and artists. "Although we remain absolutely dedicated to finding new talent, we must announce that until further notice we can no longer accept unsolicited manuscripts. We also cannot accept queries or submissions via e-mail."

◨ BRET ADAMS LTD. AGENCY

448 W. 44th St., New York NY 10036. (212)765-5630. **Contact:** Bruce Ostler, Antje Oegel. Member of AAR.
How to Contact Query with SASE.

◨ AGENTS INK!

P.O. Box 4956, Fresno CA 93744. (559)438-8289. **Contact:** Sydney H. Harriet, director. Estab. 1987. Member of APA. Represents 20 clients. 70% of clients are new/unpublished writers. Currently handles: 80% nonfiction books; 20% novels; multimedia.
- Prior to opening his agency, Dr. Harriet was a psychologist, radio and television reporter, and professor of English. Ms. McNichols has a BA in classical Greek and an MA in classics. She has more than 20 years of experience as an editor for daily and alternative newspapers, major syndicates, and independent authors.

Member Agents Sydney Harriet; Dinah McNichols.

Represents Nonfiction books, novels. **Considers these nonfiction areas:** Animals; cooking/foods/nutrition; government/politics/law; health/medicine (mind/body healing); history; language/literature/criticism; psychology; science/technology; self-help/personal improvement; sociology; sports (medicine, psychology); foreign affairs; international topics.

    0→ This agency specializes in writers who have education experience in the business, legal, and health professions. It is helpful if the writer is licensed, but not necessary. Prior nonfiction book publication is not necessary. For fiction, previously published fiction is a prerequisite for representation. Does not want memoirs, autobiographies, stories about overcoming an illness, science fiction, fantasy, religious materials, or children's books.

How to Contact Query with SASE. Considers simultaneous submissions. Responds in 1 month.

Recent Sales Sold 5 titles in the last year. *Infantry Soldier*, by George Neil (University of Oklahoma Press); *SAMe, The European Arthritis and Depression Breakthrough*, by Sol Grazi and Maria Costa (Prima); *What to Eat if You Have Diabetes*, by Danielle Chase (Contemporary); *How to Turn Your Fat Husband Into a Lean Lover*, by Maureen Keane (Random House).

Terms Agent receives 15% commission on domestic sales; 20% commission on foreign sales. Offers written contract, binding for 6-12 months (negotiable).

Writers' Conferences Scheduled as a speaker at a number of conferences across the country. Contact agency to book authors and agents for conferences.

Tips "Remember, query first. Do not call to pitch an idea. The only way we can judge the quality of your idea is to see how you write. Unsolicited manuscripts will not be read if they arrive without a SASE. Currently, we are receiving more than 200 query letters and proposals each month. Send a complete proposal/manuscript only if requested. Ask yourself why someone would be compelled to buy your book. If you think the idea is unique, spend the time to create a query and then a proposal where every word counts. Fiction writers need to understand that the craft is just as important as the idea—99% of the fiction is rejected because of sloppy, overwritten dialogue, wooden characters, predictable plotting, and lifeless narrative. Once you finish your novel, put it away and let it percolate, then take it out and work on fine-tuning it some more. A novel is never finished until you stop working on it. We would love to represent more fiction writers and probably will when we read a manuscript that has gone through a dozen or more drafts. Because of rising costs, we no longer can respond to queries, proposals, and/or complete manuscripts without receiving a return envelope and sufficient postage."

☑ THE AHEARN AGENCY, INC.

2021 Pine St., New Orleans LA 70118. E-mail: pahearn@aol.com. **Contact:** Pamela G. Ahearn. Estab. 1992. Member of MWA, RWA, ITW. Represents 25 clients. 20% of clients are new/unpublished writers. Currently handles: 10% nonfiction books; 90% novels.

    ● Prior to opening her agency, Ms. Ahearn was an agent for 8 years and an editor with Bantam Books.

Represents Nonfiction books, novels, short story collections (if stories have been previously published). **Considers these nonfiction areas:** Animals; child guidance/parenting; current affairs; ethnic/cultural interests; gay/lesbian issues; health/medicine; history; music/dance; popular culture; self-help/personal improvement; theater/film; true crime/investigative; women's issues/studies. **Considers these fiction areas:** Action/adventure; contemporary issues; detective/police/crime; ethnic; family saga; feminist; gay/lesbian; glitz; historical; humor/satire; literary; mainstream/contemporary; mystery/suspense; psychic/supernatural; regional; romance; thriller.

    0→ This agency specializes in historical romance and is also very interested in mysteries and suspense fiction. Does not want to receive category romance, science fiction, or fantasy.

How to Contact Query with SASE. Accepts e-mail queries (no attachments). Considers simultaneous queries. Responds in 8 weeks to queries; 10 weeks to mss. Obtains most new clients through recommendations from others, solicitations, conferences.

Recent Sales *Assassin's Touch*, by Laura Joh Rowland (St. Martin's Press); *To Pleasure a Prince*, by Sabrina Jeffries (Pocket); *The Templar Legacy*, by Steve Berry.

Terms Agent receives 15% commission on domestic sales; 20% commission on foreign sales. Offers written contract, binding for 1 year; renewable by mutual consent.

Writers' Conferences Moonlight & Magnolias; RWA National Conference; Virginia Romance Writers; Florida Romance Writers; Bouchercon; Malice Domestic.

Tips "Be professional! Always send in exactly what an agent/editor asks for—no more, no less. Keep query letters brief and to the point, giving your writing credentials and a very brief summary of your book. If one agent rejects you, keep trying—there are a lot of us out there!"

⏺ ALIVE COMMUNICATIONS, INC.

7680 Goddard St., Suite 200, Colorado Springs CO 80920. (719)260-7080. Fax: (719)260-8223. Web site: www.alivecom.com. Estab. 1989. Member of CBA, Authors Guild. Represents 200+ clients. 5% of clients are new/unpublished writers. Currently handles: 50% nonfiction books; 35% novels; 5% novellas; 10% juvenile books.

Member Agents Rick Christian, president (blockbusters, bestsellers); Don Pape (popular/commercial nonfiction and fiction, new authors with breakout potential); Beth Jusino (thoughtful/inspirational nonfiction, women's fiction/nonfiction, Christian living); Lee Hough (popular/commercial nonfiction and fiction, thoughtful spirituality, children's).

Represents Nonfiction books, novels, short story collections, novellas. **Considers these nonfiction areas:** Biography/autobiography; business/economics; child guidance/parenting; how-to; memoirs; religious/inspirational; self-help/personal improvement; women's issues/studies. **Considers these fiction areas:** Action/adventure; contemporary issues; detective/police/crime; family saga; historical; humor/satire; literary; mainstream/contemporary; mystery/suspense; religious/inspirational; thriller.

 O⚊ This agency specializes in fiction, Christian living, how-to, and commercial nonfiction. Actively seeking inspirational, literary and mainstream fiction, and work from authors with established track records and platforms. Does not want poetry, young adult paperbacks, scripts, or dark themes.

How to Contact Works primarily with well-established, bestselling, and career authors. Returns materials only with SASE. Obtains most new clients through recommendations from others.

Recent Sales Sold 300+ titles in the last year. Left Behind series, by Tim LaHaye and Jerry B. Jenkins (Tyndale); *Let's Roll*, by Lisa Beamer (Tyndale); *The Message*, by Eugene Peterson (NavPress); Every Man series, by Stephen Arterburn (Waterbrook); *One Tuesday Morning*, by Karen Kingsbury (Zondervan).

Terms Agent receives 15% commission on domestic and foreign sales. Offers written contract; 2-month written notice must be given to terminate contract.

Tips "Rewrite and polish until the words on the page shine. Endorsements and great connections may help, provided you can write with power and passion. Network with publishing professionals by making contacts, joining critique groups, and attending writers' conferences in order to make personal connections and to get feedback. Alive Communications, Inc., has established itself as a premiere literary agency. We serve an elite group of authors who are critically acclaimed and commercially successful in both Christian and general markets."

⏺ MIRIAM ALTSHULER LITERARY AGENCY

53 Old Post Rd. N., Red Hook NY 12571. (845)758-9408. **Contact:** Miriam Altshuler. Estab. 1994. Member of AAR. Represents 40 clients. Currently handles: 45% nonfiction books; 45% novels; 5% story collections; 5% juvenile books.

 ● Ms. Altshuler has been an agent since 1982.

Represents Nonfiction books, novels, short story collections, juvenile books. **Considers these nonfiction areas:** Biography/autobiography; ethnic/cultural interests; history; language/literature/criticism; memoirs; multicultural; music/dance; nature/environment; popular culture; psychology; sociology; theater/film; women's issues/studies. **Considers these fiction areas:** Literary; mainstream/contemporary; multicultural.

 O⚊ Does not want self-help, mystery, how-to, romance, horror, spiritual, fantasy, poetry, screenplays, science fiction, or techno-thriller.

How to Contact Query with SASE. Prefers to read materials exclusively. If no SASE is included, no response will be sent. No unsolicited mss. No e-mail or fax queries. Considers simultaneous queries. Responds in 3 weeks to mss. Returns materials only with SASE. Obtains most new clients through recommendations from others.

Terms Agent receives 15% commission on domestic sales; 20% commission on foreign sales. Charges clients for overseas mailing, photocopies, overnight mail when requested by author.

Writers' Conferences Bread Loaf Writers' Conference; Washington Independent Writers Conference; North Carolina Writers' Network Conference.

ℕ ⊕ ⏺ THE AMPERSAND AGENCY

Ryman's Cottages, Little Tew, Oxfordshire OX7 4JJ United Kingdom. (44)(16)868-3677. Fax: (44)(16)868-3449. E-mail: peter@theampersandagency.co.uk. Web site: www.theampersandagency.co.uk. **Contact:** Peter Buckman. Estab. 2003. Represents 30 clients. 75% of clients are new/unpublished writers.

 ● Prior to opening his agency, Mr. Buckman was a writer and publisher in England and America.

Member Agents Peter Buckman (literary fiction and nonfiction); Peter Janson-Smith (crime, thrillers, biography); Anne-Marie Doulton (historical and women's fiction).

Represents Nonfiction books, novels, juvenile books, scholarly books. **Considers these nonfiction areas:** Animals; biography/autobiography; cooking/foods/nutrition; current affairs; education; ethnic/cultural interests; government/politics/law; health/medicine; history; humor/satire; language/literature/criticism; memoirs; military/war; music/dance; popular culture; psychology; theater/film; translation; true crime/investigative. **Considers these fiction areas:** Action/adventure; comic books/cartoon; confession; detective/police/crime; ethnic; family saga; fantasy; historical; juvenile; literary; mainstream/contemporary; mystery/suspense; romance; thriller; young adult; glitz.

> O→ "Being a new agency, we specialize in new writers, although we also represent well-established names. We are small, experienced, and professional. We know what we like, respond quickly, and enjoy working with the writers we take on to present their work in the best possible way. We also offer a foreign rights service and have well-established contacts on both sides of the Atlantic in film, TV, broadcasting, and publishing." Actively seeking commercial and literary fiction and nonfiction. Does not want science fiction or works with only regional appeal.

How to Contact Submit outline, 1-2 sample chapters. Accepts queries via e-mail. Considers simultaneous queries. Responds in 1 week to queries; 1 month to mss. Returns materials only with SASE. Obtains most new clients through recommendations, writers' handbooks, word of mouth.

Recent Sales Sold 14 titles in the last year. *Q&A*, by Vikas Swarup (Scribner/Doubleday); *My Side of the Story*, by Will Davis (Bloomsbury); *Digging Up the Dead*, by Dr. Druin Burch (Chatoo & Windus); *Neptune's Daughter*, by Beryl Kingston (Transita). Other clients include Geoff Baker, Max Barron, Rob Buckman, Anna Crosbie, Andrew Cullen, Tom Darke, Francis Ellen, Justin Elliott, Cora Harrison, Georgette Heyer, Michael Hutchinson, Jim McKenna, Euan Macpherson, Bolaji Odofin, Rosie Orr, Philip Purser, Penny Rumble, Nick van Bloss, Mike Walters, Norman Welch, Kirby Wright.

Terms Agent receives 10-15% commission on domestic sales; 20% commission on foreign sales. Offers written contract. "By agreement with the author, we charge for extra photocopying in the case of multiple submissions and for any lawyer's or other profesional fees required by a negotiation."

⦿ BETSY AMSTER LITERARY ENTERPRISES

P.O. Box 27788, Los Angeles CA 90027-0788. **Contact:** Betsy Amster. Estab. 1992. Member of AAR. Represents over 65 clients. 35% of clients are new/unpublished writers. Currently handles: 65% nonfiction books; 35% novels.

> • Prior to opening her agency, Ms. Amster was an editor at Pantheon and Vintage for 10 years, and served as editorial director for the Globe Pequot Press for 2 years. "This experience gives me a wider perspective on the business and the ability to give focused editorial feedback to my clients."

Represents Nonfiction books, novels. **Considers these nonfiction areas:** Biography/autobiography; child guidance/parenting; ethnic/cultural interests; gardening; health/medicine; history; money/finance; psychology; sociology; women's issues/studies; career. **Considers these fiction areas:** Ethnic; literary; mystery/suspense (quirky); thriller (quirky); women's (high quality).

> O→ Actively seeking strong narrative nonfiction, particularly by journalists; outstanding literary fiction (the next Michael Chabon or Jhumpa Lahiri); witty, intelligent, commercial women's fiction (the next Elinor Lipman or Jennifer Weiner); and high-profile self-help and psychology, preferably research based. Does not want to receive poetry, children's books, romances, westerns, science fiction, or action/adventure.

How to Contact For fiction, send query, first 3 pages, SASE. For nonfiction, send query or proposal with SASE. No e-mail or fax queries. Considers simultaneous queries. Responds in 1 month to queries; 2 months to mss. Obtains most new clients through recommendations from others, solicitations, conferences.

Recent Sales *Wild Indigo* and *Wild Inferno*, by Sandi Ault (Berkley Prime Crime); *Famous Writers School*, by Steven Carter (Counterpoint); *The Great Black Way: L.A.'s Central Avenue in the 1940s and the Rise of African American Pop Culture*, by RJ Smith (PublicAffairs); *Rejuvenile: The Reinvention of the American Grown-Up*, by Christopher Noxon (Crown); *The Renaissance Soul: Life Design for People with Too Many Passions to Pick Just One*, by Margaret Lobenstine (Broadway). Other clients include Dr. Linda Acredolo, Dr. Susan Goodwyn, Dwight Allen, Lynette Brasfield, Dr. Elaine N. Aron, Barbara DeMarco-Barrett, Robin Chotzinoff, Rob Cohen, David Wollock, Phil Doran, María Amparo Escandón, Paul Mandelbaum, Wendy Mogel, Sharon Montrose, Joy Nicholson, Lynette Padwa, Diana Wells, Dr. Edward Schneider, Leigh Ann Hirschman.

Terms Agent receives 15% commission on domestic sales; 20% commission on foreign sales. Offers written contract, binding for 1 year; 3-month notice must be given to terminate contract. Charges for photocopying, postage, long distance phone calls, messengers, galleys/books used in submissions to foreign and film agents and to magazines for first serial rights.

Writers' Conferences Squaw Valley Writers Workshop; San Diego State University Writers' Conference; UCLA Extension Writers' Program; The Loft Literary Center.

N ◐ THE ANDERSON LITERARY AGENCY

435 Convent Ave., Suite 5, New York NY 10031. (212)234-0692. E-mail: gilesa@rcn.com. **Contact:** Giles Anderson.

Represents Nonfiction books. **Considers these nonfiction areas:** Biography; memoir; religion; science; true crime.

How to Contact Send brief query via e-mail.

N ⊕ ◐ ANUBIS LITERARY AGENCY

7 Birdhaven Close Lighthorne Heath, Banbury Rd., Warwick Warwickshire CV35 0BE Great Britain. Phone/Fax: (44)(192)664-2588. E-mail: anubis.agency2@btopenworld.com. **Contact:** Steve Calcutt. Estab. 1994. Represents 15 clients. 50% of clients are new/unpublished writers. Currently handles: 100% novels.

• In addition to being an agent, Mr. Calcutt teaches creative writing and American history (US Civil War) at Warwick University.

Represents Novels. **Considers these fiction areas:** Horror; science fiction; dark fantasy.

    O⊸ Actively seeking horror fiction. Does not want to receive children's books, nonfiction, journalism, or TV/film scripts.

How to Contact Query with proposal package, outline, SASE/IRCs. Returns materials only with SASE/IRCs. No e-mail or fax queries. Responds in 6 weeks to queries; 3 months to mss. Obtains most new clients through personal recommendation.

Recent Sales *Berserk* and *Dusk*, by Tim Lebbon (Dorchester); *The Beloved*, by J.F. Gonzalez; *Breeding Ground*, by Sarah Pinborough (Dorchester); *Gradisil*, by Adam Roberts (Orion). Other clients include Steve Savile, Lesley Asquith, Anthea Ingham, Brett A. Savory.

Terms Agent receives 15% commission on domestic sales; 20% commission on foreign sales.

◐ APPLESEEDS MANAGEMENT

200 E. 30th St., Suite 302, San Bernardino CA 92404. (909)882-1667. **Contact:** S. James Foiles. Estab. 1988. 40% of clients are new/unpublished writers. Currently handles: 15% nonfiction books; 85% novels.

Represents Nonfiction books, novels. **Considers these nonfiction areas:** True crime/investigative. **Considers these fiction areas:** Detective/police/crime; mystery/suspense.

How to Contact Query with SASE. Responds in 2 weeks to queries; 2 months to mss.

Recent Sales This agency prefers not to share information on specific sales.

Terms Agent receives 10-15% commission on domestic sales; 20% commission on foreign sales. Offers written contract, binding for 1-7 years.

Tips "Because readership of mysteries is expanding, Appleseeds specializes in mysteries with a detective who could be in a continuing series."

◐ ARCADIA

31 Lake Place N., Danbury CT 06810. E-mail: arcadialit@att.net. **Contact:** Victoria Gould Pryor. Member of AAR.

Represents Nonfiction books, literary and commercial fiction. **Considers these nonfiction areas:** Biography/autobiography; business/economics; current affairs; history; memoirs; psychology; science/technology; true crime/investigative; women's issues/studies; medicine; investigative journalism; culture; classical music; life transforming self-help.

    O⊸ "I'm a very hands-on agent, which is necessary in this competitive marketplace. I work with authors on revisions until whatever we present to publishers is as perfect as it can be. I represent talented, dedicated, intelligent, and ambitious writers who are looking for a long-term relationship based on professional success and mutual respect." No science fiction/fantasy, horror, humor, or children's/YA. "We are only able to read fiction submissions from previously published authors."

How to Contact Query with SASE. Accepts e-mail queries (no attachments).

Recent Sales This agency prefers not to share information on specific sales.

N ◐ ARTISTS AND ARTISANS INC.

104 W. 29th St., 11th Floor, New York NY 10001. Fax: (212)931-8377. E-mail: adam@artistsandartisans.com. Web site: www.artistsandartisans.com. **Contact:** Adam Chromy. Estab. 2002. Represents 40 clients. 80% of clients are new/unpublished writers. Currently handles: 63% nonfiction books; 35% novels; 2% scholarly books.

• Prior to becoming an agent, Mr. Chromy was an entrepreneur in the technology field for nearly a decade.

Represents Nonfiction books, novels. **Considers these nonfiction areas:** Biography/autobiography; business/economics; child guidance/parenting; cooking/foods/nutrition; current affairs; ethnic/cultural interests; health/medicine; how-to; humor/satire; language/literature/criticism; memoirs; money/finance; music/dance; popular culture; religious/inspirational; science/technology; self-help/personal improvement; sports; theatre/film; true crime/investigative; women's issues/studies; fashion/style. **Considers these fiction areas:** Confession; family saga; humor/satire; literary; mainstream/contemporary.

> O⟶ "My education and experience in the business world ensure that my clients' enterprise as authors gets as much attention and care as their writing." Actively seeking working journalists for nonfiction books. Does not want to receive scripts.

How to Contact Query with SASE. Considers simultaneous queries. Responds in 2 weeks to queries and mss. Returns materials only with SASE. Obtains most new clients through queries, referrals, conferences.

Recent Sales Sold 12 titles in the last year.

Terms Agent receives 15% commission on domestic sales; 25% commission on foreign sales. Offers written contract; 1-month notice must be given to terminate contract. "We only charge for extraordinary expenses (e.g., client requests check via FedEx instead of regular mail)."

Writers' Conferences ASJA Writers Conference.

Tips "Please make sure you are ready before approaching us or any other agent. If you write fiction, make sure it is the best work you can do and get objective criticism from a writing group. If you write nonfiction, make sure the proposal exhibits your best work and a comprehensive understanding of the market."

N ◪ THE AUGUST AGENCY LLC

E-mail: submissions@augustagency.com. Web site: www.augustagency.com. **Contact:** Cricket Pechstein, Jefferey McGraw. Estab. 2004. Represents 25-40 clients. 50% of clients are new/unpublished writers. Currently handles: 75% nonfiction books; 20% novels; 5% other.

> • Before opening The August Agency, Ms. Pechstein was a freelance writer, magazine editor, and independant literary agent; Mr. McGraw worked for magazines and book publishers doing editorial, public relations, publicity, advertising, and promotional work.

Member Agents Jeffery McGraw (narrative/commercial nonfiction, chick lit, women's fiction, self-help, literary fiction); Cricket Pechstein (mystery/crime fiction, chick lit, thrillers).

Represents Nonfiction books, novels. **Considers these nonfiction areas:** Biography/autobiography; business/economics; child guidance/parenting; cooking/foods/nutrition; current affairs; ethnic/cultural interests; gay/lesbian issues; government/politics/law; health/medicine; history; how-to; humor/satire; interior design/decorating; memoirs; military/war; money/finance; music/dance; popular culture; psychology; self-help/personal improvement; sociology; sports; theater/film; true crime/investigative; women's issues/studies; inspirational. **Considers these fiction areas:** Action/adventure; detective/police/crime; ethnic; family saga; gay/lesbian; historical; humor/satire; literary; mainstream/contemporary; mystery/suspense; psychic/supernatural; thriller; smart chick lit (non-genre romance).

> O⟶ "We actively pursue an array of fiction and nonfiction writers to represent, with an emphasis in media (seasoned journalists receive special favor here), popular culture/entertainment, political science, diet/fitness, health, cookbooks, psychology, business, memoir, highly creative nonfiction, accessible literary fiction, women's fiction, and high-concept mysteries and thrillers. When it comes to nonfiction, we favor persuasive and prescriptive works with a full-bodied narrative command and an undeniable contemporary relevance. Our favorite novelists are as eclectic as our minds are broad, yet they all share one common denominator that might explain a peculiar predisposition for what we prefer to call "emotion fiction"—a brand of storytelling defined not so much by a novel's category as by its extraordinary power to resonate universally on a deeply emotional level." Does not want to receive academic textbooks, children's books, cozy mysteries, horror, poetry, science fiction/fantasy, short story collections, westerns, or genre romance.

How to Contact Submit book summary (1-2 paragraphs), chapter outline (nonfiction only), first 1,000 words or first chapter, total page/word count, brief paragraph on why you have chosen to write the book. Send via e-mail only (no attachments). Considers simultaneous queries. Responds in 2-3 weeks to queries; 3 months to mss. Obtains most new clients through recommendations from others, solicitations, conferences.

Terms Agent receives 15% commission on domestic sales; 20% commission on foreign sales. Offers written contract; 1-month notice must be given to terminate contract.

Writers' Conferences Surrey International Writers' Conference.

N ◉ ◪ AUSTRALIA LITERARY MANAGEMENT

2-A Booth St., Balmain NSW 2041 Australia. (61)(2)9818-8557. Fax: (61)(2)9818-8569. E-mail: alpha@austlit.com. Web site: www.austlit.com. Estab. 1980.

Represents Nonfiction books, novels. **Considers these nonfiction areas:** Art/architecture/design; biography/autobiography; memoirs; money/finance; diet/food preparation. **Considers these fiction areas:** Comic books/cartoon; fantasy; historical; juvenile; young adult; crime; travel.

O— No screenplays, plays, poetry, or short stories.

How to Contact Call first. If requested, send synopsis, 2 sample chapters, SASE. Responds in 4-6 weeks to queries.

Recent Sales *Organisations Behaving Badly*, by Leon Gettler (John Wiley & Sons); *Not Happy, John!*, by Margo Kingston (Penguin); *The Hythrun Chronicles*, by Jennifer Fallong (Tor).

Terms Agent receives 15% commission on domestic sales.

AUTHENTIC CREATIONS LITERARY AGENCY

911 Duluth Hwy., Suite D3-144, Lawrenceville GA 30043. (770)339-3774. Fax: (770)339-7126. E-mail: ron@authenticcreations.com. Web site: www.authenticcreations.com. **Contact:** Mary Lee Laitsch. Estab. 1993. Member of AAR, Authors Guild. Represents 70 clients. 30% of clients are new/unpublished writers. Currently handles: 60% nonfiction books; 40% novels.

• Prior to becoming an agent, Ms. Laitsch was a librarian and an elementary school teacher; Mr. Laitsch was an attorney and a writer.

Member Agents Mary Lee Laitsch; Ronald Laitsch; Jason Laitsch.

Represents Nonfiction books, novels, scholarly books. **Considers these nonfiction areas:** Anthropology/archaeology; biography/autobiography; child guidance/parenting; crafts/hobbies; current affairs; history; how-to; science/technology; self-help/personal improvement; sports; true crime/investigative; women's issues/studies. **Considers these fiction areas:** Action/adventure; detective/police/crime; family saga; literary; mainstream/contemporary; mystery/suspense; romance; sports; thriller.

How to Contact Query with SASE. No e-mail or fax queries. Considers simultaneous queries. Responds in 2 weeks to queries; 2 months to mss.

Recent Sales Sold 20 titles in the last year. *Secret Agent*, by Robyn Spizman and Mark Johnston (Simon & Schuster); *Beauchamp Beseiged*, by Elaine Knighton (Harlequin); *Visible Differences*, by Dominic Pulera (Continuum).

Terms Agent receives 15% commission on domestic and foreign sales. Charges clients for photocopying.

Tips "We thoroughly enjoy what we do. What makes being an agent so satisfying for us is having the opportunity to work with authors who are as excited about the works they write as we are about representing them."

THE AXELROD AGENCY

55 Main St., P.O. Box 357, Chatham NY 12037. (518)392-2100. Fax: (518)392-2944. E-mail: steve@axelrodagency.com. **Contact:** Steven Axelrod. Estab. 1983. Member of AAR. Represents 20-30 clients. 1% of clients are new/unpublished writers. Currently handles: 5% nonfiction books; 95% novels.

• Prior to becoming an agent, Mr. Axelrod was a book club editor.

Represents Nonfiction books, novels. **Considers these fiction areas:** Mystery/suspense; romance; women's.

How to Contact Query with SASE. Considers simultaneous queries. Responds in 3 weeks to queries; 6 weeks to mss. Returns materials only with SASE. Obtains most new clients through recommendations from others.

Recent Sales This agency prefers not to share information on specific sales.

Terms Agent receives 15% commission on domestic sales; 20% commission on foreign sales. No written contract.

Writers' Conferences RWA National Conference

BALKIN AGENCY, INC.

P.O. Box 222, Amherst MA 01004. (413)548-9835. Fax: (413)548-9836. **Contact:** Rick Balkin, president. Estab. 1972. Member of AAR. Represents 50 clients. 10% of clients are new/unpublished writers. Currently handles: 85% nonfiction books; 5% scholarly books; 5% textbooks; 5% reference books.

• Prior to opening his agency, Mr. Balkin served as executive editor with Bobbs-Merrill Company.

Represents Nonfiction books, scholarly books, textbooks. **Considers these nonfiction areas:** Animals; anthropology/archaeology; current affairs; health/medicine; history; how-to; language/literature/criticism; music/dance; nature/environment; popular culture; science/technology; sociology; translation; biography.

O— This agency specializes in adult nonfiction. Does not want to receive fiction, poetry, screenplays, or computer books.

How to Contact Query with SASE, proposal package, outline. No e-mail or fax queries. Responds in 1 week to queries; 2 weeks to mss. Returns materials only with SASE. Obtains most new clients through recommendations from others.

Recent Sales Sold 30 titles in the last year. *The Liar's Tale* (W.W. Norton Co.); *Adolescent Depression* (Henry Holt); *Eliz. Van Lew: A Union Spy in the Heart of the Confederacy* (Oxford University Press).

Terms Agent receives 15% commission on domestic sales; 20% commission on foreign sales. Offers written contract, binding for 1 year. Charges clients for photocopying and express or foreign mail.

Tips "I do not take on books described as bestsellers or potential bestsellers. Any nonfiction work that is either unique, paradigmatic, a contribution, truly witty, or a labor of love is grist for my mill."

◢ BARER LITERARY, LLC

156 Fifth Ave., Suite 1134, New York NY 10010. Web site: www.barerliterary.com. **Contact:** Julie Barer. Member of AAR.

Represents Nonfiction books, novels, short story collections. **Considers these nonfiction areas:** Biography/autobiography; ethnic/cultural interests; history; memoirs; popular culture; women's issues/studies. **Considers these fiction areas:** Ethnic; family saga; historical; literary; mainstream/contemporary; young adult.

How to Contact Query with SASE.

Recent Sales *Jupiter's Palace*, by Lauren Fox (Knopf); *Then We Came to the End*, by Joshua Ferris (Little, Brown); *Why Can't We Be Friends*, by Megan Crane (Warner Books); *The Time It Takes to Fall*, by Margaret Lazarus Dean (Simon & Schuster).

Terms Agent receives 15% commission on domestic sales; 20% commission on foreign sales. Offers written contract. Charges for photocopying and books ordered.

◢ LORETTA BARRETT BOOKS, INC.

101 Fifth Ave., New York NY 10003. (212)242-3420. Fax: (212)807-9579. E-mail: mail@lorettabarrettbooks.com. **Contact:** Loretta A. Barrett, Nick Mullendore. Estab. 1990. Member of AAR. Currently handles: 60% nonfiction books; 40% novels.

• Prior to opening her agency, Ms. Barrett was vice president and executive editor at Doubleday and editor-in-chief of Anchor Books.

Represents Nonfiction books, novels. **Considers these nonfiction areas:** Biography/autobiography; business/economics; child guidance/parenting; current affairs; ethnic/cultural interests; gay/lesbian issues; government/politics/law; health/medicine; history; language/literature/criticism; memoirs; money/finance; multicultural; nature/environment; philosophy; popular culture; psychology; religious/inspirational; science/technology; self-help/personal improvement; sociology; spirituality; sports; women's issues/studies; nutrition; creative nonfiction. **Considers these fiction areas:** Action/adventure; contemporary issues; detective/police/crime; ethnic; family saga; historical; literary; mainstream/contemporary; mystery/suspense; psychic/supernatural; thriller.

O━ This agency specializes in general interest books. No children's, juvenile, science fiction, or fantasy.

How to Contact Query with SASE. No e-mail or fax queries. Considers simultaneous queries. Responds in 2-3 weeks to queries. Returns materials only with SASE.

Recent Sales *Dark Circles*, by Lila Shaara (Ballantine); *The Secret Power of Yoga*, by Nischala Joy Devi (Harmony); *Riverside Park*, by Laura Van Wormer (Mira); *Healing the Schism*, by Mark Judge (Doubleday); The Truth series, by Mariah Stewart (Ballantine); The Reincarnationist series, by M.J. Rose (Mira).

Terms Agent receives 15% commission on domestic sales; 20% commission on foreign sales. Offers written contract. Charges clients for shipping and photocopying.

Writers' Conferences San Diego State University Writers' Conference; Pacific Northwest Writers Conference; SEAK Medical & Legal Fiction Writing Conference.

N ◢ FAYE BENDER LITERARY AGENCY

337 W. 76th St., #E1, New York NY 10023. E-mail: info@fbliterary.com. Web site: www.fbliterary.com. **Contact:** Faye Bender. Estab. 2004. Member of AAR. Currently handles: 50% nonfiction books; 50% novels.

Represents Nonfiction books, novels. **Considers these nonfiction areas:** Memoirs; popular culture; women's issues/studies; narrative; health; biography; popular science. **Considers these fiction areas:** Literary; young adult (middle-grade); women's; commercial.

O━ "I choose books based on the narrative voice and strength of writing. I work with previously published and first-time authors." Does not want genre fiction (westerns, romance, horror, fantasy, science fiction).

How to Contact Query with SASE, 10 sample pages via mail or e-mail.

◢ MEREDITH BERNSTEIN LITERARY AGENCY

2095 Broadway, Suite 505, New York NY 10023. (212)799-1007. Fax: (212)799-1145. Estab. 1981. Member of AAR. Represents 85 clients. 20% of clients are new/unpublished writers. Currently handles: 50% nonfiction books; 50% fiction.

• Prior to opening her agency, Ms. Bernstein served at another agency for 5 years.

Represents Nonfiction books, novels. **Considers these nonfiction areas:** Any area of nonfiction in which the author has an established platform. **Considers these fiction areas:** Literary; mystery/suspense; romance; thriller; women's.

0— This agency does not specialize. It is very eclectic.

How to Contact Query with SASE. No e-mail or fax queries. Considers simultaneous queries. Obtains most new clients through recommendations from others, conferences, developing/packaging ideas.

Recent Sales *No Cry Discipline Solution*, by Elizabeth Pantley (McGraw-Hill); *Asking For It*, by Tory Johnson and Robyn Spizman (St. Martin's Press); *The House of Night*, by P.C. Cast (St. Martin's press).

Terms Agent receives 15% commission on domestic sales; 20% commission on foreign sales. Charges clients $75 disbursement fee/year.

Writers' Conferences Southwest Writers Conference; Rocky Mountain Fiction Writers Colorado Gold; Pacific Northwest Writers' Conference; Willamette Writers Conference; Surrey International Writers Conference; San Diego State University Writers' Conference.

⬤ DANIEL BIAL AGENCY

41 W. 83rd St., Suite 5-C, New York NY 10024-5246. (212)721-1786. Fax: (309)405-0525. E-mail: dbialagency@j uno.com. **Contact:** Daniel Bial. Estab. 1992. Represents under 50 clients. 15% of clients are new/unpublished writers. Currently handles: 95% nonfiction books; 5% novels.

● Prior to opening his agency, Mr. Bial was an editor for 15 years.

Represents Nonfiction books, novels. **Considers these nonfiction areas:** Animals; anthropology/archaeology; biography/autobiography; business/economics; child guidance/parenting; cooking/foods/nutrition; current affairs; ethnic/cultural interests; government/politics/law; history; how-to; humor/satire; language/literature/criticism; memoirs; military/war; money/finance; music/dance; nature/environment; New Age/metaphysics; popular culture; psychology; religious/inspirational; science/technology; self-help/personal improvement; sociology; spirituality; sports; theater/film; travel; true crime/investigative; women's issues/studies. **Considers these fiction areas:** Action/adventure; contemporary issues; detective/police/crime; erotica; ethnic; humor/satire; literary.

How to Contact Submit proposal package, outline. Responds in 2 weeks to queries. Returns materials only with SASE. Obtains most new clients through recommendations from others, solicitations, "good rolodex."

Recent Sales *Osama Bin Ladin: The Man Who Delcared War on America*, by Yossef Bodansky.

Terms Agent receives 15% commission on domestic sales; 25% commission on foreign sales. Offers written contract, binding for 1 year with cancellation clause. Charges clients for overseas calls, overnight mailing, photocopying, messenger expenses.

Tips "Publishers want their authors to have platforms. In other words, they want authors to have the ability to sell their work or get themselves in the media even before the book comes out. And successful agents get publishers what they want."

⬤ BIGSCORE PRODUCTIONS, INC.

P.O. Box 4575, Lancaster PA 17604. (717)293-0247. E-mail: bigscore@bigscoreproductions.com. Web site: www.bigscoreproductions.com. **Contact:** David A. Robie. Estab. 1995. Represents 50-75 clients. 25% of clients are new/unpublished writers.

Represents Nonfiction and fiction (see Web site for categories of interest).

0— Mr. Robie specializes in inspirational and self-help nonfiction and fiction, and has been in the publishing and agenting business for over 20 years.

How to Contact See Web site for submission guidelines. Query by e-mail only. Do not fax or mail queries. Considers simultaneous queries. Only responds if interested.

Terms Agent receives 15% commission on domestic sales. Offers written contract, binding for 6 months. Charges clients for expedited shipping, ms photocopying and preparation, books for subsidiary rights submissions.

Tips "We are very open to taking on new nonfiction clients. We only consider established fiction writers. Submit a well-prepared proposal that will take minimal fine-tuning for presentation to publishers. Nonfiction writers must be highly marketable and media savvy—the more established in speaking or in your profession, the better. Bigscore Productions works with all major general and Christian publishers."

◖ VICKY BIJUR LITERARY AGENCY

333 West End Ave., Apt. 5B, New York NY 10023. E-mail: assistant@vickybijuragency.com. Member of AAR.

Represents Nonfiction books, novels. **Considers these nonfiction areas:** Cooking/foods/nutrition; government/politics/law; health/medicine; history; psychology (psychiatry); science/technology; self-help/personal improvement; sociology; biography; child care/development; environmental studies; journalism; nursing/dentistry; social sciences.

How to Contact Accepts e-mail queries.

DAVID BLACK LITERARY AGENCY

156 Fifth Ave., Suite 608, New York NY 10010-7002. (212)242-5080. Fax: (212)924-6609. **Contact:** David Black, owner. Estab. 1990. Member of AAR. Represents 150 clients. Currently handles: 90% nonfiction books; 10% novels.

Member Agents David Black; Susan Raihofer (general nonfiction, literary fiction); Gary Morris (commercial fiction, psychology); Joy E. Tutela (general nonfiction, literary fiction); Leigh Ann Eliseo; Linda Loewenthal (general nonfiction, health, science, psychology, narrative).

Represents Nonfiction books, novels. **Considers these nonfiction areas:** Biography/autobiography; business/economics; government/politics/law; health/medicine; history; memoirs; military/war; money/finance; multicultural; psychology; religious/inspirational; sports; women's issues/studies. **Considers these fiction areas:** Literary; mainstream/contemporary; commercial.

O⇥ This agency specializes in business, sports, politics, and novels.

How to Contact Query with SASE, outline. No e-mail or fax queries. Considers simultaneous queries. Responds in 2 months to queries. Returns materials only with SASE.

Recent Sales *Body for Life*, by Bill Phillips with Mike D'Orso (HarperCollins); *Devil in the White City*, by Erik Larson; The Don't Know Much About series, by Ken Davis; *Tuesdays with Morrie*, by Mitch Albom.

Terms Agent receives 15% commission on domestic sales. Charges clients for photocopying and books purchased for sale of foreign rights.

BLEECKER STREET ASSOCIATES, INC.

532 LaGuardia Place, #617, New York NY 10012. (212)677-4492. Fax: (212)388-0001. **Contact:** Agnes Birnbaum. Estab. 1984. Member of AAR, RWA, MWA. Represents 60 clients. 20% of clients are new/unpublished writers. Currently handles: 75% nonfiction books; 25% novels.

• Prior to becoming an agent, Ms. Birnbaum was a senior editor at Simon & Schuster, Dutton/Signet, and other publishing houses.

Represents Nonfiction books, novels. **Considers these nonfiction areas:** Animals; biography/autobiography; business/economics; child guidance/parenting; computers/electronic; cooking/foods/nutrition; current affairs; ethnic/cultural interests; government/politics/law; health/medicine; history; how-to; memoirs; military/war; money/finance; nature/environment; New Age/metaphysics; popular culture; psychology; religious/inspirational; science/technology; self-help/personal improvement; sociology; sports; true crime/investigative; women's issues/studies. **Considers these fiction areas:** Ethnic; historical; literary; mystery/suspense; romance; thriller; women's.

O⇥ "We're very hands-on and accessible. We try to be truly creative in our submission approaches. We've had especially good luck with first-time authors." Does not want to receive science fiction, westerns, poetry, children's books, academic/scholarly/professional books, plays, scripts, or short stories.

How to Contact Query with SASE. No email, phone, or fax queries. Considers simultaneous queries. Responds in 2 weeks to queries; 1 month to mss. Returns materials only with SASE. Obtains most new clients through recommendations from others, solicitations, conferences, "plus, I will approach someone with a letter if his/ her work impresses me."

Recent Sales Sold 20 titles in the last year. *How America Got It Right*, by Bevin Alexander (Crown); *Buddha Baby*, by Kim Wong Keltner (Morrow/Avon); *American Bee*, by James Maguire (Rodale); *Guide to the Galaxy*, by Pat Barnes-Svarney (Sterling); *Phantom Warrior*, by Bryant Johnson (Berkley).

Terms Agent receives 15% commission on domestic sales; 25% commission on foreign sales. Offers written contract; 1-month notice must be given to terminate contract. Charges for postage, long distance, fax, messengers, photocopies (not to exceed $200).

Tips "Keep query letters short and to the point; include only information pertaining to the book or your background as a writer. Try to avoid superlatives in description. Work needs to stand on its own, so how much editing it may have received has no place in a query letter."

THE BLUMER LITERARY AGENCY, INC.

350 Seventh Ave., Suite 2003, New York NY 10001-5013. (212)947-3040. **Contact:** Olivia B. Blumer. Estab. 2002. Board member of AAR. Represents 34 clients. 60% of clients are new/unpublished writers. Currently handles: 67% nonfiction books; 33% novels.

• Prior to becoming an agent, Ms. Blumer spent 25 years in publishing (subsidiary rights, publicity, editorial).

Represents Nonfiction books, novels. **Considers these nonfiction areas:** Agriculture/horticulture; animals; anthropology/archaeology; art/architecture/design; biography/autobiography; business/economics; cooking/foods/nutrition; ethnic/cultural interests; health/medicine; how-to; humor/satire; language/literature/criticism; memoirs; money/finance; nature/environment; photography; popular culture; psychology; religious/inspirational; self-help/personal improvement; true crime/investigative; women's issues/studies; New Age/metaphysics; crafts/hobbies; interior design/decorating. **Considers these fiction areas:** Detective/police/crime; ethnic; family saga; feminist; historical; humor/satire; literary; mainstream/contemporary; mystery/suspense; regional; thriller.

O↝ Actively seeking quality fiction, practical nonfiction, and memoir with a larger purpose.

How to Contact Query with SASE. No e-mail or fax queries. Responds in 2 weeks to queries; 4-6 weeks to mss. Returns materials only with SASE. Obtains most new clients through recommendations from others, but significant exceptions have come from the slush pile.

Recent Sales *The Color of Law*, by Mark Gimenez; *Still Life with Chickens*, by Catherine Goldhammer. Other clients include Joan Anderson, Marialisa Calta, Ellen Rolfes, Mark Forstater, Laura Karr, Liz McGregor, Constance Snow, Lauri Ward, Michelle Curry Wright, Susann Cokal, Dennis L. Smith, Sharon Pywell, Sarah Turnbull, Naomi Duguid, Jeffrey Alford.

Terms Agent receives 15% commission on domestic sales; 20% commission on foreign sales. Charges for photocopying, overseas shipping, FedEx/UPS.

⊘ REID BOATES LITERARY AGENCY

69 Cooks Crossroad, Pittstown NJ 08867. (908)730-8523. Fax: (908)730-8931. E-mail: boatesliterary@att.net. **Contact:** Reid Boates. Estab. 1985. Represents 45 clients. 5% of clients are new/unpublished writers. Currently handles: 85% nonfiction books; 15% novels; very rarely story collections.

How to Contact No unsolicited queries of any kind. Obtains new clients by personal referral only.

Recent Sales Sold 20 titles in the last year. This agency prefers not to share information on specific sales.

Terms Agent receives 15% commission on domestic sales; 20% commission on foreign sales.

⊘ BOOKENDS, LLC

136 Long Hill Rd., Gillette NJ 07933. E-mail: editor@bookends-inc.com. Web site: www.bookends-inc.com. **Contact:** Jessica Faust, Jacky Sach, Kim Lionetti. Estab. 1999. Represents 50+ clients. 20% of clients are new/unpublished writers. Currently handles: 50% nonfiction books; 50% novels.

Represents Nonfiction books, novels. **Considers these nonfiction areas:** Business/economics; child guidance/parenting; ethnic/cultural interests; gay/lesbian issues; health/medicine; how-to; money/finance; New Age/metaphysics; psychology; religious/inspirational; self-help/personal improvement; spirituality; true crime/investigative; women's issues/studies. **Considers these fiction areas:** Detective/police/crime (cozies); mainstream/contemporary; mystery/suspense; romance; thriller; chick lit.

O↝ BookEnds does not want to receive children's books, screenplays, science fiction, poetry, or technical/military thrillers.

How to Contact Review Web site for guidelines.

⊘ BOOKS & SUCH

52 Mission Circle, Suite 122, PMB 170, Santa Rosa CA 95409. E-mail: representative@booksandsuch.biz. Web site: www.booksandsuch.biz. **Contact:** Janet Kobobel Grant, Wendy Lawton. Estab. 1996. Member of CBA (associate), American Christian Fiction Writers. Represents 80 clients. 5% of clients are new/unpublished writers. Currently handles: 49% nonfiction books; 50% novels; 1% children's picture books.

● Prior to becoming an agent, Ms. Grant was an editor for Zondervan and managing editor for *Focus on the Family*; Ms. Lawton was an author, sculptor, and designer of porcelein dolls.

Represents Nonfiction books, novels, children's picture books. **Considers these nonfiction areas:** Child guidance/parenting; humor/satire; juvenile nonfiction; religious/inspirational; self-help/personal improvement; women's issues/studies. **Considers these fiction areas:** Contemporary issues; family saga; historical; juvenile; mainstream/contemporary; picture books; religious/inspirational; romance; African American adult.

O↝ This agency specializes in general and inspirational fiction, romance, and in the Christian booksellers market. Actively seeking well-crafted material that presents Judeo-Christian values, if only subtly.

How to Contact Query with SASE. Considers simultaneous queries. Responds in 1 month to queries; 2 months to mss. Returns materials only with SASE. Obtains most new clients through recommendations from others, conferences.

Recent Sales Sold 112 titles in the last year. *My Life As a Doormat (In Three Acts)*, by Rene Gutterridge; *Having a Mary Spirit*, by Joanna Weaver; *Finding Father Christmas*, by Robin Jones Gunn; *No More Mr. Christian Nice Guy*, by Paul Coughlin. Other clients include Janet McHenry, Jane Orcutt, Gayle Roper, Stephanie Grace Whitson, Dale Cramer, Patti Hill, Gayle Roper, Sara Horn.

Terms Agent receives 15% commission on domestic and foreign sales. Offers written contract; 2-month notice must be given to terminate contract. Charges clients for postage, photocopying, telephone calls, fax, express mail.

Writers' Conferences Mount Hermon Christian Writers Conference; Wrangling With Writing; Glorieta Christian

Writers' Conference; Writing for the Soul; Blue Ridge Mountains Christian Writers Conference; Write! Canada; American Christian Fiction Writers Conference; Sandy Cove Christian Writers Conference.

Tips ''The heart of our agency's motivation is to develop relationships with the authors we serve, to do what we can to shine the light of success on them, and to help be a caretaker of their gifts and time.''

☺ GEORGES BORCHARDT, INC.

136 E. 57th St., New York NY 10022. Estab. 1967. Member of AAR.

Member Agents Anne Borchardt; Georges Borchardt; Valerie Borchardt.

○➝ This agency specializes in literary fiction and outstanding nonfiction.

How to Contact *No unsolicited mss.* Obtains most new clients through recommendations from others.

Terms Agent receives 15% commission on domestic sales; 20% commission on foreign sales. Offers written contract.

☺ THE BARBARA BOVA LITERARY AGENCY

P.O. Box 770365, Naples FL 34107. (941)649-7237. Fax: (239)649-7263. E-mail: barbarabova@barbarabovaliter aryagency.com. Web site: www.barbarabovaliteraryagency.com. **Contact:** Barbara Bova. Estab. 1974. Represents 30 clients. Currently handles: 20% nonfiction books; 80% novels.

Represents Nonfiction books, novels. **Considers these nonfiction areas:** Biography/autobiography; science/technology; self-help/personal improvement; true crime/investigative; women's issues/studies; social sciences. **Considers these fiction areas:** Action/adventure; detective/police/crime; glitz; mystery/suspense; science fiction; thriller; women's; chick lit; teen lit.

○➝ This agency specializes in fiction and nonfiction, hard and soft science.

How to Contact Query through Web site. Obtains most new clients through recommendations from others.

Recent Sales Sold 13 titles in the last year. *Powersat* and *Titan*, by Ben Bova; *So Lyrical* and *Overnight Sensation*, by Patricia Cook; *Springheel Jack*, by Virginia Baker; *Written on the Wind*, by Joyce Henderson.

Terms Agent receives 15% commission on domestic sales; 20% commission on foreign sales.

Tips ''We also handle foreign, movie, television, and audio rights.''

ℕ ◎ BRANDS-TO-BOOKS, INC.

419 Lafayette St., New York NY 10003. (646)723-4583. Fax: (212)874-2892. E-mail: agents@brandstobooks.c om. Web site: www.brandstobooks.com. **Contact:** Kathleen Spinelli, Robert Allen. Estab. 2004. 70% of clients are new/unpublished writers. Currently handles: 100% nonfiction books.

- Prior to co-founding Brands-to-Books, Mr. Allen was president and publisher of the Random House Audio Division; Ms. Spinelli was vice president/director of marketing for Ballantine Books.

Member Agents Kathleen Spinelli (lifestyle, design, business, personal finance, health, pop culture, sports, travel, cooking, crafts, how-to, reference); Robert Allen (business, motivation, psychology, how-to, pop culture, self-help/personal improvement, narrative nonfiction).

Represents Nonfiction books, ghostwriters. **Considers these nonfiction areas:** Anthropology/archaeology; art/architecture/design; biography/autobiography; business/economics; child guidance/parenting; computers/electronic; cooking/foods/nutrition; crafts/hobbies; current affairs; ethnic/cultural interests; gay/lesbian issues; government/politics/law; health/medicine; history; how-to; humor/satire; interior design/decorating; language/literature/criticism; memoirs; money/finance; music/dance; photography; popular culture; psychology; self-help/personal improvement; sports; theater/film; books based from brands.

○➝ ''We concentrate on brand-name businesses, products, and personalities whose platform, passion, and appeal translate into successful publishing ventures. We offer more than literary representation—we provide clients a true marketing partner, pursuing and maximizing every opportunity for promotion and sales within the publishing process.'' Actively seeking nonfiction proposals supported by strong media platforms and experienced ghostwriters—especially those who have worked with brands/personalities. Does not want fiction or poetry.

How to Contact Query with book overview, résumé/platform. Considers simultaneous queries. Responds in 3 weeks to queries. Obtains most new clients through recommendations from others, outreach to brand managers and the licensing industry.

Recent Sales *The Travel Mom's Ultimate Book of Family Travel*, by Emily Kaufman (Broadway Books); *TV Guide: TV on DVD 2006*, by the editors of *TV Guide* (St. Martin's Press); *Weddings: Create a Day Uniquely Your Own*, by Michelle Rago (Gotham Books); *A Passion for Jewelry*, by Temple St. Clair (Regan Books).

Terms Agent receives 15% commission on domestic sales; 20% commission on foreign sales. Offers written contract; 3-month written notice must be given to terminate contract. Charges for office expenses (copying, messengers, express mail).

Tips ''In your query, clearly show your passion for the subject and why you are the best person to write this book. Establish your media experience and platform. Indicate you have done your market research and demonstrate how this book is different from what is already on the shelves.''

BRANDT & HOCHMAN LITERARY AGENTS, INC.

1501 Broadway, Suite 2310, New York NY 10036. (212)840-5760. Fax: (212)840-5776. Estab. 1913. Member of AAR. Represents 200 clients.
Member Agents Carl Brandt; Gail Hochman; Marianne Merola; Charles Schlessiger.
Represents Nonfiction books, novels, short story collections, juvenile books, journalism. **Considers these nonfiction areas:** Biography/autobiography; current affairs; ethnic/cultural interests; government/politics/law; history; women's issues/studies. **Considers these fiction areas:** Contemporary issues; ethnic; historical; literary; mainstream/contemporary; mystery/suspense; romance; thriller; young adult.
How to Contact Query with SASE. No e-mail or fax queries. Considers simultaneous queries. Responds in 1 month to queries. Returns materials only with SASE. Obtains most new clients through recommendations from others.
Recent Sales This agency prefers not to share information on specific sales.
Terms Agent receives 15% commission on domestic sales; 20% commission on foreign sales. Charges clients for ms duplication or other special expenses agreed to in advance.
Tips "Write a letter which will give the agent a sense of you as a professional writer—your long-term interests as well as a short description of the work at hand.''

THE HELEN BRANN AGENCY, INC.

94 Curtis Rd., Bridgewater CT 06752. Fax: (860)355-2572. Member of AAR.
How to Contact Query with SASE.

BARBARA BRAUN ASSOCIATES, INC.

104 Fifth Ave., 7th Floor, New York NY 10011. Fax: (212)604-9041. E-mail: bba230@earthlink.net. Web site: www.barbarabraunagency.com. **Contact:** Barbara Braun. Member of AAR.
Member Agents Barbara Braun; John F. Baker.
Represents Nonfiction books, novels.

> "Our fiction is strong on women's stories, historical and multicultural stories, as well as mysteries and thrillers. We're interested in narrative nonfiction and books by journalists. We do not represent poetry, science fiction, fantasy, horror, or screenplays." Look online for more details.

How to Contact Query with SASE. Accepts e-mail queries (no full mss).
Recent Sales *Life Studies*, by Susan Vreeland (Viking/Penguin); *The Lost Van Gogh*, by A.J. Zerries (Tor/ Forge); *Sakharov: Science and Freedom*, by Gennady Gorelik and Antonina Bouis (Oxford University Press); *A Strand of Corpses* and *A Friend of Need*, by J.R. Benn (Soho Press).
Terms Agent receives 15% commission on domestic sales; 20% commission on foreign sales.

BRICK HOUSE LITERARY AGENTS

80 Fifth Ave., Suite 1101, New York NY 10011. Web site: www.brickhouselit.com. **Contact:** Sally Wofford-Girand. Member of AAR.
Member Agents Sally Wofford-Girand; Judy Heiblum; Margaret Kopp, assistant.
Represents Nonfiction books, novels. **Considers these nonfiction areas:** Ethnic/cultural interests; history; memoirs; women's issues/studies; biography; science; natural history. **Considers these fiction areas:** Literary.
How to Contact Query via mail or e-mail.

RICK BROADHEAD & ASSOCIATES LITERARY AGENCY

501-47 St. Clair Ave. W., Toronto ON M4V 3A5 Canada. (416)929-0516. Fax: (416)927-8732. E-mail: rba@rbalite rary.com. Web site: www.rbaliterary.com. **Contact:** Rick Broadhead, president. Estab. 2002. Member of Authors Guild. Represents 20 clients. 50% of clients are new/unpublished writers. Currently handles: 85% nonfiction books; 5% novels; 10% juvenile books.

> • Mr. Broadhead discovered his passion for books when he co-authored his first bestseller at the age of 23. His vast knowledge of the publishing industry, both as an author and an agent, and his relationships with American publishers and editors, have allowed the agency to consistently negotiate excellent deals for its clients. Mr. Broadhead brings a passion, tenacity, and energy to agenting that his clients love.

Represents Nonfiction books. **Considers these nonfiction areas:** Animals; anthropology/archaeology; art/ architecture/design; biography/autobiography; business/economics; child guidance/parenting; computers/ electronic; cooking/foods/nutrition; crafts/hobbies; current affairs; education; ethnic/cultural interests; government/politics/law; health/medicine; history; how-to; humor/satire; interior design/decorating; juvenile nonfiction; language/literature/criticism; memoirs; military/war; money/finance; music/dance; nature/environment;

popular culture; psychology; religious/inspirational; science/technology; self-help/personal improvement; sociology; sports; true crime/investigative; women's issues/studies.

　　O→ This established agency represents American authors to American and foreign publishers in a wide variety of nonfiction genres, including narrative nonfiction, business, self-help, parenting, memoir, reference, history/politics, sports, science, current affairs, health/medicine, pop culture, humor, and gift books. The agency is deliberately small, which allows clients to receive personalized service to maximize the success of their book projects and brands. The agency works with Hollywood agents on book projects with film/TV potential and sells projects directly to foreign publishers (United Kingdom, Australia/New Zealand) and in partnership with co-agents. Actively seeking compelling nonfiction proposals, especially narrative nonfiction (history, current affairs, business) from authors with relevant credentials and an established media platform (TV, radio, print exposure). Does not want television scripts, movie scripts, or poetry.

How to Contact If sending by mail, include a complete proposal, 1-2 sample chapters. If sending by e-mail, include a short description of the project, credentials/bio. E-mail queries preferred. Do not paste entire proposal or ms into e-mail. Agency will reply only to projects of interest. Considers simultaneous queries. Obtains most new clients through solicitations, e-mail queries, referrals from existing clients.

Recent Sales Sold 16 titles in the last year. *The Secret Life of Meat*, by Susan Bourette (Putnam/Penguin); *The Subway Chronicles*, by Jacquelin Cangro (Plume/Penguin); *The Trouble With Africa*, by Robert Calderisi (St. Martin's Press); *101 Foods That Could Save Your Life*, by Dave Grotto (Bantam/Random House); *Talk Isn't Cheap: The Elements of Great Public Speaking*, by Lyman MacInnis (Ten Speed Press); *When the Lights Went Out: The Last Battle in Hockey's Cold War*, by Gare Joyce (Random House/Doubleday Canada). Other clients include Sarah Smiley, David Katz, Michael Weiss, Sheldon Wagner, Gary Sutton, Terence Denman.

Terms Agent receives 15% commission on domestic sales; 20-25% commission on foreign sales. Offers written contract.

Tips ''The agency has excellent relationships with New York publishers and editors and many of the agency's clients are American authors. The agency has sold numerous unsolicited submissions to large publishers and welcomes queries by e-mail.''

◙ MARIE BROWN ASSOCIATES, INC.

412 W. 154th St., New York NY 10032. (212)939-9725. Fax: (212)939-9728. E-mail: mbrownlit@aol.com. **Contact:** Marie Brown. Estab. 1984. Represents 60 clients. Currently handles: 75% nonfiction books; 10% juvenile books; 15% other.

Member Agents Janell Walden Agyeman (Miami, Florida).

Represents Nonfiction books, juvenile books. **Considers these nonfiction areas:** Biography/autobiography; business/economics; ethnic/cultural interests; history; juvenile nonfiction; music/dance; religious/inspirational; women's issues/studies. **Considers these fiction areas:** Ethnic; juvenile; literary; mainstream/contemporary.

　　O→ This agency specializes in multicultural and African-American writers.

How to Contact Query with SASE. Prefers to read materials exclusively. Responds in 6-10 to queries. Obtains most new clients through recommendations from others.

Recent Sales *Kwanzaa*, by Maetefa Angana; *Kinky Gazpacho*, by Lori Tharps; *Lovers Rock*, by Colin Channer; *Succulent Tales*, by Valinda Brown.

Terms Agent receives 15% commission on domestic sales; 20% commission on foreign sales. Offers written contract.

N ◙ BROWN LITERARY AGENCY

410 7th St. NW, Naples FL 34120. (239)455-7190. E-mail: broagent@aol.com. Web site: www.brownliteraryagency.com. **Contact:** Roberta Brown. Estab. 1996. Member of AAR, RWA, Author's Guild. Represents 35 clients. 5% of clients are new/unpublished writers.

　　● Prior to becoming an agent, Ms. Brown worked in a literacy program at a local high school.

Represents Novels. **Considers these fiction areas:** Erotica; romance (single title and category); women's.

How to Contact Submit synopsis, 3 sample chapters. No e-mail or fax queries. Considers simultaneous queries. Responds in 4-6 weeks to queries; 2 months to mss. Obtains most new clients through recommendations from others, conferences, visitors to Web site.

Recent Sales Sold 35 titles in the last year. Clients include Emma Holly, Angela Knight, Karen Kay, Jenna Mills, Dianne Castell, Lora Leigh, Shiloh Walker, Kate Angell, Sue-Ellen Welfonder.

Terms Agent receives 15% commission on domestic and foreign sales. Offers written contract; 30-day notice must be given to terminate contract.

Writers' Conferences RWA National Conference; Romantic Times Convention.

Tips ''Polish your manuscript. Be professional.''

ANDREA BROWN LITERARY AGENCY, INC.

560 San Antonio Rd., Suite 105, Palo Alto CA 94306. E-mail: andrea@andreabrownlit.com. Web site: www.andr eabrownlit.com. **Contact:** Andrea Brown, president. Estab. 1981. 10% of clients are new/unpublished writers.

- Prior to opening her agency, Ms. Brown served as an editorial assistant at Random House and Dell Publishing and as an editor with Alfred A. Knopf.

Member Agents Andrea Brown; Laura Rennert; Caryn Wiseman; Jennifer Jaeger; Robert Welsh; Michelle Andelman.

Represents Nonfiction books, novels. **Considers these nonfiction areas:** Memoirs; young adult; narrative; juvenile. **Considers these fiction areas:** Juvenile; literary; picture books; thriller; young adult; women's.

How to Contact For picture books, submit complete ms, SASE. For fiction, submit short synopsis, SASE, first 3 chapters. For nonfiction, submit proposal, 1-2 sample chapters. For illustrations, submit 4-5 color samples (no originals). Accepts e-mail queries. No fax queries. Considers simultaneous queries. Obtains most new clients through referrals from editors, clients, and agents.

Terms Agent receives 15% commission on domestic sales; 20% commission on foreign sales. Offers written contract. Charges clients for shipping costs.

Writers' Conferences SCBWI; Asilomar; Maui Writers Conference; Southwest Writers Conference; San Diego State University Writers' Conference; Big Sur Children's Writing Workshop; William Saroyan Writers' Conference; Columbus Writers Conference; Willamette Writers Conference; La Jolla Writers Conference; San Francisco Writers Conference; Hilton Head Writers Conference.

CURTIS BROWN, LTD.

10 Astor Place, New York NY 10003-6935. (212)473-5400. Alternate address: Peter Ginsberg, president at CBF, 1750 Montgomery St., San Fancisco CA 94111. (415)954-8566. Member of AAR; signatory of WGA.

Member Agents Laura Blake Peterson; Emilie Jacobson, senior vice president; Maureen Walters, senior vice president; Ginger Knowlton, vice president (children's); Timothy Knowlton, CEO (film, screenplays); Ed Wintle; Mitchell Waters; Elizabeth Harding.

Represents Nonfiction books, novels, short story collections, juvenile books. **Considers these nonfiction areas:** Agriculture/horticulture; Americana; animals; anthropology/archaeology; art/architecture/design; biography/ autobiography; business/economics; child guidance/parenting; computers/electronic; cooking/foods/nutrition; crafts/hobbies; current affairs; education; ethnic/cultural interests; gardening; gay/lesbian issues; government/politics/law; health/medicine; history; how-to; humor/satire; interior design/decorating; juvenile nonfiction; language/literature/criticism; memoirs; military/war; money/finance; multicultural; music/dance; nature/environment; New Age/metaphysics; philosophy; photography; popular culture; psychology; recreation; regional; religious/inspirational; science/technology; self-help/personal improvement; sex; sociology; software; spirituality; sports; theater/film; translation; travel; true crime/investigative; women's issues/studies; young adult; creative nonfiction. **Considers these fiction areas:** Action/adventure; comic books/cartoon; confession; contemporary issues; detective/police/crime; erotica; ethnic; experimental; family saga; fantasy; feminist; gay/ lesbian; glitz; gothic; hi-lo; historical; horror; humor/satire; juvenile; literary; mainstream/contemporary; military/war; multicultural; multimedia; mystery/suspense; New Age; occult; picture books; plays; poetry; psychic/ supernatural; regional; religious/inspirational; romance; science fiction; short story collections; spiritual; sports; thriller; translation; westerns/frontier; young adult; women's.

How to Contact Query individual agent with SASE. Prefers to read materials exclusively. *No unsolicited mss.* No e-mail or fax queries. Responds in 3 weeks to queries; 5 weeks to mss. Obtains most new clients through recommendations from others, solicitations, conferences.

Recent Sales This agency prefers not to share information on specific sales.

Terms Offers written contract. Charges for photocopying and some postage.

BROWNE & MILLER LITERARY ASSOCIATES

410 S. Michigan Ave., Suite 460, Chicago IL 60605-1465. (312)922-3063. E-mail: mail@browneandmiller.com. **Contact:** Danielle Egan-Miller. Estab. 1971. Member of AAR, RWA, MWA, Author's Guild. Represents 150 clients. 2% of clients are new/unpublished writers. Currently handles: 40% nonfiction books; 60% novels.

Represents Nonfiction books, novels. **Considers these nonfiction areas:** Agriculture/horticulture; animals; anthropology/archaeology; biography/autobiography; business/economics; child guidance/parenting; cooking/foods/nutrition; crafts/hobbies; creative nonfiction; current affairs; ethnic/cultural interests; health/medicine; how-to; humor/satire; memoirs; money/finance; nature/environment; popular culture; psychology; religious/inspirational; science/technology; self-help/personal improvement; sociology; sports; true crime/investigative; women's issues/studies. **Considers these fiction areas:** Detective/police/crime; ethnic; family saga; glitz; historical; literary; mainstream/contemporary; mystery/suspense; religious/inspirational; romance (contemporary, gothic, historical, regency); sports; thriller.

O₋ᴨ "We are generalists looking for professional writers with finely honed skills in writing. We are partial to authors with promotion savvy. We work closely with our authors through the whole publishing process, from proposal to after publication." Actively seeking highly commercial mainstream fiction and nonfiction. Does not represent poetry, short stories, plays, screenplays, articles, or children's books.

How to Contact Query with SASE. *No unsolicited mss.* Prefers to read material exclusively. Responds in 6 weeks to queries. Returns materials only with SASE. Obtains most new clients through referrals, queries by professional/marketable authors.

Terms Agent receives 15% commission on domestic sales; 20% commission on foreign sales. Offers written contract, binding for 2 years. Charges clients for photocopying, overseas postage, faxes, phone calls.

Writers' Conferences BookExpo America; Frankfurt Book Fair; RWA National Conference; CBA National Conference; London Book Fair; Bouchercon.

Tips "If interested in agency representation, be well informed."

☑ PEMA BROWNE, LTD.

11 Tena Place, Valley Cottage NY 10989. Web site: www.pemabrowneltd.com. **Contact:** Pema Browne. Estab. 1966. Member of SCBWI, RWA; signatory of WGA. Represents 30 clients. Currently handles: 25% nonfiction books; 50% novels/romance novels; 25% juvenile books.

• Prior to opening her agency, Ms. Browne was an artist and art buyer.

Represents Nonfiction books, novels, juvenile books, reference books. **Considers these nonfiction areas:** Business/economics; child guidance/parenting; cooking/foods/nutrition; ethnic/cultural interests; gay/lesbian issues; health/medicine; how-to; juvenile nonfiction; military/war; money/finance; New Age/metaphysics; popular culture; psychology; religious/inspirational; self-help/personal improvement; spirituality; true crime/investigative; women's issues/studies; reference. **Considers these fiction areas:** Action/adventure; contemporary issues; detective/police/crime; feminist; gay/lesbian; glitz; historical; humor/satire; juvenile; literary; mainstream/contemporary (commercial); mystery/suspense; picture books; psychic/supernatural; religious/inspirational; romance (contemporary, gothic, historical, regency); young adult.

O₋ᴨ "We are not accepting any new projects or authors until further notice."

How to Contact Query with SASE. No e-mail or fax queries. Responds in 6 weeks to queries; 6-8 weeks to mss. Returns materials only with SASE. Obtains most new clients through editors, authors, *LMP, Guide to Literary Agents.*"

Recent Sales *The Daring Harriet Quimby*, by Suzane Whitaker (Holiday House); *One Night to Be Sinful*, by Samantha Garver (Kensington); *Point Eyes of the Dragon*, by Linda Cargill (Cora Verlag).

Terms Agent receives 20% commission on domestic and foreign sales.

Tips "We do not review manuscripts that have been sent out to publishers. If writing romance, be sure to receive guidelines from various romance publishers. In nonfiction, one must have credentials to lend credence to a proposal. Make sure of margins, double-space, and use clean, dark type."

🆔 ⊕ ☑ BRYSON AGENCY AUSTRALIA

(61)(3)9620-9100. Fax: (61)(3)9621-2788. E-mail: agency@bryson.com.au. Web site: www.bryson.com.au. **Contact:** Fran Bryson, John Timlin.

Represents Nonfiction books, novels, movie scripts, TV scripts, stage plays.

O₋ᴨ "We are not accepting submissions at this time."

Recent Sales *The Lost Thoughts of Soldiers*, by Delia Falconer (Picador); *After the Party*, by Jesse Blackadder (Hardie Grant Books); *Judy Cassab: A Portrait*, by Brenda Niall (Allen & Unwin).

☑ KNOX BURGER ASSOCIATES, LTD.

10 W. 15th St., Suite 1914, New York NY 10011. Member of AAR.

O₋ᴨ "We are not taking on new clients at this time."

◖ SHEREE BYKOFSKY ASSOCIATES, INC.

16 W. 36th St., 13th Floor, New York NY 10018. E-mail: shereebee@aol.com. Web site: www.shereebee.com. **Contact:** Sheree Bykofsky. Estab. 1984; incorporated 1991. Member of AAR, ASJA, WNBA. Currently handles: 80% nonfiction books; 20% novels.

• Prior to opening her agency, Ms. Bykofsky served as executive editor of The Stonesong Press and managing editor of Chiron Press. She is also the author or co-author of more than 20 books, including *The Complete Idiot's Guide to Getting Published*. Ms. Bykofsky teaches publishing at NYU and SEAK, Inc.

Member Agents Janet Rosen, associate; Caroline Woods, associate.

Represents Nonfiction books, novels. **Considers these nonfiction areas:** Americana; animals; art/architecture/design; biography/autobiography; business/economics; child guidance/parenting; cooking/foods/nutrition; crafts/hobbies; current affairs; education; ethnic/cultural interests; gardening; gay/lesbian issues; government/

politics/law; health/medicine; history; how-to; humor/satire; interior design/decorating; language/literature/criticism; memoirs; military/war; money/finance (personal finance); multicultural; music/dance; nature/environment; New Age/metaphysics; philosophy; photography; popular culture; psychology; recreation; regional; religious/inspirational; science/technology; self-help/personal improvement; sex; sociology; spirituality; sports; theater/film; translation; travel; true crime/investigative; women's issues/studies; anthropolgy; creative nonfiction. **Considers these fiction areas:** Literary; mainstream/contemporary; mystery/suspense.

O—┐ This agency specializes in popular reference nonfiction, commercial fiction with a literary quality, and mysteries. "I have wide-ranging interests, but it really depends on quality of writing, originality, and how a particular project appeals to me (or not). I take on fiction when I completely love it—it doesn't matter what area or genre." Does not want to receive poetry, material for children, screenplays, westerns, horror, science fiction, or fantasy.

How to Contact Query with SASE. No unsolicited mss, e-mail queries, or phone calls. Considers simultaneous queries. Responds in 3 weeks to queries with SASE. Responds in 1 month to requested mss. Returns materials only with SASE. Obtains most new clients through recommendations from others.

Recent Sales Sold 100 titles in the last year. *Self-Esteem Sickness*, by Albert Ellis (Prometheus); *When the Ghost Screams*, by Leslie Rule (Andrews McMeel); *225 Squares*, by Matt Gaffney (Avalon).

Terms Agent receives 15% commission on domestic sales; 20% commission on foreign sales. Offers written contract, binding for 1 year. Charges for postage, photocopying, fax.

Writers' Conferences ASJA Writers Conference; Asilomar; Florida Suncoast Writers' Conference; Whidbey Island Writers' Conference; Florida First Coast Writers' Festibal; Agents and Editors Conference; Columbus Writers Conference; Southwest Writers Conference; Willamette Writers Conferece; Dorothy Canfield Fisher Conference; Maui Writers Conference; Pacific Northwest Writers Conference; IWWG.

Tips "Read the agent listing carefully and comply with guidelines."

⊘ CYNTHIA CANNELL LITERARY AGENCY

833 Madison Ave., New York NY 10021. **Contact:** Cynthia Cannell. Member of AAR.

O—┐ Not accepting new clients at this time.

⊘ CANTON SMITH AGENCY

194 Broadway, Amityville NY 11701. (631)842-9476 or (210)379-5961. E-mail: bookhold2@yahoo.com; esmith167@hotmail.com. Alternate address: 11955 Parliament Rd., #1008, San Antonio TX 78216. **Contact:** Eric Smith, senior partner; Chamein Canton, partner. Estab. 2001. Represents 28 clients. 100% of clients are new/unpublished writers.

• Prior to becoming agents, Mr. Smith was in advertising and bookstore retail; Ms. Canton was a writer and a paralegal.

Member Agents Eric Smith (science fiction, sports, literature); Chamein Canton (how-to, reference, literary, women's, multicultural, ethnic, crafts, cooking, health); Melissa Falcone (childrens, juvenile, young adult, teen, fantasy).

Represents Nonfiction books, novels, juvenile books, scholarly books, textbooks, movie scripts. **Considers these nonfiction areas:** Art/architecture/design; business/economics; child guidance/parenting; cooking/foods/nutrition; education; ethnic/cultural interests; health/medicine; history; how-to; humor/satire; language/literature/criticism; memoirs; military/war; music/dance; photography; psychology; sports; translation; women's issues/studies. **Considers these fiction areas:** Fantasy; humor/satire; juvenile; multicultural; romance; young adult; Latina fiction; chick lit; African-American fiction; entertainment. **Considers these script subject areas:** Action/adventure; comedy; romantic comedy; romantic drama; science fiction.

O—┐ "We specialize in helping new and established writers expand their marketing potential for prospective publishers. We are currently focusing on women's fiction (chick lit), Latina fiction, African American fiction, multicultural, romance, memoirs, humor, and entertainment, in addition to more nonfiction titles (cooking, how to, fashion, home improvement, etc)."

How to Contact Query with SASE or e-mail query with synopsis (preferred); include the title and genre in the subject line. Send nonfiction snail mail to Chamein Canton at New York address. Send all other snail mail queries to Eric Smith at Texas address. Considers simultaneous queries. Responds in 3 weeks to queries; 6 weeks to mss. Obtains most new clients through recommendations from others.

Recent Sales Sold 7 titles in the last year. Clients include Robert Koger, Olivia, Jennifer DeWit, Sheila Smestad, James Weil, Jaime Nava, JC Miller, Diana Smith, Robert Beers, Marcy Gannon, Keith Maxwell, Dawn Jackson, Jeannine Carney, Mark Barlow, Robert Marsocci, Anita Ballard Jones, Deb Mohr, Seth Ahonen, Melissa Graf, Robert Zavala, Cliff Webb, John and Carolyn Osborne.

Terms Agent receives 15% commission on domestic sales; 20% commission on foreign sales. Offers written contract; 2-month notice must be given to terminate contract.

Tips "Know your market. Agents, as well as publishers, are keenly interested in writers with their finger on the pulse of their market."

[N] [✏] CARNICELLI LITERARY MANAGEMENT

108 E. 17th St., New York NY 10003. (212)979-0101. E-mail: matthew@carnicellilit.com. **Contact:** Matthew Carnicelli. Estab. 2004. Represents 30 clients. 40% of clients are new/unpublished writers. Currently handles: 90% nonfiction books; 5% novels; 5% scholarly books.

- Prior to opening his agency, Mr. Carnicelli held senior editorial positions at the Penguin Group, Contemporary Books, and McGraw-Hill.

Represents Nonfiction books, novels. **Considers these nonfiction areas:** Anthropology/archaeology; biography/autobiography; business/economics; child guidance/parenting; current affairs; education; ethnic/cultural interests; gay/lesbian issues; government/politics/law; health/medicine; history; memoirs; money/finance; popular culture; psychology; religious/inspirational; science/technology; sociology; sports. **Considers these fiction areas:** Literary.

  ⚷ "Our main areas of interest are popular and serious nonfiction, including current events, history, biography/memoir, science, business, sports, health, spirituality, and psychology. We only consider fiction from authors who have had their work published in established literary journals or magazines. Our goal is to discover important new voices that have something unique and important to contribute to the world, be they experts in their fields or simply great storytellers. We are involved with the author's work every step of the way, from refining an idea and developing a strong book proposal, to selling the project to the right publisher and monitoring the book's progress after publication."

How to Contact Query with SASE or via e-mail (no attachments). Accepts simultaneous submissions. Returns materials only with SASE. Obtains most new clients through referrals from other writers.

Recent Sales Sold 15 titles in the last year. *Religion Gone Bad: The Hidden Dangers of the Christian Right*, by Mel White (Tarcher/Penguin); *Bloody Island: The East St. Louis Race Riot of 1917*, by Harper Barnes (Walker & Company); *With Eyes Shut Tight: A Mother, A Daughter, and a Journey Past Addiction*, by Felicia Sullivan (Algonquin Books); *Foxes in the Henhouse: How the Republicans Stole the South and the Heartland and What the Democrats Must Do to Run 'em Out*, by Steve Jarding and Dave "Mudcat" Saunders (Touchstone/Simon & Schuster). Other clients include Joseph Minton Amann, Tom Breuer, Emerson Baker, Anat Baniel, Abigail Brenner, Dean M. Brenner, Dara Colwell, Kalena Cook, Margaret Christensen, Paul Donahue, Jim Gorant, Pam Grout, Fran Harris, Brigitte Humbert, Brad Karsh, Roland Lazenby, Michele Simon, Jim Taylor, Donna Vinson.

Terms Agent receives 15% commission on domestic sales; 20% commission on foreign sales. Offers written contract; 30-day notice must be given to terminate contract. Charges for photocopying/messenger and express mail services.

Tips "It's very important that authors present themselves to agents in a formal, professional, and specific way. I simply ignore mass e-mails and most queries, though I will pay more attention if it's clear the author has actually researched the types of books I represent. It's also very important for authors to be as focused and as specific as possible about their writing. Ask yourself: Why am I the only one who can write this book? What are my unique credentials? How will my book be different from the many other books already published on this subject? What is my big idea, why is it relevant, and why will people want to read about it?

[✏] MARIA CARVAINIS AGENCY, INC.

1350 Avenue of the Americas, Suite 2905, New York NY 10019. (212)245-6365. Fax: (212)245-7196. E-mail: mca@mariacarvainisagency.com. **Contact:** Maria Carvainis, Donna Bagdasarian. Estab. 1977. Member of AAR, Authors Guild, Women's Media Group, ABA, MWA, RWA; signatory of WGA. Represents 75 clients. 10% of clients are new/unpublished writers. Currently handles: 34% nonfiction books; 65% novels; 1% poetry.

- Prior to opening her agency, Ms. Carvainis spent more than 10 years in the publishing industry as a senior editor with Macmillan Publishing, Basic Books, Avon Books, and Crown Publishers. Ms. Carvainis has served as a member of the AAR Board of Directors and AAR Treasurer, as well as serving as chair of the AAR Contracts Committee. She presently serves on the AAR Royalty Committee. Ms. Bagdasarian began her career as an academic at Boston University, then spent 5 years with Addison Wesley Longman as an acquisitions editor before joining the William Morris Agency in 1998. She has represented a breadth of projects, ranging from literary fiction to celebrity memoir.

Member Agents Maria Carvainis, president/literary agent; Donna Bagdasarian, literary agent; Moira Sullivan, literary associate/subsidiary rights manager; Peter Senftleben, literary assistant.

Represents Nonfiction books, novels. **Considers these nonfiction areas:** Biography/autobiography; business/economics; history; memoirs; science/technology (pop science); women's issues/studies. **Considers these fiction areas:** Historical; literary; mainstream/contemporary; mystery/suspense; thriller; young adult; women's; middle grade.

  ⚷ Does not want to receive science fiction or children's picture books.

How to Contact Query with SASE. Responds in 1 week to queries; 3 months to mss. Obtains most new clients through recommendations from others, conferences, query letters.

Recent Sales *Simply Love*, by Mary Balogh (Bantam Dell); *Save Your Own*, by Elizabeth Brink (Houghton Mifflin); *Chill Factor*, by Sandra Brown (Simon & Schuster); *A Dangerous Man*, by Candace Camp (Mira); *A Minister's Ghost*, by Phillip DePoy (St. Martin's Press); *You Didn't Hear It From Us: Two Bartenders Serve Up the Cold Truth About Men* (Atria); *The Grail Bird: Hot on the Trail of the Ivory-Billed Woodpecker*, by Tim Gallgher (Houghton Mifflin); *Over the Line*, by Cindy Gerard (St. Martin's Press); *Semiprecious*, by D. Anne Love (Simon & Schuster Children's Publishing); *An Unquiet Grave*, by P.J. Parrish (Kensington); *Mr. Lincoln's Boys*, by Staton Rabin (Viking Children's Books); *The Limehouse Text*, by Will Thomas (Touchstone/Fireside). Other clients include Sue Erikson Bloland, David Bottoms, Pam Conrad, S.V. Date, Michael Downs, Kristan Higgins, John Faunce, Samantha James, Merline Lovelace.

Terms Agent receives 15% commission on domestic sales; 20% commission on foreign sales. Offers written contract. Charges clients for foreign postage and bulk copying.

Writers' Conferences Frankfurt Book Fair; London Book Fair; BookExpo America.

◙ CASTIGLIA LITERARY AGENCY

1155 Camino Del Mar, Suite 510, Del Mar CA 92014. (858)755-8761. Fax: (858)755-7063. Estab. 1993. Member of AAR, PEN. Represents 50 clients. Currently handles: 55% nonfiction books; 45% novels.

Member Agents Julie Castiglia; Winifred Golden; Sally Van Haitsma.

Represents Nonfiction books, novels. **Considers these nonfiction areas:** Animals; anthropology/archaeology; biography/autobiography; business/economics; child guidance/parenting; cooking/foods/nutrition; current affairs; ethnic/cultural interests; health/medicine; history; language/literature/criticism; money/finance; nature/environment; psychology; religious/inspirational; science/technology; self-help/personal improvement; women's issues/studies. **Considers these fiction areas:** Ethnic; literary; mainstream/contemporary; mystery/suspense; women's.

　0-ᴙ Does not want to receive horror, screenplays, poetry, or academic nonfiction.

How to Contact Query with SASE. No fax queries. Returns materials only with SASE. Obtains most new clients through recommendations from others, solicitations, conferences.

Recent Sales Sold 26 titles in the last year. *Never Bet the Farm*, by Anthony Iaquinto and Stephen Spinelli Jr. (Wiley); *Invisible Lives*, by Anjali Banerjee (Pocket Books); *Orphan's Destiny*, by Robert Buettner (Warner); *What Should I Eat*, by Tershia d'Elgin (Random House); *Urban Gardens*, by Brian Coleman (Gibbs Smith).

Terms Agent receives 15% commission on domestic sales; 25% commission on foreign sales. Offers written contract; 6-week notice must be given to terminate contract.

Writers' Conferences Santa Barbara Writers Conference; Southern California Writers' Conference; Surrey International Writers' Conference; San Diego State University Writers' Conference; Willamette Writers Conference.

Tips "Be professional with submissions. Attend workshops and conferences before you approach an agent."

◙ JANE CHELIUS LITERARY AGENCY

548 Second St., Brooklyn NY 11215. (718)499-0236. Fax: (718)832-7335. E-mail: queries@janechelius.com. Web site: www.janechelius.com. Member of AAR.

Represents Nonfiction books, novels. **Considers these nonfiction areas:** Humor/satire; women's issues/studies; science; parenting; medicine; biography; military history; narrative. **Considers these fiction areas:** Fantasy; literary; mystery/suspense; science fiction; women's; men's adventure.

　0-ᴙ Does not want to receive children's books, stage plays, screenplays, or poetry.

How to Contact Query with synopsis, cover letter, SASE. Accepts e-mail queries. *No unsolicited chapters or mss.* Responds in 3-4 weeks to queries.

Ⓝ ◙ THE CHOATE AGENCY, LLC

1320 Bolton Rd., Pelham NY 10803. E-mail: choateagency@optonline.net. **Contact:** Mickey Choate. Member of AAR.

Represents Nonfiction books, novels. **Considers these nonfiction areas:** History; memoirs; biography; cookery/food; journalism; military science; narrative; politics; general science; wine/spirits. **Considers these fiction areas:** Historical; literary; mystery/suspense; thriller.

How to Contact Query with SASE, brief synopsis. Accepts e-mail queries.

Recent Sales *The King of Lies*, by John Hart (St. Martin's Minotaur); *Heart-Shaped Box*, by Joe Hill (William Morrow); *Simply Michael Mina*, by Michael Mina (Bulfinch/Little Brown).

◙ CINE/LIT REPRESENTATION

P.O. Box 802918, Santa Clarita CA 91380-2918. Fax: (661)513-0915. E-mail: cinelit@msn.com. **Contact:** Mary Alice Kier. Member of AAR.

How to Contact Accepts e-mail queries.

◙ WM CLARK ASSOCIATES

154 Christopher St., Suite 3C, New York NY 10014. (212)675-2784. Fax: (646)349-1658. E-mail: query@wmclark .com. Web site: www.wmclark.com. Estab. 1997. Member of AAR. 50% of clients are new/unpublished writers. Currently handles: 50% nonfiction books; 50% novels.

• Prior to opening WCA, Mr. Clark was an agent at the William Morris Agency.

Represents Nonfiction books, novels. **Considers these nonfiction areas:** Art/architecture/design; biography/ autobiography; current affairs; ethnic/cultural interests; history; memoirs; music/dance; popular culture; religious/inspirational (Eastern philosophy only); science/technology; sociology; theater/film; translation. **Considers these fiction areas:** Contemporary issues; ethnic; historical; literary; mainstream/contemporary; Southern fiction.

    O┓ "Building on a reputation for moving quickly and strategically on behalf of his clients, and offering individual focus and a global presence, William Clark practices an aggressive, innovative, and broad-ranged approach to the representation of content and the talent that creates it. His clients range from authors of first fiction and award-winning bestselling narrative nonfiction, to international authors in translation, musicians, and artists."

How to Contact E-mail queries only. Prefers to read requested materials exclusively. Responds in 1-2 months to queries.

Recent Sales Sold 25 titles in the last year. *Fallingwater Rising: E.J. Kaufman and Frank Lloyd Wright Create the Most Exciting House in the World*, by Franklin Toker (Alfred A. Knopf); *The Balthazar Cookbook*, by Riad Nasr, Lee Hanson, and Keith McNally (Clarkson Potter); *The Book of 'Exodus': The Making and Meaning of Bob Marley's Album of the Century*, by Vivien Goldman (Crown/Three Rivers Press); *Hungry Ghost*, by Keith Kachtick (HarperCollins). Other clients include Russell Martin, Daye Haddon, Bjork, Mian Mian, Jonathan Stone, Jocko Weyland, Peter Hessler, Rev. Billy (Billy Talen).

Terms Agent receives 15% commission on domestic sales; 20% commission on foreign sales. Offers written contract.

Tips "WCA works on a reciprocal basis with Ed Victor Ltd. (UK) in representing select properties to the US market and vice versa. Translation rights are sold directly in the German, Italian, Spanish, Portuguese, Latin American, French, Dutch, and Scandinavian territories in association with Andrew Nurnberg Associates Ltd. (UK); through offices in China, Bulgaria, Czech Republic, Latvia, Poland, Hungary, and Russia; and through corresponding agents in Japan, Greece, Israel, Turkey, Korea, Taiwan, and Thailand."

◙ FRANCES COLLIN, LITERARY AGENT

P.O. Box 33, Wayne PA 19087-0033. Web site: www.francescollin.com. **Contact:** Frances Collin. Estab. 1948. Member of AAR. Represents 90 clients. 1% of clients are new/unpublished writers. Currently handles: 50% nonfiction books; 48% novels; 1% textbooks; 1% poetry.

Represents Nonfiction books, fiction.

    O┓ "We are accepting almost no new clients unless recommended by publishing professionals or current clients." Does not want cookbooks, crafts, children's books, software, or original screenplays.

How to Contact Query with SASE, brief proposal. No phone, fax, or e-mail inquiries. Enclose sufficient IRCs if outside the US. Considers simultaneous queries.

Terms Agent receives 15% commission on domestic sales; 20% commission on foreign sales. Offers written contract. Charges clients for overseas postage for books mailed to foreign agents; photocopying of mss, books, proposals; copyright registration fees; registered mail fees; passes along cost of any books purchased.

Ⓝ ◙ COLLINS LITERARY AGENCY

30 Bond St., New York NY 10012. (212)529-4909. Fax: (212)358-1055. E-mail: nina@collinsliterary.com. Web site: www.collinsliterary.com. **Contact:** Nina Collins. Estab. 2005. Represents 30 clients. 40% of clients are new/unpublished writers. Currently handles: 70% nonfiction books; 20% novels; 5% story collections; 5% juvenile books.

• Prior to opening her agency, Ms. Collins was a literary scout for foreign publishers and American film companies.

Represents Nonfiction books, novels. **Considers these nonfiction areas:** Biography/autobiography; child guidance/parenting; cooking/foods/nutrition; crafts/hobbies; current affairs; health/medicine; history; humor/satire; language/literature/criticism; memoirs; popular culture; psychology; self-help/personal improvement; women's issues/studies. **Considers these fiction areas:** Literary; mainstream/contemporary; young adult.

    O┓ Actively seeking nonfiction in the areas of history, psychology, health, women's studies, and lifestyle. Does not want any genre fiction.

How to Contact Query with SASE. Accepts e-mail queries. Considers simultaneous queries. Responds in 1 week to queries; 1 month to mss. Returns materials only with SASE. Obtains most new clients through referrals.

Recent Sales Sold 10 titles in the last year. *The Mother Daughter Project*, by Hamkins & Schulz (Hudson St.

Press); *Over the Hill and Between the Sheets*, by Gail Belsky (Warner); *Evo-lution*, by Stephanie Staal (Bloomsbury); *Gonzo Gardening*, by Katherine Whiteside (Clarkson Potter).

Terms Agent receives 15% commission on domestic sales; 20% commission on foreign sales. Offers written contract; 1-month notice must be given to terminate contract.

◉ DON CONGDON ASSOCIATES INC.

156 Fifth Ave., Suite 625, New York NY 10010-7002. (212)645-1229. Fax: (212)727-2688. E-mail: dca@doncongdon.com. **Contact:** Don Congdon, Michael Congdon, Susan Ramer, Cristina Concepcion. Estab. 1983. Member of AAR. Represents 100 clients. Currently handles: 60% nonfiction books; 40% fiction.

Represents Nonfiction books, fiction. **Considers these nonfiction areas:** Anthropology/archaeology; biography/autobiography; child guidance/parenting; cooking/foods/nutrition; current affairs; government/politics/law; health/medicine; history; humor/satire; language/literature/criticism; memoirs; military/war; music/dance; nature/environment; popular culture; psychology; science/technology; theater/film; travel; true crime/investigative; women's issues/studies; creative nonfiction. **Considers these fiction areas:** Action/adventure; detective/police/crime; literary; mainstream/contemporary; mystery/suspense; short story collections; thriller; women's.

   ○⟶ Especially interested in narrative nonfiction and literary fiction.

How to Contact Query with SASE or via e-mail (no attachments). Responds in 3 weeks to queries; 1 month to mss. Obtains most new clients through recommendations from other authors.

Terms Agent receives 15% commission on domestic sales; 19% commission on foreign sales. Charges client for extra shipping costs, photocopying, copyright fees, book purchases.

Tips "Writing a query letter with a self-addressed stamped envelope is a must. We cannot guarantee replies to foreign queries via e-mail. No phone calls. We never download attachments to e-mail queries for security reasons, so please copy and paste material into your e-mail."

◉ CONNOR LITERARY AGENCY

2911 W. 71st St., Minneapolis MN 55423. Phone/Fax: (612)866-1486. E-mail: coolmkc@aol.com. **Contact:** Marlene Connor Lynch. Estab. 1985. Represents 50 clients. 30% of clients are new/unpublished writers. Currently handles: 50% nonfiction books; 50% novels.

   • Prior to opening her agency, Ms. Connor served at the Literary Guild of America, Simon & Schuster, and Random House. She is author of *Welcome to the Family: Memories of the Past for a Bright Future* (Broadway Books) and *What is Cool: Understanding Black Manhood in America* (Crown).

Member Agents Deborah Coker; Nichole Shields; Ralph Crowder.

Represents Nonfiction books, novels (especially with a minority slant). **Considers these nonfiction areas:** Child guidance/parenting; cooking/foods/nutrition; crafts/hobbies; current affairs; ethnic/cultural interests; government/politics/law; health/medicine; how-to; humor/satire; interior design/decorating; language/literature/criticism; money/finance; photography; popular culture; self-help/personal improvement; sports; true crime/investigative; women's issues/studies; relationships. **Considers these fiction areas:** Historical; horror; literary; mainstream/contemporary; multicultural; thriller; women's; suspense.

How to Contact All unsolicited mss returned unopened. Obtains most new clients through recommendations from others, conferences, grapevine.

Recent Sales *Outrageous Commitments*, by Dr. Ronn Elmore (HarperCollins); *Seductions*, by Snow Starborn (Sourcebooks); *Simplicity's Simply the Best Sewing Book, Revised Edition; Beautiful Hair at Any Age*, by Lisa Akbari.

Terms Agent receives 15% commission on domestic sales; 25% commission on foreign sales. Offers written contract, binding for 1 year.

Writers' Conferences National Writers Union, Midwest Chapter; Agents, Agents, Agents; Texas Writer's Conference; Detroit Writer's Conference.

Tips "We are seeking previously published writers with good sales records and new writers with real talent."

✣ ◉ THE COOKE AGENCY

278 Bloor St. E., Suite 305, Toronto ON M4W 3M4 Canada. E-mail: agents@cookeagency.ca. Web site: www.cookeagency.ca. **Contact:** Elizabeth Griffin. Estab. 1992. Represents 60 clients. 30% of clients are new/unpublished writers. Currently handles: 50% nonfiction books; 50% novels.

Represents Nonfiction books, literary novels. **Considers these nonfiction areas:** Biography/autobiography; business/economics; child guidance/parenting; current affairs; gay/lesbian issues; health/medicine; popular culture; science/technology; young adult. **Considers these fiction areas:** Literary; women's.

   ○⟶ "The Cooke Agency represents some of the best Canadian writers in the world. Through our contacts and sub-agents, we have built an international reputation for quality. Curtis Brown Canada is jointly owned by Dean Cooke and Curtis Brown New York. It represents Curtis Brown New York authors in Canada." Does not want to receive how-to, self-help, spirituality, or genre fiction (science fiction, fantasy, mystery, thriller, horror).

How to Contact Query with SASE. Accepts e-mail and fax queries. Considers simultaneous queries. Responds in 6-8 weeks to queries. Returns materials only with SASE. Obtains most new clients through recommendations from others.

Recent Sales Sold 20 titles in the last year. *Last Crossing*, by Guy Vanderhaeghe (Grove/Atlantic); *The Juggler's Children*, by Carolyn Abraham (Random House); *I Was a Child of Holocaust Survivors*, by Bernice Eisenstein (McClelland & Stewart); Belgian rights to *The Englishmen's Boy*, by Guy Vanderhaeghe; Indian rights to *Brahma's Dream*, by Shree Ghatage (Rol Books); Belgian rights to *Clara Callan*, by Richard B. Wright (Perseus Books). Other clients include Lauren B. Davis, Doug Hunter, Andrew Podnieks, Steven Hayward, Robertson Davies, Neil Smith.

Terms Agent receives 15% commission on domestic sales; 20% commission on foreign sales. Offers written contract. Charges clients for postage, photocopying, courier.

Tips "Check our Web site for complete guidelines rather than calling for them."

◉ THE DOE COOVER AGENCY

P.O. Box 668, Winchester MA 01890. (781)721-6000. Fax: (781)721-6727. Estab. 1985. Represents more than 100 clients. Currently handles: 80% nonfiction books; 20% novels.

Member Agents Doe Coover (general nonfiction, cooking); Colleen Mohyde (literary and commercial fiction, general and narrative nonfiction); Amanda Lewis (children's books); Frances Kennedy, associate.

    O➠ This agency specializes in nonfiction, particularly books on history, popular science, biography, social issues, and narrative nonfiction, as well as cooking, gardening, and literary and commercial fiction. Does not want romance, fantasy, science fiction, poetry, or screenplays.

How to Contact Query with SASE, outline. No e-mail or fax queries. Considers simultaneous queries. Returns materials only with SASE. Obtains most new clients through recommendations from others, solicitations.

Recent Sales Sold 25-30 titles in the last year. *The Gourmet Cookbook, Vol. II* (Houghton Mifflin); *The Power of Play*, by David Elkind (Houghton Mifflin); *Teaching Your Dog to Read*, by Bonnie Bergin (Broadway Books); *The Assassin's Accomplice*, by Kate Clifford Larson (Basic Books); *Liberal Arts*, by Michael Berube (W.W. Norton); *Cooking from the Hip*, by Cat Cora with Anne Krueger Spivack (Houghton Mifflin). ***Movie/TV MOW scripts optioned/sold:*** *A Crime in the Neighborhood*, by Suzanne Berne; *Mr. White's Confession*, by Robert Clark. Other clients include WGBH, New England Aquarium, Blue Balliett, Deborah Madison, Rick Bayless, Molly Stevens, David Allen, Adria Bernardi, Paula Poundstone.

Terms Agent receives 15% commission on domestic sales; 10% of original advance on foreign sales.

◉ CORNERSTONE LITERARY, INC.

4500 Wilshire Blvd., 3rd Floor, Los Angeles CA 90010. (323)930-6037. Fax: (323)930-0407. Web site: www.cornerstoneliterary.com. **Contact:** Helen Breitwieser. Estab. 1998. Member of AAR, Authors Guild, MWA, RWA, PEN, Poets & Writers. Represents 40 clients. 30% of clients are new/unpublished writers.

    ● Prior to founding her own boutique agency, Ms. Breitwieser was a literary agent at The William Morris Agency.

Represents Nonfiction books, novels. **Considers these fiction areas:** Detective/police/crime; erotica; ethnic; family saga; glitz; historical; literary; mainstream/contemporary; multicultural; mystery/suspense; romance; thriller; women's.

    O➠ "We are not taking new clients at this time. We do not respond to unsolicited e-mail inquiries. All unsolicited manuscripts will be returned unopened." Does not want to receive science fiction, westerns, poetry, screenplays, fantasy, gay/lesbian, horror, self-help, psychology, business, or diet.

How to Contact Query with SASE. Responds in 6-8 weeks to queries; 2 months to mss. Returns materials only with SASE. Obtains most new clients through recommendations from others.

Recent Sales Sold 37 titles in the last year. *How Was It For You*, by Carmen Reid (Pocket); *Sisters in Pink*, by Kayla Perrin (St. Martin's Press); *When Gods Die*, by Candice Proctor (NAL). Other clients include Elaine Coffman, Danielle Girard, Rachel Lee, Marilyn Jaye Lewis, Carole Matthews, Ahmet Zappa.

Terms Agent receives 15% commission on domestic sales; 20% commission on foreign sales. Offers written contract, binding for 1 year; 2-month notice must be given to terminate contract.

◉ THE CREATIVE CULTURE, INC.

72 Spring St., Suite 304, New York NY 10012. Web site: www.thecreativeculture.com. **Contact:** Debra Goldstein. Estab. 1998. Member of AAR.

    ● Prior to opening her agency, Ms. Goldstein was an agent at the William Morris Agency; Ms. Naples was a senior editor at Simon & Schuster.

Member Agents Debra Goldstein (sel-help, creativity, fitness, inspiration, lifestyle); Mary Ann Naples (health/nutrition, lifestyle, narrative nonfiction, practical nonfiction, literary fiction, animals/vegetarianism); Lauren Nolan (literary fiction, parenting, self-help, psychology, women's studies, current affairs, science).

Represents Nonfiction books, novels. **Considers these nonfiction areas:** Animals (vegetarianism); child guidance/parenting; current affairs; health/medicine; psychology; science/technology; self-help/personal improvement; women's issues/studies. **Considers these fiction areas:** Literary.

O┳ Does not want children's, poetry, screenplays, science fiction, or romance.

How to Contact Query with bio, book description, 3-5 sample pages (fiction only), SASE. Responds in 2 months to queries.

Recent Sales Clients include David Awbrey, Domonique Dierickx, Tom Hughes, Brenda McClain, Paula Chaffee Scardamalia.

Ⓝ Ⓩ SHA-SHANA CRICHTON

6940 Carroll Ave., Takoma Park MD 20912. (301)495-9663. Fax: (202)318-0050. E-mail: cricht1@aol.com; queries@crichton-associates.com. Web site: www.crichton-associates.com. **Contact:** Sha-Shana Crichton. Estab. 2002. 90% of clients are new/unpublished writers. Currently handles: 20% nonfiction books; 80% novels.

● Prior to becoming an agent, Ms. Crichton did commercial litigation for a major law firm.

Represents Nonfiction books, novels. **Considers these nonfiction areas:** Child guidance/parenting; ethnic/cultural interests; gay/lesbian issues; government/politics/law; true crime/investigative; women's issues/studies. **Considers these fiction areas:** Ethnic; feminist; literary; mainstream/contemporary; mystery/suspense; religious/inspirational; romance.

O┳ Seeking women's fiction, romance, and chick lit. No poetry.

How to Contact Accepts e-mail queries (no attachments). Responds in 3-5 weeks to queries. Returns materials only with SASE.

Recent Sales *Charmed and Dangerous*, by Candace Havens (Berkley); *After the Storm*, by Cassandra Darden-Bell (BET); *Dark Desire*, by Eve Silver (Kensington); *Weapons of Seduction*, by Maureen Smith (Kensington). Other clients include Dirk Gibson, Kimberley White, Beverly Long, Jessica Trap, Altonya Washington, Ann Christopher.

Terms Agent receives 15% commission on domestic sales; 20% commission on foreign sales. Offers written contract, binding for 45 days. Only charges fees for postage and photocopying.

Writers' Conferences Silicon Valley RWA; BookExpo America.

Ⓜ RICHARD CURTIS ASSOCIATES, INC.

171 E. 74th St., New York NY 10021. (212)772-7363. Fax: (212)772-7393. Web site: www.curtisagency.com. Estab. 1979. Member of RWA, MWA, SFWA; signatory of WGA. Represents 100 clients. 1% of clients are new/unpublished writers. Currently handles: 70% nonfiction books; 20% genre fiction, 10% fiction.

● Prior to opening his agency, Mr. Curtis was an agent with the Scott Meredith Literary Agency for 7 years. He has also authored over 50 published books.

Represents Commercial nonfiction and fiction. **Considers these nonfiction areas:** Health/medicine; history; science/technology.

How to Contact Send 1-page query letter and no more than a 5-page synopsis. Don't send ms unless specifically requested. If requested, submission must be accompanied by a SASE. No e-mail or fax queries. Returns materials only with SASE.

Recent Sales Sold 150 titles in the last year. *Olympos*, by Dan Simmons; *The Side-Effects Solution*, by Dr. Frederic Vagnini and Barry Fox; *Quantico*, by Greg Bear. Other clients include Janet Dailey, Jennifer Blake, Leonard Maltin, D.J. MacHale, John Altman, Beverly Barton, Earl Mindell, Barbara Parker.

Terms Agent receives 15% commission on domestic sales; 25% commission on foreign sales. Offers written contract. Charges for photocopying, express mail, international freight, book orders.

Writers' Conferences SFWA Conference; HWA Conference; RWA National Conference; World Fantasy Convention; Backspace Writers Conference.

Ⓩ JAMES R. CYPHER, THE CYPHER AGENCY

816 Wolcott Ave., Beacon NY 12508-4261. Phone/Fax: (845)831-5677. E-mail: jim@jimcypher.com. Web site: www.jimcypher.com. **Contact:** James R. Cypher. Estab. 1993. Member of AAR, Authors Guild. Represents 30 clients. 35% of clients are new/unpublished writers. Currently handles: 100% nonfiction books.

● Prior to opening his agency, Mr. Cypher worked as a corporate public relations manager for a Fortune 500 multi-national computer company for 28 years.

Represents Nonfiction books. **Considers these nonfiction areas:** Current affairs; health/medicine; history; memoirs; popular culture; science/technology; sports (NASCAR, golf, baseball); true crime/investigative; Biography.

O┳ Actively seeking a variety of topical nonfiction. Does not want to receive humor, sewing, computer books, children's, gardening, cookbooks, spiritual, religious, or New Age topics.

How to Contact Query with SASE, proposal package, 2 sample chapters. Accepts e-mail queries. Considers simultaneous queries. Responds in 2 weeks to queries; 6 weeks to mss. Obtains most new clients through recommendations from others, conferences, networking on online computer service.

Recent Sales Sold 9 titles in the last year. *The Man Who Predicts Earthquakes*, by Cal Orey (Sentient Publications); *No Good Deed: A True Story of Jealousy, Deceit, Rage and Fiery Murder*, by Tom Basinski (Berkley Books); *True to the Roots: Excursions Off Country Music's Beaten Path*, by Monte Dutton (University of Nebraska Press); *Minds on Trial; 20 Great Cases in Forensic Psychology*, by Charles Patrick Ewing and Joseph T. McCann (Oxford University Press). Other clients include Walter Harvey, Mark Horner, Charles Hustmyre, Glenn Puit, Robert L. Snow.

Terms Agent receives 15% commission on domestic sales; 20% commission on foreign sales. Offers written contract; 1-month notice must be given to terminate contract. 100% of business is derived from commissions on ms sales. Charges clients for postage, photocopying, overseas phone calls/faxes.

ᴺ ☑ D4EO LITERARY AGENCY

7 Indian Valley Rd., Weston CT 06883. (203)544-7180. Fax: (203)544-7160. E-mail: d4eo@optonline.net. Web site: www.publishersmarketplace.com/members/d4eo. **Contact:** Bob Diforio. Estab. 1991. Represents 150 clients. 90% of clients are new/unpublished writers. Currently handles: 70% nonfiction books; 25% novels; 5% juvenile books.

• Prior to opening his agency, Mr. Diforio was a publisher.

Represents Nonfiction books, novels. **Considers these nonfiction areas:** Art/architecture/design; biography/autobiography; business/economics; child guidance/parenting; current affairs; gay/lesbian issues; health/medicine; history; how-to; humor/satire; juvenile nonfiction; memoirs; military/war; money/finance; psychology; religious/inspirational; science/technology; self-help/personal improvement; sports; true crime/investigative; women's issues/studies. **Considers these fiction areas:** Action/adventure; detective/police/crime; erotica; historical; horror; humor/satire; juvenile; literary; mainstream/contemporary; mystery/suspense; picture books; romance; science fiction; sports; thriller; westerns/frontier; young adult.

How to Contact Query with SASE. Accepts e-mail queries. Prefers to read material exclusively. Responds in 1 week to queries; several weeks to mss. Returns materials only with SASE. Obtains most new clients through recommendations from others.

Recent Sales Sold 75 titles in the last year. *The Worry Cure*, by Robert L. Leahy (Harmony); *Havoc*, by Jack DuBrul (NAL); *Application Suicide*, by Don Dunbar (Gotham); *Thunderhorse Six*, by Wess Roberts and Doc Bahnsen (Citadel). Other clients include Robert K. Tanenbaum, Andrea DaRif, Tawny Stokes, Cathy Verge, Lynn Kerston, Bob Bly, Michael Levine, Mark Wiskup, George Parker, Michael Stodther, Evie Rhoder, Charlie Stella, Kathy Tracy.

Terms Agent receives 15% commission on domestic sales; 25% commission on foreign sales. Offers written contract, binding for 2 years; 60-day notice must be given to terminate contract. Charges for photocopying and submission postage.

☑ LAURA DAIL LITERARY AGENCY, INC.

350 7th Ave., Suite 2003, New York NY 10010. (212)239-7477. Fax: (212)947-0460. E-mail: tellman@ldlainc.com. Web site: www.ldlainc.com. Member of AAR.

Member Agents Talia Cohen; Laura Dail; Tamar Ellman.

Represents Nonfiction books, novels.

☞ "Due to the volume of queries and manuscripts received, we apologize for not answering every e-mail and letter." Specializes in historical, literary, and some young adult fiction, as well as both practical and idea-driven nonfiction.

How to Contact Query with SASE.

Recent Sales *Bras & Broomsticks*, by Sarah Mlynowski (Delacorte); *Hide Yourself Away*, by Mary Jane Clark (St. Martin's Press); *Eating in the Raw*, by Carol Alt (Clarkson Potter).

☑ DARHANSOFF, VERRILL, FELDMAN LITERARY AGENTS

236 W. 26th St., Suite 802, New York NY 10001. (917)305-1300. Fax: (917)305-1400. Estab. 1975. Member of AAR. Represents 120 clients. 10% of clients are new/unpublished writers. Currently handles: 25% nonfiction books; 60% novels; 15% story collections.

Member Agents Liz Darhansoff; Charles Verrill; Leigh Feldman.

Represents Nonfiction books, novels, short story collections.

How to Contact Obtains most new clients through recommendations from others.

☑ LIZA DAWSON ASSOCIATES

240 W. 35th St., Suite 500, New York NY 10001. (212)465-9071. **Contact:** Liza Dawson, Caitlin Blasdell. Member of AAR, MWA, Women's Media Group. Represents 50 clients. 15% of clients are new/unpublished writers. Currently handles: 60% nonfiction books; 40% novels.

- Prior to becoming an agent, Ms. Dawson was an editor for 20 years, spending 11 years at William Morrow as vice president and 2 years at Putnam as executive editor; Ms. Blasdell was a senior editor at HarperCollins and Avon.

Represents Nonfiction books, novels. **Considers these nonfiction areas:** Biography/autobiography; health/medicine; history; memoirs; psychology; sociology; women's issues/studies; politics; business; parenting. **Considers these fiction areas:** Fantasy (Blasdell only); historical; literary; mystery/suspense; regional; science fiction (Blasdell only); thriller.

    O→ This agency specializes in readable literary fiction, thrillers, mainstream historicals, women's fiction, academics, historians, business, journalists, and psychology. Does not want to receive westerns, sports, computers, or juvenile.

How to Contact Query with SASE. Responds in 3 weeks to queries; 6 weeks to mss. Obtains most new clients through recommendations from others, conferences.

Recent Sales Sold 40 titles in the last year. *Going for It*, by Karen E. Quinones Miller (Warner); *Mayada: Daughter of Iraq*, by Jean Sasson (Dutton); *It's So Much Work to Be Your Friend: Social Skill Problems at Home and at School*, by Richard Lavoie (Touchstone); *WORDCRAFT: How to Write Like a Professional*, by Jack Hart (Pantheon); *...And a Time to Die: How Hospitals Shape the End of Life Experience*, by Dr. Sharon Kaufman (Scribner); *Zeus: A Biography*, by Tom Stone (Bloomsbury).

Terms Agent receives 15% commission on domestic sales; 20% commission on foreign sales. Offers written contract. Charges clients for photocopying and overseas postage.

[N] [◻] THE JENNIFER DECHIARA LITERARY AGENCY

254 Park Ave. S., Suite 2L, New York NY 10010. Phone/Fax: (212)777-2702. E-mail: jenndec@aol.com. Web site: www.jdlit.com. **Contact:** Jennifer DeChiara. Estab. 2001. Represents 100 clients. 50% of clients are new/unpublished writers. Currently handles: 50% nonfiction books; 25% novels; 25% juvenile books.

    - Prior to becoming an agent, Ms. DeChiara was a writing consultant, freelance editor at Simon & Schuster and Random House, and a ballerina and an actress.

Represents Nonfiction books, novels, juvenile books. **Considers these nonfiction areas:** Biography/autobiography; child guidance/parenting; cooking/foods/nutrition; crafts/hobbies; current affairs; education; ethnic/cultural interests; gay/lesbian issues; government/politics/law; health/medicine; history; how-to; humor/satire; interior design/decorating; juvenile nonfiction; language/literature/criticism; memoirs; military/war; money/finance; music/dance; nature/environment; photography; popular culture; psychology; science/technology; self-help/personal improvement; sociology; sports; theater/film; true crime/investigative; women's issues/studies. **Considers these fiction areas:** Confession; detective/police/crime; ethnic; family saga; fantasy; feminist; gay/lesbian; historical; horror; humor/satire; juvenile; literary; mainstream/contemporary; mystery/suspense; picture books; regional; sports; thriller; young adult; chick lit; psychic/supernatural; glitz.

    O→ "We represent both children's and adult books in a wide range of ages and genres. We are a full-service agency and fulfill the potential of every book in every possible medium—stage, film, television, etc. We help writers every step of the way, from creating book ideas to editing and promotion. We are passionate about helping writers further their careers, but are just as eager to discover new talent, regardless of age or lack of prior publishing experience. This agency is committed to managing a writer's entire career. For us, it's not just about selling books, but about making dreams come true. We are especially attracted to the downtrodden, the discouraged, and the downright disgusted." Actively seeking literary fiction, chick lit, young adult fiction, self-help, pop culture, and celebrity biographies. Does not want westerns, poetry, or short stories.

How to Contact Query with SASE. Considers simultaneous queries. Responds in 3-6 months to queries and mss. Returns materials only with SASE. Obtains most new clients through recommendations from others, conferences, query letters.

Recent Sales Sold 30 titles in the last year. *I Was a Teenage Popsicle*, by Bev Katz Rosenbaum (Berkley/JAM); *Hazing Meri Sugarman*, by M. Apostolina (Simon Pulse); *The 10-Minute Sexual Solution* and *Virgin Sex: A Guy's Guide to Sex*, by Dr. Darcy Luadzers (Hatherleigh Press). ***Movie/TV MOW scripts optioned/sold:*** *Geography Club*, by Brent Hartinger (East of Doheny). Other clients include Adam Meyer, Herbie J. Pilato, Chris Demarest, Jeff Lenburg, Joe Cadora, Tiffani Amber Thiessen, Bonnie Neubauer.

Terms Agent receives 15% commission on domestic sales; 20% commission on foreign sales. Offers written contract.

[◻] DEFIORE & CO.

72 Spring St., Suite 304, New York NY 10012. (212)925-7744. Fax: (212)925-9803. E-mail: info@defioreandco.com. Web site: www.defioreandco.com. **Contact:** Brian DeFiore. Estab. 1999. Represents 55 clients. 50% of clients are new/unpublished writers. Currently handles: 70% nonfiction books; 30% novels.

• Prior to becoming an agent, Mr. DeFiore was publisher of Villard Books (1997-1998), editor-in-chief of Hyperion (1992-1997), and editorial director of Delacorte Press (1988-1992).

Member Agents Brian DeFiore (popular nonfiction, business, pop culture, parenting, commercial fiction); Laurie Abkemeier (memoir, parenting, business, how-to/self-help, popular science); Kate Garrick (literary fiction, crime, pop culture, politics, history, psychology, narrative nonfiction).

Represents Nonfiction books, novels. **Considers these nonfiction areas:** Biography/autobiography; business/economics; child guidance/parenting; cooking/foods/nutrition; money/finance; multicultural; popular culture; psychology; religious/inspirational; self-help/personal improvement; sports. **Considers these fiction areas:** Ethnic; literary; mainstream/contemporary; mystery/suspense; thriller.

How to Contact Query with SASE. Considers simultaneous queries. Responds in 3 weeks to queries; 2 months to mss. Returns materials only with SASE. Obtains most new clients through recommendations from others.

Recent Sales Sold 35 titles in the last year. *Marley and Me*, by John Grogan; *Post Secret*, by Frank Warren; *Bitter Is the New Black*, by Jen Lancaster; *All for a Few Perfect Waves*, by David Rensin; *Seemed Like a Good Idea at the Time*, by David Goodwillie; *Lights Out*, by Jason Starr; *The Alpha Solution*, by Dr. Ronald Glassman; *The $64 Tomato*, by Bill Alexander; *The Extraordinary Adventures of Alfred Kropp*, by Rick Yancey. Other clients include Loretta LaRoche, Joel Engel, Robin McMillan, Jessica Teich, Ronna Lichtenberg, Jimmy Lerner, Lou Manfredini, Norm Green, Lisa Kusel, Michael Walter, Stephen Graham Jones.

Terms Agent receives 15% commission on domestic sales; 20% commission on foreign sales. Offers written contract; 10-day notice must be given to terminate contract. Charges clients for photocopying and overnight delivery (deducted only after a sale is made).

Writers' Conferences Maui Writers Conference; Pacific Northwest Writers Conference; North Carolina Writers' Network Fall Conference.

N ☺ JOËLLE DELBOURGO ASSOCIATES, INC.

516 Bloomfield Ave., Suite 5, Montclair NJ 07042. (973)783-6800. Fax: (973)783-6802. E-mail: info@delbourgo.com. Web site: www.delbourgo.com. **Contact:** Joëlle Delbourgo, Molly Lyons. Estab. 2000. Represents 80 clients. 40% of clients are new/unpublished writers. Currently handles: 75% nonfiction books; 25% novels.

• Prior to becoming an agent, Ms. Delbourgo was an editor and senior publishing executive at HarperCollins and Random House.

Member Agents Joëlle Delbourgo (parenting, self-help, psychology, business, serious nonfiction, narrative nonfiction, quality fiction); Molly Lyons (practical and narrative nonfiction, memoir, quality fiction).

Represents Nonfiction books, novels, short story collections. **Considers these nonfiction areas:** Biography/autobiography; business/economics; child guidance/parenting; cooking/foods/nutrition; current affairs; education; ethnic/cultural interests; gay/lesbian issues; government/politics/law; health/medicine; history; how-to; money/finance; music/dance; nature/environment; popular culture; psychology; religious/inspirational; science/technology; self-help/personal improvement; sociology; theater/film; true crime/investigative; women's issues/studies; New Age/metaphysics, interior design/decorating. **Considers these fiction areas:** Historical; literary; mainstream/contemporary; mystery/suspense; regional (southern).

○━ "We are former publishers and editors, with deep knowledge and an insider perspective. We have a reputation for individualized attention to clients, strategic management of authors' careers, and creating strong partnerships with publishers for our clients." Actively seeking history, narrative nonfiction, science/medicine, memoir, literary fiction, psychology, parenting, and biographies. Does not want to receive genre fiction or screenplays.

How to Contact Query with SASE. No e-mail or fax queries. Considers simultaneous queries. Responds in 3 weeks to queries; 2 months to mss. Returns materials only with SASE.

Recent Sales Sold 18 titles and 2 scripts in the last year. *Journey of a Lifetime: The Remarkable Story of Human Development from Prebirth to Death*, by Thomas Armstrong, PhD (Sterling); *Reporting the War: Freedom of the Press in Wartime From the American Revolution to the War on Terror*, by John Byrne Cooke (Palgrave/Macmillan); *Julius Caesar, A Biography*, by Philip Freeman, PhD (Simon & Schuster); *Sex Lives of Wives: The Quest for Missing Passion*, by Helarie Hollenbeck (Springboard); *He's Just Not in the Stars: Wicked Astrology and Uncensored Advice for Getting the (Almost) Perfect Guy*, by Jenni Kosarin (HarperEntertainment). Other clients include Phyllis Chesler, Pamela Duncan, Geeta Anand, Philip Mitchell Freeman, Roy Hoffman, Chris Farrell, David Cole, Marc Siegel, Joan Wester Anderson, Julie Fenster.

Terms Agent receives 15% commission on domestic sales; 20% commission on foreign sales. Offers written contract. Charges clients for postage and photocopying. "We match writers with specific editors or co-writers as needed."

Tips "Do your homework. Do not cold call. Read and follow submission guidelines before contacting us. Do not call to find out if we received your material. No e-mail queries. Treat agents with respect, as you would any other professional, such as a doctor, lawyer, or financial advisor."

⊘ DH LITERARY, INC.

P.O. Box 805, Nyack NY 10960-0990. (845)358-7364. E-mail: dhendin@aol.com. **Contact:** David Hendin. Estab. 1993. Member of AAR. Represents 5 clients. Currently handles: 80% nonfiction books; 10% novels; 10% scholarly books.

- Prior to opening his agency, Mr. Hendin served as president and publisher for Pharos Books/World Almanac, as well as senior VP and COO at sister company United Feature Syndicate.

○─┓ "We are not accepting new clients."

Recent Sales *No Vulgar Hotel,* by Judith Martin (Norton); *Murder Between the Covers,* by Elaine Viets (Penguin/ Putnam); *Coined by God,* by Jeffrey McQuain and Stanley Malless (Norton).

Terms Agent receives 15% commission on domestic sales; 20% commission on foreign sales. Offers written contract, binding for 1 year. Charges for out-of-pocket expenses for overseas postage specifically related to the sale.

◑ DHS LITERARY, INC.

10711 Preston Rd., Suite 100, Dallas TX 75230. (214)363-4422. Fax: (214)363-4423. E-mail: submissions@dhslit erary.com. Web site: www.dhsliterary.com. **Contact:** David Hale Smith, president. Estab. 1994. Represents 35 clients. 15% of clients are new/unpublished writers. Currently handles: 60% nonfiction books; 40% novels.

- Prior to opening his agency, Mr. Smith was an agent at Dupree/Miller & Associates.

Represents Nonfiction books, novels. **Considers these nonfiction areas:** Biography/autobiography; business/ economics; child guidance/parenting; cooking/foods/nutrition; current affairs; ethnic/cultural interests; popular culture; sports; true crime/investigative. **Considers these fiction areas:** Detective/police/crime; ethnic; literary; mainstream/contemporary; mystery/suspense; thriller; westerns/frontier.

○─┓ This agency specializes in commercial fiction and nonfiction for the adult trade market. Actively seeking thrillers, mysteries, suspense, etc., and narrative nonfiction. Does not want to receive poetry, short fiction, or children's books.

How to Contact Accepts new material by referral only. *No unsolicited mss.*

Recent Sales Sold 40 + titles in the last year. *Officer Down,* by Theresa Schwegel; *Private Wars,* by Greg Rucka; *The Lean Body Promise,* by Lee Labrada.

Terms Agent receives 15% commission on domestic sales; 25% commission on foreign sales. Offers written contract; 10-day notice must be given to terminate contract. Charges for postage and photocopying. 100% of business is derived from commissions on sales.

Tips "Remember to be courteous and professional, and to treat marketing your work and approaching an agent as you would any formal business matter. If you have a referral, always query first via e-mail. Sorry, but we cannot respond to queries sent via mail, even with a SASE. Visit our Web site for more information."

◔ SANDRA DIJKSTRA LITERARY AGENCY

1155 Camino del Mar, PMB 515, Del Mar CA 92014. (858)755-3115. Fax: (858)794-2822. E-mail: sdla@dijkstraag ency.com. **Contact:** Elise Capron. Estab. 1981. Member of AAR, Authors Guild, PEN West, Poets and Editors, MWA. Represents 100+ clients. 30% of clients are new/unpublished writers. Currently handles: 50% nonfiction books; 45% novels; 5% juvenile books.

Member Agents Sandra Dijkstra; Jill Marsal; Taryn Fagerness

Represents Nonfiction books, novels. **Considers these nonfiction areas:** Americana; animals (pets); anthropology/archaeology; business/economics; child guidance/parenting; cooking/foods/nutrition; ethnic/cultural interests; gay/lesbian issues; government/politics/law; health/medicine; history; juvenile nonfiction; language/ literature/criticism; military/war; money/finance; nature/environment; psychology; regional; religious/inspirational; science/technology; self-help/personal improvement; sociology; travel; women's issues/studies; Asian studies; art; accounting; biography; environmental studies; technology; transportation. **Considers these fiction areas:** Erotica; ethnic; literary; mainstream/contemporary; mystery/suspense; picture books; thriller.

How to Contact Submit author bio, brief synopsis, 50 sample pages, SASE. No e-mail or fax queries. Responds in 4-6 weeks to queries. Obtains most new clients through recommendations from others, solicitations, conferences.

Recent Sales *Firewife,* by Tinling Choong; *Palace of Illusions,* by Chitra Divakaruni; *The Longevity Bible,* by Dr. Gary Small; *The American Resting Place,* by Marilyn Yalom.

Terms Agent receives 15% commission on domestic sales; 20% commission on foreign sales. Offers written contract. Charges clients for expenses "to cover domestic costs so that we can spend time selling books instead of accounting expenses. We also charge for the photocopying of the full manuscript or nonfiction proposal and for foreign postage."

Writers' Conferences "I have attended Squaw Valley Writers Workshop, Santa Barbara Writers' Conference, Asilomar, Southern California Writers' Conference, and Rocky Mountain Fiction Writers Colorado Gold, to name a few. We also speak regularly for writers groups such as PEN West and the Independent Writers Association."

Tips "Be professional and learn the standard procedures for submitting your work. Be a regular patron of bookstores, and study what kind of books are being published. Read. Check out your local library and bookstores—you'll find lots of books on writing and the publishing industry that will help you. At conferences, ask published writers about their agents. Don't believe the myth that an agent has to be in New York to be successful—we've already disproved it!"

◙ THE JONATHAN DOLGER AGENCY

49 E. 96th St., Suite 9B, New York NY 10128. Estab. 1980. Member of AAR.

Represents Illustrated books.

How to Contact Query with SASE. No e-mail queries.

Recent Sales This agency prefers not to share information on specific sales.

Terms Agent receives 15% commission on domestic sales; 25% commission on foreign sales.

Tips "Writer must have been previously published if submitting fiction. Prefers to work with published/established authors; works with a small number of new/previously unpublished writers."

◙ DONADIO & OLSON, INC.

121 W. 27th St., Suite 704, New York NY 10001. (212)691-8077. Fax: (212)633-2837. E-mail: mail@donadio.com. Member of AAR.

Member Agents Neil Olson; Ira Silverberg; Edward Hibbert.

　O⇥ Represents nonfiction books and literary fiction.

How to Contact Obtains most new clients through recommendations from others.

◙ JANIS A. DONNAUD & ASSOCIATES, INC.

525 Broadway, 2nd Floor, New York NY 10012. (212)431-2664. Fax: (212)431-2667. E-mail: jdonnaud@aol.com. **Contact:** Janis A. Donnaud. Member of AAR; signatory of WGA. Represents 40 clients. 5% of clients are new/unpublished writers. Currently handles: 100% nonfiction books.

　• Prior to opening her agency, Ms. Donnaud was vice president and associate publisher of Random House Adult Trade Group.

Represents Nonfiction books. **Considers these nonfiction areas:** Biography/autobiography; child guidance/parenting; cooking/foods/nutrition; current affairs; health/medicine; humor/satire; psychology (pop); women's issues/studies; lifestyle.

　O⇥ This agency specializes in health, medical, cooking, humor, pop psychology, narrative nonfiction, biography, parenting, and current affairs. "We give a lot of service and attention to clients." Actively seeking serious narrative nonfiction, cookbooks, and books on health and medical topics—all written by experts with an already established national platform in their area of specialty. Does not want to receive fiction, poetry, mysteries, juvenile books, romances, science fiction, young adult, religious, or fantasy.

How to Contact Query with SASE, description of book, 2-3 pages of sample material. Prefers to read materials exclusively. No phone calls. Responds in 1 month to queries and mss. Obtains most new clients through recommendations from others.

Recent Sales Sold 25 titles in the last year. *Inventing the Rest of Our Lives*, by Suzanne Braun Levine; major deals for the Food Network's Paula Deen.

Terms Agent receives 15% commission on domestic sales; 20% commission on foreign and dramatic rights sales. Offers written contract; 1-month notice must be given to terminate contract. Charges clients for messengers, photocopying, purchase of books.

◙ DOYEN LITERARY SERVICES, INC.

1931 660th St., Newell IA 50568-7613. (712)272-3300. Web site: www.barbaradoyen.com. **Contact:** (Ms.) B.J. Doyen, president. Estab. 1988. Represents over 100 clients. 20% of clients are new/unpublished writers. Currently handles: 95% nonfiction books; 5% novels.

　• Prior to opening her agency, Ms. Doyen worked as a published author, teacher, guest speaker, and wrote and appeared in her own weekly TV show airing in 7 states. She is also the co-author of *The Everything Guide to Writing a Book Proposal* (Adams 2005) and *The Everything Guide to Getting Published* (Adams 2006).

Represents Nonfiction books, novels. **Considers these nonfiction areas:** Agriculture/horticulture; Americana; animals; anthropology/archaeology; art/architecture/design; biography/autobiography; business/economics; child guidance/parenting; computers/electronic; cooking/foods/nutrition; crafts/hobbies; current affairs; education; ethnic/cultural interests; gardening; government/politics/law; health/medicine; history; how-to; humor/satire; interior design/decorating; language/literature/criticism; memoirs; military/war; money/finance; multicultural; music/dance; nature/environment; New Age/metaphysics; philosophy; photography; popular culture; psychology; recreation; regional; religious/inspirational; science/technology; self-help/personal improvement; sex; sociology; software; spirituality; theater/film; travel; true crime/investigative; women's issues/studies; young adult; creative nonfiction. **Considers these fiction areas:** Family saga; historical; literary; mainstream/contemporary.

○━ This agency specializes in nonfiction and occasionally handles mainstream fiction for adults. Actively seeking business, health, how-to, self-help—all kinds of adult nonfiction suitable for the major trade publishers. Does not want to receive pornography, children's books, or poetry.

How to Contact Query with SASE. No e-mail or fax queries. Considers simultaneous queries. Responds in 3 weeks to mss. Responds immediately to queries. Returns materials only with SASE.

Recent Sales *The Birth Order Effect for Couples*, by Isaacson/Schneider (Fairwinds); *1,000 Best Casino Tips*, by Bill Burton (Sourcebooks).

Terms Agent receives 15% commission on domestic sales; 20% commission on foreign sales. Offers written contract, binding for 2 years.

Tips "Our authors receive personalized attention. We market aggressively, undeterred by rejection. We get the best possible publishing contracts. We are very interested in nonfiction book ideas at this time and will consider most topics. Many writers come to us from referrals, but we also get quite a few who initially approach us with query letters. Do not call us regarding queries. It is best if you do not collect editorial rejections prior to seeking an agent, but if you do, be upfront and honest about it. Do not submit your manuscript to more than 1 agent at a time—querying first can save you (and us) much time. We're open to established or beginning writers—just send us a terrific letter with a SASE!"

✪ DUNHAM LITERARY, INC.

156 Fifth Ave., Suite 625, New York NY 10010-7002. (212)929-0994. Web site: www.dunhamlit.com. **Contact:** Jennie Dunham. Estab. 2000. Member of AAR. Represents 50 clients. 15% of clients are new/unpublished writers. Currently handles: 25% nonfiction books; 25% novels; 50% juvenile books.

● Prior to opening her agency, Ms. Dunham worked as a literary agent for Russell & Volkening. The Rhoda Weyr Agency is now a division of Dunham Literary, Inc.

Represents Nonfiction books, novels, short story collections, juvenile books. **Considers these nonfiction areas:** Anthropology/archaeology; biography/autobiography; ethnic/cultural interests; government/politics/law; health/medicine; history; language/literature/criticism; nature/environment; popular culture; psychology; science/technology; women's issues/studies. **Considers these fiction areas:** Ethnic; juvenile; literary; mainstream/contemporary; picture books; young adult.

How to Contact Query with SASE. No e-mail or fax queries. Responds in 1 week to queries; 2 months to mss. Obtains most new clients through recommendations from others, solicitations.

Recent Sales *America the Beautiful*, by Robert Sabuda; *Dahlia*, by Barbara McClintock; *Living Dead Girl*, by Tod Goldberg; *In My Mother's House*, by Margaret McMulla; *Black Hawk Down*, by Mark Bowden; *Look Back All the Green Valley*, by Fred Chappell; *Under a Wing*, by Reeve Lindbergh; *I Am Madame X*, by Gioia Diliberto.

Terms Agent receives 15% commission on domestic sales; 20% commission on foreign sales.

✪ DUNOW, CARLSON, & LERNER AGENCY

27 W. 20th St., #1107, New York NY 10011. **Contact:** Rolph Blythe, Jennifer Carlson, Henry Dunow, Betsy Lerner. Member of AAR.

How to Contact Query with SASE.

✪ DUPREE/MILLER AND ASSOCIATES INC. LITERARY

100 Highland Park Village, Suite 350, Dallas TX 75205. (214)559-BOOK. Fax: (214)559-PAGE. E-mail: dmabook @aol.com. **Contact:** Submissions Department. Estab. 1984. Member of ABA. Represents 200 clients. 20% of clients are new/unpublished writers. Currently handles: 90% nonfiction books; 10% novels.

Member Agents Jan Miller, president/CEO; Shannon Miser-Marven, senior executive VP; Annabelle Baxter; Jennifer Holder; Nena Madonia.

Represents Nonfiction books, novels, scholarly books, syndicated material. **Considers these nonfiction areas:** Americana; animals; anthropology/archaeology; art/architecture/design; biography/autobiography; business/economics; child guidance/parenting; cooking/foods/nutrition; crafts/hobbies; creative nonfiction; current affairs; education; ethnic/cultural interests; gardening; gay/lesbian issues; government/politics/law; health/medicine; history; how-to; humor/satire; interior design/decorating; language/literature/criticism; memoirs; money/finance; multicultural; music/dance; nature/environment; New Age/metaphysics; philosophy; photography; popular culture; psychology; recreation; regional; religious/inspirational; science/technology; self-help/personal improvement; sex; sociology; spirituality; sports; theater/film; translation; true crime/investigative; women's issues/studies. **Considers these fiction areas:** Action/adventure; detective/police/crime; ethnic; experimental; family saga; feminist; gay/lesbian; glitz; historical; humor/satire; literary; mainstream/contemporary; mystery/suspense; picture books; psychic/supernatural; religious/inspirational; sports; thriller.

Literary Agents

O━ This agency specializes in commercial fiction and nonfiction.

How to Contact Submit 1-page query, outline, SASE. Obtains most new clients through recommendations from others, conferences, lectures.

Recent Sales Sold 30 titles in the last year. *Love Smart*, by Dr. Phil McGraw (Simon & Schuster); *And One More Thing Before You Go*, by Maria Shriver; *The New Health Insurance Solution*, by Paul Zane Pilzer; *The Truth About Diamonds*, by Nicole Richie. Other clients include Anthony Robbins, Catherine Crier, Dr. Stephen Covey.

Terms Agent receives 15% commission on domestic sales. Offers written contract.

Writers' Conferences Aspen Summer Words Literary Festival.

Tips "If interested in agency representation, it is vital to have the material in the proper working format. As agents' policies differ, it is important to follow their guidelines. The best advice I can give is to work on establishing a strong proposal that provides sample chapters, an overall synopsis (fairly detailed), and some biographical information on yourself. Do not send your proposal in pieces; it should be complete upon submission. Remember you are trying to sell your work, and it should be in its best condition."

☑ DWYER & O'GRADY, INC.

P.O. Box 790, Cedar Key FL 32625. (352)543-9307. Web site: www.dwyerogrady.com. **Contact:** Elizabeth O'Grady. Estab. 1990. Member of SCBWI. Represents 20 clients. Currently handles: 100% juvenile books.

• Prior to opening their agency, Mr. Dwyer and Ms. O'Grady were booksellers and publishers.

Member Agents Elizabeth O'Grady; Jeff Dwyer.

Represents Juvenile books. **Considers these nonfiction areas:** Juvenile nonfiction. **Considers these fiction areas:** Juvenile; picture books; young adult.

O━ "We are not accepting new clients at this time." This agency represents only writers and illustrators of children's books. Does not want to receive submissions that are not for juvenile audiences.

How to Contact *No unsolicited mss.* Obtains most new clients through recommendations from others, direct approach by agent to writer whose work they've read.

Recent Sales Sold 22 titles in the last year. Clients include Kim Ablon Whitney, Mary Azarian, Tom Bodett, Odds Bodkin, E.B. Lewis, Steve Schuch, Virginia Stroud, Natasha Tarpley, Zong-Zhou Wang, Rich Michelson, Barry Moser, Peter Sylvada, James Rumford, Clemence McLaren, Nat Tripp, Lita Judge, Geoffrey Norman, Stan Fellows, Irving Toddy.

Terms Agent receives 15% commission on domestic sales; 20% commission on foreign sales. Offers written contract; 1-month notice must be given to terminate contract. Charges clients for photocopying of longer mss or mutually agreed upon marketing expenses.

Writers' Conferences BookExpo America; American Library Association Annual Conference; SCBWI.

☑ DYSTEL & GODERICH LITERARY MANAGEMENT

1 Union Square W., Suite 904, New York NY 10003. (212)627-9100. Fax: (212)627-9313. E-mail: miriam@dystel.com. Web site: www.dystel.com. **Contact:** Miriam Goderich. Estab. 1994. Member of AAR. Represents 300 clients. 50% of clients are new/unpublished writers. Currently handles: 65% nonfiction books; 25% novels; 10% cookbooks.

• Dystel & Goderich Literary Management recently acquired the client list of Bedford Book Works.

Member Agents Stacey Glick; Jane Dystel; Miriam Goderich; Michael Bourret; Jim McCarthy; Kate McKean; Lauren Abramo.

Represents Nonfiction books, novels, cookbooks. **Considers these nonfiction areas:** Animals; anthropology/archaeology; biography/autobiography; business/economics; child guidance/parenting; cooking/foods/nutrition; current affairs; education; ethnic/cultural interests; gay/lesbian issues; government/politics/law; health/medicine; history; humor/satire; military/war; money/finance; New Age/metaphysics; popular culture; psychology; religious/inspirational; science/technology; true crime/investigative; women's issues/studies. **Considers these fiction areas:** Action/adventure; detective/police/crime; ethnic; family saga; gay/lesbian; literary; mainstream/contemporary; mystery/suspense; thriller.

O━ This agency specializes in cookbooks and commercial and literary fiction and nonfiction.

How to Contact Query with SASE. Considers simultaneous queries. Responds in 1 month to queries; 6 weeks to mss. Obtains most new clients through recommendations from others, solicitations, conferences.

Terms Agent receives 15% commission on domestic sales; 19% commission on foreign sales. Offers written contract. Charges for photocopying. Galley charges and book charges from the publisher are passed on to the author.

Writers' Conferences Whidbey Island Writers' Conference; Iowa Summer Writing Festival; Pacific Northwest Writer's Association; Pike's Peak Writers Conference; Santa Barbara Writers' Conference; Harriette Austin Writers Conference; Sandhills Writers Conference; Denver Publishing Institute; Love Is Murder.

Tips ''Work on sending professional, well-written queries that are concise and addressed to the specific agent the author is contacting. No dear Sirs/Madam.''

ANNE EDELSTEIN LITERARY AGENCY

20 W. 22nd St., Suite 1603, New York NY 10010. (212)414-4923. Fax: (212)414-2930. E-mail: info@aeliterary.com. Web site: www.aeliterary.com. Estab. 1990. Member of AAR.

Member Agents Anne Edelstein; Emilie Stewart.

Represents Nonfiction books, novels. **Considers these nonfiction areas:** History; memoirs; psychology; Buddhist thought. **Considers these fiction areas:** Commercial.

How to Contact Query with SASE, 25 sample pages. No e-mail queries.

EDUCATIONAL DESIGN SERVICES LLC

7238 Treviso Ln., Boynton Beach FL 33437-7338. (561)739-9402. **Contact:** Bertram L. Linder, president. Estab. 1979. Represents 17 clients. 70% of clients are new/unpublished writers. Currently handles: 100% textbooks and teacher education materials.

Represents Scholarly books, textbooks. **Considers these nonfiction areas:** Anthropology/archaeology; business/economics; child guidance/parenting; current affairs; education; ethnic/cultural interests; government/politics/law; history; language/literature/criticism; military/war; money/finance; science/technology; sociology; women's issues/studies.

    ○ₐ This agency specializes in textual material for the educational (K-12) market.

How to Contact Query with SASE, proposal package, outline, 1-2 sample chapters. Considers simultaneous queries. Responds in 1 month to queries; 6 weeks to mss. Returns materials only with SASE. Obtains most new clients through recommendations from others, solicitations, conferences.

Recent Sales Sold 4 titles in the last year. *Minority Report*, by H. Gunn and J. Singh (Scarecrow Press); *Spreadsheets for School Administrators & Supervisors* (Scarecrow Press); *How to Solve the Word Problems in Arithmetic Grades 6-8*, by P. Pullman (McGraw-Hill/Schaum); *How to Solve Math Word Problems on Standardized Tests*, by D. Wayne (McGraw-Hill/Schaum); *First Principles of Cosmology*, by E.V. Linder (Addison-Wesley Longman); *Preparing for the 8th Grade Test in Social Studies*, by E. Farren and A. Paci (AMSCO School Publications).

Terms Agent receives 15% commission on domestic sales; 25% commission on foreign sales. Offers written contract. Charges clients for photocopying and postage/shipping costs.

LISA EKUS PUBLIC RELATIONS CO., LLC

57 North St., Hatfield MA 01038. (413)247-9325. Fax: (413)247-9873. E-mail: lcecooks@lisaekus.com. Web site: www.lisaekus.com. **Contact:** Lisa Ekus. Estab. 1982. Member of AAR.

Represents Nonfiction books. **Considers these nonfiction areas:** Cooking/foods/nutrition; occasionally health/well-being and women's issues.

How to Contact Submit a hard copy proposal with title page, proposal contents, concept, author bio, marketing and promotion, competition, TOC, chapter summaries, complete sample chapter (include tested recipes).

Recent Sales *Weeknight Grilling with the BBQ Queens*, by Karen Adler and Judith Fertig (Harvard Common Press); *The Berghoff Family Cookbook*, by Carlyn and Jan Berghoff with Nancy Ross Ryan (Andrews McMeel); *Passione di Sardinia*, by Efisio Farris with Jim Eber (Rizzoli); *1,000 Gluten-Free Recipes*, by Carol Fenster (John Wiley & Sons); *New Orleans Food*, by Tom Fitzmorris (Stewart, Tabori & Chang); *Fit and Fast Meals in Minutes*, by Linda Gassenheimer (Rodale); *The Food Synergy Handbook*, by Elaine Magee (Rodale).

ETHAN ELLENBERG LITERARY AGENCY

548 Broadway, #5-E, New York NY 10012. (212)431-4554. Fax: (212)941-4652. E-mail: agent@ethanellenberg.com. Web site: www.ethanellenberg.com. **Contact:** Ethan Ellenberg. Estab. 1983. Represents 80 clients. 10% of clients are new/unpublished writers. Currently handles: 25% nonfiction books; 75% novels.

    ● Prior to opening his agency, Mr. Ellenberg was contracts manager of Berkley/Jove and associate contracts manager for Bantam.

Represents Nonfiction books, novels, children's books. **Considers these nonfiction areas:** Biography/autobiography; health/medicine; history; military/war; New Age/metaphysics; religious/inspirational; science/technology. **Considers these fiction areas:** Fantasy; mystery/suspense; picture books; romance (all genres); science fiction; thriller; young adult; women's; middle grade.

    ○ₐ This agency specializes in commercial fiction—especially thrillers, romance/women's, and specialized nonfiction. ''We also do a lot of children's books.'' Actively seeking commercial and literary fiction, children's books, and breakthrough nonfiction. Does not want to receive poetry, short stories, westerns, autobiographies, or screenplays.

How to Contact For fiction, send introductory letter, outline, first 3 chapters, SASE. For nonfiction, send query letter, proposal, 1 sample chapter, SASE. For children's books, send introductory letter, up to 3 picture book mss, outline, first 3 chapters, SASE. No fax queries. Accepts e-mail queries (no attachments). Will only respond to e-mail queries if interested. Considers simultaneous queries. Responds in 4-6 weeks to mss. Returns materials only with SASE.

Recent Sales Has sold over 100 titles in the last 3 years. *Ghost Brigades*, by John Scalzi (Tor); *Dark Moon Descender*, by Sharon Shinn (Ace); *Deep, Dark and Dangerous*, by Jaid Black (Pocket Books); *The Alien in the Supermarket*, by Susan Grant (HQN); *Beyond the Limit*, by Lindsay McKenna (HQN); *Master of Darkness*, by Susan Sizemore (Pocket Books); *Peach Hill*, by Marthe Jocelyn (Random House/Wendy Lamb Books). Other clients include Mel Odom, MaryJanice Davidson, Amanda Ashley, Rebecca York, Bertrice Small, Eric Rohmann.

Terms Agent receives 15% commission on domestic sales; 10% commission on foreign sales. Offers written contract. Charges clients (with their consent) for direct expenses limited to photocopying and postage.

Writers' Conferences RWA National Conference; Novelists, Inc; and other regional conferences.

Tips "We do consider new material from unsolicited authors. Write a good, clear letter with a succinct description of your book. We prefer the first 3 chapters when we consider fiction. For all submissions, you must include a SASE or the material will be discarded. It's always hard to break in, but talent will find a home. Check our Web site for complete submission guidelines. We continue to see natural storytellers and nonfiction writers with important books."

◨ NICHOLAS ELLISON, INC.

Affiliated with Sanford J. Greenburger Associates, 55 Fifth Ave., 15th Floor, New York NY 10003. (212)206-6050. Fax: (212)463-8718. Web site: www.greenburger.com. **Contact:** Nicholas Ellison. Estab. 1983. Represents 70 clients. Currently handles: 50% nonfiction books; 50% novels.

   • Prior to becoming an agent, Mr. Ellison was an editor at Minerva Editions and Harper & Row, and editor-in-chief at Delacorte.

Member Agents Nicholas Ellison; Jennifer Cayea.

Represents Nonfiction books, novels. **Considers these nonfiction areas:** Considers most nonfiction areas. **Considers these fiction areas:** Literary; mainstream/contemporary.

How to Contact Query with SASE. Responds in 6 weeks to queries.

Recent Sales *A Dirty Job*, by Christopher Moore (HarperCollins); *I'm Not Myself*, by Sarah Dunn (Little, Brown); *The Girl from Charnelle*, by K.L. Cook (HarperCollins); next 3 Nelson DeMille Books (Warner). Other clients include Olivia Goldsmith, P.T. Deutermann, Nancy Geary, Jeff Lindsay, Lee Gruenfeld, Thomas Christopher Greene, Bill Mason; Mario Boxquez, Father Albert Cutié, Geoff Emerick, Howard Massey, Sofia Quintero.

Terms Agent receives 15% commission on domestic sales; 20% commission on foreign sales.

◨ ANN ELMO AGENCY, INC.

60 E. 42nd St., New York NY 10165. (212)661-2880. Fax: (212)661-2883. **Contact:** Lettie Lee. Estab. 1959. Member of AAR, Authors Guild.

Member Agents Lettie Lee; Mari Cronin (plays); A.L. Abecassis (nonfiction).

Represents Nonfiction books, novels. **Considers these nonfiction areas:** Biography/autobiography; current affairs; health/medicine; history; how-to; popular culture; science/technology. **Considers these fiction areas:** Ethnic; family saga; mainstream/contemporary; romance (contemporary, gothic, historical, regency); thriller; women's.

How to Contact Only accepts mailed queries with SASE. Do not send full ms unless requested. No fax queries. Responds in 3 months to queries. Obtains most new clients through recommendations from others.

Recent Sales This agency prefers not to share information on specific sales.

Terms Agent receives 15% commission on domestic sales; 20% commission on foreign sales. Offers written contract. Charges clients for special mailings, shipping, multiple international calls. There is no charge for usual cost of doing business.

Tips "Query first, and only when asked send properly prepared manuscript. A double-spaced, readable manuscript is the best recommendation. Include a SASE, of course."

◨ THE ELAINE P. ENGLISH LITERARY AGENCY

4701 41st St. NW, Suite D, Washington DC 20016. (202)362-5190. Fax: (202)362-5192. E-mail: elaineengl@aol.com. Web site: www.elaineenglish.com. **Contact:** Elaine English. Member of AAR. Represents 16 clients. 50% of clients are new/unpublished writers. Currently handles: 100% novels.

   • Ms. English has been working in publishing for over 15 years. She is also an attorney specializing in media and publishing law.

Represents Novels. **Considers these fiction areas:** Historical; multicultural; mystery/suspense; romance (single title, historical, contemporary, romantic, suspense, chick lit, erotic); thriller; women's.

O-π Actively seeking women's fiction, including single-title romances. Does not want to receive any science fiction, time travel, children's, or young adult.

How to Contact Prefers e-mail queries. If requested, submit synopsis, first 3 chapters, SASE. Responds in 6-12 weeks to queries; 6 months to requested ms. Returns materials only with SASE. Obtains most new clients through recommendations from others, conferences, submissions.

Terms Agent receives 15% commission on domestic sales; 20% commission on foreign sales. Offers written contract; 30-day notice must be given to terminate contract. Charges only for expenses directly related to sales of ms (long distance phone calls, postage, copying).

Writers' Conferences RWA National Conference; SEAK Medical & Legal Fiction Writing Conference; Novelists, Inc; Washington Romance Writers Retreat.

🖉 FELICIA ETH LITERARY REPRESENTATION

555 Bryant St., Suite 350, Palo Alto CA 94301-1700. (650)375-1276. Fax: (650)401-8892. E-mail: feliciaeth@aol.c om. **Contact:** Felicia Eth. Estab. 1988. Member of AAR. Represents 25-35 clients. Currently handles: 85% nonfiction books; 15% adult novels.

Represents Nonfiction books, novels. **Considers these nonfiction areas:** Animals; anthropology/archaeology; biography/autobiography; business/economics; child guidance/parenting; current affairs; ethnic/cultural interests; gay/lesbian issues; government/politics/law; health/medicine; history; nature/environment; popular culture; psychology; science/technology; sociology; true crime/investigative; women's issues/studies. **Considers these fiction areas:** Ethnic; feminist; gay/lesbian; literary; mainstream/contemporary; thriller.

O-π This agency specializes in high-quality fiction (preferably mainstream/contemporary) and provocative, intelligent, and thoughtful nonfiction on a wide array of commercial subjects.

How to Contact Query with SASE, outline. Considers simultaneous queries. Responds in 3 weeks to queries; 4-6 weeks to mss.

Recent Sales Sold 7-10 titles in the last year. *Jane Austen in Boca*, by Paula Marantz Cohen (St. Martin's Press); *Why Gender Matters*, by Dr. Leonard Sax (Doubleday/Random House); *Anna Maria Violino*, by Barbara Quick (HarperCollins).

Terms Agent receives 15% commission on domestic sales; 20% commission on foreign and dramatic rights sales. Charges clients for photocopying and express mail service.

Writers' Conferences National Coalition of Independent Scholars Conference.

Tips "For nonfiction, established expertise is certainly a plus—as is magazine publication—though not a prerequisite. I am highly dedicated to those projects I represent, but highly selective in what I choose."

🖉 MARY EVANS INC.

242 E. Fifth St., New York NY 10003. (212)979-0880. Member of AAR.

Member Agents Mary Evans; Tanya McKinnon.

How to Contact Query with SASE.

🖉 FARBER LITERARY AGENCY, INC.

14 E. 75th St., #2E, New York NY 10021. (212)861-7075. Fax: (212)861-7076. E-mail: farberlit@aol.com. Web site: www.donaldfarber.com. **Contact:** Ann Farber, Dr. Seth Farber. Estab. 1989. Represents 40 clients. 50% of clients are new/unpublished writers. Currently handles: 25% nonfiction books; 15% scholarly books; 25% stage plays; 35% novels.

Member Agents Ann Farber (novels); Seth Farber (plays, scholarly books, novels); Donald C. Farber (attorney, all entertainment media).

Represents Nonfiction books, novels, juvenile books, textbooks, stage plays. **Considers these nonfiction areas:** Child guidance/parenting; cooking/foods/nutrition; music/dance; psychology; theater/film. **Considers these fiction areas:** Action/adventure; humor/satire; juvenile; literary; mainstream/contemporary; mystery/suspense; thriller; young adult.

How to Contact Submit outline, 3 sample chapters, SASE. Prefers to read materials exclusively. Responds in 1 month to queries; 2 months to mss. Obtains most new clients through recommendations from others.

Terms Agent receives 15% commission on domestic sales; 20% commission on foreign sales. Offers written contract, binding for 1 year. Client must furnish copies of ms, treatments, and any other items for submission.

Tips "Our attorney, Donald C. Farber, is the author of many books. His services are available to the agency's clients as part of the agency service at no additional charge."

🖉 FARRIS LITERARY AGENCY, INC.

P.O. Box 570069, Dallas TX 75357. (972)203-8804. E-mail: farris1@airmail.net. Web site: www.farrisliterary.c om. **Contact:** Mike Farris, Susan Morgan Farris. Estab. 2002. Represents 30 clients. 60% of clients are new/ unpublished writers.

• Both Mr. Farris and Ms. Farris are attorneys.

Represents Nonfiction books, novels. **Considers these nonfiction areas:** Biography/autobiography; business/economics; child guidance/parenting; cooking/foods/nutrition; current affairs; government/politics/law; health/medicine; history; how-to; humor/satire; memoirs; military/war; music/dance; popular culture; religious/inspirational; self-help/personal improvement; sports; women's issues/studies. **Considers these fiction areas:** Action/adventure; detective/police/crime; historical; humor/satire; literary; mainstream/contemporary; mystery/suspense; religious/inspirational; romance; sports; thriller; westerns/frontier.

   O─ "We specialize in both fiction and nonfiction books. We are particularly interested in discovering unpublished authors. We adhere to AAR guidelines" Does not consider science fiction, fantasy, gay and lesbian, erotica, young adult, or children's.

How to Contact Query with SASE. Considers simultaneous queries. Responds in 2-3 weeks to queries; 4-8 weeks to mss. Returns materials only with SASE. Obtains most new clients through recommendations from others, solicitations, conferences.

Recent Sales Sold 4 titles in the last year. *Detachment Fault* and *Untitled*, by Susan Cummins Miller (Berkley); *Creed*, by Sheldon Russell (Oklahoma University Press); *How to Understand Autism: The Easy Way*, by Dr. Alexander Durig (Jessica Kingsley Publishers Ltd.).

Terms Agent receives 15% commission on domestic sales; 20% commission on foreign sales. Offers written contract; 30-day notice must be given to terminate contract. Charges clients for postage and photocopying.

Writers' Conferences Oklahoma Writers Federation Conference; The Screenwriting Conference in Santa Fe; Pikes Peak Writers Conference; Women Writing the West Annual Conference.

◢ DIANA FINCH LITERARY AGENCY

116 W. 23rd St., Suite 500, New York NY 10011. (646)375-2081. E-mail: diana.finch@verizon.net. **Contact:** Diana Finch. Estab. 2003. Member of AAR. Represents 45 clients. 20% of clients are new/unpublished writers. Currently handles: 65% nonfiction books; 25% novels; 5% juvenile books; 5% multimedia.

   • Prior to opening her agency, Ms. Finch worked at Ellen Levine Literary Agency for 18 years.

Represents Nonfiction books, novels, scholarly books. **Considers these nonfiction areas:** Biography/autobiography; business/economics; child guidance/parenting; computers/electronic; current affairs; ethnic/cultural interests; government/politics/law; health/medicine; history; how-to; humor/satire; juvenile nonfiction; memoirs; military/war; money/finance; music/dance; nature/environment; photography; popular culture; psychology; science/technology; self-help/personal improvement; sports; theater/film; translation; true crime/investigative; women's issues/studies. **Considers these fiction areas:** Action/adventure; detective/police/crime; ethnic; historical; literary; mainstream/contemporary; thriller; young adult.

   O─ Actively seeking narrative nonfiction, popular science, and health topics. Does not want romance, mysteries, or children's picture books.

How to Contact Query with SASE or via e-mail (no attachments). No phone or fax queries. Considers simultaneous queries. Returns materials only with SASE. Obtains most new clients through recommendations from others.

Recent Sales *Armed Madhouse*, by Greg Palast (Penguin US/UK); *Journey of the Magi*, by Tudor Parfitt (Farrar, Straus & Giroux); *The Queen's Soprano*, by Carol Dines (Harcourt Young Adult); *Was the 2004 Election Stolen?*, by Steven Freeman and Joel Bleifuss (Seven Stories); *Lipstick Jihad*, by Azadeh Moaveni (Public Affairs); *Great Customer Connections*, by Rich Gallagher (Amacom). Other clients include Keith Devlin, Daniel Duane, Thomas Goltz, Hugh Pope, Owen Matthews, Joan Lambert, Dr. Robert Marion.

Terms Agent receives 15% commission on domestic sales; 20% commission on foreign sales. Offers written contract. "I charge for photocopying, overseas postage, galleys, and books purchased, and try to recap these costs from earnings received for a client, rather than charging outright."

Tips "Do as much research as you can on agents before you query. Have someone critique your query letter before you send it. It should be only 1 page and describe your book clearly—and why you are writing it—but also demonstrate creativity and a sense of your writing style."

◢ FLAMING STAR LITERARY ENTERPRISES

320 Riverside Dr., New York NY 10025. E-mail: flamingstarlit@aol.com. Web site: flamingstarlit.com. **Contact:** Joseph B. Vallely, Janis C. Vallely. Estab. 1985. Represents 100 clients. 25% of clients are new/unpublished writers. Currently handles: 100% nonfiction books.

   • Prior to opening the agency, Mr. Vallely served as national sales manager for Dell; Ms. Vallely was vice president of Doubleday.

Represents Nonfiction books. **Considers these nonfiction areas:** Current affairs; government/politics/law; health/medicine; nature/environment; science/technology; self-help/personal improvement; spirituality; sports.

   O─ This agency specializes in upscale commercial nonfiction.

How to Contact E-mail only (no attachments). Obtains most new clients through recommendations from others, solicitations.

Terms Agent receives 15% commission on domestic sales; 20% commission on foreign sales. Offers written contract. Charges clients for photocopying and postage only.

◙ FLANNERY LITERARY

1155 S. Washington St., Suite 202, Naperville IL 60540. (630)428-2682. Fax: (630)428-2683. **Contact:** Jennifer Flannery. Estab. 1992. Represents 40 clients. 50% of clients are new/unpublished writers. Currently handles: 100% juvenile books.

　　O→ This agency specializes in children's and young adult fiction and nonfiction. It also accepts picture books.

How to Contact Query with SASE. No fax or e-mail queries. Responds in 2 weeks to queries; 1 month to mss. Obtains most new clients through recommendations from others, submissions.

Recent Sales Sold 50 titles in the last year. This agency prefers not to share information on specific sales.

Terms Agent receives 15% commission on domestic sales; 20% commission on foreign sales. Offers written contract, binding for life of book in print; 1-month notice must be given to terminate contract. 100% of business is derived from commissions on ms sales.

Tips "Write an engrossing, succinct query describing your work. We are always looking for a fresh new voice."

◙ PETER FLEMING AGENCY

P.O. Box 458, Pacific Palisades CA 90272. (310)454-1373. **Contact:** Peter Fleming. Estab. 1962. Currently handles: 100% nonfiction books.

　　O→ This agency specializes in nonfiction books that unearth innovative and uncomfortable truths with bestseller potential. Greatly interested in journalists in the free press (the Internet).

How to Contact Query with SASE. Obtains most new clients through "a different, one-of-a-kind idea for a book often backed by the writer's experience in that area of expertise."

Recent Sales *Rulers of Evil*, by F. Tupper Saussy (HarperCollins); *Why Is It Always About You—Saving Yourself from the Narcissists in Your Life*, by Sandy Hotchkiss (Free Press).

Terms Agent receives 15% commission on domestic sales; 25% commission on foreign sales. Offers written contract, binding for 1 year. Charges clients only those fees agreed to in writing. "We may ask for a TV contract, too."

Tips "You can begin by self-publishing, test marketing with direct sales, and starting your own Web site."

N̄ ◙ FLETCHER & PARRY

78 Fifth Ave., 3rd Floor, New York NY 10011. (212)614-0778. Fax: (212)614-0728. **Contact:** Christy Fletcher, Emma Parry. Estab. 2003. Member of AAR.

Represents Nonfiction books, novels. **Considers these nonfiction areas:** Current affairs; history; memoirs; sports; travel; African American; narrative; science; biography; business; health; lifestyle. **Considers these fiction areas:** Literary; young adult; commercial.

　　O→ Does not want genre fiction.

How to Contact Query with SASE. Responds in 4-6 weeks to queries.

◙ B.R. FLEURY AGENCY

P.O. Box 149352, Orlando FL 32814-9352. (407)895-8494. Fax: (407)898-3923 or (888)310-8142. E-mail: brfleury agency@juno.com. Estab. 1994. Signatory of WGA.

　　O→ "We are not accepting queries until further notice."

◙ THE FOGELMAN LITERARY AGENCY

5420 LBJ Feeway to Lincoln Center, Suite 1900, Dallas TX 75240. (972)661-5114. Fax: (972)661-5691. E-mail: info@fogelman.com. Web site: www.fogelman.com. Alternate address: 415 Park Ave., New York NY 10022. (212)836-4803. **Contact:** Evan Fogelman. Estab. 1990. Member of AAR. Represents 100 clients. 2% of clients are new/unpublished writers. Currently handles: 40% nonfiction books; 40% novels; 10% scholarly books; 10% TV scripts.

　　● Prior to opening his agency, Mr. Fogelman was an entertainment lawyer. He is still active in the field and serves as chairman of the Texas Entertainment and Sports Lawyers Association. The Fogelman Literary Agency is associated with the law firm Underwood, Perkins & Ralstan.

Member Agents Evan Fogelman (nonfiction, women's fiction); Linda Kruger (women's fiction, nonfiction); Helen Brown (literary fiction, nonfiction).

Represents Nonfiction books, novels. **Considers these nonfiction areas:** Biography/autobiography; business/ economics; child guidance/parenting; current affairs; education; ethnic/cultural interests; government/politics/ law; health/medicine; popular culture; psychology; sports; true crime/investigative; women's issues/studies. **Considers these fiction areas:** Historical; literary; mainstream/contemporary; romance (all genres).

O-- This agency specializes in women's fiction and nonfiction. "Zealous advocacy makes this agency stand apart from others." Does not want to receive children's/juvenile.

How to Contact Query with SASE. Accepts e-mail queries (no attachments). Considers simultaneous queries. Responds in 1 week to queries; 3 months to mss. Returns materials only with SASE. Obtains most new clients through recommendations from others.

Recent Sales *Bulletproof Princess*, by Vicki Hinze (Silhouette Bombshell); *Surf Girl School*, by Cathy Yardley (Harlequin Signature Spotlight); *The Dark One*, by Ronda Thompson (St. Martin's Press).

Terms Agent receives 15% commission on domestic sales; 10% commission on foreign sales. Offers written contract.

Writers' Conferences RWA National Conference; Novelists, Inc.

Tips "Finish your manuscript, then see our Web site."

◖ THE FOLEY LITERARY AGENCY

34 E. 38th St., New York NY 10016-2508. (212)686-6930. **Contact:** Joan Foley, Joseph Foley. Estab. 1961. Represents 10 clients. Currently handles: 75% nonfiction books; 25% novels.

Represents Nonfiction books, novels.

How to Contact Query with letter, brief outline, SASE. Responds promptly to queries. Obtains most new clients through recommendations from others (rarely taking on new clients).

Recent Sales This agency prefers not to share information on specific sales.

Terms Agent receives 10% commission on domestic sales; 15% commission on foreign sales. 100% of business is derived from commissions on ms sales.

[N] ◖ FOLIO LITERARY MANAGEMENT, LLC

508 8th Ave., Suite 603, New York NY 10018. Web site: www.foliolit.com. Alternate address: 1627 K St. NW, Suite 1200, Washington DC 20006. Estab. 2006. Member of AAR. Represents 100+ clients.

● Prior to creating Folio Literary Management, Mr. Hoffman was an agent at PMA Literary and Film Management; Mr. Kleinman was an agent at Graybill & English; Ms. Wheeler was an agent at Creative Media Agency; Ms. Culver worked in foreign rights at Lowenstein-Yost; Ms. Cartwright-Niumata was an editor at Simon & Schuster, HarperCollins, and Avalon Books; Ms. Rappaport graduated from Carnegie Mellon University.

Member Agents Scott Hoffman; Jeff Kleinman; Paige Wheeler; Julie Culver; Erin Cartwright-Niumata, associate agent; Jenny Rappaport, associate agent.

Represents Nonfiction books, novels, short story collections. **Considers these nonfiction areas:** Animals (equestrian); business/economics; child guidance/parenting; creative nonfiction; history; how-to; humor/satire; memoirs; military/war; nature/environment; popular culture; psychology; religious/inspirational; science/technology; self-help/personal improvement; women's issues/studies; narrative nonfiction; art; espionage; biography; crime; politics; health/fitness; lifestyle; relationship; culture; cookbooks. **Considers these fiction areas:** Erotica; fantasy; literary; mystery/suspense; religious/inspirational; romance; science fiction; thriller (psychological); young adult; women's; Southern; legal; edgy crime; middle grade.

How to Contact Query with SASE or via e-mail (no attachments). Read agent bios online for specific submission guidelines. Responds in 1 month to queries.

Recent Sales Sold over 30 titles in the last year. *Finn*, by Will Murphy (Random House); *A Killing Tide*, by P.J. Alderman (Dorchester); *Color of the Sea*, by John Hamamura (Thomas Dunne Books/St. Martin's Press); *Meow Is for Murder*, by Linda O. Johnston (Berkley Prime Crime); *Wildlife's Scotland Yard*, by Laurel Neme (Joseph Henry Press); *Mockingbird*, by Charles J. Shields (Henry Holt); *Under the Mask*, by Heidi Ardizzone (Norton); *The Culture Code*, by Dr. Clotaire Rapaille (Doubleday).

◖ FOX CHASE AGENCY, INC.

701 Lee Rd., Suite 102, Chesterbrook Corporate Center, Chesterbrook PA 19087. Estab. 1972. Member of AAR.
Member Agents A.L. Hart; Jo C. Hart.

◖ LYNN C. FRANKLIN ASSOCIATES, LTD.

1350 Broadway, Suite 2015, New York NY 10018. (212)868-6311. Fax: (212)868-6312. **Contact:** Lynn Franklin, Claudia Nys. Estab. 1987. Member of PEN America. Represents 30-35 clients. 50% of clients are new/unpublished writers. Currently handles: 90% nonfiction books; 10% novels.

Represents Nonfiction books, novels. **Considers these nonfiction areas:** Biography/autobiography; current affairs; health/medicine; history; memoirs; New Age/metaphysics; psychology; religious/inspirational; self-help/personal improvement; spirituality. **Considers these fiction areas:** Literary; mainstream/contemporary (commercial).

O→ This agency specializes in general nonfiction with a special interest in self-help, biography/memoir, alternative health, and spirituality.

How to Contact Query with SASE. *No unsolicited mss.* Considers simultaneous queries. Responds in 2 weeks to queries; 6 weeks to mss. Obtains most new clients through recommendations from others, solicitations.

Recent Sales *Rabble-Rouser for Peace: The Authorized Biography of Desmond Tutu*, by John Allen (The Free Press); *Alexander II: Russia Between Hope and Terror*, by Edvard Radzinsky (The Free Press); *The Tao of Poop: Growing Yourself While Growing Your Baby*, by Vivian Glyck (Shambhala); *Healing Invisible Wounds*, by Richard Mollica (Harcourt); *The 10 Commitments: Translating Good Intentions into Great Choices*, by David Simon (Health Communications); *The Dalai Lama: Man, Monk, Mystic*, by Mayank Chhaya (Doubleday); *Grandmothers Counsel Our World: Indigenous Women Elders Offer Their Vision for Our Planet*, by Carol Schaefer (Shambhala Publications).

Terms Agent receives 15% commission on domestic sales; 20% commission on foreign sales. Offers written contract. 100% of business is derived from commissions on ms sales. Charges clients for postage, photocopying, long distance telephone (if significant).

◖ JEANNE FREDERICKS LITERARY AGENCY, INC.

221 Benedict Hill Rd., New Canaan CT 06840. (203)972-3011. Fax: (203)972-3011. E-mail: jfredrks@optonline.n et. **Contact:** Jeanne Fredericks. Estab. 1997. Member of AAR, Authors Guild. Represents 90 clients. 10% of clients are new/unpublished writers. Currently handles: 100% nonfiction books.

• Prior to opening her agency, Ms. Fredericks was an agent and acting director with the Susan P. Urstadt, Inc. Agency. In an earlier career she held editorial positions in trade publishing, most recently as editorial director of Ziff-Davis Books.

Represents Nonfiction books. **Considers these nonfiction areas:** Animals; biography/autobiography; child guidance/parenting; cooking/foods/nutrition; gardening; health/medicine (alternative health); history; how-to; interior design/decorating; money/finance; nature/environment; photography; psychology; self-help/personal improvement; sports (not spectator sports); women's issues/studies.

O→ This agency specializes in quality adult nonfiction by authorities in their fields. No children's books or fiction.

How to Contact Query first with SASE, then send outline/proposal, 1-2 sample chapters, SASE. No fax queries. Accepts short e-mail queries (no attachments). Considers simultaneous queries. Responds in 3-5 weeks to queries; 2-4 months to mss. Returns materials only with SASE. Obtains most new clients through recommendations from others, solicitations, conferences.

Recent Sales *Lilias! Yoga Gets Better with Age*, by Lilias Folan (Rodale); *Homescaping*, by Anne Halpin (Rodale); *Stealing with Style*, by Emyl Jenkins (Algonquin); *Creating Optimism in Your Child*, by Bob Murray, PhD, and Alice Fortinberry, MS (McGraw-Hill); *Waking the Warrior Goddess*, by Christine Horner, MD (Basic Health); *Healing the Heart with EECP*, by Debra Braverman, MD (Celestial Arts); *Melanoma*, by Catherine Poole and Dupont Guerry, MD (Yale); *Bodywork*, by Thomas Claire (Basic Health); *Jonathan's Treasure: The Quest, Risks, and Conflicts Over a Historical Ship's Gold*, by Dennis M. Powers (Citadel); *Integral Health*, by Elliott Dacher, MD (Basic Health); *Informatica: The Deep History of Computer Science*, by Alex Wright (Joseph Henry Press); *Building Within Nature*, by Andy and Sally Wasowski (University of Minnesota Press); *The Art of War for Executives, Revised Edition*, by Donald Krause (Perigee); *Into Brown Bear Country*, by Will Troyer (University of Alaska Press).

Terms Agent receives 15% commission on domestic sales; 25% commission on foreign sales with co-agent (20% without co-agent). Offers written contract, binding for 9 months; 2-month notice must be given to terminate contract. Charges client for photocopying proposals and mss, overseas postage, priority mail, express mail services.

Writers' Conferences Connecticut Press Club Biennial Writer's Conference; ASJA Writers Conference; BookExpo America; Garden Writers Association Annual Symposium.

Tips ''Be sure to research the competition for your work and be able to justify why there's a need for it. I enjoy building an author's career, particularly if he/she is professional, hardworking, and courteous. Aside from 15 years of agenting experience, I've had 10 years of editorial experience in adult trade book publishing that enables me to help an author polish a proposal so that it's more appealing to prospective editors. My MBA in marketing also distinguishes me from other agents.''

◲ ◖ SARAH JANE FREYMANN LITERARY AGENCY

59 W. 71st St., Suite 9B, New York NY 10023. (212)362-9277. Fax: (212)501-8240. E-mail: sjfs@aol.com. **Contact:** Sarah Jane Freymann. Represents 100 clients. 20% of clients are new/unpublished writers. Currently handles: 75% nonfiction books; 23% novels; 2% juvenile books.

Represents Nonfiction books, novels, illustrated books. **Considers these nonfiction areas:** Animals; anthropology/archaeology; art/architecture/design; biography/autobiography; business/economics; child guidance/parenting; cooking/foods/nutrition; current affairs; ethnic/cultural interests; health/medicine; history; interior design/decorating; memoirs (narrative); nature/environment; psychology; religious/inspirational; self-help/personal improvement; women's issues/studies; lifestyle. **Considers these fiction areas:** Ethnic; literary; mainstream/contemporary.

How to Contact Query with SASE. Responds in 2 weeks to queries; 6 weeks to mss. Obtains most new clients through recommendations from others.

Recent Sales *Girl Stories*, by Lauren Weinstein (Henry Holt); *The Good, Good Pig*, by Sy Montgomery (Ballantine/Random House); *The Man Who Killed the Whale*, by Linda Hogan (W.W. Norton); *Writing the Fire! Yoga and the Art of Making Your Words Come Alive*, by Gail Sher (Harmoney/Bell Tower); *Mexicocina*, by Melba Levick and Betsy McNair (Chronicle); *Holy Play*, by Kirk Byron Jones (Jossey Bass).

Terms Agent receives 15% commission on domestic sales; 20% commission on foreign sales. Offers written contract. Charges clients for long distance, overseas postage, photocopying. 100% of business is derived from commissions on ms sales.

Tips "I love fresh, new, passionate works by authors who love what they are doing and have both natural talent and carefully honed skill."

N ☑ FULL CIRCLE LITERARY, LLC

7676 Hazard Center Dr., Suite 500, San Diego CA 92108. E-mail: info@fullcircleliterary.com. Web site: www.full circleliterary.com. **Contact:** Lilly Ghahremani, Stefanie Von Borstel. Estab. 2004. Represents 30 clients. 90% of clients are new/unpublished writers. Currently handles: 80% nonfiction books; 5% novels; 10% juvenile books; 5% scholarly books.

● Before forming Full Circle, Ms. Von Borstel worked in both marketing and editorial capacities at Putnam and Harcourt; Ms. Ghahremani received her law degree from UCLA, specializing in representing authors.

Member Agents Lilly Ghahremani (pop culture, crafts, useful humor, how-to, narrative nonfiction, Middle Eastern interest, multicultural); Stefanie Von Borstel (Latino interest, crafts, cookbooks, parenting, wedding/relationships, middle grade/teen fiction, multicultural/bilingual picture books).

Represents Nonfiction books, juvenile books, graphic novels. **Considers these nonfiction areas:** Animals; biography/autobiography; business/economics; child guidance/parenting; cooking/foods/nutrition; crafts/hobbies; current affairs; ethnic/cultural interests; health/medicine; how-to; humor/satire; juvenile nonfiction; music/dance; popular culture; religious/inspirational; self-help/personal improvement; sports; theater/film; translation; women's issues/studies. **Considers these fiction areas:** Comic books/cartoon; ethnic; literary; young adult.

○─┐ "Our full-service boutique agency, representing a range of nonfiction and children's books (limited fiction), provides a one-stop resource for authors. Our expertise in the realms of law and marketing provide Full Circle clients with a unique edge." Actively seeking nonfiction by authors with a unique and strong platform, projects that offer new and diverse viewpoints, and literature with a global or multicultural perspective. "We are particularly interested in books with a Latino or Middle Eastern angle and books related to pop culture, music, or the arts." No screenplays, poetry, or genre fiction (horror, thriller, mystery, western, sci-fi, fantasy, romance)

How to Contact For nonfiction, send hard copy of outline, 1 sample chapter. Send children's/middle grade/YA queries to kidsquery@fullcircleliterary.com; fiction/nonfiction queries to query@fullcircleliterary.com. Considers simultaneous queries. Responds in 1-2 weeks to queries; 4-6 weeks to mss. Returns materials only with SASE. Obtains most new clients through recommendations from others, solicitations, conferences.

Recent Sales Sold 9 titles in the last year. *The Grilled Cheese Madonna & 99 Other of the Weirdest, Wackiest, Most Famous eBay Auctions Ever*, by Christopher Cihlar (Broadway/Random House); *Baby Read-Aloud Basics*, by Caroline Blakemore and Barbara Weston Ramirez (Amacom); *The Craftster Guide to Nifty, Thrifty & Kitschy Crafts*, by Leah Kramer (Ten Speed Press); *Poetry Zoo/Zoológico de Poemas*, by Margarita Montalvo (Scholastic en español).

Terms Agent receives 15% commission on domestic sales; 20% commission on foreign sales. Offers written contract; up to 60-day notice must be given to terminate contract. Charges for copying and postage.

Writers' Conferences San Diego State University Writers; Conference, San Francisco Writers Conference; Pikes Peak Writers Conference; National Latino Writers Conference; Santa Barbara Writers' Conference; Willamette Writers Conference; La Jolla Writers Conference; Surrey International Writers Conference.

Tips "Put your best foot forward. Contact us when you simply can't make your project any better on your own, and please be sure your work fits with what the agent you're approaching represents. Little things count, so copyedit your work. Join a writing group and attend conferences to get objective and constructive feedback before submitting. Be active about building your platform as an author before, during, and after publication. Remember this is a business and your agent is a business partner. Be prepared to work together every step of the way. Be patient—this publishing thing takes time."

❂ MAX GARTENBERG LITERARY AGENCY

912 N. Pennsylvania Ave., Yardley PA 19067. (215)295-9230. Web site: www.maxgartenberg.com. **Contact:** Max Gartenberg (gartenbook@att.net), Anne Devlin (agdevlin@aol.com), Will Devlin (wad411@hotmail.com). Estab. 1954. Represents 30 clients. 5% of clients are new/unpublished writers. Currently handles: 90% nonfiction books; 10% novels.

Represents Nonfiction books, novels. **Considers these nonfiction areas:** Agriculture/horticulture; animals; art/architecture/design; biography/autobiography; child guidance/parenting; current affairs; health/medicine; history; military/war; money/finance; music/dance; nature/environment; psychology; science/technology; self-help/personal improvement; sports; theater/film; true crime/investigative; women's issues/studies.

How to Contact Query with SASE. Considers simultaneous queries. Responds in 2 weeks to queries; 6 weeks to mss. Obtains most new clients through recommendations from others, following up on good query letters.

Recent Sales *What Patients Taught Me*, by Audrey Young, MD (Sasquatch Books); *Unorthodox Warfare: The Chinese Experience*, by Ralph D. Sawyer (Westview Press); *Encyclopedia of Earthquakes and Volcanoes*, by Alexander E. Gates (Facts on File).

Terms Agent receives 15% commission on domestic sales; 15-20% commission on foreign sales.

Tips "This agency has recently expanded to allow more access for new writers."

❂ GELFMAN, SCHNEIDER, LITERARY AGENTS, INC.

250 W. 57th St., Suite 2515, New York NY 10107. (212)245-1993. Fax: (212)245-8678. E-mail: mail@gelfmanschneider.com. **Contact:** Jane Gelfman, Deborah Schneider. Estab. 1981. Member of AAR. Represents 300+ clients. 10% of clients are new/unpublished writers.

Represents Nonfiction books, novels. **Considers these nonfiction areas:** Biography; health; lifestyle; politics; science. **Considers these fiction areas:** Literary; mainstream/contemporary; mystery/suspense.

    ○➡ Does not want to receive romance, science fiction, westerns, or children's books.

How to Contact Query with SASE. No e-mail queries accepted. Responds in 1 month to queries; 2 months to mss. Obtains most new clients through recommendations from others.

Terms Agent receives 15% commission on domestic and dramatic rights sales; 20% commission on foreign sales. Offers written contract. Charges clients for photocopying and messengers/couriers.

❂ THE GISLASON AGENCY

219 Main St. SE, Suite 506, Minneapolis MN 55414-2160. (612)331-8033. Fax: (612)331-8115. E-mail: gislasonbj@aol.com. Web site: www.thegislasonagency.com. **Contact:** Barbara J. Gislason. Estab. 1992. Member of Minnesota State Bar Association, American Bar Association, Art & Entertainment Law Section, Animal Law, Internet Committee, Minnesota Intellectual Property Law Association Copyright Committee; SFWA, MWA, Sisters in Crime, Icelandic Association of Minnesota, American Academy of Acupuncture and Oriental Medicine. 80% of clients are new/unpublished writers. Currently handles: 10% nonfiction books; 90% novels.

    ● Ms. Gislason became an attorney in 1980, and continues to practice art and entertainment law. She has been nationally recognized as a Leading American Attorney and a Super Lawyer. She is also the owner of Blue Raven Press, which publishes fiction and nonfiction about animals.

Member Agents Deborah Sweeney (fantasy, science fiction); Kellie Hultgren (fantasy, science fiction); Lisa Higgs (mystery, literary fiction); Kris Olson (mystery); Kevin Hedman (fantasy, science fiction, mystery, literary fiction).

Represents Nonfiction books, novels. **Considers these nonfiction areas:** Animals (behavior/communications). **Considers these fiction areas:** Fantasy; literary; mystery/suspense; science fiction; thriller (legal).

    ○➡ Do not send personal memoirs, poetry, short stories, screenplays, or children's books.

How to Contact For fiction, query with synopsis, first 3 chapters, SASE. For nonfiction, query with proposal, sample chapters. Published authors may submit complete ms. No e-mail or fax queries. Responds in 2 months to queries; 3 months to mss. Obtains most new clients through recommendations from others, conferences, *Guide to Literary Agents*, *Literary Market Place*, other reference books.

Recent Sales *Historical Romance #4*, by Linda Cook (Kensington); *Dancing Dead*, by Deborah Woodworth (HarperCollins); *Owen Keane's Lonely Journey*, by Terence Faherty (Harlequin).

Terms Agent receives 15% commission on domestic sales; 20% commission on foreign sales. Offers written contract, binding for 1 year with option to renew. Charges clients for photocopying and postage.

Writers' Conferences Southwest Writers Conference; Willamette Writers Conference; Wrangling with Writing; other state and regional conferences.

Tips "Your cover letter should be well written and include a detailed synopsis (fiction) or proposal (nonfiction), the first 3 chapters, and author bio. Appropriate SASE required. We are looking for a great writer with a poetic, lyrical, or quirky writing style who can create intriguing ambiguities. We expect a well-researched, imaginative, and fresh plot that reflects a familiarity with the applicable genre. If submitting nonfiction work, explain how the submission differs from and adds to previously published works in the field. Scenes with sex and violence must be intrinsic to the plot. Remember to proofread. If the work was written with a specific publisher in mind, this should be communicated."

◢ BARRY GOLDBLATT LITERARY AGENCY, INC.

320 7th Ave., #266, Brooklyn NY 11215. **Contact:** Barry Goldblatt. Member of AAR.
Represents Juvenile books. **Considers these fiction areas:** Picture books; young adult; middle grade.
How to Contact Query with SASE. No e-mail queries.

◗ GOLDFARB & ASSOCIATES

721 Gibbon St., Alexandria VA 22314. (202)466-3030. Fax: (703)836-5644. E-mail: rglawlit@aol.com. Web site: www.ronaldgoldfarb.com. **Contact:** Ronald Goldfarb. Estab. 1966. Currently handles: 85-90% nonfiction books; 10-15% novels; roster of TV and movie projects is rapidly growing (works closely with MainStreet Media, a production company owned by Mr. Goldfarb).

• Mr. Goldfarb is an experienced trial lawyer and a veteran literary agent, as well as the author of 10 books and over 275 articles. He spends December-March at his Miami office. Ms. Hare, a native Australian currently residing in both Israel and the US, is a literary agent with experience as a reporter, writer, and radio and television producer. Ms. Wheatley, whose background is teaching English literature, is an editor who also works with new authors.

Member Agents Ronald Goldfarb; Robbie Anna Hare; Louise Wheatley.
Represents Nonfiction books, novels.

O— "Serious nonfiction is our must active area (with all publishing houses and editors), though we do handle fiction selectively. Our location in the nation's capital enables us to represent many well-known print journalists, TV correspondents, politicians, and policymakers in both fiction and nonfiction fields, but many of our clients come from all over this country and some from abroad."

How to Contact The firm is accepting select new projects, usually on the basis of personal referrals.
Tips "We are a law firm and a literary agency. Through our work with writers' organizations, we are constantly adding new and talented writers to our list of literary clients, and matching collaborators with projects in need of authors or editors. We have found writers to develop book ideas at the request of publishers."

◖ FRANCES GOLDIN LITERARY AGENCY, INC.

57 E. 11th St., Suite 5B, New York NY 10003. (212)777-0047. Fax: (212)228-1660. E-mail: agency@goldinlit.com. Web site: www.goldinlit.com. Estab. 1977. Member of AAR. Represents over 100 clients.
Member Agents Frances Goldin, principal/agent; Ellen Geiger, agent (commercial and literary fiction and non-fiction, cutting-edge topics of all kinds); Matt McGowan, agent/rights director (innovative works of fiction and nonfiction); Sam Stoloff, agent (literary fiction, memoir, history, accessible sociology and philosophy, cultural studies, serious journalism, narrative and topical nonfiction with a progressive orientation); David Csontos, agent/office manager (literary fiction, biography, memoir, psychology, spirituality, gay and social studies, the arts).
Represents Nonfiction books, novels. **Considers these nonfiction areas:** Serious, controversial nonfiction with a progressive political orientation. **Considers these fiction areas:** Adult literary.

O— "We are hands on and we work intensively with clients on proposal and manuscript development." Does not want anything that is racist, sexist, agist, homophobic, or pornographic. No screenplays, children's books, art books, cookbooks, business books, diet books, self-help, or genre fiction.

How to Contact Query with SASE. No unsolicited mss or work previously submitted to publishers. Prefers hard-copy queries. Responds in 4-6 weeks to queries.
Recent Sales *Skin Deep*, by Dalton Conley (Pantheon); *Conned: How Millions Have Lost the Right to Vote*, by Sasha Abramsky (New Press); *Gotham II*, by Mike Wallace; *Animal, Vegetable, Miracle*, by Barbara Kingslover; an untitled memoir by Staceyann Chin.

N ⊕ ◢ GOLVAN ARTS MANAGEMENT

P.O. Box 766, Kew VIC 3101 Australia. E-mail: golvan@ozemail.com.au. Web site: www.golvanarts.com.au.
Contact: Colin Golvan.
Represents Nonfiction books, novels, juvenile books, poetry books, movie scripts, TV scripts, stage plays.
How to Contact Query with author bio, SASE.

Recent Sales *The Runaway Circus*, by Gordon Reece (Lothian Books); *Two for the Road*, by Shirly Hardy-Rix and Brian Rix (Macmillan); *The Catch*, by Marg Vandeleur (Penguin).
Terms Agent receives 11% commission on domestic sales.

☻ GOODMAN ASSOCIATES

500 West End Ave., New York NY 10024-4317. (212)873-4806. **Contact:** Elise Simon Goodman. Estab. 1976. Member of AAR. Represents 50 clients.

• Mr. Goodman is the former chair of the AAR Ethics Committee.

Member Agents Elise Simon Goodman; Arnold P. Goodman.

Represents Nonfiction books, novels.

O━ Accepting new clients by recommendation only. Does not want to receive poetry, articles, individual stories, children's, or young adult material.

How to Contact Query with SASE. Responds in 10 days to queries; 1 month to mss.

Terms Agent receives 15% commission on domestic sales; 20% commission on foreign sales. Charges clients for certain expenses: faxes, toll calls, overseas postage, photocopying, book purchases.

☻ IRENE GOODMAN LITERARY AGENCY

80 Fifth Ave., Suite 1101, New York NY 10011. Web site: www.irenegoodman.com. **Contact:** Irene Goodman, Miriam Kriss. Member of AAR.

Represents Novels. **Considers these fiction areas:** Historical; literary; mystery/suspense; romance; thriller; young adult; women's; chick lit; modern urban fantasies.

How to Contact Query with 1-3 chapters, synopsis, SASE. No e-mail or fax queries. Responds in 1 month.

☻ ASHLEY GRAYSON LITERARY AGENCY

1342 18th St., San Pedro CA 90732. Fax: (310)514-1148. E-mail: graysonagent@earthlink.net. Estab. 1976. Member of AAR. Represents 100 clients. 5% of clients are new/unpublished writers. Currently handles: 20% nonfiction books; 50% novels; 30% juvenile books.

Member Agents Ashley Grayson (fantasy, mystery, thrillers, young adult); Carolyn Grayson (chick lit, mystery, children's, nofiction, women's fiction, thrillers); Denise Dumars (mind/body/spirit, women's fiction, dark fantasy/horror); Lois Winston (women's fiction, chick lit, mystery).

Represents Nonfiction books, novels. **Considers these nonfiction areas:** Business/economics; computers/electronic; history; popular culture; science/technology; self-help/personal improvement; sports; true crime/investigative; investing/finance; mind/body/spirit; health; lifestyle. **Considers these fiction areas:** Fantasy; juvenile; multicultural; mystery/suspense; romance; science fiction; young adult; women's; chick lit.

O━ "We prefer to work with published (traditional print), established authors. We will give first consideration to authors who come recommended to us by our clients or other publishing professionals. We accept a very small number of new, previously unpublished authors."

How to Contact Query with SASE, first 3 pages of ms or overview of the nonfiction proposal. Accepts e-mail queries (no attachments).

Recent Sales *Ball Don't Lie*, by Matt de la Peña (Delacorte); *Heaven*, by Jack Cohen and Ian Stewart (Warner Books); *I Wish I Never Met You*, by Denise Wheatley (Touchstone/Simon & Schuster).

Terms Agent receives 15% commission on domestic sales; 20% commission on foreign sales.

☻ SANFORD J. GREENBURGER ASSOCIATES, INC.

55 Fifth Ave., New York NY 10003. (212)206-5600. Fax: (212)463-8718. Web site: www.greenburger.com. **Contact:** Heide Lange. Estab. 1932. Member of AAR. Represents 500 clients.

Member Agents Heide Lange; Faith Hamlin; Dan Mandel; Peter McGuigan; Matthew Bialer; Jeremy Katz.

Represents Nonfiction books, novels. **Considers these nonfiction areas:** Agriculture/horticulture; Americana; animals; anthropology/archaeology; art/architecture/design; biography/autobiography; business/economics; child guidance/parenting; computers/electronic; cooking/foods/nutrition; crafts/hobbies; current affairs; education; ethnic/cultural interests; gardening; gay/lesbian issues; government/politics/law; health/medicine; history; how-to; humor/satire; interior design/decorating; juvenile nonfiction; language/literature/criticism; memoirs; military/war; money/finance; multicultural; music/dance; nature/environment; New Age/metaphysics; philosophy; photography; popular culture; psychology; recreation; regional; religious/inspirational; science/technology; self-help/personal improvement; sex; sociology; software; sports; theater/film; translation; travel; true crime/investigative; women's issues/studies; young adult. **Considers these fiction areas:** Action/adventure; detective/police/crime; ethnic; family saga; feminist; gay/lesbian; glitz; historical; humor/satire; literary; mainstream/contemporary; mystery/suspense; psychic/supernatural; regional; sports; thriller.

O━ Does not want to receive romances or westerns.

How to Contact Submit query, first 3 chapters, synopsis, brief bio, SASE. Accepts fax queries. No e-mail queries. Considers simultaneous queries. Responds in 2 months to queries and mss.

Recent Sales Sold 200 titles in the last year. This agency prefers not to share information on specific sales.
Terms Agent receives 15% commission on domestic sales; 20% commission on foreign sales. Charges for photocopying and books for foreign and subsidiary rights submissions.

GREGORY & CO. AUTHORS' AGENTS

3 Barb Mews, London W6 7PA England. (44)(207)610-4676. Fax: (44)(207)610-4686. E-mail: info@gregoryandcompany.co.uk; maryjones@gregoryandcompany.co.uk. Web site: www.gregoryandcompany.co.uk. Estab. 1987. Member of AAA. Represents 60 clients. Currently handles: 10% nonfiction books; 90% novels.

- Prior to becoming an agent, Ms. Gregory was rights director for Chatto & Windus. Ms. Gregory is successful at selling rights all over the world, including film and television rights.

Member Agents Jane Gregory, sales; Emma Dunford, editorial; Claire Morris, rights.
Represents Nonfiction books, novels. **Considers these nonfiction areas:** Biography/autobiography; history. **Considers these fiction areas:** Detective/police/crime; historical; literary; mainstream/contemporary; thriller; contemporary women's fiction.

- "As a British agency we do not generally take on American authors." Actively seeking well-written, accessible modern novels. Does not want to receive horror, science fiction, fantasy, mind/body/spirit, children's books, screenplays, plays, short stories, or poetry.

How to Contact Query with outline, 3 sample chapters, SASE. Considers simultaneous queries. Returns materials only with SASE. Obtains most new clients through recommendations from others, conferences.
Recent Sales Sold 100 titles in the last year. *Tokyo*, by Mo Hayder (Bantam UK/Gove Atlantic); *The Torment of Others*, by Val McDermid (HarperCollins UK/St. Martin's Press); *Disordered Minds*, by Minette Walters (MacMillan UK/Putnam USA); *The Lover*, by Laura Wilson (Orion UK/Bantam USA); *Gagged & Bound*, by Natasha Cooper (Simon & Schuster UK/St. Martin's Press); *Demon of the Air*, by Simon Levack (Simon & Schuster/St. Martin's Press).
Terms Agent receives 15% commission on domestic sales; 20% commission on foreign sales. Offers written contract; 3-month notice must be given to terminate contract. Charges clients for photocopying typescripts and copies of book for submissions.
Writers' Conferences CWA Conference; Bouchercon.

BLANCHE C. GREGORY, INC.

2 Tudor City Place, New York NY 10017. (212)697-0828. E-mail: info@bcgliteraryagency.com. Web site: www.bcgliteraryagency.com. Member of AAR.
Member Agents Gertrude Bregman; Merry Gregory Pantano.

- Adult fiction and nonfiction and children's literature are considered. Does not want screen, stage, or teleplays.

How to Contact Submit query, synopsis, SASE. No e-mail queries.

JILL GROSJEAN LITERARY AGENCY

1390 Millstone Rd., Sag Harbor NY 11963-2214. (631)725-7419. Fax: (631)725-8632. E-mail: jill6981@aol.com. Web site: www.hometown.aol.com/jill6981/myhomepage/index.html. **Contact:** Jill Grosjean. Estab. 1999. Represents 33 clients. 100% of clients are new/unpublished writers.

- Prior to becoming an agent, Ms. Grosjean was manager of an independent bookstore. She has also worked in publishing and advertising.

Represents Novels. **Considers these fiction areas:** Historical; literary; mainstream/contemporary; mystery/suspense; regional; romance.

- This agency offers some editorial assistance (i.e., line-by-line edits). Actively seeking literary novels and mysteries.

How to Contact Query with SASE. No cold calls, please. Considers simultaneous queries. Responds in 1 week to queries; 1 month to mss. Returns materials only with SASE. Obtains most new clients through recommendations from others, solicitations.
Recent Sales *Stealing the Dragon*, by Tim Maleeny (Midnight Ink); *I Love You Like a Tomato*, by Marie Giordano (Forge Books); *Nectar*, by David C. Fickett (Forge Books); *Cycling* and *Sanctuary*, by Greg Garrett (Kensington); *The Smoke*, by Tony Broadbent (St. Martin's Press/Minotaur); *Fields of Gold*, by Marie Bostwick (Kensington); Spectres in the Smoke, by Tony Broadbent (St. Martin's Press/Minotaur).
Terms Agent receives 15% commission on domestic sales; 20% commission on foreign sales. No written contract. Charges clients for photocopying and mailing expenses.
Writers' Conferences Book Passage's Mystery Writers Conference; Agents and Editors Conference.

THE GROSVENOR LITERARY AGENCY

5510 Grosvenor Ln., Bethesda MD 20814. Fax: (301)581-9401. E-mail: deb@gliterary.com. Web site: www.gliterary.com. Alternate address: 1627 K St., Suite 1200, Washington DC 20006. **Contact:** Deborah C. Grosvenor.

Estab. 1996. Member of National Press Club. Represents 30 clients. 10% of clients are new/unpublished writers. Currently handles: 80% nonfiction books; 20% novels.

- Prior to opening her agency, Ms. Grosvenor was a book editor for 16 years.

Represents Nonfiction books, novels. **Considers these nonfiction areas:** Animals; anthropology/archaeology; art/architecture/design; biography/autobiography; business/economics; child guidance/parenting; current affairs; government/politics/law; health/medicine; history; how-to; language/literature/criticism; military/war; money/finance; music/dance; nature/environment; photography; popular culture; psychology; religious/inspirational; science/technology; self-help/personal improvement; sociology; spirituality; theater/film; translation; true crime/investigative; women's issues/studies. **Considers these fiction areas:** Detective/police/crime; family saga; historical; literary; mainstream/contemporary; mystery/suspense; romance (contemporary, gothic, historical); thriller.

How to Contact For nonfiction, send outline/proposal. For fiction, send query, 3 sample chapters. No fax queries. Responds in 1 month to queries; 2 months to mss. Returns materials only with SASE. Obtains most new clients through recommendations from others.

Terms Agent receives 15% commission on domestic sales; 20% commission on foreign sales. Offers written contract; 10-day notice must be given to terminate contract.

◙ REECE HALSEY NORTH

98 Main St., #704, Tiburon CA 94920. Fax: (415)789-9177. E-mail: info@reecehalseynorth.com. Web site: www.reecehalseynorth.com. **Contact:** Kimberley Cameron. Estab. 1957 (Reece Halsey Agency); 1993 (Reece Halsey North). Member of AAR. Represents 40 clients. 30% of clients are new/unpublished writers. Currently handles: 25% nonfiction books; 75% fiction.

- The Reece Halsey Agency has an illustrious client list of established writers, including the estate of Aldous Huxley, and has represented Upton Sinclair, William Faulkner, and Henry Miller.

Member Agents Dorris Halsey (Reece Halsey Agency, Los Angeles); Kimberley Cameron, Adam Marsh (Reece Halsey North).

Represents Nonfiction books, novels. **Considers these nonfiction areas:** Biography/autobiography; current affairs; history; language/literature/criticism; popular culture; science/technology; true crime/investigative; women's issues/studies. **Considers these fiction areas:** Action/adventure; contemporary issues; detective/police/crime; ethnic; family saga; historical; literary; mainstream/contemporary; mystery/suspense; science fiction; thriller; women's.

O➡ "We are looking for a unique and heartfelt voice."

How to Contact Query with SASE, first 10 pages of novel. Please do not fax queries. Responds in 3-6 weeks to queries; 3 months to mss. Obtains most new clients through recommendations from others, solicitations.

Terms Agent receives 15% commission on domestic sales; 10% commission on dramatic rights sales. Offers written contract, binding for 1 year. Requests 6 copies of ms if representing an author.

Writers' Conferences Maui Writers Conference; Aspen Summer Words Literary Festival; Willamette Writers Conference.

Tips "Always send a well-written query and include a SASE with it."

◙ THE MITCHELL J. HAMILBURG AGENCY

149 S. Barrington Ave., #732, Los Angeles CA 90049-2930. (310)471-4024. Fax: (310)471-9588. **Contact:** Michael Hamilburg. Estab. 1937. Signatory of WGA. Represents 70 clients. Currently handles: 70% nonfiction books; 30% novels.

Represents Nonfiction books, novels. **Considers these nonfiction areas:** Anthropology/archaeology; biography/autobiography; business/economics; child guidance/parenting; cooking/foods/nutrition; current affairs; education; government/politics/law; health/medicine; history; memoirs; military/war; money/finance; psychology; recreation; regional; self-help/personal improvement; sex; sociology; spirituality; sports; travel; women's issues/studies; creative nonfiction; romance; architecture; inspirational; true crime. **Considers these fiction areas:** Action/adventure; experimental; feminist; glitz; humor/satire; military/war; mystery/suspense; New Age; occult; regional; religious/inspirational; romance; sports; thriller; crime; mainstream; psychic.

How to Contact Query with outline, 2 sample chapters, SASE. Responds in 1 month to mss. Obtains most new clients through recommendations from others, conferences, personal search.

Terms Agent receives 10-15% commission on domestic sales.

◙ THE JOY HARRIS LITERARY AGENCY, INC.

156 Fifth Ave., Suite 617, New York NY 10010. (212)924-6269. Fax: (212)924-6609. E-mail: agentname@jhlitagent.com. **Contact:** Joy Harris. Member of AAR. Represents over 100 clients. Currently handles: 50% nonfiction books; 50% novels.

Member Agents Joy Harris; Cheryl Pientica; Robin London.

Represents Nonfiction books, novels. **Considers these fiction areas:** Ethnic; experimental; family saga; feminist; gay/lesbian; glitz; hi-lo; historical; humor/satire; literary; mainstream/contemporary; multicultural; multimedia; mystery/suspense; regional; short story collections; spiritual; translation; young adult; women's.

    O⫨ Does not want to receive screenplays.

How to Contact Query with sample chapter, outline/proposal, SASE. Considers simultaneous queries. Responds in 2 months to queries. Obtains most new clients through recommendations from clients and editors.

Recent Sales This agency prefers not to share information on specific sales.

Terms Agent receives 15% commission on domestic sales; 20% commission on foreign sales. Charges clients for some office expenses.

◉ HARTLINE LITERARY AGENCY

123 Queenston Dr., Pittsburgh PA 15235-5429. (412)829-2495. Fax: (412)829-2450. E-mail: joyce@hartlinelitera ry.com. Web site: www.hartlineliterary.com. **Contact:** Joyce A. Hart. Estab. 1990. Represents 40 clients. 20% of clients are new/unpublished writers. Currently handles: 40% nonfiction books; 60% novels.

Member Agents Joyce A. Hart, principal agent; Janet Benrey; Tamela Hancock Murray; Andrea Boeshaar.

Represents Nonfiction books, novels. **Considers these nonfiction areas:** Business/economics; child guidance/ parenting; cooking/foods/nutrition; money/finance; religious/inspirational; self-help/personal improvement; women's issues/studies. **Considers these fiction areas:** Action/adventure; contemporary issues; family saga; historical; literary; mystery/suspense (amateur sleuth, cozy); regional; religious/inspirational; romance (contemporary, gothic, historical, regency); thriller.

    O⫨ This agency specializes in the Christian bookseller market. Actively seeking adult fiction, self-help, nutritional books, devotional, and business. Does not want to receive erotica, gay/lesbian, fantasy, horror, etc.

How to Contact Submit summary/outline, author bio, 3 sample chapters. Accepts e-mail and fax queries. Considers simultaneous queries. Responds in 2 months to queries; 3 months to mss. Returns materials only with SASE. Obtains most new clients through recommendations from others.

Recent Sales *I'm Not OK and Neither Are You*, by David E. Clarke, PhD (Barbour Publishers); *Along Came Love*, by Carrie Turansky (Steeple Hill); *Glory Be*, by Ron and Janet Benrey (Steeple Hill); *Overcoing the Top Ten Reasons Singles Stay Single*, by Tom and Beverly Rodgers (NavPress); *A Clearing in the Wild*, by Jane Kirkpatrick (Waterbrook); *The Mothers-in-Law*, by Andrea Boeshaar and Jeri Odel (Focus on the Family); *Ties to Home*, by Kim Sawyer (Bethany House); The Reluctant 3-book series, by Jill Nelson (Harvest House).

Terms Agent receives 15% commission on domestic sales. Offers written contract.

⬛ ◉ ◪ ANTONY HARWOOD LIMITED

103 Walton St., Oxford OX2 6EB England. (44)(186)555-9615. Fax: (44)(186)531-0660. E-mail: mail@antonyhar wood.com. Web site: www.antonyharwood.com. **Contact:** Antony Harwood, James Macdonald Lockhart. Estab. 2000. Represents 52 clients.

    • Prior to starting this agency, Mr. Harwood and Mr. Lockhart worked at publishing houses and other literary agencies.

Represents Nonfiction books, novels. **Considers these nonfiction areas:** Agriculture/horticulture; Americana; animals; anthropology/archaeology; art/architecture/design; biography/autobiography; business/economics; child guidance/parenting; computers/electronic; cooking/foods/nutrition; creative nonfiction; current affairs; education; ethnic/cultural interests; gardening; gay/lesbian issues; government/politics/law; health/medicine; history; how-to; humor/satire; language/literature/criticism; memoirs; military/war; money/finance; multicultural; music/dance; nature/environment; philosophy; photography; popular culture; psychology; recreation; regional; religious/inspirational; science/technology; self-help/personal improvement; sex; sociology; software; spirituality; sports; theater/film; translation; travel; true crime/investigative; women's issues/studies. **Considers these fiction areas:** Action/adventure; comic books/cartoon; confession; detective/police/crime; erotica; ethnic; experimental; family saga; fantasy; feminist; gay/lesbian; gothic; hi-lo; historical; horror; humor/satire; literary; mainstream/contemporary; military/war; multicultural; multimedia; mystery/suspense; occult; picture books; plays; regional; religious/inspirational; romance; science fiction; spiritual; sports; thriller; translation; westerns/frontier; young adult.

    O⫨ "We accept every genre of fiction and nonfiction except for children's fiction for readers ages 10 and younger. We also do not accept poetry or screenplays."

How to Contact Submit outline, 2-3 sample chapters via e-mail or postal mail (include SAE). Responds in 2 months to queries.

Recent Sales *Learning to Swim*, by Clare Chambers; *The Dark Fields*, by Alan Glynn; *Jimmy Corrigan*, by Chris Ware; *The Proposal*, by Owen Slot.

Terms Agent receives 15% commission on domestic sales; 20% commission on foreign sales.

✪ JOHN HAWKINS & ASSOCIATES, INC.

71 W. 23rd St., Suite 1600, New York NY 10010. (212)807-7040. Fax: (212)807-9555. E-mail: jha@jhalit.com. Web site: www.jhalit.com. **Contact:** Moses Cardona (moses@jhalit.com). Estab. 1893. Member of AAR. Represents over 100 clients. 5-10% of clients are new/unpublished writers. Currently handles: 40% nonfiction books; 40% novels; 20% juvenile books.

Member Agents Moses Cardona; Warren Frazier; Anne Hawkins; John Hawkins; William Reiss.

Represents Nonfiction books, novels, juvenile books. **Considers these nonfiction areas:** Agriculture/horticulture; Americana; anthropology/archaeology; art/architecture/design; biography/autobiography; business/economics; current affairs; education; ethnic/cultural interests; gardening; gay/lesbian issues; government/politics/law; health/medicine; history; how-to; interior design/decorating; language/literature/criticism; memoirs; money/finance; multicultural; nature/environment; philosophy; popular culture; psychology; recreation; science/technology; self-help/personal improvement; sex; sociology; software; theater/film; travel; true crime/investigative; young adult; music, creative nonfiction. **Considers these fiction areas:** Action/adventure; detective/police/crime; ethnic; experimental; family saga; feminist; gay/lesbian; glitz; gothic; hi-lo; historical; literary; mainstream/contemporary; military/war; multicultural; multimedia; mystery/suspense; psychic/supernatural; religious/inspirational; short story collections; sports; thriller; translation; westerns/frontier; young adult; women's.

How to Contact Submit query, proposal package, outline, SASE. Considers simultaneous queries. Responds in 1 month to queries. Returns materials only with SASE. Obtains most new clients through recommendations from others.

Recent Sales *And Only to Deceive*, by Tasha Alexander; *The Dream Life of Sukhanov*, by Olga Grushin; *The Method Actors*, by Carl Shuker.

Terms Agent receives 15% commission on domestic sales; 20% commission on foreign sales. Charges clients for photocopying.

✪ RICHARD HENSHAW GROUP

127 W. 24th St., 4th Floor, New York NY 10011. (212)414-1172. Fax: (212)414-1182. E-mail: submissions@henshaw.com. Web site: www.rich.henshaw.com. **Contact:** Rich Henshaw. Estab. 1995. Member of AAR, SinC, MWA, HWA, SFWA, RWA. Represents 35 clients. 20% of clients are new/unpublished writers. Currently handles: 35% nonfiction books; 65% novels.

• Prior to opening his agency, Mr. Henshaw served as an agent with Richard Curtis Associates, Inc.

Represents Nonfiction books, novels. **Considers these nonfiction areas:** Animals; biography/autobiography; business/economics; child guidance/parenting; computers/electronic; cooking/foods/nutrition; current affairs; gay/lesbian issues; government/politics/law; health/medicine; how-to; humor/satire; military/war; money/finance; music/dance; nature/environment; New Age/metaphysics; popular culture; psychology; science/technology; self-help/personal improvement; sociology; sports; true crime/investigative; women's issues/studies. **Considers these fiction areas:** Action/adventure; detective/police/crime; ethnic; family saga; fantasy; glitz; historical; horror; humor/satire; literary; mainstream/contemporary; mystery/suspense; psychic/supernatural; romance; science fiction; sports; thriller.

○┮ This agency specializes in thrillers, mysteries, science fiction, fantasy, and horror.

How to Contact Query with SASE. Responds in 3 weeks to queries; 6 weeks to mss. Obtains most new clients through recommendations from others, solicitations, conferences.

Recent Sales *Blindfold Game*, by Dana Stabenow (St. Martin's Press); *Eye of the Wolf*, by Margaret Coel (Berkely); *The Well-Educated Mind*, by Susan Wise Bauer (Norton); *Shadow Man*, by James D. Doss (St. Martin's Press); *Box Like the Pros*, by Joe Frazier and William Dettloff (HarperCollins). Other clients include Jessie Wise, Peter van Dijk, Jay Caselberg, Judith Laik.

Terms Agent receives 15% commission on domestic sales; 20% commission on foreign sales. No written contract. 100% of business is derived from commissions on ms sales. Charges clients for photocopying mss and book orders.

Tips "While we do not have any reason to believe that our submission guidelines will change in the near future, writers can find up-to-date submission policy information on our Web site. Always include a SASE with correct return postage."

✪ THE JEFF HERMAN AGENCY, LLC

P.O. Box 1522, Stockbridge MA 01262. (413)298-0077. Fax: (413)298-8188. E-mail: jeff@jeffherman.com. Web site: www.jeffherman.com. **Contact:** Jeffrey H. Herman. Estab. 1985. Represents 100 clients. 10% of clients are new/unpublished writers. Currently handles: 85% nonfiction books; 5% scholarly books; 5% textbooks.

• Prior to opening his agency, Mr. Herman served as a public relations executive.

Member Agents Deborah Levine, vice president (nonfiction book doctor); Jeff Herman.

Represents Nonfiction books. **Considers these nonfiction areas:** Business/economics; government/politics/

law; health/medicine (recovery issues); history; how-to; self-help/personal improvement; spirituality; popular reference; technology; popular psychology.

    O─ₐ This agency specializes in adult nonfiction.

How to Contact Query with SASE. Accepts e-mail and fax queries. Considers simultaneous queries.

Recent Sales Sold 35 titles in the last year. This agency prefers not to share information on specific sales.

Terms Agent receives 15% commission on domestic sales. Offers written contract. Charges clients for copying and postage.

FREDERICK HILL BONNIE NADELL, INC.

1842 Union St., San Francisco CA 94123. (415)921-2910. Fax: (415)921-2802. **Contact:** Elise Proulx. Estab. 1979. Represents 100 clients.

Member Agents Fred Hill, president; Bonnie Nadell, vice president; Elise Proulx, associate.

Represents Nonfiction books, novels. **Considers these nonfiction areas:** Current affairs; language/literature/criticism; nature/environment; biography; government/politics. **Considers these fiction areas:** Literary; mainstream/contemporary.

How to Contact Query with SASE. No e-mail or fax queries. Considers simultaneous queries. Returns materials only with SASE.

Recent Sales *It Might Have Been What He Said*, by Eden Collinsworth; *Consider the Lobster and Other Essays*, by David Foster Wallace; *The Underdog*, by Joshua Davis.

Terms Agent receives 15% commission on domestic and dramatic rights sales; 20% commission on foreign sales. Charges clients for photocopying.

JOHN L. HOCHMANN BOOKS

320 E. 58th St., New York NY 10022-2220. (212)319-0505. **Contact:** Theodora Eagle. Director: John L. Hochmann. Estab. 1976. Member of PEN. Represents 23 clients. Currently handles: 100% nonfiction books.

Member Agents Theodora Eagle (popular medical and nutrition books).

Represents Nonfiction books, college textbooks. **Considers these nonfiction areas:** Anthropology/archaeology; art/architecture/design; biography/autobiography; cooking/foods/nutrition; current affairs; gay/lesbian issues; government/politics/law; health/medicine; history; military/war; music/dance; sociology; theater/film.

    O─ₐ This agency specializes in nonfiction books. Writers must have demonstrable eminence in the field or in previous publications.

How to Contact Query first with detailed chapter outline, titles, sample reviews of previously published books. Responds in 1 week to queries; 1 month to solicited mss. Obtains most new clients through recommendations from authors and editors.

Recent Sales Sold 6 titles in the last year. *Granite and Rainbow: The Life of Virginia Woolf*, by Mitchell Leaska (Farrar, Straus & Giroux); *Manuel Puig and the Spider Woman*, by Suzanne Jill Levine (Farrar, Straus & Giroux); *Part-Time Vegetarian*, by Louise Lambert-Lagasse (Stoddart).

Terms Agent receives 15% commission on domestic sales.

Tips "Detailed outlines are read carefully; letters and proposals written like flap copy get chucked. We make multiple submissions to editors, but we do not accept multiple submissions from authors. Why? Editors are on salary, but we work for commission, and do not have time to read manuscripts on spec."

BARBARA HOGENSON AGENCY

165 West End Ave., Suite 19-C, New York NY 10023. (212)874-8084. Fax: (212)362-3011. E-mail: bhogenson@aol.com. **Contact:** Barbara Hogenson, Nicole Verity. Member of AAR.

How to Contact Query with SASE. No e-mail queries. Obtains most new clients through recommendations from other clients.

HOPKINS LITERARY ASSOCIATES

2117 Buffalo Rd., Suite 327, Rochester NY 14624-1507. (585)352-6268. **Contact:** Pam Hopkins. Estab. 1996. Member of AAR, RWA. Represents 30 clients. 5% of clients are new/unpublished writers. Currently handles: 100% novels.

Represents Novels. **Considers these fiction areas:** Romance (historical, contemporary, category); women's.

    O─ₐ This agency specializes in women's fiction, particularly historical, contemporary, and category romance, as well as mainstream work.

How to Contact Submit outline, 3 sample chapters. No e-mail or fax queries. Considers simultaneous queries. Responds in 2 weeks to queries; 1 month to mss. Returns materials only with SASE. Obtains most new clients through recommendations from others, solicitations, conferences.

Recent Sales Sold 50 titles in the last year. *Lady of Sin*, by Madeline Hunter (Bantam); *Silent in the Grave*, by Deanna Raybourn (Mira); *Passion*, by Lisa Valdez (Berkley).

Terms Agent receives 15% commission on domestic sales; 20% commission on foreign sales. No written contract.
Writers' Conferences RWA National Conference.

HORNFISCHER LITERARY MANAGEMENT, INC.

P.O. Box 50544, Austin TX 78763. E-mail: jim@hornfischerlit.com. Web site: www.hornfischerlit.com. **Contact:** James D. Hornfischer, president. Estab. 2001. Represents 45 clients. 20% of clients are new/unpublished writers. Currently handles: 100% nonfiction books.

- Prior to opening his agency, Mr. Hornfischer was an agent with Literary Group International and held editorial positions at HarperCollins and McGraw-Hill. "I work hard to make an author's first trip to market a successful one. That means working closely with my clients prior to submission to produce the strongest possible book proposal or manuscript. My New York editorial background working with a variety of best-selling authors, such as Erma Bombeck, Jared Diamond, and Erica Jong, is useful in this regard. In 13 years as an agent, I've handled 8 No. 1 *New York Times* nonfiction bestsellers."

Represents Nonfiction books. **Considers these nonfiction areas:** Anthropology/archaeology; biography/autobiography; business/economics; child guidance/parenting; current affairs; government/politics/law; health/medicine; history; how-to; humor/satire; memoirs; military/war; money/finance; multicultural; nature/environment; popular culture; psychology; religious/inspirational; science/technology; self-help/personal improvement; sociology; sports; true crime/investigative.

- Actively seeking the best work of terrific writers. Does not want poetry or fiction.

How to Contact Submit proposal package, outline, 2 sample chapters. Considers simultaneous queries. Responds in 6-8 weeks to queries. Returns materials only with SASE. Obtains most new clients through referrals from clients, reading books and magazines, pursuing ideas with New York editors.
Recent Sales See Web site for sales information.
Terms Agent receives 15% commission on domestic sales; 25% commission on foreign sales. Offers written contract. Reasonable expenses deducted from proceeds after book is sold.
Tips "When you query agents and send out proposals, present yourself as someone who's in command of his material and comfortable in his own skin. Too many writers have a palpable sense of anxiety and insecurity. Take a deep breath and realize that—if you're good—someone in the publishing world will want you."

IMG LITERARY

825 Seventh Ave., New York NY 10019. (212)489-5400. Web site: literary.imgworld.com. **Contact:** Lisa Queen, Lisa Hyman.

- "Our clients have ranged from bestselling and award-winning journalists to celebrities, academics, novelists, memoirists, biographers, historians, and humorists."

How to Contact Query with synopsis, bio, 1 sample chapter, SASE. *No unsolicited mss.* No e-mail or fax queries. Only responds if interested.
Recent Sales *Better Sex Through Yoga*, by Jacquie Noelle with Jennifer Langheld and Garvey Rich (Broadway); *Creativity and Personal Mastery*, by Srikumar Rao (Hyperion).

IMPRINT AGENCY, INC.

5 W. 101 St., Suite 8B, New York NY 10025. E-mail: imprintagency@earthlink.net. Web site: www.imprintagency.com. **Contact:** Stephany Evans. Member of AAR. Represents 100+ clients.
Member Agents Stephany Evans; Gary Heidt (garyheidt@yahoo.com); Meredith Phelan (mphelan@mindspring.com).
Represents Nonfiction books, novels. **Considers these nonfiction areas:** Animals; art/architecture/design; biography/autobiography; child guidance/parenting; cooking/foods/nutrition; crafts/hobbies; current affairs; ethnic/cultural interests; health/medicine; history; how-to; interior design/decorating; memoirs; music/dance; nature/environment; popular culture; psychology; self-help/personal improvement; sports; theater/film; true crime/investigative; women's issues/studies. **Considers these fiction areas:** Detective/police/crime; glitz; literary; mystery/suspense; romance; thriller; women's.
How to Contact Query with SASE. Responds in 1 week to queries; 2 months to mss.
Terms Agent receives 15% commission on domestic and foreign sales. Offers written contract. Charges clients for copying and postage if necessary.

INKWELL MANAGEMENT, LLC

521 Fifth Ave., 26th Floor, New York NY 10175. (212)922-3500. Fax: (212)922-0535. E-mail: submissions@inkwellmanagement.com. Web site: www.inkwellmanagement.com. Estab. 2004. Represents 500 clients. Currently handles: 60% nonfiction books; 40% novels.
Member Agents Michael Carlisle; Richard Pine; Kimberly Witherspoon; George Lucas; Catherine Drayton; Matthew Guma; David Forrer; Eleanor Jackson; Alexis Hurley; Pilar Queen; Celine Texier-Rose; Susanna Schell.

Represents Nonfiction books, novels.
How to Contact Query with SASE or via e-mail. Obtains most new clients through recommendations from others.
Recent Sales Sold 100 titles in the last year.
Terms Agent receives 15% commission on domestic and foreign sales. Offers written contract.
Tips "We will not read manuscripts before receiving a letter of inquiry."

⊘ INTERNATIONAL CREATIVE MANAGEMENT

40 W. 57th St., New York NY 10019. (212)556-5600. Web site: www.icmtalent.com. **Contact:** Literary Department. Member of AAR; signatory of WGA.

    O₋ "We do not accept unsolicited submissions."
How to Contact Obtains most new clients through recommendations from others.
Terms Agent receives 15% commission on domestic sales; 20% commission on foreign sales.

⊠ J DE S ASSOCIATES, INC.

9 Shagbark Rd., Wilson Point, South Norwalk CT 06854. (203)838-7571. **Contact:** Jacques de Spoelberch. Estab. 1975. Represents 50 clients. Currently handles: 50% nonfiction books; 50% novels.

    ● Prior to opening his agency, Mr. de Spoelberch was an editor with Houghton Mifflin.

Represents Nonfiction books, novels. **Considers these nonfiction areas:** Biography/autobiography; business/economics; current affairs; ethnic/cultural interests; government/politics/law; health/medicine; history; military/war; New Age/metaphysics; self-help/personal improvement; sociology; sports; translation. **Considers these fiction areas:** Detective/police/crime; historical; juvenile; literary; mainstream/contemporary; mystery/suspense; New Age; westerns/frontier; young adult.
How to Contact Query with SASE. Responds in 2 months to queries. Obtains most new clients through recommendations from authors and other clients.
Terms Agent receives 15% commission on domestic sales; 20% commission on foreign sales. Charges clients for foreign postage and photocopying.

⊠ JABBERWOCKY LITERARY AGENCY

P.O. Box 4558, Sunnyside NY 11104-0558. (718)392-5985. Web site: www.awfulagent.com. **Contact:** Joshua Bilmes. Estab. 1994. Member of SFWA. Represents 40 clients. 15% of clients are new/unpublished writers. Currently handles: 15% nonfiction books; 75% novels; 5% scholarly books; 5% other.
Represents Nonfiction books, novels, scholarly books. **Considers these nonfiction areas:** Biography/autobiography; business/economics; cooking/foods/nutrition; current affairs; gay/lesbian issues; government/politics/law; health/medicine; history; humor/satire; language/literature/criticism; military/war; money/finance; nature/environment; popular culture; science/technology; sociology; sports; theater/film; true crime/investigative; women's issues/studies. **Considers these fiction areas:** Action/adventure; contemporary issues; detective/police/crime; ethnic; family saga; fantasy; gay/lesbian; glitz; historical; horror; humor/satire; literary; mainstream/contemporary; psychic/supernatural; regional; science fiction; sports; thriller.

    O₋ This agency represents quite a lot of genre fiction and is actively seeking to increase the amount of nonfiction projects. It does not handle juvenile or young adult. Book-length material only—no poetry, articles, or short fiction.

How to Contact Query with SASE. Do not send mss unless requested. No e-mail or fax queries. Considers simultaneous queries. Responds in 2 weeks to queries. Returns materials only with SASE. Obtains most new clients through solicitations, recommendation by current clients.
Recent Sales Sold 25 US and 100 foreign titles in the last year. *Definitely Dead*, by Charlaine Harris (ACE); *Engaging the Enemy*, by Elizabeth Moon (Del Rey); *Mistborn*, by Brandon Sanderson (Tor); *Greywalker*, by Kathleen Richardson. Other clients include Simon Green, Tanya Huff, Tobias Buckell.
Terms Agent receives 15% commission on domestic sales; 20% commission on foreign sales. Offers written contract, binding for 1 year. Charges clients for book purchases, photocopying, international book/ms mailing.
Writers' Conferences Malice Domestic; World Fantasy Convention.
Tips "In approaching with a query, the most important things to me are your credits and your biographical background to the extent it's relevant to your work. I (and most agents) will ignore the adjectives you may choose to describe your own work."

⊠ JAMES PETER ASSOCIATES, INC.

P.O. Box 358, New Canaan CT 06840. (203)972-1070. E-mail: gene_brissie@msn.com. **Contact:** Gene Brissie. Estab. 1971. Represents 75 individual and 6 corporate clients. 15% of clients are new/unpublished writers. Currently handles: 100% nonfiction books.
Represents Nonfiction books. **Considers these nonfiction areas:** Anthropology/archaeology; art/architecture/

design; biography/autobiography; business/economics; child guidance/parenting; current affairs; ethnic/cultural interests; gay/lesbian issues; government/politics/law; health/medicine; history; language/literature/criticism; memoirs (political, business); military/war; money/finance; music/dance; popular culture; psychology; self-help/personal improvement; theater/film; travel; women's issues/studies.

> O→ "We are especially interested in general, trade, and reference nonfiction." Does not want to receive children's/young adult books, poetry, or fiction.

How to Contact Submit proposal package, outline, SASE. Prefers to read materials exclusively. No e-mail or fax queries. Responds in 1 month to queries. Returns materials only with SASE. Obtains most new clients through recommendations from others, solicitations, contact with people who are doing interesting things.

Recent Sales Sold 50 titles in the last year. *Nothing to Fear*, by Dr. Alan Axelrod (Prentice-Hall); *The Right Way*, by Mark Smith (Regnery); *Churchill's Folly*, by Christopher Catherwood (Carroll & Graf); *The Encyclopedia of Cancer*, by Carol Turkington (Facts on File); *The Lazy Person's Guide to Investing*, by Paul Farrell (Warner Books); *The Subject Is Left-Handed*, by Barney Rosset (Algonquin Books); *It's OK to Be Neurotic*, by Dr. Frank Bruno (Adams Media).

Terms Agent receives 15% commission on domestic sales; 20% commission on foreign sales. Offers written contract.

⊘ JANKLOW & NESBIT ASSOCIATES

445 Park Ave., New York NY 10022. (212)421-1700. Fax: (212)980-3671. **Contact:** Morton L. Janklow, Lynn Nesbit. Estab. 1989.

Member Agents Tina Bennett; Luke Janklow; Richard Morris; Eric Simonoff; Anne Sibbald; Cullen Stanley; Rebecca Gradinger.

Represents Commercial and literary nonfiction and novels.

> O→ No unsolicited submissions.

⊘ JCA LITERARY AGENCY

174 Sullivan St., New York NY 10012. (212)807-0888. E-mail: tom@jcalit.com. Web site: www.jcalit.com. **Contact:** Tom Cushman. Estab. 1978. Member of AAR. Represents 100 clients. 10% of clients are new/unpublished writers. Currently handles: 20% nonfiction books; 75% novels; 5% scholarly books.

Member Agents Tom Cushman; Melanie Meyers Cushman; Tony Outhwaite.

Represents Nonfiction books, novels. **Considers these nonfiction areas:** Biography/autobiography; current affairs; government/politics/law; history; language/literature/criticism; memoirs; popular culture; sociology; sports; theater/film; translation; true crime/investigative. **Considers these fiction areas:** Action/adventure; contemporary issues; detective/police/crime; family saga; historical; literary; mainstream/contemporary; mystery/suspense; sports; thriller.

> O→ Does not want to receive screenplays, poetry, children's books, science fiction/fantasy, or genre romance.

How to Contact Query with SASE. No e-mail or fax queries. Considers simultaneous queries. Responds in 1 month to queries; 10 weeks to mss. Returns materials only with SASE. Obtains most new clients through recommendations from others, solicitations, conferences.

Recent Sales *Jury of One*, by David Ellis (Putnam); *The Heaven of Mercury*, by Brad Watson (Norton); *The Rope Eater*, by Ben Jones; *The Circus in Winter*, by Cathy Dial. Other clients include Ernest J. Gaines, Gwen Hunter.

Terms Agent receives 15% commission on domestic sales; 20% commission on foreign sales. No written contract. "We work with our clients on a handshake basis." Charges for postage on overseas submissions, photocopying, mss for submission, books purchased for subrights submission, bank charges. "We deduct the cost from payments received from publishers."

Tips "We do not provide legal, accounting, or public relations services for our clients, although some of the advice we give falls into these realms. In cases where it seems necessary, we will recommend obtaining outside advice or assistance in these areas from professionals who are not in any way connected to the agency."

⊘ JELLINEK & MURRAY LITERARY AGENCY

2024 Muana Place, Honolulu HI 96822. (808)521-4057. Fax: (808)521-4058. E-mail: r.jellinek@verizon.net. **Contact:** Roger Jellinek. Estab. 1995. Represents 75 clients. 90% of clients are new/unpublished writers. Currently handles: 70% nonfiction books; 30% novels.

> ● Prior to becoming an agent, Mr. Jellinek was deputy editor, *New York Times Book Review* (1966-1974); editor-in-chief, New York Times Book Co. (1975-1981); editor/packager of book/TV projects (1981-1995); editorial director, Inner Ocean Publishing (2000-2003).

Member Agents Roger Jellinek; Eden Lee Murray. Literary Associates: Grant Ching; Lavonne Leong; Jeremy Colvin.

Represents Nonfiction books, novels, textbooks, movie scripts (from book clients), TV scripts (from book clients). **Considers these nonfiction areas:** Animals; anthropology/archaeology; art/architecture/design; biography/autobiography; business/economics; child guidance/parenting; computers/electronic; cooking/foods/nutrition; current affairs; ethnic/cultural interests; gay/lesbian issues; government/politics/law; health/medicine; history; how-to; memoirs; military/war; money/finance; nature/environment; New Age/metaphysics; popular culture; psychology; religious/inspirational; science/technology; self-help/personal improvement; travel; true crime/investigative; women's issues/studies. **Considers these fiction areas:** Action/adventure; confession; contemporary issues; detective/police/crime; erotica; ethnic; family saga; feminist; gay/lesbian; glitz; historical; horror; humor/satire; literary; mainstream/contemporary; multicultural; mystery/suspense; New Age; picture books; psychic/supernatural; regional (specific to Hawaii); thriller.

> ⊶ This is the only literary agency in Hawaii. "Half our clients are based in Hawaii and half are from all over the world. We prefer submissions (after query) via e-mail attachment. We only send out fully-edited proposals and manuscripts." Actively seeking first-rate writing.

How to Contact Query with SASE, outline, author bio, 2 sample chapters, credentials/platform. Accepts e-mail and fax queries. Considers simultaneous queries. Responds in 2-3 weeks to queries; 2 months to mss. Returns materials only with SASE. Obtains most new clients through recommendations from others, solicitations, conferences.

Recent Sales Sold 10 titles and 1 script in the last year.

Terms Agent receives 15% commission on domestic sales; 25% commission on foreign sales. Offers written contract, binding for indefinite period; 30-day notice must be given to terminate contract. Charges clients for photocopies and postage. May refer to editing services if author asks for recommendation. "We derive no income from our referrals. Referrals to editors do not imply representation."

Writers' Conferences Mr. Jellinek manages the publishing program at the Maui Writers Conference.

Tips "Would-be authors should be well read and knowledgeable about their field and genre."

◙ JETREID LITERARY AGENCY

Am Co Center #106, 201 E. 10th St., New York NY 10003. (718)821-4996. E-mail: jetreidliterary@earthlink.net. Web site: www.jetreidliterary.com. **Contact:** Janet Reid. Estab. 2003. Represents 22 clients. Currently handles: 50% nonfiction books; 50% novels.

> • Prior to becoming an agent, Ms. Reid spent 15 years in book publicity with national and regional clients.

Represents Nonfiction books, novels. **Considers these nonfiction areas:** Animals; art/architecture/design; biography/autobiography; business/economics; current affairs; ethnic/cultural interests; history; language/literature/criticism; memoirs; music/dance; nature/environment; popular culture; science/technology; true crime/investigative. **Considers these fiction areas:** Action/adventure; detective/police/crime; ethnic; experimental; literary; mainstream/contemporary; mystery/suspense; regional; thriller; young adult.

> ⊶ "JetReid Literary has an eclectic list of interesting, original, and imaginative voices. We look for authors of compelling work in both fiction and nonfiction. Our mysteries range from smart girls with guns to rat pack noir best read with a martini and a sardonic sneer at danger. Our nonfiction runs from the narrative of living on an Oregon commune to the prescriptive help of what to do if you work with an abuser." Actively seeking narrative fiction and nonfiction, along with an original voice and subject matter. Does not want to receive poems, screenplays, romance, westerns, self-help, or previously published work.

How to Contact Query with SASE. Considers simultaneous queries. Responds in 10 days to queries; 2-3 months to mss. Obtains most new clients through recommendations from others, query letters.

Recent Sales Sold 7 titles in the last year. *The Greening of Ben Brown*, by Michael Strelow (Hawthorne Press); *The Electric Church*, by Jeff Somers (Warner Aspect); *Lost Dog*, by Bill Cameron (Midnight Ink); *Becoming a Great Musician*, by Stan Munslow (Schirmer Trade Books); *Master Detective: The Life and Crimes of Ellis Parker*, by John Reisinger (Kensington); *Million Dollar Baby*, by Amy Meade (Midnight Ink). Other clients include Tim Anderson, Adam Eisenberg, Kari Dell, Jeanne Erickson, Kennedy Foster, Katy King, Evan Mandery, Dan Tomasulo, Garry Wang.

Terms Agent receives 15% commission on domestic and foreign sales. Offers written contract; 30-day written notice must be given to terminate contract. Charges up to $300 for office expenses when the project is sold. Most projects don't come close to reaching the $300 maximum.

Tips "Check the Web site for guidelines that will help you send the right material. We do not accept e-mail queries."

◙ NATASHA KERN LITERARY AGENCY

P.O. Box 1069, White Salmon WA 98672. (509)493-3803. Web site: www.natashakern.com. **Contact:** Natasha Kern. Estab. 1986. Member of RWA, MWA, SinC.

• Prior to opening her agency, Ms. Kern worked as an editor and publicist for Simon & Schuster, Bantam, and Ballantine. "This agency has sold over 700 books."

Represents Adult commercial nonfiction and fiction. **Considers these nonfiction areas:** Animals; child guidance/parenting; current affairs; ethnic/cultural interests; gardening; health/medicine; nature/environment; New Age/metaphysics; popular culture; psychology; religious/inspirational; self-help/personal improvement; spirituality; women's issues/studies; investigative journalism. **Considers these fiction areas:** Women's; chick lit; lady lit; romance (contemporary, historical); historical; mainstream/contemporary; multicultural; mystery/ suspense; religious/inspirational; thriller.

O— This agency specializes in commercial fiction and nonfiction for adults. "We are a full-service agency." Does not represent sports, true crime, scholarly works, coffee table books, war memoirs, software, scripts, literary fiction, photography, poetry, short stories, children's, horror, fantasy, genre science fiction, stage plays, or traditional westerns.

How to Contact See submission instructions online. Query with SASE, submission history, writing credits, length of ms. Considers simultaneous queries. Responds in 3 weeks to queries.

Recent Sales Sold 56 titles in the last year. *Wicked Pleasure*, by Nina Bangs (Berkley); *Inviting God In*, by David Aaron (Shambhala); *Perfect Killer*, by Lewis Perdue (Tor); *The Secret Lives of the Sushi Club*, by Christy Yorke (Penguin); *Extreme Exposure*, by Pamela Clare (Berkley); *Dead End Dating*, by Kimberly Raye (Ballantine); *Under the Jacaranda Tree*, by Nikki Arana (Baker Book House); *My True Love's Name*, by Diana Holquist (Warner Books).

Terms Agent receives 15% commission on domestic and dramatic rights sales; 20% commission on foreign sales.

Writers' Conferences RWA National Conference; MWA National Conference; and many regional conferences.

Tips "Your chances of being accepted for representation will be greatly enhanced by going to our Web site first. Our idea of a dream client is someone who participates in a mutually respectful business relationship, is clear about needs and goals, and communicates about career planning. If we know what you need and want, we can help you achieve it. A dream client has a storytelling gift, a commitment to a writing career, a desire to learn and grow, and a passion for excellence. We want clients who are expressing their own unique voice and truly have something of their own to communicate. This client understands that many people have to work together for a book to succeed and that everything in publishing takes far longer than one imagines. Trust and communication are truly essential."

LOUISE B. KETZ AGENCY

1485 First Ave., Suite 4B, New York NY 10021-1363. (212)535-9259. Fax: (212)249-3103. E-mail: ketzagency@aol.com. **Contact:** Louise B. Ketz. Estab. 1983. Represents 25 clients. 15% of clients are new/unpublished writers. Currently handles: 100% nonfiction books.

Represents Nonfiction books. **Considers these nonfiction areas:** Current affairs; history; military/war; science/ technology; economics.

O— This agency specializes in science, history, and reference.

How to Contact Submit outline, 2 sample chapters, author bio (with qualifications for authorship of work). Responds in 6 weeks to mss. Obtains most new clients through recommendations from others, idea development.

Terms Agent receives 15% commission on domestic sales.

VIRGINIA KIDD AGENCY, INC.

538 E. Harford St., P.O. Box 278, Milford PA 18337. (570)296-6205. Fax: (570)296-7266. Web site: www.vk-agency.com. Estab. 1965. Member of SFWA, SFRA. Represents 80 clients.

Member Agents Christine Cohen; Vaughne Hansen; Brian Townsell.

Represents Novels. **Considers these fiction areas:** Fantasy; historical; mystery/suspense; science fiction; women's; speculative; mainstream.

O— This agency specializes in science fiction and fantasy.

How to Contact Submit synopsis (1-3 pages), cover letter, first chapter, SASE. Responds in 4-6 weeks to queries.

Recent Sales *The Wizard* and *Starwater Strains*, by Gene Wolfe (Tor); *Gifts* and *Voices*, by Ursula K. Le Guin (Harcourt); *The Galileo's Children*, by Gardner Dozois (Pry); *The Light Years Beneath My Feet* and *Running From the Deity*, by Alan Dean Foster (Del Ray); *From the Files of the Time Rangers*, by Rick Bowes (Golden Gryphon); *Chasing Fire*, by Michelle Welch. Other clients include Eleanor Arnason, Ted Chiang, Jack Skillinsgread, Kage Baker, Patricia Briggs, and the estates for James Tiptree Jr., Murray Leinster, E.E. "Doc" Smith, R.A. Lafferty.

Terms Agent receives 15% commission on domestic sales; 20-25% commission on foreign sales; 20% commission on dramatic rights sales. Offers written contract; 2-month notice must be given to terminate contract. Charges clients occasionally for extraordinary expenses.

Tips "If you have a completed novel that is of extraordinary quality, please send us a query."

◎ KIRCHOFF/WOHLBERG, INC., AUTHORS' REPRESENTATION DIVISION

866 United Nations Plaza, #525, New York NY 10017. (212)644-2020. Fax: (212)223-4387. **Contact:** Liza Pulitzer Voges. Director of Operations: John R. Whitman. Estab. 1930s. Member of AAR, AAP, Society of Illustrators, SPAR, Bookbuilders of Boston, New York Bookbinders' Guild, AIGA. Represents 50 clients. 10% of clients are new/unpublished writers. Currently handles: 5% nonfiction books; 25% novels; 5% young adult; 65% picture books.

- Kirchoff/Wohlberg has been in business for over 60 years.
- O→ This agency specializes in only juvenile through young adult trade books.

How to Contact For novels, query with SASE, outline, a few sample chapters. For picture books, send entire ms, SASE. No e-mail or fax queries. Considers simultaneous queries. Responds in 1 month to queries; 2 months to mss. Returns materials only with SASE. Obtains most new clients through recommendations from authors, illustrators, and editors.

Recent Sales Sold over 50 titles in the last year. *Three Nasty Gnarlies*, by Keith Graves (Scholastic); *Listening for Lions*, by Gloria Whelan (HarperCollins); My Weird School series, by Dan Gutman (HarperCollins); *Biscuit*, by Alyssa Capucilli (HarperCollins).

Terms Offers written contract, binding for at least 1 year. Agent receives standard commission, depending upon whether it is an author only, illustrator only, or an author/illustrator book.

◑ HARVEY KLINGER, INC.

300 W. 55th St., New York NY 10019. (212)581-7068. E-mail: queries@harveyklinger.com. Web site: www.harveyklinger.com. **Contact:** Harvey Klinger. Estab. 1977. Member of AAR. Represents 100 clients. 25% of clients are new/unpublished writers. Currently handles: 50% nonfiction books; 50% novels.

Member Agents David Dunton (popular culture, music-related books, literary fiction, crime novels, thrillers); Sara Crowe (children's and young adult authors, some adult authors, foreign rights sales); Andrea Somberg (literary fiction, commercial fiction, quality narrative nonfiction, popular culture, how-to, self-help, humor, interior design, cookbooks, health/fitness); Nikki Van De Car (science fiction/fantasy, horror, romance, literary fiction, popular culture, how-to, memoir).

Represents Nonfiction books, novels. **Considers these nonfiction areas:** Biography/autobiography; cooking/foods/nutrition; health/medicine; psychology; science/technology; self-help/personal improvement; spirituality; sports; true crime/investigative; women's issues/studies. **Considers these fiction areas:** Action/adventure; detective/police/crime; family saga; glitz; literary; mainstream/contemporary; mystery/suspense; thriller.

- O→ This agency specializes in big, mainstream, contemporary fiction and nonfiction.

How to Contact Query with SASE. No phone or fax queries. Accepts e-mail queries. Responds in 2 months to queries and mss. Obtains most new clients through recommendations from others.

Recent Sales *The Red Hat Society: Fun & Friendship After Fifty*, by Sue Ellen Cooper; *Wilco: Learning How to Die*, by Greg Kot; *A Window Across the River*, by Brian Morton; *The Sweet Potato Queen's Field Guide to Men: Every Man I Love Is Either Gay, Married, or Dead*, by Jill Conner Browne; *Get Your Share: A Guide to Striking it Rich in the Stock Market*, by Julie Stav; *Wink: The Incredible Life & Epic Journey of Jimmy Winkfield*, by Ed Hotaling. Other clients include Barbara Wood, Terry Kay, Barbara De Angelis, Jeremy Jackson.

Terms Agent receives 15% commission on domestic sales; 25% commission on foreign sales. Offers written contract. Charges for photocopying mss and overseas postage for mss.

Ⓝ ◑ KNEERIM & WILLIAMS

225 Franklin St., Boston MA 02110. (617)542-5070. Fax: (617)542-8906. Web site: www.fr.com/kwfr. **Contact:** Melissa Grella. Estab. 1990. Represents 200 clients. 5% of clients are new/unpublished writers. Currently handles: 80% nonfiction books; 15% novels; 5% movie scripts.

- Prior to becoming an agent, Mr. Williams was a lawyer; Ms. Kneerim was a publisher and editor; Mr. Wasserman was an editor and journalist.

Member Agents Elaine Rogers (film/TV agent and entertainment lawyer).

Represents Nonfiction books, novels. **Considers these nonfiction areas:** Anthropology/archaeology; biography/autobiography; business/economics; child guidance/parenting; current affairs; government/politics/law; health/medicine; history; language/literature/criticism; memoirs; nature/environment; popular culture; psychology; religious/inspirational; science/technology; sociology; sports; women's issues/studies. **Considers these fiction areas:** Historical; literary; mainstream/contemporary.

- O→ This agency specializes in narrative nonfiction, history, science, business, women's issues, commercial and literary fiction, film, and television. "We have 7 agents and 2 scouts in Boston, New York, and Santa Fe." Actively seeking distinguished authors, experts, professionals, intellectuals, and serious writers. Does not want to receive blanket multiple submissions, genre fiction, children's literature, or original screenplays.

How to Contact Query with SASE. Responds in 2 weeks to queries; 2 months to mss. Returns materials only with SASE. Obtains most new clients through recommendations from others.

Recent Sales See Web site for a list of clients and recent sales.

🌙 LINDA KONNER LITERARY AGENCY

10 W. 15th St., Suite 1918, New York NY 10011-6829. (212)691-3419. E-mail: ldkonner@cs.com. **Contact:** Linda Konner. Estab. 1996. Member of AAR, ASJA; signatory of WGA. Represents 85 clients. 30-35% of clients are new/unpublished writers. Currently handles: 100% nonfiction books.

Represents Nonfiction books. **Considers these nonfiction areas:** Biography/autobiography (celebrity); gay/lesbian issues; health/medicine (diet/nutrition/fitness); how-to; money/finance (personal finance); popular culture; psychology; self-help/personal improvement; women's issues; African American and Latino issues; business; parenting; relationships.

    O₋ This agency specializes in health, self-help, and how-to books.

How to Contact Query with SASE, synopsis, author bio, sufficient return postage. Prefers to read materials exclusively for 2 weeks. Considers simultaneous queries. Obtains most new clients through recommendations from others, occasional solicitation among established authors/journalists.

Recent Sales Sold 28 titles in the last year. *The 3-Apple-A-Day Plan*, by Tammi Flynn (Broadway Books); *Diabetes-Free Kids*, by Sheri Colberg (Avery/Penguin); *Like a Lampshade in a Whorehouse: My Life in Comedy*, by Phyllis Diller (Tarcher/Penguin).

Terms Agent receives 15% commission on domestic sales; 25% commission on foreign sales. Offers written contract. Charges $85 one-time fee for domestic expenses; additional expenses may be incurred for foreign sales.

Writers' Conferences ASJA Writers Conference.

🌙 ELAINE KOSTER LITERARY AGENCY, LLC

55 Central Park W., Suite 6, New York NY 10023. (212)362-9488. Fax: (212)712-0164. **Contact:** Elaine Koster, Stephanie Lehmann. Member of AAR, MWA. Represents 40 clients. 10% of clients are new/unpublished writers. Currently handles: 30% nonfiction books; 70% novels.

    • Prior to opening her agency in 1998, Ms. Koster was president and publisher of Dutton NAL, part of the Penguin Group.

Represents Nonfiction books, novels. **Considers these nonfiction areas:** Biography/autobiography; business/economics; child guidance/parenting; cooking/foods/nutrition; current affairs; ethnic/cultural interests; health/medicine; history; how-to; money/finance; nature/environment; popular culture; psychology; self-help/personal improvement; spirituality; women's issues/studies. **Considers these fiction areas:** Contemporary issues; detective/police/crime; ethnic; family saga; feminist; historical; literary; mainstream/contemporary; mystery/suspense (amateur sleuth, cozy, culinary, malice domestic); regional; thriller; chick lit.

    O₋ This agency specializes in quality fiction and nonfiction. Does not want to receive juvenile, screenplays, or science fiction.

How to Contact Query with SASE, outline, 3 sample chapters. Prefers to read materials exclusively. No e-mail or fax queries. Responds in 3 weeks to queries; 1 month to mss. Returns materials only with SASE. Obtains most new clients through recommendations from others.

Recent Sales Sold 29 titles in the last year. *A Rock and a Hard Place*, by Kimberla Lawson Roby (Morrow); *Mine to Keep*, by Sheridan Hay (Doubleday); *Body Count*, by P.D. Martin (Mira).

Terms Agent receives 15% commission on domestic sales. Bills back specific expenses incurred doing business for a client.

Tips "We prefer exclusive submissions. Don't e-mail or fax submissions. Please include biographical information and publishing history."

☑ BARBARA S. KOUTS, LITERARY AGENT

P.O. Box 560, Bellport NY 11713. (631)286-1278. Fax: (631) 286-1538. **Contact:** Barbara Kouts. Estab. 1980. Member of AAR. Represents 50 clients. 10% of clients are new/unpublished writers.

    O₋ This agency specializes in children's books.

How to Contact Query with SASE. Considers simultaneous queries. Responds in 1 week to queries; 2 months to mss. Obtains most new clients through recommendations from others, solicitations, conferences.

Terms Agent receives 10% commission on domestic sales; 20% commission on foreign sales. Charges clients for photocopying.

Tips "Write, do not call. Be professional in your writing."

☑ KRAAS LITERARY AGENCY

13514 Winter Creek Ct., Houston TX 77077. (281)870-9770. Fax: (281)679-1655. **Contact:** Irene Kraas. Alternate address: 3447 NE 23rd Ave., Portland OR 97212. (503)319-0900. **Contact:** Ashley Kraas. Estab. 1990. Represents

40 clients. 75% of clients are new/unpublished writers. Currently handles: 5% nonfiction books; 95% novels.
Member Agents Irene Kraas, principal (psychological thrillers, medical thrillers, literary fiction, young adult); Ashley Kraas, associate (romance, women's fiction, historical fiction, memoirs, biographies, self-help, spiritual). Please send appropriate submissions to the correct address (Ashley in Portland; Irene in Houston).

O⃛ This agency specializes in adult fiction. Actively seeking books that are well written with commercial potential. Does not want to receive short stories, plays, or poetry.

How to Contact Submit cover letter, first 50 pages of a completed ms, SASE. No e-mail or fax queries. Considers simultaneous queries. Returns materials only with SASE.

Recent Sales *Words to Die By*, by Kyra Davis (Harlequin); St. Germain series, by Chelsea Quinn Yarbro (Tor); *Shriker*, by Janet Lee Carey (Atheneum); *Crazy Quilt*, by Paula Paul (University of New Mexico Press); *The Sword*, *The Shield* and *The Crown*, a trilogy by Hilari Bell (Simon & Schuster).

Terms Agent receives 15% commission on domestic sales. Offers written contract. Charges clients for photocopying and postage.

Writers' Conferences Irene: Southwest Writers Conference; Wrangling with Writing. Ashley: Surrey International Writers Conference; Wrangling with Writing; Willamette Writers Conference.

Tips "Material by unpublished authors will be accepted in the above areas only. Published authors seeking representation may contact us regarding any material in any area except children's picture books and chapter books."

⌬ STUART KRICHEVSKY LITERARY AGENCY, INC.

381 Park Ave. S., Suite 914, New York NY 10016. Fax: (212)725-5275. E-mail: query@skagency.com. Member of AAR.

Member Agents Stuart Krichevsky; Shana Cohen (science fiction, fantasy); Elizabeth Kellermeyer.

Represents Nonfiction books, novels.

How to Contact Submit query, synopsis, 1 sample page via e-mail (no attachments).

🅽 ◯ KT PUBLIC RELATIONS & LITERARY SERVICES

1905 Cricklewood Cove, Fogelsville PA 18051. (610)395-6298. Fax: (610)395-6299. E-mail: kae@ktpublicrelations.com. Web site: www.ktpublicrelations.com. **Contact:** Kae Tienstra, Jon Tienstra. Estab. 2005. Represents 5 clients. 75% of clients are new/unpublished writers. Currently handles: 50% nonfiction books; 50% novels.

● Prior to becoming an agent, Ms. Tienstra was publicity director for Rodale, Inc. for 13 years and then founded her own publicity agency; Mr. Tienstra joined the firm in 1995 with varied corporate experience and a master's degree in library science.

Member Agents Kae Tienstra (health, parenting, psychology, how-to, crafts, foods/nutrition, beauty, women's fiction, general fiction); Jon Tienstra (nature/environment, history, cooking/foods/nutrition, war/military, automotive, health/medicine, gardening, general fiction, science fiction/fantasy, popular fiction).

Represents Nonfiction books, novels, novellas. **Considers these nonfiction areas:** Agriculture/horticulture; animals; child guidance/parenting; cooking/foods/nutrition; crafts/hobbies; health/medicine; history; how-to; military/war; nature/environment; popular culture; psychology; science/technology; self-help/personal improvement; interior design/decorating. **Considers these fiction areas:** Action/adventure; detective/police/crime; family saga; fantasy; historical; literary; mainstream/contemporary; mystery/suspense; romance; science fiction; thriller.

O⃛ "We have worked with a variety of authors and publishers over the years and have learned what individual publishers are looking for in terms of new acquisitions. We are both mad about books and authors, and we look forward to finding publishing success for all our clients." Specializes in parenting, history, cooking/foods/nutrition, crafts, beauty, war, health/medicine, psychology, how-to, gardening, science fiction, fantasy, women's fiction, and popular fiction. Does not want to see unprofessional material.

How to Contact Query with SASE. Accepts e-mail and fax queries. Considers simultaneous queries. Responds in 2 weeks to queries; 3 months to mss. Returns materials only with SASE. Obtains most new clients through recommendations from others.

Terms Agent receives 15% commission on domestic sales; 20% commission on foreign sales. No written contract. Charges clients for long-distance phone calls, fax, postage, photocopying (only when incurred). No advance payment for these out-of-pocket expenses.

❤ THE LA LITERARY AGENCY

P.O. Box 46370, Los Angeles CA 90046. (323)654-5288. E-mail: laliteraryag@aol.com. **Contact:** Ann Cashman, Eric Lasher. Estab. 1980.

● Prior to becoming an agent, Mr. Lasher worked in publishing in New York and Los Angeles.

Represents Nonfiction books, novels. **Considers these nonfiction areas:** Animals; anthropology/archaeology; art/architecture/design; biography/autobiography; business/economics; child guidance/parenting; cooking/

foods/nutrition; current affairs; ethnic/cultural interests; government/politics/law; health/medicine; history; how-to; nature/environment; popular culture; psychology; science/technology; self-help/personal improvement; sociology; sports; true crime/investigative; women's issues/studies; narrative nonfiction. **Considers these fiction areas:** Action/adventure; detective/police/crime; family saga; feminist; historical; literary; mainstream/contemporary; sports; thriller.

How to Contact Query with SASE, outline, 1 sample chapter. No e-mail or fax queries.

Recent Sales *Full Bloom: The Art and Life of Georgia O'Keeffe*, by Hunter Drohojowska-Philp (Norton); *And the Walls Came Tumbling Down*, by H. Caldwell (Scribner); *Italian Slow & Savory*, by Joyce Goldstein (Chronicle); *A Field Guide to Chocolate Chip Cookies*, by Dede Wilson (Harvard Common Press); *Teen Knitting Club* (Artisan); *The Framingham Heart Study*, by Dr. Daniel Levy (Knopf).

☑ PETER LAMPACK AGENCY, INC.

551 Fifth Ave., Suite 1613, New York NY 10176-0187. (212)687-9106. Fax: (212)687-9109. E-mail: alampack@verizon.net. **Contact:** Andrew Lampack. Estab. 1977. Represents 50 clients. 10% of clients are new/unpublished writers. Currently handles: 20% nonfiction books; 80% novels.

Member Agents Peter Lampack (psychological suspense, action/adventure, literary fiction, nonfiction, contemporary relationships); Rema Delanyan (foreign rights); Andrew Lampack (new writers).

Represents Nonfiction books, novels. **Considers these fiction areas:** Action/adventure; detective/police/crime; family saga; historical; literary; mainstream/contemporary; mystery/suspense; thriller; contemporary relationships.

> O→ This agency specializes in commercial fiction and nonfiction by recognized experts. Actively seeking literary and commercial fiction, thrillers, mysteries, suspense, and psychological thrillers. Does not want to receive horror, romance, science fiction, westerns, or academic material.

How to Contact Query with SASE. *No unsolicited mss.* Accepts e-mail queries. No fax queries. Considers simultaneous queries. Responds in 2 months to queries and mss. Obtains most new clients through referrals made by clients.

Recent Sales *Slow Man*, by J.M. Coetzee; *Black Wind*, by Clive Cussler and Dirk Cussler; *Sacred Stone*, by Clive Cussler and Craig Dirgo; *Lost City*, by Clive Cussler with Paul Kemprecos.

Terms Agent receives 15% commission on domestic sales; 20% commission on foreign sales.

Writers' Conferences BookExpo America.

Tips "Submit only your best work for consideration. Have a very specific agenda of goals you wish your prospective agent to accomplish for you. Provide the agent with a comprehensive statement of your credentials—educational and professional."

Ⓝ ☑ LAURA LANGLIE, LITERARY AGENT

275 President St., Suite 3, Brooklyn NY 11231. (718)858-0659. Fax: (718)858-6161. E-mail: laura@lauralanglie.com. **Contact:** Laura Langlie. Estab. 2001. Represents 25 clients. 50% of clients are new/unpublished writers. Currently handles: 25% nonfiction books; 48% novels; 2% story collections; 25% juvenile books.

> • Prior to opening her agency, Ms. Langlie worked in publishing for 7 years and as an agent at Kidde, Hoyt & Picard for 6 years.

Represents Nonfiction books, novels, short story collections, novellas, juvenile books. **Considers these nonfiction areas:** Animals (not how-to); anthropology/archaeology; biography/autobiography; current affairs; ethnic/cultural interests; gay/lesbian issues; government/politics/law; history; humor/satire; memoirs; nature/environment; popular culture; psychology; theater/film; women's issues/studies; history of medicine and science; language/literature. **Considers these fiction areas:** Detective/police/crime; ethnic; feminist; gay/lesbian; historical; humor/satire; juvenile; literary; mystery/suspense; romance; thriller; young adult; mainstream.

> O→ "I love working with first-time authors. I'm very involved with and committed to my clients. I also employ a publicist to work with all my clients to make the most of each book's publication. Most of my clients come to me via recommendations from other agents, clients, and editors. I've met very few at conferences. I've often sought out writers for projects, and I still find new clients via the traditional query letter." Does not want science fiction, poetry, men's adventure, or erotica.

How to Contact Query with SASE. Accepts queries via fax. Considers simultaneous queries. Responds in 1 week to queries; 1 month to mss. Returns materials only with SASE. Obtains most new clients through recommendations, submissions.

Recent Sales Sold 40 titles in the last year. *How to Be Popular*, by Meg Cabot (HarperCollins Children's); *It's About Your Husband*, by Lauren Lipton (Warner Books); *Fix*, by Leslie Margolis (Simon Pulse); Untitled work about Muslims in America since September 11, by Geneive Abdo (Oxford University Press). Other clients include Renée Ashley, Mignon F. Ballard, Jessica Benson, Joan Druett, Jack El-Hai, Sarah Elliott, Fiona Gibson, Robin Hathaway, Melanie Lynne Hauser, Mary Hogan, Jonathan Neale, Eric Pinder, Delia Ray, Cheryl L. Reed, Jennifer Sturman.

Terms Agent receives 15% commission on domestic sales; 20% commission on foreign sales. No written contract.
Tips "Be complete, forthright, and clear in your communications. Do your research as to what a particular agent represents."

◢ MICHAEL LARSEN/ELIZABETH POMADA, LITERARY AGENTS

1029 Jones St., San Francisco CA 94109-5023. (415)673-0939. E-mail: larsenpoma@aol.com. Web site: www.lar sen-pomada.com. **Contact:** Mike Larsen, Elizabeth Pomada. Estab. 1972. Member of AAR, Authors Guild, ASJA, PEN, WNBA, California Writers Club, National Speakers Association. Represents 100 clients. 40-45% of clients are new/unpublished writers. Currently handles: 70% nonfiction books; 30% novels.

- Prior to opening their agency, Mr. Larsen and Ms. Pomada were promotion executives for major publishing houses. Mr. Larsen worked for Morrow, Bantam, and Pyramid (now part of Berkley); Ms. Pomada worked at Holt, David McKay, and The Dial Press.

Member Agents Michael Larsen (nonfiction); Elizabeth Pomada (fiction, narrative nonfiction, nonfiction for women).

Represents Adult book-length fiction and nonfiction that will interest New York publishers or are irresistibly written or conceived. **Considers these nonfiction areas:** Anthropology/archaeology; art/architecture/design; biography/autobiography; business/economics; cooking/foods/nutrition; current affairs; ethnic/cultural interests; gay/lesbian issues; government/politics/law; health/medicine; history; how-to; humor/satire; memoirs; money/finance; music/dance; nature/environment; New Age/metaphysics; popular culture; psychology; religious/inspirational; science/technology; self-help/personal improvement; sociology; sports; theater/film; travel; true crime/investigative; women's issues/studies; futurism. **Considers these fiction areas:** Action/adventure; contemporary issues; detective/police/crime; ethnic; experimental; family saga; fantasy; feminist; gay/lesbian; glitz; historical; humor/satire; literary; mainstream/contemporary; mystery/suspense; religious/inspirational; romance (contemporary, gothic, historical); chick lit.

- ○┐ "We have diverse tastes. We look for fresh voices and new ideas. We handle literary, commercial, and genre fiction, and the full range of nonfiction books." Actively seeking commercial and literary fiction. Does not want to receive children's books, plays, short stories, screenplays, pornography, poetry, or stories of abuse.

How to Contact Query with SASE, first 10 pages of completed novel, 2-page synopsis, SASE. "For nonfiction, send title, promotion plan and proposal done according to our plan (see Web site)." No e-mail or fax queries. Responds in 2 days to queries; 2 months to mss.

Recent Sales Sold at least 15 titles in the last year. *The Blonde Theory*, by Kristin Harmel (Warner 5 Spot); *The Shadowed Isle*, by Katharine Kerr (Daw); *Making Documentary Movies*, by Barry Hampe (Holt); *Hit By a Farm*, by Catherine Friend (Marlowe).

Terms Agent receives 15% commission on domestic sales; 20% commission on foreign sales (30% for Asia). May charge for printing, postage for multiple submissions, foreign mail, foreign phone calls, galleys, books, legal fees.

Writers' Conferences BookExpo America; Santa Barbara Writers' Conference; San Francisco Writers Conference.

Tips "If you can write books that meet the needs of the marketplace and you can promote your books, now is the best time ever to be a writer. We must find new writers to make a living, so we are very eager to hear from new writers whose work will interest large houses, and nonfiction writers who can promote their books. For a list of recent sales, helpful info, and three ways to make yourself irresistible to any publisher, please visit our Web site."

◎ THE STEVE LAUBE AGENCY

5501 N. 7th Ave., #502, Phoenix AZ 85013. (602)336-8910. Fax: (602)532-7123. E-mail: krichards@stevelaube.c om. Web site: www.stevelaube.com. **Contact:** Steve Laube. Estab. 2004. Member of CBA. Represents 50 clients. 20% of clients are new/unpublished writers. Currently handles: 48% nonfiction books; 48% novels; 2% novellas; 2% scholarly books.

- Prior to becoming an agent, Mr. Laube worked 11 years as a bookseller and 11 years as editorial director of nonfiction with Bethany House Publishers.

Represents Nonfiction books, novels. **Considers these nonfiction areas:** Religious/inspirational. **Considers these fiction areas:** Religious/inspirational.

- ○┐ "We primarily serve the Christian market (CBA). However, we have had success representing books in a variety of fields." Actively seeking fiction and religious nonfiction. Does not want children's picture books, poetry, or cookbooks.

How to Contact Submit proposal package, outline, 3 sample chapters, SASE. No e-mail submissions. Consult Web site for guidelines. Considers simultaneous queries. Responds in 6-8 weeks. Returns materials only with SASE. Obtains most new clients through recommendations from others, solicitations, conferences.

Recent Sales Sold 80 titles in the last year. Clients include Deborah Raney, Bright Media, Allison Bottke, H. Norman Wright, Ellie Kay, Jack Cavanaugh, Karen Ball, Tracey Bateman, Clint Kelly, Susan May Warren, Lori Copeland, Martha Bolton, Lisa Bergren.

Terms Agent receives 15% commission on domestic sales; 20% commission on foreign sales. Offers written contract; 30-day notice must be given to terminate contract.

Writers' Conferences Mount Hermon Christian Writers Conference; American Christian Fiction Writers Conference; Glorieta Christian Writers Conference.

⬛ LAZEAR AGENCY, INC.

431 2nd St., Suite 300, Hudson WI 54016. (715)531-0012. Fax: (715)531-0016. E-mail: info@lazear.com. Web site: www.lazear.com. **Contact:** Editorial Board. Estab. 1984. Represents 250 clients. Currently handles: 60% nonfiction books; 30% novels; 10% juvenile books.

- The Lazear Agency opened a New York office in September 1997.

Member Agents Jonathon Lazear; Christi Cardenas; Julie Mayo; Anne Blackstone.

Represents Nonfiction books, novels, juvenile books, licensing, new media with connection to book project. **Considers these nonfiction areas:** Agriculture/horticulture; Americana; animals; anthropology/archaeology; art/architecture/design; biography/autobiography; business/economics; child guidance/parenting; computers/electronic; cooking/foods/nutrition; crafts/hobbies; current affairs; education; ethnic/cultural interests; gardening; gay/lesbian issues; government/politics/law; health/medicine; history; how-to; humor/satire; interior design/decorating; juvenile nonfiction; language/literature/criticism; memoirs; military/war; money/finance; multicultural; music/dance; nature/environment; New Age/metaphysics; philosophy; photography; popular culture; psychology; recreation; regional; religious/inspirational; science/technology; self-help/personal improvement; sex; sociology; software; spirituality; sports; theater/film; translation; travel; true crime/investigative; women's issues/studies; young adult; creative nonfiction. **Considers these fiction areas:** Action/adventure; comic books/cartoon; confession; detective/police/crime; erotica; ethnic; experimental; family saga; fantasy; feminist; gay/lesbian; glitz; gothic; hi-lo; historical; horror; humor/satire; juvenile; literary; mainstream/contemporary; military/war; multicultural; multimedia; mystery/suspense; New Age; occult; picture books; plays; poetry; poetry in translation; psychic/supernatural; regional; religious/inspirational; romance; science fiction; short story collections; spiritual; sports; thriller; translation; westerns/frontier; young adult; women's.

How to Contact Query with SASE, outline/proposal. No phone calls or faxes. Responds in 3 weeks to queries; 1 month to mss. Returns materials only with SASE. Obtains most new clients through recommendations from others, bestseller lists, word of mouth.

Recent Sales Sold over 50 titles in the last year. *The Truth (with Jokes)*, by Al Franken (Dutton); *Harvest for Hope*, by Jane Goodall with Gary McAvoy and Gail Hudson (Warner); *Mommy Knows Worst*, by James Lileks (Crown); *The Prop*, by Pete Hautman (Simon & Schuster); *One Phone Call Away: Secrets of a Master Networker*, by Jeffrey Meshel (Portfolio); *Full Service*, by Will Weaver (Farrar, Straus & Giroux); *101 Ways to Help Birds*, by Laura Erickson (Stackpole).

Terms Agent receives 15% commission on domestic sales; 20% commission on foreign sales. Offers written contract. Charges clients for photocopying, international express mail, bound galleys, books used for subsidiary rights sales. No fees charged if book is not sold.

Tips "The writer should first view himself as a salesperson in order to obtain an agent. Sell yourself, your idea, your concept. Do your homework. Notice what is in the marketplace. Be sophisticated about the arena in which you are writing."

⬛ SARAH LAZIN BOOKS

126 Fifth Ave., Suite 300, New York NY 10011. (212)989-5757. Fax: (212)989-1393. Member of AAR.

Member Agents Paula Balzer; Sarah Lazin.

How to Contact Query with SASE. No e-mail queries.

⬛ THE NED LEAVITT AGENCY

70 Wooster St., Suite 4F, New York NY 10012. (212)334-0999. Web site: www.nedleavittagency.com/agency.html. **Contact:** Ned Leavitt. Member of AAR.

Represents Nonfiction books, novels.

How to Contact For fiction, submit cover letter, 1-2 chapters, brief synopsis, author bio. For nonfiction, submit cover letter, TOC, brief chapter synopsis or outline, 1-2 sample chapters, author bio. No materials will be returned.

Tips "See Web site for more information on what we need."

🔣 🖊 ROBERT LECKER AGENCY

4055 Melrose Ave., Montreal QC H4A 2S5 Canada. (514)830-4818. Fax: (514)483-1644. E-mail: leckerlink@aol.c om. Web site: www.leckeragency.com. **Contact:** Robert Lecker. Estab. 2004. Represents 15 clients. 20% of clients are new/unpublished writers. Currently handles: 80% nonfiction books; 10% novels; 10% scholarly books.

- Prior to becoming an agent, Mr. Lecker was the co-founder and publisher of ECW Press and professor of English literature at McGill University. He has 30 years of experience in book and magazine publishing.

Member Agents Robert Lecker (popular culture, music); Mary Williams (travel, food, popular science).

Represents Nonfiction books, novels, scholarly books, syndicated material. **Considers these nonfiction areas:** Biography/autobiography; cooking/foods/nutrition; ethnic/cultural interests; how-to; language/literature/criticism; music/dance; popular culture; science/technology; theater/film. **Considers these fiction areas:** Action/adventure; detective/police/crime; erotica; literary; mainstream/contemporary; mystery/suspense; thriller.

- ⊶ RLA specializes in books about popular culture, music, entertainment, food, and travel. The agency responds to articulate, innovative proposals within 2 weeks. Actively seeking original book mss only after receipt of outlines and proposals. *No unsolicited mss.*

How to Contact Submit proposal package, outline. Accepts e-mail queries. No fax queries. Considers simultaneous queries. Responds in 2 weeks to queries; 1 month to mss. Obtains most new clients through recommendations from others, conferences, interest in Web site.

Terms Agent receives 15% commission on domestic sales; 15-20% commission on foreign sales. Offers written contract, binding for 1 year; 6-month notice must be given to terminate contract.

🖊 LESCHER & LESCHER, LTD.

47 E. 19th St., New York NY 10003. (212)529-1790. Fax: (212)529-2716. **Contact:** Robert Lescher, Susan Lescher. Estab. 1966. Member of AAR. Represents 150 clients. Currently handles: 80% nonfiction books; 20% novels.

Represents Nonfiction books, novels. **Considers these nonfiction areas:** Current affairs; history; memoirs; popular culture; biography; cookbooks/wines; law; contemporary issues; narrative nonfiction. **Considers these fiction areas:** Literary; mystery/suspense; commercial.

- ⊶ Does not want to receive screenplays, science fiction, or romance.

How to Contact Query with SASE. Obtains most new clients through recommendations from others.

Recent Sales Sold 35 titles in the last year. This agency prefers not to share information on specific sales. Clients include Neil Sheehan, Madeleine L'Engle, Calvin Trillin, Judith Viorst, Thomas Perry, Anne Fadiman, Frances FitzGerald, Paula Fox, Robert M. Parker Jr.

Terms Agent receives 15% commission on domestic sales; 20-25% commission on foreign sales.

🖊 LEVINE GREENBERG LITERARY AGENCY, INC.

307 7th Ave., Suite 2407, New York NY 10001. (212)337-0934. Fax: (212)337-0948. Web site: www.levinegreenb erg.com. Estab. 1989. Member of AAR. Represents 250 clients. 33% of clients are new/unpublished writers. Currently handles: 70% nonfiction books; 30% novels.

- Prior to opening his agency, Mr. Levine served as vice president of the Bank Street College of Education.

Member Agents James Levine; Arielle Eckstut; Daniel Greenberg; Stephanie Kip Roston; Jenoyne Adams.

Represents Nonfiction books, novels. **Considers these nonfiction areas:** Animals; art/architecture/design; biography/autobiography; business/economics; child guidance/parenting; computers/electronic; cooking/foods/nutrition; gardening; gay/lesbian issues; health/medicine; money/finance; nature/environment; New Age/metaphysics; psychology; religious/inspirational; science/technology; self-help/personal improvement; sociology; spirituality; sports; women's issues/studies. **Considers these fiction areas:** Literary; mainstream/contemporary; mystery/suspense; thriller (psychological); women's.

- ⊶ This agency specializes in business, parenting, health/medicine, narrative nonfiction, spirituality, religion, women's issues, and commercial fiction.

How to Contact See Web site for full submission procedure. Prefers e-mail queries. Obtains most new clients through recommendations from others.

Recent Sales *The Onion: Our Dumb Century*; *Alternadad*, by Neal Pollack; *The Opposite of Death Is Love*, by Nando Parrado.

Terms Agent receives 15% commission on domestic sales; 20% commission on foreign sales. Offers written contract. Charges clients for out-of-pocket expenses—telephone, fax, postage, photocopying—directly connected to the project.

Writers' Conferences ASJA Writers Conference.

Tips "We focus on editorial development, business representation, and publicity and marketing strategy."

🖊 PAUL S. LEVINE LITERARY AGENCY

1054 Superba Ave., Venice CA 90291-3940. (310)450-6711. Fax: (310)450-0181. E-mail: pslevine@ix.netcom.c om. Web site: www.paulslevine.com. **Contact:** Paul S. Levine. Estab. 1996. Member of the State Bar of California. Represents over 100 clients. 75% of clients are new/unpublished writers. Currently handles: 30% nonfiction books; 30% novels; 10% movie scripts; 30% TV scripts.

Represents Nonfiction books, novels, movie scripts, feature film, TV scripts, TV movie of the week, episodic drama, sitcom, animation, documentary, miniseries, syndicated material. **Considers these nonfiction areas:** Art/architecture/design; biography/autobiography; business/economics; child guidance/parenting; computers/electronic; cooking/foods/nutrition; crafts/hobbies; current affairs; education; ethnic/cultural interests; gay/lesbian issues; government/politics/law; health/medicine; history; how-to; humor/satire; interior design/decorating; language/literature/criticism; memoirs; military/war; money/finance; music/dance; nature/environment; New Age/metaphysics; photography; popular culture; psychology; religious/inspirational; science/technology; self-help/personal improvement; sociology; sports; theater/film; true crime/investigative; women's issues/studies; creative nonfiction. **Considers these fiction areas:** Action/adventure; comic books/cartoon; confession; detective/police/crime; erotica; ethnic; experimental; family saga; feminist; gay/lesbian; glitz; historical; humor/satire; literary; mainstream/contemporary; mystery/suspense; regional; religious/inspirational; romance; sports; thriller; westerns/frontier. **Considers these script subject areas:** Action/adventure; biography/autobiography; cartoon/animation; comedy; contemporary issues; detective/police/crime; erotica; ethnic; experimental; family saga; feminist; gay/lesbian; glitz; historical; horror; juvenile; mainstream; multimedia; mystery/suspense; religious/inspirational; romantic comedy; romantic drama; sports; teen; thriller; western/frontier.

○━ Actively seeking commercial fiction and nonfiction. Also handles children's and young adult fiction and nonfiction. Does not want to receive science fiction, fantasy, or horror.

How to Contact Query with SASE. Accepts e-mail and fax queries. Considers simultaneous queries. Responds in 1 day to queries; 2 months to mss. Returns materials only with SASE. Obtains most new clients through conferences, referrals, listings on various Web sites and in directories.

Recent Sales Sold 25 titles in the last year. This agency prefers not to share information on specific sales.

Terms Agent receives 15% commission on domestic sales; 20% commission on foreign sales. Offers written contract. Charges clients for messengers, long distance calls, postage (only when incurred). No advance payment necessary.

Writers' Conferences California Lawyers for the Arts Workshops; Selling to Hollywood Conference; Willamette Writers Conference; and many others.

◎ ROBERT LIEBERMAN ASSOCIATES

400 Nelson Rd., Ithaca NY 14850-9440. (607)273-8801. Fax: (801)749-9682. E-mail: rhl10@cornell.edu. Web site: www.people.cornell.edu/pages/rhl10. **Contact:** Robert Lieberman. Estab. 1993. Represents 30 clients. 50% of clients are new/unpublished writers. Currently handles: 20% nonfiction books; 80% textbooks.

Represents Nonfiction books (trade), scholarly books, textbooks (college/high school/middle school). **Considers these nonfiction areas:** Agriculture/horticulture; anthropology/archaeology; art/architecture/design; business/economics; computers/electronic; education; health/medicine; memoirs (by authors with high public recognition); money/finance; music/dance; nature/environment; psychology; science/technology; sociology; theater/film.

○━ This agency specializes in university/college-level textbooks, CD-ROM/software, and popular trade books in math, engineering, economics, and other subjects. Does not want to receive fiction, self-help, or screenplays.

How to Contact Query with SASE or by e-mail. Prefers to read materials exclusively. Prefers e-mail queries. Responds in 2 weeks to queries; 1 month to mss. Returns materials only with SASE. Obtains most new clients through referrals.

Recent Sales Sold 15 titles in the last year. *The Standard Model and the Triumph of 20th Century Physics*, by Robert Oerter (Pi Press); *Fundamentals in Voice Quality Engineering in Wireless Networks*, by Avi Perry (Cambridge University Press); *C++ Programming*, by John Mason (Prentice Hall); *College Physics*, by Giambattist and Richardson (McGraw-Hill); *Conflict Resolution*, by Baltos and Weir (Cambridge University Press).

Terms Agent receives 15% commission on domestic sales; 20% commission on foreign sales. Offers written contract; 1-month notice must be given to terminate contract. 100% of business is derived from commissions on ms sales. Fees are sometimes charged to clients for shipping and when special reviewers are required.

Tips "The trade books we handle are by authors who are highly recognized in their fields of expertise. Our client list includes Nobel Prize winners and others with high name recognition, either by the public or within a given area of expertise."

⊕ ♥ LIMELIGHT MANAGEMENT

33 Newman St., London W1T 1PY England. (44)(207)637-2529. E-mail: limelight.management@virgin.net. Web site: www.limelightmanagement.com. **Contact:** Fiona Lindsay. Estab. 1990. Member of AAA. Represents 70 clients. Currently handles: 100% nonfiction; multimedia.

• Prior to becoming an agent, Ms. Lindsay was a public relations manager at the Dorchester and was working on her law degree.

Represents Nonfiction books. **Considers these nonfiction areas:** Cooking/foods/nutrition; gardening; agriculture/horticulture; art/architecture/design; crafts/hobbies; nature/environment; New Age/metaphysics; photography; self-help; sports; travel, health/medicine; interior design/decorating.

☞ This agency specializes in lifestyle subject areas, especially celebrity chefs, gardeners journalists, and wine experts.

How to Contact Prefers to read materials exclusively. Query with SASE or submit proposal via e-mail. Responds in 1 week to queries. Return materials only with SASE. Obtains most new clients through recommendations from others.

Recent Sales This agency prefers not to share information on specific sales. Clients include Oz Clarke, Antony Worrall Thompson, David Stevens, Linda Barker, James Martin.

Terms Agent receives 15% commission on domestic sales; 20% commission on foreign sales. Offers written contract; 2-month notice must be given to terminate contract.

◉ WENDY LIPKIND AGENCY

120 E. 81st St., New York NY 10028. (212)628-9653. Fax: (212)585-1306. E-mail: lipkindag@aol.com. **Contact:** Wendy Lipkind. Estab. 1977. Member of AAR. Represents 60 clients. Currently handles: 90% nonfiction books; 10% novels.

Represents Nonfiction books, novels. **Considers these nonfiction areas:** Biography/autobiography; current affairs; health/medicine; history; science/technology; women's issues/studies; social history; narrative nonfiction. **Considers these fiction areas:** Mainstream/contemporary; mystery/suspense (psychological).

☞ This agency specializes in adult nonfiction. Does not want to receive mass market originals.

How to Contact Prefers to read materials exclusively. Accepts e-mail queries only (no attachments). Obtains most new clients through recommendations from others.

Recent Sales Sold 10 titles in the last year. *One Small Step*, by Robert Mauner (Workman); *Classroom Tinderbox*, by Dr. Ross Green.

Terms Agent receives 15% commission on domestic sales; 20% commission on foreign sales. Sometimes offers written contract. Charges clients for foreign postage, messenger service, photocopying, transatlantic calls, faxes.

Tips "Send intelligent query letter first. Let me know if you've submitted to other agents."

N ◉ LIPPINCOTT MASSIE MCQUILKIN

80 Fifth Ave., Suite 1101, New York NY 10011. (212)337-2044. Fax: (212)352-2059. E-mail: rob@lmqlit.com; will@lmqlit.com; maria@lmqlit.com. Web site: www.lmqlit.com. **Contact:** Makila Sands, assistant. Estab. 2003. Represents 90 clients. 30% of clients are new/unpublished writers. Currently handles: 40% nonfiction books; 40% novels; 10% story collections; 5% scholarly books; 5% poetry.

Member Agents Maria Massie (fiction, memoir, cultural criticism); Will Lippincott (politics, current affairs, history); Rob McQuilkin (fiction, history, psychology, sociology, graphic material).

Represents Nonfiction books, novels, short story collections, scholarly books, graphic novels. **Considers these nonfiction areas:** Animals; anthropology/archaeology; art/architecture/design; biography/autobiography; business/economics; child guidance/parenting; current affairs; ethnic/cultural interests; gay/lesbian issues; government/politics/law; health/medicine; history; language/literature/criticism; memoirs; military/war; money/finance; music/dance; nature/environment; popular culture; psychology; religious/inspirational; science/technology; self-help/personal improvement; sociology; theater/film; true crime/investigative; women's issues/studies. **Considers these fiction areas:** Action/adventure; comic books/cartoon; confession; family saga; feminist; gay/lesbian; historical; humor/satire; literary; mainstream/contemporary; regional.

☞ LMQ focuses on bringing new voices in literary and commercial fiction to the market, as well as popularizing the ideas and arguments of scholars in the fields of history, psychology, sociology, political science, and current affairs. Seeks fiction writers who already have credits in magazines and quarterlies, as well as nonfiction writers who already have a media platform or some kind of a university affiliation. No romance, genre fiction, or children's material.

How to Contact Send query via e-mail. Only send additional materials if requested. Considers simultaneous queries. Responds in 1 week to queries; 1 month to mss. Obtains most new clients through recommendations from others, solicitations, conferences.

Recent Sales Sold 27 titles in the last year. *The Abstinence Teacher*, by Tom Perrotta (St. Martins); *Queen of Fashion*, by Caroline Weber (Henry Holt); *Whistling Past Dixie*, by Tom Schaller (Simon & Schuster); *Pretty Little Dirty*, by Amanda Boyden (Vintage). Other clients include Peter Ho Davies, Kim Addonizio, Don Lee, Natasha Trethewey, Anotol Lieven, Sir Michael Marmot, Anne Carson, Liza Ward, David Sirota, Anne Marie Slaughter, Marina Belozerskaya, Kate Walbert.

Terms Agent receives 15% commission on domestic sales; 30% commission on foreign sales. Offers written contract; 30-day notice must be given to terminate contract. Only charges for reasonable business expenses upon successful sale.

◉ LITERARY AND CREATIVE ARTISTS, INC.

3543 Albemarle St. NW, Washington DC 20008-4213. (202)362-4688. Fax: (202)362-8875. E-mail: query@lcadc. com. Web site: www.lcadc.com. **Contact:** Muriel Nellis. Estab. 1981. Member of AAR, Authors Guild, American Bar Association. Represents 75 clients. Currently handles: 70% nonfiction books; 15% novels.

Member Agents Muriel Nellis; Jane Roberts; Stephen Ruwe.

Represents Nonfiction books, novels. **Considers these nonfiction areas:** Biography/autobiography; business/ economics; cooking/foods/nutrition; government/politics/law; health/medicine; how-to; memoirs; philosophy; human drama; lifestyle.

How to Contact Query with SASE. *No unsolicited mss.* Responds in 3 months to queries.

Recent Sales *Lady Cottington's Pressed Fairy Book*, by Brian Froud and Terry Jones (Pavilion); *The New Feminine Brain*, by Mona Lisa Schulz (Free Press); *Al Qaeda in Europe*, by Lorenzo Vidino (Prometheus Books); *What Type of Leader Am I?*, by Ginger Lapid-Bogda (McGraw-Hill); *The Longest Ride*, by Emilio Scotto (MBI Publishing).

Terms Agent receives 15% commission on domestic sales; 20% commission on foreign sales; 25% commission on dramatic rights sales. Charges clients for long-distance phone/fax, photocopying, shipping.

Tips ''While we prefer published writers, it is not required if the proposed work has great merit.''

◉ THE LITERARY GROUP

270 Lafayette St., Suite 1505, New York NY 10012. (212)274-1616. Fax: (212)274-9876. E-mail: fweimann@thelit erarygroup.com. Web site: www.theliterarygroup.com. **Contact:** Frank Weimann. Estab. 1985. 65% of clients are new/unpublished writers. Currently handles: 50% nonfiction books; 50% fiction.

Member Agents Frank Weimann; Ian Kleinert.

Represents Nonfiction books, novels. **Considers these nonfiction areas:** Animals; anthropology/archaeology; biography/autobiography; business/economics; child guidance/parenting; crafts/hobbies; current affairs; education; ethnic/cultural interests; government/politics/law; health/medicine; history; how-to; humor/satire; juvenile nonfiction; language/literature/criticism; memoirs; military/war; money/finance; multicultural; music/ dance; nature/environment; popular culture; psychology; religious/inspirational; science/technology; self-help/personal improvement; sociology; sports; theater/film; true crime/investigative; women's issues/studies; creative nonfiction. **Considers these fiction areas:** Action/adventure; contemporary issues; detective/police/ crime; ethnic; family saga; fantasy; feminist; horror; humor/satire; mystery/suspense; psychic/supernatural; romance (contemporary, gothic, historical, regency); sports; thriller; westerns/frontier.

   ⚏ This agency specializes in nonfiction (memoir, military, history, biography, sports, how-to).

How to Contact Query with SASE, outline, 3 sample chapters. Prefers to read materials exclusively. Only responds if interested. Returns materials only with SASE. Obtains most new clients through referrals, writers' conferences, query letters.

Recent Sales Sold 150 titles in the last year. *There and Back Again: An Actor's Tale*, by Sean Astin; *The Ambassador's Son*, by Homer Hickam; *Idiot*, by Johnny Damon; *Lemons Are Not Red*, by Laura Vaccaro Seeger; *The Good Guys*, by Bill Bonanno and Joe Pistone; *Flags of Our Fathers*, by James Bradley; *One Minute Wellness*, by Dr. Ben Lerner. Other clients include Robert Anderson, Michael Reagan, J.L. King.

Terms Agent receives 15% commission on domestic sales; 20% commission on foreign sales. Offers written contract; 30-day notice must be given to terminate contract.

Writers' Conferences San Diego State University Writers' Conference; Maui Writers Conference; Agents and Editors Conference.

◉ LITERARY MANAGEMENT GROUP, INC.

407 NW 122nd St., Gainesville FL 32607. (615)812-4445. E-mail: brucebarbour@literarymanagementgroup. com; brb@brucebarbour.com. Web site: www.literarymanagementgroup.com; www.brucebarbour.com. **Contact:** Bruce Barbour. Estab. 1995.

   ● Prior to becoming an agent, Mr. Barbour held executive positions at several publishing houses, including Revell, Barbour Books, Thomas Nelson, and Random House.

Represents Nonfiction books, novels. **Considers these nonfiction areas:** Biography/autobiography; Christian living; spiritual growth; women's and men's issues; prayer; devotional; meditational; Bible study; marriage; business; family/parenting. **Considers these fiction areas:** Accepts a few works of adult fiction each year.

   ⚏ No gift books, poetry, children's books, short stories, or juvenile/young adult fiction. No unsolicited mss or proposals from unpublished authors.

How to Contact E-mail proposal as an attachment.

Terms Agent receives 15% commission on domestic sales.

◉ LITERARY & MEDIA REPRESENTATION

240 W. 35th St., Suite 500, New York NY 10001. **Contact:** Nancy Coffey. Member of AAR.
Represents Nonfiction books, novels. **Considers these nonfiction areas:** True crime/investigative. **Considers these fiction areas:** Family saga; fantasy; gay/lesbian; military/war (espionage); mystery/suspense; romance; science fiction; thriller; women's.
How to Contact Query with SASE.

◉ JULIA LORD LITERARY MANAGEMENT

38 W. Ninth St., #4, New York NY 10011. (212)995-2333. Fax: (212)995-2332. E-mail: julialordliterary@nyc.rr.com. Estab. 1999. Member of AAR.
Member Agents Julia Lord, owner; Riley Kellogg, subagent.
Represents Nonfiction books, novels. **Considers these nonfiction areas:** Biography/autobiography; history; sports; travel; African-American; lifestyle; narrative nonfiction. **Considers these fiction areas:** Action/adventure; historical; literary; mainstream/contemporary; mystery/suspense.
How to Contact Query with SASE or via e-mail. Obtains most new clients through recommendations from others, solicitations.

◉ STERLING LORD LITERISTIC, INC.

65 Bleecker St., 12th Floor, New York NY 10012. (212)780-6050. Fax: (212)780-6095. E-mail: info@sll.com. Web site: www.sll.com. Estab. 1952. Member of AAR; signatory of WGA. Represents 600 clients. Currently handles: 50% nonfiction books; 50% novels.
Member Agents Marcy Posner; Philippa Brophy; Laurie Liss; Chris Calhoun; Peter Matson; Sterling Lord; Claudia Cross; Neeti Madan; George Nicholson; Jim Rutman; Charlotte Sheedy (affiliate); Douglas Stewart; Paul Rodeen; Robert Guinsler.
Represents Nonfiction books, novels.
How to Contact Query with SASE. Responds in 1 month to mss. Obtains most new clients through recommendations from others.
Recent Sales This agency prefers not to share information on specific sales. Clients include Kent Haruf, Dick Francis, Mary Gordon, Sen. John McCain, Simon Winchester, James McBride, Billy Collins, Richard Paul Evans, Dave Pelzer.
Terms Agent receives 15% commission on domestic sales; 20% commission on foreign sales. Offers written contract. Charges clients for photocopying.

◉ NANCY LOVE LITERARY AGENCY

250 E. 65th St., New York NY 10021-6614. (212)980-3499. Fax: (212)308-6405. E-mail: nloveag@aol.com. **Contact:** Nancy Love. Estab. 1984. Member of AAR. Represents 60-80 clients. 25% of clients are new/unpublished writers. Currently handles: 90% nonfiction books; 10% novels.
Represents Nonfiction books, fiction. **Considers these nonfiction areas:** Biography/autobiography; child guidance/parenting; cooking/foods/nutrition; current affairs; ethnic/cultural interests; government/politics/law; health/medicine; history; how-to; nature/environment; popular culture; psychology; religious/inspirational; science/technology; self-help/personal improvement; sociology; spirituality; travel (armchair only, no how-to); true crime/investigative; women's issues/studies. **Considers these fiction areas:** Mystery/suspense; thriller.

    ⊶ This agency specializes in adult nonfiction and mysteries. Actively seeking narrative nonfiction. Does not want to receive novels other than mysteries and thrillers.

How to Contact For nonfiction, send proposal, chapter summary, sample chapter. For fiction, query first. No e-mail or fax queries. Considers simultaneous queries. Responds in 3 weeks to queries; 6 weeks to mss. Returns materials only with SASE. Obtains most new clients through recommendations from others, solicitations.
Recent Sales Sold 18 titles in the last year. *Indian Pipes*, by Cynthia Riggs (St. Martin's Press); *Overthrow*, by Stephen Kinzer (Henry Holt); *Don't Panic*, by Stanton Peele, PhD (Crown); *Overcoming Obesity with Surgery*, by James Weber, MD (M. Evans/Rowman & Littlefield); *How to Think Like a Terrorist*, by Mike German (Potomac Books).
Terms Agent receives 15% commission on domestic sales; 20% commission on foreign sales. Offers written contract. Charges clients for photocopying if it runs over $20.
Tips "Nonfiction authors and/or collaborators must be an authority in their subject area and have a platform. Send a SASE if you want a response."

◉ LOWENSTEIN-YOST ASSOCIATES

121 W. 27th St., Suite 601, New York NY 10001. (212)206-1630. Fax: (212)727-0280. Web site: www.lowensteinyost.com. **Contact:** Barbara Lowenstein. Estab. 1976. Member of AAR. Represents 150 clients. 20% of clients are new/unpublished writers. Currently handles: 60% nonfiction books; 40% novels.

Member Agents Barbara Lowenstein, president; Nancy Yost, vice president; Norman Kurz, business affairs; Rachel Vater.

Represents Nonfiction books, novels. **Considers these nonfiction areas:** Animals; anthropology/archaeology; biography/autobiography; business/economics; child guidance/parenting; creative nonfiction; current affairs; education; ethnic/cultural interests; government/politics/law; health/medicine; history; how-to; language/literature/criticism; memoirs; money/finance; multicultural; nature/environment; popular culture; psychology; self-help/personal improvement; sociology; travel; women's issues/studies; music; narrative nonfiction; science; film. **Considers these fiction areas:** Detective/police/crime; erotica; ethnic; feminist; historical; literary; mainstream/contemporary; mystery/suspense; romance (contemporary, historical, regency); thriller; women's.

    O₋ This agency specializes in health, business, creative nonfiction, literary fiction, and commercial fiction—especially suspense, crime, and women's issues. "We are a full-service agency, handling domestic and foreign rights, film rights, and audio rights to all of our books."

How to Contact Query with SASE. Prefers to read materials exclusively. For fiction, send outline and first chapter. *No unsolicited mss.* Responds in 6 weeks to queries. Returns materials only with SASE. Obtains most new clients through recommendations from others, solicitations, conferences.

Recent Sales Sold 75 titles in the last year. *6 Day Body Makeover*, by Michael Thurmond (Warner); *House of Dark Delights*, by Louisa Burton. Other clients include Ishmael Reed, Deborah Crombie, Stephanie Laurens, Perri O'Shaughnessy, Tim Cahill, Liz Carlyle, Valerie Frankel, Suzanne Enoch, Cordelia Fine, Rovenia Brock, Barbara Keerling.

Terms Agent receives 15% commission on domestic sales; 20% commission on foreign sales. Offers written contract. Charges for large photocopy batches, messenger service, international postage.

Writers' Conferences Malice Domestic; Bouchercon; RWA National Conference.

Tips "Know the genre you are working in and read!"

🌐 ✉ ANDREW LOWNIE LITERARY AGENCY, LTD.

17 Sutherland St., London SW1V4JU England. (44)(207)828-1274. Fax: (44)(207)828-7608. E-mail: lownie@glo balnet.co.uk. Web site: www.andrewlownie.co.uk. **Contact:** Andrew Lownie. Estab. 1988. Member of AAA. Represents 130 clients. 20% of clients are new/unpublished writers. Currently handles: 90% nonfiction books; 10% novels.

    • Prior to becoming an agent, Mr. Lownie was a journalist, bookseller, publisher, author of 12 books, and director of the Curtis Brown Agency.

Represents Nonfiction books. **Considers these nonfiction areas:** Biography/autobiography; current affairs; government/politics/law; history; memoirs; military/war; popular culture; true crime/investigative.

    O₋ This agent has wide publishing experience, extensive journalistic contacts, and a specialty in showbiz/celebrity memoir. Actively seeking showbiz memoirs, narrative histories, and biographies. Does not want to receive poetry, short stories, children's fiction, academic, or scripts.

How to Contact Query with SASE and/or IRCs. Submit outline, 1 sample chapter. Accepts e-mail and fax queries. Considers simultaneous queries. Responds in 1 week to queries; 1 month to mss. Returns materials only with SASE. Obtains most new clients through recommendations from others.

Recent Sales Sold 50 titles in the last year. *Avenging Justice*, by David Stafford (Time Warner); *Shadow of Solomon*, by Laurence Gardner; David Hasselhoff's autobiography. Other clients include Norma Major, Guy Bellamy, Joyce Cary estate, Lawrence James, Juliet Barker, Patrick McNee, Sir John Mills, Peter Evans, Desmond Seward, Laurence Gardner, Richard Rudgley, Timothy Good, Tom Levine.

Terms Agent receives 15% commission on domestic and foreign sales. Offers written contract; 30-day notice must be given to terminate contract. Charges clients for copying, postage, books for submission.

Tips "I prefer submissions in writing by letter."

✉ DONALD MAASS LITERARY AGENCY

121 W. 27th St., Suite 801, New York NY 10001. (212)727-8383. Web site: www.maassagency.com. Estab. 1980. Member of AAR, SFWA, MWA, RWA. Represents over 100 clients. 5% of clients are new/unpublished writers. Currently handles: 100% novels.

    • Prior to opening his agency, Mr. Maass served as an editor at Dell Publishing (New York) and as a reader at Gollancz (London). He also served as the president of AAR.

Member Agents Donald Maass (mainstream, literary, mystery/suspense, science fiction); Jennifer Jackson (commercial fiction, romance, science fiction, fantasy, mystery/suspense); Cameron McClure (literary, historical, mystery/suspense, fantasy, women's fiction, narrative nonfiction and projects with multicultural, international, and environmental themes); Stephen Barbara (literary fiction, young adult novels, narrative nonfiction, historical nonfiction, commercial fiction, topical nonfiction).

Represents Novels. **Considers these fiction areas:** Detective/police/crime; fantasy; historical; horror; literary;

mainstream/contemporary; mystery/suspense; psychic/supernatural; romance (historical, paranormal, time travel); science fiction; thriller; women's.

○⇥ This agency specializes in commercial fiction, especially science fiction, fantasy, romance, and suspense. Actively seeking to expand in literary fiction and women's fiction. Does not want to receive nonfiction, children's material, or poetry.

How to Contact Query with SASE, synopsis, first 5 pages. Returns material only with SASE. Considers simultaneous queries. Responds in 2 weeks to queries; 3 months to mss.

Recent Sales Sold over 100 titles in the last year. *The Shifting Tide*, by Anne Perry (Ballantine); *Midnight Plague*, by Gregg Keizer (G.P. Putnam's Sons).

Terms Agent receives 15% commission on domestic sales; 20% commission on foreign sales.

Writers' Conferences Donald Maass: World Science Fiction Convention; Frankfurt Book Fair; Pacific Northwest Writers Conference; Bouchercon. Jennifer Jackson: World Science Fiction Convention; RWA National Conference.

Tips "We are fiction specialists, also noted for our innovative approach to career planning. Few new clients are accepted, but interested authors should query with a SASE. Works with subagents in all principle foreign countries and Hollywood. No nonfiction or juvenile works will be considered."

⬤ GINA MACCOBY LITERARY AGENCY

P.O. Box 60, Chappaqua NY 10514. (914)238-5630. **Contact:** Gina Maccoby. Estab. 1986. Represents 25 clients. Currently handles: 33% nonfiction books; 33% novels; 33% juvenile books; illustrators of children's books.

Represents Nonfiction books, novels, juvenile books. **Considers these nonfiction areas:** Biography/autobiography; current affairs; ethnic/cultural interests; history; juvenile nonfiction; popular culture; women's issues/studies. **Considers these fiction areas:** Juvenile; literary; mainstream/contemporary; mystery/suspense; thriller; young adult.

How to Contact Query with SASE. Considers simultaneous queries. Responds in 3 months to queries. Returns materials only with SASE. Obtains most new clients through recommendations from clients and publishers.

Recent Sales Sold 21 titles in the last year.

Terms Agent receives 15% commission on domestic sales; 25% commission on foreign sales. Charges clients for photocopying. May recover certain costs, such as legal fees or the cost of shipping books by air to Europe or Japan.

⬤ CAROL MANN AGENCY

55 Fifth Ave., New York NY 10003. (212)206-5635. Fax: (212)675-4809. E-mail: will@carolmannagency.com. **Contact:** Will Sherlin. Estab. 1977. Member of AAR. Represents 200 clients. 15% of clients are new/unpublished writers. Currently handles: 70% nonfiction books; 30% novels.

Member Agents Carol Mann; Will Sherlin; Laura Yorke.

Represents Nonfiction books, novels. **Considers these nonfiction areas:** Anthropology/archaeology; art/architecture/design; biography/autobiography; business/economics; child guidance/parenting; current affairs; ethnic/cultural interests; government/politics/law; health/medicine; history; money/finance; psychology; self-help/personal improvement; sociology; sports; women's issues/studies; music. **Considers these fiction areas:** Literary; commercial.

○⇥ This agency specializes in current affairs, self-help, popular culture, psychology, parenting, and history. Does not want to receive genre fiction (romance, mystery, etc.).

How to Contact Query with outline/proposal, SASE. Responds in 3 weeks to queries.

Recent Sales Clients include novelists Paul Auster and Marita Golden; journalists Tim Egan, Hannah Storm, and Willow Bay; Pulitzer Prize-winner Fox Butterfield; bestselling essayist Shelby Steele; sociologist Dr. William Julius Wilson; economist Thomas Sowell; bestselling diet doctors Mary Dan and Michael Eades; ACLU president Nadine Strossen; pundit Mona Charen; memoirist Lauren Winner; photography project editors Rick Smolan and David Cohen (*America 24/7*); and Kevin Liles, executive vice president of Warner Music Group and former president of Def Jam Records.

Terms Agent receives 15% commission on domestic sales; 20% commission on foreign sales. Offers written contract.

Ⓝ 🌐 Ⓖ SARAH MANSON LITERARY AGENT

6 Totnes Walk, London N2 0AD United Kingdom. (44)(208)442-0396. E-mail: info@sarahmanson.com. Web site: www.sarahmanson.com. **Contact:** Sarah Manson. Estab. 2002. Currently handles: 100% juvenile books.

● Prior to opening her agency, Ms. Manson worked in academic and children's publishing for 10 years and was a chartered school librarian for 8 years.

○⇥ This agency specializes in fiction for children and young adults. No picture books. Does not want to receive submissions from writers outside the UK and the Republic of Ireland.

How to Contact See Web site for full submission guidelines.

Recent Sales This agency prefers not to give information on specific sales.

Terms Agent receives 10% commission on domestic sales; 20% commission on foreign sales. Offers written contract, binding for 1-month.

☑ MANUS & ASSOCIATES LITERARY AGENCY, INC.

425 Sherman Ave., Suite 200, Palo Alto CA 94306. (650)470-5151. Fax: (650)470-5159. E-mail: manuslit@manus lit.com. Web site: www.manuslit.com. **Contact:** Jillian Manus, Jandy Nelson, Stephanie Lee, Donna Levin, Penny Nelson. Alternate address: 445 Park Ave., New York NY 10022. (212)644-8020. Fax (212)644-3374. **Contact:** Janet Manus. Estab. 1985. Member of AAR. Represents 75 clients. 30% of clients are new/unpublished writers. Currently handles: 70% nonfiction books; 30% novels.

● Prior to becoming an agent, Jillian Manus was associate publisher of two national magazines and director of development at Warner Bros. and Universal Studios; Janet Manus has been a literary agent for 20 years.

Member Agents Jandy Nelson (self-help, health, memoirs, narrative nonfiction, women's fiction, literary fiction, multicultural fiction, thrillers); Stephanie Lee (self-help, narrative nonfiction, commercial literary fiction, quirky/edgy fiction, pop culture, pop science); Jillian Manus (political, memoirs, self-help, history, sports, women's issues, Latin fiction and nonfiction, thrillers); Penny Nelson (memoirs, self-help, sports, nonfiction); Dena Fischer (literary fiction, mainstream/commercial fiction, chick lit, women's fiction, historical fiction, ethnic/cultural fiction, narrative nonfiction, parenting, relationships, pop culture, health, sociology, psychology).

Represents Nonfiction books, novels. **Considers these nonfiction areas:** Biography/autobiography; business/economics; child guidance/parenting; current affairs; ethnic/cultural interests; health/medicine; how-to; memoirs; money/finance; nature/environment; popular culture; psychology; science/technology; self-help/personal improvement; women's issues/studies; Gen X and Gen Y issues; creative nonfiction. **Considers these fiction areas:** Literary; mainstream/contemporary; multicultural; mystery/suspense; thriller; women's; quirky/edgy fiction.

○─┐ This agency specializes in commercial literary fiction, narrative nonfiction, thrillers, health, pop psychology, and women's empowerment. "Our agency is unique in the way that we not only sell the material, but we edit, develop concepts, and participate in the marketing effort. We specialize in large, conceptual fiction and nonfiction, and always value a project that can be sold in the TV/feature film market." Actively seeking high-concept thrillers, commercial literary fiction, women's fiction, celebrity biographies, memoirs, multicultural fiction, popular health, women's empowerment, and mysteries. Does not want to receive horror, romance, science fiction/fantasy, westerns, young adult, children's, poetry, cookbooks, or magazine articles.

How to Contact Query with SASE. If requested, submit outline, 2-3 sample chapters. All queries should be sent to the California office. Accepts e-mail queries. No fax queries. Considers simultaneous queries. Responds in 3 months to queries and mss. Returns materials only with SASE. Obtains most new clients through recommendations from others, solicitations, conferences.

Recent Sales *Nothing Down for the 2000s* and *Multiple Streams of Income for the 2000s*, by Robert Allen; *Missed Fortune* and *Missed Fortune 101*, by Doug Andrew; *Cracking the Millionaire Code*, by Mark Victor Hansen and Robert Allen; *Stress Free for Good*, by Dr. Fred Luskin and Dr. Ken Pelletier; *The Mercy of Thin Air*, by Ronlyn Domangue; *The Fine Art of Small Talk*, by Debra Fine; *Bone Man of Bonares*, by Terry Tarnoff. Other clients include Dr. Lorraine Zappart, Marcus Allen, Carlton Stowers, Alan Jacobson, Ann Brandt, Dr. Richard Marrs, Mary LoVerde, Lisa Huang Fleishman, Judy Carter, Daryl Ott Underhill, Glen Kleier, Andrew X. Pham, Alexander Sanger, Lalita Tademy, Frank Baldwin, Katy Robinson, K.M. Soehnlein, Joelle Fraser, James Rogan, Jim Schutze, Deborah Santana, Karen Neuburger, Mira Tweti, Newt Gingrich, William Forstchen, Ken Walsh, Doug Wead, Nadine Schiff, Deborah Santana, Tom Dolby, Laurie Lynn Drummond, Christine Wicker, Wendy Dale, Mineko Iwasaki, Dorothy Ferebee, Reverand Run.

Terms Agent receives 15% commission on domestic sales; 20-25% commission on foreign sales. Offers written contract, binding for 2 years; 60-day notice must be given to terminate contract. Charges for photocopying and postage/UPS.

Writers' Conferences Maui Writers Conference; San Diego State University Writers' Conference; Willamette Writers Conference; BookExpo America; MEGA Book Marketing University.

Tips "Research agents using a variety of sources, including *LMP*, guides, *Publishers Weekly*, conferences, and even acknowledgements in books similar in tone to yours."

◐ MARCH TENTH, INC.

4 Myrtle St., Haworth NJ 07641-1740. (201)387-6551. Fax: (201)387-6552. E-mail: hchoron@aol.com. Web site: www.marchtenthinc.com. **Contact:** Harry Choron, vice president. Estab. 1982. Represents 40 clients. 30% of clients are new/unpublished writers. Currently handles: 75% nonfiction books; 25% novels.

Represents Nonfiction books, novels. **Considers these nonfiction areas:** Biography/autobiography; current affairs; health/medicine; history; humor/satire; language/literature/criticism; music/dance; popular culture; theater/film. **Considers these fiction areas:** Confession; ethnic; family saga; historical; humor/satire; literary; mainstream/contemporary.

o—₁ Writers must have professional expertise in their field. "We prefer to work with published/established writers."

How to Contact Query with SASE. Considers simultaneous queries. Responds in 1 month to queries. Returns materials only with SASE.

Recent Sales Sold 24 titles in the last year. *Art of the Chopper*, by Tom Zimberoff; *Bruce Springstein Live*, by Dave Marsh; *Complete Annotated Grateful Dead Lyrics*, by David Dodd.

Terms Agent receives 15% commission on domestic sales; 20% commission on foreign and dramatic rights sales. Charges clients for postage, photocopying, overseas phone expenses. Does not require expense money upfront.

◖ THE DENISE MARCIL LITERARY AGENCY, INC.

156 Fifth Ave., Suite 625, New York NY 10010. (212)337-3402. Fax: (212)727-2688. **Contact:** Denise Marcil, Maura Kye-Casella. Estab. 1977. Member of AAR. Represents 50 clients. 10% of clients are new/unpublished writers.

● Prior to opening her agency, Ms. Marcil served as an editorial assistant with Avon Books and as an assistant editor with Simon & Schuster.

Represents Commercial fiction and nonfiction books.

o—₁ Denise Marcil specializes in women's commercial fiction, thrillers, suspense, popular reference, how-to, self-help, health, business, and parenting. "I am looking for fresh, new voices in commercial women's fiction: chick lit, mom lit—stories that capture women's experiences today. I'd love to find a well-written historical novel about a real-life woman from another century." Maura Kye-Casella is seeking narrative nonfiction (adventure, pop culture, parenting, cookbooks, humor, memoir) and fiction (multicultural, paranormal, suspense, chick lit, well-written novels with an edgy voice, quirky characters, and/or unique plots and settings).

How to Contact Query with SASE.

Recent Sales Sold 43 titles in the last year. *My Grandmother's Bones*, by Jill Althouse Wood (Algonquin); *Silent Wager*, by Anita Bunkley (Kensington/Dafina); *Duke of Scandal*, by Adele Ashworth (Avon); *Big City, Bad Blood*, by Sean Chercover (Avon/Morrow); *Consigned to Death*, by Jane Cleland (St. Martin's Press); *The Liars Club*, by Peter Spiegelman (Knopf); *Tales from the Top: Ten Crucial Questions from the World's #1 Executive Coach*, by Graham Alexander (Nelson Business Books).

Terms Agent receives 15% commission on domestic sales; 20% commission on foreign sales. Offers written contract, binding for 2 years. 100% of business is derived from commissions on ms sales. Charges $100/year for postage, photocopying, long-distance calls, etc.

Writers' Conferences Pacific Northwest Writers Conference; RWA National Conference; Oregon Writers Colony.

◖ THE EVAN MARSHALL AGENCY

Six Tristam Place, Pine Brook NJ 07058-9445. (973)882-1122. Fax: (973)882-3099. E-mail: evanmarshall@theno velist.com. Web site: www.publishersmarketplace.com/members/evanmarshall. **Contact:** Evan Marshall. Estab. 1987. Member of AAR, MWA, RWA, Sisters in Crime. Currently handles: 100% novels.

● Prior to opening his agency, Mr. Marshall served as an editor with Houghton Mifflin, New American Library, Everest House, and Dodd, Mead & Co., and then worked as a literary agent at The Sterling Lord Agency.

Represents Novels. **Considers these fiction areas:** Action/adventure; erotica; ethnic; historical; horror; humor/satire; literary; mainstream/contemporary; mystery/suspense; religious/inspirational; romance (contemporary, gothic, historical, regency); science fiction; westerns/frontier.

How to Contact Query first with SASE; do not enclose material. No e-mail queries. Responds in 1 week to queries; 3 months to mss. Obtains most new clients through recommendations from others.

Recent Sales *Copycat*, by Erica Spindler (Mira); *The Closing*, by Rebecca Drake (Kensington); *Desperately Seeking Sushi*, by Jerrilyn Farmer (Morrow).

Terms Agent receives 15% commission on domestic sales; 20% commission on foreign sales. Offers written contract.

◖ MARTIN LITERARY MANAGEMENT

17328 Ventura Blvd., Suite 138, Encino CA 91316. (818)595-1130. Fax: (818)715-0418. E-mail: sharlene@martin literarymanagement.com. Web site: www.martinliterarymanagement.com. **Contact:** Sharlene Martin. Estab. 2002. 75% of clients are new/unpublished writers. Currently handles: 100% nonfiction books.

• Prior to becoming an agent, Ms. Martin worked in film/TV production and acquisitions.
Represents Nonfiction books. **Considers these nonfiction areas:** Biography/autobiography; business/economics; child guidance/parenting; current affairs; health/medicine; history; how-to; humor/satire; memoirs; popular culture; psychology; religious/inspirational; self-help/personal improvement; true crime/investigative; women's issues/studies.

Oₙ This agency has strong ties to film/TV. Actively seeking nonfiction that is highly commercial and that can be adapted to film.
How to Contact Query with SASE, outline, 2 sample chapters. Accepts e-mail queries. No fax queries. Considers simultaneous queries. Responds in 1 week to queries; 3-4 weeks to mss. Returns materials only with SASE. Obtains most new clients through recommendations from others.
Terms Agent receives 15% commission on domestic sales; 25% commission on foreign sales. Offers written contract, binding for 1 year; 1-month notice must be given to terminate contract. Charges author for postage and copying if material is not sent electronically.
Tips "Have a strong platform for nonfiction. Don't call. I gladly welcome e-mail. Do your homework prior to submission and only submit your best efforts."

HAROLD MATSON CO. INC.
276 Fifth Ave., New York NY 10001. (212)679-4490. Fax: (212)545-1224. **Contact:** Jonathan Matson. Estab. 1937. Member of AAR.
Member Agents Jonathan Matson (literary, adult); Ben Camardi (literary, adult, dramatic).

JED MATTES, INC.
2095 Broadway, Suite 302, New York NY 10023-2895. (212)595-5228. Fax: (212)595-5232. E-mail: general@jed mattes.com. **Contact:** Fred Morris. Member of AAR.
How to Contact Query with SASE.

MARGRET MCBRIDE LITERARY AGENCY
7744 Fay Ave., Suite 201, La Jolla CA 92037. (858)454-1550. Fax: (858)454-2156. E-mail: staff@mcbridelit.com. Web site: www.mcbrideliterary.com. **Contact:** Michael Daley, submissions manager. Estab. 1980. Member of AAR, Authors Guild. Represents 55 clients.
• Prior to opening her agency, Ms. McBride worked at Random House, Ballantine Books, and Warner Books.
Represents Nonfiction books, novels. **Considers these nonfiction areas:** Biography/autobiography; business/economics; cooking/foods/nutrition; current affairs; ethnic/cultural interests; government/politics/law; health/medicine; history; how-to; money/finance; music/dance; popular culture; psychology; science/technology; self-help/personal improvement; sociology; women's issues/studies; style. **Considers these fiction areas:** Action/adventure; detective/police/crime; ethnic; historical; humor/satire; literary; mainstream/contemporary; mystery/suspense; thriller; westerns/frontier.
Oₙ This agency specializes in mainstream fiction and nonfiction. Does not want to receive screenplays, romance, poetry, or children's/young adult.
How to Contact Query with synopsis, bio, SASE. No e-mail or fax queries. Considers simultaneous queries. Responds in 4-6 weeks to queries; 6-8 weeks to mss. Returns materials only with SASE.
Recent Sales *If Harry Potter Ran General Electric*, by Tom V. Morris (Doubleday/Currency); *Letting Go of Your Bananas*, by Dr. Daniel Drubin (Warner Business); *Become Who You Were Born to Be*, by Brian Souza (Harmony).
Terms Agent receives 15% commission on domestic sales; 25% commission on foreign sales. Charges for overnight delivery and photocopying.

THE MCCARTHY AGENCY, LLC
7 Allen St., Rumson NJ 07660. Phone/Fax: (732)741-3065. E-mail: mccarthylit@aol.com; ntfrost@hotmail.com. **Contact:** Shawna McCarthy. Estab. 1999. Member of AAR. Currently handles: 25% nonfiction books; 75% novels.
Member Agents Shawna McCarthy; Nahvae Frost.
Represents Nonfiction books, novels. **Considers these nonfiction areas:** Biography/autobiography; history; philosophy; science/technology. **Considers these fiction areas:** Fantasy; juvenile; mystery/suspense; romance; science fiction; women's.
How to Contact Query via e-mail or mail submission to 101 Clinton Ave., Apt. #2, Brooklyn NY 11205.

HELEN MCGRATH
1406 Idaho Ct., Concord CA 94521. (925)672-6211. Fax: (925)672-6383. E-mail: hmcgrath_lit@yahoo.com. **Contact:** Helen McGrath. Estab. 1977. Currently handles: 50% nonfiction books; 50% novels.

Represents Nonfiction books, novels. **Considers these nonfiction areas:** Biography/autobiography; business/economics; current affairs; health/medicine; history; how-to; military/war; psychology; self-help/personal improvement; sports; women's issues/studies. **Considers these fiction areas:** Detective/police/crime; literary; mainstream/contemporary; mystery/suspense; psychic/supernatural; romance; science fiction; thriller.

How to Contact Submit proposal with SASE. *No unsolicited mss.* Responds in 2 months to queries. Obtains most new clients through recommendations from others.

Terms Agent receives 15% commission on domestic sales. Offers written contract. Charges clients for photocopying.

MCINTOSH & OTIS

353 Lexington Ave., 15th Floor, New York NY 10016. Member of AAR.

Member Agents Jonathan Lyons; Elizabeth A. Winick; Eugene Winick; Edward Necarsulmer IV.

How to Contact Query with SASE, outline, sample chapters.

SALLY HILL MCMILLAN & ASSOCIATES, INC.

429 E. Kingston Ave., Charlotte NC 28203. (704)334-0897. Fax: (704)334-1897. **Contact:** Sally Hill McMillan. Member of AAR.

- ⚷ "We are not seeking new clients at this time." Agency specializes in Southern fiction, women's fiction, mystery, and practical nonfiction. No scripts, plays, poetry, children's books, cookbooks, fantasy, science fiction, or horror.

MENDEL MEDIA GROUP LLC

254 Canal St., Suite 4018, New York NY 10013. (646)239-9896. Fax: (212)697-7777. E-mail: scott@mendelmedia.com. Web site: www.mendelmedia.com. Estab. 2002. Member of AAR. Represents 40-60 clients.

- ● Prior to becoming an agent, Mr. Mendel was an academic. "I taught American literature, Yiddish, Jewish studies, and literary theory at the University of Chicago and the University of Illinois at Chicago while working on my PhD in English. I also worked as a freelance technical writer and as the managing editor of a healthcare magazine. In 1998, I began working for the late Jane Jordan Browne, a long-time agent in the book publishing world."

Represents Nonfiction books, novels, scholarly books (with potential for broad/popular appeal). **Considers these nonfiction areas:** Americana; animals; anthropology/archaeology; art/architecture/design; biography/autobiography; business/economics; child guidance/parenting; cooking/foods/nutrition; current affairs; education; ethnic/cultural interests; gardening; gay/lesbian issues; government/politics/law; health/medicine; history; how-to; humor/satire; language/literature/criticism; memoirs; military/war; money/finance; multicultural; music/dance; nature/environment; philosophy; popular culture; psychology; recreation; regional; religious/inspirational; science/technology; self-help/personal improvement; sex; sociology; software; spirituality; sports; true crime/investigative; women's issues/studies; Jewish topics; creative nonfiction. **Considers these fiction areas:** Action/adventure; contemporary issues; detective/police/crime; erotica; ethnic; feminist; gay/lesbian; glitz; historical; humor/satire; juvenile; literary; mainstream/contemporary; mystery/suspense; picture books; religious/inspirational; romance; sports; thriller; young adult; Jewish fiction.

- ⚷ "I am interested in major works of history, current affairs, biography, business, politics, economics, science, major memoirs, narrative nonfiction, and other sorts of general nonfiction. Actively seeking new, major, or definitive work on a subject of broad interest, or a controversial, but authoritative, new book on a subject that affects many people's lives. I also represent more light-hearted nonfiction projects, such as gift or novelty books, when they suit the market particularly well." Does not want queries about projects written years ago that were unsuccessfully shopped to a long list of trade publishers by either the author or another agent. "I am specifically not interested in reading short, category romances (regency, time travel, paranormal, etc.), horror novels, supernatural stories, poetry, original plays, or film scripts."

How to Contact Query with SASE. Do not e-mail or fax queries. For nonfiction, include a complete, fully-edited book proposal with sample chapters. For fiction, include a complete synopsis and no more than 20 pages of sample text. Responds in 2 weeks to queries; 4-6 weeks to mss. Returns materials only with SASE. Obtains most new clients through recommendations from others.

Terms Agent receives 15% commission on domestic sales; 20% commission on foreign sales. Offers written contract, binding for 2 years; 1-month notice must be given to terminate contract. Charges clients for ms duplication, expedited delivery services (when necessary), any overseas shipping, telephone calls/faxes necessary for marketing the author's foreign rights.

Writers' Conferences BookExpo America; Frankfurt Book Fair; London Book Fair; RWA National Conference; Modern Language Association Convention; Jerusalem Book Fair.

Tips "While I am not interested in being flattered by a prospective client, it does matter to me that she knows why she is writing to me in the first place. Is one of my clients a colleague of hers? Has she read a book by one of my clients that led her to believe I might be interested in her work? Authors of descriptive nonfiction should have real credentials and expertise in their subject areas, either as academics, journalists, or policy experts, and authors of prescriptive nonfiction should have legitimate expertise and considerable experience communicating their ideas in seminars and workshops, in a successful business, through the media, etc.''

⬤ MENZA-BARRON AGENCY

1170 Broadway, Suite 807, New York NY 10001. (212)889-6850. **Contact:** Claudia Menza, Manie Barron. Estab. 1983. Member of AAR. Represents 100 clients. 50% of clients are new/unpublished writers.
Represents Nonfiction books, novels. **Considers these nonfiction areas:** Current affairs; education; ethnic/cultural interests (especially African-American); health/medicine; history; multicultural; music/dance; photography; psychology; theater/film.

　　O⊸ This agency specializes in editorial assistance and African-American fiction and nonfiction.
How to Contact Query with SASE. Responds in 2-4 weeks to queries; 2-4 months to mss. Returns materials only with SASE.
Recent Sales This agency prefers not to share information on specific sales.
Terms Agent receives 15% commission on domestic sales; 20% commission on foreign and dramatic rights sales. Offers written contract.

⬤ DORIS S. MICHAELS LITERARY AGENCY, INC.

1841 Broadway, Suite 903, New York NY 10023. (212)265-9474. Fax: (212)265-9480. E-mail: query@dsmagenecy.com. Web site: www.dsmagency.com. **Contact:** Doris S. Michaels, president. Estab. 1994. Member of AAR, WNBA.
Represents Novels. **Considers these fiction areas:** Literary (with commercial appeal and strong screen potential).
How to Contact Query by e-mail; see submission guidelines on Web site. Obtains most new clients through recommendations from others, conferences.
Terms Agent receives 15% commission on domestic sales; 20% commission on foreign sales. Offers written contract, binding for 1 year; 1-month notice must be given to terminate contract. 100% of business is derived from commissions on ms sales. Charges clients for office expenses, not to exceed $150 without written permission.
Writers' Conferences BookExpo America; Frankfurt Book Fair; London Book Fair; Maui Writers Conference.

⬤ MARTHA MILLARD LITERARY AGENCY

50 W. 67th St., #1G, New York NY 10023. (212)787-7769. Fax: (212)787-7867. E-mail: marmillink@aol.com. **Contact:** Martha Millard. Estab. 1980. Member of AAR, SFWA. Represents 50 clients. Currently handles: 25% nonfiction books; 65% novels; 10% story collections.

　　● Prior to becoming an agent, Ms. Millard worked in editorial departments of several publishers and was vice president at another agency for 4½ years.
Represents Nonfiction books, novels. **Considers these nonfiction areas:** Art/architecture/design; biography/autobiography; business/economics; child guidance/parenting; cooking/foods/nutrition; current affairs; education; ethnic/cultural interests; health/medicine; history; how-to; juvenile nonfiction; memoirs; money/finance; music/dance; New Age/metaphysics; photography; popular culture; psychology; self-help/personal improvement; theater/film; true crime/investigative; women's issues/studies. **Considers these fiction areas:** Fantasy; mystery/suspense; romance; science fiction.
How to Contact No unsolicited queries. No e-mail or fax queries. Returns materials only with SASE. Obtains most new clients through recommendations from others.
Recent Sales *Nazi Art: The Secret of Post-War History*, by Gregory Maertz (Yale University Press); *Playing With the HP Way*, by Peter Burrows (John Wiley & Sons); *Restore Yourself*, by James Simm and Victoria Houston (Berkley).
Terms Agent receives 15% commission on domestic sales; 20% commission on foreign sales. Offers written contract.

⬤ THE MILLER AGENCY

One Sheridan Square, #32, New York NY 10014. (212) 206-0913. Fax: (212) 206-1473. E-mail: angela@milleragency.net. Web site: www.milleragency.net. **Contact:** Angela Miller, Sharon Bowers. Estab. 1990. Represents 100 clients. 5% of clients are new/unpublished writers.
Represents Nonfiction books. **Considers these nonfiction areas:** Anthropology/archaeology; art/architecture/design; biography/autobiography; business/economics; child guidance/parenting; cooking/foods/nutrition; current affairs; ethnic/cultural interests; gay/lesbian issues; health/medicine; language/literature/criticism; New Age/metaphysics; psychology; self-help/personal improvement; sports; women's issues/studies.

0━ This agency specializes in nonfiction, multicultural arts, psychology, self-help, cookbooks, biography, travel, memoir, and sports. Fiction is considered selectively.

How to Contact Query with SASE, outline, a few sample chapters. Considers simultaneous queries. Responds in 1 week to queries. Obtains most new clients through referrals.

Recent Sales Sold 25 titles in the last year.

Terms Agent receives 15% commission on domestic sales; 20-25% commission on foreign sales. Offers written contract, binding for 2 years; 2-month notice must be given to terminate contract. 100% of business is derived from commissions on ms sales. Charges clients for postage (express mail or messenger services) and photocopying.

◎ MOORE LITERARY AGENCY

10 State St., Newburyport MA 01950. (978)465-9015. Fax: (978)465-8817. E-mail: cmoore@moorelit.com. **Contact:** Claudette Moore. Estab. 1989. 10% of clients are new/unpublished writers. Currently handles: 100% nonfiction books.

Represents Nonfiction books. **Considers these nonfiction areas:** Computers/electronic; technology.

0━ This agency specializes in trade computer books (90% of titles).

How to Contact Submit outline. Obtains most new clients through recommendations from others, conferences.

Recent Sales *Windows XP Timesaving Techniques for Dummies*, by Woody Leonhard (Wiley); *Expert One-on-One Microsoft Access Application Development*, by Helen Feddema (Wiley); *Thinking in C++, Vol. 2*, by Bruce Eckel and Chuck Allison (Prentice Hall); *Microsoft Windows XP Inside Out, 2nd Ed.*, by Ed Bolt, Carl Siechert, and Craig Stinson (Microsoft Press).

Terms Agent receives 15% commission on domestic sales; 15% commission on foreign sales and dramatic rights sales. Offers written contract.

◙ PATRICIA MOOSBRUGGER LITERARY AGENCY

165 Bennet Ave., #6M, New York NY 10040. **Contact:** Patricia Moosbrugger. Member of AAR.

How to Contact Query with SASE.

◙ HOWARD MORHAIM LITERARY AGENCY

11 John St., Suite 407, New York NY 10038-4067. (212)529-4433. Fax: (212)995-1112. Member of AAR.

Represents Young adult fiction.

How to Contact Query with SASE.

◙ WILLIAM MORRIS AGENCY, INC.

1325 Avenue of the Americas, New York NY 10019. (212)586-5100. Fax: (212)246-3583. Web site: www.wma.c om. Alternate address: One William Morris Place, Beverly Hills CA 90212. (310)859-4000. Fax: (310)859-4462. Member of AAR.

Member Agents Owen Laster; Jennifer Rudolph Walsh; Suzanne Gluck; Joni Evans; Tracy Fisher; Mel Berger; Jay Mandel; Peter Franklin; Lisa Grubka; Jonathan Pecursky.

Represents Nonfiction books, novels.

How to Contact Query with synopsis, publication history, SASE. Considers simultaneous queries.

Recent Sales This agency prefers not to share information on specific sales.

Terms Agent receives 15% commission on domestic sales; 20% commission on foreign sales.

◙ HENRY MORRISON, INC.

105 S. Bedford Rd., Suite 306A, Mt. Kisco NY 10549. (914)666-3500. Fax: (914)241-7846. **Contact:** Henry Morrison. Estab. 1965. Signatory of WGA. Represents 53 clients. 5% of clients are new/unpublished writers. Currently handles: 5% nonfiction books; 95% novels.

Represents Nonfiction books, novels. **Considers these nonfiction areas:** Anthropology/archaeology; biography/autobiography; government/politics/law; history. **Considers these fiction areas:** Action/adventure; detective/police/crime; family saga; historical.

How to Contact Query with SASE. Responds in 2 weeks to queries; 3 months to mss. Obtains most new clients through recommendations from others.

Recent Sales Sold 16 titles in the last year. *The Ambler Warning*, by Robert Ludlum (St. Martin's Press); *The Bravo Testament*, by Eric Van Lustbader (Forge); *White Flag Down*, by Joel N. Ross (Doubleday); *Encyclopedia of World War II*, by Alan Axelrod (Facts on File); *The Lucifer Gospel*, by Paul Christopher (Signet); *The Midas Touch*, by Jon J. Land (Tor); *Your Cat Is Into You*, by Molly Katz (Morrow); *Son of a Gun*, by Randye Lordon (St. Martin's Press); *Rage Therapy*, by Dan Kalla (Forge). Other clients include Samuel R. Delany, Daniel Cohen, Brian Garfield, Gayle Lynds, Christopher Hyde.

Terms Agent receives 15% commission on domestic sales; 25% commission on foreign sales. Charges clients for ms copies, bound galleys, finished books for submissions to publishers, movie producers and foreign publishers.

◙ DEE MURA LITERARY

269 West Shore Dr., Massapequa NY 11758-8225. (516)795-1616. Fax: (516)795-8797. E-mail: samurai5@ix.netc om.com. **Contact:** Dee Mura, Karen Roberts, Frank Nakamura, Brian Hertler, Kimiko Nakamura. Estab. 1987. Signatory of WGA. 50% of clients are new/unpublished writers.

• Prior to opening her agency, Ms. Mura was a public relations executive with a roster of film and entertainment clients and worked in editorial for major weekly news magazines.

Represents Nonfiction books, novels, juvenile books, scholarly books, feature film, TV scripts, episodic drama, sitcom, animation, documentary, miniseries, variety show. **Considers these nonfiction areas:** Agriculture/ horticulture; animals; anthropology/archaeology; biography/autobiography; business/economics; child guidance/parenting; computers/electronic; current affairs; education; ethnic/cultural interests; gay/lesbian issues; government/politics/law; health/medicine; history; how-to; humor/satire; juvenile nonfiction; memoirs; military/war; money/finance; nature/environment; science/technology; self-help/personal improvement; sociology; sports; travel; true crime/investigative; women's issues/studies. **Considers these fiction areas:** Action/ adventure; contemporary issues; detective/police/crime; ethnic; experimental; family saga; fantasy; feminist; gay/lesbian; glitz; historical; humor/satire; juvenile; literary; mainstream/contemporary; mystery/suspense; psychic/supernatural; regional; romance (contemporary, gothic, historical, regency); science fiction; sports; thriller; westerns/frontier; young adult; espionage; political. **Considers these script subject areas:** Action/ adventure; cartoon/animation; comedy; contemporary issues; detective/police/crime; family saga; fantasy; feminist; gay/lesbian; glitz; historical; horror; juvenile; mainstream; mystery/suspense; psychic/supernatural; religious/inspirational; romantic comedy; romantic drama; science fiction; sports; teen; thriller; western/frontier.

Oー "We work on everything, but are especially interested in literary fiction, commercial fiction/nonfiction, thrillers/espionage, humor/drama (we love to laugh and cry), self-help, inspirational, medical, scholarly, true life stories, true crime, and women's stories/issues." Actively seeking unique nonfiction mss and proposals, novelists who are great storytellers, and contemporary writers with distinct voices and passion. Does not want to receive ideas for sitcoms, novels, films, etc., or queries without SASEs.

How to Contact Query with SASE. Accepts e-mail queries (no attachments). No fax queries. Considers simultaneous queries. Only responds if interested. Returns materials only with SASE. Obtains most new clients through recommendations from others, queries.

Recent Sales Sold over 40 titles and 35 scripts in the last year.

Terms Agent receives 15% commission on domestic sales; 20% commission on foreign sales. Offers written contract. Charges clients for photocopying, mailing expenses, overseas/long distance phone calls/faxes.

Tips "Please include a paragraph on the writer's background, even if the writer has no literary background, and a brief synopsis of the project. We enjoy well-written query letters that tell us about the project and the author."

◙ ERIN MURPHY LITERARY AGENCY

2700 Woodlands Village, #300-458, Flagstaff AZ 86001-7172. (928)525-2056. Fax: (928)525-2480. **Contact:** Erin Murphy. Member of AAR.

Oー This agency only represents children's books. "We do not accept unsolicited manuscripts or queries. We consider new clients by referral or personal contact only."

▒ ◙ MUSE LITERARY MANAGEMENT

189 Waverly Place, #4, New York NY 10014. (212)925-3721. E-mail: museliterarymgmt@aol.com. **Contact:** Deborah Carter. Estab. 1998. Member of Author's Guild, SCBWI, International Thriller Writers. Represents 10 clients. 80% of clients are new/unpublished writers. Currently handles: 9% nonfiction books; 55% novels; 9% story collections; 27% juvenile books.

• Prior to starting her agency, Ms. Carter trained with an AAR literary agent and worked in the music business in artist management and as a talent scout for record companies. She has a BA in English and music from Washington Square University College at NYU.

Represents Novels, short story collections, novellas, juvenile books. **Considers these nonfiction areas:** Narrative-only nonfiction (memoir, sports, outdoors, music, writing). Please query other narrative nonfiction subjects. **Considers these fiction areas:** Action/adventure; detective/police/crime; experimental; juvenile; literary; mainstream/contemporary; mystery/suspense; picture books; thriller; young adult; espionage; middle-grade novels; literary short story collections.

Oー Specializes in ms development, the sale and administration of print, performance, and foreign rights to literary works, and post-publication publicity and appearances. Actively seeking progressive, African-American, and multicultural fiction for adults and children in the US market. Does not want category fiction (romance, chick lit, fantasy, science fiction), or books with any religious or spiritual matter.

How to Contact Query via e-mail (no attachments). Discards unwanted queries. Responds in 2 weeks to queries; 2-3 weeks to mss. Obtains most new clients through recommendations from others, conferences.

Recent Sales Sold 3 titles in the last year. *Heat Sync* and *The Fund*, by Wes DeMott (Leisure Books); foreign rights sales. Other clients include Anne Shelby, Samantha Talbot.

Terms Agent receives 15% commission on domestic sales; 20% commission on foreign sales. Offers written contract, binding for 1 year; 1-day notice must be given to terminate contract. Sometimes charges for postage and photocopying. All expenses are subject to client approval.

Writers' Conferences BookExpo America; Bouchercon; SCBWI Winter Conference.

◙ JEAN V. NAGGAR LITERARY AGENCY, INC.

216 E. 75th St., Suite 1E, New York NY 10021. (212)794-1082. **Contact:** Jean Naggar. Estab. 1978. Member of AAR, PEN, Women's Media Group, Women's Forum. Represents 80 clients. 20% of clients are new/unpublished writers. Currently handles: 35% nonfiction books; 45% novels; 15% juvenile books; 5% scholarly books.

• Ms. Naggar has served as president of AAR.

Member Agents Jennifer Weltz, director (subsidiary rights, children's books); Alice Tasman, senior agent (commercial and literary fiction, thrillers, narrative nonfiction); Mollie Glick, agent (literary and commercial fiction with a unique premise/voice, literary and practical nonfiction); Jessica Regel, agent (young adult fiction and nonfiction).

Represents Nonfiction books, novels. **Considers these nonfiction areas:** Biography/autobiography; child guidance/parenting; current affairs; government/politics/law; health/medicine; history; juvenile nonfiction; memoirs; New Age/metaphysics; psychology; religious/inspirational; self-help/personal improvement; sociology; travel; women's issues/studies. **Considers these fiction areas:** Action/adventure; detective/police/crime; ethnic; family saga; feminist; historical; literary; mainstream/contemporary; mystery/suspense; psychic/supernatural; thriller.

○┅ This agency specializes in mainstream fiction and nonfiction and literary fiction with commercial potential.

How to Contact Query with SASE. Prefers to read materials exclusively. No e-mail or fax queries. Responds in 1 day to queries; 2 months to mss. Returns materials only with SASE. Obtains most new clients through recommendations from others.

Recent Sales *Dark Angels*, by Karleen Koen; *Poison*, by Susan Fromberg Schaeffer; *Unauthorized*, by Kristin McCloy; *Voyage of the Sea Turtle: The Search for the Last Dinosaurs*, by Carl Safina; *Enola Holmes*, by Nancy Springer; *The Liar's Diary*, by Patry Francis; *Closing Costs*, by Seth Margolis; *Blind Faith*, by Richard Sloan.

Terms Agent receives 15% commission on domestic sales; 20% commission on foreign sales. Offers written contract. Charges for overseas mailing, messenger services, book purchases, long-distance telephone, photocopying—all deductible from royalties received.

Writers' Conferences Willamette Writers Conference; Pacific Northwest Writers Conference; Bread Loaf Writers Conference; Marymount Manhattan Writers Conference; SEAK Medical & Legal Fiction Writing Conference.

Tips "Use a professional presentation. Because of the avalanche of unsolicited queries that flood the agency every week, we have had to modify our policy. We will now only guarantee to read and respond to queries from writers who come recommended by someone we know. Our areas are general fiction and nonfiction—no children's books by unpublished writers, no multimedia, no screenplays, no formula fiction, and no mysteries by unpublished writers. We recommend patience and fortitude: the courage to be true to your own vision, the fortitude to finish a novel and polish it again and again before sending it out, and the patience to accept rejection gracefully and wait for the stars to align themselves appropriately for success."

◙ NELSON LITERARY AGENCY

1020 15th St., Suite 26L, Denver CO 80202. (303)463-5301. E-mail: query@nelsonagency.com. Web site: www.nelsonagency.com. **Contact:** Kristin Nelson. Estab. 2002. Member of AAR.

• Prior to opening her own agency, Ms. Nelson worked as a literary scout and subrights agent for agent Jody Rein.

Represents Novels, select nonfiction. **Considers these nonfiction areas:** Memoirs; narrative nonfiction. **Considers these fiction areas:** Literary; romance (includes fantasy with romantic elements, science fiction, young adult); women's; chick lit (includes mysteries); commercial/mainstream.

○┅ NLA specializes in representing commercial fiction and high caliber literary fiction. Actively seeking Latina writers who tackle contemporary issues in a modern voice (think *Dirty Girls Social Club*). Does not want short story collections, mysteries (except chick lit), thrillers, Christian, horror, or children's picture books.

How to Contact Query by e-mail only.

Recent Sales *Plan B*, by Jennifer O'Connell (MTV/Pocket Books); *Code of Love*, by Cheryl Sawyer (NAL/Penguin Group); *Once Upon Stilettos*, by Shanna Swendson (Ballantine); *I'd Tell You I Love You But Then I'd Have to Kill You*, by Ally Carter (Hyperion Children's); *An Accidental Goddess*, by Linnea Sinclair (Bantam Spectra). Other clients include Paula Reed, Becky Motew, Jack McCallum, Jana Deleon.

◪ NEW BRAND AGENCY GROUP, LLC

E-mail: mark@literaryagent.net. Web site: www.literaryagent.net. **Contact:** Mark Ryan. Estab. 1994. Represents 3 clients. Currently handles: 33% nonfiction books; 33% novels; 33% juvenile books.

- Mr. Ryan handles fiction and nonfiction with bestseller and/or high commercial potential.

Represents Nonfiction books, novels, juvenile books. **Considers these nonfiction areas:** Biography/autobiography; business/economics; juvenile nonfiction; memoirs; popular culture; psychology; religious/inspirational; self-help/personal improvement; sex; spirituality; women's issues/studies; body and soul; health; humor; family; finance; fitness; gift/novelty; leadership; men's issues; parenting; relationships; success. **Considers these fiction areas:** Fantasy; historical; horror; juvenile; literary; mainstream/contemporary; mystery/suspense; romance (mainstream); science fiction; thriller; cross-genre; magical realism; supernatural.

  ○▄ New Brand Agency is currently closed to submissions. Check Web site for more details. "We only work with authors we are passionate about."

How to Contact Accepts e-mail queries only (submit online). Responds in 1 week to mss; 2 days to queries if interested. Obtains most new clients through queries.

Recent Sales *Black Valley*, by Jim Brown (Ballantine); *The Marriage Plan*, by Aggie Jordan, PhD (Broadway/Bantam); *Mother to Daughter*, by Harry Harrison (Workman); *The She*, by Carol Plum-Ucci (Harcourt).

Terms Agent receives 15% commission on domestic sales. Offers written contract, binding for 6 months; 1-month notice must be given to terminate contract. Charges for postage and phone costs after sale of the project.

◐ NEW ENGLAND PUBLISHING ASSOCIATES, INC.

P.O. Box 5, Chester CT 06412-0645. (860)345-READ or (860)345-4976. Fax: (860)345-3660. E-mail: nepa@nepa.com. Web site: www.nepa.com. **Contact:** Elizabeth Frost-Knappman, Edward W. Knappman, Kristine Schiavi, Victoria Harlow. Estab. 1983. Member of AAR. Represents 125-150 clients. 15% of clients are new/unpublished writers.

Represents Nonfiction books. **Considers these nonfiction areas:** Biography/autobiography; business/economics; child guidance/parenting; government/politics/law; health/medicine; history; language/literature/criticism; military/war; money/finance; nature/environment; psychology; science/technology; self-help/personal improvement; sports; true crime/investigative; women's issues/studies; reference.

  ○▄ This agency specializes in adult nonfiction of serious purpose.

How to Contact Send outline/proposal, SASE. Accepts e-mail and fax queries. Considers simultaneous queries. Responds in 1 month to queries; 5 weeks to mss. Returns materials only with SASE.

Recent Sales Sold 45 titles in the last year. *The Rise of the Animal Kingdom*, by Wallace Arthur (Farrar, Straus & Giroux); *Honor the Devil: The Secret Alliance Between the World's Most Notorious Pirates and America's First Governors*, by Doug Burgess (McGraw-Hill); *The Financial Founding Fathers*, by David Cohen and Robert Wrights (University of Chicago Press); *The Low Glycemic Shock Diet*, by Dr. Rob Thompson (Contemporary).

Terms Agent receives 15% commission on domestic sales; 20% commission on foreign sales. Offers written contract, binding for 6 months. Charges clients for copying.

Writers' Conferences BookExpo America; London Book Fair.

Tips "Send us a well-written proposal that clearly identifies your audience—who will buy this book and why. Check our Web site for tips on proposals and advice on how to market your books. Revise, revise, revise, but never give up. We don't."

◖ HAROLD OBER ASSOCIATES

425 Madison Ave., New York NY 10017. (212)759-8600. Fax: (212)759-9428. Estab. 1929. Member of AAR. Represents 250 clients. 10% of clients are new/unpublished writers. Currently handles: 35% nonfiction books; 50% novels; 15% juvenile books.

Member Agents Phyllis Westberg; Pamela Malpas; Knox Burger; Craig Tenney (not accepting new clients).

Represents Nonfiction books, novels, juvenile books.

  ○▄ "We consider all subjects/genres of fiction and nonfiction."

How to Contact Submit query letter only with SASE. No e-mail or fax queries. Responds as promptly as possible. Obtains most new clients through recommendations from others.

Terms Agent receives 15% commission on domestic sales; 20% commission on foreign sales. Charges clients for photocopying and express mail/package services.

◖ FIFI OSCARD AGENCY, INC.

110 W. 40th St., 16th Floor, New York NY 10018. (212)764-1100. Fax: (212)840-5019. E-mail: agency@fifioscard.com. Web site: www.fifioscard.com. **Contact:** Literary Department. Estab. 1978. Signatory of WGA.

Member Agents Peter Sawyer; Carmen La Via; Kevin McShane; Ivy Fischer Stone; Carolyn French; Jerry Rudes; Laura R. Paperny.

Represents Nonfiction books, novels, stage plays. **Considers these nonfiction areas:** Business/economics (finance); history; religious/inspirational; science/technology; sports; women's issues/studies; African American; biography; body/mind/spirit; health; lifestyle; cookbooks. **Considers these fiction areas:** Fantasy; mystery/suspense; science fiction.

How to Contact Query through online submission form. *No unsolicited mss.* Responds in 2 weeks to queries.

Recent Sales *Beating Around the Bush*, by Art Buchwald (Seven Stories); *To the Mountaintop*, by Stewart Burns (HarperSanFrancisco); *Perfect . . . I'm Not*, by David Wells and Chris Kreski (Wm. Morrow).

Terms Agent receives 15% commission on domestic sales; 20% commission on foreign sales; 10% commission on dramatic rights sales. Charges clients for photocopying expenses.

◗ PARAVIEW, INC.

40 Florence Circle, Bracey VA 23919. Phone/Fax: (434)636-4138. E-mail: lhagan@paraview.com. Web site: www.paraview.com. **Contact:** Lisa Hagan. Estab. 1988. Represents 75 clients. 15% of clients are new/unpublished writers. Currently handles: 100% nonfiction books.

Represents Nonfiction books. **Considers these nonfiction areas:** Agriculture/horticulture; animals; anthropology/archaeology; art/architecture/design; biography/autobiography; business/economics; cooking/foods/nutrition; current affairs; education; ethnic/cultural interests; gay/lesbian issues; government/politics/law; health/medicine; history; how-to; humor/satire; language/literature/criticism; memoirs; military/war; money/finance; multicultural; nature/environment; New Age/metaphysics; philosophy; popular culture; psychology; recreation; regional; religious/inspirational; science/technology; self-help/personal improvement; sex; sociology; spirituality; travel; true crime/investigative; women's issues/studies; Americana; creative nonfiction.

　　O╕ This agency specializes in business, science, gay/lesbian, spiritual, New Age, and self-help nonfiction.

How to Contact Submit query, synopsis, author bio via e-mail. Responds in 1 month to queries; 3 months to mss. Obtains most new clients through recommendations from editors and current clients.

Recent Sales Sold 40 titles in the last year. *The High Purpose Company*, by Christine Arena (Collins Business); *Never Throw Rice at a Pisces*, by Stacey Wolf (Thomas Dunne Books); *The Whole World Was Watching*, by Romaine Patterson and Patrick Hinds (Alyson Books); *Babylon's Ark*, by Graham Spence and Lawrence Anthony (Thomas Dunne Books); *From Zero to Zillionaire*, by Chellie Campbell (Sourcebooks); *The Encyclopedia of Magickal Ingredients*, by Lexa Rosean (Pocket Books).

Terms Agent receives 15% commission on domestic sales; 20% commission on foreign sales.

Writers' Conferences BookExpo America; London Book Fair; E3—Electronic Entertainment Exposition.

Tips "New writers should have their work edited, critiqued, and carefully reworked prior to submission. First contact should be via e-mail."

◗ THE RICHARD PARKS AGENCY

Box 693, Salem NY 12865. Web site: www.richardparksagency.com. **Contact:** Richard Parks. Estab. 1988. Member of AAR. Currently handles: 55% nonfiction books; 40% novels; 5% story collections.

Represents Nonfiction books, novels. **Considers these nonfiction areas:** Animals; anthropology/archaeology; art/architecture/design; biography/autobiography; business/economics; child guidance/parenting; cooking/foods/nutrition; crafts/hobbies; current affairs; ethnic/cultural interests; gardening; gay/lesbian issues; government/politics/law; health/medicine; history; how-to; humor/satire; language/literature/criticism; memoirs; military/war; money/finance; music/dance; nature/environment; popular culture; psychology; science/technology; self-help/personal improvement; sociology; theater/film; travel; women's issues/studies.

　　O╕ Actively seeking nonfiction. Considers fiction by referral only. Does not want to receive unsolicited material.

How to Contact Query with SASE. No e-mail or fax queries. Considers simultaneous queries Responds in 2 weeks to queries. Returns materials only with SASE. Obtains most new clients through recommendations.

Terms Agent receives 15% commission on domestic sales; 20% commission on foreign sales. Charges clients for photocopying or any unusual expense incurred at the writer's request.

◗ L. PERKINS ASSOCIATES

5800 Arlington Ave., Riverdale NY 10471. (718)543-5344. Fax: (718)543-5354. E-mail: lperkinsagency@yahoo.com. **Contact:** Lori Perkins, Amy Stout (astoutlperkinsagency@yahoo.com). Estab. 1990. Member of AAR. Represents 50 clients. 10% of clients are new/unpublished writers.

　　• Ms. Perkins has been an agent for 18 years. She is also the author of *The Insider's Guide to Getting an Agent* (Writer's Digest Books).

Represents Nonfiction books, novels. **Considers these nonfiction areas:** Popular culture. **Considers these fiction areas:** Fantasy; horror; literary (dark); science fiction.

　　O╕ Most of Ms. Perkins' clients write both fiction and nonfiction. "This combination keeps my clients
　　　　publishing for years. I am also a published author, so I know what it takes to write a good book."

Actively seeking a Latino *Gone With the Wind* and *Waiting to Exhale,* and urban ethnic horror. Does not want to receive anything outside of the above categories (westerns, romance, etc.).

How to Contact Query with SASE. Considers simultaneous queries. Responds in 6 weeks to queries; 3 months to mss. Returns materials only with SASE. Obtains most new clients through recommendations from others, solicitations, conferences.

Recent Sales Sold 100 titles in the last year. *How to Make Love Like a Porn Star: A Cautionary Tale*, by Jenna Jameson (Reagan Books); *Dear Mom, I Always Wanted You to Know*, by Lisa Delman (Perigee Books); *The Illustrated Ray Bradbury*, by Jerry Weist (Avon); *The Poet in Exile*, by Ray Manzarek (Avalon); *Behind Sad Eyes: The Life of George Harrison*, by Marc Shapiro (St. Martin's Press).

Terms Agent receives 15% commission on domestic sales; 20% commission on foreign sales. No written contract. Charges clients for photocopying.

Writers' Conferences San Diego State University Writers' Conference; NECON; BookExpo America; World Fantasy Convention.

Tips ''Research your field and contact professional writers' organizations to see who is looking for what. Finish your novel before querying agents. Read my book, *An Insider's Guide to Getting an Agent*, to get a sense of how agents operate.''

☑ STEPHEN PEVNER, INC.

382 Lafayette St., 8th Floor, New York NY 10003. (212)674-8403. Fax: (212)529-3692. E-mail: spevner@aol.com. **Contact:** Stephen Pevner.

Represents Nonfiction books, novels, feature film, TV scripts, TV movie of the week, episodic drama, animation, documentary, miniseries. **Considers these nonfiction areas:** Biography/autobiography; ethnic/cultural interests; gay/lesbian issues; history; humor/satire; language/literature/criticism; memoirs; music/dance; New Age/metaphysics; photography; popular culture; religious/inspirational; sociology; travel. **Considers these fiction areas:** Comic books/cartoon; erotica; ethnic; experimental; gay/lesbian; glitz; horror; humor/satire; literary; mainstream/contemporary; psychic/supernatural; thriller; urban. **Considers these script subject areas:** Comedy; contemporary issues; detective/police/crime; gay/lesbian; glitz; horror; romantic comedy; romantic drama; thriller.

 ☞ This agency specializes in motion pictures, novels, humor, pop culture, urban fiction, and independent filmmakers.

How to Contact Query with SASE, outline/proposal. Prefers to read materials exclusively. No e-mail or fax queries. Responds in 2 weeks to queries; 1 month to mss. Obtains most new clients through recommendations from others.

Recent Sales *Matt and Ben*, by Mindy Kaling and Brenda Withers; *In the Company of Men* and *Bash: Latterday Plays*, by Neil Labote; *The Vagina Monologues*, by Eve Ensler; *Guide to Life*, by The Five Lesbian Brothers; *Noise From Underground*, by Michael Levine. Other clients include Richard Linklater, Gregg Araki, Tom DiCillo, Genvieve Turner/Rose Troche, Todd Solondz, Neil LaBute.

Terms Agent receives 15% commission on domestic sales; 20% commission on foreign sales. Offers written contract, binding for 1 year; 6-week notice must be given to terminate contract. 100% of business is derived from commissions on ms sales.

Tips ''Be persistent, but civilized.''

☑ ALISON J. PICARD, LITERARY AGENT

P.O. Box 2000, Cotuit MA 02635. Phone/Fax: (508)477-7192. E-mail: ajpicard@aol.com. **Contact:** Alison Picard. Estab. 1985. Represents 48 clients. 30% of clients are new/unpublished writers. Currently handles: 40% nonfiction books; 40% novels; 20% juvenile books.

 • Prior to becoming an agent, Ms. Picard was an assistant at a literary agency in New York.

Represents Nonfiction books, novels, juvenile books. **Considers these nonfiction areas:** Animals; biography/autobiography; business/economics; child guidance/parenting; cooking/foods/nutrition; current affairs; education; ethnic/cultural interests; gay/lesbian issues; government/politics/law; health/medicine; history; how-to; humor/satire; juvenile nonfiction; memoirs; military/war; money/finance; multicultural; nature/environment; New Age/metaphysics; popular culture; psychology; religious/inspirational; science/technology; self-help/personal improvement; travel; true crime/investigative; women's issues/studies; young adult. **Considers these fiction areas:** Action/adventure; contemporary issues; detective/police/crime; erotica; ethnic; family saga; feminist; gay/lesbian; glitz; historical; horror; humor/satire; juvenile; literary; mainstream/contemporary; multicultural; mystery/suspense; New Age; picture books; psychic/supernatural; romance; sports; thriller; young adult.

 ☞ ''Many of my clients have come to me from big agencies, where they felt overlooked or ignored. I communicate freely with my clients and offer a lot of career advice, suggestions for revising manuscripts, etc. If I believe in a project, I will submit it to a dozen or more publishers, unlike some agents who give up after four or five rejections.'' Does not want to receive science fiction/fantasy, westerns, poetry, plays, or articles.

How to Contact Query with SASE. Considers simultaneous queries. Responds in 2 weeks to queries; 4 months to mss. Returns materials only with SASE. Obtains most new clients through recommendations from others, solicitations.

Recent Sales Sold 32 titles in the last year. *A Hard Ticket Home*, by David Housewright (St. Martin's Press); *Indigo Rose*, by Susan Miller (Bantam Books/Random House); *Fly Fishing & Funerals*, by Mary Bartek (Henry Holt & Co.); *Stage Fright*, by Dina Friedman (Farrar, Straus & Giroux); *Fashion Slaves*, by Louise de Teliga (Kensington). Other clients include Osha Gray Davidson, Amy Dean, David Housewright, Nancy Means Wright.

Terms Agent receives 15% commission on domestic sales; 20% commission on foreign sales. Offers written contract, binding for 1 year; 1-week notice must be given to terminate contract.

Tips ''Please don't send material without sending a query first via mail or e-mail. I don't accept phone or fax queries. Always enclose a SASE with a query.''

◖ PINDER LANE & GARON-BROOKE ASSOCIATES, LTD.

159 W. 53rd St., Suite 14C, New York NY 10019. Member of AAR; signatory of WGA.

Member Agents Dick Duane; Robert Thixton.

>   ☞ This agency specializes in mainstream fiction and nonfiction. Does not want to receive screenplays, TV series teleplays, or dramatic plays.

How to Contact Query with SASE. *No unsolicited mss.* Obtains most new clients through referrals.

Terms Agent receives 15% commission on domestic sales; 30% commission on foreign sales. Offers written contract.

Ⓝ ◎ PIPPIN PROPERTIES, INC.

155 E. 38th St., Suite 2H, New York NY 10016. (212)338-9310. Fax: (212)338-9579. Web site: www.pippinproper ties.com. **Contact:** Emily van Beek, Holly McGhee. Estab. 1998. Represents 40 clients. 45% of clients are new/unpublished writers. Currently handles: 100% juvenile books.

>   • Prior to becoming an agent, Ms. McGhee was an editor for 7 years and in book marketing for 4 years.

Represents Juvenile books.

>   ☞ ''We are strictly a children's literary agency devoted to the management of authors and artists in all media. We are small and discerning in choosing our clientele.'' Actively seeking middle-grade novels.

How to Contact Query with SASE. Accepts e-mail queries. Considers simultaneous queries. Responds in 6 weeks to queries; 10 weeks to mss. Obtains most new clients through recommendations from others.

Terms Agent receives 15% commission on domestic sales; 25% commission on foreign sales. Offers written contract; 30-day notice must be given to terminate contract. Charges for color copying and UPS/FedEx.

Tips ''Please do not start calling after sending a submission.''

◖ ALICKA PISTEK LITERARY AGENCY, LLC

302A W. 12th St., #124, New York NY 10014. E-mail: info@apliterary.com. Web site: www.apliterary.com. **Contact:** Alicka Pistek. Estab. 2003. Represents 15 clients. 50% of clients are new/unpublished writers. Currently handles: 60% nonfiction books; 40% novels.

>   • Prior to opening her agency, Ms. Pistek worked at ICM and as an agent at Nicholas Ellison, Inc.

Represents Nonfiction books, novels. **Considers these nonfiction areas:** Animals; anthropology/archaeology; biography/autobiography; business/economics; child guidance/parenting; cooking/foods/nutrition; current affairs; government/politics/law; health/medicine; history; how-to; language/literature/criticism; memoirs; military/war; money/finance; nature/environment; psychology; religious/inspirational; science/technology; self-help/personal improvement; translation; travel; creative nonfiction. **Considers these fiction areas:** Detective/police/crime; ethnic; family saga; historical; literary; mainstream/contemporary; mystery/suspense; romance; thriller.

>   ☞ Does not want to receive fantasy, science fiction, or westerns.

How to Contact Query with SASE, outline, 2 sample chapters. Considers simultaneous queries. Responds in 2 months to queries; 8 weeks to mss. Returns materials only with SASE.

Recent Sales *Mommy Yoga*, by Julie Tilsner; *The Pajamaist*, by Matthew Zapruder; *900 Miles From Nowhere*, by Steve Kinsella. Other clients include Michael Christopher Carroll, Alex Boese, Quinton Skinner, Erin Grady, Marcelle DiFalco, Jocelyn Herz, John Fulton.

Terms Agent receives 15% commission on domestic sales; 20% commission on foreign sales. Offers written contract. Charges for photocopying over 40 pages and international postage.

Writers' Conferences Frankfurt Book Fair.

Tips ''Be sure you are familiar with the genre you are writing in and learn standard procedures for submitting your work. A good query will go a long way.''

◙ JULIE POPKIN

725 Richmond Ave., Silver Spring MD 20910. (301)585-3676. **Contact:** Julie Popkin, Joel Mandelbaum. Estab. 1989. Represents 35 clients. 30% of clients are new/unpublished writers. Currently handles: 70% nonfiction books; 30% novels.

- Prior to opening her agency, Ms. Popkin taught at the university level and did freelance editing and writing.

Member Agents Julie Popkin (fiction, memoirs, biography); Alyson Sena (nonfiction).

Represents Nonfiction books, novels, translations. **Considers these nonfiction areas:** Art/architecture/ design; ethnic/cultural interests; government/politics/law; history; memoirs; philosophy; women's issues/ studies (feminist); criticism. **Considers these fiction areas:** Literary; mainstream/contemporary; mystery/ suspense.

- This agency specializes in selling book-length fiction and nonfiction mss. Especially interested in social issues, ethnic and minority subjects, and Latin American authors. Does not want to receive New Age, spiritual, romance, or science fiction.

How to Contact Query with SASE. No e-mail or fax queries. Responds in 1 month to queries; 2 months to mss. Obtains most new clients through personal contacts and guidebooks.

Recent Sales *Out of the Shadows: Contributions of 20th Century Women to Physics*, edited by Nina Byers (Cambridge University Press); *The End of Romance: Love, Sex and Violins*, by Norma Barzman (Nation Books); *In the Dark Cave*, by Richard Watson, illustrated by Dean Norman (Star Bright); *The Docks*, by Bill Sharpsteen (Gibbs Smith); *That Inferno*, translated from Spanish by Gretta Siebentritt (Vanderbilt University Press).

Terms Agent receives 15% commission on domestic sales; 20% commission on foreign sales; 10% commission on dramatic rights sales. Sometimes asks for fee if ms requires extensive copying and mailing.

Writers' Conferences BookExpo America; Santa Barbara Writers' Conference.

Tips "Keep your eyes on the current market. Publishing responds to changes very quickly and often works toward perceived and fresh subject matter. Historical fiction seems to be rising in interest after a long, quiet period."

◙ HELEN F. PRATT INC.

1165 Fifth Ave., New York NY 10029. (212)722-5081. Fax: (212)722-8569. **Contact:** Helen F. Pratt. Member of AAR.

How to Contact Query with SASE.

◙ AARON M. PRIEST LITERARY AGENCY

708 Third Ave., 23rd Floor, New York NY 10017-4103. (212)818-0344. Fax: (212)573-9417. Estab. 1974. Member of AAR. Currently handles: 25% nonfiction books; 75% novels.

Member Agents Lisa Erbach Vance (levance@aaronpriest.com); Aaron Priest (apriest@aaronpriest.com); Lucy Childs (lchilds@aaronpriest.com).

Represents Commercial fiction, literary fiction, some nonfiction.

How to Contact No e-mail or fax queries. Considers simultaneous queries. Responds in 1 month if interested.

Terms Agent receives 15% commission on domestic sales. Charges for photocopying and postage expenses.

Ⓝ ◙ PROSPECT AGENCY LLC

285 Fifth Ave., PMB 445, Brooklyn NY 11215. Phone/Fax: (718)788-3217. E-mail: esk@prospectagency.com. Web site: www.prospectagency.com. **Contact:** Emily Sylvan Kim. Estab. 2005. Represents 15 clients. 50% of clients are new/unpublished writers. Currently handles: 66% novels; 33% juvenile books.

- Prior to starting her agency, Ms. Kim briefly attended law school and worked for another literary agency.

Represents Nonfiction books, novels, juvenile books. **Considers these nonfiction areas:** Memoirs; science/ technology; juvenile. **Considers these fiction areas:** Action/adventure; detective/police/crime; erotica; ethnic; family saga; fantasy; juvenile; literary; mainstream/contemporary; mystery/suspense; picture books; romance; science fiction; thriller; westerns/frontier; young adult.

- "We are currently looking for the next generation of writers to shape the literary landscape. Our clients receive professional and knowledgeable representation. We are committed to offering skilled editorial advice and advocating our clients in the marketplace." Actively seeking romance, literary fiction, and young adult submissions. Does not want to receive poetry, short stories, textbooks, or most nonfiction.

How to Contact Upload outline and 3 sample chapters to the Web site. Considers simultaneous queries. Responds in 3 weeks to queries; 1 month to mss. Returns materials only with SASE. Obtains most new clients through recommendations from others, conferences, unsolicited mss.

Recent Sales Clients include Diane Perkins, Kate Rothwell, Regina Scott.

Terms Agent receives 15% commission on domestic sales; 20% commission on foreign sales. Offers written contract.

Writers' Conferences SCBWI Annual Winter Conference; Pikes Peak Writers Conference; RWA National Conference.

⬤ SUSAN ANN PROTTER, LITERARY AGENT

110 W. 40th St., Suite 1408, New York NY 10018. **Contact:** Susan Protter. Estab. 1971. Member of AAR, Authors Guild.

- Prior to opening her agency, Ms. Protter was associate director of subsidiary rights at Harper & Row Publishers.
- ⟳ Writers must have a book-length project or ms that is ready to sell. Does not want westerns, romance, children's books, young adult novels, screenplays, plays, poetry, Star Wars, or Star Trek.

How to Contact Currently looking for a limited number of new clients. Query with SASE. *No unsolicited mss.*

Terms Agent receives 15% commission on domestic and dramatic rights sales.

⬤ MICHAEL PSALTIS

200 Bennett Ave., New York NY 10040. E-mail: michael@mpsaltis.com. **Contact:** Michael Psaltis. Member of AAR. Represents 30 clients.

Represents Nonfiction books, novels. **Considers these nonfiction areas:** Biography/autobiography; business/economics; cooking/foods/nutrition; health/medicine; history; psychology. **Considers these fiction areas:** Mainstream/contemporary.

How to Contact Submit outline/proposal. Responds in 2 weeks to queries; 6 weeks to mss.

Recent Sales *Turning the Tables*, by Steven Shaw (HarperCollins); *Why We Hate*, by David Smith (St. Martin's Press); *A Life in Twilight*, by Mark Wolverton (Joseph Henry Press); *Under a Passionate Moon*, by Donna Simpson (Berkley).

Terms Agent receives 15% commission on domestic sales; 20% commission on foreign sales. Offers written contract.

⬤ QUICKSILVER BOOKS—LITERARY AGENTS

508 Central Park Ave., #5101, Scarsdale NY 10583. Phone/Fax: (914)722-4664. Web site: www.quicksilverbooks .com. **Contact:** Bob Silverstein. Estab. 1973 as packager; 1987 as literary agency. Represents 50 clients. 50% of clients are new/unpublished writers. Currently handles: 75% nonfiction books; 25% novels.

- Prior to opening his agency, Mr. Silverstein served as senior editor at Bantam Books and Dell Books/Delacorte Press.

Represents Nonfiction books, novels. **Considers these nonfiction areas:** Anthropology/archaeology; biography/autobiography; business/economics; child guidance/parenting; cooking/foods/nutrition; current affairs; ethnic/cultural interests; health/medicine; history; how-to; language/literature/criticism; memoirs; nature/environment; New Age/metaphysics; popular culture; psychology; religious/inspirational; science/technology; self-help/personal improvement; sociology; sports; true crime/investigative; women's issues/studies. **Considers these fiction areas:** Action/adventure; glitz; mystery/suspense; thriller.

- ⟳ This agency specializes in literary and commercial mainstream fiction and nonfiction, especially psychology, New Age, holistic healing, consciousness, ecology, environment, spirituality, reference, cookbooks, and narrative nonfiction. Does not want to receive science fiction, pornography, poetry, or single-spaced mss.

How to Contact Query with SASE. Authors are expected to supply SASE for return of ms and for query letter responses. No e-mail or fax queries. Considers simultaneous queries. Responds in 2 weeks to queries; 1 month to mss. Returns materials only with SASE. Obtains most new clients through recommendations, listings in sourcebooks, solicitations, workshop participation.

Recent Sales Sold over 20 titles in the last year. *Nice Girls Don't Get Rich*, by Lois P. Frankel, PhD (Warner Books); *The Young Patriots*, by Charles Cerami (Sourcebooks); *The Coming of the Beatles*, by Martin Goldsmith (Wiley); *The Real Food Daily Cookbook*, by Ann Gentry (Ten Speed Press); *The Complete Book of Vinyasa Yoga*, by Srivatsa Ramaswami (Marlowe & Co.).

Terms Agent receives 15% commission on domestic sales; 20% commission on foreign sales. Offers written contract.

Writers' Conferences National Writers Union.

Tips "Write what you know. Write from the heart. Publishers print, authors sell."

⬤ SUSAN RABINER, LITERARY AGENT, INC.

240 W. 35th St., Suite 500, New York NY 10001. (212)279-0316. Fax: (212)279-0932. E-mail: susan@rabiner.net. Web site: www.rabiner.net. **Contact:** Susan Rabiner.

● Prior to becoming an agent, Ms. Rabiner was editorial director of Basic Books. She is also the co-author of *Thinking Like Your Editor: How to Write Great Serious Nonfiction and Get it Published* (W.W. Norton).

Member Agents Susan Rabiner; Susan Arellano; Sydelle Kramer; Alfred Fortunato; Helena Schwarz.

Represents Nonfiction books, textbooks. **Considers these nonfiction areas:** Business/economics; education; history; philosophy; psychology; science/technology; biography, law/politics.

⛎ Does not want to receive fiction or self-help.

How to Contact Query with proposal, sample chapter, SASE. No fax or phone queries. Considers simultaneous queries. Responds in 3 weeks to queries. Returns materials only with SASE. Obtains most new clients through recommendations from editors.

Recent Sales *Madness: A Life*, by Marya Hornbaeher (Houghton Mifflin); *Is God a Mathematician?*, by Mario Livio (Simon & Schuster); *Teapot in a Tempest: The Boston Tea Party*, by Benjamin Carp (Yale University Press).

Terms Agent receives 15% commission on domestic sales; 20% commission on foreign sales. Offers written contract; 1-month notice must be given to terminate contract.

⦿ RAINES & RAINES

103 Kenyon Rd., Medusa NY 12120. (518)239-8311. Fax: (518)239-6029. **Contact:** Theron Raines (member of AAR); Joan Raines; Keith Korman. Represents 100 clients.

Represents Nonfiction books, novels. **Considers these nonfiction areas:** Any. **Considers these fiction areas:** Action/adventure; detective/police/crime; fantasy; historical; mystery/suspense; picture books; science fiction; thriller; westerns/frontier.

How to Contact Query with SASE. Responds in 2 weeks to queries.

Terms Agent receives 15% commission on domestic sales; 20% commission on foreign sales. Charges for photocopying.

⦿ CHARLOTTE CECIL RAYMOND, LITERARY AGENT

32 Bradlee Rd., Marblehead MA 01945. **Contact:** Charlotte Cecil Raymond. Estab. 1983. Currently handles: 90% nonfiction books; 10% novels.

Represents Nonfiction books. **Considers these nonfiction areas:** Current affairs; ethnic/cultural interests; history; nature/environment; psychology; sociology; biography, gender interests.

⛎ Does not want to receive self-help/personal improvement, science fiction, fantasy, young adult, juvenile, poetry, or screenplays.

How to Contact Query with SASE, proposal package, outline. Responds in 2 weeks to queries; 6 weeks to mss.

Terms Agent receives 15% commission on domestic sales. 100% of business is derived from commissions on ms sales.

⦿ HELEN REES LITERARY AGENCY

376 North St., Boston MA 02113-2013. (617)227-9014. Fax: (617)227-8762. E-mail: reesagency@reesagency.com. **Contact:** Joan Mazmanian, Ann Collette, Helen Rees, Lorin Rees. Estab. 1983. Member of AAR, PEN. Represents 98 clients. 50% of clients are new/unpublished writers. Currently handles: 60% nonfiction books; 40% novels.

Member Agents Ann Collette (literary fiction, women's studies, health, biography, history); Helen Rees (business, money/finance/economics, government/politics/law, contemporary issues, literary fiction); Lorin Rees (business, money/finance, management, history, narrative nonfiction, science, literary fiction, memoir).

Represents Nonfiction books, novels. **Considers these nonfiction areas:** Biography/autobiography; business/economics; current affairs; government/politics/law; health/medicine; history; money/finance; women's issues/studies. **Considers these fiction areas:** Historical; literary; mainstream/contemporary; mystery/suspense; thriller.

How to Contact Query with SASE, outline, 2 sample chapters. No unsolicited e-mail submissions. No multiple submissions. No e-mail or fax queries. Responds in 3-4 weeks to queries. Obtains most new clients through recommendations from others, conferences, submissions.

Recent Sales Sold over 35 titles in the last year. *Get Your Shipt Together*, by Capt. D. Michael Abrashoff; *Overpromise and Overdeliver*, by Rick Berrara; *Opacity*, by Joel Kurtzman; *America the Broke*, by Gerald Swanson; *Murder at the B-School*, by Jeffrey Cruikshank; *Bone Factory*, by Steven Sidor; *Father Said*, by Hal Sirowitz; *Winning*, by Jack Welch; *The Case for Israel*, by Alan Dershowitz; *As the Future Catches You*, by Juan Enriquez; *Killing Haji: A Travelogue*, by Johnny Rico; *DVD Video Movie Guide*, by Mick Martin and Marsha Porter; *Killer Words*, by Frank Luntz.

Terms Agent receives 15% commission on domestic sales; 20% commission on foreign sales.

⦿ REGAL LITERARY AGENCY

1140 Broadway, Penthouse, New York NY 10001. (212)684-7900. Fax: (212)684-7906. E-mail: office@regal-literary.com. Web site: www.regal-literary.com. **Contact:** Bess Reed, Lauren Schott Pearson. Estab. 2002. Member of AAR. Represents 90 clients. 20% of clients are new/unpublished writers. Currently handles: 48% nonfiction books; 46% novels; 2% story collections; 2% novellas; 2% poetry.

- Prior to becoming agents, Mr. Regal was a musician; Mr. Steinberg was a filmmaker and screenwriter; Ms. Reid and Ms. Schott Pearson were magazine editors.

Member Agents Joseph Regal (literary fiction, science, history, memoir); Peter Steinberg (literary and commercial fiction, history, humor, memoir, narrative nonfiction, young adult); Bess Reed (literary fiction, narrative nonfiction, self-help); Lauren Schott Pearson (literary fiction, commercial fiction, memoir, narrative nonfiction, thrillers, mysteries). Michael Psaltis of Psaltis Literary also works with Regal Literary agents to form the Culinary Cooperative—a joint-venture agency dedicated to food writing, cookbooks, and all things related to cooking. Recent sales include *The Fat Guy's Manifatso* (Bloomsbury USA); *Fish On a First-Name Basis* (St. Martin's Press); *The Reverse Diet* (John Wiley & Sons); and *The Seasoning of a Chef* (Doubleday/Broadway).

Represents Nonfiction books, novels, short story collections, novellas. **Considers these nonfiction areas:** Anthropology/archaeology; art/architecture/design; biography/autobiography; business/economics; cooking/foods/nutrition; current affairs; ethnic/cultural interests; gay/lesbian issues; history; humor/satire; language/literature/criticism; memoirs; military/war; music/dance; nature/environment; photography; popular culture; psychology; religious/inspirational; science/technology; sports; translation; women's issues/studies. **Considers these fiction areas:** Comic books/cartoon; detective/police/crime; ethnic; historical; literary; mystery/suspense; thriller; contemporary.

- O➔ "We have discovered more than a dozen successful literary novelists in the last 5 years. We are small, but are extraordinarily responsive to our writers. We are more like managers than agents, with an eye toward every aspect of our writers' careers, including publicity and other media." Actively seeking literary fiction and narrative nonfiction. Does not want romance, science fiction, horror, or screenplays.

How to Contact Query with SASE, 5-15 sample pages. No phone calls. No e-mail or fax queries. Considers simultaneous queries. Responds in 2-3 weeks to queries; 4-12 weeks to mss. Returns materials only with SASE. Obtains most new clients through recommendations from others, unsolicited submissions.

Recent Sales Sold 20 titles in the last year. *The Stolen Child*, by Keith Donohue (Nan Talese/Doubleday); *What Elmo Taught Me*, by Kevin Clash (HarperCollins); *The Affected Provincial's Companion*, by Lord Breaulove Swells Whimsy (Bloomsbury); *The Three Incestuous Sisters*, by Audrey Niffenegger (Abrams); *The Traveler*, by John Twelve Hawks (Doubleday). Other clients include James Reston Jr., Tony Earley, Dennie Hughes, Mark Lee, Jake Page, Cheryl Bernard, Daniel Wallace, John Marks, Keith Scribner, Cathy Day, Alicia Erian, Gregory David Roberts, Dallas Hudgens, Tim Winton, Ian Spiegelman, Brad Barkley, Heather Hepler, Gavin Edwards, Sara Voorhees, Alex Abella.

Terms Agent receives 15% commission on domestic sales; 20% commission on foreign sales. No written contract. Charges clients for typical/major office expenses, such as photocopying and foreign postage.

◑ JODY REIN BOOKS, INC.

7741 S. Ash Ct., Centennial CO 80122. (303)694-4430. Fax: (303)694-0687. Web site: www.jodyreinbooks.com. **Contact:** Winnefred Dollar. Estab. 1994. Member of AAR, Authors' Guild. Currently handles: 70% nonfiction books; 30% novels.

- Prior to opening her agency, Ms. Rein worked for 13 years as an acquisitions editor for Contemporary Books and as executive editor for Bantam/Doubleday/Dell and Morrow/Avon.

Represents Nonfiction books, novels. **Considers these nonfiction areas:** Business/economics; child guidance/parenting; current affairs; ethnic/cultural interests; government/politics/law; history; humor/satire; music/dance; nature/environment; popular culture; psychology; science/technology; sociology; theater/film; women's issues/studies. **Considers these fiction areas:** Literary; mainstream/contemporary.

- O➔ This agency specializes in commercial and narrative nonfiction and literary/commercial fiction.

How to Contact Query with SASE. No e-mail or fax queries. Considers simultaneous queries. Responds in 6 weeks to queries; 2 months to mss. Obtains most new clients through recommendations from others, solicitations.

Recent Sales *How to Remodel a Man*, by Bruce Cameron (St. Martin's Press); *8 Simple Rules for Dating My Teenage Daughter*, by Bruce Cameron (ABC/Disney); *Skeletons on the Zahara*, by Dean King (Little, Brown); *The Big Year*, by Mark Obmascik (The Free Press).

Terms Agent receives 15% commission on domestic sales; 25% commission on foreign sales; 20% commission on dramatic rights sales. Offers written contract. Charges clients for express mail, overseas expenses, photocopying mss.

Tips "Do your homework before submitting. Make sure you have a marketable topic and the credentials to write about it. We want well-written books on fresh and original nonfiction topics that have broad appeal, as well as novels written by authors who have spent years developing their craft. Authors must be well established in their fields and have strong media experience."

◙ JODIE RHODES LITERARY AGENCY

8840 Villa La Jolla Dr., Suite 315, La Jolla CA 92037-1957. **Contact:** Jodie Rhodes, president. Estab. 1998. Member of AAR. Represents 50 clients. 60% of clients are new/unpublished writers. Currently handles: 60% nonfiction books; 35% novels; 5% middle grade/young adult books.

• Prior to opening her agency, Ms. Rhodes was a university-level creative writing teacher, workshop director, published novelist, and vice president/media director at the N.W. Ayer Advertising Agency.

Member Agents Jodie Rhodes; Clark McCutcheon (fiction); Bob McCarter (nonfiction).

Represents Nonfiction books, novels. **Considers these nonfiction areas:** Biography/autobiography; child guidance/parenting; ethnic/cultural interests; government/politics/law; health/medicine; history; memoirs; military/war; science/technology; women's issues/studies. **Considers these fiction areas:** Ethnic; family saga; historical; literary; mainstream/contemporary; mystery/suspense; thriller; young adult; women's.

O→ Actively seeking writers passionate about their books with a talent for richly textured narrative, an eye for details, and a nose for research. Nonfiction writers must have recognized credentials and expert knowledge of their subject matter. Does not want to receive erotica, horror, fantasy, romance, science fiction, religious/inspirational, or children's books (does accept young adult/teen).

How to Contact Query with brief synopsis, first 30-50 pages, SASE. No e-mail or fax queries. Considers simultaneous queries. Responds in 10 days to queries. Returns materials only with SASE. Obtains most new clients through recommendations from others, agent sourcebooks.

Recent Sales Sold 40 titles in the last year. *Chloe Doe*, by Suzanne Phillips (Little, Brown US/MacMillan UK); *Memory Matters*, by Scott Hagwood (Simon & Schuster); *Diagnosis of Love*, by Maggie Martin (Bantam); *Salaam, Paris*, by Kavita Daswani (Putnam); *Preventing Alzheimer's*, by Marwan Sabbagh (John Wiley & Sons); *Japanland*, by Karin Muller (Rodale); *Raising Drug Free Kids*, by Aletha Solter (Da Capo Press).

Terms Agent receives 15% commission on domestic sales; 20% commission on foreign sales. Offers written contract; 1-month notice must be given to terminate contract. Charges clients for fax, photocopying, phone calls, postage. Charges are itemized and approved by writers upfront.

Tips "Think your book out before you write it. Do your research, know your subject matter intimately, and write vivid specifics, not bland generalities. Care deeply about your book. Don't imitate other writers. Find your own voice. We never take on a book we don't believe in, and we go the extra mile for our writers. We welcome talented, new writers."

Ⓝ ⊕ ◙ RICHARDS LITERARY AGENCY

P.O. Box 31 240, Milford Auckland 1309 New Zealand. (64)(9)410-5681. E-mail: rla.richards@clear.net.nz. **Contact:** Ray Richards. Estab. 1977. Member of NZALA. Represents 100 clients. 20% of clients are new/unpublished writers. Currently handles: 20% nonfiction books; 15% novels; 5% story collections; 30% juvenile books; 5% scholarly books; 15% movie scripts;

• Prior to opening his agency, Mr. Richards was a book publisher, managing director, and vice chairman.

O→ "We offer a high quality of experience, acceptances, and client relationships." Does not want short stories, articles, or poetry. Do not send full ms until requested.

How to Contact Submit outline/proposal. Responds in 1 week to queries; 1 month to mss. Returns materials only with SASE. Obtains most new clients through referrals.

Recent Sales *Blindsights*, by Maurice Gee (Penguin/Faber); *The Whale Rider*, by Witi Ihimaera (Reed Publishing); *Margaret Moby: A Writer's Life*, by Tessa Duder (HarperCollins); *New Zealand Centenaries*, by John Dunmore (New Holland). *Movie/TV MOW scripts optioned/sold:* Buzzy Bee TV animation series.

Terms Agent receives 15% commission on domestic and foreign sales. Offers written contract. Charges clients for postage and photocopying.

Tips "We first need a full book proposal, outline of 2-10 pages, author statement of experience, and published works."

◙ RIGHTS UNLIMITED, INC.

6 W. 37th St., 4th Floor, New York NY 10018. (212)246-0900. Fax: (212)246-2114. E-mail: submissions@rightsu nlimited.com. Web site: www.rightsunlimited.com. Estab. 1985. Member of AAR.

Member Agents Al Longden; Raymond Kurman; Diane Dreher; Ben Salmon.

Represents Nonfiction books, novels. **Considers these nonfiction areas:** Business/economics; current affairs; health/medicine; history; humor/satire; memoirs; popular culture; self-help/personal improvement; sociology; travel; women's issues/studies; celebrity biography; career development; alternative culture; diet/fitness; alternative medicine; inspiration; relationships; gender/sexuality; lifestyle; cookbooks; gift books. **Considers these fiction areas:** Fantasy; literary; multicultural; mystery/suspense; romance (contemporary); science fiction; thriller (international); women's (mainstream); chick lit; mommy lit; quirky/edgy fiction; crime.

How to Contact Query with SASE or via e-mail (no attachments). For nonfiction, send query letter, bio, outline, SASE. For fiction, send query letter, bio, synopsis, first 10 pages, SASE. Responds in 1 month to queries.

⊿ ANGELA RINALDI LITERARY AGENCY

P.O. Box 7877, Beverly Hills CA 90212-7877. (310)842-7665. Fax: (310)837-8143. E-mail: amr@rinaldiliterary.c
om. Estab. 1994. Member of AAR. Represents 50 clients. Currently handles: 30% nonfiction books; 70% novels.

- Prior to opening her agency, Ms. Rinaldi was an editor at NAL/Signet, Pocket Books, and Bantam, and the manager of book development for *The Los Angeles Times.*

Represents Nonfiction books, novels, TV and motion picture rights (for clients only). **Considers these nonfiction areas:** Biography/autobiography; business/economics; health/medicine; money/finance; self-help/personal improvement; true crime/investigative; women's issues/studies; books by journalists and academics. **Considers these fiction areas:** Literary; commercial; upmarket women's fiction; suspense.

- ○┐ Actively seeking commercial and literary fiction. Does not want to receive scripts, poetry, category romances, children's books, westerns, science fiction/fantasy, technothrillers, or cookbooks.

How to Contact For fiction, send first 3 chapters, brief synopsis, SASE. For nonfiction, query with SASE or send outline/proposal, SASE. Do not send certified or metered mail. Brief e-mail inquiries are OK (no attachments). Considers simultaneous queries. Please advise if it is a multiple submission. Responds in 6 weeks to queries. Returns materials only with SASE.

Recent Sales *My First Crush,* by Linda Kaplan (Lyons Press); *Rescue Me,* by Megan Clark (Kensington); *The Blood Orange Tree,* by Drusilla Campbell (Kensington); *Some Writers Deserve to Starve: 31 Brutal Truths About the Publishing Industry,* by Elaura Niles (Writer's Digest Books); *Indivisible by Two: Great Tales of Twins, Triplets and Quads,* by Dr. Nancy Segal (Harvard University Press); *Zen Putting,* by Dr. Joseph Parent (Gotham Books).

Terms Agent receives 15% commission on domestic sales; 20% commission on foreign sales. Offers written contract. Charges clients for photocopying.

◖ ANN RITTENBERG LITERARY AGENCY, INC.

30 Bond St., New York NY 10012. (212)684-6936. **Contact:** Ann Rittenberg, president. Estab. 1992. Member of AAR. Represents 35 clients. 40% of clients are new/unpublished writers. Currently handles: 50% nonfiction books; 50% novels.

Represents Nonfiction books, novels. **Considers these nonfiction areas:** Biography/autobiography; history (social/cultural); memoirs; women's issues/studies. **Considers these fiction areas:** Literary.

- ○┐ This agent specializes in literary fiction and literary nonfiction.

How to Contact Submit outline, 3 sample chapters, SASE. Considers simultaneous queries. Responds in 6 weeks to queries; 2 months to mss. Obtains most new clients through referrals from established writers and editors.

Recent Sales Sold 20 titles in the last year. *Bad Cat,* by Jim Edgar (Workman); *A Certain Slant of Light,* by Laura Whitcomb (Houghton Mifflin); *New York Night,* by Mark Caldwell (Scribner); *In Plain Sight,* by C.J. Box (Putnam); *Improbable,* by Adam Fawer; *Colleges That Change Lives,* by Loren Pope.

Terms Agent receives 15% commission on domestic sales; 20% commission on foreign sales. Offers written contract. Charges clients for photocopying only.

◖ RIVERSIDE LITERARY AGENCY

41 Simon Keets Rd., Leyden MA 01337. (413)772-0067. Fax: (413)772-0969. E-mail: rivlit@sover.net. **Contact:** Susan Lee Cohen. Estab. 1990. Represents 40 clients. 20% of clients are new/unpublished writers.

Represents Adult nonfiction, adult novels.

How to Contact Query with SASE, outline. Accepts e-mail queries. No fax queries. Considers simultaneous queries. Responds in 2 weeks to queries. Obtains most new clients through referrals.

Recent Sales *Writing to Change the World,* by Mary Pipher, PhD (Riverhead/Penguin Putnam); *The Sociopath Next Door: The Ruthless Versus the Rest of Us,* by Dr. Martha Stout (Broadway); *Letting Go of the Person You Used to Be,* by Lama Surya Das (Broadway); *The Secret Magdalene,* by Ki Longfellow (Crown); *Right, Wrong, and Risky: A Dictionary of Today's American English Usage,* by Mark Davidson (Norton).

Terms Agent receives 15% commission on domestic sales. Offers written contract. Charges clients for foreign postage, photocopying large mss, express mail deliveries, etc.

Tips "We are very selective."

⊿ RLR ASSOCIATES, LTD.

Literary Department, 7 W. 51st St., New York NY 10019. (212)541-8641. Fax: (212)541-6052. E-mail: info@rlrass
ociates.net. Web site: www.rlrliterary.net. **Contact:** Jennifer Unter, Tara Mark, Scott Gould. Member of AAR. Represents 50 clients. 25% of clients are new/unpublished writers. Currently handles: 70% nonfiction books; 25% novels; 5% story collections.

Represents Nonfiction books, novels, short story collections, scholarly books. **Considers these nonfiction areas:** Animals; anthropology/archaeology; art/architecture/design; biography/autobiography; business/economics; child guidance/parenting; cooking/foods/nutrition; current affairs; education; ethnic/cultural interests; gay/lesbian issues; government/politics/law; health/medicine; history; humor/satire; interior design/decorating; language/literature/criticism; memoirs; money/finance; multicultural; music/dance; nature/environment; photography; popular culture; psychology; religious/inspirational; science/technology; self-help/personal improvement; sociology; sports; translation; travel; true crime/investigative; women's issues/studies. **Considers these fiction areas:** Action/adventure; comic books/cartoon; detective/police/crime; ethnic; experimental; family saga; feminist; gay/lesbian; historical; horror; humor/satire; literary; mainstream/contemporary; multicultural; mystery/suspense; sports; thriller.

    O⌐ "We provide a lot of editorial assistance to our clients and have connections." Actively seeking fiction, current affairs, history, art, popular culture, health, and business. Does not want to receive science fiction, fantasy, screenplays, or illustrated children's stories.

How to Contact Query with SASE. Considers simultaneous queries. Responds in 4-8 weeks. Returns materials only with SASE. Obtains most new clients through recommendations from others.

Recent Sales Sold 20 titles in the last year. Clients include Shelby Foote, The Grief Recovery Institute, Don Wade, Don Zimmer, The Knot.com, David Plowden, PGA of America, Danny Peary, Goerge Kalinsky, Peter Hyman, Daniel Parker, Lee Miller, Elise Miller, Nina Planck, Karyn Bosnak.

Terms Agent receives 15% commission on domestic sales; 20% commission on foreign sales. Offers written contract.

Tips "Please check out our Web site for more details on our agency. No e-mail submissions, please."

☑ B.J. ROBBINS LITERARY AGENCY

5130 Bellaire Ave., North Hollywood CA 91607-2908. (818)760-6602. Fax: (818)760-6616. E-mail: robbinsliterary@aol.com. **Contact:** (Ms.) B.J. Robbins. Estab. 1992. Member of AAR. Represents 40 clients. 50% of clients are new/unpublished writers. Currently handles: 50% nonfiction books; 50% novels.

Represents Nonfiction books, novels. **Considers these nonfiction areas:** Biography/autobiography; child guidance/parenting; current affairs; ethnic/cultural interests; health/medicine; how-to; humor/satire; memoirs; music/dance; popular culture; psychology; self-help/personal improvement; sociology; sports; theater/film; travel; true crime/investigative; women's issues/studies. **Considers these fiction areas:** Detective/police/crime; ethnic; literary; mainstream/contemporary; mystery/suspense; sports; thriller; young adult.

How to Contact Submit outline/proposal, 3 sample chapters, SASE. Accepts e-mail queries (no attachments). No fax queries. Considers simultaneous queries. Responds in 2-6 weeks to queries; 6-8 weeks to mss. Returns materials only with SASE. Obtains most new clients through conferences, referrals.

Recent Sales Sold 15 titles in the last year. *Getting Stoned with Savages*, by J. Maarten Troost (Broadway); *Hot Water*, by Kathryn Jordan (Berkley); *Between the Bridge and the River*, by Craig Ferguson (Chronicle); *I'm Proud of You*, by Tim Madigan (Gotham); *Man of the House*, by Chris Erskine (Rodale); *Bird of Another Heaven*, by James D. Houston (Knopf); *Tomorrow They Will Kiss*, by Eduardo Santiago (Little, Brown).

Terms Agent receives 15% commission on domestic sales; 20% commission on foreign sales. Offers written contract; 3-month notice must be given to terminate contract. 100% of business is derived from commissions on ms sales. Charges clients for postage and photocopying (only after sale of ms).

Writers' Conferences Squaw Valley Writers Workshop; San Diego State University Writers' Conference; Santa Barbara Writers' Conference.

☑ LINDA ROGHAAR LITERARY AGENCY, INC.

133 High Point Dr., Amherst MA 01002. (413)256-1921. Fax: (413)256-2636. E-mail: contact@lindaroghaar.com. Web site: www.lindaroghaar.com. **Contact:** Linda L. Roghaar. Estab. 1996. Represents 50 clients. 40% of clients are new/unpublished writers. Currently handles: 90% nonfiction books; 10% novels.

    ● Prior to opening her agency, Ms. Roghaar worked in retail bookselling for 5 years and as a publisher's sales rep for 15 years.

Represents Nonfiction books, novels. **Considers these nonfiction areas:** Animals; anthropology/archaeology; biography/autobiography; education; history; nature/environment; popular culture; religious/inspirational; self-help/personal improvement; women's issues/studies. **Considers these fiction areas:** Mystery/suspense (amateur sleuth, cozy, culinary, malice domestic).

How to Contact Query with SASE. Accepts e-mail queries. No fax queries. Considers simultaneous queries. Responds in 2 months to queries; 4 months to mss.

Recent Sales *Yarn Harlot*, by Stephanie Pearl-McPhee (Andrews McMeel); *Inspired Cable Knits*, by Fiona Ellis (Potter Craft); *Authentic Beauty the Dr. Hauschka Way*, by Susan West Kurz (Clarkson Potter).

Terms Agent receives 15% commission on domestic sales; negotiable commission on foreign sales. Offers written contract.

⦿ THE ROSENBERG GROUP

23 Lincoln Ave., Marblehead MA 01945. (781)990-1341. Fax: (781)990-1344. Web site: www.rosenberggroup.c om. **Contact:** Barbara Collins Rosenberg. Estab. 1998. Member of AAR, recognized agent of the RWA. Represents 32 clients. 25% of clients are new/unpublished writers. Currently handles: 30% nonfiction books; 30% novels; 10% scholarly books; 30% textbooks.

• Prior to becoming an agent, Ms. Rosenberg was a senior editor for Harcourt.

Represents Nonfiction books, novels, textbooks. **Considers these nonfiction areas:** Current affairs; popular culture; psychology; sports; women's issues/studies; women's health; food/wine/beverages. **Considers these fiction areas:** Romance; women's.

⚷ Ms. Rosenberg is well-versed in the romance market (both category and single title). She is a frequent speaker at romance conferences. Actively seeking romance category or single title in contemporary chick lit, romantic suspense, and the historical subgenres. Does not want to receive time travel, paranormal, or inspirational/spiritual romances.

How to Contact Query with SASE. No e-mail or fax queries. Responds in 2 weeks to queries; 4-6 weeks to mss. Returns materials only with SASE. Obtains most new clients through recommendations from others, solicitations, conferences.

Recent Sales Sold 24 titles in the last year.

Terms Agent receives 15% commission on domestic and foreign sales. Offers written contract; 1-month notice must be given to terminate contract. Charges maximum of $350/year for postage and photocopying.

Writers' Conferences RWA National Conference; BookExpo America.

⦿ RITA ROSENKRANZ LITERARY AGENCY

440 West End Ave., Suite 15D, New York NY 10024-5358. (212)873-6333. **Contact:** Rita Rosenkranz. Estab. 1990. Member of AAR. Represents 30 clients. 20% of clients are new/unpublished writers. Currently handles: 99% nonfiction books; 1% novels.

• Prior to opening her agency, Ms. Rosenkranz worked as an editor in major New York publishing houses.

Represents Nonfiction books. **Considers these nonfiction areas:** Animals; anthropology/archaeology; art/architecture/design; biography/autobiography; business/economics; child guidance/parenting; computers/electronic; cooking/foods/nutrition; crafts/hobbies; current affairs; ethnic/cultural interests; gay/lesbian issues; government/politics/law; health/medicine; history; how-to; humor/satire; interior design/decorating; language/literature/criticism; military/war; money/finance; music/dance; nature/environment; New Age/metaphysics; photography; popular culture; psychology; religious/inspirational; science/technology; self-help/personal improvement; sports; theater/film; women's issues/studies.

⚷ This agency focuses on adult nonfiction, stresses strong editorial development and refinement before submitting to publishers, and brainstorms ideas with authors. Actively seeking authors who are well paired with their subject, either for professional or personal reasons.

How to Contact Submit proposal package, outline, SASE. No e-mail or fax queries. Considers simultaneous queries. Responds in 2 weeks to queries. Obtains most new clients through solicitations, conferences, word of mouth.

Recent Sales Sold 35 titles in the last year. *Forbidden Fruit: True Love Stories from the Underground Railroad*, by Betty DeRamus (Atria Books); *Business Class: Etiquette Essentials for Success at Work*, by Jacqueline Whitmore (St. Martin's Press); *Olive Trees and Honey: A Treasury of Vegetarian Recipes from Jewish Communities Around the World*, by Gil Marks (Wiley); *Branded Customer Service*, by Janelle Barlow and Paul Stewart (Berrett-Koehler).

Terms Agent receives 15% commission on domestic sales; 20% commission on foreign sales. Offers written contract, binding for 3 years; 3-month written notice must be given to terminate contract. 100% of business is derived from commissions on ms sales. Charges clients for photocopying. Makes referrals to editing services.

Tips ''Identify the current competition for your project to make sure the project is valid. A strong cover letter is very important.''

⦿ ROSENSTONE/WENDER

38 E. 29th St., 10th Floor, New York NY 10016. (212)725-9445. Fax: (212)725-9447. Member of AAR.

Member Agents Howard Rosenstone; Phyllis Wender; Sonia Pabley; Ronald Gwiazda, associate member.

⚷ Interested in literary, adult, and dramatic material.

How to Contact Query with SASE.

⦿ THE GAIL ROSS LITERARY AGENCY

1666 Connecticut Ave. NW, #500, Washington DC 20009. (202)328-3282. Fax: (202)328-9162. E-mail: jennifer@gailross.com. Web site: www.gailross.com. **Contact:** Jennifer Manguera. Estab. 1988. Member of AAR. Represents 200 clients. 75% of clients are new/unpublished writers. Currently handles: 95% nonfiction books.

Represents Nonfiction books. **Considers these nonfiction areas:** Anthropology/archaeology; biography/auto-biography; business/economics; education; ethnic/cultural interests; gay/lesbian issues; government/politics/law; health/medicine; money/finance; nature/environment; psychology; religious/inspirational; science/technology; self-help/personal improvement; sociology; sports; true crime/investigative.

O— This agency specializes in adult trade nonfiction.

How to Contact Query with SASE. Considers simultaneous queries. Responds in 1 month to queries. Obtains most new clients through recommendations from others.

Recent Sales Sold 50 titles in the last year. This agency prefers not to share information on specific sales.

Terms Agent receives 15% commission on domestic sales; 25% commission on foreign sales. Charges for office expenses.

☑ CAROL SUSAN ROTH, LITERARY & CREATIVE

P.O. Box 620337, Woodside CA 94062. (650)323-3795. E-mail: carol@authorsbest.com. **Contact:** Carol Susan Roth. Estab. 1995. Represents 47 clients. 15% of clients are new/unpublished writers. Currently handles: 100% nonfiction books.

• Prior to becoming an agent, Ms. Roth was trained as a psychotherapist and worked as a motivational coach, conference producer, and promoter for best-selling authors (e.g., Scott Peck, Bernie Siegal, John Gray) and the 1987 Heart of Business conference (the first business and spirituality conference).

Represents Nonfiction books. **Considers these nonfiction areas:** Business/economics; money/finance (personal finance/investing); popular culture; religious/inspirational; self-help/personal improvement; spirituality; Buddhism; wellness/health/medicine; yoga; humor.

O— This agency specializes in pop culture, spirituality, health, personal growth, personal finance, and business. Actively seeking previously published journalists, authors, and experts with an established audience in pop culture, health, spirituality, personal growth, and business. Does not want to receive fiction.

How to Contact Submit proposal package, media kit, promotional video, SASE. Accepts e-mail queries (no attachments). Considers simultaneous queries. Responds in 1 week to queries. Returns materials only with SASE. Obtains most new clients through recommendations from others, solicitations.

Recent Sales Sold 17 titles in the last year. *Bird Signs*, by Gwen Carbone (New World Library); *Snooze or Lose!*, by Helene Emsellem (Joseph Henry Press); *Living Wisdom of the Dalai Lama* (Soundstrue); *Busting Out!*, by Shirley Archer (Chronicle Books).

Terms Agent receives 15% commission on domestic and foreign sales. Offers written contract, binding for 3 years (only for work with the acquiring publisher); 60-day notice must be given to terminate contract. This agency asks the client to provide postage (FedEx airbills) and do copying. Refers to book doctor for proposal development and publicity service on request.

Writers' Conferences MEGA Book Marketing University; Maui Writers Conference.

Tips "Have charisma, content, and credentials—solve an old problem in a new way. I prefer experts with extensive seminar and media experience."

☑ JANE ROTROSEN AGENCY LLC

318 E. 51st St., New York NY 10022. (212)593-4330. Fax: (212)935-6985. E-mail: firstinitiallastname@janerotrosen.com. Estab. 1974. Member of AAR, Authors Guild. Represents over 100 clients. Currently handles: 30% nonfiction books; 70% novels.

Member Agents Jane R. Berkey; Andrea Cirillo; Annelise Robey; Margaret Ruley; Kelly Harms; Christina Hogrebe; Peggy Gordijn, director of translation rights.

Represents Nonfiction books, novels. **Considers these nonfiction areas:** Biography/autobiography; business/economics; child guidance/parenting; cooking/foods/nutrition; current affairs; health/medicine; how-to; humor/satire; money/finance; nature/environment; popular culture; psychology; self-help/personal improvement; sports; true crime/investigative; women's issues/studies. **Considers these fiction areas:** Action/adventure; detective/police/crime; family saga; historical; horror; mainstream/contemporary; mystery/suspense; romance; thriller; women's.

How to Contact Query with SASE. No e-mail or fax queries. Responds in 2 months to mss; 2 weeks to writers who have been referred by a client or colleague. Returns materials only with SASE. Obtains most new clients through referrals.

Recent Sales This agency prefers not to share information on specific sales.

Terms Agent receives 15% commission on domestic sales; 20% commission on foreign sales. Offers written contract, binding for 3-5 years; 2-month notice must be given to terminate contract. Charges clients for photocopying, express mail, overseas postage, book purchase.

◐ THE DAMARIS ROWLAND AGENCY

5 Cooper Rd., Apt. 13H, New York NY 10010. **Contact:** Damaris Rowland. Estab. 1994. Member of AAR.

O⇁ This agency specializes in women's fiction.

How to Contact Query with SASE. Obtains most new clients through recommendations from others, solicitations, conferences.

Terms Agent receives 15% commission on domestic sales; 20% commission on foreign sales. Offers written contract.

◩ THE PETER RUBIE LITERARY AGENCY

240 W. 35th St., Suite 500, New York NY 10001. (212)279-1776. Fax: (212)279-0927. E-mail: peterrubie@prlit.com. Web site: www.prlit.com. **Contact:** Peter Rubie, June Clark (pralit@aol.com). Estab. 2000. Member of AAR. Represents 130 clients. 20% of clients are new/unpublished writers.

• Prior to opening his agency, Mr. Rubie was a founding partner of another literary agency (Perkins, Rubie & Associates), and the fiction editor at Walker and Co.; Ms. Clark is the author of several books and plays, and previously worked in cable TV marketing and promotion.

Member Agents Peter Rubie (crime, science fiction, fantasy, literary fiction, thrillers, narrative/serious nonfiction, business, self-help, how-to, popular, food/wine, history, commercial science, music, education, parenting); June Clark (celebrity biographies, parenting, pets, women's issues, teen nonfiction, how-to, self-help, offbeat business, food/wine, commercial New Age, pop culture, entertainment, gay/lesbian).

Represents Nonfiction books, novels. **Considers these nonfiction areas:** Business/economics; current affairs; ethnic/cultural interests; gay/lesbian issues; how-to; popular culture; science/technology; self-help/personal improvement; TV; creative nonfiction (narrative); health/nutrition; cooking/food/wine; music; theater/film; prescriptive New Age; parenting/education; pets; commercial academic material. **Considers these fiction areas:** Fantasy; historical; literary; science fiction; thriller.

How to Contact For fiction, submit short synopsis, first 30-40 pages. For nonfiction, submit 1-page overview of the book, TOC, outline, 1-2 sample chapters. Responds in 2 months to queries; 3 months to mss. Returns materials only with SASE. Obtains most new clients through recommendations from others.

Recent Sales Sold 50 titles in the last year. *Walking Money*, by James Born (Putnam); *Dark Hills Divide*, by Patrick Carman; *One Nation Under God*, by James P. Moore; *28 Days*, by Gabrielle Lichterman (Adams); *Shattered Dreams*, by Harlan Ullman (Carroll & Graf); *Chef on Fire*, by Joseph Carey (Taylor); *Laughing with Lucy*, by Madelyn Pugh Davis (Emis); *Read My Hips*, by Eve Marx (Adams); *King Kong: The History of a Movie Icon*, by Ray Morton (Applause).

Terms Agent receives 15% commission on domestic sales; 20% commission on foreign sales. Offers written contract. Charges clients for photocopying and some foreign mailings.

Tips "We look for writers who are experts, have a strong platform and reputation in their field, and have an outstanding prose style. Be professional and open-minded. Know your market and learn your craft. Go to our Web site for up-to-date information on clients and sales."

◩ RUSSELL & VOLKENING

50 W. 29th St., #7E, New York NY 10001. (212)684-6050. Fax: (212)889-3026. **Contact:** Timothy Seldes, Jesseca Salky. Estab. 1940. Member of AAR. Represents 140 clients. 20% of clients are new/unpublished writers. Currently handles: 45% nonfiction books; 50% novels; 3% story collections; 2% novellas.

Represents Nonfiction books, novels, short story collections. **Considers these nonfiction areas:** Anthropology/archaeology; art/architecture/design; biography/autobiography; business/economics; cooking/foods/nutrition; current affairs; education; ethnic/cultural interests; gay/lesbian issues; government/politics/law; health/medicine; history; language/literature/criticism; military/war; money/finance; music/dance; nature/environment; photography; popular culture; psychology; science/technology; sociology; sports; theater/film; true crime/investigative; women's issues/studies; creative nonfiction. **Considers these fiction areas:** Action/adventure; detective/police/crime; ethnic; literary; mainstream/contemporary; mystery/suspense; picture books; sports; thriller.

O⇁ This agency specializes in literary fiction and narrative nonfiction.

Recent Sales *Digging to America*, by Anne Tyler (Knopf); *Get a Life*, by Nadine Gardiner; *The Franklin Affair*, by Jim Lehrer (Random House).

Terms Agent receives 15% commission on domestic sales; 20% commission on foreign sales. Charges clients for standard office expenses relating to the submission of materials.

Tips "If the query is cogent, well written, well presented, and is the type of book we'd represent, we'll ask to see the manuscript. From there, it depends purely on the quality of the work."

◐ REGINA RYAN PUBLISHING ENTERPRISES, INC.

251 Central Park W., 7D, New York NY 10024. (212)787-5589. E-mail: queryreginaryanbooks@rcn.com. **Contact:** Regina Ryan. Estab. 1976. Currently handles: 100% nonfiction books.

Literary Agents

- Prior to becoming an agent, Ms. Ryan was an editor at Alfred A. Knopf, editor-in-chief of Macmillan Adult Trade, and a book producer.

Represents Nonfiction books. **Considers these nonfiction areas:** Gardening; history; psychology; travel; women's issues/studies; narrative nonfiction; natural history (especially birds and birding); popular science; parenting; adventure; architecture.

How to Contact Query by e-mail or mail with SASE. No telephone queries. Does not accept queries for juvenile or fiction. Considers simultaneous queries. Tries to respond in 1 month to queries. Returns materials only with SASE. Obtains most new clients through recommendations from others.

Recent Sales *The Serotonin Diet*, by Judith Wurtman, PhD and Nina Marquis, MD (Rodale); *Autopsy of a Suicidal Mind*, by Edwin Shneidman, PhD (Oxford University Press); *Surviving Hitler*, by Andrea Warren (HarperCollins Books for Young Readers); *The Bomb in the Basement: The Israeli Nuclear Option*, by Michael Karpin (Simon & Schuster).

Terms Agent receives 15% commission on domestic and foreign sales. Offers written contract. Charges clients for all out-of-pocket expenses (e.g., long distance calls, messengers, freight, copying) if it's more than just a nominal amount.

Tips "An analysis of why your proposed book is different and better than the competition is essential; a sample chapter is helpful."

THE SAGALYN AGENCY

7201 Bethesda Ave., Suite 675, Bethesda MD 20814. (301)718-6440. Fax: (301)718-6444. E-mail: query@sagalyn .com. Web site: sagalyn.com. Estab. 1980. Member of AAR. Currently handles: 85% nonfiction books; 5% novels; 10% scholarly books.

Member Agents Raphael Sagalyn.

Represents Nonfiction books. **Considers these nonfiction areas:** Business/economics; history; science/technology.

- Does not want to receive stage plays, screenplays, poetry, science fiction, fantasy, romance, children's books, or young adult books.

How to Contact Please send e-mail queries only (no attachments). Include 1 of these words in the subject line: query, submission, inquiry.

Recent Sales See Web site for sales information.

Tips "We receive 1,000-1,200 queries a year, which in turn lead to 2 or 3 new clients."

VICTORIA SANDERS & ASSOCIATES

241 Avenue of the Americas, Suite 11H, New York NY 10014. (212)633-8811. Fax: (212)633-0525. E-mail: queriesvsa@hotmail.com. Web site: www.victoriasanders.com. **Contact:** Victoria Sanders, Diane Dickensheid. Estab. 1993. Member of AAR; signatory of WGA. Represents 135 clients. 25% of clients are new/unpublished writers. Currently handles: 50% nonfiction books; 50% novels.

Represents Nonfiction books, novels. **Considers these nonfiction areas:** Biography/autobiography; current affairs; ethnic/cultural interests; gay/lesbian issues; government/politics/law; history; humor/satire; language/literature/criticism; music/dance; popular culture; psychology; theater/film; translation; women's issues/studies. **Considers these fiction areas:** Action/adventure; contemporary issues; ethnic; family saga; feminist; gay/lesbian; literary; thriller.

How to Contact Query by e-mail only.

Recent Sales Sold 20+ titles in the last year. *Faithless* and *Triptych*, by Karin Slaughter (Delacorte); *Jewels: 50 Phenomenal Black Women Over 50*, by Connie Briscoe and Michael Cunningham (Bulfinch); *B Mother*, by Maureen O'Brien (Harcourt); *Vagablonde*, by Kim Green (Warner); *Next Elements*, by Jeff Chang (Basic Civitas); *The Ties That Bind*, by Dr. Bertice Berry.

Terms Agent receives 15% commission on domestic sales; 20% commission on foreign sales. Offers written contract. Charges for photocopying, messenger, express mail. If in excess of $100, client approval is required.

Tips "Limit query to letter (no calls) and give it your best shot. A good query is going to get a good response."

SCHIAVONE LITERARY AGENCY, INC.

236 Trails End, West Palm Beach FL 33413-2135. (561)966-9294. Fax: (561)966-9294. E-mail: profschia@aol.c om. Web site: www.publishersmarketplace.com/members/profschia. **Contact:** James Schiavone. Estab. 1996. Member of National Education Association. Represents 60 clients. 2% of clients are new/unpublished writers. Currently handles: 50% nonfiction books; 49% novels; 1% textbooks.

- Prior to opening his agency, Dr. Schiavone was a full professor of developmental skills at the City University of New York and author of 5 trade books and 3 textbooks.

Represents Nonfiction books, novels, juvenile books, scholarly books, textbooks. **Considers these nonfiction**

areas: Animals; anthropology/archaeology; biography/autobiography; child guidance/parenting; current affairs; education; ethnic/cultural interests; gay/lesbian issues; government/politics/law; health/medicine; history; how-to; humor/satire; juvenile nonfiction; language/literature/criticism; military/war; nature/environment; popular culture; psychology; science/technology; self-help/personal improvement; sociology; true crime/investigative. **Considers these fiction areas:** Ethnic; family saga; historical; horror; humor/satire; juvenile; literary; mainstream/contemporary; science fiction; young adult.

> O⊸ This agency specializes in celebrity biography and autobiography. Actively seeking serious nonfiction, literary fiction, and celebrity biography. Does not want to receive poetry.

How to Contact Query with SASE. One-page e-mail queries with no attachments are accepted and encouraged for a fast response. Does not accept phone or fax queries. Considers simultaneous queries. Responds in 2 weeks to queries; 6 weeks to mss. Returns materials only with SASE. Obtains most new clients through recommendations from others, solicitations, conferences.

Terms Agent receives 15% commission on domestic sales; 20% commission on foreign sales. Offers written contract. Charges clients for postage only.

Writers' Conferences Key West Literary Seminar; South Florida Writer's Conference.

Tips "I prefer to work with established authors published by major houses in New York. I will consider marketable proposals from new/previously unpublished writers."

◓ HAROLD SCHMIDT

415 W. 23rd St., #6F, New York NY 10011. **Contact:** Harold Schmidt. Member of AAR.
How to Contact Query with SASE.

◓ SUSAN SCHULMAN, A LITERARY AGENCY

454 W. 44th St., New York NY 10036-5205. (212)713-1633. Fax: (212)581-8830. E-mail: schulman@aol.com. Web site: www.susanschulmanagency.com. **Contact:** Susan Schulman, president. Estab. 1979. Member of AAR, Dramatists Guild, Women's Media Group; signatory of WGA. 10-15% of clients are new/unpublished writers. Currently handles: 70% nonfiction books; 20% novels; 10% stage plays.

Member Agents Susan Schulman (women's issues/interests, self-help, health, business, spirituality); Linda Migalti (children's books, ecology, natural sciences, business books); Emily Uhry (plays, pitches for films).

Represents Nonfiction books, novels. **Considers these nonfiction areas:** Anthropology/archaeology; biography/autobiography; child guidance/parenting; current affairs; education; ethnic/cultural interests; gay/lesbian issues; government/politics/law; health/medicine; history; how-to; juvenile nonfiction; money/finance; music/dance; nature/environment; popular culture; psychology; self-help/personal improvement; sociology; theater/film; translation; true crime/investigative; women's issues/studies. **Considers these fiction areas:** Detective/police/crime; gay/lesbian; historical; literary; mainstream/contemporary; mystery/suspense; young adult. **Considers these script subject areas:** Comedy; contemporary issues; detective/police/crime; feminist; historical; mainstream; mystery/suspense; psychic/supernatural; teen.

> O⊸ This agency specializes in books for, by, and about women's issues, including family, careers, health and spiritual development, business, sociology, history, and economics. Emphasizing contemporary women's fiction and nonfiction books of interest to women.

How to Contact Query with SASE, outline/proposal. Accepts e-mail and fax queries. Considers simultaneous queries. Responds in 1 week to queries; 6 weeks to mss. Returns materials only with SASE.

Recent Sales Sold 30 titles in the last year. *Heritage*, by Judy Nunn (Random House); *The Velvet Rage*, by Alan Downs (Da Capo Press); *The Walls Around Us*, by David Owen (Simon & Schuster); *Flight of the Creative Class*, by Richard Florida (HarperBusiness); *Bi Coastal Babe*, by Cynthia Langston (NAL); *Better Than Yesterday*, by Robyn Schneider (Delacrote); *Pinned*, by Alfred Martino (Harcourt); *The Grammar of the Heart*, by Miriam Udell Lambert (Shambhala). ***Movie/TV MOW scripts optioned/sold:*** *The Man Who Fell to Earth*, by Walter Tevis (Warner Independent); *Sideways Stories from Wayside School*, by Louis Sachar (Nickelodeon); *Blue Movie*, by Terry Southern (Mark Toberoff Productions).

Terms Agent receives 15% commission on domestic sales; 15-20% commission on foreign sales; 10-20% commission on dramatic rights sales. Charges client for special messenger or copying services, foreign mail, any other service requested by client.

◓ SCOVIL CHICHAK GALEN LITERARY AGENCY

381 Park Ave. S., Suite 1020, New York NY 10016. (212)679-8686. Fax: (212)679-6710. E-mail: info@scglit.com. Web site: www.scglit.com. **Contact:** Russell Galen. Estab. 1992. Member of AAR. Represents 300 clients. Currently handles: 70% nonfiction books; 30% novels.

Member Agents Russell Galen; Jack Scovil; Anna Ghosh; Danny Baror.

How to Contact Query with SASE or via e-mail. Considers simultaneous queries.

Recent Sales *The Last True Story I'll Ever Tell: An Accidental Soldier's Account of the War in Iraq*, by John

Crawford (Riverhead); *Naked Empire*, by Terry Goodkind (Tor); *Meant to Be*, by Walter Anderson (HarperCollins).
Terms Charges clients for photocopying and postage.

☑ SCRIBBLERS HOUSE LLC LITERARY AGENCY

P.O. Box 1007, Cooper Station, New York NY 10276-1007. E-mail: query@scribblershouse.net. Web site: www.s
cribblershouse.net. **Contact:** Stedman Mays, Garrett Gambino. Estab. 2003. 25% of clients are new/unpublished
writers.

Represents Nonfiction books, novels (occasionally). **Considers these nonfiction areas:** Business/economics;
health/medicine; history; how-to; language/literature/criticism; memoirs; popular culture; psychology; self-
help/personal improvement; sex; spirituality; diet/nutrition; the brain; personal finance; biography; politics;
writing books; relationships; gender issues; parenting. **Considers these fiction areas:** Historical; literary; wom-
en's; suspense; crime; thrillers.

How to Contact Query via e-mail. Put "Nonfiction Query" or "Fiction Query" in the subject line followed by
the title of your project. Considers simultaneous queries.

Recent Sales *Perfect Balance: Dr. Robert Greene's Breakthrough Program for Getting the Hormone Health You
Deserve*, by Robert Greene and Leah Feldon (Clarkson Potter/Random House); *Age-Proof Your Mind*, by Zaldy
Tan (Warner); *The Okinawa Program* and *The Okinawa Diet Plan*, by Bradley Willcox, Craig Willcox, and
Makoto Suzuki (Clarkson Potter/Random House); *The Emotionally Abusive Relationship*, by Beverly Engel
(Wiley); *Help Your Baby Talk*, by Dr. Robert Owens with Leah Feldon (Perigee).

Terms Agent receives 15% commission on domestic sales. Charges clients for postage, shipping, copying.

Tips "We prefer e-mail queries, but if you must send by snail mail, we will return material or respond to a
United States Postal Service-accepted SASE. (No international coupons or outdated mail strips, please.) Presentation means a lot. A well-written query letter with a brief author bio and your credentials is important. For query
letter models, go to the bookstore or online and look at the cover copy and flap copy on other books in your
general area of interest. Emulate what's best. Have an idea of other notable books that will be perceived as
being in the same vein as yours. Know what's fresh about your project and articulate it in as few words as
possible. Consult our Web site for the most up-to-date information on submitting."

☐ SCRIBE AGENCY, LLC

5508 Joylynne Dr., Madison WI 53716. E-mail: queries@scribeagency.com. Web site: www.scribeagency.com.
Contact: Kristopher O'Higgins. Estab. 2004. Represents 5 clients. 60% of clients are new/unpublished writers.
Currently handles: 100% novels.
- "We have 14 years of experience in publishing and have worked on both agency and editorial sides in
  the past, with marketing expertise to boot. We love books as much or more than anyone you know. Check
  our Web site to see what we're about."

Member Agents Kristopher O'Higgins; Jesse Vogel.

Represents Nonfiction books, novels, short story collections, novellas, juvenile books, poetry books. **Considers
these nonfiction areas:** Cooking/foods/nutrition; ethnic/cultural interests; gay/lesbian issues; humor/satire;
memoirs; music/dance; popular culture; true crime/investigative; women's issues/studies. **Considers these
fiction areas:** Action/adventure; comic books/cartoon; detective/police/crime; erotica; ethnic; experimental;
fantasy; feminist; gay/lesbian; horror; humor/satire; juvenile; literary; mainstream/contemporary; mystery/
suspense; psychic/supernatural; science fiction; thriller; young adult.
- ⚡ Actively seeking excellent writers with ideas and stories to tell. Does not want cat mysteries or anything
  not listed above.

How to Contact Query with SASE. Responds in 3-4 weeks to queries; 3-4 months to mss. Returns materials
only with SASE.

Recent Sales Sold 2 titles in the last year.

Terms Agent receives 17% commission on domestic sales; 25% commission on foreign sales. Offers written
contract. Charges for postage and photocopying.

Writers' Conferences BookExpo America; The Writer's Institute; Spring Writer's Festival; WisCon; Wisconsin
Book Festival; World Fantasy Convention.

☑ LYNN SELIGMAN, LITERARY AGENT

400 Highland Ave., Upper Montclair NJ 07043. (973)783-3631. **Contact:** Lynn Seligman. Estab. 1985. Member
of Women's Media Group. Represents 32 clients. 15% of clients are new/unpublished writers. Currently han-
dles: 70% nonfiction books; 30% novels.
- Prior to opening her agency, Ms. Seligman worked in the subsidiary rights department of Doubleday and
  Simon & Schuster, and served as an agent with Julian Bach Literary Agency (which became IMG Literary
  Agency). Foreign rights are represented by Books Crossing Borders, Inc.

Represents Nonfiction books, novels. **Considers these nonfiction areas:** Anthropology/archaeology; art/architecture/design; biography/autobiography; business/economics; child guidance/parenting; cooking/foods/nutrition; current affairs; education; ethnic/cultural interests; government/politics/law; health/medicine; history; how-to; humor/satire; interior design/decorating; language/literature/criticism; money/finance; music/dance; nature/environment; photography; popular culture; psychology; science/technology; self-help/personal improvement; sociology; theater/film; true crime/investigative; women's issues/studies. **Considers these fiction areas:** Detective/police/crime; ethnic; fantasy; feminist; gay/lesbian; historical; horror; humor/satire; literary; mainstream/contemporary; mystery/suspense; romance (contemporary, gothic, historical, regency); science fiction.

O— This agency specializes in general nonfiction and fiction. "I also do illustrated and photography books and have represented several photographers for books." This agency does not handle children's or young adult books.

How to Contact Query with SASE, sample chapters, outline/proposal. Prefers to read materials exclusively. No e-mail or fax queries. Considers simultaneous queries. Responds in 2 weeks to queries; 2 months to mss. Returns materials only with SASE. Obtains most new clients through referrals from other writers and editors.

Recent Sales Sold 15 titles in the last year. *20,001 Names for Baby, GEM edition*, by Carol McD. Wallace; *A House Divided*, by Deborah Leblanc.

Terms Agent receives 15% commission on domestic sales; 25% commission on foreign sales. Charges clients for photocopying, unusual postage, express mail, telephone expenses (checks with author first).

◪ SERENDIPITY LITERARY AGENCY, LLC

305 Gates Ave., Brooklyn NY 11216. (718)230-7689. Fax: (718)230-7829. E-mail: rbrooks@serendipitylit.com. Web site: www.serendipitylit.com. **Contact:** Regina Brooks. Estab. 2000. Represents 50 clients. 50% of clients are new/unpublished writers. Currently handles: 50% nonfiction books; 50% fiction.

• Prior to becoming an agent, Ms. Brooks was an acquisitions editor for John Wiley & Sons, Inc. and McGraw-Hill Companies.

Represents Nonfiction books, novels, juvenile books, scholarly books, children's books. **Considers these nonfiction areas:** Business/economics; current affairs; education; ethnic/cultural interests; history; juvenile nonfiction; memoirs; money/finance; multicultural; New Age/metaphysics; popular culture; psychology; religious/inspirational; science/technology; self-help/personal improvement; sports; women's issues/studies; health/medical; narrative; popular science, biography; politics; crafts/design; food/cooking; contemporary culture. **Considers these fiction areas:** Action/adventure; confession; ethnic; historical; juvenile; literary; multicultural; picture books; thriller; chick lit; lady lit; suspense; mystery; romance.

O— Actively seeking African-American nonfiction, commercial fiction, young adult novels with an urban flair, and juvenile books. "We do not represent original stage plays, screenplays, or poetry."

How to Contact Prefers to read materials exclusively. For nonfiction, submit outline, 1 sample chapter, SASE. Responds in 2 months to queries; 3 months to mss. Obtains most new clients through conferences, referrals.

Recent Sales This agency prefers not to share information on specific sales. Recent sales available upon request.

Terms Agent receives 15% commission on domestic sales; 20% commission on foreign sales. Offers written contract; 2-month notice must be given to terminate contract. Charges clients for office fees, which are taken from any advance. Does not make referrals to editing services.

Tips "We are eagerly looking for young adult books and fiction and nonfiction targeted to 20 and 30 year olds. We also represent illustrators."

◪ THE SEYMOUR AGENCY

475 Miner St., Canton NY 13617. (315)386-1831. Fax: (315)386-1037. E-mail: marysue@slic.com. Web site: www.theseymouragency.com. **Contact:** Mary Sue Seymour. Estab. 1992. Member of AAR, RWA, Authors Guild; signatory of WGA. Represents 50 clients. 5% of clients are new/unpublished writers. Currently handles: 50% nonfiction books; 50% fiction.

• Ms. Seymour is a retired New York State certified teacher.

Represents Nonfiction books, novels. **Considers these nonfiction areas:** Business/economics; health/medicine; how-to; self-help/personal improvement; Christian books; cookbooks; any well-written nonfiction that includes a proposal in standard format and 1 sample chapter. **Considers these fiction areas:** Literary; religious/inspirational (Christian books); romance (any type).

How to Contact Query with SASE, synopsis, first 50 pages for romance. Accepts e-mail queries. No fax queries. Considers simultaneous queries. Responds in 1 month to queries; 3 months to mss. Returns materials only with SASE.

Recent Sales *Interference*, by Shelley Wernlein; *The Doctor's Daughter*, by Donna MacQuigg; 2-book historical romance deal for Tracy Willouer.

Terms Agent receives 12-15% commission on domestic sales.

Writers' Conferences BookExpo America; Start Your Engines; Romantic Times Convention; ICE Escape Writers Conference; Spring Into Romance; Silicon Valley RWA Conference; Put Your Heart in a Book.

Literary Agents

N ◐ DENISE SHANNON LITERARY AGENCY, INC.

20 W. 22nd St., Suite 1603, New York NY 10010. (212)414-2911. Fax: (212)414-2930. E-mail: info@deniseshann onagency.com. Web site: www.deniseshannonagency.com. **Contact:** Denise Shannon. Estab. 2002. Member of AAR.

- Prior to opening her agency, Ms. Shannon worked for 16 years with Georges Borchardt and International Creative Management.

Represents Nonfiction books, novels. **Considers these nonfiction areas:** Biography/autobiography; business/economics; health/medicine; narrative nonfiction; politics; journalism; social history. **Considers these fiction areas:** Literary.

- ○━ "We are a boutique agency with a distinguished list of fiction and nonfiction authors."

How to Contact Submit query with description of project, bio, SASE. Accepts e-mail queries (submissions@deni seshannonagency.com).

Recent Sales *Tête À Tête: Simone de Beauvoir and Jean-Paul Sartre*, by Hazel Rowley (HarperCollins); *Organic, Inc.: The Marketing of Innocence*, by Samuel Fromartz (Harcourt); *Absurdistan*, by Gary Shteyngart (Random House); *Giving It Up*, by Stephen McCauley (Simon & Schuster).

◐ THE ROBERT E. SHEPARD AGENCY

1608 Dwight Way, Berkeley CA 94703-1804. (510)849-3999. E-mail: mail@shepardagency.com. Web site: www. shepardagency.com. **Contact:** Robert Shepard. Estab. 1994. Member of Authors Guild. Represents 60 clients. 15% of clients are new/unpublished writers. Currently handles: 90% nonfiction books; 10% scholarly books.

- Prior to opening his agency, Mr. Shepard was an editor and a sales and marketing manager in book publishing; he now writes, teaches courses for nonfiction authors, and speaks at many writers' conferences.

Represents Nonfiction books, scholarly books (appropriate for trade publishers). **Considers these nonfiction areas:** Business/economics; current affairs; gay/lesbian issues; government/politics/law; history; popular culture; sports; Judaica; narrative nonfiction; health; cultural issues; science for laypeople.

- ○━ This agency specializes in nonfiction, particularly key issues facing society and culture. Actively seeking works by experts recognized in their fields whether or not they're well-known to the general public, and books that offer fresh perspectives or new information even when the subject is familiar. Does not want to receive autobiographies, art books, or fiction.

How to Contact Query with SASE. E-mail queries encouraged. Fax and phone queries strongly discouraged. Considers simultaneous queries. Responds in 2-3 weeks to queries; 6 weeks to proposals or mss. Returns materials only with SASE. Obtains most new clients through recommendations from others, solicitations.

Recent Sales Sold 10 titles in the last year. *Night Draws Near*, by Anthony Shadid (Henry Holt); *Champagne: How the World's Most Glamorous Wine Overcame War and Hard Times*, by Don and Petie Kladstrup (William Morrow); *Word Freak: Heartbreak, Triumph, Genius, and Obsession in the World of Competitive Scrabble Players*, by Stefan Fatsis (Houghton Mifflin HC/Penguin PB); *Find More Time*, by Laura Stack (Broadway Books); *The Root of Wild Madder: Chasing the History, Mystery, and Lore of the Persian Carpet*, by Brian Murphy (Simon & Schuster).

Terms Agent receives 15% commission on domestic sales; 20% commission on foreign sales. Offers written contract, binding for term of project or until canceled; 30-day notice must be given to terminate contract. Charges clients for phone/fax, photocopying, postage (if and when the project sells).

Tips "We pay attention to detail. We believe in close working relationships between the author and agent, and in building better relationships between the author and editor. Please do your homework! There's no substitute for learning all you can about similar or directly competing books and presenting a well-reasoned competitive analysis in your proposal. Be sure to describe what's new and fresh about your work, why you are the best person to be writing on your subject, and how the book will serve the needs or interests of your intended readers. Don't work in a vacuum: Visit bookstores, talk to other writers about their experiences, and let the information you gather inform the work that you do as an author."

◐ WENDY SHERMAN ASSOCIATES, INC.

450 Seventh Ave., Suite 2307, New York NY 10123. (212)279-9027. Fax: (212)279-8863. Web site: www.wsherm an.com. **Contact:** Wendy Sherman. Estab. 1999. Member of AAR. Represents 50 clients. 30% of clients are new/unpublished writers. Currently handles: 50% nonfiction books; 50% novels.

- Prior to opening the agency, Ms. Sherman worked for The Aaron Priest agency and served as vice president, executive director, associate publisher, subsidary rights director, and sales and marketing director in the publishing industry.

Member Agents Tracy Brown; Wendy Sherman; Michelle Brower.

Represents Nonfiction books, novels. **Considers these nonfiction areas:** Psychology; narrative; practical. **Considers these fiction areas:** Literary; women's (suspense).

Literary Agents

○━ "We specialize in developing new writers, as well as working with more established writers. My experience as a publisher has proven to be a great asset to my clients."

How to Contact Query with SASE or send outline/proposal, 1 sample chapter. No e-mail queries. Considers simultaneous queries. Responds in 1 month to queries. Returns materials only with SASE. Obtains most new clients through recommendations from others.

Recent Sales Fiction clients include: William Lashner, Nani Power, DW Buffa, Howard Bahr, Suzanne Chazin, Sarah Stonich, Ad Hudler, Mary Sharratt, Libby Street, Heather Estay, Darri Stephens, Megan Desales. Nonfiction clients include: Rabbi Mark Borovitz, Alan Eisenstock, Esther Perel, Clifton Leaf, Maggie Estep, Greg Baer, Martin Friedman, Lundy Bancroft, Alvin Ailey Dance, Lise Friedman, Liz Landers, Vicky Mainzer.

Terms Agent receives 15% commission on domestic sales; 20% commission on foreign sales. Offers written contract.

◑ ROSALIE SIEGEL, INTERNATIONAL LITERARY AGENCY, INC.

1 Abey Dr., Pennington NJ 08543. (609)737-1007. Fax: (609)737-3708. **Contact:** Rosalie Siegel. Estab. 1977. Member of AAR. Represents 35 clients. 10% of clients are new/unpublished writers. Currently handles: 45% nonfiction books; 45% novels; 10% young adult books; short story collections for current clients.

How to Contact Obtains most new clients through referrals from writers and friends.

Terms Agent receives 15% commission on domestic sales; 20% commission on foreign sales. Offers written contract; 2-month notice must be given to terminate contract. Charges clients for photocopying.

Tips "I'm not looking for new authors in an active way."

⊕ ◑ JEFFREY SIMMONS LITERARY AGENCY

15 Penn House, Mallory St., London NW8 8SX England. (44)(207)224-8917. E-mail: jasimmons@btconnect.com. **Contact:** Jeffrey Simmons. Estab. 1978. Represents 43 clients. 40% of clients are new/unpublished writers. Currently handles: 65% nonfiction books; 35% novels.

● Prior to becoming an agent, Mr. Simmons was a publisher. He is also an author.

Represents Nonfiction books, novels. **Considers these nonfiction areas:** Biography/autobiography; current affairs; government/politics/law; history; language/literature/criticism; memoirs; music/dance; popular culture; sociology; sports; theater/film; translation; true crime/investigative. **Considers these fiction areas:** Action/adventure; confession; detective/police/crime; family saga; literary; mainstream/contemporary; mystery/suspense; thriller.

○━ This agency seeks to handle good books and promising young writers. "My long experience in publishing and as an author and ghostwriter means I can offer an excellent service all around, especially in terms of editorial experience where appropriate." Actively seeking quality fiction, biography, autobiography, showbiz, personality books, law, crime, politics, and world affairs. Does not want to receive science fiction, horror, fantasy, juvenile, academic books, or specialist subjects (e.g., cooking, gardening, religious).

How to Contact Submit sample chapter, outline/proposal, SASE (IRCs if necessary). Prefers to read materials exclusively. Responds in 1 week to queries; 1 month to mss. Obtains most new clients through recommendations from others, solicitations.

Recent Sales Sold 16 titles in the last year. *The Masks of Christ*, by Picknett & Prince (Time Warner UK/Simon & Schuster US); *The Complete One Foot in the Grave*, by Webber (Orion).

Terms Agent receives 10-15% commission on domestic sales; 15% commission on foreign sales. Offers written contract, binding for lifetime of book in question or until it becomes out of print.

Tips "When contacting us with an outline/proposal, include a brief biographical note (listing any previous publications, with publishers and dates). Preferably tell us if the book has already been offered elsewhere."

✤ ◑ BEVERLEY SLOPEN LITERARY AGENCY

131 Bloor St. W., Suite 711, Toronto ON M5S 1S3 Canada. (416)964-9598. Fax: (416)921-7726. E-mail: beverly@slopenagency.ca. Web site: www.slopenagency.ca. **Contact:** Beverley Slopen. Estab. 1974. Represents 70 clients. 20% of clients are new/unpublished writers. Currently handles: 60% nonfiction books; 40% novels.

● Prior to opening her agency, Ms. Slopen worked in publishing and as a journalist.

Represents Nonfiction books, novels, scholarly books, textbooks (college). **Considers these nonfiction areas:** Anthropology/archaeology; biography/autobiography; business/economics; current affairs; psychology; sociology; true crime/investigative; women's issues/studies. **Considers these fiction areas:** Literary; mystery/suspense.

○━ This agency has a strong bent toward Canadian writers. Actively seeking serious nonfiction that is accessible and appealing to the general reader. Does not want to receive fantasy, science fiction, or children's books.

How to Contact Query with SAE and IRCs. Returns materials only with SASE (Canadian postage only). Accepts short e-mail queries. Considers simultaneous queries. Responds in 2 months to queries.

Recent Sales Sold over 40 titles in the last year. *Court Lady* and *Country Wife*, by Lita-Rose Betcherman (HarperCollins Canada/Morrow/Wiley UK); *Vermeer's Hat*, by Timothy Brook (HarperCollins Canada); *Midnight Cab*, by James W. Nichol (Canongate US/Droemer); *Lady Franklin's Revenge*, by Ken McGoogan (HarperCollins Canada/Bantam UK); *Understanding Uncertainty*, by Jeffrey Rosenthal (HarperCollins Canada); *Damaged Angels*, by Bonnie Buxton (Carroll & Graf US); *Sea of Dreams*, by Adam Mayers (McClelland & Stewart Canada); *Memory Book*, by Howard Engel (Carroll & Graf); *Written in the Flesh*, by Edward Shorter (University of Toronto Press); *Punch Line*, by Joey Slinger. Other clients include Modris Eksteins, Michael Marrus, Robert Fulford, Morley Torgov, Elliott Leyton, Don Gutteridge, Joanna Goodman, Roberta Rich, Jennifer Welsh, Margaret Wente, Frank Wydra.

Terms Agent receives 15% commission on domestic sales; 10% commission on foreign sales. Offers written contract, binding for 2 years; 3-month notice must be given to terminate contract.

Tips "Please, no unsolicited manuscripts."

▦ ◷ ROBERT SMITH LITERARY AGENCY, LTD.

12 Bridge Wharf, 156 Caledonian Rd., London NI 9UU England. (44)(207)278-2444. Fax: (44)(207)833-5680. E-mail: robertsmith.literaryagency@virgin.net. **Contact:** Robert Smith. Estab. 1997. Member of AAA. Represents 25 clients. 10% of clients are new/unpublished writers. Currently handles: 80% nonfiction books; 20% syndicated material.

• Prior to becoming an agent, Mr. Smith was a book publisher.

Represents Nonfiction books, syndicated material. **Considers these nonfiction areas:** Biography/autobiography; cooking/foods/nutrition; health/medicine; memoirs; music/dance; New Age/metaphysics; popular culture; self-help/personal improvement; theater/film; true crime/investigative.

O—ᴙ This agency offers clients full management service in all media. Clients are not necessarily book authors. "Our special expertise is in placing newspaper series internationally." Actively seeking autobiographies.

How to Contact Submit outline/proposal, SASE (IRCs if necessary). Prefers to read materials exclusively. Accepts e-mail and fax queries. Responds in 1 week to queries. Returns materials only with SASE. Obtains most new clients through recommendations from others, direct approaches to prospective authors.

Recent Sales Sold 25 titles in the last year. *Bill Hicks*, by Kevin Booth and Michael Bertin (HarperCollins); *For Better or Worse: Her Story*, by Christine Hamilton (Robson Books); *Warlord (Himmler)*, by Martin Allen (Constable and Robinson). Other clients include Stewart Evans, Neil Hamilton, James Haspiel, Geoffrey Guiliano, Roberta Kray, Norman Parker, Mike Reid, Donald Rumbelow, Douglas Thompson.

Terms Agent receives 15% commission on domestic sales; 20% commission on foreign sales. Offers written contract, binding for 3 months; 3-month notice must be given to terminate contract. Charges clients for couriers, photocopying, overseas mailings of mss (subject to client authorization).

◷ MICHAEL SNELL LITERARY AGENCY

P.O. Box 1206, Truro MA 02666-1206. (508)349-3718. **Contact:** Michael Snell. Estab. 1978. Represents 200 clients. 25% of clients are new/unpublished writers. Currently handles: 90% nonfiction books; 10% novels.

• Prior to opening his agency, Mr. Snell served as an editor at Wadsworth and Addison-Wesley for 13 years.

Member Agents Michael Snell (business, leadership, pets, sports); Patricia Snell (pets, relationships, health, communication, parenting, self-help, how-to).

Represents Nonfiction books. **Considers these nonfiction areas:** Agriculture/horticulture; animals (pets); anthropology/archaeology; art/architecture/design; business/economics; child guidance/parenting; computers/electronic; cooking/foods/nutrition; crafts/hobbies; current affairs; education; ethnic/cultural interests; gardening; gay/lesbian issues; government/politics/law; health/medicine; history; how-to; humor/satire; interior design/decorating; language/literature/criticism; military/war; money/finance; music/dance; nature/environment; New Age/metaphysics; photography; popular culture; psychology; recreation; religious/inspirational; science/technology; self-help/personal improvement; sex; spirituality; sports (fitness); theater/film; travel; true crime/investigative; women's issues/studies; creative nonfiction.

O—ᴙ This agency specializes in how-to, self-help, and all types of business and computer books, from low-level how-to to professional and reference. Especially interested in business, health, law, medicine, psychology, science, and women's issues. Actively seeking strong book proposals in any nonfiction area where a clear need exists for a new book—especially self-help and how-to books on all subjects, from business to personal well-being. Does not want to receive fiction, children's books, or complete mss (considers proposals only).

How to Contact Query with SASE. Prefers to read materials exclusively. Responds in 1 week to queries; 2 weeks to mss. Obtains most new clients through unsolicited mss, word of mouth, *Literary Market Place, Guide to Literary Agents*.

Recent Sales *The Ultimate Book of Small Business Lists*, by Gene Marks (Adams Media); *Customer Service Made Easy*, by Paul Levesque (Entrepreneur Press); *How Your Horse Wants You to Ride*, by Gincy Bucklin (Wiley).
Terms Agent receives 15% commission on domestic and foreign sales.
Tips "Send a maximum 1-page query with SASE. Brochure on 'How to Write a Book Proposal' is available on request with SASE. We suggest prospective clients read Michael Snell's book, *From Book Idea to Bestseller* (Prima 1997), or purchase a model propodal directly from the company."

SPECTRUM LITERARY AGENCY

320 Central Park W., Suite 1-D, New York NY 10025. Web site: www.spectrumliteraryagency.com. **Contact:** Eleanor Wood, president. Represents 90 clients. Currently handles: 10% nonfiction books; 90% novels.
Member Agents Lucienne Diver.
Represents Nonfiction books, novels. **Considers these fiction areas:** Fantasy; historical; mainstream/contemporary; mystery/suspense; romance; science fiction.
How to Contact Query with SASE, include publishing credits and background information. No phone, e-mail, or fax queries. Responds in 1-3 months to queries. Obtains most new clients through recommendations from authors.
Recent Sales Sold over 100 titles in the last year. This agency prefers not to share information on specific sales.
Terms Agent receives 15% commission on domestic sales. Deducts for photocopying and book orders.

SPENCERHILL ASSOCIATES

P.O. Box 374, Chatham NY 12037. (518)392-9293. Fax: (518)392-9554. E-mail: ksolem@klsbooks.com. **Contact:** Karen Solem. Estab. 2001. Member of AAR. Represents 40 clients. 5% of clients are new/unpublished writers. Currently handles: 5% nonfiction books; 90% novels; 5% novellas.
• Prior to becoming an agent, Ms. Solem was editor-in-chief at HarperCollins and an associate publisher.
Represents Nonfiction books, novels. **Considers these nonfiction areas:** Animals; religious/inspirational. **Considers these fiction areas:** Detective/police/crime; historical; mainstream/contemporary; religious/inspirational; romance; thriller.
• "I handle mostly commercial women's fiction, romance, thrillers, and mysteries. I also represent Christian fiction and nonfiction." No poetry, science fiction, juvenile, or scripts.
How to Contact Query with SASE, proposal package, outline. Responds in 1 month to queries. Returns materials only with SASE.
Recent Sales Sold 115 titles in the last year.
Terms Agent receives 15% commission on domestic sales; 20% commission on foreign sales. Offers written contract; 3-month notice must be given to terminate contract.

THE SPIELER AGENCY

154 W. 57th St., 13th Floor, Room 135, New York NY 10019. **Contact:** Katya Balter. Estab. 1981. Represents 160 clients. 2% of clients are new/unpublished writers.
• Prior to opening his agency, Mr. Spieler was a magazine editor.
Member Agents Joe Spieler; John Thornton (nonfiction); Lisa M. Ross (fiction, nonfiction); Deirdre Mullane (nonfiction); Eric Myers (nonfiction, fiction); Victoria Shoemaker (fiction, nonfiction).
Represents Nonfiction books, novels, children's books. **Considers these nonfiction areas:** Biography/autobiography; business/economics; child guidance/parenting; current affairs; gay/lesbian issues; government/politics/law; history; memoirs; money/finance; music/dance; nature/environment; religious/inspirational; sociology; spirituality; theater/film; travel; women's issues/studies. **Considers these fiction areas:** Feminist; gay/lesbian; literary.
How to Contact Query with SASE. Prefers to read materials exclusively. Returns materials only with SASE; otherwise materials are discarded when rejected. No fax queries. Considers simultaneous queries. Responds in 2 weeks to queries; 2 months to mss. Obtains most new clients through recommendations, listing in *Guide to Literary Agents*.
Recent Sales *What's the Matter with Kansas*, by Thomas Frank (Metropolitan/Holt); *Natural History of the Rich*, by Richard Conniff (W.W. Norton); *Juicing the Game*, by Howard Bryant (Viking).
Terms Agent receives 15% commission on domestic sales. Charges clients for messenger bills, photocopying, postage.
Writers' Conferences London Book Fair.

PHILIP G. SPITZER LITERARY AGENCY, INC

50 Talmage Farm Ln., East Hampton NY 11937. (631)329-3650. Fax: (631)329-3651. E-mail: spitzer516@aol.com. **Contact:** Philip Spitzer. Estab. 1969. Member of AAR. Represents 60 clients. 10% of clients are new/unpublished writers. Currently handles: 50% nonfiction books; 50% novels.

• Prior to opening his agency, Mr. Spitzer served at New York University Press, McGraw-Hill, and the John Cushman Associates literary agency.

Represents Nonfiction books, novels. **Considers these nonfiction areas:** Biography/autobiography; business/economics; current affairs; ethnic/cultural interests; government/politics/law; health/medicine; history; language/literature/criticism; military/war; music/dance; nature/environment; popular culture; psychology; sociology; sports; theater/film; true crime/investigative. **Considers these fiction areas:** Detective/police/crime; literary; mainstream/contemporary; mystery/suspense; sports; thriller.

   O→ This agency specializes in mystery/suspense, literary fiction, sports, and general nonfiction (no how-to).

How to Contact Query with SASE, outline, 1 sample chapter. Responds in 1 week to queries; 6 weeks to mss. Obtains most new clients through recommendations from others.

Recent Sales *The Narrows* and *Lost Light*, by Michael Connelly; *Shadow Man*, by Jonathon King; *Something's Down There*, by Mickey Spillane; *Missing Justice*, by Alafair Burke; *Last Car to Elysian Fields*, by James Lee Burke; *Shattered*, by Deborah Puglisi Sharp with Marjorie Perston.

Terms Agent receives 15% commission on domestic sales; 20% commission on foreign sales. Charges clients for photocopying.

Writers' Conferences BookExpo America.

☺ NANCY STAUFFER ASSOCIATES

P.O. Box 1203, Darien CT 06820. (203)655-3717. Fax: (203)655-3704. E-mail: nanstauf@optonline.net. **Contact:** Nancy Stauffer Cahoon. Estab. 1989. Member of Authors Guild. 5% of clients are new/unpublished writers. Currently handles: 15% nonfiction books; 85% novels.

Represents Nonfiction books, novels. **Considers these nonfiction areas:** Current affairs; ethnic/cultural interests; creative nonfiction (narrative). **Considers these fiction areas:** Contemporary issues; literary; regional.

How to Contact Obtains most new clients through referrals from existing clients.

Recent Sales New novels by Sherman Alexie, Mark Spragg, and William C. Harris.

Terms Agent receives 15% commission on domestic and dramatic rights sales; 20% commission on foreign sales.

Tips "We work with foreign agents in all major markets."

☺ STEELE-PERKINS LITERARY AGENCY

26 Island Ln., Canandaigua NY 14424. (585)396-9290. Fax: (585)396-3579. E-mail: pattiesp@aol.com. **Contact:** Pattie Steele-Perkins. Member of AAR, RWA. Currently handles: 100% novels.

Represents Novels. **Considers these fiction areas:** Mainstream/contemporary; multicultural; romance (inspirational); women's.

How to Contact Submit outline, 3 sample chapters, SASE. Considers simultaneous queries. Responds in 6 weeks to queries. Returns materials only with SASE. Obtains most new clients through recommendations from others, queries/solicitations.

Recent Sales This agency prefers not to share information on specific sales.

Terms Agent receives 15% commission on domestic sales. Offers written contract, binding for 1 year; 1-month notice must be given to terminate contract.

Writers' Conferences RWA National Conference; BookExpo America; CBA Convention; Romance Slam Jam.

Tips "Be patient. E-mail rather than call. Make sure what you are sending is the best it can be."

☺ STERNIG & BYRNE LITERARY AGENCY

2370 S. 107th St., Apt. #4, Milwaukee WI 53227-2036. (414)328-8034. Fax: (414)328-8034. E-mail: jackbyrne@hotmail.com. Web site: www.sff.net/people/jackbyrne. **Contact:** Jack Byrne. Estab. 1950s. Member of SFWA, MWA. Represents 30 clients. 10% of clients are new/unpublished writers. Currently handles: 5% nonfiction books; 85% novels; 10% juvenile books.

Represents Nonfiction books, novels, juvenile books. **Considers these fiction areas:** Fantasy; horror; mystery/suspense; science fiction.

   O→ "Our client list is comfortably full and our current needs are therefore quite limited." Actively seeking science fiction/fantasy by established writers. Does not want to receive romance, poetry, textbooks, or highly specialized nonfiction.

How to Contact Query with SASE. Accepts e-mail queries (no attachments). Responds in 3 weeks to queries; 3 months to mss. Returns materials only with SASE.

Recent Sales Sold 13 new titles and 40+ reprints/foreign rights in the last year. *Magic Bites*, by Ilona Andrews; *Webmage*, by Kelly McCullough. Other clients include Lyn McConche, Betty Ren Wright, Jo Walton, Moira Moore, Sarah Monette, John C. Wright, Naomi Kritzer.

Terms Agent receives 15% commission on domestic sales; 20% commission on foreign sales. Offers written contract; 2-month notice must be given to terminate contract.

Tips "Don't send first drafts, have a professional presentation (including cover letter), and know your field. Read what's been done—good and bad."

◐ STIMOLA LITERARY STUDIO

308 Chase Ct., Edgewater NJ 07020. Phone/Fax: (201)945-9353. E-mail: ltrystudio@aol.com. **Contact:** Rosemary B. Stimola. Member of AAR.

Represents Preschool through young adult fiction and nonfiction.

How to Contact Query with SASE or via e-mail (no unsolicited attachments). Responds in 3 weeks to queries; 2 months to mss. Obtains most new clients through referrals. Unsolicted submissions are still accepted.

Recent Sales *Gregor and the Marks of Secret*, by Suzanne Collins (Scholastic); *Rooftop*, by Paul Volponi (Viking); *The Wizard, the Witch & Two Girls from Jersey*, by Lisa Papademetriou (Razorbill); *Swords*, by Ben Boos (Candlewick); *Max and Pinky*, by Maxwell Eaton III (Random House); *An Orange in January*, by Dianna Hutts Aston (Dial Books).

Terms Agent receives 15% commission on domestic sales; 20% commission on foreign sales (if subagents are employed).

Tips "Offers written contract covering all children's literary work not previously published or under agreement. No phone inquiries."

◑ PAM STRICKLER AUTHOR MANAGEMENT

1 Water St., New Paltz NY 12561. (845)255-0061. Web site: www.pamstrickler.com. **Contact:** Pamela Dean Strickler. Member of AAR.

- Prior to opening her agency, Ms. Strickler was senior editor at Ballantine Books.

- ⊶ Specializes in romance and women's fiction. No nonfiction or children's books.

How to Contact Query via e-mail with 1-page letter of plot description and first 10 pages of ms (no attachments). *No unsolicited mss.*

Recent Sales *Lady Dearing's Masquerade*, by Elena Greene (New American Library); *Her Body of Work*, by Marie Donovan (Harlequin/Blaze); *Deceived*, by Nicola Cornick (Harlequin/HQN).

⟦N⟧ ◐ REBECCA STRONG INTERNATIONAL LITERARY AGENCY

235 W. 108th St., #35, New York NY 10025. (212)865-1569. **Contact:** Rebecca Strong. Estab. 2003. 95% of clients are new/unpublished writers. Currently handles: 50% nonfiction books; 40% novels; 10% story collections.

- Prior to opening her agency, Ms. Strong was an industry executive with experience editing and licensing in the US and UK. She has worked at Crown/Random House, Harmony/Random House, Bloomsbury, and Harvill.

Represents Nonfiction books, novels, short story collections. **Considers these nonfiction areas:** Biography/autobiography; cooking/foods/nutrition; current affairs; how-to; interior design/decorating; memoirs; self-help/personal improvement. **Considers these fiction areas:** Detective/police/crime; experimental; historical; humor/satire; literary; mainstream/contemporary; mystery/suspense; thriller.

- ⊶ "We are a consciously small agency dedicated to established and buidling writers' book publishing careers rather than representing one-time projects." Does not want poetry, screenplays, or any unsolicited mss.

How to Contact Query with SASE. No e-mail or fax queries. Considers simultaneous queries. Responds in 2 months to queries. Returns materials only with SASE. Obtains most new clients through recommendations from others, conferences.

Terms Agent receives 15% commission on domestic sales; 20% commission on foreign sales. Offers written contract, binding for 10 years; 30-day notice must be given to terminate contract.

Tips "I represent writers with prior publishing experience only: journalists, magazine writers, or writers of fiction who have been published in anthologies or literary magazines. There are exceptions to this guideline, but not many."

◐ THE STROTHMAN AGENCY, LLC

One Faneuil Hall Marketplace, 3rd Floor, Boston MA 02109. (617)742-2011. Fax: (617)742-2014. **Contact:** Wendy Strothman, Dan O'Connell. Estab. 2003. Represents 50 clients. Currently handles: 60% nonfiction books; 15% novels; 5% juvenile books; 20% scholarly books.

- Prior to becoming an agent, Ms. Strothman was head of Beacon Press (1983-1995) and executive vice president of Houghton Mifflin's Trade & Reference Division (1996-2002).

Member Agents John Ryden; Wendy Strothman; Dan O'Connell.

Represents Nonfiction books, novels, scholarly books. **Considers these nonfiction areas:** Current affairs;

government/politics/law; history; language/literature/criticism; nature/environment. **Considers these fiction areas:** Literary.

○┓ "Because we are highly selective in the clients we represent, we increase the value publishers place on our properties. We seek out public figures, scholars, journalists, and other acknowledged and emerging experts in their fields. We specialize in narrative nonfiction, memoir, history, science and nature, arts and culture, literary travel, current affairs, and some business. We have a highly selective practice in literary fiction and children's literature." Actively seeking scholarly nonfiction written to appeal to several audiences. Does not want commercial fiction, romance, science fiction, or self-help.

How to Contact Query with SASE. Considers simultaneous queries. Responds in 3 weeks to queries; 1 month to mss. Returns materials only with SASE. Obtains most new clients through recommendations from others.

Recent Sales Sold 16 titles in the last year. *Iran Awakening: A Memoir of Revolution and Hope*, by Shirin Ebadi (Random House); *The Race Card*, by Richard T. Ford (Farrar, Straus & Giroux); *High Crimes: How a Mountain of Money Draws Thievery, Extortion, Fraud and Death to the Top of the World*, by Michael Kodas (Hyperion); *Errors and Omissions*, by Paul Goldstein (Doubleday); *IP Rules: How Law and Legal Change Drive the Risk and Reward of Intellectual Assets*, by Paul Goldstein (Viking/Portfolio); *The Collapse of the Conservative Case*, by James Galbraith (Holt); *Righteous Warrior: Jesse Helms and the Rise of Modern Conservatism*, by William A. Link (St. Martin's Press); *Addled*, by JoeAnn Hart (Little, Brown).

Terms Agent receives 15% commission on domestic sales; 20% commission on foreign sales. Offers written contract; 30-day notice must be given to terminate contract.

🌐 ◙ THE SUSIJN AGENCY

64 Great Titchfield St., London W1W 7QH England. (44)(207)580-6341. Fax: (44)(207)580-8626. Web site: www.thesusijnagency.com. **Contact:** Laura Susijn, Nicola Barr. Currently handles: 25% nonfiction books; 75% novels.

● Prior to becoming an agent, Ms. Susijn was a rights director at Sheil Land Associates and at Fourth Estate; Ms. Barr was a commissioning editor at Flamingo (literary imprint of HarperCollins).

Represents Nonfiction books, novels. **Considers these nonfiction areas:** Biography/autobiography; memoirs; multicultural; popular culture; science/technology; travel. **Considers these fiction areas:** Literary.

○┓ Does not want romance, sagas, fantasy, or screenplays.

How to Contact Submit outline, 2 sample chapters, SASE/IRC. Returns materials only with SASE. Obtains most new clients through recommendations from others.

Recent Sales Sold 120 titles in the last year. Clients include Dubravka Ugresic, Peter Ackroyd, Robin Baker, BI Feiyu, Jeffrey Moore, Anita Nair, Podium, De Arbeiderspers, Van Oorschot.

Terms Agent receives 15% commission on domestic sales; 15-20% commission on foreign sales. Offers written contract; 6-week notice must be given to terminate contract. Charges clients for photocopying (only if sale is made).

Ⓝ ◙ THE SWETKY AGENCY

2150 Balboa Way, No. 29, St. George UT 84770. E-mail: fayeswetky@amsaw.org. Web site: www.amsaw.org/swetkyagency/index-agency.html. **Contact:** Faye M. Swetky. Estab. 2000. Member of American Society of Authors and Writers. Represents 40+ clients. 80% of clients are new/unpublished writers. Currently handles: 10% nonfiction books; 30% novels; 10% juvenile books; 40% movie scripts; 10% TV scripts.

● Prior to becoming an agent, Ms. Swetky was an editor and corporate manager. She has also raised and raced thoroughbred horses.

Represents Nonfiction books, novels, short story collections, juvenile books, movie scripts, feature film, TV scripts, TV movie of the week, sitcom, documentary. **Considers these nonfiction areas:** Agriculture/horticulture; Americana; animals; anthropology/archaeology; art/architecture/design; biography/autobiography; business/economics; child guidance/parenting; computers/electronic; cooking/foods/nutrition; creative nonfiction; current affairs; education; ethnic/cultural interests; gardening; gay/lesbian issues; government/politics/law; health/medicine; history; how-to; humor/satire; language/literature/criticism; memoirs; military/war; money/finance; multicultural; music/dance; nature/environment; philosophy; photography; popular culture; psychology; recreation; regional; religious/inspirational; science/technology; self-help/personal improvement; sex; sociology; software; spirituality; sports; theater/film; translation; travel; true crime/investigative; women's issues/studies. **Considers these fiction areas:** Action/adventure; comic books/cartoon; confession; detective/police/crime; erotica; ethnic; experimental; family saga; fantasy; feminist; gay/lesbian; gothic; hi-lo; historical; horror; humor/satire; juvenile; literary; mainstream/contemporary; military/war; multicultural; multimedia; mystery/suspense; occult; picture books; plays; poetry; poetry in translation; regional; religious/inspirational; romance; science fiction; short story collections; spiritual; sports; thriller; translation; westerns/frontier; young adult. **Considers these script subject areas:** Action/adventure; biography/autobiography; cartoon/animation; comedy; contemporary issues; detective/police/crime; erotica; ethnic; experimental; family saga; fantasy; feminist;

gay/lesbian; glitz; historical; horror; juvenile; mainstream; multicultural; multimedia; mystery/suspense; psychic/supernatural; regional; religious/inspirational; romantic comedy; romantic drama; science fiction; sports; teen; thriller; western/frontier.

○┱ ''I handle only book-length fiction and nonfiction and feature-length movie and television scripts. Please visit our Web site before submitting. All agency-related information is there, including a sample contract, e-mail submission forms, policies, clients, etc.'' Actively seeking young adult material. Do not send unprofessionally prepared mss and/or scripts.

How to Contact See Web site for submission instructions. Accepts e-mail queries only. Considers simultaneous queries. Response time varies. Obtains most new clients through queries from the Web site.

Recent Sales Sold 6 titles and 8 scripts in the last year. *Solid Stiehl*, by D.J. Herda (Archebooks); *24/7*, by Susan Diplacido (Zumaya Publications); *House on the Road to Salisbury*, by Lisa Adams (Archebooks). *Movie/ TV MOW scripts optioned/sold:* *Demons 5*, by Jim O'Rear (Katzir Productions); *Detention* and *Instinct Vs. Reason*, by Garrett Hargrove (Filmjack Productions).

Terms Agent receives 15% commission on domestic sales; 20% commission on foreign and dramatic rights sales. Offers written contract, binding for 1 year; 30-day notice must be given to terminate contract.

Tips ''Be professional. Have a professionally prepared product. See the Web site for instructions beofre making any queries or submissions.''

MARY M. TAHAN LITERARY, LLC

P.O. Box 1060 Gracie Station, New York NY 10028. E-mail: querymarytahan@earthlink.net. Web site: www.tah anliterary.com. **Contact:** Mary M. Tahan. Member of AAR, Authors Guild.

Member Agents Mary M. Tahan; Jena H. Anderson.

Represents Nonfiction books, novels, rights for books optioned for TV movies and feature films. **Considers these nonfiction areas:** Biography/autobiography; cooking/foods/nutrition; health/medicine; history; how-to; memoirs; money/finance; psychology; writing books; fashion/beauty/style; relationships.

How to Contact Accepts submissions via mail or e-mail. For nonfiction, submit query or proposal package with outline, SASE. For fiction, submit brief synopsis (1-2 pages), first 3 chapters, SASE. Responds in 1 month to queries. Returns materials only with SASE.

Recent Sales *A Few Good Women: A History of the Rise of Women in the Military*, by Evelyn Monahan and Rosemary Neidel-Greenlee (Knopf); *The Siren of Solace Glen*, by Susan S. James (Berkley); *Finding the Right Words for the Holidays*, by J. Beverly Daniels (Pocket); *The Stinking Rose Restaurant Cookbook*, by Andrea Froncillo with Jennifer Jeffrey (Ten Speed Press).

Tips ''For nonfiction, it's crucial to research how to write a proposal, especially how to analyze your book's competing titles. For both fiction and nonfiction, do not send a full manuscript. Please do not phone or fax queries.''

TALCOTT NOTCH LITERARY

276 Forest Rd., Milford CT 06460. (203)877-1146. Fax: (203)876-9517. E-mail: gpanettieri@talcottnotch.net; editorial@talcottnotch.net. Web site: www.talcottnotch.net. **Contact:** Gina Panettieri. Estab. 2003. Represents 25 clients. 30% of clients are new/unpublished writers.

● Prior to becoming an agent, Ms. Panettieri was a freelance writer and editor.

Represents Nonfiction books, novels, juvenile books, scholarly books, textbooks. **Considers these nonfiction areas:** Agriculture/horticulture; animals; anthropology/archaeology; art/architecture/design; biography/autobiography; business/economics; child guidance/parenting; computers/electronic; cooking/foods/nutrition; current affairs; education; ethnic/cultural interests; gay/lesbian issues; government/politics/law; health/medicine; history; how-to; memoirs; military/war; money/finance; music/dance; nature/environment; popular culture; psychology; science/technology; self-help/personal improvement; sociology; sports; true crime/investigative; women's issues/studies; New Age/metaphysics, interior design/decorating, juvenile nonfiction. **Considers these fiction areas:** Action/adventure; detective/police/crime; juvenile; mystery/suspense; thriller; young adult.

○┱ Actively seeking prescriptive nonfiction and mysteries. Does not want poetry or picture books.

How to Contact Query via e-mail (preferred) or with SASE. Considers simultaneous queries. Responds in 1 week to queries; 2 weeks to mss. Returns materials only with SASE. Obtains most new clients through ''our listings with publishing-related Web sites or from writers seeing our sales listed in Publishers Marketplace.''

Recent Sales Sold 24 titles in the last year. *Your Plus-Size Pregnancy*, by Dr. Bruce Rodgers and Brette Sember (Barricade Books); *The Healing Parent*, by Dr. Karyn Purvis, Dr. David Cross, and Wendy Sunshine (McGraw-Hill); *Multiple Job Offers in Ten Days*, by Jonathan Price (Career Books). Other clients include Mark Ellis (writing as James Axler), Wayne Wilson, Ron Franscell, Dr. Dawn-Michelle Baude, Gloria Petersen, Ira Berkowitz.

Terms Agent receives 15% commission on domestic sales; 20% commission on foreign sales. Offers written contract, binding for 1 year.

Tips "Present your book or project effectively in your query. Don't include links to a Web page rather than a traditional query, and take the time to prepare a thorough but brief synopsis of the material. Make the effort to prepare a thoughtful analysis of comparison titles. How is your work different, yet would appeal to those same readers?"

◉ ROSLYN TARG LITERARY AGENCY, INC.

105 W. 13th St., New York NY 10011. (212)206-9390. Fax: (212)989-6233. E-mail: roslyn@roslyntargagency.c om. **Contact:** Roslyn Targ. Estab. 1945. Member of AAR. Represents 100 clients.

How to Contact Query with SASE, outline/proposal, curriculum vitae. No mss without query first. Obtains most new clients through recommendations from others, solicitations.

Terms Agent receives 15% commission on domestic sales; 20% commission on foreign sales. Charges standard agency fees (bank charges, long distance, postage, photocopying, shipping of books, overseas long distance, shipping, etc.).

◉ PATRICIA TEAL LITERARY AGENCY

2036 Vista Del Rosa, Fullerton CA 92831-1336. Phone/Fax: (714)738-8333. **Contact:** Patricia Teal. Estab. 1978. Member of AAR. Represents 20 clients. Currently handles: 10% nonfiction books; 90% fiction.

Represents Nonfiction books, novels. **Considers these nonfiction areas:** Animals; biography/autobiography; child guidance/parenting; health/medicine; how-to; psychology; self-help/personal improvement; true crime/ investigative; women's issues/studies. **Considers these fiction areas:** Glitz; mainstream/contemporary; mystery/suspense; romance (contemporary, historical).

    Oー This agency specializes in women's fiction, commercial how-to, and self-help nonfiction. Does not want to receive poetry, short stories, articles, science fiction, fantasy, or regency romance.

How to Contact Published authors only may query with SASE. No e-mail or fax queries. Considers simultaneous queries. Responds in 10 days to queries; 6 weeks to mss. Returns materials only with SASE. Obtains most new clients through conferences, recommendations from authors and editors.

Recent Sales Sold 20 titles in the last year. *Texas Rose*, by Marie Ferrarella (Silhouette); *Watch Your Language*, by Sterling Johnson (St. Martin's Press); *The Black Sheep's Baby*, by Kathleen Creighton (Silhouette); *Man With a Message*, by Muriel Jensen (Harlequin).

Terms Agent receives 10-15% commission on domestic sales; 20% commission on foreign sales. Offers written contract, binding for 1 year. Charges clients for postage.

Writers' Conferences RWA Conferences; Asilomar; BookExpo America; Bouchercon; Maui Writers Conference.

Tips "Include SASE with all correspondence. I am taking on published authors only."

◙ TESSLER LITERARY AGENCY, LLC

27 W. 20th St., Suite 1003, New York NY 10011. (212)242-0466. Fax: (212)242-2366. Web site: www.tessleragen cy.com. **Contact:** Michelle Tessler. Member of AAR.

    ● Prior to forming her own agency, Ms. Tessler worked at Carlisle & Co. (now a part of Inkwell Management). She has also worked at the William Morris Agency and the Elaine Markson Literary Agency.

    Oー The Tessler Agency is a full-service boutique agency that represents writers of high-quality nonfiction and literary and commercial fiction.

How to Contact Submit query through Web site only.

🅽 ⊕ ◙ THE TFS LITERARY AGENCY

P.O. Box 46-031, Lower Hutt, New Zealand. E-mail: tfs@elseware.co.nz. Web site: www.elseware.co.nz. **Contact:** Chris Else, Barbara Else. Estab. 1988. Member of NZALA.

    Oー Seeks general fiction, nonfiction, and children's books from New Zealand authors only. No poetry, individual short stories, or articles.

How to Contact Send query and brief author bio via e-mail.

◙ 3 SEAS LITERARY AGENCY

P.O. Box 7038, Madison WI 53708. (608)221-4306. E-mail: threeseaslit@aol.com. Web site: www.threeseaslit.c om. **Contact:** Michelle Grajkowski. Estab. 2000. Member of RWA, Chicago Women in Publishing. Represents 40 clients. 15% of clients are new/unpublished writers. Currently handles: 5% nonfiction books; 80% novels; 15% juvenile books.

    ● Prior to becoming an agent, Ms. Grajkowski worked in both sales and purchasing for a medical facility. She has a degree in journalism from the University of Wisconsin-Madison.

Represents Nonfiction books, novels, juvenile books, scholarly books.

    Oー 3 Seas focuses on romance (including category, historical, regency, western, romantic suspense, paranormal), women's fiction, mysteries, nonfiction, young adult, and children's stories. Does not want to receive poetry, screenplays, or short stories.

How to Contact For fiction, query with first 3 chapters, synopsis, bio, SASE. For nonfiction, query with complete proposal, first 3 chapters, word count, bio, SASE. Considers simultaneous queries. Responds in 1 month to queries. Responds in 3 months to partials. Returns materials only with SASE. Obtains most new clients through recommendations from others, conferences.

Recent Sales Sold 75 titles in the last year. *Fire Me Up, Sex, Lies & Vampires* and *Hard Day's Knight*, by Katie MacAlister; *Calendar Girl*, by Naomi Neale; *To Die For*, by Stephanie Rowe; *The Phantom in the Bathtub*, by Eugenia Riley; *The Unknown Daughter*, by Anna DeStefano. Other clients include Winnie Griggs, Diane Amos, Pat Pritchard, Barbara Jean Hicks, Carrie Weaver, Robin Popp, Kerrelyn Sparks, Sandra Madden.

Terms Agent receives 15% commission on domestic sales; 20% commission on foreign sales. Offers written contract, binding for 1 month.

Writers' Conferences RWA National Conference.

ANN TOBIAS—A LITERARY AGENCY FOR CHILDREN'S BOOKS

520 E. 84th St., Apt. 4L, New York NY 10028. **Contact:** Ann Tobias. Estab. 1988. Represents 25 clients. 50% of clients are new/unpublished writers. Currently handles: 100% juvenile books.

• Prior to opening her agency, Ms. Tobias worked as a children's book editor at Harper, William Morrow, and Scholastic.

Represents Juvenile books. **Considers these nonfiction areas:** Juvenile nonfiction; young adult. **Considers these fiction areas:** Picture books; poetry (for children); young adult; illustrated mss; mid-level novels.

O— This agency specializes in books for children.

How to Contact For picture books, submit entire ms. For longer fiction and nonfiction, submit 30 pages, synopsis. No phone queries. All queries must be in writing and accompanied by a SASE. No overnight mail or mail by private carrier that requires a signature. No e-mail or fax queries. Considers simultaneous queries, but requires 1-month exclusive on all requested mss. Responds in 2 months to mss. Returns materials only with SASE. Obtains most new clients through recommendations from editors.

Recent Sales Sold 12 titles in the last year. This agency prefers not to share information on specific sales.

Terms Agent receives 15% commission on domestic sales; 20% commission on foreign sales. No written contract. Charges clients for photocopying, overnight mail, foreign postage, foreign telephone.

Tips ''Read at least 200 children's books in the age group and genre in which you hope to be published. Follow this by reading another 100 children's books in other age groups and genres so you will have a feel for the field as a whole.''

LYNDA TOLLS LITERARY AGENCY

P.O. Box 1785, Bend OR 97709. (541)388-3510. E-mail: blswarts@juno.com. **Contact:** Lynda Tolls Swarts. Estab. 1995. Represents 8 clients. 20% of clients are new/unpublished writers. Currently handles: 90% nonfiction books; 10% novels.

Represents Nonfiction books, novels. **Considers these nonfiction areas:** Education; ethnic/cultural interests; health/medicine; history; self-help/personal improvement; travel; biography; global interests; religious/spiritual. **Considers these fiction areas:** Mystery/suspense (and its subgenres).

How to Contact For nonfiction, query with book concept, market, competing titles, author expertise. For fiction, query with synopsis, first 10 pages.

Writers' Conferences Willamette Writers Conference; Surrey International Writers' Conference; Idaho Writers' Conference.

SCOTT TREIMEL NY

434 Lafayette St., New York NY 10003. (212)505-8353. Fax: (212)505-0664. E-mail: st.ny@verizon.net. Estab. 1995. Member of AAR, Authors Guild, SCBWI. 10% of clients are new/unpublished writers. Currently handles: 100% junvenile/teen books.

• Prior to becoming an agent, Mr. Treimel was an assistant to Marilyn E. Marlow at Curtis Brown, a rights agent for Scholastic, a book packager and rights agent for United Feature Syndicate, a freelance editor, a rights consultant for HarperCollins Children's Books, and the founding director of Warner Bros. Worldwide Publishing.

O— This agency specializes in tightly focused segments of the trade and institutional markets. Wants career clients. Does not consider activity or coloring books. No new picture books.

How to Contact Send query/outline, SASE, sample chapters of no more than 50 pages. No multiple submissions. Queries without SASE will be recycled. No fax queries.

Recent Sales Sold 23 titles in the last year. *What Happened to Cass McBride?*, by Gail Gailes (Little, Brown); *Fragments*, by Jeff Johnston (Simon & Schuster); *The Ugliest Beast*, by Pat Hughes (Farrar, Straus & Giroux); *But That's Another Story*, by Mary Hanson (Random House/Schwartz & Wade); *Megiddo's Shadow*, by Arthur Slade (Random House/Wendy Lamb Books); *Death & Me*, by Richard Scrimger (Tundra Books).

Terms Agent receives 15% commission on domestic sales; 20% commission on foreign sales. Offers verbal or written contract. Charges clients for photocopying, express postage, messengers, and books ordered to sell foreign, film, and other rights.

Writers' Conferences SCBWI; The New School; Southwest Writers Conference; Pikes Peak Writers Conference.

Tips "Keep cover letters short and do not pitch."

TRIADA U.S. LITERARY AGENCY, INC.

P.O. Box 561, Sewickley PA 15143. (412)401-3376. E-mail: uwe@triadaus.com. Web site: www.triadaus.com. **Contact:** Dr. Uwe Stender. Estab. 2004. Represents 44 clients. 62% of clients are new/unpublished writers. Currently handles: 35% nonfiction books; 57% novels; 6% juvenile books; 2% scholarly books.

Member Agents Paul Hudson (science fiction, fantasy).

Represents Nonfiction books, novels, short story collections, juvenile books, scholarly books. **Considers these nonfiction areas:** Biography/autobiography; business/economics; child guidance/parenting; education; how-to; humor/satire; memoirs; popular culture; self-help/personal improvement; sports. **Considers these fiction areas:** Action/adventure; detective/police/crime; ethnic; fantasy; historical; horror; juvenile; literary; mainstream/contemporary; mystery/suspense; romance; science fiction; sports; thriller; young adult.

> "We are now focusing on self-help and how-to. Additionally, we specialize in literary novels and suspense. Education, business, popular culture, and narrative nonfiction are other strong suits. Our response time is fairly unique. We recognize that neither we nor the authors have time to waste, so we guarantee a 5-day response time. We usually respond within 24 hours." Actively looking for nonfiction, especially self-help, how-to, and prescriptive nonfiction. De-emphasizing fiction, although great writing will always be considered.

How to Contact E-mail queries preferred; otherwise query with SASE. Considers simultaneous queries. Responds in 1-5 weeks to queries; 2-4 weeks to mss. Returns materials only with SASE. Obtains most new clients through recommendations from others, conferences.

Recent Sales *Out of the Pocket*, by Tony Moss (University of Nebraska Press); *Lost World*, by Lynnette Porter and David Lavery (Sourcebooks).

Terms Agent receives 15% commission on domestic sales; 20% commission on foreign sales. Offers written contract; 30-day notice must be given to terminate contract.

Tips "I comment on all requested manuscripts which I reject."

TRIDENT MEDIA GROUP

41 Madison Ave., 36th Floor, New York NY 10010. E-mail: levine.assistant@tridentmediagroup.com. Web site: www.tridentmediagroup.com. **Contact:** Ellen Levine. Member of AAR.

Member Agents Jenny Bent; Scott Miller; Paul Fedarko; Alex Glass; Melissa Flashman; Eileen Cope.

> Actively seeking new or established authors in a variety of fiction and nonfiction genres.

How to Contact Query with SASE or via e-mail. Check Web site for more details.

2M COMMUNICATIONS, LTD.

121 W. 27 St., #601, New York NY 10001. (212)741-1509. Fax: (212)691-4460. E-mail: morel@bookhaven.com. Web site: www.2mcommunications.com. **Contact:** Madeleine Morel. Estab. 1982. Represents 50 clients. 20% of clients are new/unpublished writers. Currently handles: 100% nonfiction books.

• Prior to becoming an agent, Ms. Morel worked at a publishing company.

Represents Nonfiction books. **Considers these nonfiction areas:** Biography/autobiography; child guidance/parenting; ethnic/cultural interests; health/medicine; history; self-help/personal improvement; women's issues/studies; music; cookbooks.

> This agency specializes in ghostwriters.

How to Contact Query with SASE, outline, 3 sample chapters. Considers simultaneous queries. Responds in 1 week to queries; 1 month to mss. Obtains most new clients through recommendations from others, solicitations.

Recent Sales Sold 25 titles in the last year. *How Do You Compare?*, by Andy Williams (Penguin Putnam); *Hormone Wisdom*, by Theresa Dale (John Wiley); *Irish Dessert Cookbook*, by Margaret Johnson (Chronicle).

Terms Agent receives 15% commission on domestic sales; 20% commission on foreign sales. Offers written contract, binding for 2 years. Charges clients for postage, photocopying, long-distance calls, faxes.

ⓝ UNITED TRIBES MEDIA, INC.

240 W. 35th St., Suite 500, New York NY 10001. (212)244-4166. E-mail: janguerth@aol.com. **Contact:** Jan-Erik Guerth. Estab. 1998. Currently handles: 100% nonfiction books.

• Prior to becoming an agent, Mr. Guerth was a comedian, journalist, radio producer, and film distributor.

Represents Nonfiction books. **Considers these nonfiction areas:** Anthropology/archaeology; art/architecture/design; biography/autobiography; business/economics; child guidance/parenting; cooking/foods/nutrition;

current affairs; education; ethnic/cultural interests; gay/lesbian issues; government/politics/law; health/medicine; history; how-to; language/literature/criticism; memoirs; money/finance; music/dance; nature/environment; popular culture; psychology; religious/inspirational; science/technology (popular); self-help/personal improvement; sociology; theater/film; translation; women's issues/studies.

> O— This agency represents serious nonfiction, comparative religions, self-help, spirituality and wellness, science and arts, history and politics, nature and travel, any fascinating future trends, and ethnic, social, gender, and cultural issues.

How to Contact Submit outline, résumé, SASE. Agent prefers e-mail queries. Considers simultaneous queries. Responds in 1 month to queries. Returns materials only with SASE. Obtains most new clients through recommendations from others, solicitations, conferences.

Recent Sales *Shadow Cities*, by Robert Neuwirth (Routledge); *A Revolution in Eating*, by James McWilliams (Columbia University Press).

Terms Agent receives 15% commission on domestic sales; 20% commission on foreign sales.

THE RICHARD R. VALCOURT AGENCY, INC.

177 E. 77th St., PHC, New York NY 10021-1934. Phone/Fax: (212)570-2340. **Contact:** Richard R. Valcourt, president. Estab. 1995. Represents 25 clients. 20% of clients are new/unpublished writers. Currently handles: 100% nonfiction books.

> • Prior to opening his agency, Mr. Valcourt was a journalist, editor, and college political science instructor. He is also editor-in-chief of the *International Journal of Intelligence* and faculty member at American Military University in West Virginia.

Represents Scholarly books.

> O— Not accepting new clients at this time. This agency specializes in intelligence and other national security affairs. Represents exclusively academics, journalists, and professionals in the categories listed.

How to Contact Prefers to read materials exclusively. No e-mail or fax queries. Responds in 1 week to queries; 1 month to mss. Returns materials only with SASE. Obtains most new clients through recommendations from others.

Terms Agent receives 15% commission on domestic sales; 20% commission on foreign sales. Offers written contract. Charges clients for excessive photocopying, express mail, overseas telephone expenses.

VENTURE LITERARY

8895 Towne Centre Dr., Suite 105, #141, San Diego CA 92122. (619)807-1887. Fax: (772)365-8321. E-mail: submissions@ventureliterary.com. Web site: www.ventureliterary.com. **Contact:** Frank R. Scatoni. Estab. 1999. Represents 30 clients. 50% of clients are new/unpublished writers. Currently handles: 95% nonfiction books; 5% novels.

> • Prior to becoming an agent, Mr. Scatoni worked as an editor at Simon & Schuster.

Member Agents Frank R. Scatoni (general nonfiction, biography, memoir, narrative nonfiction, sports, serious nonfiction, graphic novels, narratives); Greg Dinkin (general nonfiction, business, gambling); Byrd Leavell (fiction, general nonfiction, pop culture).

Represents Nonfiction books, novels, grahpic novels, narratives. **Considers these nonfiction areas:** Animals; anthropology/archaeology; biography/autobiography; business/economics; current affairs; ethnic/cultural interests; government/politics/law; history; memoirs; military/war; money/finance; multicultural; music/dance; nature/environment; popular culture; psychology; science/technology; sports; true crime/investigative; gambling. **Considers these fiction areas:** Action/adventure; detective/police/crime; literary; mainstream/contemporary; mystery/suspense; sports; thriller.

> O— Specializes in nonfiction, sports, biography, gambling, and nonfiction narratives. Actively seeking nonfiction, graphic novels, and narratives.

How to Contact Considers e-mail queries only. *No unsolicited mss.* See Web site for complete submission guidelines. Obtains most new clients through recommendations from others.

Recent Sales *Phil Gordon's Little Green Book*, by Phil Gordon (Simon & Schuster); *The Summer of 1941*, by Mike Vaccaro (Doubleday); *Valvano*, by Adrian Wojnarowski (Gotham); *Look at My Striped Shirt!*, by The Phat Phree (Broadway); *The 9/11 Commission Report, Illustrated Edition*, by Sid Jacobsen and Ernie Colon (FSG).

Terms Agent receives 15% commission on domestic sales; 20% commission on foreign sales. Offers written contract.

VERITAS LITERARY AGENCY

1157 Valencia, Suite 4, San Francisco CA 94110. E-mail: agent@veritasliterary.com. Web site: www.veritasliterary.com. **Contact:** Katherine Boyle. Member of AAR.

How to Contact Query with SASE.

Literary Agents

⊠ ⊘ BETH VESEL LITERARY AGENCY

80 Fifth Ave., Suite 1101, New York NY 10011. (212)924-4252. Fax: (212)675-1381. E-mail: bvesel@bvlit.com. **Contact:** Makila Sands, assistant. Estab. 2003. Represents 65 clients. 10% of clients are new/unpublished writers. Currently handles: 75% nonfiction books; 10% novels; 5% story collections; 10% scholarly books.

• Prior to becoming an agent, Ms. Vesel was a poet and a journalist.

Represents Nonfiction books, novels. **Considers these nonfiction areas:** Biography/autobiography; business/ economics; ethnic/cultural interests; health/medicine; how-to; memoirs; photography; psychology; self-help/ personal improvement; true crime/investigative; women's issues/studies; cultural criticism. **Considers these fiction areas:** Detective/police/crime; literary.

○━ "My specialties include serious nonfiction, psychology, cultural criticism, memoir, and women's issues." Actively seeking cultural criticism, literary psychological thrillers, and sophisticated memoirs. No uninspired psychology or run-of-the-mill first novels.

How to Contact Query with SASE. Considers simultaneous queries. Responds in 2 weeks to queries; 1 month to mss. Returns materials only with SASE. Obtains most new clients through referrals, reading good magazines, contacting professionals with ideas.

Recent Sales Sold 10 titles in the last year. *The Female Complaint*, by Laura Kipnis (Pantheon); *Uses of Literature*, by Marge Garber (Pantheon); *Inside the Mind of Scott Peterson*, by Keith Ablow (St. Martin's Press); *The Other Mother*, by Gina Hyans and Susan Davis (The Hudson Press). Other clients include Martha Beck, Linda Carroll, Tracy Thompson, Vicki Robin, Paul Raeburn, John Head, Joe Graves.

Terms Agent receives 15% commission on domestic sales; 20% commission on foreign sales. Offers written contract.

Writers' Conferences Squaw Valley Writers Workshop, Iowa Summer Writing Festival.

Tips "Try to find out if you fit on a particular agent's list by looking at his/her books and comparing yours. You can almost always find who represents a book by looking at the acknowledgements."

⊘ RALPH VICINANZA, LTD.

303 W. 18th St., New York NY 10011. (212)924-7090. Fax: (212)691-9644. Member of AAR.

Member Agents Ralph M. Vicinanza; Chris Lotts; Chris Schelling.

○━ This agency specializes in foreign rights.

How to Contact This agency takes on new clients by professional recommendation only.

Recent Sales This agency prefers not to share information on specific sales.

Terms Agent receives 15% commission on domestic sales; 20% commission on foreign sales.

⊠ ⊘ VRATTOS LITERARY AGENCY

708 Gravenstein Hwy., Suite 185, Sebastopol CA 95472. Phone/Fax: (707)570-2720. E-mail: vrattoslitagency@aol.c om. Web site: www.vrattosliteraryagency.com. **Contact:** John Vrattos, Francesca Vrattos. Estab. 2003. Represents 16 clients. 80% of clients are new/unpublished writers. Currently handles: 60% nonfiction books; 40% novels.

• Prior to becoming an agent, Ms. Vrattos worked at Penguin Putnam and co-founded Writer's Showplace, Inc.

Represents Nonfiction books, novels. **Considers these nonfiction areas:** Agriculture/horticulture; animals; art/architecture/design; biography/autobiography; business/economics; child guidance/parenting; cooking/ foods/nutrition; crafts/hobbies; current affairs; education; ethnic/cultural interests; gay/lesbian issues; government/politics/law; health/medicine; history; how-to; humor/satire; interior design/decorating; language/literature/criticism; memoirs; military/war; money/finance; nature/environment; New Age/metaphysics; photography; popular culture; psychology; religious/inspirational; self-help/personal improvement; sociology; sports; true crime/investigative; women's issues/studies. **Considers these fiction areas:** Comic books/cartoon; confession; detective/police/crime; ethnic; family saga; feminist; gay/lesbian; glitz; historical; humor/satire; literary; mainstream/contemporary; mystery/suspense; psychic/supernatural; regional; religious/inspirational; romance; sports; thriller; westerns/frontier.

○━ Actively seeking sports, humor, mystery, thriller, and mainstream. No horror, young adult, children's, or erotica.

How to Contact Query with SASE. Accepts e-mail queries. Considers simultaneous queries. Responds in 2 weeks to queries; 6 weeks to mss. Obtains most new clients through recommendations from others, conferences.

Recent Sales Sold 3 titles in the last year. *You Don't Say!*, by Hartley Miller (Andrews McMeel); *Spoiled Sports*, by Garret Kolb (Andrews McMeel); *Ultimate Betrayal*, by Danine Manette (Square One). Other clients include Sherry Rowlands, Bob Mann, Bob Stewart, Dawn Patitucci, Marcel Pincince, Brad Stanhope, Liz Holzemer, Nick Anderson, Sharon Anderson, Mitch Haudelsman, Guy Mirabello.

Terms Agent receives 15% commission on domestic sales; 20% commission on foreign sales. Offers written contract; 30-day notice must be given to terminate contract. Charges for postage and phone calls.

Writers' Conferences San Francisco Writers Conference; Willamette Writers Conference.

Tips "Be professional and patient."

N ⊕ ⊘ WADE & DOHERTY LITERARY AGENCY

33 Cormorant Lodge, Thomas Moore St., London E1W 1AU England. (44)(20)7488-4171. Fax: (44)(20)7488-4172. E-mail: rw@rwla.com. Web site: www.rwla.com. **Contact:** Robin Wade. Estab. 2001.

- Prior to opening his agency, Mr. Wade was an author; Ms. Doherty worked as a production assistant, editor, and editorial director.

Member Agents Mark Barty-King, chairman; Robin Wade, agent; Broo Doherty, agent.

Represents Nonfiction books, novels, juvenile books.

- ⊶ "We are young and dynamic and actively seek new writers across the literary spectrum." No poetry, plays, or short stories.

How to Contact Submit synopsis (2-6 pages), bio, first 10,000 words via e-mail (Word or PDF documents only). If sending by post, include SASE or IRC. Responds in 1 week to queries; 1 month to mss.

Recent Sales *A Spin Doctor's Diary*, by Lance Price; *The Icarus Girl*, by Helen Oyeyemi; *Benedict XVI*, by Rupert Shortt; *The Truth Will Out: Unmasking the Real Shakespeare*, by Brenda James.

Terms Agent receives 10% commission on domestic sales; 20% commission on foreign sales. Offers written contract; 1-month notice must be given to terminate contract.

Tips "We seek manuscripts that are well written, with strong characters and an original narrative voice. Our absolute priority is giving the best possible service to the authors we choose to represent, as well as maintaining routine friendly contact with them as we help develop their careers."

⊘ MARY JACK WALD ASSOCIATES, INC.

111 E. 14th St., New York NY 10003. (212)254-7842. **Contact:** Danis Sher. Estab. 1985. Member of AAR, Authors Guild, SCBWI. Represents 35 clients. 5% of clients are new/unpublished writers.

Member Agents Mary Jack Wald; Danis Sher; Alvin Wald; Lynne Rabinoff Agency (association who represents foreign rights).

Represents Nonfiction books, novels, short story collections, novellas, juvenile books, clients' movie/TV scripts. **Considers these nonfiction areas:** Biography/autobiography; current affairs; ethnic/cultural interests; history; juvenile nonfiction; language/literature/criticism; music/dance; nature/environment; photography; sociology; theater/film; translation; true crime/investigative. **Considers these fiction areas:** Action/adventure; contemporary issues; detective/police/crime; ethnic; experimental; family saga; feminist; gay/lesbian; glitz; historical; juvenile; literary; mainstream/contemporary; mystery/suspense; picture books; thriller; young adult; satire.

- ⊶ This agency is not accepting mss at this time. This agency specializes in literary works and juvenile works.

Recent Sales *Hey, Cowgirl, Need a Ride?*, by Baxter Black (Random House); *Two-Time*, by Chris Knopf (Permanent Press).

Terms Agent receives 15% commission on domestic sales; 15-30% commission on foreign sales. Offers written contract, binding for 1 year.

⊘ WALES LITERARY AGENCY, INC.

P.O. Box 9428, Seattle WA 98109-0428. (206)284-7114. E-mail: waleslit@waleslit.com. Web site: www.waleslit.com. **Contact:** Elizabeth Wales, Josie di Bernardo. Estab. 1988. Member of AAR, Book Publishers' Northwest, Pacific Northwest Booksellers Association, PEN. Represents 65 clients. 10% of clients are new/unpublished writers. Currently handles: 60% nonfiction books; 40% novels.

- Prior to becoming an agent, Ms. Wales worked at Oxford University Press and Viking Penguin.

Member Agents Elizabeth Wales; Adrienne Reed.

- ⊶ This agency specializes in narrative nonfiction and quality mainstream and literary fiction. Does not handle screenplays, children's literature, genre fiction, or most category nonfiction.

How to Contact Query with cover letter, writing sample (about 30 pages), SASE. No phone or fax queries. Prefers regular mail queries, but accepts 1-page e-mail queries with no attachments. Considers simultaneous queries. Responds in 3 weeks to queries; 6 weeks to mss. Returns materials only with SASE.

Recent Sales *Breaking Ranks*, by Norman H. Stamper (Nation Books); *Birds of Central Park*, photographs by Cal Vornberger (Abrams); *Against Gravity*, by Farnoosh Moshiri (Penguin).

Terms Agent receives 15% commission on domestic sales; 20% commission on foreign sales.

Writers' Conferences Pacific Northwest Writers Conference; Willamette Writers Conference.

Tips "We are especially interested in work that espouses a progressive cultural or political view, projects a new voice, or simply shares an important, compelling story. We also encourage writers living in the Pacific Northwest, West Coast, Alaska, and Pacific Rim countries, and writers from historically underrepresented groups, such as gay and lesbian writers and writers of color, to submit work (but does not discourage writers outside these areas). Most importantly, whether in fiction or nonfiction, the agency is looking for talented storytellers."

ⓐ JOHN A. WARE LITERARY AGENCY

392 Central Park W., New York NY 10025-5801. (212)866-4733. Fax: (212)866-4734. **Contact:** John Ware. Estab. 1978. Represents 60 clients. 40% of clients are new/unpublished writers. Currently handles: 75% nonfiction books; 25% novels.

• Prior to opening his agency, Mr. Ware served as a literary agent with James Brown Associates/Curtis Brown, Ltd., and as an editor for Doubleday & Co.

Represents Nonfiction books, novels. **Considers these nonfiction areas:** Anthropology/archaeology; biography/autobiography; current affairs; health/medicine (academic credentials required); history (oral history, Americana, folklore); language/literature/criticism; music/dance; nature/environment; popular culture; psychology (academic credentials required); science/technology; sports; true crime/investigative; women's issues/studies; social commentary; investigative journalism; bird's eye views of phenomena. **Considers these fiction areas:** Detective/police/crime; mystery/suspense; thriller; accessible literary noncategory fiction.

O→ Does not want personal memoirs.

How to Contact Query with SASE. No e-mail or fax queries. Considers simultaneous queries. Responds in 2 weeks to queries.

Recent Sales *The Butterfly Hunter*, by Chris Ballard (Broadway); *Velva Jean Learns to Drive*, by Jennifer Niven (Plume); *Sunday*, by Craig Harline (Doubleday); *Man O'War*, by Dorothy Ours (St. Martin's Press); *The Family Business: A History of Tobacco*, by Jeffrey Rothfeder (HarperCollins); *Ledyard*, by William Gifford (Harcourt).

Terms Agent receives 15% commission on domestic and dramatic rights sales; 20% commission on foreign sales. Charges clients for messenger service and photocopying.

Tips "Writers must have appropriate credentials for authorship of proposal (nonfiction) or manuscript (fiction); no publishing track record required. Open to good writing and interesting ideas by new or veteran writers."

ⓐ HARRIET WASSERMAN LITERARY AGENCY

137 E. 36th St., New York NY 10016. **Contact:** Harriet Wasserman. Member of AAR.

ⓦ WATERSIDE PRODUCTIONS, INC.

2367 Oxford Ave., Cardiff-by-the-Sea CA 92007. (760)632-9190. Fax: (760)632-9295. E-mail: admin@waterside.com. Web site: www.waterside.com. Estab. 1982.

Member Agents Bill Gladstone; Margot Maley Hutchison; Carole McClendon; William E. Brown; Lawrence Jackel; Ming Russell; Neil Gudovitz; Kimberly Valentini.

Represents Nonfiction books. **Considers these nonfiction areas:** Art/architecture/design; biography/autobiography; business/economics; child guidance/parenting; computers/electronic; ethnic/cultural interests; health/medicine; how-to; humor/satire; money/finance; nature/environment; popular culture; psychology; sociology; sports; cookbooks.

O→ Specializes in computer books, how-to, business, and health titles.

How to Contact Query via mail or online form. Phone queries are not accepted. Obtains most new clients through referrals from established client and publisher list.

Recent Sales "We have represented bestselling authors ranging from Eckhart Tolle to Kevin Trudeau, Kevin Mitnick, Ron Mansfield, Ken Milbern, Randy Fitzgerald, and David Karlins."

Tips "For new writers, a quality proposal and a strong knowledge of the market you're writing for goes a long way toward helping us turn you into a published author. We like to see a strong author platform."

ⓦ WATKINS LOOMIS AGENCY, INC.

133 E. 35th St., Suite 1, New York NY 10016. (212)532-0080. Fax: (212)889-0506. **Contact:** Katherine Fausset. Estab. 1908. Represents 150 clients.

Member Agents Gloria Loomis, president; Katherine Fausset, agent.

Represents Nonfiction books, novels, short story collections. **Considers these nonfiction areas:** Art/architecture/design; biography/autobiography; current affairs; ethnic/cultural interests; history; nature/environment; popular culture; science/technology; true crime/investigative; journalism. **Considers these fiction areas:** Literary.

O→ This agency specializes in literary fiction and nonfiction.

How to Contact *No unsolicited mss.*

Recent Sales This agency prefers not to share information on specific sales. Clients include Walter Mosley and Cornel West.

Terms Agent receives 15% commission on domestic sales; 20% commission on foreign sales.

ⓐ WAXMAN LITERARY AGENCY, INC.

80 Fifth Ave., Suite 1101, New York NY 10011. Web site: www.waxmanagency.com. Estab. 1997. Represents 60 clients. 50% of clients are new/unpublished writers. Currently handles: 80% nonfiction books; 20% novels.

● Prior to opening his agency, Mr. Waxman was an editor at HarperCollins for 5 years.
Member Agents Scott Waxman (all categories of nonfiction, commercial fiction).
Represents Nonfiction books, novels. **Considers these nonfiction areas:** Narrative nonfiction. **Considers these fiction areas:** Literary.

O━ "Looking for serious journalists and novelists with published works."

How to Contact Query through Web site. All unsolicited mss returned unopened. Considers simultaneous queries. Responds in 2 weeks to queries; 6 weeks to mss. Returns materials only with SASE. Obtains most new clients through recommendations from others, solicitations, conferences.

Terms Agent receives 15% commission on domestic sales; 25% commission on foreign sales. Offers written contract; 2-month notice must be given to terminate contract.

⬤ THE WENDY WEIL AGENCY, INC.

232 Madison Ave., Suite 1300, New York NY 10016. (212)685-0030. Fax: (212)685-0765. E-mail: wweil@wendyweil.com. Web site: www.wendyweil.com. Member of AAR.

Member Agents Wendy Weil; Emily Forland; Emma Patterson.

How to Contact Query with SASE.

⬤ CHERRY WEINER LITERARY AGENCY

28 Kipling Way, Manalapan NJ 07726-3711. (732)446-2096. Fax: (732)792-0506. E-mail: cherry8486@aol.com. **Contact:** Cherry Weiner. Estab. 1977. Represents 40 clients. 10% of clients are new/unpublished writers. Currently handles: 10-20% nonfiction books; 80-90% novels.

Represents Nonfiction books, novels. **Considers these nonfiction areas:** Self-help/personal improvement. **Considers these fiction areas:** Action/adventure; contemporary issues; detective/police/crime; family saga; fantasy; historical; mainstream/contemporary; mystery/suspense; psychic/supernatural; romance; science fiction; thriller; westerns/frontier.

O━ This agency is currently not looking for new clients except by referral or by personal contact at writers' conferences. Specializes in fantasy, science fiction, westerns, mysteries (both contemporary and historical), historical novels, Native American works, mainstream, and all genre romances.

How to Contact Query with SASE. Prefers to read materials exclusively. No fax queries. Responds in 1 week to queries; 2 months to mss. Returns materials only with SASE.

Recent Sales Sold 75 titles in the last year.

Terms Agent receives 15% commission on domestic and foreign sales. Offers written contract. Charges clients for extra copies of mss, first-class postage for author's copies of books, express mail for important documents/mss.

Writers' Conferences Western writers conventions; science fiction conventions; fantasy conventions; romance conventions.

Tips "Meet agents and publishers at conferences. Establish a relationship, then get in touch with them and remind them of the meeting and conference."

⬤ THE WEINGEL-FIDEL AGENCY

310 E. 46th St., 21E, New York NY 10017. (212)599-2959. **Contact:** Loretta Weingel-Fidel. Estab. 1989. Currently handles: 75% nonfiction books; 25% novels.

● Prior to opening her agency, Ms. Weingel-Fidel was a psychoeducational diagnostician.

Represents Nonfiction books, novels. **Considers these nonfiction areas:** Art/architecture/design; biography/autobiography; memoirs; music/dance; psychology; science/technology; sociology; women's issues/studies; investigative journalism. **Considers these fiction areas:** Literary; mainstream/contemporary.

O━ This agency specializes in commercial and literary fiction and nonfiction. Actively seeking investigative journalism. Does not want to receive genre fiction, self-help, science fiction, or fantasy.

How to Contact Accepts writers by referral only. *No unsolicited mss.*

Terms Agent receives 15% commission on domestic sales; 20% commission on foreign sales. Offers written contract, binding for 1 year with automatic renewal. Bills sent back to clients are all reasonable expenses, such as UPS, express mail, photocopying, etc.

Tips "A very small, selective list enables me to work very closely with my clients to develop and nurture talent. I only take on projects and writers about which I am extremely enthusiastic."

⬤ TED WEINSTEIN LITERARY MANAGEMENT

35 Stillman St., Suite 203, Dept. GL, San Francisco CA 94107. Web site: www.twliterary.com. **Contact:** Ted Weinstein. Estab. 2001. Member of AAR. Represents 50 clients. 75% of clients are new/unpublished writers. Currently handles: 100% nonfiction books.

Represents Nonfiction books by a wide range of journalists, academics, and other experts. **Considers these**

nonfiction areas: Biography/autobiography; business/economics; current affairs; government/politics/law; health/medicine; history; popular culture; science/technology; self-help/personal improvement; travel; lifestyle.

How to Contact Please visit Web site for detailed guidelines before submitting. Considers simultaneous queries. Responds in 3 weeks to queries.

Terms Agent receives 15% commission on domestic sales; 20% commission on foreign and dramatic rights sales. Offers written contract, binding for 1 year. Charges clients for photocopying and express shipping.

◙ WIESER & ELWELL, INC.

80 Fifth Ave., Suite 1101, New York NY 10010. (212)260-0860. **Contact:** Jake Elwell. Estab. 1975. 30% of clients are new/unpublished writers. Currently handles: 50% nonfiction books; 50% novels.

Member Agents Jake Elwell (history, military, mysteries, romance, sports, thrillers, psychology, fiction, pop medical).

Represents Nonfiction books, novels. **Considers these nonfiction areas:** Business/economics; cooking/foods/nutrition; current affairs; health/medicine; history; money/finance; nature/environment; psychology; sports; true crime/investigative. **Considers these fiction areas:** Detective/police/crime; historical; literary; mainstream/contemporary; mystery/suspense; romance; thriller.

  ○━ This agency specializes in mainstream fiction and nonfiction.

How to Contact For nonfiction, query with proposal, SASE. For fiction, query with synopsis, first 2-10 pages, SASE. Responds in 2 weeks to queries. Obtains most new clients through queries, authors' recommendations, industry professionals.

Recent Sales *Stolen Tomorrows*, by Steven Levenkron (Norton); *The Wire: Truth Be Told*, by Rafael Alvarez (Pocket); *Freemasons*, by H. Paul Jeffers (Citadel).

Terms Agent receives 15% commission on domestic sales; 20% commission on foreign sales. Offers written contract. Charges clients for photocopying and overseas mailing.

Writers' Conferences BookExpo America; Frankfurt Book Fair.

◖ WINSUN LITERARY AGENCY

3706 NE Shady Lane Dr., Gladstone MO 64119. Phone/Fax: (816)459-8016. E-mail: mlittleton@earthlink.net. Estab. 2004. Represents 20 clients. 50% of clients are new/unpublished writers. Currently handles: 75% nonfiction books; 20% novels; 5% juvenile books.

  ● Prior to becoming an agent, Mr. Littleton was a writer and a speaker.

Represents Nonfiction books, novels, juvenile books. **Considers these nonfiction areas:** Biography/autobiography; child guidance/parenting; current affairs; how-to; humor/satire; memoirs; religious/inspirational; self-help/personal improvement. **Considers these fiction areas:** Action/adventure; detective/police/crime; family saga; humor/satire; juvenile; literary; mainstream/contemporary; mystery/suspense; picture books; psychic/supernatural; religious/inspirational; romance; thriller.

  ○━ "We mainly serve Christian clients in the CBA."

How to Contact Query with SASE. Considers simultaneous queries. Responds in 6 weeks to queries; 3 months to mss. Returns materials only with SASE. Obtains most new clients through recommendations from others, conferences.

Recent Sales Sold 8 titles in the last year. *Footsteps* and *When the Lion Roars*, by Diann Mills; *Rockets, Rebels, and Rescue*, by Mark and Jeanette Littleton.

Terms Agent receives 15% commission on domestic sales; 20% commission on foreign sales. Offers written contract, binding for 1 year; 30-day notice must be given to terminate contract.

◙ AUDREY A. WOLF LITERARY AGENCY

2510 Virginia Ave. NW, #702N, Washington DC 20037. Member of AAR.

How to Contact Query with SASE.

ⓝ ◖ WOLGEMUTH & ASSOCIATES, INC.

8600 Crestgate Circle, Orlando FL 32819. (407)909-9445. Fax: (407)909-9446. E-mail: rwolgemuth@cfl.rr.com. **Contact:** Dr. Robert D. Wolgemuth. Estab. 1992. Member of AAR. Represents 25 clients. 10% of clients are new/unpublished writers. Currently handles: 90% nonfiction books; 2% novellas; 5% juvenile books; 3% multimedia.

  ● "We have been in the publishing business since 1976, having been a marketing executive at a number of houses, a publisher, an author, and a founder and owner of a publishing company."

Member Agents Robert D. Wolgemuth; Andrew D. Wolgemuth; Erik S. Wolgemuth.

  ○━ "I am not considering any new material at this time."

Recent Sales Sold 25-30 titles in the last year. Clients include Joni Eareckson Tada, Dr. Ravi Zacharias, Dr.

John MacArthur, Dr. James MacDonald, Dr. Henry Blackaby, Dr. Mel Blackaby, Dr. Norm Blackaby, Dr. Tom Blackaby, Nancy Leigh DeMoss, Dr. Ted Baehr, Dr. Gordon MacDonald, Dr. Max Anders, Ronald Blue, Jeremy White, Dale Buss, Don Cousins, Bruce Bugbee, Dr. Al Mohler, Dr. Patrick Morley, Ellen Santilli Vaughn, Chad Williams, Melissa Schrader.

Terms Agent receives 15% commission on domestic sales. Offers written contract, binding for 2-3 years; 30-day notice must be given to terminate contract.

⊚ WORDSERVE LITERARY GROUP

10152 S. Knoll Circle, Highlands Ranch CO 80130. (303)471-6675. Fax: (303)471-1297. Web site: www.wordserv eliterary.com. **Contact:** Greg Johnson. Estab. 2003. Represents 30 clients. 25% of clients are new/unpublished writers. Currently handles: 30% nonfiction books; 40% novels; 10% story collections; 5% novellas; 10% juvenile books; 5% multimedia.

- Prior to becoming an agent in 1994, Mr. Johnson was a magazine editor and freelance writer of more than 20 books and 200 articles.

Represents Primarily religious books in these categories: nonfiction, fiction, short story collections, novellas. **Considers these nonfiction areas:** Biography/autobiography; business/economics; child guidance/parenting; current affairs; how-to; humor/satire; memoirs; religious/inspirational; self-help/personal improvement; sports. **Considers these fiction areas:** Action/adventure; detective/police/crime; family saga; historical; humor/satire; religious/inspirational; romance; sports; thriller.

How to Contact Query with SASE, proposal package, outline, 2-3 sample chapters. Considers simultaneous queries. Responds in 1 week to queries; 2 months to mss. Returns materials only with SASE. Obtains most new clients through recommendations from others, solicitations.

Recent Sales Sold 1,300 titles in the last 10 years. Redemption series, by Karen Kingsbury (Tyndale); *Loving God Up Close*, by Calvin Miller (Warner Faith); *Christmas in My Heart*, by Joe Wheeler (Tyndale). Other clients include Gilbert Morris, Calvin Miller, Robert Wise, Jim Burns, Ed Young Sr., Wayne Cordeiro, Denise George, Susie Shellenberger, Tim Smith, Joe Wheeler, Athol Dickson, Bob DeMoss, Patty Kirk, John Shore.

Terms Agent receives 15% commission on domestic sales; 10-15% commission on foreign sales. Offers written contract; up to 60-day notice must be given to terminate contract.

Tips ''We are looking for good proposals, great writing, and authors willing to market their books, as appropriate.''

◙ WRITERS HOUSE

21 W. 26th St., New York NY 10010. (212)685-2400. Fax: (212)685-1781. Web site: www.writershouse.com. Estab. 1974. Member of AAR. Represents 440 clients. 50% of clients are new/unpublished writers. Currently handles: 25% nonfiction books; 40% novels; 35% juvenile books.

Member Agents Albert Zuckerman (major novels, thrillers, women's fiction, important nonfiction); Amy Berkower (major juvenile authors, women's fiction, art/decorating, psychology); Merrilee Heifetz (quality children's fiction, science fiction/fantasy, popular culture, literary fiction); Susan Cohen (juvenile/young adult fiction and nonfiction, Judaism, women's issues); Susan Ginsburg (serious and popular fiction, true crime, narrative nonfiction, personality books, cookbooks); Michele Rubin (serious nonfiction); Robin Rue (commercial fiction and nonfiction, young adult fiction); Jodi Reamer (juvenile/young adult fiction and nonfiction, adult commercial fiction, popular culture); Simon Lipskar (literary and commercial fiction, narrative nonfiction); Steven Malk (juvenile/young adult fiction and nonfiction); Dan Lazar (pop culture, hip/edgy fiction and nonfiction).

Represents Nonfiction books, novels, juvenile books. **Considers these nonfiction areas:** Animals; art/architecture/design; biography/autobiography; business/economics; child guidance/parenting; cooking/foods/nutrition; health/medicine; history; humor/satire; interior design/decorating; juvenile nonfiction; military/war; money/finance; music/dance; nature/environment; psychology; science/technology; self-help/personal improvement; theater/film; true crime/investigative; women's issues/studies. **Considers these fiction areas:** Action/adventure; contemporary issues; detective/police/crime; erotica; ethnic; family saga; fantasy; feminist; gay/lesbian; gothic; hi-lo; historical; horror; humor/satire; juvenile; literary; mainstream/contemporary; military/war; multicultural; mystery/suspense; New Age; occult; picture books; psychic/supernatural; regional; romance; science fiction; short story collections; spiritual; sports; thriller; translation; westerns/frontier; young adult; women's; cartoon.

- ⟳ This agency specializes in all types of popular fiction and nonfiction. Does not want to receive scholarly, professional, poetry, plays, or screenplays.

How to Contact Query with SASE. No e-mail or fax queries. Responds in 1 month to queries. Obtains most new clients through recommendations from authors and editors.

Recent Sales Sold 200-300 titles in the last year. *Moneyball*, by Michael Lewis (Norton); *Cut and Run*, by Ridley Pearson (Hyperion); *Report from Ground Zero*, by Dennis Smith (Viking); *Northern Lights*, by Nora

Roberts (Penguin/Putnam); Captain Underpants series, by Dav Pilkey (Scholastic); Junie B. Jones series, by Barbara Park (Random House). Other clients include Francine Pascal, Ken Follett, Stephen Hawking, Linda Howard, F. Paul Wilson, Neil Gaiman, Laurel Hamilton, V.C. Andrews, Lisa Jackson, Michael Gruber, Chris Paolini, Barbara Delinsky, Ann Martin, Bradley Trevor Greive, Erica Jong, Kyle Mills.

Terms Agent receives 15% commission on domestic sales; 20% commission on foreign sales. Offers written contract, binding for 1 year. Agency charges fees for copying mss/proposals and overseas airmail of books.

Tips "Do not send manuscripts. Write a compelling letter. If you do, we'll ask to see your work."

ℕ⃞ ⊘ WRITERS' PRODUCTIONS

P.O. Box 630, Westport CT 06881-0630. (203)227-8199. Fax: (203)227-6349. E-mail: dlm67@mac.com. **Contact:** David L. Meth. Estab. 1982. Represents 25 clients. Currently handles: 40% nonfiction books; 60% novels. **Represents** Nonfiction books, novels, quality literary fiction.

○━ "We are not accepting new clients at this time."

How to Contact No e-mail or fax queries. Obtains most new clients through recommendations from others.

Recent Sales This agency prefers not to share information on specific sales.

Terms Agent receives 15% commission on domestic sales; 25% commission on foreign sales. Offers written contract. Charges clients for electronic transmissions, long-distance phone calls, express or overnight mail, courier service, etc.

Tips "Send only your best, most professionally prepared work. Do not send it before it is ready. We must have a SASE for all correspondence and return of manuscripts. Do not waste time sending work to agencies or editors who are not accepting new clients."

◉ WRITERS' REPRESENTATIVES, INC.

116 W. 14th St., 11th Floor, New York NY 10011-7305. (212)620-9009. Fax: (212)620-0023. E-mail: transom@wr itersreps.com. Web site: www.writersreps.com. Estab. 1985. Represents 130 clients. 5% of clients are new/ unpublished writers. Currently handles: 90% nonfiction books; 10% novels.

● Prior to becoming an agent, Ms. Chu was a lawyer; Mr. Hartley worked at Simon & Schuster, Harper & Row, and Cornell University Press.

Member Agents Lynn Chu; Glen Hartley; Farah Peterson.

Represents Nonfiction books, novels. **Considers these fiction areas:** Literary.

○━ Actively seeking serious nonfiction and quality fiction. Does not want to receive motion picture or television screenplays.

How to Contact Query with SASE. Prefers to read materials exclusively. Considers simultaneous queries, but must be informed at time of submission.

Recent Sales Sold 30 titles in the last year. *The Surrender*, by Toni Bentley; *War Like No Other*, by Victor Davis Hanson; *Jesus and Yahweh*, by Harold Bloom; *To Rule the Waves*, by Arthur Herman.

Terms Agent receives 15% commission on domestic sales; 20% commission on foreign sales.

Tips "Always include a SASE—it will ensure a response from the agent and the return of your submitted material."

◉ WYLIE-MERRICK LITERARY AGENCY

1138 S. Webster St., Kokomo IN 46902-6357. (765)459-8258. E-mail: smartin@wylie-merrick.com; rbrown@wy lie-merrick.com. Web site: www.wylie-merrick.com. **Contact:** Sharene Martin, Robert Brown. Estab. 1999. Member of SCBWI.

● Ms. Martin holds a master's degree in language education and is a writing and technology curriculum specialist; Mr. Brown holds a degree in communication and English.

Member Agents Sharene Martin (juvenile, picture books, young adult); Robert Brown (adult fiction and nonfiction, young adult).

○━ "We prefer writers who understand the writing craft and have thoroughly researched and have a firm understanding of the publishing industry. We specialize in highly commercial literature. Because our needs are constantly changing, please always consult our Web site to see what we are currently seeking."

How to Contact Correspond via e-mail only. No phone queries, please. Obtains most new clients through recommendations from others, conferences.

Recent Sales *Blackbelly*, by Heather Sharfeddin (Bridge Works); *Whiskey on the Rocks*, by Nina Wright (Llewellyn); *Derailed*, by Jon Ripslinger; *Boy Meets Earl*, by M.J. Pearson; *If You Were Not You*, by Hanna Coffer (Roaring Brook).

Terms Agent receives 15% commission on domestic sales; 20% commission on foreign and dramatic rights sales. Offers written contract.

☑ ZACHARY SHUSTER HARMSWORTH

1776 Broadway, Suite 1405, New York NY 10019. (212)765-6900. Fax: (212)765-6490. E-mail: kfleury@zshlitera ry.com. Web site: www.zshliterary.com. Alternate address: 535 Boylston St., 11th Floor. (617)262-2400. Fax: (617)262-2468. **Contact:** Kathleen Fleury. Estab. 1996. Represents 125 clients. 20% of clients are new/unpublished writers. Currently handles: 45% nonfiction books; 45% novels; 5% story collections; 5% scholarly books.

    ● "Our principals include 2 former publishing and entertainment lawyers, a journalist, and an editor/agent." Lane Zachary was an editor at Random House before becoming an agent.

Member Agents Esmond Harmsworth (commercial mysteries, literary fiction, history, science, adventure, business); Todd Shuster (narrative and prescriptive nonfiction, biography, memoirs); Lane Zachary (biography, memoirs, literary fiction); Jennifer Gates (literary fiction, nonfiction).

Represents Nonfiction books, novels. **Considers these nonfiction areas:** Animals; biography/autobiography; business/economics; current affairs; gay/lesbian issues; government/politics/law; health/medicine; history; how-to; language/literature/criticism; memoirs; money/finance; music/dance; psychology; science/technology; self-help/personal improvement; sports; true crime/investigative; women's issues/studies. **Considers these fiction areas:** Detective/police/crime; ethnic; feminist; gay/lesbian; historical; literary; mainstream/contemporary; mystery/suspense; thriller.

    O→ This agency specializes in journalist-driven narrative nonfiction and literary and commercial fiction. Interested in narrative nonfiction, mystery, commercial and literary fiction, memoirs, history, and biographies. Does not want to receive poetry.

How to Contact *No unsolicited submissions.* No e-mail or fax queries. Obtains most new clients through recommendations from others, solicitations, conferences.

Recent Sales *Christmas Hope*, by Donna Van Liere; *Female Chauvinist Pigs*, by Ariel Levy; *War Trash*, by Ha Jin; *Women Who Think Too Much*, by Susan Nolen-Hoeksema, PhD; *The Red Carpet*, by Lavanya Sankaran; *Grapevine*, by David Balter and John Butman.

Terms Agent receives 15% commission on domestic sales; 20% commission on foreign sales. Offers written contract, binding for 1 work only; 30-day notice must be given to terminate contract. Charges clients for postage, copying, courier, telephone. "We only charge expenses if the manuscript is sold."

Tips "We work closely with all our clients on all editorial and promotional aspects of their works."

☑ SUSAN ZECKENDORF ASSOC., INC.

171 W. 57th St., New York NY 10019. (212)245-2928. **Contact:** Susan Zeckendorf. Estab. 1979. Member of AAR. Represents 15 clients. 25% of clients are new/unpublished writers. Currently handles: 50% nonfiction books; 50% novels.

    ● Prior to opening her agency, Ms. Zeckendorf was a counseling psychologist.

Represents Nonfiction books, novels. **Considers these nonfiction areas:** Biography/autobiography; child guidance/parenting; health/medicine; history; music/dance; psychology; science/technology; sociology; women's issues/studies. **Considers these fiction areas:** Detective/police/crime; ethnic; historical; literary; mainstream/contemporary; mystery/suspense; thriller.

    O→ Actively seeking mysteries, literary fiction, mainstream fiction, thrillers, social history, parenting, classical music, and biography. Does not want to receive science fiction, romance, or children's books.

How to Contact Query with SASE. No e-mail or fax queries. Considers simultaneous queries. Responds in 10 days to queries; 3 weeks to mss. Returns materials only with SASE.

Recent Sales *How to Write a Damn Good Mystery*, by James N. Frey (St. Martin's Press); *The Handscrabble Chronicles* (Berkley); *Something to Live For* (University of Michigan Press).

Terms Agent receives 15% commission on domestic sales; 20% commission on foreign sales. Charges for photocopying and messenger services.

Writers' Conferences Frontiers in Writing Conference; Oklahoma Festival of Books.

Tips "We are a small agency giving lots of individual attention. We respond quickly to submissions."

Script Agents

This section contains agents who sell feature film scripts, television scripts and theatrical stage plays. Many of the script agents listed here are signatories to the Writers Guild of America (WGA) Artists' Manager Basic Agreement. They have paid a membership fee and agree to abide by the WGA's standard code of behavior.

It's a good idea to register your script before sending it out, and the WGA offers a registration service to members and nonmembers alike. Membership in the WGA is earned through the accumulation of professional credits and carries a number of significant benefits.

A few of the listings in this section are actually management companies. The role of managers is quickly changing in Hollywood. Actors and the occasional writer were once the only ones to use them. Now many managers are actually selling scripts to producers.

Like the literary agents listed in this book, some script agencies ask that clients pay for some or all of the office fees accrued when sending out scripts. Some agents ask for a one-time up-front "handling" fee, while others deduct office expenses after a script has been sold. Always have a clear understanding of any fee an agent asks you to pay.

SUBHEADS

Each listing is broken down into subheads to make locating specific information easier. In the first section, you'll find contact information for each agency. You'll also learn if the agent is a WGA signatory or a member of any other professional organizations. Other information provided indicates the agency's size, its willingness to work with a new or unpublished writer, and a percentage breakdown of the general types of scripts the agency will consider.

Member Agents: Agencies comprised of more than one agent list member agents and their individual specialties. This information will help you determine the person to whom you should send your query letter.

Represents: In this section, agents specify what type of scripts they represent. Make sure you query only agents who represent the type of material you write.

○━ Look for the key icon to quickly learn an agent's areas of specialization. In this portion of the listing, agents mention the specific subject areas they're currently seeking, as well as those subject areas they do not consider.

How to Contact: Most agents open to submissions prefer an initial query letter that briefly describes your work. Script agents usually discard material sent without a SASE. In this section, agents also mention if they accept queries by fax or e-mail; if they consider simultaneous submissions; and how they prefer to solicit new clients.

Recent Sales: Reflecting the different ways scriptwriters work, agents list scripts optioned or sold and scripting assignments procured for clients. The film industry is very secretive about sales, but you may be able to get a list of clients or other references upon request—especially if the agency is interested in representing your work.

Terms: Most agents' commissions range from 10-15 percent, and WGA signatories may not earn more than 10 percent from WGA members.

Writers' Conferences: A great way to meet an agent is at a writers' conference. Here agents list the conferences they usually attend. For more information about a specific conference, check the Conferences section starting on page 230.

Tips: In this section, agents offer advice and additional instructions for writers seeking representation.

SPECIAL INDEXES

Script Agents Specialties Index: This index (page 324) organizes agencies according to the subjects they are interested in receiving. This index should help you compose a list of agents specializing in your areas. Cross-referencing categories and concentrating on agents interested in two or more aspects of your manuscript might increase your chances of success.

Script Agents Format Index: This index (page 329) organizes agents according to the script types they consider, such as TV movie of the week (MOW), sitcom or episodic drama.

Openness to Submissions Index: This index (page 331) lists agencies according to how receptive they are to new clients.

Geographic Index: For writers seeking an agent close to home or in a specific area, this index (page 336) lists agents by state.

Agents Index: This index (page 342) provides a list of agents' names in alphabetical order along with the name of the agency for which they work. Find the name of the person you would like to contact, and then check the agency listing.

General Index: This index (page 354) lists all agencies, publicists and conferences appearing in the book.

Quick Reference Icons

At the beginning of some listings, you will find one or more of the following symbols:

N Agency new to this edition

Canadian agency

International agency

Agency actively seeking clients

Agency seeking both new and established writers

Agency seeking mostly established writers through referrals

Agency specializing in certain types of work

Agency not currently seeking new clients

Find a pull-out bookmark with a key to symbols on the inside cover of this book.

⌗ ☻ ABOVE THE LINE AGENCY

468 N. Camden Dr., #200, Beverly Hills CA 90210. (310)859-6115. Fax: (310)859-6119. **Contact:** Bruce Bartlett. Owner: Rima Bauer Greer. Estab. 1994. Signatory of WGA. Represents 35 clients. 10% of clients are new/unpublished writers. Currently handles: 95% movie scripts; 5% TV scripts.

• Prior to opening her agency, Ms. Greer served as president of Writers & Artists Agency.

Represents Feature film, TV movie of the week. **Considers these script subject areas:** Cartoon/animation.

How to Contact This agency accepts clients by referral only and does not guarantee a response.

Recent Sales *The Great Cookie Wars*, by Greg Taylor and Jim Strain (Fox); *Velveteen Rabbit*, by Greg Taylor (Disney); *Wing and a Prayer*, by David Engelbach and John Wolff (Franchise).

Terms Agent receives 10% commission on domestic and foreign sales.

☻ ABRAMS ARTISTS AGENCY

275 Seventh Ave., 26th Floor, New York NY 10001.

Member Agents Maura Teitelbaum; Sarah Douglas; Charles Kopelman; Beth Blickers; Morgan Jenness.

Represents Stage plays, screenplays, books. **Considers these script subject areas:** Action/adventure; biography/autobiography; comedy; contemporary issues; detective/police/crime; ethnic; experimental; family saga; fantasy; feminist; gay/lesbian; glitz; historical; horror; juvenile; mainstream; multicultural; multimedia; mystery/suspense; psychic/supernatural; regional; religious/inspirational; romantic comedy; romantic drama; science fiction; sports; teen; thriller; western/frontier.

○ₙ This agency specializes in musical stage plays.

How to Contact Query with SASE. Prefers to read materials exclusively. Referrals needed for new materials. *No unsolicited mss.* No e-mail or fax queries.

☻ ACME TALENT & LITERARY

4727 Wilshire Blvd., Suite #333, Los Angeles CA 90010. (323)954-2263. Fax: (323)954-2262. **Contact:** Mickey Frieberg, head of literary division. Estab. 1993. Signatory of WGA. Represents 50 clients. Currently handles: movie scripts; TV scripts; video game rights.

Member Agents Mickey Freiberg (books, film scripts).

Represents Feature film. **Considers these script subject areas:** Action/adventure; biography/autobiography; cartoon/animation; comedy; contemporary issues; detective/police/crime; erotica; ethnic; experimental; family saga; fantasy; feminist; gay/lesbian; glitz; historical; horror; juvenile; mainstream; multicultural; multimedia; mystery/suspense; psychic/supernatural; regional; religious/inspirational; romantic comedy; romantic drama; science fiction; sports; teen; thriller; western/frontier.

○ₙ This agency specializes in feature films and completed specs or pitches by established/produced writers and new writers. Actively seeking great feature scripts. *No unsolicited material.*

How to Contact No e-mail or fax queries. Obtains most new clients through recommendations from established industry contacts, production companies of note, reputable entertainment attorneys.

Terms Agent receives 10% commission on domestic sales; 15% commission on foreign sales. Offers written contract, binding for 2 years.

⌗ ☻ THE ALPERN GROUP

15645 Royal Oak Rd., Encino CA 91436. (818)528-1111. E-mail: mail@alperngroup.com. **Contact:** Jeff Alpern. Estab. 1994. Represents 50 clients. 10% of clients are new/unpublished writers. Currently handles: 30% movie scripts; 60% TV scripts; 10% stage plays.

• Prior to opening his agency, Mr. Alpern was an agent with William Morris.

Member Agents Jeff Alpern, president; Elana Trainoff; Jeff Aghassi.

Represents Movie scripts, feature film, TV scripts, TV movie of the week, episodic drama, miniseries. **Considers these script subject areas:** Action/adventure; biography/autobiography; comedy; contemporary issues; detective/police/crime; ethnic; fantasy; feminist; gay/lesbian; horror; juvenile; mainstream; multicultural; mystery/suspense; regional; romantic comedy; science fiction; teen; thriller; family; supernatural.

How to Contact Query with SASE or via e-mail. Only responds to e-mail queries if interested. Responds to all mail queries that include a SASE. Responds in 1 month to queries.

Terms Agent receives 10% commission on domestic sales. Offers written contract.

☻ MICHAEL AMATO AGENCY

1650 Broadway, Suite 307, New York NY 10019. (212)247-4456 or (212)247-4457. **Contact:** Michael Amato. Estab. 1970. Member of SAG, AFTRA. Represents 6 clients. 2% of clients are new/unpublished writers.

Represents Feature film, TV movie of the week, episodic drama, animation, documentary, miniseries. **Considers these script subject areas:** Action/adventure.

How to Contact Query with SASE. Responds in 1 month to queries. Obtains most new clients through recommendations from others.
Recent Sales This agency prefers not to share information on specific sales.

◑ THE ARTISTS AGENCY
1180 S. Beverly, Suite 400, Los Angeles CA 90035. (310)277-7779. Fax: (310)785-9338. **Contact:** Richard Shepherd. Estab. 1974. Signatory of WGA. Represents 50 clients. 20% of clients are new/unpublished writers. Currently handles: 70% movie scripts; 30% TV scripts.
Represents Movie scripts (feature film), TV movie of the week. **Considers these script subject areas:** Action/adventure; comedy; contemporary issues; detective/police/crime; mystery/suspense; romantic comedy; romantic drama; thriller.
How to Contact Query with SASE. Responds in 2 weeks to queries. Obtains most new clients through recommendations from others.
Recent Sales This agency prefers not to share information on specific sales.
Terms Agent receives 10% commission on dramatic rights sales. Offers written contract, binding for 1-2 years.

ⓝ ◑ BASKOW AGENCY
2948 E. Russell Rd., Las Vegas NV 89120. (702)733-7818. Fax: (702)733-2052. E-mail: jaki@baskow.com. **Contact:** Jaki Baskow. Estab. 1976. Represents 8 clients. 40% of clients are new/unpublished writers. Currently handles: 5% nonfiction books; 5% novels; 20% movie scripts; 70% TV scripts.
Member Agents Crivolus Sarulus (scripts); Jaki Baskow.
Represents Feature film, TV movie of the week, episodic drama, sitcom, documentary, miniseries, variety show. **Considers these script subject areas:** Action/adventure; biography/autobiography; comedy; contemporary issues; family saga; glitz; mystery/suspense; religious/inspirational; romantic comedy; romantic drama; science fiction (juvenile only); thriller.
> O⇥ Actively seeking unique scripts, all-American true stories, kids' projects, and movies of the week. Does not want to receive heavy violence.
How to Contact Submit outline, proposal, treatments. Accepts e-mail and fax queries. Responds in 1 month to queries. Obtains most new clients through recommendations from others.
Recent Sales Sold 3 movie/TV MOW scripts in the last year. *Malpractice*, by Larry Leirketen (Blakely); *Angel of Death* (CBS). Other clients include Cheryl Anderson, Camisole Prods, Michael Store.
Terms Agent receives 10% commission on domestic and foreign sales. Offers written contract.

⊘ BEACON ARTISTS AGENCY INC.
120 E. 56th St., Suite 540, New York NY 10022. (212)736-6630. **Contact:** Patricia McLaughlin. Member of AAR. Represents 20-25 clients.
Represents Movie scripts, TV movie of the week, episodic drama, stage plays. **Considers these script subject areas:** Mainstream.
> O⇥ "We are not seeking new clients at this time. We handle theatre writers and screenwriters, as well as some TV and the occasional book. We are a small agency with very personal service."
Terms Agent receives 10% commission on domestic sales; 15-20% commission on foreign sales. Offers written contract, binding for 2-3 years (renewable). Client pays own legal fees and any extraordinary office costs.

◑ THE BOHRMAN AGENCY
8899 Beverly Blvd., Suite 811, Los Angeles CA 90048. **Contact:** Michael Hruska, Caren Bohrman. Signatory of WGA.
Represents Novels, feature film, TV scripts. **Considers these script subject areas:** Action/adventure; biography/autobiography; cartoon/animation; comedy; contemporary issues; detective/police/crime; erotica; ethnic; experimental; family saga; fantasy; feminist; gay/lesbian; glitz; historical; horror; juvenile; mainstream; multicultural; multimedia; mystery/suspense; psychic/supernatural; regional; religious/inspirational; romantic comedy; romantic drama; science fiction; sports; teen; thriller; western/frontier.
How to Contact Query with self-addressed postcard. *No unsolicited mss.* No phone calls. Obtains most new clients through recommendations from others.
Recent Sales This agency prefers not to share information on specific sales.

▦ ◑ ALAN BRODIE REPRESENTATION LTD.
Fairgate House, 78 New Oxford St., 6th Floor, London WC1A 1HB England. E-mail: info@alanbrodie.com. Web site: www.alanbrodie.com. Member of PMA. 10% of clients are new/unpublished writers.
Member Agents Alan Brodie; Sarah McNair; Lisa Foster.
> O⇥ This agency specializes in stage, film, TV, and radio.
How to Contact Does not accept unsolicited mss. North American writers accepted only in exceptional circum-

stances. Accepts e-mail and fax queries. Responds in 3 months to queries. Obtains most new clients through recommendations from others.

Recent Sales This agency prefers not to share information on specific sales.

Terms Charges clients for photocopying.

Tips "Biographical details can be helpful. Generally only playwrights whose work has been performed will be considered, provided they come recommended by an industry professional."

🌑 DON BUCHWALD & ASSOCIATES, INC.

6500 Wilshire Blvd., 22nd Floor, Los Angeles CA 90048. (323)655-7400. Fax: (323)655-7470. E-mail: info@buch wald.com. Web site: www.donbuchwald.com. Estab. 1977. Signatory of WGA. Represents 50 clients.

Member Agents Debbie Deuble Hill; Sheryl Petersen; Max Stubblefield.

Represents Movie scripts, feature film, TV scripts, TV movie of the week, episodic drama, sitcom, documentary, miniseries.

How to Contact Query with SASE. Considers simultaneous queries. Obtains most new clients through recommendations from others.

N ☑ KELVIN C. BULGER AND ASSOCIATES

1525 E. 53rd St., Suite 534, Chicago IL 60615. (773)256-1501. Fax: (773)256-1503. E-mail: kcbwoi@aol.com. **Contact:** Kelvin Bulger. Estab. 1992. Signatory of WGA. Represents 25 clients. 90% of clients are new/unpublished writers. Currently handles: 75% movie scripts; 25% TV scripts.

Represents Feature film, TV movie of the week, documentary, syndicated material. **Considers these script subject areas:** Action/adventure; cartoon/animation; comedy; contemporary issues; ethnic; family saga; religious/inspirational.

How to Contact Query with SASE, 1-page logline, 1-page plot synopsis (beginning/middle/end), first 10 pages of screenplay. Accepts e-mail and fax queries. Considers simultaneous queries. Responds in 3 weeks to queries; 2 months to mss. Returns materials only with SASE. Obtains most new clients through recommendations from others, solicitations.

Recent Sales *Severed Ties* (Maverick Entertainment).

Terms Agent receives 10% commission on domestic and foreign sales. Offers written contract, binding for 6-12 months.

Tips "Proofread before submitting to an agent. We only reply to letters of inquiry if a SASE is enclosed."

☑ CEDAR GROVE AGENCY ENTERTAINMENT

P.O. Box 1692, Issaquah WA 98027-0068. (425)837-1687. E-mail: cedargroveagency@juno.com. **Contact:** Samantha Powers. Estab. 1995. Member of Cinema Seattle. Represents 7 clients. 100% of clients are new/unpublished writers. Currently handles: 90% movie scripts; 10% TV scripts.

- Prior to becoming an agent, Ms. Taylor worked for Morgan Stanley Dean Witter. She is also a member of Bellevue Community College's media advisory board.

Member Agents Amy Taylor, senior vice president of motion picture division; Samantha Powers, executive vice president of motion picture division.

Represents Feature film, TV movie of the week, sitcom. **Considers these script subject areas:** Action/adventure; biography/autobiography; comedy; detective/police/crime; family saga; juvenile; mystery/suspense; romantic comedy; science fiction; sports; thriller; western/frontier.

- ⚬⚖ Cedar Grove Agency Entertainment was formed in the Pacific Northwest to take advantage of the rich and diverse culture, as well as the many writers who reside there. Does not want period pieces, horror genres, children's scripts dealing with illness, or scripts with excessive substance abuse.

How to Contact Submit 1-page synopsis via mail with SASE or via e-mail (no attachments). No phone calls, please. Responds in 10 days to queries; 2 months to mss. Obtains most new clients through referrals, Web site.

Recent Sales This agency prefers not to share information on specific sales.

Terms Agent receives 10% commission on domestic sales. Offers written contract, binding for 6-12 months; 30-day notice must be given to terminate contract.

Tips "We focus on finding that rare gem, the undiscovered, multi-talented writer, no matter where they live. Write, write, write! Find time every day to write. Network with other writers when possible, and write what you know. Learn the craft through books. Read scripts of your favorite movies. Enjoy what you write!"

🔳 ☑ THE CHARACTERS TALENT AGENCY

8 Elm St., Toronto ON M5G 1G7 Canada. (416)964-8522. Fax: (416)964-6349. E-mail: clib5@aol.com. **Contact:** Carl Liberman. Estab. 1968. Signatory of WGC. Represents 1,000 clients (writers, actors, directors). 5% of clients are new/unpublished writers.

- Before becoming an agent, Mr. Liberman was an advertising executive, writer and actor.

Member Agents Brent Jordan Sherman (film/TV writers and directors); Geoff Brooks (animation, children's writers); Ben Silverman (writers).

Represents Movie scripts, feature film, TV scripts, TV movie of the week, episodic drama, sitcom, animation, documentary, miniseries, soap opera, syndicated material. **Considers these script subject areas:** Action/adventure; biography/autobiography; cartoon/animation; comedy; contemporary issues; detective/police/crime; erotica (no porn); ethnic; family saga; fantasy; feminist; gay/lesbian; glitz; historical; horror; juvenile; mainstream; mystery/suspense; psychic/supernatural; romantic comedy; romantic drama; science fiction; sports; teen; thriller; western/frontier.

    O— Actively seeking romantic comedy features, comedy features, family comedy features, and strong female leads in thrillers (MOW/features). Does not represent playwrights.

How to Contact Query with SASE. Accepts e-mail and fax queries. Considers simultaneous queries. Responds in 2 days to queries if by e-mail; 60 days to ms if query is accepted. Obtains most new clients through recommendations from others.

Recent Sales *Ada*, by Ronalda Jones (Milagro Films); *13th Apostle*, by Paul Margolis (Stallion Films); *Drake Diamond: Exorcist for Hire*, by Arne Olsen (Montecito Pictures); *Grounded in Eire*, by Ralph Keefer (Amaze Film & TV). Other clients include Tim Burns, Robert C. Cooper, Paul Margolis, Gerald Sanford.

Terms Agent receives 10% commission on domestic and foreign sales. No written contract.

Tips "To reach or get information about each individual agent, please call for an e-mail address. All agents are based in Toronto, except one in Vancouver."

◙ CIRCLE OF CONFUSION

E-mail: queries@circleofconfusion.com. Web site: www.circleofconfusion.com. Estab. 1990.

    O— This agency specializes in comic books, video games, and screenplays (science fiction, action, fantasy, thrillers, urban, horror).

How to Contact Submit brief synopsis via e-mail. Obtains most new clients through recommendations from others, writing contests, queries.

Terms Agent receives 10% commission on domestic and foreign sales. Offers written contract, binding for 1 year.

Tips "We look for writing that shows a unique voice, especially one which puts a fresh spin on commercial Hollywood genres."

◙ COMMUNICATIONS AND ENTERTAINMENT, INC.

2851 S. Ocean Blvd., #5K, Boca Raton FL 33432-8407. (561)391-9575. Fax: (561)391-7922. E-mail: jlbearde@bell south.net. **Contact:** James L. Bearden. Estab. 1989. Represents 10 clients. 50% of clients are new/unpublished writers. Currently handles: 10% novels; 5% juvenile books; 40% movie scripts; 40% TV scripts.

    • Prior to opening his agency, Mr. Bearden worked as a producer/director and an entertainment attorney.

Member Agents James Bearden (TV, film); Joyce Daniels (literary).

Represents Novels, juvenile books, movie scripts, TV scripts, syndicated material. **Considers these nonfiction areas:** History; music/dance; theater/film. **Considers these fiction areas:** Action/adventure; comic books/cartoon; fantasy; historical; mainstream/contemporary; science fiction; thriller.

How to Contact For scripts, query with SASE. For books, query with outline/proposal or send entire ms. Responds in 1 month to queries; 3 months to mss. Obtains most new clients through recommendations from others.

Recent Sales This agency prefers not to share information on specific sales.

Terms Agent receives 10% commission on domestic sales; 5% commission on foreign sales. Offers written contract.

Tips "Be patient."

◪ ◙ THE CORE GROUP TALENT AGENCY, INC.

89 Bloor St. W., Suite 300, Toronto ON M5S 1M1 Canada. (416)955-0819. Fax: (416)955-0825. E-mail: literary@c oregroupta.com. **Contact:** Charles Northcote, literary agent/co-owner. Estab. 1989. Member of WGC. Represents 60 clients. 10% of clients are new/unpublished writers. Currently handles: 25% movie scripts; 25% TV scripts; 50% stage plays.

Represents Movie scripts, feature film, TV scripts, TV movie of the week, episodic drama, sitcom, animation, documentary, miniseries, soap opera, stage plays. **Considers these script subject areas:** Action/adventure; biography/autobiography; cartoon/animation; comedy; contemporary issues; detective/police/crime; erotica; ethnic; experimental; family saga; fantasy; feminist; gay/lesbian; glitz; historical; horror; juvenile; mainstream; multicultural; mystery/suspense; psychic/supernatural; regional; romantic comedy; romantic drama; sports; teen; thriller; western/frontier.

    O— Seeks previously-produced writers with Canadian status. Doesn't want international writers without Canadian status.

How to Contact Query with SASE. Responds in 1 week to queries. Returns materials only with SASE.

Terms Agent receives 10% commission on domestic sales. Offers written contract, binding for 1 year; 60-day notice must be given to terminate contract.

Script Agents

⌷ Ⓓ DRAMATIC PUBLISHING

311 Washington St., Woodstock IL 60098. (815)338-7170. Fax: (815)338-8981. E-mail: plays@dramaticpublishin g.com. Web site: www.dramaticpublishing.com. **Contact:** Linda Habjan. Estab. 1885. Currently handles: 2% textbooks; 98% stage plays.

Represents Stage plays.

> ○➼ This agency specializes in a full range of stage plays, musicals, adaptations, and instructional books about theater.

How to Contact Submit complete ms, SASE. Responds in 10-12 weeks to mss.

Recent Sales This agency prefers not to share information on specific sales.

Ⓓ THE E S AGENCY

6612 Pacheco Way, Citrus Heights CA 95610. (916)723-2794. Fax: (916)723-2796. E-mail: edley07@cs.com. **Contact:** Ed Silver, president. Estab. 1995. Represents 50-75 clients. 70% of clients are new/unpublished writers. Currently handles: 50% nonfiction books; 25% novels; 25% movie scripts.

> ● Prior to becoming an agent, Mr. Silver was an entertainment business manager.

Represents Nonfiction books, novels, movie scripts, feature film, TV movie of the week. **Considers these nonfiction areas:** General nonfiction. **Considers these fiction areas:** Action/adventure; detective/police/crime; erotica; experimental; historical; humor/satire; literary; mainstream/contemporary; mystery/suspense; thriller; young adult. **Considers these script subject areas:** Action/adventure; comedy; contemporary issues; detective/ police/crime; erotica; ethnic; experimental; family saga; mainstream; mystery/suspense; romantic comedy; romantic drama; sports; thriller.

> ○➼ This agency specializes in theatrical screenplays, MOW, and miniseries. Actively seeking anything unique and original.

How to Contact Query with SASE. Considers simultaneous queries. Returns materials only with SASE. Obtains most new clients through recommendations from others, queries from WGA agency list.

Terms Agent receives 15% commission on domestic sales; 20% commission on foreign sales; 10% commission on dramatic rights sales. Offers written contract; 30-day notice must be given to terminate contract.

Ⓓ EVATOPIA, INC.

400 S. Beverly Dr., Suite 214, Beverly Hills CA 90212. E-mail: submissions@evatopia.com. Web site: www.evato pia.com. **Contact:** Margery Walshaw. Estab. 2004. Represents 15 clients. 85% of clients are new/unpublished writers. Currently handles: 100% movie scripts.

> ● Prior to becoming an agent, Ms. Walshaw was a writer and publicist for the entertainment industry.

Member Agents Mary Kay (story development); Stacy Glenn (story development); Jamie Davis (story assistant); Jill Jones (story editor).

Represents Movie scripts. **Considers these script subject areas:** Action/adventure; biography/autobiography; cartoon/animation; comedy; contemporary issues; detective/police/crime; ethnic; family saga; fantasy; historical; horror; juvenile; mainstream; mystery/suspense; psychic/supernatural; romantic comedy; romantic drama; science fiction; sports; teen; thriller.

> ○➼ "We specialize in promoting and developing the careers of first-time screenwriters. All of our staff members have strong writing and entertainment backgrounds, making us sympathetic to the needs of our clients." Actively seeking dedicated and hard-working writers.

How to Contact Submit via online submission form. Considers simultaneous queries. Responds in 2 weeks to queries; 3 weeks to mss. Returns materials only with SASE. Obtains most new clients through recommendations from others, solicitations.

Terms Agent receives 15% commission on domestic and foreign sales. Offers written contract, binding for up to 2 years; 30-day notice must be given to terminate contract.

Tips "Remember that you only have one chance to make that important first impression. Make your loglines original and your synopses concise. The secret to a screenwriter's success is creating an original story and telling it in a manner that we haven't heard before."

Ⓓ FILMWRITERS LITERARY AGENCY

4932 Long Shadow Dr., Midlothian VA 23112. (804)744-1718. **Contact:** Helene Wagner. Signatory of WGA.

> ● Prior to opening her agency, Ms. Wagner was director of the Virginia Screenwriter's Forum for 7 years and taught college-level screenwriting classes. "As a writer myself, I have won or been a finalist in most major screenwriting competitions throughout the country and have a number of my screenplays optioned. Through the years, I have enjoyed helping and working with other writers. Some have gone on to have their movies made, their work optioned, and won national contests."

Represents Feature film, TV movie of the week, miniseries. **Considers these script subject areas:** Action/

adventure; comedy; contemporary issues; detective/police/crime; historical; juvenile; mystery/suspense; psychic/supernatural; romantic comedy; romantic drama; teen; thriller.

    ○⊶ This agency does not accept unsolicited queries and is currently not accepting new clients.

How to Contact No e-mail or fax queries. Obtains most new clients through recommendations from others.

Recent Sales *Woman of His Dreams*, by Jeff Rubin (Ellenfreyer Productions).

Terms Agent receives 10% commission on domestic and foreign sales. Offers written contract. Clients supply photocopying and postage. Writers are reimbursed for office fees after the sale of the ms.

Tips "Professional writers should wait until they have at least 4 drafts done before they send out their work because they know it takes that much hard work to make a story and characters work. Show me something I haven't seen before with characters that I care about and that jump off the page. I not only look at a writer's work, I look at the writer's talent. If I believe in a writer, even though a piece may not sell, I'll stay with the writer and help nurture that talent, which a lot of the big agencies won't do."

◉ FITZGERALD LITERARY MANAGEMENT

84 Monte Alto Rd., Santa Fe NM 87505. (505)466-1186. **Contact:** Lisa FitzGerald. Estab. 1994. Represents 12 clients. 75% of clients are new/unpublished writers. Currently handles: 15% film rights novels; 85% movie scripts.

    ● Prior to opening her agency, Ms. FitzGerald headed development at Universal Studios for Oscar-nominated writers/producers Bruce Evans and Raynold Gideon. She also served as executive story analyst at CBS, and held positions at Curtis Brown Agency in New York and Adams, Ray & Rosenberg Talent Agency in Los Angeles.

Represents Feature film, TV movie of the week, film rights to novels. **Considers these fiction areas:** Mainstream/contemporary (novels with film potential). **Considers these script subject areas:** Action/adventure; biography/autobiography; comedy; contemporary issues; detective/police/crime; ethnic; family saga; fantasy; historical; horror; mainstream; mystery/suspense; psychic/supernatural; romantic comedy; romantic drama; science fiction; sports; teen; thriller; western/frontier.

    ○⊶ This agency specializes in screenwriters and selling film rights to novels. Actively seeking mainstream feature film scripts. Does not want to receive true stories.

How to Contact We are not accepting new clients except by referral.

Recent Sales Sold 7 titles and 5 scripts in the last year.

Terms Agent receives 15% commission on domestic sales. Offers written contract, binding for 1-2 years. Charges clients for photocopying and postage.

Tips "Know your craft. Read produced screenplays. Enter screenplay contests. Educate yourself on the business in general (read *The Hollywood Reporter* or *Daily Variety*). Learn how to pitch. Keep writing and don't be afraid to get your work out there."

◉ ROBERT A. FREEDMAN DRAMATIC AGENCY, INC.

1501 Broadway, Suite 2310, New York NY 10036. (212)840-5760. Fax: (212)840-5776. **Contact:** Robert A. Freedman. Estab. 1928. Member of AAR; signatory of WGA.

    ● Mr. Freedman has served as vice president of the dramatic division of AAR.

Member Agents Robert A. Freedman, president; Selma Luttinger, senior vice president; Robin Kaver, vice president (movie/TV scripts); Marta Praeger, agent (stage plays).

Represents Movie scripts, TV scripts, stage plays.

    ○⊶ This agency works with both new and established authors who write plays and movie and TV scripts.

How to Contact Query with SASE. All unsolicited mss returned unopened. Responds in 2 weeks to queries; 3 months to mss.

Recent Sales "We will speak directly with any prospective client concerning sales that are relevant to his/her specific script."

Terms Agent receives 10% commission on domestic sales. Charges clients for photocopying.

◉ SAMUEL FRENCH, INC.

45 W. 25th St., New York NY 10010-2751. (212)206-8990. Fax: (212)206-1429. E-mail: samuelfrench@earthlink. net. Web site: samuelfrench.com. **Contact:** Lawrence Harbison, senior editor. Estab. 1830. Member of AAR.

Member Agents Charles R. Van Nostrand.

Represents Theatrical stage play, musicals. **Considers these script subject areas:** Comedy; contemporary issues; detective/police/crime; ethnic; fantasy; horror; mystery/suspense; thriller.

    ○⊶ This agency specializes in publishing plays which it also licenses for production.

How to Contact Query with SASE, or submit complete ms to Lawrence Harbison. Accepts e-mail and fax queries. Considers simultaneous queries. Responds immediately to queries. Responds in 2-8 months to mss.

Recent Sales This agency prefers not to share information on specific sales.

Terms Agent receives variable commission on domestic sales.

N ☑ THE GAGE GROUP

14724 Ventura Blvd., Suite 505, Sherman Oaks CA 91403. (818)905-3800. Fax: (818)905-3322. E-mail: gagegroup la@yahoo.com. Estab. 1976. Member of DGA; signatory of WGA.

Member Agents Jonathan Westover (feature, television).

Represents Movie scripts, feature film, TV scripts, theatrical stage play.

   O➤ Considers all script subject areas.

How to Contact Query with SASE. Considers simultaneous queries. Responds in 1 month to queries and mss.

Recent Sales This agency prefers not to share information on specific sales.

Terms Agent receives 10% commission on domestic and foreign sales. Agency charges clients for photocopying.

☑ THE GERSH AGENCY

41 Madison Ave., 33rd Floor, New York NY 10010. (212)997-1818. Web site: www.gershcomedy.com. Estab. 1949. Member of AAR.

Member Agents John Buzzetti; Peter Franklin; Peter Hagan.

☑ GRAHAM AGENCY

311 W. 43rd St., New York NY 10036. **Contact:** Earl Graham. Estab. 1971. Represents 40 clients. 30% of clients are new/unpublished writers.

Represents Theatrical stage play, musicals.

   O➤ This agency specializes in playwrights. "We're interested in commercial material of quality." Does not want to receive one-acts or material for children.

How to Contact Query with SASE. No e-mail or fax queries. Responds in 3 months to queries; 6 weeks to mss. Obtains most new clients through recommendations from others, solicitations.

Recent Sales This agency prefers not to share information on specific sales.

Terms Agent receives 10% commission on dramatic rights sales.

Tips "Write a concise, intelligent letter giving the gist of what you are offering."

☑ THE SUSAN GURMAN AGENCY, LLC

865 West End Ave., # 15A, New York NY 10025. (212)749-4618. Fax: (212)864-5055. E-mail: susan@gurmanage ncy.com. Web site: www.gurmanagency.com. Estab. 1993. Signatory of WGA.

Represents Playwrights, screenwriters, directors, composers, lyricists.

How to Contact Obtains new clients by referral only. No e-mail or fax queries.

N ☑ JARET ENTERTAINMENT

6973 Birdview Ave., Malibu CA 90265. (310)589-9600. Fax: (310)589-9602. Web site: www.jaretentertainment.c om. **Contact:** Seth Jaret. Represents 20 clients. 10% of clients are new/unpublished writers. Currently handles: 75% movie scripts; 25% TV scripts.

Represents Movie scripts, TV scripts, books. **Considers these script subject areas:** Action/adventure; comedy; horror; romantic comedy; science fiction; thriller.

   O➤ This management company specializes in creative, out-of-the-box thinking. "We're willing to take a chance on well-written materials." Actively seeking high concept action and comedies. Does not want westerns, serial killer, black comedy, or period pieces.

How to Contact Accepts fax queries only. Discards unwanted material. Obtains most new clients through recommendations from others.

Recent Sales Sold 5 scripts in the last year. *Bumper to Bumper* (Fox); *The Fraud Prince* (Warner Brothers); *The Path*; *The Cold*; *Girl in the Curl* (Paramount).

Terms Agent receives 10% commission on domestic sales. Offers written contract, binding for 2 years.

☑ CHARLENE KAY AGENCY

901 Beaudry St., Suite 6, St.Jean/Richelieu QC J3A 1C6 Canada. E-mail: lmchakay@hotmail.com. **Contact:** Louise Meyers, director of development. Estab. 1992. Member of BMI; signatory of WGA. 50% of clients are new/unpublished writers. Currently handles: 50% movie scripts; 50% TV scripts.

   • Prior to opening her agency, Ms. Kay was a screenwriter.

Member Agents Louise Meyers; Karen Forsyth.

Represents Feature film, TV scripts, TV movie of the week, episodic drama, sitcom. **Considers these script subject areas:** Action/adventure; biography/autobiography; family saga; fantasy; psychic/supernatural; romantic comedy; romantic drama; science fiction.

   O➤ This agency specializes in teleplays and screenplays. "We seek stories that are out of the ordinary, something we don't see too often. A well-written and well-constructed script is important." Does not want to receive thrillers, barbaric/erotic films, novels, books, or mss.

How to Contact Query with SASE, outline/proposal. Does not return materials. Rejected mss are shredded. Responds in 1 month to queries; 10 weeks to mss.
Recent Sales This agency prefers not to share information on specific sales.
Terms Agent receives 10% commission on domestic and foreign sales. Offers written contract, binding for 1 year.
Tips "This agency is on the WGA lists, and query letters arrive by the dozens every week. As our present clients understand, success comes with patience. A sale rarely happens overnight, especially when you are dealing with totally unknown writers. We are not impressed by the credentials of a writer, amateur, or professional, or by his/her pitching techniques, but by his/her story ideas and ability to build a well-crafted script."

☑ THE JOYCE KETAY AGENCY

630 Ninth Ave., Suite 706, New York NY 10036. (212)354-6825. Fax: (212)354-6732. **Contact:** Joyce Ketay, Carl Mulert. Signatory of WGA.
Represents Feature film, TV movie of the week, episodic drama, sitcom, theatrical stage play. **Considers these script subject areas:** Comedy; contemporary issues; ethnic; experimental; feminist; gay/lesbian; historical; juvenile; mainstream; romantic comedy; romantic drama.
      ⚬━ This agency specializes in playwrights and screenwriters only. Does not want to receive novels.
Recent Sales This agency prefers not to share information on specific sales.

☑ EDDIE KRITZER PRODUCTIONS

8484 Wilshire Blvd., Suite 205, Beverly Hills CA 90211. (323)655-5696. Fax: (323)655-5173. E-mail: producedby @aol.com. Web site: www.eddiekritzer.com. **Contact:** Executive Story Editor. Estab. 1974.
Member Agents Eddie Kritzer (producer who also secures publishing agreements).
Represents Nonfiction books, movie scripts, feature film, TV scripts, TV movie of the week.
How to Contact Query with SASE. Prefers to read materials exclusively. Discards unwanted queries and mss. Obtains most new clients through recommendations from others, solicitations.
Recent Sales *Gmen & Gangsters* (Seven Locks Press/in development at Mandeville Films); *The Practical Patient* (Seven Locks Press); *The Making of a Surgeon in the 21st Century*, by Dr. Craig Miller (Blue Dolphin Press); *Kids Say the Darndest Things*, by Art Linkletter (Ten Speed Press/produced by Nick@Nite); *Live Ten Years Longer*, by Dr. Clarence Agrees (Ten Speed Press); *Take Back a Scary Movie* (currently at auction).
Terms Agent receives 15% commission on domestic sales; 20% commission on foreign sales. Offers written contract.
Tips "I am only looking for the most compelling stories. Be succinct, but be compelling."

⃞Ⓝ ☑ THE CANDACE LAKE AGENCY

9200 Sunset Blvd., Suite 820, Los Angeles CA 90069. (310)476-2882. Fax: (310)476-8283. E-mail: candace@lakel iterary.com. **Contact:** Candace Lake. Estab. 1977. Signatory of WGA, DGA. 50% of clients are new/unpublished writers. Currently handles: 10% novels; 70% movie scripts; 20% TV scripts.
Member Agents Candace Lake, president; Richard Ryba, agent; Ryan Lewis, agent.
Represents Novels, feature film, TV movie of the week, episodic drama. **Considers these fiction areas:** Action/ adventure; detective/police/crime; fantasy; gothic; historical; horror; humor/satire; literary; mainstream/con- temporary; military/war; multicultural; multimedia; mystery/suspense; New Age; occult; psychic/supernatural; science fiction; thriller; westerns/frontier; young adult. **Considers these script subject areas:** Action/adventure; comedy; contemporary issues; detective/police/crime; fantasy; historical; horror; mainstream; mystery/sus- pense; psychic/supernatural; romantic comedy; romantic drama; science fiction; teen; thriller.
      ⚬━ This agency specializes in screenplay and teleplay writers.
How to Contact *No unsolicited material.* Obtains most new clients through recommendations from others.
Recent Sales This agency prefers not to share information on specific sales.
Terms Agent receives 10% commission on domestic and foreign sales. Offers written contract, binding for 2 years.

◯ THE LANTZ OFFICE

200 W. 57th St., Suite 503, New York NY 10019. E-mail: rlantz@lantzoffice.com. **Contact:** Robert Lantz. Member of AAR.
Represents Movie scripts, feature film, theatrical stage play.
How to Contact Query with SASE.
Terms Agent receives 10% commission on domestic sales; 10% commission on foreign sales.

☑ LEGACIES . . . A LITERARY AGENCY

501 Woodstork Circle, Bradenton FL 34209-7393. **Contact:** MaryAnn Amato, executive director. Estab. 1992. Member of Licensed State of Florida Dept. of Business & Professional Regulations; signatory of WGA. Currently handles: 90% movie scripts; 10% stage plays.

Represents Feature film. **Considers these script subject areas:** Comedy; contemporary issues; family saga; feminist; historical.

　Oя This agency is not accepting new clients at this time.

Recent Sales *Death's Parallel*, by Dr. Oakley Jordan (Rainbow Books); *A Bench on Which to Rest*, by Maria Phillips; *Progress of the Sun* and *Journey from the Jacarandas*, by Patricia Friedberg; *Elsie Venner*, by Raleigh Marcell; *Glass House*, by Dan Guardino (adapted from *Glass House*, by Ari and Max Overton); *Dawn's Glory*, by Czerny Lee Miller.

Terms Agent receives 15% commission on domestic and foreign sales. Offers written contract.

❷ LEONARDS CORP.

(formerly International Leonards Corp.), 3612 N. Washington Blvd., Indianapolis IN 46205-3534. (317)926-7566. **Contact:** David Leonards. Estab. 1972. Signatory of WGA. Currently handles: 50% movie scripts; 50% TV scripts.

Represents Feature film, TV movie of the week, sitcom, animation, variety show. **Considers these script subject areas:** Action/adventure; cartoon/animation; comedy; contemporary issues; detective/police/crime; horror; mystery/suspense; romantic comedy; science fiction; sports; thriller.

　Oя All unsolicited mss are discarded.

Recent Sales This agency prefers not to share information on specific sales.

Terms Agent receives 10% commission on domestic and foreign sales. Offers written contract.

❷ THE MANAGEMENT CO.

1337 Ocean Ave., Suite F, Santa Monica CA 90401. (310)963-5670. **Contact:** Tom Klassen. Represents 15 clients.

　• Prior to starting his agency, Mr. Klassen was an agent with International Creative Management.

Member Agents Tom Klassen; Helene Taber; Paul Davis; Steve Gamber; Veronica Hernandez.

Represents Feature film, TV scripts, episodic drama, sitcom, miniseries.

　Oя Actively seeking studio-quality, action-drama scripts and really good comedies. Does not want horror scripts.

How to Contact Submit query letter with synopsis. No e-mail or fax queries. Responds in 2-3 weeks to queries. Returns materials only with SASE. Obtains most new clients through recommendations from others, conferences.

Recent Sales Sold 11 scripts in the last year.

Terms Agent receives 10% commission on domestic and foreign sales. Offers written contract, binding for 2 years.

Writers' Conferences Sundance Film Festival; film festivals in New York, Telluride, Atlanta, Chicago, Minnesota.

Tips "We only accept query letters with a short, 1-page synopsis. We will request a full manuscript with a SASE if interested. We rarely take on nonreferred material, but do review query letters and occasionally take on new writers. We have done very well with those we have taken on."

❷ THE MARTON AGENCY, INC.

One Union Square W., Suite 815, New York NY 10003-3303. Fax: (212)691-9061. E-mail: info@martonagency.com. **Contact:** Tonda Marton. Member of AAR.

Member Agents Tonda Marton; Anne Reingold.

　Oя This agency specializes in foreign-language licensing.

❷ THE STUART M. MILLER CO.

11684 Ventura Blvd., #225, Studio City CA 91604-2699. (818)506-6067. Fax: (818)506-4079. E-mail: smmco@aol.com. **Contact:** Stuart Miller. Estab. 1977. Signatory of WGA, DGA. Currently handles: 50% movie scripts; 6% multimedia; 40% books.

Represents Nonfiction books, novels, movie scripts. **Considers these nonfiction areas:** Biography/autobiography; computers/electronic; current affairs; government/politics/law; health/medicine; history; how-to; memoirs; military/war; self-help/personal improvement; true crime/investigative. **Considers these fiction areas:** Action/adventure; detective/police/crime; historical; literary; mainstream/contemporary; mystery/suspense; science fiction; sports; thriller. **Considers these script subject areas:** Action/adventure; biography/autobiography; cartoon/animation; comedy; contemporary issues; detective/police/crime; family saga; historical; mainstream; multimedia; mystery/suspense; romantic comedy; romantic drama; science fiction; sports; teen; thriller.

How to Contact For screenplays, query with SASE, narrative outline (2-3 pages). For books, submit narrative outline (5-10 pages). Accepts e-mail and fax queries. Considers simultaneous queries. Responds in 3 days to queries; 4-6 weeks to screenplays and mss. Returns materials only with SASE.

Recent Sales This agency prefers not to share information on specific sales.

Terms Offers written contract, binding for 2 years. Agent receives 10% commission on screenplay sales; 15% commission on motion picture/TV rights sales for books and other non-screenplay literary properties.

Tips "Always include a SASE, e-mail address, or fax number with query letters. Make it easy to respond."

🔘 MONTEIRO ROSE DRAVIS AGENCY, INC.

17514 Ventura Blvd., Suite 205, Encino CA 91316. (818)501-1177. Fax: (818)501-1194. Web site: www.monte iro-rose.com. **Contact:** Candy Monteiro. Estab. 1987. Signatory of WGA. Represents 50 clients. Currently handles: 40% movie scripts; 20% TV scripts; 40% animation.

Member Agents Candace Monteiro; Fredda Rose; Jason Dravis.

Represents Feature film, TV movie of the week, episodic drama, animation. **Considers these script subject areas:** Action/adventure; cartoon/animation; comedy; contemporary issues; detective/police/crime; ethnic; family saga; historical; juvenile; mainstream; mystery/suspense; psychic/supernatural; romantic comedy; romantic drama; science fiction; teen; thriller.

    O➡ This agency specializes in scripts for animation, TV, and film.

How to Contact Query with SASE. Accepts e-mail and fax queries. Responds in 1 week to queries; 2 months to mss. Returns materials only with SASE. Obtains most new clients through recommendations from others, solicitations.

Recent Sales This agency prefers not to share information on specific sales.

Terms Agent receives 10% commission on domestic sales. Offers written contract, binding for 2 years; 3-month notice must be given to terminate contract. Charges for photocopying.

Tips "We prefer to receive inquiries by e-mail, although by mail is OK with a SASE. We do not return manuscripts. We suggest that all feature manuscripts be no longer than 120 pages."

🔘 NIAD MANAGEMENT

15030 Ventura Blvd., Bldg. 19 #860, Sherman Oaks CA 91403. (818)981-2505. Fax: (818)386-2082. E-mail: queries@niadmanagement.com. Web site: www.niadmanagement.com. Estab. 1997. Represents 20 clients. 2% of clients are new/unpublished writers. Currently handles: 99% movie scripts; 1% stage plays.

Represents Movie scripts, feature film, TV movie of the week, miniseries, stage plays. **Considers these nonfiction areas:** Biography/autobiography. **Considers these fiction areas:** Action/adventure; detective/police/crime; family saga; literary; mainstream/contemporary; multicultural; mystery/suspense; psychic/supernatural; romance; thriller. **Considers these script subject areas:** Action/adventure; biography/autobiography; comedy; contemporary issues; detective/police/crime; ethnic; family saga; historical; horror; mainstream; multicultural; mystery/suspense; psychic/supernatural; romantic comedy; romantic drama; sports; teen; thriller.

How to Contact Query with SASE. Accepts e-mail and fax queries. Considers simultaneous queries. Responds in 1 week to queries; 3 months to mss. Returns materials only with SASE. Obtains most new clients through recommendations from others.

Recent Sales *MacGyver* (the feature film), by Lee Zlotoff; *Moebius*, by Neil Cohen (Mandate); *Winter Woke Up*, by Aaron Garcia and Melissa Emery; *Homecoming*, by Katie Fetting (Armada); *Stage Mom*, by Katie Fetting (Lightstorm); *Under the Bed*, by Susan Sandler (Caldwell Theater).

Terms Offers written contract, binding for 1 year; 30-day notice must be given to terminate contract. Agent receives 15% commission on all gross monies received.

🔘 OMNIQUEST ENTERTAINMENT

1416 N. La Brae Ave., Hollywood CA 90028. Fax: (303)802-1633. E-mail: mk@omniquestmedia.com. Web site: www.omniquestmedia.com. **Contact:** Michael Kaliski. Estab. 1997. Currently handles: 5% novels; 5% juvenile books; 40% movie scripts; 20% TV scripts; 10% multimedia; 15% stage plays.

Member Agents Michael Kaliski; Traci Belushi.

Represents Screenwriters, established playwrights. **Considers these script subject areas:** Action/adventure; biography/autobiography; comedy; contemporary issues; detective/police/crime; experimental; family saga; fantasy; historical; mainstream; multimedia; mystery/suspense; psychic/supernatural; romantic comedy; romantic drama; science fiction; thriller.

    O➡ Does not accept unsolicited material at this time.

How to Contact Obtains most new clients through recommendations from others.

Recent Sales This agency prefers not to share information on specific sales.

Terms Agent receives 15% commission on domestic and foreign sales. Offers written contract.

🔘 DOROTHY PALMER

235 W. 56 St., New York NY 10019. (212)765-4280. Fax: (212)977-9801. Estab. 1968 (talent agency); 1990 (literary agency). Signatory of WGA. Represents 12 clients. Currently handles: 70% movie scripts; 30% TV scripts.

    ● In addition to being a literary agent, Ms. Palmer has worked as a talent agent for 36 years.

Represents Feature film, TV movie of the week, episodic drama, sitcom, miniseries. **Considers these script subject areas:** Action/adventure; comedy; contemporary issues; detective/police/crime; family saga; feminist; mainstream; mystery/suspense; romantic comedy; romantic drama; thriller.

O— This agency specializes in screenplays and TV. Actively seeking successful, published writers (screenplays only). Does not want to receive work from new or unpublished writers.

How to Contact Query with SASE. Prefers to read materials exclusively. Returns materials only with SASE. Obtains most new clients through recommendations from others.

Recent Sales This agency prefers not to share information on specific sales.

Terms Agent receives 10% commission on domestic and foreign sales. Offers written contract, binding for 1 year. Charges clients for postage and photocopies.

Tips "Do not telephone. When I find a script that interests me, I call the writer. Calls to me are a turn-off because they cut into my reading time. The only ones who can call are serious investors of independent films."

ⓐ BARRY PERELMAN AGENCY

1155 N. La Cienega Blvd., Suite 412, W. Hollywood CA 90069. (310)659-1122. Fax: (310)659-1122. Estab. 1982. Signatory of WGA, DGA. Represents 40 clients. 15% of clients are new/unpublished writers. Currently handles: 100% movie scripts.

Member Agents Barry Perelman.

Represents Movie scripts, TV scripts, reality shows. **Considers these script subject areas:** Action/adventure; biography/autobiography; contemporary issues; detective/police/crime; historical; horror; mystery/suspense; romantic comedy; romantic drama; science fiction; thriller.

O— This agency specializes in motion pictures/packaging.

How to Contact Query with SASE, proposal package, outline. Responds in 1 month to queries. Obtains most new clients through recommendations from others, solicitations.

Recent Sales This agency prefers not to share information on specific sales.

Terms Agent receives 10% commission on domestic and foreign sales. Offers written contract, binding for 1-2 years. Charges clients for postage and photocopying.

ⓐ THE QUILLCO AGENCY

3104 W. Cumberland Ct., Westlake Village CA 91362. (805)495-8436. Fax: (805)373-9868. E-mail: quillco2@aol. com. **Contact:** Sandy Mackey. Estab. 1993. Signatory of WGA. Represents 7 clients.

Represents Feature film, TV movie of the week, animation, documentary.

How to Contact Prefers to read materials exclusively. Not accepting query letters at this time.

Recent Sales This agency prefers not to share information on specific sales.

Terms Agent receives 10% commission on domestic and foreign sales.

ⓜ KEN SHERMAN & ASSOCIATES

9507 Santa Monica Blvd., Beverly Hills CA 90210. (310)273-3840. Fax: (310)271-2875. E-mail: ksassociates@ear thlink.com. **Contact:** Ken Sherman. Estab. 1989. Member of BAFTA, PEN International; signatory of WGA, DGA. Represents approximately 50 clients. 10% of clients are new/unpublished writers.

● Prior to opening his agency, Mr. Sherman was with The William Morris Agency, The Lantz Office, and Paul Kohner, Inc.

Represents Nonfiction books, novels, movie scripts, TV scripts, teleplays, video games, life rights to books, film/TV rights to books. **Considers these nonfiction areas:** Agriculture/horticulture; Americana; animals; anthropology/archaeology; art/architecture/design; biography/autobiography; business/economics; child guidance/parenting; computers/electronic; cooking/foods/nutrition; crafts/hobbies; current affairs; education; ethnic/cultural interests; gardening; gay/lesbian issues; government/politics/law; health/medicine; history; how-to; humor/satire; interior design/decorating; language/literature/criticism; memoirs; military/war; money/finance; multicultural; music/dance; nature/environment; New Age/metaphysics; philosophy; photography; popular culture; psychology; recreation; regional; religious/inspirational; science/technology; self-help/personal improvement; sex; sociology; software; spirituality; sports; theater/film; translation; travel; true crime/investigative; women's issues/studies; young adult; creative nonfiction. **Considers these fiction areas:** Action/adventure; comic books/cartoon; confession; detective/police/crime; erotica; ethnic; experimental; family saga; fantasy; feminist; gay/lesbian; glitz; gothic; hi-lo; historical; horror; humor/satire; literary; mainstream/contemporary; military/war; multicultural; multimedia; mystery/suspense; New Age; occult; picture books; plays; poetry; poetry in translation; psychic/supernatural; regional; religious/inspirational; romance; science fiction; short story collections; spiritual; sports; thriller; translation; westerns/frontier; young adult. **Considers these script subject areas:** Action/adventure; biography/autobiography; cartoon/animation; comedy; contemporary issues; detective/police/crime; erotica; ethnic; experimental; family saga; fantasy; feminist; gay/lesbian; glitz; historical; horror; mainstream; multicultural; multimedia; mystery/suspense; psychic/supernatural; regional; religious/inspirational; romantic comedy; romantic drama; science fiction; sports; teen; thriller; western/frontier.

O— This agency specializes in television rights to books and solid writers for TV, books, and film.

How to Contact Contact by referral only. Responds in 1 month to mss. Obtains most new clients through recommendations from others.

Recent Sales Sold over 20 scripts in the last year. *Back Roads*, by Tawni O'Dell (Dreamworks); *Priscilla Salyers Story*, produced by Andrea Baynes (ABC); *Toys of Glass*, by Martin Booth (ABC/Saban Entertainment); *Brazil*, by John Updike (film rights to Glaucia Carmagos); *Fifth Sacred Thing*, by Starhawk (Bantam); *Questions From Dad*, by Dwight Twilly (Tuttle); *Snow Falling on Cedars*, by David Guterson (Universal Pictures); *The Witches of Eastwick—The Musical*, by John Updike (Cameron Macintosh, Ltd.).

Terms Agent receives 15% commission on domestic, foreign, and dramatic rights sales. Offers written contract. Charges clients for reasonable office expenses (postage, photocopying, etc.).

Writers' Conferences Maui Writers Conference; Squaw Valley Writers Workshop; Santa Barbara Writers' Conference; Screenwriting Conference in Santa Fe; Aspen Summer Words Literary Festival.

☻ MARK CHRISTIAN SUBIAS AGENCY

331 W. 57th St., #462, New York NY 10019. (212)445-1091. Fax: (212)898-0375. E-mail: marksubias@earthlink. net. **Contact:** Mark Subias. Estab. 2002. Represents 18 clients. Currently handles: movie scripts; stage plays. **How to Contact** Query with SASE.

☻ SUITE A MANAGEMENT TALENT & LITERARY AGENCY

120 El Camino Dr., Suite 202, Beverly Hills CA 90212. (310)278-0801. Fax: (310)278-0807. E-mail: suite-a@juno. com. **Contact:** Lloyd Robinson. Estab. 1996. Signatory of WGA, DGA. Represents 76 clients. 10% of clients are new/unpublished writers. Currently handles: 15% novels; 40% movie scripts; 40% TV scripts; 5% stage plays.

- Prior to becoming an agent, Mr. Robinson worked as a manager.

Member Agents Lloyd Robinson (adaptation of books and plays for development as features or TV MOW); Kevin Douglas (scripts for film and TV); Judy Jacobs (feature development).

Represents Feature film, TV movie of the week, episodic drama, documentary, miniseries, variety show, stage plays, CD-ROM. **Considers these script subject areas:** Action/adventure; cartoon/animation; comedy; contemporary issues; detective/police/crime; erotica; ethnic; experimental; family saga; fantasy; mainstream; mystery/suspense; psychic/supernatural; religious/inspirational; romantic comedy; romantic drama; science fiction; sports; teen; thriller; western/frontier.

- ⚷ "We represent screenwriters, playwrights, novelists, producers, and directors."

How to Contact Submit synopsis, outline/proposal, logline. Obtains most new clients through recommendations from others.

Recent Sales This agency prefers not to share information on specific sales or client names.

Terms Agent receives 10% commission on domestic and foreign sales. Offers written contract, binding for minimum 1 year. Charges clients for photocopying, messenger, FedEx, postage.

Tips "We are a talent agency specializing in the copyright business. Fifty percent of our clients generate copyright (screenwriters, playwrights, and novelists). Fifty percent of our clients service copyright (producers and directors). We represent produced, published, and/or WGA writers who are eligible for staff TV positions, as well as novelists and playwrights whose works may be adapted for film or TV."

◖ TALENT SOURCE

1711 Dean Forest Rd., Suite H, Savannah GA 31408. (912)963-0941. Fax: (912)963-0944. E-mail: michael@talent source.com. Web site: www.talentsource.com. **Contact:** Michael L. Shortt. Estab. 1991. Signatory of WGA. 35% of clients are new/unpublished writers. Currently handles: 85% movie scripts; 15% TV scripts.

- Prior to becoming an agent, Mr. Shortt was a TV program producer/director.

Represents Feature film, TV movie of the week, episodic drama, sitcom. **Considers these script subject areas:** Comedy; contemporary issues; detective/police/crime; erotica; family saga; juvenile; mainstream; mystery/suspense; romantic comedy; romantic drama; teen.

- ⚷ Actively seeking character-driven stories (e.g., *Sling Blade* or *Sex, Lies, and Videotape*). Does not want to receive science fiction or scripts with big budget special effects.

How to Contact Query with SASE, synopsis. No e-mail or fax queries. Responds in 10 weeks to queries. Obtains most new clients through recommendations from others.

Recent Sales This agency prefers not to share information on specific sales.

Terms Agent receives 10% commission on domestic sales; 15% commission on foreign sales. Offers written contract.

Tips "See the literary button on our Web site for complete submissions details. No exceptions."

◖ TALENTWORKS

3500 W. Olive Ave., Suite 1400, Burbank CA 91505. (818)972-4300. Fax: (818)972-4313. **Contact:** Kimber Wheeler. Estab. 1985. Signatory of WGA. 60% of clients are new/unpublished writers. Currently handles: 70% movie scripts; 30% TV scripts.

Represents Movie scripts, TV scripts. **Considers these script subject areas:** Action/adventure; biography/

autobiography; comedy; contemporary issues; detective/police/crime; ethnic; family saga; fantasy; feminist; gay/lesbian; mystery/suspense; psychic/supernatural; romantic comedy; romantic drama; science fiction; sports; thriller.

How to Contact Query with SASE, outline/proposal.

Recent Sales This agency prefers not to share information on specific sales.

Terms Agent receives 10% commission on domestic sales. Offers written contract, binding for 1 year; WGA rules on termination apply.

Tips "Be who you are and write from your heart."

✏ PEREGRINE WHITTLESEY AGENCY

279 Central Park W., New York NY 10024. (212)787-1802. Fax: (212)787-4985. E-mail: pwwagy@aol.com. **Contact:** Peregrine Whittlesey. Estab. 1986. Signatory of WGA. Represents 30 clients. 50% of clients are new/unpublished writers. Currently handles: 2% movie scripts; 98% stage plays.

   ➔ This agency specializes in playwrights who also write for screen and TV.

How to Contact Query with SASE. Prefers to read materials exclusively. Accepts e-mail and fax queries. Responds in 1 week to queries; 1 month to mss. Obtains most new clients through recommendations from others.

Recent Sales Sold 20 scripts in the last year. *Christmas Movie*, by Darrah Cloud (CBS). Scripts are also in production at Arena Stage in Washington, New Theatre in Miami, La Jolla Playhouse, Seattle Repertory Theatre, Oregon Shakespeare Festival, South Coast Repertory.

Terms Agent receives 10% commission on domestic sales; 15% commission on foreign sales. Offers written contract, binding for 2 years.

Publicists

Most publishing houses have in-house publicists, but their time is often limited and priority is usually given to big-name authors who have already proven they will make money for the publisher. Often writers feel their books aren't getting the attention they deserve, so many decide to work with an independent publicist.

Like agents, publicists view publishing as a business. Usually, they are more than happy to work in conjunction with your editor, your publisher, and your agent. Together they can form a strong team that will help make you a publishing sensation.

When choosing a publicist, you'll want someone who has a good business sense and experience in sales. And, you'll want someone who is enthusiastic about you and your writing and is interested in your subject area. By focusing on specific areas, publicists can actually do more for their clients. If a publicist is interested in cookbooks, she can send her clients to contacts she has on Food Network shows, editors at gourmet cooking magazines, bookstores that have cafes, and culinary conferences. The more knowledge a publicist has about your subject, the more opportunities she will find to publicize your work.

Contacting publicists should be much less stressful than the query process you've gone through to find an agent. Most publicists are open to a phone call or e-mail. Often an agent, an editor, or even another writer can refer you to a publicist. Of course, not every publicist you call will be the best fit for you. Be prepared to hear that the publicist already has a full client load or that she doesn't have the necessary level of interest in your work.

As you read over the listings of publicists, you'll quickly notice that many charge a substantial amount of money for their services. You should only pay what you feel comfortable paying and what you can reasonably afford. Keep in mind, however, that any money you spend on publicity will come back to you in the form of more books sold. A general rule of thumb is to budget one dollar for every copy of your book that is printed. For a print run of 10,000, you should expect to spend $10,000.

There are ways you can make working with a publicist less of a strain on your wallet. If you received an advance for your book, you can use part of it to help with your marketing expenses. Some publishers will agree to match the amount of money an author pays on outside publicity. If your publicist's bill is $2,000, you would pay half and your publisher would pay the other half. Be sure to ask your publishing house if this option is available to you. Most publicists are very willing to work with their clients on a marketing budget.

SUBHEADS

Each listing is broken down into subheads to make locating specific information easier. In the first paragraph, you'll find contact information for each publicist. Other information indicates the company's size and the publicist's experience in the publishing industry.

Members: This section includes the publicists' names and the year they joined their agency.

Specializations: Similar to the agents listed in this book, most publicists have specific areas of interest. A publicist with knowledge of your book's subject will have contacts in your field and a solid sense of your audience.

Services: This subhead provides a list of services available for clients, including book tour information, television shows on which clients have appeared, and contents of media kits.

⊶ Look for the key icon to quickly learn the publicist's areas of specialization and specific marketing strengths.

How to Contact: Most publicists are open to phone calls, letters, and e-mail; check this subhead to see the individual publicist's preference. Also pay close attention to the time frame the publicist needs between your initial contact and your book's publication date.

Clients: Here, publicists list authors they have helped promote and indicate if they are willing to provide references to potential clients.

Costs: Specific details are provided on how publicists charge their clients. Publicists also indicate if they work with clients on a marketing budget, and if they offer a written contract.

Writers' Conferences: Here publicists list the conferences they attend. For more information about a specific conference, check the Conferences section starting on page 230.

Tips: This section provides advice and additional instructions for working with a publicist.

SPECIAL INDEXES

Openness to Submissions Index: This index (page 331) lists agents and publicists according to how open they are to accepting new clients.

Geographic Index: For writers seeking a publicist close to home or in a specific area, this index (page 336) lists publicists by state.

General Index: This index (page 354) lists all agencies, publicists and conferences listed in the book.

Quick Reference Icons

At the beginning of some listings, you will find one or more of the following symbols:

N Publicist new to this edition

Canadian publicist

International publicist

Publicist actively seeking clients

Publicist seeking both new and established writers

Publicist seeking mostly established writers through referrals

Publicist specializing in certain types of work

Publicist not currently seeking new clients

Find a pull-out bookmark with a key to symbols on the inside cover of this book.

ACHESON-GREUB, INC.
P.O. Box 735, Friday Harbor WA 98250-0735. (360)378-2815. Fax: (360)378-2841. E-mail: aliceba@aol.com. **Contact:** Alice B. Acheson. Estab. 1981; specifically with books for 31 years. Currently works with 9 clients. 20% of clients are new/first-time writers.
- Prior to becoming a publicist, Ms. Acheson was a trade book editor, associate publicity director (Simon & Schuster and Crown Publishers), and high school Spanish teacher.

Specializations Nonfiction, fiction, children's books. **Considers these nonfiction areas:** Art/architecture/design; biography/autobiography; juvenile nonfiction; language/literature/criticism; memoirs; multicultural; music/dance/theater/film; nature/environment; photography. **Considers these fiction areas:** Contemporary issues; historical; juvenile; literary; mainstream; multicultural; mystery/suspense.

Services Media training, market research, sends material to magazines/newspapers for reviews, brochures. Book tours include bookstores, radio interviews, TV interviews, newspaper interviews, magazine interviews. Assists in coordinating travel plans. Clients have appeared on CBS-TV, *Early Show*, CNN, and innumerable radio and TV shows nationwide. Media kit includes author's biography, testimonials, articles about author, basic information on book, professional photos, sample interview questions. Clients are responsible for assisting with promotional material. Helps writer obtain endorsements.

- "We mentor so writers can do the work on their own for their next projects."

How to Contact Call, e-mail, or send letter with SASE. Responds in 2 weeks, unless on a teaching trip. Returns materials only with SASE. Obtains most new clients through recommendations from others, conferences. Contact 8 months prior to book's publication.

Clients *Africa*, by Art Wolfe (Wildlands Press); *Eating Heaven*, by Jennie Shortridge (NAL Accent/Penguin Group); Bel Barrett mystery series, by Jane Isenberg (Avon). References and contact numbers are available to potential clients.

Costs Clients charged hourly fee. Works with clients on marketing budget. Offers written contract; written notice must be given to terminate contract.

ADVENTURES IN MEDIA, INC.
4927 Bridgeville Ln., Spring TX 77038. Phone/Fax: (281)350-9005. E-mail: mediarod@aol.com. Web site: www.aimpress.com; www.talkguests.com. **Contact:** Rod Mitchell. Estab. 1984; specifically with books for 15 years. Currently works with 7 clients. 45% of clients are new/first-time writers.
- Prior to becoming a publicist, Mr. Mitchell did radio and TV news broadcasting and was a public relations executive.

Specializations Nonfiction. **Considers these nonfiction areas:** Business; child guidance/parenting; current affairs; government/politics/law; history; military/war; money/finance/economics; music/dance/theater/film; popular culture; psychology; science/technology; women's issues/studies.

Services Media training, fax news releases, electronic news releases, Web site publicity. Book tours include bookstores, radio interviews, TV interviews, newspaper interviews, magazine interviews. Firm is responsible for writing promotional material.

- "We take full advantage of my news background and tie in clients who are experts (as contributors) with timely news items and news breaking stories. We regularly schedule clients with major network talk and news programs."

How to Contact Call or send letter. Responds in 10 days. Discards unwanted materials. Obtains most new clients through publishers, Web site presence, literary services directories. Contact 1 month prior to book's publication.

Clients *Legion of the Lost*, by Jaime Salazar (Penguin Group); *The Tax Wars*, by Michael Louis Minns (Baracade Books); *The Master of Disguise*, by Tony Mendez (Simon & Schuster); *Black Gold*, by Steven Roby (Billboard Books). References and contact numbers are available to potential clients.

Costs Clients charged flat fee of $1,500-5,000/month. Offers written contract.

Tips "Always look at the publicist's track record and ask for references. Ask these questions: How will my publicist be accountable for the work performed? How long has the publicist been in business? Does the publicist work with national media outlets? What national success has the publicist accumulated in his/her work?"

AMERICAN BLACKGUARD, INC.
P.O. Box 680686, Franklin TN 37068-0686. (615)599-4032. E-mail: media@americanblackguard.com. Web site: www.americanblackguard.com. **Contact:** Eddie Lightsey. Estab. 1977.
- Prior to becoming a publicist, Mr. Lightsey was the senior publicist for an award-winning country music PR firm.

Specializations Nonfiction, fiction, children's books. **Considers these nonfiction areas:** Animals; art/architecture/design; biography/autobiography; cooking/food; history; how-to; interior design/decorating; music/

dance/theater/film; nature/environment; popular culture; self-help/personal improvement; sports; travel. **Interested in these fiction areas:** Action/adventure; fantasy; historical; horror; mystery/suspense; science fiction; thriller/espionage; westerns/frontier. Other types of clients include publishers, record labels, theater companies, screenwriters, entertainment companies, financial institutions, physicians, nonprofits, corporations.

Services Provides national publicity, creates and services press releases, sends material to magazines/newspapers for reviews. Book tours include bookstores, specialty stores, radio interviews, TV interviews, newspaper interviews, magazine interviews, speaking engagements. Clients have appeared on Discovery Channel, History Channel, ABC, CBS, NBC, PBS, NPR. Media kit includes author's biography, testimonials, articles about author, basic information on book, professional photos. Clients are responsible for assisting with promotional material.

How to Contact Call, e-mail, or fax. Responds in less than 1 week. Returns materials only with SASE. Obtains most new clients through recommendations from others, queries/solicitations. Contact 4 months prior to book's publication.

Clients *Queen of Diamonds*, by Carol Ann Rapp and Joseph Gregory (Providence House); *Genealogy 101*, by Barbara Ann Ranick (Rutledge Hill Press); *A Family Affair*, by Sandra Clunies (Rutledge Hill Press).

Costs Clients charged a monthly retainer. Offers a written contract, binding for 3 months.

Writers' Conferences Council for the Written Word Fall Writers' Seminar.

Tips ''American Blackguard will work on your behalf to handle all the promotional details of your career so you can focus on what you do best—being an author. We will be involved in your campaign as much or as little as you choose.''

N ◢ AUTHOR MARKETING EXPERTS, INC.

P.O. Box 421156, San Diego CA 92142. (858)560-0121. Fax: (858)560-1231. E-mail: penny@amarketingexpert.com. Web site: www.amarketingexpert.com. **Contact:** Penny C. Sansevieri. Estab. 1999; specifically with books for 6 years. Currently works with 5 clients. 5% of clients are new/first-time writers.

• Prior to becoming a publicist, Ms. Sansevieri worked in corporate PR and media relations.

Members Paula Krapf (media relations/virtual tours, at firm 1 year); Penny C. Sansevieri (marketing/media relations/virtual promotion, at firm 6 years).

Specializations Nonfiction, fiction, children's books. **Considers these nonfiction areas:** Animals; business; child guidance/parenting; computers/electronics; cooking/food/nutrition; health/medicine; history; how-to; humor; military/war; money/finance/economics; New Age/metaphysics; popular culture; psychology; religious/inspirational; self-help/personal improvement; travel; women's issues/studies. **Interested in these fiction areas:** Action/adventure; contemporary issues; detective/police/crime; historical; literary; mystery/suspense; New Age/metaphysical; religious/inspirational; romance.

Services Media training, international publicity, market research, fax news releases, electronic news release, sends material to magazines/newspapers for reviews, brochures, Web site assistance, Web site publicity. Book tours include bookstores, specialty stores, radio interviews, TV interviews, newspaper interviews, magazine interviews, virtual author tours, speaking engagements, conferences, libraries, schools, universities. Clients have appeared on *The Today Show*, NPR, MSNBC, *NBC Nightly News*, CNN, *Something You Should Know*. Media kit includes author's biography, testimonials, articles about author, basic information on book, professional photos, sample interview questions, book request information, review copy, reviews and mock reviews, tip sheets, book highlights, one-paragraph description of the book. Firm is responsible for writing promotional material. Helps writer obtain endorsements.

☞ ''Because our initial background was in self-published or small press authors, we've developed a team of creative people with an entrepreneurial bent. Our team has a unique ability to bring books that might have been overlooked into the spotlight. We regularly attend writers' conferences and other publishing, media, and marketing events that help to keep us fresh and in touch with our markets. We do not accept every book we receive—only those we absolutely love and feel we can deliver the client's media goals and objectives.''

How to Contact Call or e-mail. Responds in 1 week. Returns materials only with SASE. Obtains most new clients through recommendations from others, conferences. Contact 3-6 months prior to book's publication (preferred) or after book's publication.

Clients *Awakening the Mystic Gift*, by Jane Doherty (Hummel/Solvarr Publishing); *Cookin' for Love*, by Sharon Boorstin (iUniverse/Star Imprint); *Personal Budget Planner*, by Eric Gelb (PublishingGold.com). Other clients include Susie Galvez, Carol Welsh, Austin Camacho, Phil Goscienski. References and contact numbers are available to potential clients.

Costs Clients charged hourly retainer fee of $125-250; per service fee of $450-2,200; or monthly retainer of $750-3,500. Works with clients on marketing budget. Offers written contract, binding for 3-6 months; 1-month notice must be given to terminate contract.

Writers' Conferences Whidbey Island Writers' Conference; PMA University; Express Yourself Writers Conference.

Tips "Try to determine your criteria for hiring a publicist before you start your search and be wary of the publicist who promises too much over the phone. It is essential that you make sure there's chemistry because you're going to be working closely with this person. If your account will be handed off to an associate, contact that associate before you sign the contract. Also, never enter into an agreement with a publicist unless their marketing efforts are detailed in a contract; you want to know what this person will be doing for you in detail, not in general terms."

N ☑ BISSON BARCELONA

124 Hall Rd., Barrington NH 03825-3169. Phone/Fax: (603)664-5776. E-mail: info@bissonbarcelona.com. Web site: www.bissonbarcelona.com. **Contact:** Traci Bisson. Estab. 2000; specifically with books for 3 years. Currently works with 12 clients. 60% of clients are new/first-time writers.

• Prior to becoming a publicist, Ms. Bisson was marketing director for an international company.

Members Heather-Dale Barcelona (business development, at firm 2 years); Penny Maurer (creative director, at firm 2 years); Traci Bisson (senior publicist, at firm 5 years).

Specializations Nonfiction, fiction, children's books. **Considers these nonfiction areas:** Animals; biography/autobiography; business; child guidance/parenting; cooking/food/nutrition; crafts/hobbies; gay/lesbian issues; health/medicine; memoirs; nature/environment; self-help/personal improvement; travel; women's issues/studies. **Considers these fiction areas:** Action/adventure; detective/police/crime; mainstream; mystery/suspense.

Services Market research, fax news releases, electronic news release, sends material to magazines/newspapers for reviews, brochures, Web site assistance, Web site publicity. Book tours include bookstores, specialty stores, radio interviews, TV interviews, newspaper interviews, magazine interviews, speaking engagements, conferences, libraries, schools, universities. Assists in coordinating travel plans. Clients have appeared on KISS 106.1 (Seattle WA), 105.1 Lite FM (Miami FL), New Hampshire Public Radio, WMUR Channel 9 News (ABC affiliate), WVNY ABC 22 (Burlington VT). Media kit includes résumé, author's biography, testimonials, articles about author, basic information on book, professional photos, sample interview questions, book request information, speaker materials. Firm is responsible for writing promotional material.

○⊸ "Our employees have a strong background in strategic marketing, public relations, and branding. This expertise helps us to create unique promotional campaigns for clients. We also have a published writer of several articles on staff."

How to Contact Call, e-mail, or fax. "We require an author questionnaire to be completed prior to acceptance." Responds in 1 day. Returns materials only with SASE. Obtains most new clients through recommendations from others, queries/solicitations, seminars/workshops. Contact 4 months prior to book's publication (preferred) or after book's publication.

Clients *Mountain Peril*, by Tom Eslick (Viking); *The Taming of the Chew*, by Denise Lamothe (Penguin Putnam); *Far East Down East*, by Bruce de Mustchine (Down East Books); *Sisters By Heart*, by Mary Lou Fuller (KALM Publishing). Other clients include Tom Chase, Kathy Brodsky, Nancy Hanger. References and contact numbers are available to potential clients.

Costs Clients charged flat fee, $90/hour, or $500-1,500/month depending on the scope of the project. Works with clients on marketing budget. Offers written contract; suggested contract period is 4 months (not binding).

Writers' Conferences New Hampshire Writer's Project Writer's Day.

Tips "Seek out referrals from other authors. Ask for and check references prior to hiring. Ask about their specializations, if any, and ask them to give examples of other campaign promotions."

☑ BRICKMAN MARKETING

395 Del Monte Center, #250, Monterey CA 93940. (831)633-4444. E-mail: brickman@redshift.net. Web site: www.brickmanmarketing.com. **Contact:** Wendy Brickman. Estab. 1990; specifically with books for 15 years. Currently works with 30 clients. 10% of clients are new/first-time writers.

• Prior to becoming a publicist, Ms. Brickman worked in public relations in the home video industry.

Specializations Nonfiction, children's book, academic. **Considers these nonfiction areas:** Biography/autobiography; business; education; ethnic/cultural interests; health/medicine; history; how-to; interior design/decorating; music/dance/theater/film; nature/environment; New Age/metaphysics; popular culture; self-help/personal improvement; travel; women's issues/studies. **Considers these fiction areas:** Children's. Other types of clients include home video producers and a wide variety of businesses.

Services Media training, market research, fax news releases, sends material to magazines/newspapers for reviews. Book tours include bookstores, specialty stores, radio interviews, TV interviews, newspaper interviews, magazine interviews, speaking engagements, conferences, libraries, schools, universities. Clients have appeared on *Howie Mandel*, CNN, Bloomberg TV, HGTV, *Fox & Friends*, local TV, syndicated radio, and in hundreds of national and local magazines and newspapers. Media kit includes author's biography, testimonials, articles about author, basic information on book, professional photos, sample interview questions, book request information. Helps writer obtain endorsements.

O— "My wide variety of clients and contacts makes me a valuable publicist."

How to Contact E-mail. Responds in 1 week. Discards unwanted materials. Obtains most new clients through recommendations from others. Contact 4 months prior to book's publication.

Clients *What Do They Say When You Leave the Room*, by Brigid McGrath Massie (Eudemonia); *Diet for Allergies*, by Raphael Rethner; *Listening: It Will Change Your Life*, by Charles Page; *Writers and Artists Hideouts: Great Getaways for Seducing the Muse*, by Andrea Brown.

Costs Clients charged hourly retainer or monthly retainer. No written contract.

◑ BRODY PUBLIC RELATIONS

145 Route 519, Stockton NJ 08559-1711. (609)397-3737. Fax: (609)397-3666. E-mail: bebrody@aol.com. Web site: www.brodypr.com. **Contact:** Beth Brody. Estab. 1988; specifically with books for 17 years. Currently works with 8-10 clients. 10% of clients are new/first-time writers.

Specializations Nonfiction. **Considers these nonfiction areas:** Business; child guidance/parenting; education; entertainment; health/medicine; how-to; money/finance/economics; music/dance/theater/film; popular culture; psychology; self-help/personal improvement; travel.

Services Fax news releases, electronic news releases, sends material to magazines/newspapers for reviews, brochures, Web site assistance, Web site publicity. Book tours include bookstores, specialty stores, radio interviews, TV interviews, newspaper interviews, magazine interviews, speaking engagements, conferences, libraries, schools, universities. Assists in coordinating travel plans. Clients have appeared on *Oprah, Good Morning America, The Today Show*. Media kit includes author's biography, testimonials, articles about author, basic information on book, sample interview questions, book request information. Helps writer obtain endorsements.

How to Contact Call or e-mail. Responds in 48 hours. Obtains most new clients through recommendations from others. Contact 6 months prior to book's publication.

Clients Music Sales Corporation, Crown Business, Random House, Berkeley Publishing, Free Spirit Publishing. Other clients include Dow Jones, Don & Bradstreet, Foundations Behavioral Health, JVC Music, Mack Avenue Records, Magweb.com. References and contact numbers are available to potential clients.

Costs Clients charged hourly fee or monthly retainer. Offers written contract.

Tips "Contact a publicist after you have secured a publisher and distributor."

ℕ ◐ LAUREN CERAND

111 Worth St., 14X, New York NY 10013. (347)273-9364. E-mail: lcerand@gmail.com. Web site: www.laurencerand.com. **Contact:** Lauren Cerand. Estab. 2004; specifically with books for 1 year. Currently works with 12 clients. 25% of clients are new/first-time writers.

Specializations Nonfiction, fiction. **Considers these nonfiction areas:** Art/architecture/design; current affairs; language/literature/criticism; photography; popular culture; travel. **Considers these fiction areas:** Literary.

Services Media training, international publicity, market research, electronic news release, sends material to magazines/newspapers for reviews, Web site assistance, Web site publicity. Book tours include bookstores, specialty stores, radio interviews, TV interviews, speaking engagements. Clients have appeared on *The Daily Show*, CNBC's *Dennis Miller*, MSNBC's *Lester Holt Live*, Air America Radio's *Morning Edition*, NPR's *On The Media*. Media kit includes author's biography, basic information on book, professional photos. Firm is responsible for writing promotional material. Helps writer obtain endorsements.

O— "I embrace innovation, am always willing to take risks, work tirelessly on behalf of my clients, and endeavor to help them use the most technologically advanced methods of connecting with potential readers and finding the natural audience for their work."

How to Contact E-mail. Responds in 1-2 weeks. Discards unwanted materials. Obtains most new clients through recommendations from others. Contact 2 months prior to book's publication.

Clients *All The President's Spin: George W. Bush, the Media, and the Truth*, by Bryan Keefer (Touchstone); *Bulletproof Girl*, by Quinn Dalton (Washington Square Press); *The Untelling*, by Tayari Jones (Warner Books); *Twins*, by Marcy Dermansky (William Morrow).

Costs Clients charged hourly retainer fee. Works with clients on marketing budget. No written contract.

Tips "The best advice I can give authors is to talk to as many people as possible and take advantage of the level of expertise around you that you can draw on informally—your agent, editor, in-house publicist—to determine what amount of outside publicity would best serve your goals and aspirations for your book in the marketplace. It really is a team effort."

ℕ ◎ CLASS PROMOTIONAL SERVICES, LLC

3830 Sienna St., Oceanside CA 92056-7282. (760)630-2677. Fax: (760)630-9355. E-mail: classinterviews@cox.net. Web site: www.classervices.com. **Contact:** Kim Garrison. Estab. 1996; specifically with books for 10 years. Currently works with 20 clients. 50% of clients are new/first-time writers.

• Prior to becoming a publicist, Ms. Garrison managed the speakers bureau and publicity services of CLAS-Services, Inc. (parent company). Before that, she worked as support staff with the Dale Carnegie organization.

Specializations Nonfiction, adult Christian Living or issue-oriented books. **Considers these nonfiction areas:** Child guidance/parenting; current affairs; education; health; money/finance; psychology; religious; self-help; women's issues/studies (all from a biblical Christian point of view). Other types of clients include ministries, video/film producers.

Services Electronic news releases, pitches to Christian radio and TV outlets. Book tours include radio interviews, TV interviews. Clients have appeared on *The 700 Club*, *Life Today*, *At Home—Live with Chuck and Jenni*. Media kit includes author's biography, basic information on book, sample interview questions, book request information. Firm is responsible for writing promotional material.

How to Contact Read Web site and then send an e mail. Responds in 2-4 weeks. Discards unwanted materials. Obtains most new clients through recommendations from others, conferences, Internet searches. Contact 3 months prior to book's publication.

Clients *Blended Families Workbook*, by Maxine Marsolini (Wine Press); *Finding Financial Freedom*, by Grant Jeffrey (Waterbrook Press); *Think Before You Look*, by Daniel Henderson (AMG Publishers); *Where is the God of Justice*, by Dr. Warren McWilliams (Hendrickson Publishers). Other clients include Florence Littauer, Marita Littauer, Jill Swanson, Elgin Husbeck Jr. References and contact numbers are available to potential clients.

Costs Clients charged flat fee of $2,700. Offers written contract; 1-month notice must be given to terminate contract.

Writers' Conferences Glorieta Christian Writers Conference.

Tips "Understand about publicity niches these days. Look for someone who specializes in the market you need to reach."

N 🌐 ☑ COLMAN GETTY PR

Middlesex House, 34 Cleveland St., London W1T 4JE United Kingdom. (44)(20)7631-2666. Fax: (44)(20)7631-2699. E-mail: pr@colmangettypr.co.uk. Web site: www.colmangettypr.co.uk. **Contact:** Dotti Irving. Estab. 1987; specifically with books 18 years. Currently works with 30 clients. 10% of clients are new/first-time writers.

Specializations Nonfiction, fiction, children's books, academic. **Interested in all subject areas.**

Services Audio/video tapes, media training, international publicity, market research, fax news releases, electronic news release, sends material to magazines/newspapers for reviews, brochures, Web site assistance, Web site publicity. Book tours include bookstores, specialty stores, radio interviews, TV interviews, newspaper interviews, magazine interviews, speaking engagements, conferences. Assists in coordinating travel plans. Clients have appeared on *The Today Programme*, BBC Radio 4, *News At 10*, *Newsnight*, BBC1, BBC2, CNN. Media kit includes author's biography, basic information on book, professional photos. Firm is responsible for writing promotional material. Helps writer obtain endorsements.

How to Contact Call, e-mail, or fax.

Clients Clients include Ruby Wax, Scott Turow, JK Rowling, Nigella Lawson, Kathy Lette, Germaine Greer, Philippa Gregory, and many more.

☑ GARIS AGENCY—NATIONAL PUBLICISTS

100 E. San Marcos Blvd., Suite 400, San Marcos CA 92069. (760)471-4807. Fax: (760)454-1814. E-mail: publicists @garis-agency.com. Web site: www.nationalpublicist.com. **Contact:** R.J. Garis. Estab. 1989. Currently works with 50 clients. 20% of clients are new/first-time writers.

• Prior to becoming a publicist, Mr. Garis was a promoter and producer.

Members Taryn Roberts (associate national publicist, at firm 9 years); R.J. Garis.

Specializations Nonfiction, fiction, script. **Considers these nonfiction areas:** Animals; biography/autobiography; business; child guidance/parenting; current affairs; gay/lesbian issues; government/politics/law; health/medicine; how-to; humor; interior design/decorating; juvenile nonfiction; memoirs; military/war; money/finance/economics; multicultural; music/dance/theater/film; nature/environment; New Age/metaphysics; photography; popular culture; psychology; science/technology; self-help/personal improvement; sociology; sports; travel; true crime/investigative; women's issues/studies; young adult. **Considers these fiction areas:** Action/adventure; cartoon/comic; contemporary issues; detective/police/crime; erotica; ethnic; family saga; fantasy; feminist; gay/lesbian; glitz; horror; humor/satire; juvenile; literary; mainstream; multicultural; mystery/suspense; New Age/metaphysical; picture book; psychic/supernatural; romance; science fiction; sports; thriller/espionage; westerns/frontier; young adult.

Services Media training, nationwide publicity, fax news releases, electronic news release, sends material to magazines/newspapers for reviews, Web site assistance, Web site publicity. Book tours include bookstores, specialty stores, radio interviews, TV interviews, newspaper interviews, magazine interviews, speaking engagements, conferences. Assists in coordinating travel plans. Clients have appeared on *Oprah*, *Dateline*, *Larry King Live*, *The Sally Jessy Raphael Show*, *Extra*, *48 Hours*, *Good Morning America*, *The Montel Williams Show*, *Inside Edition*, *20/20*, *The Today Show*. Media kits include résumé, author's biography, testimonials, articles about author, basic infomation on book, professional photos, sample interview questions, book request information. Helps writer obtain endorsements. "We designed media information for author Missy Cummings, which resulted in TV interviews on *Extra* and *Inside Edition*, and a print feature in *The Star*."

    O— This company specializes in quality media that works—morning radio, national TV, regional TV, major newspapers, and national magazines. "We currently book over 2,000 media interviews a year."

How to Contact E-mail. Responds in 3 days. Discards unwanted materials. Obtains most new clients through recommendations from others. Contact 3 months prior to book's publication.

Clients *Hornet's Nest*, by Missy Cummings (iUniverse); *Little Kids Big Questions*, by Dr. Judi Craig (Hearst Books); *There Are No Accidents*, by Robert Hopcke (Penguin Putnam); *Anger Work*, by Dr. Robert Puff (Vantage Press). References and contact numbers are available to potential clients.

Costs Clients charged monthly retainer or contract fee based on the project. Offers written contract, binding for a minimum of 6 months; 1-month notice must be given to terminate contract.

Tips "Check references. Look for a publicist with a long history. It takes many years to establish powerful media contacts."

GREATER TALENT NETWORK, INC.

437 Fifth Ave., New York NY 10016-2205. (212)645-4200. Fax: (212)627-1471. E-mail: info@greatertalent.com. Web site: www.gtnspeakers.com. **Contact:** Don Epstein. Estab. 1980; specifically with books for over 20 years. Currently works with more than 100 clients.

Members Don Epstein (corporate/literary, at firm 20+ years); Debra Greene (corporate/literary, at firm 21 years); Kenny Rahtz (corporate/associations, at firm 21 years); Barbara Solomon (health/hospitals/public relations, at firm 16 years); David Evenchick (Fortune 1000, at firm 8 years); Josh Yablon (technology/corporate management, at firm 9 years); Lisa Bransdorf (college/university, at firm 7 years).

Specializations Nonfiction, fiction, academic. **Considers these nonfiction areas:** Business; computers/electronics; current affairs; education; government/politics/law; humor; money/finance/economics; multicultural; popular culture; science/technology; sports; women's issues/studies. Other types of clients include government officials, athletes, CEO's, technology, media.

Services International publicity, fax news releases, brochures, Web site publicity. Book tours include radio interviews, TV interviews, newspaper interviews, speaking engagements. Assists in coordinating travel plans. Clients have appeared on all major networks. Media kit includes author's biography, testimonials, articles about author, professional photos, book request information.

    O— "We understand authors' needs and publishers' wants."

How to Contact Call, e-mail, or fax. Discards unwanted materials. Obtains most new clients through recommendations from others. Contact once a platform is started.

Clients *The CEO of the Sofa*, by P.J. O'Rourke (Atlantic Monthly Press); *Dude, Where's My Country*, by Michael Moore (Warner Books); *Hidden Power*, by Kati Marton (Pantheon); *The Travel Detective*, by Peter Greenberg (Villard); *American Gods*, by Neil Gaiman (William Morrow). Other clients include Homer Hickman, Tom Wolfe, John Douglas, Christopher Buckley, Erica Jong, Michael Lewis. References and contact numbers are available to potential clients.

Costs Clients charged variable commission. Offers written contract.

THE IDEA NETWORK

P.O. Box 38, Whippany NJ 07981. (973)560-0333. Fax: (973)560-0960. E-mail: esaxton@theideanetwork.net. Web site: www.theideanetwork.net. **Contact:** Erin Saxton, founder. Estab. 2000; specifically with books for 6 years. Currently works with 20-30 clients. Less than 5 clients are new/first-time writers.

    • Prior to starting her media/public relations firm, Ms. Saxton was a 4-time Emmy-nominated TV producer.

Members Jen Urezzio (vice president of media relations, at firm 5 years); Allyson Klavens (senior account executive, at firm 3 years); Anders Bjornson (vice president of business operations, at firm 4 years).

Specializations Nonfiction. **Considers these nonfiction areas:** Child guidance/parenting; cooking/food/nutrition; crafts/hobbies; current affairs; health/medicine; how-to; interior design/decorating; money/finance/economics; psychology; women's issues/studies. "We don't work with many fiction writers."

Services Full-service public relations agency. Every client's media and publicity plans differ. Call for more information. Book tours include radio interviews, TV interviews, newspaper interviews, magazine interviews. Clients have appeared on *The View*, *The Today Show*, Fox News Channel, *Good Morning America*, *The Early Show*, *Ellen*.

    O— "This company is founded by a TV producer and therefore knows what a producer is looking for in a pitch. Because of our background, our clients have an advantage." Specializes in creating hooks that reporters, editors, and producers find useful for their programs and outlets.

Publicists

How to Contact Call, e-mail, or fax. Responds in 1 week. Discards unwanted materials. Obtains most new clients through recommendations from others, queries/solicitations. Contact 6 months prior to book's publication. **Clients** Please call for an updated author list.
Costs Clients charged monthly retainer ($3,500-10,000) or by project. Offers written contract; 1-month notice must be given to terminate contract.

⊠ ◙ MICHELE KARLSBERG MARKETING AND MANAGEMENT

47 Dongan Hills Ave., Staten Island NY 10306. (718)351-9599. Fax: (718)980-4262. E-mail: karlsbergm@aol.com. **Contact:** Michele Karlsberg. Estab. 1989; specifically with books for 16 years. Currently works with 7 clients.

• Prior to becoming a publicist, Ms. Karlsberg was production coordinator for a magazine company.

Specializations Nonfiction, fiction. **Considers these nonfiction areas:** Biography/autobiography; ethnic/cultural interests; gay/lesbian issues; memoirs; women's issues/studies. **Considers these fiction areas:** Action/adventure; cartoon/comic; detective/police/crime; erotica; ethnic; feminist; gay/lesbian; humor/satire; literary; romance.
Services International publicity, market research, sends material to magazines/newspapers for reviews, brochures, Web site assistance, Web site publicity. Book tours include bookstores, specialty stores, radio interviews, TV interviews, newspaper interviews, magazine interviews, speaking engagements, conferences, libraries, schools, universities. Assists in coordinating travel plans. Clients have appeared on CNN, Logo, QTV, Air America, Sirius. Media kit includes résumé, author's biography, testimonials, articles about author, basic information on book, professional photos, sample interview questions, book request information. Clients are responsible for writing promotional material.

○⇥ "We specialize in the lesbian, gay, and feminist market."

How to Contact Call or e-mail. Responds in 1 week. Returns unwanted materials. Obtains most new clients through recommendations from others. Contact 4 months prior to book's publication, after book's publication, or once a platform is started.
Clients *What the L?*, by Kate Clinton (Avalon); *Whose Eye Is on the Sparrow*, by Robert Taylor (Haworth); *Hancock Park*, by Katherine Forrest (Haworth); *Flight of Aquavit*, by Anthony Bidulka (Insomniac). References and contact numbers are available to potential clients.
Costs Clients charged flat fee of $500-20,000. Works with clients on marketing budget. Offers written contract; 1-month notice must be given to terminate contract.
Writers' Conferences Saints & Sinners Literary Festival.

◙ KSB PROMOTIONS

55 Honey Creek NE, Ada MI 49301-9768. (616)676-0758. Fax: (616)676-0759. E-mail: pr@ksbpromotions.com. Web site: www.ksbpromotions.com. **Contact:** Kate Bandos. Estab. 1988. Currently works with 20-40 clients. 25% of clients are new/first-time writers.

• Prior to becoming a publicist, Ms. Bandos was a PR director for several publishers.

Members Kate Bandos (travel/cookbooks, at firm 18 years); Doug Bandos (radio/TV, at firm 17 years).
Specializations Nonfiction, children's books. **Considers these nonfiction areas:** Child guidance/parenting; cooking/food/nutrition; health/medicine; travel; gardening; home/how-to; general lifestyle.
Services Sends material to magazines/newspapers for reviews. Book tours include radio interviews, TV interviews, newspaper interviews, magazine interviews. Clients have appeared on *Inside Edition, Good Morning America*, CNN, Business News Network, *The Parent's Journal*, and many regional shows. Media kit includes author's biography, testimonials, basic information on book, sample interview questions, book request information, recipes for cookbooks, other excerpts as appropriate. Helps writers obtain endorsements.

○⇥ This company specializes in cookbooks, travel guides, parenting books, and other general lifestyle books. "Our specialty has allowed us to build relationships with key media in these areas. We limit ourselves to those clients we can personally help."

How to Contact Call or e-mail. Responds in 2 weeks. Returns unwanted material only with SASE. Obtains most new clients through recommendations from others, conferences, listings in books on publishing. Contact 6-8 months prior to book's publication. Can do limited PR after book's publication.
Clients Long-term clients include Morris Communications, Smart Travel, and Mile Oak Publishing. Other clients include Vanderwyk & Burnham, Parent Positive Press, Bayou Publishing, PassPorter, Travel Guides, Barnesyard Books. References and contact numbers are available to potential clients.
Costs Clients charged per service fee ($500 minimum). Total of contracted services is divided into monthly payments. Offers written contract; 1-month notice must be given to terminate contract.
Writers' Conferences PMA University; BookExpo America.
Tips "Find a publicist who has done a lot with books in the same area of interest since they will know the key media, etc."

ⓘ GAIL LEONDAR PUBLIC RELATIONS

21 Belknap St., Arlington MA 02474-6605. (781)648-1658. E-mail: gail@glprbooks.com. Web site: www.glprboo ks.com. **Contact:** Gail Leondar-Wright. Estab. 1992; specifically with books for 14 years. Currently works with 16 clients. 50% of clients are new/first-time writers.

• Prior to becoming a publicist, Ms. Leondar-Wright directed theater.

Specializations Nonfiction, fiction, academic, any books on progressive social issues. **Interested in these non-fiction areas:** Biography/autobiography; current affairs; education; ethnic/cultural interests; gay/lesbian issues; government/politics/law; history; multicultural; music/dance/theater/film; sociology; women's issues/studies. **Considers these fiction areas:** Feminist; gay/lesbian/transgender.

Services Book tours include bookstores, radio interviews, TV interviews, newspaper interviews. Clients have appeared on *Fresh Air, Morning Edition, Weekend Edition*, CNN, C-SPAN. Media kit includes author's biography, testimonials, articles about author, basic information on book, professional photos, sample interview questions.

Oₜ "GLPR promotes only books on progressive social issues. Our contacts give excellent interviews, primarily on noncommercial radio, including NPR."

How to Contact Call or e-mail. Responds in less than 1 week. Returns materials only with SASE. Obtains most new clients through recommendations from others. Contact 6 months prior to book's publication.

Clients *A Desperate Passion*, by Dr. Helen Caldicott (Norton); *The Good Heart*, by The Dalai Lama (Wisdom); *Love Canal*, by Lois Gibbs (New Society Publishers); *Gender Outlaw*, by Kate Bornstein (Routledge). References and contact numbers are available to potential clients.

Costs Clients charged flat fee of $2,000-15,000. Works with clients on marketing budget. Offers written contract, usually binding for 3 months.

ⓘ MEDIA MASTERS PUBLICITY

17600 S. Richmond Rd., Plainfield IL 60554. (815)254-7383. Fax: (815)254-1948. E-mail: tracey@mmpublicity.c om. Web site: www.mmpublicity.com. **Contact:** Tracey Daniels. Estab. 1998. Currently works with 10 clients. 10% of clients are new/first-time writers.

• Prior to becoming a publicist, Ms. Daniels worked in English education at the middle school and high school levels.

Members Karen Wadsworth (marketing/events, at firm 5 years).

Specializations Children's books, nonfiction. **Considers these nonfiction areas:** Biography/autobiography; child guidance/parenting; education; how-to; juvenile nonfiction; young adult. **Considers these fiction areas:** Juvenile; picture book; young adult.

Services Fax news releases, electronic news release, sends material to magazines/newspapers for reviews, brochures, Web site assistance, Web site publicity. Book tours include bookstores, specialty stores, radio interviews, TV interviews, newspaper interviews, magazine interviews, schools. Clients have appeared on CNN, *Talk America*, CBS, ABC, VOA, USA Radio Network, AP Radio Network, *20/20*. Each media kit varies depending on focus, client needs, and budget. Helps writer obtain endorsements.

Oₜ "We have over 18 years of book publicity experience. Our company delivers publicity with personality— we go beyond just covering the basics."

How to Contact E-mail or send letter with outline/proposal, sample chapters. Responds in 2 weeks. Returns materials only with SASE. Obtains most new clients through recommendations from others. Contact 3 months prior to book's publication.

Clients Clients include Roaring Brook, HarperCollins Children's Books, Kingfisher Books, NorthSouth Books, Henry Holt Children's Books, Candlewick Press, Hyperion, plus individual authors. Reference and contact numbers are available to potential clients.

Costs Fees depend on client's needs and budget. Offers written contract; 1-month notice must be given to terminate contract.

Writers' Conferences BookExpo America, ALA Annual Conference.

Ⓝ ⓘ S.J. MILLER COMMUNICATIONS

10 Turning Mill Ln., Randolph MA 02368. (781)986-0732. E-mail: sjmiller@bookpr.com. Web site: www.bookpr .com. **Contact:** Stacey J. Miller. Estab. 1992; specifically with books for 15 years. Currently works with 6 clients. 50% of clients are new/first-time writers.

• Prior to becoming a publicist, Ms. Miller was a marketing director.

Specializations Nonfiction, fiction, children's books, academic. **Considers these nonfiction areas:** Business; child guidance/parenting; crafts/hobbies; education; health/medicine; humor; personal finance; popular culture; psychology; relationships; women's issues/studies. **Considers these fiction areas:** Contemporary issues. **Services** "We provide full-service publicity, including traditional media kit creation, electronic news release creation, sending materials to magazines/newspapers for reviews, Web site assistance, Web site publicity, and bylined article placement. Through an associate, we provide media training.'' Clients have appeared on *Oprah*, *Good Morning America*, *The Today Show*, *Early Show*, Westwood One, National Public Radio, Associated Press Broadcasting. Media kit includes author's biography, testimonials, basic information on book, sample interview questions, etc. Clients are responsible for assisting with promotional material.

How to Contact Call or e-mail. Responds in 1 week. Returns materials only with SASE. Obtains most new clients through recommendations from others. Contact 6 months prior to book's publication, if possible.

Clients References and contact numbers are available to potential clients.

Costs Clients charged per service fee of $2,500-20,000. Offers written contract, binding for 2 months.

📋 ◎ MINISTRY MARKETING SOLUTIONS, INC.

33011 Tall Oaks St., Farmington MI 48336. (248)426-2300. Fax: (248)471-2422. E-mail: info@ministrymarketing solutions.com. Web site: www.ministrymarketingsolutions.com. **Contact:** Pamela Perry. Estab. 2000; specifically with books for 4 years. Currently works with 21 clients. 35% of clients are new/first-time writers.

• Prior to becoming a publicist, Ms. Perry was PR director for The Salvation Army and a fundraiser for Joy of Jesus.

Members Stephanie Jones (broadcast); Kanatte Worlos (print); Natasha Robinson (print).

Specializations Christian and African American nonfiction. **Considers these nonfiction areas:** Multicultural; religious/inspirational; self-help/personal improvement.

Services Media training, fax news releases, electronic news release, sends material to magazines/newspapers for reviews, Web site assistance, Web site publicity. Book tours include bookstores, radio interviews, TV interviews, newspaper interviews, magazine interviews, speaking engagements, conferences, libraries, schools, online tours/chats. Assists in coordinating travel plans. Clients have appeared on *700 Club*, *Life Today*, SGN ''The Light'' Radio, CTN, Atlanta Live, Radio One, JET. Media kit includes author's biography, testimonials, articles about author, basic information on book, professional photos, sample interview questions, book request information, chapter summary, tip sheets, book review. Firm is responsible for writing promotional material.

⊶ ''We have direct/daily contact with the Black Press and Christian media. We also produce an author event called Chocolate Pages.''

How to Contact E-mail or send letter with outline/proposal. Responds in 1 week. Discards unwanted materials. Obtains most new clients through recommendations from others, conferences. Contact 6 months prior to book's publication.

Clients *The Walk at Work*, by Andria Hall (WaterBrook Press); *Women Risk Takers*, by Dr. Pat Bailey (Harrison House); *He's Fine . . . But Is He Saved*, by Kim Brooks (Driven Enterprise); *In The Grip of His Mercy*, by Bishop Donald Hilliard (HCI). Other clients include Bishop Paul Morton, Bishop Thomas Weeks, Walk Worthy Press, Judson Press, Legacy Publishers. References and contact numbers are available to potential clients.

Costs Clients charged flat fee of $5,000-10,000. Also does book PR coaching for $500/month. Works with clients on marketing budget. Offers written contract, binding for 90 days; 1-month notice must be given to terminate contract.

Writers' Conferences Greater Philadelphia Christian Writers Conference; American Christian Writers Conferences.

Tips ''Know your target market and find a publicist who has contacts in the same market. Do your homework!''

📋 ⚡ ◐ PR DIVA

1264 W. Cordova St., Vancouver BC V6C 3R4 Canada. (604)716-8243. E-mail: gg@prdiva.com. Web site: www.p rdiva.com. **Contact:** Gwendolynn Gawlick. Estab. 1998; specifically with books for 7 years. Currently works with 4 clients. 25% of clients are new/first-time writers.

• Prior to becoming a publicist, Ms. Gawlick worked in traditional advertising in client services.

Specializations Nonfiction, fiction, children's books.

Services Market research, electronic news release, sends material to magazines/newspapers for reviews, Web site assistance, Web site publicity. Book tours include bookstores, specialty stores, radio interviews, TV interviews, newspaper interviews, magazine interviews, conferences, libraries, schools, universities. Clients have appeared on NPR, local radio, Seattle radio, local news shows, breakfast shows, Book TV. Media kit includes author's biography, testimonials, articles about author, basic information on book, professional photos, sample interview questions, book request information. Firm is responsible for writing promotional material. Helps writer obtain endorsements.

⊶ ''We offer personal attention to the client, unusual attention to detail, and 10 years expertise in online publicity.''

How to Contact Call or e-mail. Responds in 1 week. Discards unwanted materials. Obtains most new clients through recommendations from others, queries/solicitations.

Costs Clients charged flat fee of $2,000.

◎ RAAB ASSOCIATES

345 Millwood Rd., Chappaqua NY 10514. (914)241-2117. Fax: (914)241-0050. E-mail: info@raabassociates.c om. Web site: www.raabassociates.com. **Contact:** Susan Salzman Raab. Estab. 1986. Currently works with 15-20 clients. 10% of clients are new/first-time writers.

• Prior to becoming an independent publicist, Ms. Salzman Raab worked on staff at major publishing houses in the children's book industry.

Members Susanna Reich, associate (at firm 6 years); Susan Salzman Raab, partner (at firm 20 years); Tara Koppel, associate (at firm 2 years); Joyce Stein, associate (at firm 1 year).

Specializations Children's books, parenting books/products. **Considers these nonfiction areas:** Child guidance/parenting; juvenile nonfiction; young adult. **Considers these fiction areas:** Juvenile: picture book; young adult; parenting. Other types of clients include publishers, toy companies, audio companies.

Services Market research, sends material to magazines/newspapers for review, Web site assistance, Web site development, extensive online publicity. Book tours include bookstores, specialty stores, radio interviews, TV interviews, newspaper interviews, magazine interviews, schools, libraries. Assists in coordinating travel plans. Clients have appeared on NPR, CNN, C-Span, Radio-Disney, PRI. Media kit includes author's biography, testimonials, articles about author, basic information on book, sample interview questions, book request information. Helps writer obtain endorsements.

○➥ "We are the only PR agency to specialize in children's and parenting books."

How to Contact Call or e-mail. Responds in 2 weeks. Returns materials only with SASE. Obtains most new clients through recommendations from others, conferences. Contact 4 months prior to book's publication.

Costs Clients charged per service fee. Offers written contract; 3-month notice must be given to terminate contract.

Writers' Conferences SCBWI; BookExpo America; ALA Annual Conferences; Bologna Children's Book Fair.

◘ ROCKS-DEHART PUBLIC RELATIONS

306 Marberry Dr., Pittsburgh PA 15215. (412)784-8811. Fax: (412)784-8610. E-mail: celiarocks@aol.com. Web site: www.rdpr.com. **Contact:** Celia Rocks. Estab. 1993. Currently works with 10 clients. 20% of clients are new/first-time writers.

• Prior to becoming a publicist, Ms. Rocks was a publicity specialist at Burson Marsteller.

Members Dottie DeHart, principal (at firm 13 years); 8 other staff members.

Specializations Nonfiction, business, lifestyle. **Considers these nonfiction areas:** Biography/autobiography; business; cooking/food/nutrition; current affairs; health/medicine; how-to; humor; popular culture; psychology; religious/inspirational; self-help/personal improvement; sociology; travel; women's issues/women's studies. Other types of clients include major publishing houses.

Services Book tours include bookstores, specialty stores, radio interviews, TV interviews, newspaper interviews, magazine interviews, speaking engagements, conferences, libraries, schools, universities. Clients have appeared on *ABC World News* and *Oprah*, as well as in *Time* and *Newsweek*. Media kit includes author's biography, testimonials, articles about author, basic information on book, professional photos, sample interview questions, book request information, breakthrough-plan materials. Helps writers obtain endorsements. Recent promotions include taking a book like *Fishing for Dummies* and sending gummy worms with packages.

○➥ This company specializes in IDG *Dummies* books and business, management, and lifestyle titles. "We are a highly creative firm that understands the best way to obtain maximum publicity."

How to Contact Call or e-mail. Responds in 1 day. Obtains most new clients through recommendations from others. Contact 2-4 months prior to book's publication.

Clients Clients include John Wiley & Sons, AAA Publishing, Dearborn, Jossey-Bass, Yale University Press, New World Library.

Costs Clients charged monthly retainer of $3,000-5,000. Works with clients on marketing budget. Offers written contract; 1-month notice must be given to terminate contract.

◘ SHERRI ROSEN PUBLICITY LLC

15 Park Row, Suite 25C, New York NY 10038. Phone/Fax: (212)587-0296. E-mail: sherri@sherrirosen.com. Web site: www.sherrirosen.com. **Contact:** Sherri Rosen. Estab. 1997; specifically with books for 13 years. Currently works with 6 clients. 75% of clients are published authors; 25% are self-published authors.

• Ms. Rosen's first client, Naura Hayden, was on the *New York Times* bestseller list for 63 weeks. The book made millions of dollars.

Specializations Sex, relationship, spirituality. **Considers these nonfiction areas:** Child guidance/parenting; cooking/food/nutrition; current affairs; education; ethnic/cultural interests; gay/lesbian issues; health/medicine; how-to; humor; juvenile nonfiction; memoirs; music/dance/theater/film; New Age/metaphysics; popular culture; psychology; religious/inspirational; self-help/personal improvement; travel; women's issues/studies; young adult. **Considers these fiction areas:** Action/adventure; confessional; erotica; ethnic; experimental;

family saga; fantasy; feminist; humor/satire; literary; mainstream; multicultural; New Age/metaphysical; psychic/supernatural; religious/inspirational; romance; young adult.

Services Audio/video tapes, international publicity, sends material to magazines/newspapers for reviews, brochures. Book tours include bookstores, radio interviews, TV interviews, newspaper interviews, magazine interviews, speaking engagements, conferences, libraries, schools, universities. Assists in coordinating travel plans. Clients have appeared on *Oprah*, *The Montel Williams Show*, *Politically Incorrect*, *Leeza*, *Men are from Mars*, *The Sally Jessy Raphael Show*, *The Other Half*, *Howard Stern*, 5-page spread in *Playboy* magazine. Media kit includes author's biography, testimonials, articles about author, basic information on book, professional photos, sample interview questions, book request information. Will write all of the promotional material or collaborate with client. Helps writer obtain endorsements.

> O— "I work with eclectic clientele—sex books, spiritual books, personal inspirational, self-help books. What is distinct is I will only work with people I like, and I have to like and respect what they are doing."

How to Contact E-mail. Responds immediately. Discards unwanted materials or returns materials only with SASE. Obtains most new clients through recommendations from others, listings with other services in the industry. Contact 3 months prior to book's publication (preferred) or after book's publication once a platform is started. Likes to work on a book for at least 6 months.

Clients *How to Satisfy a Woman*, by Naura Hayden; *Men Who Can't Love*, by Steven Carten (HarperCollins); *Rebirth of the Goddess*, by Carol Christ (Addison-Wesley); *Buddhism Without Belief*, by Stephen Batchelor (Riverhead). Other clients include Eli Jaxon-Bear, Sandra Rothenberger, Elizabeth Ayres. References and contact numbers are available to potential clients.

Costs Clients charged $250 hourly fee/consultation fee. Monthly retainer fee is $5,000-8,000 (3-month minimum). Business expenses aren't included. Offers written contract; 1-month notice must be given to terminate contract.

Tips "Not only are contacts important, but make sure you like who you will be working with, because you work so closely."

⚫ ROYCE CARLTON, INC.

866 United Nations Plaza, Suite 587, New York, NY 10017. (212)355-7700. Fax: (212)888-8659. E-mail: info@roycecarlton.com. Web site: www.roycecarlton.com. **Contact:** Carlton Sedgeley. Estab. 1968. Currently works with 74 clients.

Members Carlton S. Sedgeley, president (at firm 38 years); Lucy Lepage, executive vice president (at firm 38 years); Helen Churko, vice president (at firm 22 years).

> O— Royce Carlton, Inc., is a lecture agency and management firm for speakers who are available for lectures and speaking engagements. Royce Carlton represents all speakers exclusively.

How to Contact Call, e-mail, or fax. Discards unwanted materials. Obtains most new clients through recommendations, direct contact.

Clients *Five People You Meet in Heaven*, by Mitch Albom; *House Made of Dawn*, by N. Scott Momaday. Other clients include Joan Rivers, Elaine Pagels, Walter Mosley, David Halberstam, Tom Friedman, Fareed Zakaria. References and contact numbers are available to potential clients.

Costs Clients charged per placement. Offers written contract; 1-month notice must be given to terminate contract.

Ⓝ Ⓞ SOCAL PUBLIC RELATIONS

8130 LaMesa Blvd., Suite 137, LaMesa CA 91941. (619)460-2179. E-mail: socalpublicrelations@yahoo.com. Web site: www.socalpr.com. **Contact:** Rebecca Grose. Estab. 2003. Currently works with 4-7 clients. 20% of clients are new/first-time writers.

> ● Prior to becoming a publicist, Ms. Grose was in publicity at several major publishers (Simon & Schuster, HarperCollins, etc.).

Specializations Children's books. **Considers these nonfiction areas:** Juvenile nonfiction; young adult. **Interested in these fiction areas:** Juvenile; picture book; young adult.

Services Media training, electronic news release, sends material to magazines/newspapers for reviews, Web site assistance, online media. Book tours include bookstores, radio interviews, TV interviews, newspaper interviews, magazine interviews, libraries (no honorarium), trade shows/festivals. Media kit includes author's biography, testimonials, articles about author, professional photos, sample interview questions, press release, quote sheet, available backlist sheet. Firm is responsible for writing promotional material.

> O— "I specialize in children's books and there aren't a lot of public relations firms that do so."

How to Contact Call or e-mail. Responds in 1-2 days. Obtains most new clients through recommendations from others. Contact 3-4 months prior to book's publication.

Clients References and contact numbers are available to potential clients.

Costs Clients charged flat fee of $500/consultation or monthly retainer of $800-1,000. "I provide a detailed quote outlining my services and the length of the project." Minimum term is 90 days, then renewable every 30 days.

Writers' Conferences SCBWI; La Jolla Writers Conference.

THE SPIZMAN AGENCY

Atlanta GA 30327. (770)953-2040. Fax: (770)953-2172. E-mail: willy@spizmanagency.com. www.spizmanagency.com. **Contact:** Willy Spizman. Estab. 1981; specifically with books for 20 years. Represents a combination of new and established authors.

Specializations Nonfiction, fiction, children's books, academic. **Considers these nonfiction areas:** Business; child guidance/parenting; cooking/food/nutrition; crafts/hobbies; current affairs; education; ethnic/cultural interests; health/medicine; history; how-to; humor; interior design/decorating; juvenile nonfiction; language/literature/criticism; memoirs; money/finance/economics; multicultural; music/dance/theater/film; nature/environment; New Age/metaphysics; photography; popular culture; psychology; religious/inspirational; science/technology; self-help/personal improvement; sociology; sports; travel; true crime/investigative; women's issues/studies; young adult. **Considers these fiction areas:** Contemporary issues; mainstream; inspirational; young adult.

Services Provides complete book development and promotion, including media training, international publicity, market research, fax news releases, electronic news releases, sends material to magazines/newspapers for reviews, brochures, Web site assistance, Web site publicity. Book tours include bookstores, specialty stores, radio interviews, TV interviews, newspaper interviews, magazine interviews, satellite media tours, speaking engagements, conferences, libraries, schools, universities. Assists in coordinating travel plans. Clients have appeared on *Oprah*, CNN, *The Today Show*, HGTV, and in the *Atlanta Journal-Constitution*. Media kit includes author's biography, testimonials, articles about author, basic information on book, professional photos, sample interview questions, book request information. Helps writer obtain endorsements. Recent promotions included a 1-hour show on a client's book on CNN.

How to Contact E-mail. Responds in 1 week. Returns materials only with SASE. Obtains most new clients through recommendations from others. Contact 6 months prior to book's publication (once a platform is started).

Clients *The 12 Immutable Laws of Branding*, by Al and Laura Ries (HarperCollins); *Live, Learn & Pass It On*, by H. Jackson Brown Jr. (Rutledge Hill). Other clients include Turner Broadcasting Systems, Reproductive Biology Associates. References and contact numbers are available to potential clients.

Costs Clients charged monthly retainer. Works with clients to create a marketing budget. Offers written contract; 1-month notice must be given to terminate contract.

Tips "It gets down to one thing—who they know and what they know, plus years of successful clients. We score high on all counts."

N SPOTLIGHT PUBLICITY

2169 Pond Circle, Lincoln NE 68512. (408)817-0730. E-mail: submissions@spotlightpublicity.com. Web site: www.spotlightpublicity.com. **Contact:** Lea Toland. Estab. 2004. Currently works with 6 clients. 83% of clients are new/first-time writers.

● Prior to becoming a publicist, Ms. Toland worked in radio administration.

Specializations Nonfiction, fiction, children's books. **Considers these nonfiction areas:** Biography/autobiography; child guidance/parenting; cooking/food/nutrition; ethnic/cultural interests; government/politics/law; how-to; juvenile nonfiction; New Age/metaphysics; religious/inspirational; self-help/personal improvement; sports; true crime/investigative; women's issues/studies; young adult. **Considers these fiction areas:** Action/adventure; detective/police/crime; ethnic; family saga; fantasy; feminist; historical; juvenile; literary; mystery/suspense; New Age/metaphysics; regional; religious/inspirational; romance; science fiction; sports; thriller/espionage; young adult.

Services Media training, market research, fax news releases, electronic news release, sends material to magazines/newspapers for reviews, brochures, Web site assistance, Web site publicity. Book tours include bookstores, specialty stores, radio interviews, TV interviews, newspaper interviews, magazine interviews, speaking engagements, conferences, libraries, schools, universities. Assists in coordinating travel plans. Clients have appeared on *The David Lawrence Show*, NPR's *Trends, Tastes and Travel*, *Coast to Coast*, *Backstage Live*, *Behind the Velvet Ropes*, *CrossTalk*, local TV and radio. Media kit includes author's biography, testimonials, articles about author, basic information on book, sample interview questions, book request information. Firm is responsible for writing promotional material.

○ "We enjoy working with self-published and first-time authors since their market has the most challenges and as such are the most rewarding."

How to Contact Call, e-mail, or send letter with entire ms, cover art. Responds in 1 week. Returns materials only with SASE. Obtains most new clients through queries/solicitations. Contact 4 months prior to book's publication (preferred) or after book's publication.

Clients *Seeds of Heaven*, by Tito Abao (Trafford); *A Broken Charity*, by Jack E. George (PublishAmerica); *The Warriors Return*, by A.W.G. Coleman (VirtualBookworm.com); *Many Faces to Many Places*, by Judy Azar LeBlanc (Xolon Press). References and contact numbers are available upon request.

Costs Clients charged $37/hour. Offers written contract; 2-4 week notice must be given to terminate contract.

Tips "Just like with agents, you need to click with your publicist. If the person or firm you hire isn't excited about you, you won't get the results you deserve."

Ⓝ ◪ STRATEGIC VISION, LLC

260 Peachtree St., Suite 503, Atlanta GA 30303. (404)880-0098. Fax: (404)880-0084. E-mail: info@strategicvision .biz. Web site: www.strategicvision.biz. **Contact:** David E. Johnson. Estab. 2001. Currently works with 10 clients. 85% of clients are new/first-time writers.

- "Prior to becoming publicists, our principals and staff were in the journalism, advertising, and public relations fields."

Members David E. Johnson (media/special events); Laura N. Ward (special events/graphic and Web design).

Specializations Nonfiction, fiction, children's books. **Considers these nonfiction areas:** Biography/autobiography; business; child guidance/parenting; cooking/food/nutrition; crafts/hobbies; current affairs; ethnic/cultural interests; government/politics/law; health/medicine; history; how-to; humor; juvenile nonfiction; memoirs; military/war; money/finance/economics; popular culture; psychology; religious/inspirational; self-help/personal improvement; sports; travel; true crime/investigative; women's issues/studies; young adult. **Interested in these fiction areas:** Contemporary issues; ethnic; fantasy; historical; humor/satire; juvenile; mainstream; mystery/suspense; religious/inspirational; romance; science fiction; thriller/espionage; westerns/frontier.

Services Media training, international publicity, market research, fax news releases, electronic news release, sends material to magazines/newspapers for reviews, brochures, Web site assistance, Web site publicity. Book tours include bookstores, specialty stores, radio interviews, TV interviews, newspaper interviews, magazine interviews, speaking engagements, conferences, libraries, schools, universities. Assists in coordinating travel plans. Clients have appeared on *Fox & Friends*, *The O'Reilly Factor*, ABC Radio News, CNN Radio News, *American Morning*, *Nightline*, *CBS Sunday Morning*, *CNN Live*. Media kit includes author's biography, testimonials, articles about author, basic information on book, professional photos, sample interview questions, book request information. Firm is responsible for writing promotional material. Helps writer obtain endorsements.

How to Contact Call, e-mail, or fax. Responds in 1 week. Returns materials only with SASE. Obtains most new clients through recommendations from others, queries/solicitations, conferences. Contact 3-4 months prior to book's publication (preferred) or after book's publication.

Clients References and contact numbers are available to potential clients.

Costs Clients charged monthly retainer. Works with clients on marketing budget. Contracts range from 4-12 months and can be renewed; 1-month notice must be given to terminate contract.

Writers' Conferences BookExpo America; Texas Book Festival.

Tips "Make sure you fit well with your publicist and share the same ideas and goals."

◪ TCI-SMITH PUBLICITY

532 Old Marlton Pike, Suite 154, Marlton NJ 08053. (856)489-8654. Fax: (856)489-8652. E-mail: info@smithpubl icity.com. Web site: www.smithpublicity.com. **Contact:** Dan Smith, ext. 111. Estab. 1997; specifically with books for 7 years. Currently works with 10-17 clients. 70% of clients are new/first-time writers.

- Prior to starting TCI-Smith Publicity, Mr. Smith was a freelance writer, publicist, and public relations specialist.

Members Dan Smith, president; Deb Ruriani, senior account executive (at firm 3 years); Erin MacDonald, account executive (at firm 2 years); Nikki Bowman, director of operations (at firm 4 years); Fran Rubin, director of marketing (at firm 7 years); Sandra Diaz, account executive (at firm 2 years).

Specializations Nonfiction, fiction. **Considers these nonfiction areas:** Business; how-to; New Age; popular culture; self-help. **Considers these fiction areas:** Historical; fiction published by mainstream publishers; novels based on the author's background/experience. Other types of clients include entrepreneurs, businesses, nonprofit organizations.

Services Media training, comprehensive publicity campaigns, specialized media pitching, press release distribution, book reviews, feature stories, radio/TV interviews, book tours, special events, seminars. Clients have appeared on *The Today Show*, CNN, CNN International, *Fox News*, *Art Bell*, *The Montel Williams Show*, *Good Morning America*, *Howard Stern*, *The O'Reilly Factor*, *The Mike Gallagher Show*, *The Sally Jessy Raphael Show*, and in the *Wall Street Journal*, *New York Times*, *USA Today*, *People*, *Philadelphia Inquirer*, *Details Magazine*, *Cosmopolitan*. Media kit includes press releases, bio, sample questions, sell sheet, book information, excerpt, etc.

- "We follow the Golden Rule: We give the media what they want—good story ideas, interview topics, and compelling information. TCI-Smith is known for its unparalleled customer service and client relations."

How to Contact Call, e-mail, mail, or fax. Responds in 1 week. Returns materials only with SASE. Obtains most new clients through referrals from current or previous clients. Contact 4 months prior to book's publication (preferred) or after book's publication.

Clients *Conversations with Tom*, by Walda Woods; *The Old Boys: The American Elite and the Origins of the CIA*, by Burton Hersh; *Emotionally Intelligent Parenting*, by Dr. Steven Tobias (Random House); *Sleuthing 101: Background Checks and the Law*, by Barry Nadell; *Bright Sword of Ireland*, by Julience Osborne-McKnight (Forge); *The Numinous Legacy*, by Adair Butchins; *Perpetual Motivation*, by Dave Durand; *Invasion Within*, by Domenick Maglio (Regnery); *5 Days to a Flatter Stomach*, by Monica Grenfell (Warner); *The Zen of Tennis*, by Nancy Koran; *The Gardener's Guide to Growing Healthy Perennial Orchids*, by Dr. William Mathis.

Costs Clients charged $1,300-3,500/month for a 4-6 month agreement. Offers written contract; 3-month notice must be given to terminate contract.

Writers' Conferences BookExpo America.

Tips "Ask questions and talk to at least 3 different publicists. Have fun with your project and enjoy the ride! Only the determined make it."

Ⓝ Ⓒ KAREN VILLANUEVA

P.O. Box 25061, Albuquerque NM 87125-0061. E-mail: authorcare@aol.com. Web site: www.authorcare.com. **Contact:** Karen Villanueva. Estab. 1988; specifically with books for 12 years. Currently works with several authors at a time, usually on a short-term basis for new book launches. 70% of clients are new/first-time writers.

- Prior to becoming a publicist, Ms. Villanueva was a national buyer for a record retail chain and a freelance photographer.

Members Judy Avila, New Mexico associate; Ronnie Frankel, New York associate.

Specializations Nonfiction, fiction. **Considers these nonfiction areas:** Anthropology/archaeology; biography/autobiography; child guidance/parenting; cooking/food/nutrition; current affairs; health/medicine; history; how-to; memoirs; multicultural; music/dance/theater/film; nature/environment; New Age/metaphysics; photography; popular culture; psychology; self-help/personal improvement; true crime/investigative; women's issues/studies. **Considers these fiction areas:** Action/adventure; detective/police/crime; historical; literary; mainstream; mystery/suspense; regional; thriller/espionage; westerns/frontier.

Services Media training, electronic news release, sends material to magazines/newspapers for reviews, Web site assistance. Book tours include bookstores, specialty stores, radio interviews, TV interviews, newspaper interviews, magazine interviews, speaking engagements. Clients have appeared on *Larry King Live, Dateline NBC, A Current Affair, All Things Considered, ABC World News Tonight*, NBC, CBS, ABC. Media kit includes author's biography, testimonials, articles about author, basic information on book, professional photos, sample interview questions, book request information, calendar of events. Both the firm and clients are responsible for writing promotional material.

- ☞ "I provide personal involvement and guidance in the author's writing career. I also provide media hosting for authors and have escorted Cliver Cussler, Naomi Judd, Michael Moore, James Lee Burke, Sue Monk Kidd, Jennifer Weiner, Ron McLarty, Elizabeth Buchan, and many other bestselling and up-and-coming authors."

How to Contact Call or e-mail. Responds in 1 week. Returns materials only with SASE. Obtains most new clients through recommendations from others. Contact 3 months prior to book's publication.

Clients *The Apache Diaries*, by Neil Goodwin (University of Nebraska Press); *Turbulence*, by John Nance (Putnam); *Living Beauty Detox Program*, by Anne Louise Gittleman (HarperSanFrancisco); *September Sacrifice*, by Mark Horner (Pinnacle/Kensington); *Crazy Quilt*, by Paula Paul (University of New Mexico Press). Does not supply references and contact numbers; potential clients can view testimonials on Web site.

Costs Clients charged flat fee of $600-2,000/month, depending on client's needs. Works with clients on marketing budget. Offers written contract. "I work on a 3-month minimum basis. One-month notice must be given to terminate contract, but once a contract is signed, the client is responsible for the entire 3-month fee whether we continue to work together or not."

Tips "There are some very good books about finding an agent, editor, and/or publicist. Most will include guidelines about what the editor, agent, or publicist is looking for and what does not interest them. We're all better off for having such guides—a great service for all of us in the publishing field."

Ⓒ WARWICK ASSOCIATES

18340 Sonoma Hwy., Sonoma CA 95476. (707)939-9212. Fax: (707)938-3515. E-mail: warwick@vom.com. Web site: www.warwickassociates.net. **Contact:** Simon Warwick-Smith, president. Estab. 1983; specifically with books for 18 years. Currently works with 24 clients. 12% of clients are new/first-time writers.

● Prior to becoming a publicist, Mr. Warwick-Smith was senior vice president of marketing at Associated Publishers Group.

Members Cierra Trenery (celebrity/sports, at firm 6 years); Simon Warwick-Smith (metaphysics/business, at firm 18 years); Karen Misuraca (travel/writing, at firm 8 years).

Specializations Nonfiction, children's books, spirituality. **Considers these nonfiction areas:** Biography/autobiography; business; child guidance/parenting; computers/electronics; cooking/food/nutrition; government/politics/law; health/medicine; how-to; New Age/metaphysics; psychology; religious/inspirational; self-help/personal improvement; sports; travel.

Services Media training, market research, fax news releases, electronic news releases, sends material to magazines/newspapers for reviews, brochures, Web site assistance, Web site publicity. Book tours include bookstores, specialty stores, radio interviews, TV interviews, newspaper interviews, magazine interviews, speaking engagements, online interviews. Assists in coordinating travel plans. Clients have appeared on *Larry King Live*, *The Phil Donahue Show*, *Oprah*, *Good Morning America*. Media kit includes résumé, author's biography, testimonials, articles about author, basic information on book, professional photos, sample interview questions, book request information. Helps writer obtain endorsements.

How to Contact See Web site. Responds in 2 weeks. Returns material only with SASE. Obtains most new clients through recommendations from others, the Web site. Contact 6 months prior to book's publication.

Clients References and contact numbers are available to potential clients.

Costs Works with clients on marketing budget. Offers written contract.

⌧ WORLD CLASS SPEAKERS & ENTERTAINERS

5200 Kanan Rd., Suite 210, Aqoura Hills CA 91301. (818)991-5400. Fax: (818)991-2226. E-mail: wcse@speak.com. Web site: www.speak.com. **Contact:** Joseph I. Kessler. Estab. 1965.

Specializations Nonfiction, academic. **Considers these nonfiction areas:** Business; humor; money/finance/economics; psychology; science/technology; self-help/personal improvement; sociology; sports; women's issues/studies; high profile/famous writers.

Services Market research, sends material to magazines/newspapers for reviews, brochures, Web site publicity. Book tours include radio interviews, TV interviews, newspaper interviews, magazine interviews, speaking engagements, conferences, universities. Media kits include author's biography, testimonials, articles about author, professional photos. Helps writer obtain endorsements.

How to Contact Call, e-mail, or fax. Responds in 1 week. Discards unwanted materials. Obtains most new clients through recommendations from others. Contact prior to book's publication.

Costs Clients charged on per placement basis ($1,500 minimum); 30% commission. Works with clients on marketing budget. Offers written contract; 3-month notice must be given to terminate contract.

⌧ THE WRITE PUBLICIST & CO.

1865 River Falls Dr., Roswell GA 30076. (770)998-9911. E-mail: thewritepublicist@earthlink.net. Web site: www.thewritepublicist.com. **Contact:** Regina Lynch-Hudson. Estab. 1990; specifically with books for 10 years. Currently works with 5 clients. 50% of clients are new/first-time writers.

● Prior to becoming a publicist, Ms. Lynch-Hudson was public relations director for a 4-star resort and was a syndicated columnist to 215 newspapers, which solidifed media contacts.

Specializations Nonfiction, fiction, children's books. **Interested in these nonfiction areas:** Biography/autobiography, business, education, ethnic/cultural interests, health/medicine, how-to, juvenile nonfiction, multicultural, religious/inspirational, women's issues/studies. **Considers these fiction areas:** Confessional; contemporary issues; erotica; ethnic; family saga; humor/satire; mainstream; multicultural; religious/inspirational; romance; science fiction; sports. Other types of clients include physicians, lawyers, entertainers, artists.

Services International publicity, electronic news releases, sends material to magazines/newspapers for reviews, Web site publicity. Book tours include bookstores, radio interviews, TV interviews, newspaper interviews, magazine interviews, schools, universities. Assists in coordinating travel plans. Clients have appeared on *Oprah*, all national TV networks. Media kit includes author's biography, basic information on book, professional photos, book request information. Helps writer obtain endorsements.

How to Contact E-mail. Send book or ms. Responds in 1 week. Returns materials only with SASE. Obtains most new clients through recommendations from others (90% of clients are referred nationally). Contact 1 month prior to book's publication (preferred) or after book's publication.

Clients *Lifestyles for the 21st Century*, by Dr. Marcus Wells (Humanics Publishing); *Preconceived Notions*, by Robyn Williams (Noble Press); *Fed Up With the Fanny*, by Franklin White (Simon & Schuster). Other clients include Vernon Jones (CEO of DeKalb County), Atlanta Perinatal Associates, former NFL player-turned-sculptor George Nock. "Our clients' contracts state that they will not be solicited by prospective clients. Our Web site shows photos of clients who give their recommendation by consenting to be placed on our Web site."

Costs Clients charged flat fee of $9,500-15,000. Works with clients on marketing budget. Offers written contract.

Tips "Does the publicist have a Web site that actually pictures clients? Our award-winning Web site ranks among top 10 of all major search engines as one of the few PR sites that actually depicts clients."

☑ MERYL ZEGAREK PUBLIC RELATIONS, INC.

255 W. 108th St., Suite 9D1, New York NY 10025. (917)493-3601. Fax: (917)493-3598. E-mail: mz@mzpr.com. Web site: www.mzpr.com. **Contact:** Meryl Zegarek.

• Prior to starting her publicity agency, Ms. Zegarek was a publicity director at Pantheon/Schocken Books, Random House, and 2 divisions of The Knopf Publishing Group.

Specializations Nonfiction, fiction. **Considers these nonfiction areas:** Animals; anthropology/archaeology; art/architecture/design; current affairs; ethnic/cultural interests; government/politics/law; health/medicine; history; how-to; humor; interior design/decorating; language/literature/criticism; multicultural; music/dance/theater/film; nature/environment; photography; popular culture; psychology; religious/inspirational; science/technology; self-help/personal improvement; sociology; travel; true crime/investigative; women's issues/studies. **Considers these fiction areas:** Action/adventure; contemporary issues; detective/police/crime; ethnic; historical; literary; multicultural; mystery/suspense; religious/inspirational; science fiction; thriller/espionage. Other types of clients include theater, performance, nonprofits, human rights organizations, international publishers.

Services Expertise in nationwide media campaigns, including print features, TV, radio, World Wide Web exposure. Arranges book tours with bookstore readings and other appearances, interviews/features in newspapers, magazines, TV, and radio. Assists in travel arrangements. Also does marketing campaigns, media training, proposal advice and writing, and general publishing and publicity consulting. Clients have appeared on *Oprah*, *Good Morning America*, *The Today Show*, Fox News, *Fresh Air* (NPR), *Morning Edition* (NPR) and in the *New York Times* and *New York Times Magazine*. Media kit includes résumé, author's biography, testimonials, articles about author, basic information on book, professional photos, sample interview questions, book request information. Plans nationwide print and radio campaigns with giveaways.

○━ "I have been a publicity director for major publishing divisions at Knopf, Bantam Doubleday, and William Morrow during a 25-year career in book publicity. I have experience in every book genre with established contacts in TV, radio, and print—as well as bookstores and speaking venues." Also has unique specialty in Jewish and nonreligious spiritual books and authors of all faiths.

How to Contact Call, e-mail, or fax. Send letter with entire ms or galley, outline/proposal, sample chapters, SASE. Responds in 2 weeks. Returns material only with SASE. Obtains most new clients through recommendations from others. Contact as early as possible, ideally 4-5 months prior to book's publication.

Clients *The Piano Teacher*, by Elfriede Jelinek; *Lit From Within*, by Victoria Moran (HarperSanFrancisco); *ETZ Hayim* (Jewish Publication Society); *The Zohar: Pritzker Edition* (Stanford University Press); *Mystics, Mavericks and Merrymakers: An Inside Journey Among Hasidic Girls*, by Stephanie Levine (New York University Press); Brother Can You Spare a Dime: The Life of Composer Jay Gorney, by Sondra Gorney (Scarecrow Press). Other clients include The Paulist Press, Harmony Books, Hidden Spring, Serpent's Tail, Continuum Books. References and contact numbers are available to potential clients.

Conferences

Attending a writers' conference that includes agents gives you the opportunity to learn more about what agents do and show an agent your work. Ideally, a conference should include a panel or two with a number of agents to give writers a sense of the variety of personalities and tastes of different agents.

Not all agents are alike: Some are more personable, and sometimes you simply click better with one agent over another. When only one agent attends a conference there is a tendency for every writer at that conference to think, "Ah, this is the agent I've been looking for!" When the number of agents attending is larger, you have a wider group from which to choose and you may have less competition for the agent's time.

Besides including panels of agents discussing what representation means and how to go about securing it, many of these gatherings also include time—either scheduled or impromptu—to meet briefly with an agent to discuss your work.

If they're impressed with what they see and hear about your work, they will invite you to submit a query, a proposal, a few sample chapters, or possibly your entire manuscript. Some conferences even arrange for agents to review manuscripts in advance and schedule one-on-one sessions during which you can receive specific feedback or advice on your work. Such meetings often cost a small fee, but the input you receive is usually worth the price.

Ask writers who attend conferences and they'll tell you that at the very least you'll walk away with new knowledge about the industry. At the very best, you'll receive an invitation to send an agent your material.

Many writers try to make it to at least one conference a year, but cost and location can count as much as subject matter when determining which one to attend. There are conferences in almost every state and province that can provide answers to your questions about writing and the publishing industry. Conferences also connect you with a community of other writers. Such connections help you learn about the pros and cons of different agents, and they can also give you a renewed sense of purpose and direction in your own writing.

SUBHEADS

Each listing is divided into subheads to make locating specific information easier. In the first section, you'll find contact information for each conference. This section also lists conference dates, specific focus, and the average number of attendees. Finally, names of agents who will be speaking or have spoken in the past are listed along with details about their availability during the conference. Calling or e-mailing a conference director to verify the names of agents in attendance is always a good idea.

Costs: Looking at the price of events, plus room and board, may help writers on a tight budget narrow their choices.

Accommodations: Here conferences list overnight accommodations and travel information. Often conferences held in hotels will reserve rooms at a discount rate and may provide a shuttle bus to and from the local airport.

Additional Information: This section includes information on conference-sponsored contests, individual meetings, the availability of brochures, and more.

REGIONS

To make it easier for you to find a conference close to home—or to find one in an exotic locale that fits with your vacation plans—listings are separated into the following geographical regions:

- **Northeast** (page 235): Connecticut, Maine, Massachusetts, New Hampshire, New York, Rhode Island, Vermont.
- **Midatlantic** (page 238): Washington DC, Delaware, Maryland, New Jersey, Pennsylvania.
- **Midsouth** (page 239): North Carolina, South Carolina, Tennessee, Virginia, West Virginia.
- **Southeast** (page 242): Alabama, Arkansas, Florida, Georgia, Louisiana, Mississippi.
- **Midwest** (page 244): Illinois, Indiana, Kentucky, Michigan, Ohio.
- **North Central** (page 247): Iowa, Minnesota, Nebraska, North Dakota, South Dakota, Wisconsin.
- **South Central** (page 248): Colorado, Kansas, Missouri, New Mexico, Oklahoma, Texas.
- **West** (page 252): Arizona, California, Hawaii, Nevada, Utah.
- **Northwest** (page 258): Alaska, Idaho, Montana, Oregon, Washington, Wyoming.
- **Canada** (page 259).

CALENDAR

Check out the writers' conference calendar below for conferences listed alphabetically by the month in which they occur.

January

Key West Literary Seminar (Key West FL)
San Diego State University Writers' Conference (San Diego CA)
Wrangling With Writing (Tucson AZ)

February

Florida Suncoast Writers' Conference (St. Petersburg FL)
Love Is Murder (Rosemont IL)
San Francisco Writers Conference (San Francisco CA)
SCBWI Annual Winter Conference (New York NY)
Southern California Writers' Conference (San Diego CA)
UCLA Extension Writers' Program (Los Angeles CA)
Writing for the Soul (Colorado Springs CO)

March

Big Sur Writing Workshops (Big Sur CA)
Florida Christian Writers Conference (Bradenton FL)
Green River Writers Novels in Progress Workshop (Louisville KY)
ICE Escape Writers Conference (Mesa AZ)

Conferences

IWWG Early Spring In California Conference (Santa Cruz CA)
Oxford Conference for the Book (University MS)
The Perspectives in Children's Literature Conference (Amherst MA)
Sandhills Writers Conference (Augusta GA)
SleuthFest (Miami Beach FL)
Spring into Romance (San Diego CA)
Spring Writers' Workshop (Franklin TN)
Tea with Eleanor Roosevelt (Hyde Park NY)
Western Reserve Writers' Conference (Kirtland OH)
Whidbey Island Writers' Conference (Langley WA)
Writing Today (Birmingham AL)

April
ASJA Writers Conference (New York NY)
Desert Dreams (Scottsdale AZ)
IWWG Meet the Authors, Agents and Editors (New York NY)
Mount Hermon Christian Writers Conference (Mount Hermon CA)
Mountain Laurel Conference (Knoxville TN)
NETWO Writers Roundup (Winfield TX)
Norwescon (Seattle WA)
Pikes Peak Writers Conference (Colorado Springs CO)
Romantic Times Convention (Daytona Beach FL)
SCBWI/Hofstra University Children's Literature Conference (Hempstead NY)
Sinipee Writers' Workshop (Dubuque IA)
Spring Writer's Festival (Milwaukee WI)
TMCC Writers' Conference (Reno NV)
University of Wisconsin at Madison Writers Institute (Madison WI)
The Women Writers Conference (Lexington KY)

May
Blue Ridge Mountains Christian Writers Conference (Ridgecrest NC)
BookExpo America/Writer's Digest Books Writer's Conference (New York NY)
Oklahoma Writers' Federation Conference (Oklahoma City OK)
Pennwriters Annual Conference (Harrisburg PA)
Pima Writers' Workshop (Tucson AZ)
Wisconsin Regional Writers' Association Conferences (Montello WI)

June
Arkansas Writers' Conference (Little Rock AR)
Aspen Summer Words Literary Festival & Writing Retreat (Aspen CO)
Bloody Words (Victoria BC)
Clarion West Writers' Workshop (Seattle WA)
Frontiers in Writing (Amarillo TX)
Great Lakes Writer's Workshop (Milwaukee WI)
Highland Summer Conference (Radford VA)
Indiana University Writers' Conference (Bloomington IN)
Iowa Summer Writing Festival (Iowa City IA)
Jackson Hole Writers Conference (Jackson Hole WY)
Manhattanville Summer Writers' Week (Purchase NY)
National Writers Association Foundation Conference (Denver CO)

The New Letters Weekend Writers Conference (Kansas City MO)
No Crime Unpublished Mystery Writers' Conference (Los Angeles CA)
Of Dark & Stormy Nights (Schaumburg IL)
Remember the Magic (Saratoga Springs NY)
Santa Barbara Writers Conference (Santa Barbara CA)
The Screenwriting Conference in Santa Fe (Santa Fe NM)
Southeastern Writers Workshop (St. Simons Island GA)
Washington Independent Writers Spring Writers Conference (Washington DC)
Wesleyan Writers Conference (Middletown CT)
Write! Canada (Markham ON)
Writers Workshop in Science Fiction (Lawrence KS)

July

Antioch Writers' Workshop (Yellow Springs OH)
Festival of Words (Moose Jaw SK)
Harriette Austin Writers Conference (Athens GA)
Highlights Foundation Writers Workshop (Chautauqua NY)
Hofstra University Summer Writing Workshops (Hempstead NY)
Maritime Writers' Workshop (Fredericton NB)
Pacific Northwest Writers Conference (Seattle WA)
Romance Writers of America National Conference (Dallas TX)
Sewanee Writers' Conference (Sewanee TN)
Steamboat Springs Writers Conference (Steamboat Springs CO)

August

Bread Loaf Writers' Conference (Ripton VT)
The Columbus Writers Conference (Columbus OH)
Maui Writers Conference (Kihei HI)
Mendocino Coast Writers Conference (Fort Bragg CA)
Sage Hill Writing Experience (Saskatoon SK)
SCBWI Annual Summer Conference on Writing and Illustrating for Children
   (Los Angeles CA)
Squaw Valley Writers Workshop (Squaw Valley CA)
Sunshine Coast Festival of the Written Arts (Sechelt BC)
Willamette Writers Conference (Portland OR)
Writers' Conference at Ocean Park (Ocean Park ME)

September

ASA International Screenwriters Conference (San Diego CA)
Bouchercon 37 (Madison WI)
East of Eden Writers Conference (Santa Clara CA)
Fall Writers' Seminar (Franklin TN)
Rocky Mountain Fiction Writers Colorado Gold (Denver CO)
Southern California Writers' Conference (Palm Springs CA)
Start Your Engines—Rev Up Your Writing Career (Ithaca NY)
Western Reserve Writers' Conference (Kirtland OH)
Winnipeg International Writers Festival (Winnipeg MB)
Wisconsin Regional Writers' Association Conferences (Montello WI)

October

Austin Film Festival & Heart of Film Screenwriters Conference (Austin TX)

Flathead River Writers Conference (Whitefish MT)

Glorieta Christian Writers Conference (Glorieta NM)

IWWG Meet the Authors, Agents and Editors (New York NY)

James River Writers Conference (Richmond VA)

La Jolla Writers Conference (San Diego CA)

Magna Cum Murder XIII (Muncie IN)

New Jersey Romance Writers Put Your Heart in a Book Conference (Iselin NJ)

Ozark Creative Writers Conference (Eureka Springs AR)

Readers & Writers Holiday Conference (Columbus OH)

Sandy Cove Christian Writers Conference (North East MD)

Surrey International Writers' Conference (Surrey BC)

The Vancouver International Writers & Readers Festival (Vancouver BC)

Wisconsin Book Festival (Madison WI)

Women Writing the West (Colorado Springs CO)

November

Baltimore Writers' Conference (Towson MD)

North Carolina Writers' Network Fall Conference (Durham NC)

Sage Hill Writing Experience (Saskatoon SK)

Words & Music (New Orleans LA)

December

Big Sur Writing Workshops (Big Sur CA)

Quick Reference Icons

At the beginning of some listings, you will find one or more of the following symbols:

 Conference new to this edition

 Canadian conference

Find a pull-out bookmark with a key to symbols on the inside cover of this book.

NORTHEAST (CT, MA, ME, NH, NY, RI, VT)

ASJA WRITERS CONFERENCE

American Society of Journalists and Authors, 1501 Broadway, Suite 302, New York NY 10036. (212)997-0947. Fax: (212)768-7414. E-mail: staff@asja.org. Web site: www.asja.org. **Contact:** Brett Harvey, executive director. Estab. 1971. Annual conference held in April. Conference duration: 2 days. Average attendance: 600. Covers nonfiction and screenwriting. Held at Grand Hyatt in New York. **Previous agents/speakers have included:** Dominick Dunne, James Brady, Dana Sobel. Agents will be speaking.

Costs $195-240, depending on when you sign up (includes lunch).

Accommodations ''The hotel holding our conference always blocks out discounted rooms for attendees.''

Additional Information Brochures available in February. Registration form on Web site. Inquiries by e-mail and fax OK.

⃞ BOOKEXPO AMERICA/WRITER'S DIGEST BOOKS WRITER'S CONFERENCE

4700 E. Galbraith Rd., Cincinnati OH 45236. (513)531-2690. Fax: (513)891-7185. E-mail: publicity@fwpubs.c om. Web site: www.writersdigest.com/bea; www.bookexpoamerica.com. **Contact:** Greg Hatfield, publicity manager. Estab. 2003. Annual conference held May 30, 2007. Average attendance: 600. The conference offers instruction on the craft of writing, as well as advice for submitting work to publications, publishing houses, and agents. ''We provide breakout sessions on these topics, including expert advice from industry professionals, and offer workshops on fiction and nonfiction. We also provide agents to whom attendees can pitch their work.'' The conference is part of the BookExpo America trade show, which is geared toward publishers, booksellers, librarians, educators, and rights professionals. Registering for the conference does not allow you access to the trade show. The 2007 event will take place in New York City. **Previous agents/speakers have included:** Jonathan Karp, Steve Almond, John Warner, Heather Sellers, Noah Lukeman, Michael Cader.

BREAD LOAF WRITERS' CONFERENCE

Middlebury College, Middlebury VT 05753. (802)443-5286. Fax: (802)443-2087. E-mail: ncargill@middlebury.e du. Web site: www.middlebury.edu/blwc. **Contact:** Noreen Cargill, administrative manager. Estab. 1926. Annual conference held in late August. Conference duration: 11 days. Average attendance: 230. Offers workshops for fiction, nonfiction, and poetry. Agents, editors, publicists, and grant specialists will be in attendance.

Costs $2,164 (includes tuition, housing).

Accommodations Bread Loaf Inn in Ripton, Vermont.

HIGHLIGHTS FOUNDATION WRITERS WORKSHOP AT CHAUTAUQUA

814 Court St., Honesdale PA 18431. (570)253-1192. Fax: (570)253-0179. E-mail: contact@highlightsfoundation. org. Web site: www.highlightsfoundation.org. **Contact:** Kent Brown, executive director. Estab. 1985. Annual conference held in July. Average attendance: 100. Workshops are geared toward those who write for children at the beginner, intermediate, and advanced levels. Offers seminars, small group workshops, and one-on-one sessions with authors, editors, illustrators, critics, and publishers. Workshop site is the picturesque community of Chautauqua, New York. **Previous agents/speakers have included:** Eve Bunting, James Cross Giblin, Walter Dean Myers, Jane Yolen, Patricia Gauch, Jerry Spinelli, Joy Cowley, Ed Young.

Costs $2,200 (includes all meals, conference supplies, gate pass to Chautauqua Institution).

Accommodations ''We coordinate ground transportation to and from airports, trains, and bus stations in the Erie, Pennsylvania and Jamestown/Buffalo, New York area. We also coordinate accommodations for conference attendees.''

Additional Information ''We offer the opportunity for attendees to submit a manuscript for review at the conference.'' Workshop brochures/guidelines are available after January for SASE. Inquiries by fax OK.

HOFSTRA UNIVERSITY SUMMER WRITING WORKSHOPS

University College for Continuing Education, 250 Hofstra University, Hempstead NY 11549-2500. (516)463-5993. Fax: (516)463-4833. E-mail: uccelibarts@hofstra.edu. Web site: www.hofstra.edu/ucce/summerwriting. **Contact:** Richard Pioreck, director of the summer writing workshops, or Judith Reed. Estab. 1972. Annual conference held in mid-July. Average attendance: 65. Conference offers workshops in short fiction, nonfiction, poetry, and occasionally another genre such as screenplay writing or writing for children. Site is the university campus on Long Island, 25 miles from New York City. **Previous authors/teachers have included:** Oscar Hijuelos, Robert Olen Butler, Hilma and Meg Wolitzer, Budd Schulberg, Cynthia Ozick, Rebecca Wolff.

Costs Check Web site for current fees. Credit available to undergraduate and graduate students. Continental breakfast daily; tuition also includes cost of banquet.

Accommodations Free bus operates between Hempstead Train Station and campus for those commuting from New York City. Dormitory rooms are available for the 2-week conference.

Additional Information "All workshops include critiquing. Each participant is given one-on-one time for a half hour with workshop leader. More details will be available in March 2007. Accepts inquiries via fax and e-mail."

IWWG MEET THE AUTHORS, AGENTS AND EDITORS: THE BIG APPLE WORKSHOPS

% International Women's Writing Guild, P.O. Box 810, Gracie Station, New York NY 10028-0082. (212)737-7536. Fax: (212)737-9469. E-mail: iwwg@iwwg.org. Web site: www.iwwg.org. **Contact:** Hannelore Hahn, executive director. Estab. 1980. Workshops held October 14-15, 2006 and April 21-22, 2007. Average attendance: 200. Workshops promote creative writing and professional success. A 1-day writing workshop is offered on Saturday. Sunday morning includes a discussion with up to 10 recently published IWWG authors and a book fair during lunch. On Sunday afternoon, up to 10 literary agents introduce themselves, and then members of the audience speak to the agents they wish to meet. Many as-yet-unpublished works have found publication in this manner. **Previous agents/speakers have included:** Meredith Bernstein, Rita Rosenkranz, Jeff Herman. **Costs** $125/members for the weekend; $155/nonmembers for the weekend; $80/90 for Saturday; $75/100 for Sunday.
Additional Information Information (including accommodations) is provided in a brochure. Inquires by fax and e-mail OK.

MANHATTANVILLE SUMMER WRITERS' WEEK

2900 Purchase St., Purchase NY 10577-0940. (914)694-3425. Fax: (914)694-0348. E-mail: gps@mville.edu; dowdr@mville.edu. Web site: www.mville.edu. **Contact:** Ruth Dowd, dean of graduate and professional studies. Estab. 1983. Annual conference held in late June. Conference duration: 5 days. Average attendance: 100. Workshops are offered in fiction, nonfiction, personal narrative, poetry, children's/young adult, and literature/playwriting. Held at a suburban college campus 30 miles from New York City. Workshop sessions are held in a 19th century Norman Castle which serves as the college's administration building. **Previous agents/speakers have included:** Brian Morton, Valerie Martin, Ann Jones, Mark Matousek, Major Jackson, Linda Oatman High, Jeffrey Sweet, Alice Quinn (*The New Yorker*), Georgia Jelatis Hoke (MacIntosh & Otis, Inc.), Paul Cirone (Aaron Priest Literary Agency), Emily Saladino (Writer's House). Agents will be speaking and available for meetings with attendees.
Costs $650/noncredit (includes all workshops, craft seminars, readings, keynote lecture). $1,040/2 graduate credits. Participants may purchase meals in the college cafeteria or cafe.
Accommodations A list of hotels in the area is available upon request. Overnight accommodations are also available in the college residence halls.
Additional Information Brochures available for SASE or online by the end of February. Inquiries by e-mail and fax OK.

THE PERSPECTIVES IN CHILDREN'S LITERATURE CONFERENCE

226 Furcolo Hall, School of Education, U-Mass, Amherst MA 01003-3035. E-mail: childlit@educ.umass.edu. Web site: www.umass.edu/childlit. **Contact:** Dr. Marsha Rudman, program director. Estab. 1970. Annual conference held in late March/early April. Conference duration: 1 day. Average attendance: 500. Conference focuses on various aspects of writing and illustrating children's books. Held at the University of Massachusetts School of Management. **Past agents/speakers have included:** Jane Yolen, Jerry and Gloria Jean Pinkey, Patricia and Emily MacLachlan, Jan Cherpiko, Eric Carle, Leslea Newman.
Costs $70-75 (includes light breakfast, lunch, freebies, snacks). For an additional fee, attendees can earn academic credit.
Additional Information During lunch, authors and illustrators are given the opportunity to converse and share experiences with editors. Books will be available for sale. Inquiries by e-mail OK.

REMEMBER THE MAGIC

International Women's Writing Guild, P.O. Box 810, Gracie Station, New York NY 10028-0082. (212)737-7536. Fax: (212)737-9469. E-mail: iwwg@iwwg.org. Web site: www.iwwg.org. **Contact:** Hannelore Hahn, executive director. Estab. 1978. Annual conference held June 15-22, 2007 and June 13-20, 2008. Average attendance: 500. Conference to promote creative writing and personal growth, professional know-how and contacts, and networking. Site is the campus of Skidmore College in Saratoga Springs, New York (near Albany). Approximately 65 workshops are offered each day. Conferees have the freedom to make their own schedule. They come from all parts of the world; all ages and backgrounds are represented.
Costs $995 single/$860 double for members; $1,025 single/$890 double for nonmembers. These fees include the 7-day program and room and board for the week. Rates for a 5-day stay and a weekend stay, as well as commuter rates, are also available.
Additional Information Conference brochures/guidelines are available for SASE. Inquiries by e-mail and fax OK, or view online.

ⓃSEAK MEDICAL & LEGAL FICTION WRITING CONFERENCES

P.O. Box 729, Falmouth MA 02541. (508)548-7023. Fax: (508)540-8304. E-mail: mail@seak.com. Web site: www.seak.com. Annual conferences held on Cape Cod. The medical seminar is taught by *New York Times* bestselling authors Michael Palmer, MD and Tess Gerritsen, MD. The legal seminar is taught by *New York Times* bestselling authors Lisa Scottoline, Esq. and Stephen Horn, Esq. Session topics include writing fiction that sells, screenwriting, writing riveting dialogue, creating memorable characters, getting your first novel published, and more. Agents will be speaking and available for one-on-one meetings.

SOCIETY OF CHILDREN'S BOOK WRITERS & ILLUSTRATORS ANNUAL WINTER CONFERENCE

8271 Beverly Blvd., Los Angeles CA 90048. E-mail: conference@scbwi.org. Web site: www.scbwi.org. Estab. 1975. Annual conference held in February. Average attendance: 800. Conference promotes writing for children (picture books, fiction, nonfiction, middle grade, young adult) and allows writers to network with professionals and learn about marketing their book, children's multimedia, etc. Conference is held at the Hilton New York.
Costs Approximately $300/members; $340/nonmembers.
Accommodations See Web site.
Additional Information Conference brochures/guidelines are available online.

SOCIETY OF CHILDREN'S BOOK WRITERS & ILLUSTRATORS CONFERENCE/HOFSTRA UNIVERSITY CHILDREN'S LITERATURE CONFERENCE

University College for Continuing Education, 250 Hofstra University, Hempstead NY 11549-2500. (516)463-5993. Fax: (516)463-4833. E-mail: uccelibarts@hofstra.edu. Web site: www.hofstra.edu/ucce/childlitconf. **Contact:** Judith Reed. Estab. 1985. Annual conference held in April 2007. The conference brings together writers, illustrators, librarians, agents, publishers, teachers and other professionals who are interested in writing for children. Each year the program is organized around a theme and includes 2 general sessions, 5 break-out groups, and a panel of children's book editors who critique randomly selected first-manuscript pages submitted by registrants. The conference takes place at the Student Center Building of Hofstra University, located in Long Island.
Costs 2006 rate: $77/members; $82/nonmembers (continental breakfast and full luncheon included).

ⓃSTART YOUR ENGINES—REV UP YOUR WRITING CAREER

Southern Tier Authors of Romance (STAR), P.O. Box 496, Endicott NY 13760. E-mail: starchapter@yahoo.com. Web site: members.aol.com/starrwa. Annual conference held in early September. Features a day of workshops designed for writers at all levels, editor/agent appointments, a book fair, and more. **Previous agents/speakers have included:** Nadia Cornier, Mary Sue Seymour, Leslie Wainger, Briana St. James, Hilary Sares, Sherrilyn Kenyon, MaryJanice Davidson, Jo Beverley, Jo Ann Ferguson, Jocelyn Kelley, Rebecca York, Elizabeth Sinclair, Annette Blair, CJ Barry.
Costs $90/RWA member; $100/nonmember.
Accommodations $120/night at the Holiday Inn in Ithaca NY.

TEA WITH ELEANOR ROOSEVELT

International Women's Writing Guild, P.O. Box 810, Gracie Station, New York NY 10028-0082. (212)737-7536. Fax: (212)737-9469. E-mail: iwwg@iwwg.org. Web site: www.iwwg.org. **Contact:** Hannelore Hahn, executive director. Estab. 1980. Annual conference held March 25, 2007 and March 29, 2008. This is a traditional visit to Mrs. Roosevelt's cozy retreat cottage during Women's History Month. Conference duration: 1 day. Average attendance: 50. Held at the Eleanor Roosevelt Center at Val-Kill in Hyde Park, New York (2 hours from New York City in the Hudson Valley).
Costs $75 (includes lunch).
Additional Information Brochure/guidelines available for SASE. Inquiries by e-mail and fax OK.

WESLEYAN WRITERS CONFERENCE

Wesleyan University, Middletown CT 06459. (860)685-3604. Fax: (860)685-2441. E-mail: agreene@wesleyan.edu. Web site: www.wesleyan.edu/writers. **Contact:** Anne Greene, director. Estab. 1956. Annual conference held the third week in June. Average attendance: 100. Focuses on fiction techniques, short stories, poetry, screenwriting, nonfiction, literary journalism, and memoir. The conference is held on the campus of Wesleyan University, in the hills overlooking the Connecticut River. Features seminars and readings of new fiction, poetry, and nonfiction, and guest lectures on a range of publishing topics. Both new and experienced writers are welcome. Participants may attend seminars in all the genres. **Agents/speakers attending include:** Esmond Harmsworth (Zachary Schuster Agency), Daniel Mandel (Sanford J. Greenburger Associates), Dorian Karchmar, Amy Williams (ICM and Collins McCormick), Mary Sue Rucci (Simon & Schuster), Denise Roy (Simon & Schuster), John Kulka (Yale University Press), and many others. Participants are often successful in finding agents and publishers for their mss. Wesleyan participants are also frequently featured in the anthology *Best New American Voices.* Agents will be speaking and available for meetings with attendees.

Costs Previous years' day rate: $775 (includes meals); boarding students' rate: $910 (includes meals and room for 5 nights).

Accommodations Meals and lodging are provided on campus.

Additional Information Ms critiques are available, but not required. Scholarships and teaching fellowships are available, including the Jakobson Awards for fiction writers and poets and the Jon Davidoff Scholarships for journalists. Inquiries by e-mail, phone, and fax OK.

WRITERS' CONFERENCE AT OCEAN PARK

P.O. Box 7146, Ocean Park ME 04063-7146. E-mail: jbrosnan@jwu.edu; opmewriters@verizon.net. **Contact:** Jim Brosnan, Donna Brosnan. Estab. 1941. Annual conference held in mid-August. Conference duration: 4 days. Average attendance: 50. "We try to present a balanced and eclectic conference. In addition to time and attention given to poetry, we also have children's literature, mystery writing, travel, fiction, nonfiction, journalism, and other issues of interest to writers. Our speakers are editors, writers, and other professionals. Our concentration is, by intention, a general view of writing to publish with supportive encouragement. We are located in Ocean Park, a small seashore village 14 miles south of Portland. Ours is a summer assembly center with many buildings from the Victorian Age. The conference meets in Porter Hall, one of the assembly buildings which is listed on the National Register of Historic Places." **Previous speakers have included:** Michael C. White (novelist/short story writer), Betsy Shool (poet), Suzanne Strempek Shea (novelist), John Perrault (poet), Josh Williamson (newspaper editor), Dawn Potter (poet), Bruce Pratt (fiction writer), Amy McDonald (children's author), Anne Wescott Dodd (nonfiction writer), Kate Chadbourne (singer/songwriter), Wesley McNair (poet/Maine faculty member), and others. "We usually have about 8 guest presenters a year." Published writers/editors will be speaking, leading workshops, and available for meetings with attendees.

Costs $160 (includes the conference, reception, and Tuesday evening meal); $175 if registering after July 1. There is a reduced fee of $80 for students ages 21 and under. The fee does not include housing or meals, which must be arranged separately by the conferees.

Accommodations An accommodations list is available. "We are in a summer resort area where motels, guest houses, and restaurants abound."

Additional Information "We have 7 contests for various genres. An announcement is available in the spring. The prizes (all modest) are awarded at the end of the conference and only to those who are registered." Send SASE in June for conference program.

MIDATLANTIC (DC, DE, MD, NJ, PA)

ALGONKIAN WRITER WORKSHOPS

2020 Pennsylvania Ave. NW, Suite 43, Washington DC 20006. (800)250-8290. E-mail: algonkian@webdelsol.c om. Web site: www.webdelsol.com/algonkian. **Contact:** Michael Neff, director. Estab. 2001. Workshops on fiction, short fiction, and poetry are held 12 times/year in various locations. Conference duration: 5 days. Average attendance: 15/craft workshops; 60/pitch sessions. **Previous agents/speakers have included:** Paige Wheeler, Elise Capron, Deborah Grosvenor, Kathleen Anderson. Agents will be speaking and available for meetings with attendees.

Costs $495-1,295 (includes tuition, meals). Housing costs vary depending on the workshop's location.

Additional Information "These workshops are challenging and are not for those looking for praise." Guidelines available online or via e-mail.

BALTIMORE WRITERS' CONFERENCE

P.O. Box 410, Riderwood MD 21139. (410)371-3515. E-mail: quita@comcast.net. Web site: www.towson.edu/ writersconference. **Contact:** Tracy Miller, coordinator. Estab. 1994. Annual conference held in November. Conference duration: 1 day. Average attendance: 150-200. Covers all areas of writing and getting published. Held at Towson University. Topics have included: mystery, science fiction, poetry, children's writing, legal issues, grant funding, working with an agent, and book and magazine panels. **Previous agents/speakers have included:** Nat Sobel (Sobel/Weber Associates) and Nina Graybill (Graybill and English). Agents will be speaking.

Costs $80-100 (includes all-day conference, lunch, snacks). Ms critiques cost an additional fee.

Accommodations Hotels are close by, if required.

Additional Information Inquiries by e-mail OK. May register through BWA Web site.

NEW JERSEY ROMANCE WRITERS PUT YOUR HEART IN A BOOK CONFERENCE

E-mail: njrwconfchair@yahoo.com. Web site: www.njromancewriters.org. **Contact:** Lena Pinto. Estab. 1984. Annual conference held in October. Average attendance: 500. Workshops are offered on various topics for all

writers of romance, from beginner to multi-published. **Previous agents/speakers have included:** Nora Roberts, Kathleen Woodiwiss, Patricia Gaffney, Jill Barnett, Kay Hooper. Appointments are offered with editors/agents.
Accommodations Special rate available for conference attendees at the Sheraton at Woodbridge Place Hotel in Iselin, New Jersey.
Additional Information Conference brochures, guidelines, and membership information are available for SASE. Massive bookfair is open to the public with authors signing copies of their books.

PENNWRITERS ANNUAL CONFERENCE

E-mail: conferenceco@pennwriters.org. Web site: www.pennwriters.org. **Contact:** Vickie Fisher, conference coordinator. Estab. 1987. Annual conference held the third weekend of May. Conference duration: 3 days. Average attendance: 120. Offers agent and editor panel and workshops on marketing, fiction, romance, networking, and more. **Previous agents/speakers have included:** Evan Marshall, Nancy Martin, Evan Fogelman, Cherry Weiner, Karen Solen. Agents will be speaking and available for meetings with attendees.
Costs $145/members; $170/nonmembers (includes all workshops and panels, as well as any editor or agent appointments). There is an additional charge for Friday's keynote dinner and Saturday night's dinner activity.
Accommodations "We arrange a special rate with the hotel, and details will be in our brochure."
Additional Information "We are a multi-genre group encompassing the state of Pennsylvania and beyond." Brochures available in February for SASE. Inquiries by e-mail OK. Visit Web site for current updates and details.

SANDY COVE CHRISTIAN WRITERS CONFERENCE

Sandy Cove Ministries, 60 Sandy Cove Rd., North East MD 21901. (410)287-5433. Fax: (410)287-3196. E-mail: info@sandycove.org. Web site: www.sandycove.org. Estab. 1991. Annual conference held the first week in October. Conference duration: 4 days. Average attendance: 200. There are major workshops in fiction, article writing, and nonfiction books for beginner and advanced writers. While Sandy Cove has a strong emphasis on available markets in Christian publishing, all writers are more than welcome. **Previous agents/speakers have included:** Francine Rivers, Lisa Bergen, Ken Petersen (Tyndale House), Linda Tomblin (*Guideposts*), Karen Ball (Zondervan).
Costs Call for rates.
Accommodations Sandy Cove is a full-service conference center located on the Chesapeake Bay. All the facilities are first class with suites, single and double rooms available.
Additional Information Conference brochures/guidelines are available. "For exact dates, please visit our Web site."

WASHINGTON INDEPENDENT WRITERS (WIW) SPRING WRITERS CONFERENCE

1001 Connecticut Ave. NW, Suite 701, Washington DC 20036. (202)775-5150. Fax: (202)775-5810. E-mail: info@washwriter.org. Web site: www.washwriter.org. **Contact:** Nicci Yang, membership manager. Estab. 1975. Annual conference held June 10. Average attendance: 350. Focuses on fiction, nonfiction, screenwriting, poetry, children's writing, and technical writing. Gives participants a chance to hear from and talk with dozens of experts on book and magazine publishing, as well as on the craft, tools, and business of writing. **Previous agents/speakers have included:** Erica Jong, John Barth, Kitty Kelley, Vanessa Leggett, Diana McLellan, Brian Lamb, Stephen Hunter. New York and local agents are at every conference.
Costs See Web site.
Additional Information Brochures/guidelines available for SASE in mid-February.

MIDSOUTH (NC, SC, TN, VA, WV)

AMERICAN CHRISTIAN WRITERS CONFERENCES

P.O. Box 110390, Nashville TN 37222-0390. (800)219-7483. Fax: (615)834-7736. E-mail: acwriters@aol.com. Web site: www.acwriters.com (includes schedule of cities). **Contact:** Reg Forder, director. Estab. 1981. Conference duration: 2 days. Average attendance: 60. Annual conference promoting all forms of Christian writing (fiction, nonfiction, scriptwriting). Conferences are held throughout the year in 36 US cities.
Costs Approximately $189, plus meals and accommodations.
Accommodations Special rates are available at the host hotel (usually a major hotel chain like Holiday Inn).
Additional Information Conference brochures/guidelines are available for SASE.

⟦N⟧ BLUE RIDGE MOUNTAINS CHRISTIAN WRITERS CONFERENCE

E-mail: ylehman@bellsouth.net. Web site: www.lifeway.com/christianwriters. **Contact:** Yvonne Lehman. Annual conference held in May. Conference duration: Sunday through lunch on Thursday. A training and networking event for both seasoned and aspiring writers that allows attendees to interact with editors, agents, professional writers, and readers. Workshops and continuing classes in a variety of creative catergories are also offered.

Costs $315 (includes sessions and banquet).

Accommodations $49-84, depending on room size, at the LifeWay Ridgecrest Conference Center near Asheville, North Carolina.

Additional Information The event also features a contest for unpublished writers and ms critiques prior to the conference.

N CAPON SPRINGS WRITERS' WORKSHOP

P.O. Box 11116, Cincinnati OH 45211-0116. (513)481-9884. Fax: (513)481-2646. E-mail: beckcomm@fuse.net. **Contact:** Wendy Beckman, director. Estab. 2000. Conference is usually held in mid-June or mid-September. Conference duration: 3 days. Covers fiction, creative nonfiction, and publishing basics. Conference held at Farm Resort, a 5,000-acre secluded mountain resort in West Virginia.

Costs $500 (includes all seminars, meals, lodging).

Accommodations Facility has swimming, hiking, fishing, tennis, badminton, volleyball, basketball, ping pong, etc. A 9-hole golf course is available for an additional fee.

Additional Information Brochures available for SASE. Inquiries by fax and e-mail OK.

N FALL WRITERS' SEMINAR

Council for the Written Word, P.O. Box 298, Franklin TN 37065. (615)790-5918. E-mail: nfblume@cs.com. Web site: www.asouthernjournal.com/cww. **Contact:** Nancy Fletcher-Blume, president. Annual seminar held September 15, 2007. An all-day event with local and area authors, agents, editors, publishers, and publicists teaching the art and business of writing.

HIGHLAND SUMMER CONFERENCE

Box 7014, Radford University, Radford VA 24142-7014. (540)831-5366. Fax: (540)831-5951. E-mail: jasbury@radford.edu. Web site: www.radford.edu/~arsc. **Contact:** JoAnn Asbury, assistant to the director. Estab. 1978. Annual conference held in June. Conference duration: 14 days. Average attendance: 25. Covers fiction, nonfiction, poetry, and screenwriting. **Previous speakers/agents have included:** Bill Brown, Robert Morgan, Sharyn McCrumb, Nikki Giovanni, Wilma Dykeman, Jim Wayne Miller, David Huddle, Diane Fisher.

Costs The cost is based on current Radford tuition for 3 credit hours, plus an additional conference fee. On-campus meals and housing are available for an additional cost. In 2005, conference tuition was $594/in-state undergraduates, $1,470/out-of-state undergraduates, $678/in-state graduates, and $1,251/out-of-state graduates.

Accommodations "We do not have special rate arrangements with local hotels. We do offer accommodations on the Radford University Campus in a recently refurbished residence hall. The 2005 cost was $24-33/night."

Additional Information Conference leaders typically critique work done during the 2-week conference, but do not ask to have any writing submitted prior to the conference. Conference brochures/guidelines are available in March for SASE. Inquiries by e-mail and fax OK.

N JAMES RIVER WRITERS CONFERENCE

P.O. Box 25067, Richmond VA 23260. (804)474-3575. E-mail: info@jamesriverwriters.com. Web site: www.jamesriverwriters.com. **Contact:** Colleen Curran, executive director. Estab. 2003. Annual conference held October 6-7, 2006. Average attendance: 250. The conference is held at the Library of Virginia, located in downtown Richmond. Some events planned include panel discussions on freelancing, historical fiction, how to create dialogue, and nonfiction. Speakers discuss the craft and profession of writing and publishing and represent many genres, from fiction, nonfiction, and screenwriting, to poetry, children's literature, and science fiction. **Agents/speakers attending include:** New York agents, best selling authors, and major publishers.

Costs $150 for two days of speakers, panels/discussions, an agent meeting if available, and a continental breakfast and box lunch on both days. Parking is not included.

Accommodations Overnight accommodation information is available on the Web site. A block of hotel rooms is also reserved at the Holiday Inn Central, located near downtown.

Additional Information Brochures/guidelines available with SASE or online. Request information via e-mail.

N MOUNTAIN LAUREL CONFERENCE

The Knoxville Crowne Plaza, 401 W. Summit Hill Dr., Knoxville TN 37902-1416. (865)522-2600. Fax: (865)523-7200. E-mail: erinmhudson@comcast.net. Web site: www.smrw.org. **Contact:** Erin Hudson, conference coordinator. Estab. 1997. Conference held April 6-8, 2007. Average attendance: 80. Romantic fiction writing is the main concentration with some talk regarding the business and market of the romance sub-genres. "We will have our annual awards banquet, along with editors, agents and published authors. Workshops will focus on craft and market.'' Editors/agents will be speaking and available for meetings with attendees.

Costs $95-145 (includes all workshops, dinner Friday, breakfast, lunch and dinner Saturday, breakfast Sunday morning, entrance to the hospitality room, author autographing).

Accommodations A rate of $96/night is available at the Crowne Plaza under the Smoky Mountain Romance Writers' block. The hotel has a shuttle service.

Additional Information In 2007, the theme will be ''Now What? Taking the next step in your writing career.'' It will feature a readers' luncheon, which is a new addition to the conference. Brochures/guidelines are online, or request information via e-mail.

NORTH CAROLINA WRITERS' NETWORK FALL CONFERENCE

P.O. Box 954, Carrboro NC 27510-0954. (919)967-9540. Fax: (919)929-0535. E-mail: mail@ncwriters.org. Web site: www.ncwriters.org **Contact:** Cynthia Barnett, executive director. Estab. 1985. Annual conference held November 10-12 in Research Triangle Park (Durham NC). Average attendance: 450. The conference is a weekend full of classes, panels, book signings and readings, including open mic. There will be a keynote speaker, along with sessions on a variety of genres, including fiction, poetry, creative nonfiction, journalism, children's book writing, screenwriting, and playwriting. ''We also offer craft, editing, and marketing classes. We hold the conference at a conference center with hotel rooms available.'' **Previous agents/speakers have included:** Donald Maass, Noah Lukeman, Joe Regal, Jeff Kleinman, Evan Marshall. Some agents teach classes and some are available for meetings with attendees.

Costs Approximately $250-350 (includes 2 meals).

Accommodations Special rates are available at the Sheraton Imperial Hotel, but the conferees must make their own reservations.

Additional Information Conference brochures/guidelines are available online or by sending your street address to mail@ncwriters.org. Online secure registration is also available.

SEWANEE WRITERS' CONFERENCE

735 University Ave., Sewanee TN 37383-1000. (931)598-1141. E-mail: cpeters@sewanee.edu. Web site: www.sewaneewriters.org. **Contact:** Cheri B. Peters, creative writing programs manager. Estab. 1990. Annual conference held in July. Conference duration: 12 days. Average attendance: 110. ''We offer genre-based workshops in fiction, poetry, and playwriting—not theme-based workshops.'' The conference uses the facilities of Sewanee: the University of the South. The university is a collection of ivy-covered Gothic-style buildings located on the Cumberland Plateau in mid-Tennessee. Editors, publishers, and agents structure their own presentations, but there is always opportunity for questions from the audience. **2006 faculty members include:** Randall Kenan, Jill McCorkle, John Casey, John Hollander, Romulus Linney, Margot Livesey, Alice McDermott, Mary Jo Salter, Barry Hannah, Arlene Hutton, Erin McGraw, Clair Messud, Alan Shapiro, Dave Smith. **Visiting agents include:** Gail Hochman and Georges Borchardt.

Costs $1,560 (includes tuition, board, basic room).

Accommodations Participants are housed in university dormitory rooms. Motel or bed & breakfast housing is available, but not abundantly so. Dormitory housing costs are included in the full conference fee.

Additional Information Complimentary chartered bus service is available on a limited basis. ''We offer each participant (excepting auditors) the opportunity for a private manuscript conference with a member of the faculty. These manuscripts are due 1 month before the conference begins.'' Conference brochures/guidelines are available, but no SASE is necessary. The conference provides a limited number of fellowships and scholarships; these are awarded on a competitive basis.

N SPRING WRITERS' WORKSHOP

Council for the Written Word, P.O. Box 298, Franklin TN 37065. (615)790-5918. E-mail: kathy@asouthernjournal.com. Web site: www.asouthernjournal.com/cww. **Contact:** Kathy Rhodes, facilitator. Annual workshop held in March. An intensive, half-day event with instruction and hands-onexperience in a specific genre.

N WASHINGTON ROMANCE WRITERS RETREAT

Historic Hilltop House, Harpers Ferry WV. Web site: www.wrwdc.com. Annual conference held in April or May.

Costs $250 (all inclusive).

Additional Information You must be a registered RWA/WRW member the August prior to the event to apply for the retreat.

SOUTHEAST (AL, AR, FL, GA, LA, MS)

[N] ARKANSAS WRITERS' CONFERENCE

7713 Harmon, Little Rock AR 72227. (501)223-8633. E-mail: blm@artistotle.net. **Contact:** Helen Austin, director. Estab. 1944. Annual conference held the first weekend in June. Average attendence: 225. Covers fiction, nonfiction, scriptwriting, and poetry. "We have some general sessions and some more specific, but try to vary each year's subjects."

Costs $15/1 day; $25/2 days; $10/contest entry.

Accommodations Holiday Inn in Little Rock. The hotel has a bus to and from the airport. Rooms average $70-75.

Additional Information "We have 35 contest categories. Some are open only to Arkansans, but most are open to all writers. Judges are not announced before the conference. Conference brochures are available for SASE after February 1."

FLORIDA CHRISTIAN WRITERS CONFERENCE

2344 Armour Ct. Titusville FL 32780. (321)269-5831. Fax: (321)264-0037. E-mail: billiewilson@cfl.rr.com. Web site: www.flwriters.org. **Contact:** Billie Wilson. Estab. 1988. Annual conference held in March. Conference duration: 5 days. Average attendance: 200. Covers fiction, nonfiction, magazine writing, marketing, Internet writing, greeting cards, and more. Conference held at the Christian Retreat Center in Brandenton, Florida.

Costs $450 (includes tuition, meals).

Accommodations "We provide a shuttle from the Sarasota airport." $590/double occupancy; $825/single occupancy.

Additional Information "Each writer may submit 2 works for critique. We have specialists in every area of writing." Conference brochures/guidelines are available for SASE or online.

FLORIDA FIRST COAST WRITERS' FESTIVAL

601 W. State St., Room 304-A, FCCJ, Jacksonville FL 32202. (904)632-3042. Fax: (904)632-5092. E-mail: kclower @fccj.org. Web site: www.fccj.org/wf. **Contact:** Kathy Clower, Dana Thomas. Estab. 1985. Annual conference held in the spring. Average attendance: 300. Covers fiction, nonfiction, scriptwriting, poetry, freelancing, etc. Offers seminars on narrative structure and plotting character development. **Previous agents/speakers have included:** Andrei Codrescu, Gerald Hausman, Connie May Fowler, Leslie Schwartz, Larry Smith, Stella Suberman, Sophia Wadsworth, Amy Gash, David Hale Smith, Katharine Sands, Rita Rosenkranz, Jim McCarthy, David Poyer, Lenore Hart, Steve Berry, S.V. Date. Agents will be speaking and available for meetings with attendees. "We offer one-on-one sessions at no additional cost for attendees to speak to selected writers, editors, and agents on first-come, first served basis."

Costs 2005 early bird special: $185 (2 days with 2 meals); regular registration: $230 (2 days with 2 meals and banquet).

Accommodations Radisson Riverwalk has a special festival rate. Call (904)396-5100 or (800)333-3333.

Additional Information Conference brochures/guidelines are available for SASE. Sponsors a contest for short fiction, poetry, novels, and plays. Novel judges are David Poyer and Lenore Hart. Entry fees: $30/novels; $10/short fiction; $5/poetry. Deadline: December 1. "Visit our Web site after January 1 for current festival updates and more details."

FLORIDA SUNCOAST WRITERS' CONFERENCE

University of South Florida, Continuing Education, 4202 E. Fowler Ave., NEC16, Tampa FL 33620-6758. (813)974-2403. Fax: (813)974-5421. E-mail: dcistaff@admin.usf.edu. Web site: english.cas.usf.edu/fswc. Directors: Steve Rubin, Betty Moss, Lagretta Lenkar. Estab. 1970. Annual conference held in February. Conference duration: 3 days. Average attendance: 400. Conference covers poetry, short story, novel, nonfiction, science fiction, detective, travel writing, drama, TV scripts, photojournalism, and juvenile. Also features panels with agents and editors. "We do not focus on any one particular aspect of the writing profession, but instead offer a variety of writing-related topics." The conference is held on the picturesque university campus fronting the bay in St. Petersburg, Florida. **Previous speakers/agents have included:** Lady P.D. James, William Styron, John Updike, Joyce Carol Oates, Francine Prose, Frank McCourt, David Guterson, Jane Smiley, Auguster Burroughs, Billy Collins, Al Young, Heather Sellers.

Costs $275.

Accommodations Special rates available at area motels. "All information is contained in our brochure."

Additional Information Participants may submit work for critiquing (costs $50). Inquiries by e-mail and fax OK.

[N] HARRIETTE AUSTIN WRITERS CONFERENCE

Georgia Center for Continuing Education, The University of Georgia, Athens GA 30602-3603. (706)542-6638. Fax: (706)542-6465. E-mail: cconnor@uga.edu. Web site: www.coe.uga.edu/hawc. **Contact:** Charles Connor.

Annual conference held in July. Sessions cover fiction, nonfiction, memoirs, children's writing, publicity, Internet writing, how to get an agent, working with editors, and more. Editors and agents will be speaking. Manuscript critiques and one-on-one meetings with an evaluator are available for $50.

Costs $175-280, depending on the days registered (includes reception, sessions, lunch, book signings, cocktail party). Meals cost extra.

Accommodations $69-89 at the Georgia Center Hotel.

KEY WEST LITERARY SEMINAR

718 Love Ln., Key West FL 33040 (December-April). 16 Prayer Ridge Rd., Fairview NC 28730 (May-November). (888)293-9291. E-mail: mail@keywestliteraryseminar.org. Web site: www.keywestliteraryseminar.org. Annual conference held in January. The 2007 seminar theme is 'Wondrous Strange: Mystery, Intrigue, and Psychological Drama.''

Costs $450/seminar; $450/writers workshop; $850/seminar and workshop.

Accommodations A list of nearby lodging establishments is made available.

OXFORD CONFERENCE FOR THE BOOK

Center for the Study of Southern Culture, The University of Mississippi, P.O. Box 1848, University MS 38677-1848. (661)915-5993. Fax: (662)915-5814. E-mail: mheh@olemiss.edu. Web site: www.olemiss.edu/depts/south. **Contact:** Ann J. Abadie, associate director. Estab. 1993. Conference held March 22-24, 2007. Average attendance: 300-400. Since its inauguration, the conference has celebrated books, writing, and reading, and has also dealt with practical concerns on which the literary arts and the humanities depend, including literacy, freedom of expression, and the book trade itself. Beginning in 1999, the conference has been open to the public without charge and broadcast on cable. Each conference presents 20-50 speakers, mostly writers (poets, literary fiction, popular fiction, nonfiction authors, academic authors, children's authors, critics, reviewers), but also editors, agents, librarians, literacy volunteers/organizers, booksellers, and book technology experts. The conference is held in the university's new performing arts center, a campus facility with 1,000 seats. It is located near the town of Oxford. **Previous agents have included:** Julian Bach, Liz Darhansoff, Leigh Feldman, Sheldon Fogelman, David Gernert, Ronald Goldfarb, Wendy Weil, Amy Williams.

Accommodations ''We provide a list of local hotels and arrange for a block of rooms for speakers and early conference registrants at the Downtown Inn, a motel near the town square. We also provide a shuttle service between Oxford and Memphis International Airport, about 60 miles away.''

Additional Information Brochure for SASE or online. Inquiries by fax and e-mail OK.

OZARK CREATIVE WRITERS CONFERENCE

ETSU-Box 23115, Johnson City TN 37614. (423)929-1049. E-mail: ozarkcreativewriters@earthlink.net. Web site: www.ozarkcreativewriters.org. **Contact:** Chrissy Willis, president. Estab. 1975. Annual conference held the second weekend in October. Includes programs for all types of writing. **Previous speakers have included:** Dan Slater (Penguin Putnam); Stephan Harrigan (novelist/screenwriter); Christopher Vogler.

Accommodations Special conference rates available at the Inn of the Ozarks in Eureka Springs, Arkansas.

Additional Information ''The conference has a friendly atmosphere and conference speakers are available. Many speakers return to the conference for the companionship of writers and speakers.'' Brochures available for SASE.

ROMANTIC TIMES CONVENTION

55 Bergen St., Brooklyn NY 11201. (718)237-1097 or (800)989-8816, ext. 12. Fax: (718)624-2526. E-mail: jocarol @rtconvention.com. Web site: www.rtconvention.com. **Contact:** Jo Carol Jones. Annual conference held in April. Features 125 workshops, agent and editor appointments, a book fair, and more.

Costs $439/convention; $200/early bird registration; $150/preconvention program (only $50 if also attending the convention).

SANDHILLS WRITERS CONFERENCE

E-mail: akellman@aug.edu. Web site: www.sandhills.aug.edu. **Contact:** Anthony Kellman, director. Annual conference held the third weekend in March. Covers fiction, poetry, children's literature, nonfiction, plays, and songwriting. Located on the campus of Augusta State University in Georgia. Agents and editors will be speaking at the event.

Accommodations Several hotels are located near the university.

SLEUTHFEST

MWA Florida Chapter. E-mail: bob@bob-williamson.com; sharonpotts@aol.com. Web site: www.mwa-florida.org/sleuthfest. **Contact:** Bob Williamson, Sharon Potts. Annual conference held in March. Four-day conference for writers of mystery and crime fiction featuring hands-on workshops, 4 tracks of writing and business panels, and 2 keynote speakers. Also offers agent and editor appointments and paid manufscript critiques.

⧈ SOUTHEASTERN WRITERS WORKSHOP

P.O. Box 82115, Athens GA 30608. E-mail: purple@southeasternwriters.com. Web site: www.southeasternwriters.com. **Contact:** Tim Hudson. Estab. 1975. Held annually the third week in June at Epworth-by-the-Sea, St. Simons Island, GA. Workshop duration: 4 days. Workshop size: Limited to 100 students. Classes are offered in all areas of writing, including fiction, poetry, nonfiction, inspirational, juvenile, specialty writing, and others. The faculty is comprised of some of the most successful authors from throughout the southeast and the country. Agent-in-Residence is available to meet with participants. Up to 3 free ms evaluations and critique sessions are also available to participants.

Costs 2005 tuition was $305; on-site accommodations (including meals) ranged from $360/double to $550/single in a variety of motel-style rooms. Meals are served cafeteria style.

Additional Information Multiple contests with cash prizes are open to participants. Registration brochure available in March—e-mail or send a SASE. Full information including registration material is avilable on the Web site.

WORDS & MUSIC

624 Pirates Alley, New Orleans LA 70116. (504)586-1609. Fax: (504)522-9725. E-mail: faulkhouse@aol.com. Web site: www.wordsandmusic.org. **Contact:** Rosemary James DeSalvo. Estab. 1997. Annual conference held in November. Conference duration: 5 days. Average attendance: 350-400. Presenters include authors, agents, editors and publishers. **Agents/speakers who appear regularly include:** Deborah Grosvenor, Jenny Bent, Jeff Kleinman, Amy Williams, Michael Murphy. Agents are available for meetings with attendees.

Costs $375 tuition fee.

Accommodations Hotel Monteleone in New Orleans.

WRITING TODAY

Birmingham-Southern College, Box 549066, Birmingham AL 35254. (205)226-4922. Fax: (205)226-4931. E-mail: agreen@bsc.edu. Web site: www.writingtoday.org. **Contact:** Annie Greene. Estab. 1978. Annual conference held March 9-10, 2007. Average attendance: 300-350. "This is a 2-day conference with approximately 18 workshops, lectures, and readings. We try to offer sessions in short fiction, novels, poetry, children's literature, magazine writing, songwriting, and general information of concern to aspiring writers, such as publishing, agents, markets, and research. The conference is sponsored by Birmingham-Southern College and is held on campus in classrooms and lecture halls." **Previous agents/speakers have included:** Eudora Welty, Pat Conroy, Ernest Gaines, Ray Bradbury, Erskine Caldwell, John Barth, Galway Kinnell, Edward Albee, Horton Foote, William Styron.

Costs $150 for both days (includes lunches, reception, morning coffee and rolls).

Accommodations Attendees must arrange their own transporation and accommodations.

Additional Information For an additional charge, poetry and short story critiques are offered for interested writers who request and send mss by the deadline. The conference also sponsors the Hackney Literary Competition Awards for poetry, short stories, and novels.

MIDWEST (IL, IN, KY, MI, OH)

ANTIOCH WRITERS' WORKSHOP

P.O. Box 494, Yellow Springs OH 45387. (937)475-7357. E-mail: info@antiochwritersworkshop.com. Web site: www.antiochwritersworkshop.com. **Contact:** Laura Carlson. Estab. 1984. Annual conference held in July. Average attendance: 80. Workshop focuses on poetry, scholarly nonfiction, literary fiction, mystery, memoir, and romance. Workshop is located on the Antioch College campus in the village of Yellow Springs. **Previous faculty/speakers have included:** Sue Grafton, Mary Grimm, Lucrecia Guerrero, Jeff Gundy, Ralph Keyes, Michel Marriott, Sharon Short, Tim Waggoner, Larry Beinhart, Crystal Wilson Harris. Agents will be speaking and available for meetings with attendees.

Costs $735.

Accommodations Accommodations are available at local hotels.

Additional Information Optional ms critique is $70. Phone or e-mail for a free brochure.

⧈ BACKSPACE WRITERS CONFERENCE

P.O. Box 454, Washington MI 48094-0454. Phone/Fax: (586)532-9652. E-mail: karendionne@bksp.org. Web site: www.backspacewritersconference.com. **Contact:** Karen Dionne, Christopher Graham. Estab. 2005. Annual

2-day conference held in June or July. Average attendance: 150. Conference focuses on all genres of fiction. Offers query letter workshop, writing workshop, and panels with agents, editors, marketing experts, and authors. **Previous agents/speakers have included:** Jeff Kleinman, Richard Curtis, Jenny Bent, Dan Lazar, Miriam Goderich, Kristin Nelson, Joe Veltre, Jessica Faust.

Costs $285 (includes 2-day, 2-track program and refreshments on both days). Banquet tickets cost $95.

Accommodations The Algonquin Hotel offers a limited number of onsite rooms at $269/night, plus taxes.

Additional Information This is a high-quality conference, with much of the program geared toward agented and published authors. Afternoon mixers each day afford plenty of networking opportunities. Scheduled 10-minute one-on-one pitch sessions are also available. Brochure available online, or request information via fax or e-mail.

THE COLUMBUS WRITERS CONFERENCE

P.O. Box 20548, Columbus OH 43220. (614)451-3075. Fax: (614)451-0174. E-mail: angelapl28@aol.com. Website: www.creativevista.com. **Contact:** Angela Palazzolo, director. Estab. 1993. Annual conference held in August. Average attendance: 350. In addition to literary agent and editor consultations, the conference offers a wide variety of fiction and nonfiction topics presented by writers, editors, and literary agents. Writing topics have included novel, short story, children's, young adult, science fiction, fantasy, humor, mystery, playwriting, screenwriting, personal essay, travel, humor, cookbook, technical, magazine writing, query letter, corporate, educational, and greeting cards. Other topics for writers include finding and working with an agent, targeting markets, research, time management, obtaining grants, and writers' colonies. **Previous agents/speakers have included:** Donald Maass, Jeff Herman, Andrea Brown, Jennifer DeChiara, Jeff Kleinman, Rita Rosenkranz, Simon Lipskar, Doris S. Michaels, Sheree Bykofsky, Lee K. Abbott, Lore Segal, Mike Harden, Oscar Collier, Maureen F. McHugh, Ralph Keyes, Nancy Zafris, Karen Harper, Melvin Helitzer, Kim Meisner, Hallie Ephron, Susan Porter, Les Roberts, Tracey E. Dils, J. Patrick Lewis, Patrick Lubrutto, Brenda Copeland, Tracy Bernstein.

Costs For registration fees or to receive a brochure (available mid-summer), check the Web site or contact the conference by e-mail, phone, fax, or postal mail.

GREEN RIVER WRITERS NOVELS IN PROGRESS WORKSHOP

2011 Lauderdale Rd., Louisville KY 40205. E-mail: nipw@greenriverwriters.org. Web site: www.nipw.org. **Contact:** Jeff Yocom, director. Estab. 1991. Annual conference held the third week of March. Conference duration: 1 week. Average attendance: 50. Open to persons, college age and above, who are at any stage of writing a mainstream, genre, or literary novel. Short fiction collections are also welcome. Site is the campus of Spalding University. Meetings and classes are held in nearby classrooms. Parks, restaurants, and shopping are available nearby.

Costs $299/week of seminars; $449/seminars and personal instruction. Personal instruction includes individual mentoring with published instructor, peer critique sessions, and one-on-one meetings with visiting agents and editors. A discount is given for early registration. Does not include meals.

Accommodations Graduate dormitory housing (private rooms with shared showers and restrooms) are available for $18/night. Conference organizers can provide local hotel information if necessary.

Additional Information Participants send 50 pages of ms with 3-page synopsis and $150 deposit, which applies to tuition. Conference brochures are available on request. Visit Web site for additional details.

INDIANA UNIVERSITY WRITERS' CONFERENCE

464 Ballantine Hall, Bloomington IN 47405. (812)855-1877. E-mail: writecon@indiana.edu. Web site: www.indiana.edu/~writecon. Estab. 1940. Annual conference held in June. Participants in the week-long conference join faculty-led workshops (fiction, creative nonfiction, poetry), take classes, engage in one-on-one consultations with authors, and attend a variety of reading and social events." **Previous speakers have included:** Raymond Carver, Mark Doty, Robert Olen Butler, Aimee Bender, Brenda Hillman, Li-Young Lee.

Costs $300/classes only; $500/classes and 1 workshop (does not include food or housing). Scholarships are available.

Accommodations "We offer special conference rates for both the Indian Memorial Union Hotel and dorm facilities on site."

Additional Information "In order to be accepted in a workshop, the writer must submit the work they would like critiqued. Work is evaluated before the applicant is accepted. Conference brochures/guidelines available online or for SASE in January.

ℕ LOVE IS MURDER

E-mail: hanleyliz@aol.com. Web site: www.loveismurder.net. **Contact:** Hanley Kanar. Annual conference held in February for readers, writers, and fans of mystery, suspense, thriller, romantic suspense, dark fiction, and true crime. Published authors provide ms critiques; editors/agents participate in pitch sessions. Attorneys, criminal justice experts, forensic scientists, and phsycisans also attend.

Costs $217 before November 11; $247 after November 11 (includes conference activities, breakfast, lunch, Friday reception, Saturday banquet, late-night events, program book). Extra sessions/events and partial registration are also available.

Accommodations O'Hare Wyndham hotel in Rosemont IL.

Additional Information Sponsors Reader's Choice Awards for best first novel, historical novel, series, crime-related nonfiction, private investigator/police procedural, paranormal/science fiction/horror, traditional/amateur sleuth, suspense thriller, romance/fantasy, and short story.

ℕ MAGNA CUM MURDER XIII

The Mid America Crime Writing Festival, The E.B. and Bertha C. Ball Center, Ball State University, Muncie IN 47306. (765)285-8975. Fax: (765)747-9566. E-mail: magnacummurder@yahoo.com. Web site: www.magnacummurder.com. **Contact:** Kathryn Kennison. Estab. 1994. Annual conference held October 27-29. Average attendance: 350. Festival for readers and writers of crime writing. Held in the Horizon Convention Center and Historic Hotel Roberts.

Costs $195 (includes continental breakfasts, boxed lunches, opening reception, Saturday evening banquet).

OF DARK & STORMY NIGHTS

Mystery Writers of America—Midwest Chapter, P.O. Box 6804, South Bend IN 46660-6804. E-mail: jdams@jeannedams.com. Web site: www.mwamidwest.org; www.ofdarkandstormynights.com. **Contact:** Jeanne Dams. Estab. 1982. Annual workshop held in June. Workshop duration: 1 day. Average attendance: 200. Covers fiction, nonfiction, scriptwriting, children, and young adult. Dedicated to writing mystery fiction and crime-related nonfiction. Workshops and panels are on plotting, dialogue, promotion, writers' groups, dealing with agents, synopsis and manuscript presentation, and various technical aspects of crime and mystery. Held at a hotel in the suburbs of Chicago. **Previous agents/speakers have included:** Kimberley Cameron (Reese Halsey North), Javan Kienzle, Victoria Houston, William X. Kienzele, Jay Bonansinga, Brandon DuBois, S.J. Rozan, Barbara D'Amato, Joe Hensley, Hariette Gillem Robinet, Michael Raleigh, James Brewer, Jeremiah Healy. Agents will be speaking and available for meetings with attendees.

Additional Information ''We accept up to 30 pages of your manuscript for critique (costs $50). Writers meet with critics during the workshop for one-on-one discussions.'' Brochures available for SASE after January 1.

READERS & WRITERS HOLIDAY CONFERENCE

Central Ohio Fiction Writers, P.O. Box 1981, Westerville OH 43086-1981. E-mail: mollygbg@columbus.rr.com. Web site: www.cofw.org. **Contact:** Molly Greenberg, conference chair. Estab. 1991. Annuall conference held in October. The conference is designed to address the needs of writers in all genres of fiction. It explores fiction-writing trends and discusses the business and the craft of writing.

Accommodations Attendees are given discounted hotel accommodations.

ℕ WESTERN RESERVE WRITERS' CONFERENCE

Lakeland Community College, 7700 Clocktower Dr., Kirtland OH 44060-5198. (440)525-7116 or (800)589-8520. E-mail: deencr@aol.com. Web site: www.lakelandcc.edu. **Contact:** Deanna Adams, contest coordinator. Estab. 1983. Bi-annual conference held in March and September. Average attendance: 120. Conference covers fiction, nonfiction, business of writing, children, sci-fi/fantasy, women's fiction, mysteries, poetry, short stories, etc. Classes take place on a community college campus. Agents will be available for meetings with attendees.

Costs $55 for March mini-conference (half day); $75 for September all-day conference. Agent consultations will be an additional cost.

Additional Information Presenters are veterans in their particular genres. There will be a prestigious keynote speaker at the September conference. Brochures/guidelines available on Web site 6 weeks prior to conference. Inquiries by e-mail OK.

THE WOMEN WRITERS CONFERENCE

232 E. Maxwell St., Lexington KY 40506. (859)257-2874. E-mail: wwk.info@gmail.com. Web site: www.thewomenwritersconference.org. **Contact:** Rebecca Howell, Sarah Wylie Ammerman. Estab. 1979. Conference held April 20-23. Programming is presented in a festival atmosphere and includes small-group workshops, panel discussions, master classes, readings, film screenings, and performances. Presenters include: Sara Vowell, Patricia Smith, Hayden Herrera, Diane Gilliam Fisher, Jawole Willa Jo Zollar and the Urban Bush Woman, Sonia Sanchez, Heather Raffo, Mabel Maney, Phoebe Gloeckner, Lauren Weinstein, Kim Ganter, Jane Vandenburgh, Alex Beauchamp.

Additional Information Visit the Web site to register and get more information.

NORTH CENTRAL (IA, MN, NE, ND, SD, WI)

BOUCHERCON 37
E-mail: bouchercon2006@supranet.net. Web site: www.bouchercon.com. Estab. 1970. Annual convention held in late September. Average attendance: 1,500. Focus is on mystery, suspense, thriller, and true crime novels. **Previous agents/speakers have included:** Lawrence Block, Jeremiah Healy, James Lee Burke, Ruth Rendell, Ian Rankin, Michael Connelly, Eileen Dreyer, Earl Emerson. Agents will be speaking and available for informal meetings with attendees.
Costs $185 registration fee.
Accommodations Attendees must make their own transportation arrangements. Special room rate is available at the Madison Concourse in Madison, Wisconsin.
Additional Information The Bookroom is a focal point of the convention. Forty specialty dealers are expected to exhibit, and collectables range from hot-off-the-press bestsellers to 1930s pulp; from fine editions to reading copies. Conference brochures/guidelines are available for SASE or by telephone. Inquiries by e-mail and fax OK.

GREAT LAKES WRITER'S WORKSHOP
Alverno College, 3400 S. 43rd St., P.O. Box 343922, Milwaukee WI 53234-3922. (414)382-6176. Fax: (414)382-6332. Website: www.alverno.edu. **Contact:** Nancy Krase. Estab. 1985. Annual workshop held June 23-24. Average attendance: 100. Workshop focuses on a variety of subjects, including fiction, writing for magazines, freelance writing, writing for children, poetry, marketing, etc. Participants may select individual workshops or opt to attend the entire weekend session. The workshop is held at Alverno College in Milwaukee, Wisconsin.
Costs In the past, the entire program cost $115 (includes continental breakfast and lunch with the keynote author).
Accommodations Attendees must make their own travel arrangments. Accommodations are available on campus; rooms are in residence halls. There are also hotels in the surrounding area.
Additional Information Brochures are available online or for SASE after March. Inquiries by fax OK.

IOWA SUMMER WRITING FESTIVAL
C215 Seashore Hall, University of Iowa, Iowa City IA 52242. (319)335-4160. Fax: (319)335-4039. E-mail: iswfestival@uiowa.edu. Web site: www.uiowa.edu/~iswfest. **Contact:** Amy Margolis, director. Estab. 1987. Annual festival held in June and July. Workshops are 1 week or a weekend. Average attendance: Limited to 12 people/class, with over 1,500 participants throughout the summer. Held on the University of Iowa campus. "We offer courses across the genres: novel, short story, essay, poetry, playwriting, screenwriting, humor, travel, writing for children, memoir, and women's writing." **Previous agents/speakers have included:** Lee K. Abbott, Susan Power, Lan Samantha Chang, Gish Jen, Abraham Verghese, Robert Olen Butler, Ethan Canin, Clark Blaise, Gerald Stern, Donald Justice, Michael Dennis Browne, Marvin Bell, Hope Edelman. Guest speakers are undetermined at this time.
Costs $475-500/week; $225/weekend workshop. Housing and meals are separate.
Accommodations Iowa House: $75/night; Sheraton: $88/night (rates subject to change).
Additional Information Brochure/guidelines are available in February. Inquiries by fax and e-mail OK.

SINIPEE WRITERS' WORKSHOP
Loras College, 1450 Alta Vista, Dubuque IA 52004-0178. (563)588-7139. Fax: (563)588-4962. E-mail: chris.neuhaus@loras.edu. Web site: www.loras.edu. **Contact:** Chris Neuhaus, administrative assistant. Director Emeritus: John Tigges. Estab. 1985. Annual workshop held in April. Average attendance: 50-75. Loras College campus holds a unique atmosphere and everyone seems to love the relaxed and restful mood it inspires. This in turn carries over to the workshop, where friendships are made that last, in addition to learning and experiencing what other writers have gone through to attain success in their chosen field.
Costs $80 for advance registration; $90 at the door. Discounted rates available for persons 65 and over and for full-time college students.
Accommodations Lodging information is available for out-of-town participants.
Additional Information See Web site after February 1 for updates. Offers The John Tigges Writing Contest for short fiction, nonfiction, and poetry.

◉ SPRING WRITER'S FESTIVAL
University of Wisconsin-Milwaukee, School of Continuing Education, 161 W. Wisconsin Ave., Suite 6000, Milwaukee WI 53203. (414)227-3311. Fax: (414)227-3146. E-mail: aomeara@uwm.edu. Web site: www3.uwm.edu/sce. **Contact:** Anne O'Meara. Annual conference held in April. Features readings, craft workshops, panels, ms reviews, preconference intensive workshops, and pitch sessions with literary agents. **Previous agents/**

speakers have included: Joanna MacKenzie, Alec Yoshio MacDonald, A. Manette Ansay, Liam Callanan, C.J. Hribal, Kelly James-Enger.

Costs $234 before March 27; $259 after March 27; $270 at the door (includes Friday dinner, Saturday/Sunday breakfast and lunch, Saturday reception). Preconference intensive workshops are $89; ms reviews are $85.

Accommodations A block of rooms ($99) has been reserved at the Residence Inn by Marriot in downtown Milwaukee.

ℕ UNIVERSITY OF WISCONSIN AT MADISON WRITERS INSTITUTE

610 Langdon St., Madison WI 53703. (608)262-3447. Fax: (608)265-2475. Web site: www.dcs.wisc.edu/lsa. **Contact:** Christine DeSmet, director. Estab. 1990. Annual conference held April 28-29, 2007. Average attendance: 200. Conference on fiction and nonfiction held at University of Wisconsin at Madison. Guest speakers are published authors, editors, and agents.

Costs Approximately $205 for 2 days; critiques and pitch meetings will cost more.

Accommodations Information on accommodations is sent with registration confirmation. Critiques are available. Conference brochures/guidelines are available online.

ℕ WISCONSIN BOOK FESTIVAL

222 S. Bedford St., Suite F, Madison WI 53703. (608)262-0706. Fax: (608)263-7970. E-mail: alison@wisconsinbo okfestival.org. Web site: www.wisconsinbookfestivalorg. **Contact:** Alison Jones Chaim, director. Estab. 2002. Annual festival held in October. Conference duration: 5 days. The festival features readings, lectures, book discussions, writing workshops, live interviews, children's events, and more. **Previous authors/speakers have included:** Phillip Gourevitch, Myla Goldberg, Harvey Pekar, Audrey Niffenegger, Billy Collins, Tim O'Brien, Isabel Allende.

Costs All festival events are free.

Accommodations The Madison Concourse Hotel.

WISCONSIN REGIONAL WRITERS' ASSOCIATION CONFERENCES

E-mail: vpresident@wrwa.net. Web site: www.wrwa.net. **Contact:** Nate Scholze, vice president. Estab. 1948. Conferences held in May and September. Conference duration: 1-2 days. Provides workshops for all genres, including fiction, nonfiction, scriptwriting, and poetry. Presenters include authors, agents, editors, and publishers. **Previous agents/speakers have included:** Marcia Preston (*Byline Magazine*), Richard Lederer, Abby Frucht.

Additional Information Brochure available for SASE or online. Inquiries by e-mail OK.

SOUTH CENTRAL (CO, KS, MO, NM, OK, TX)

AGENTS AND EDITORS CONFERENCE

Writers' League of Texas, 1501 W. Fifth St., Suite E-2, Austin TX 78703. (512)499-8914. Fax: (512)499-0441. E-mail: wlt@writersleague.org. Web site: www.writersleague.org. **Contact:** Kristy Bordine, membership director. Estab. 1982. Annual 3-day conference held in the summer. Average attendance 300. Conference provides writers with the opportunity to meet top literary agents and editors from New York and the West Coast. Topics include: finding and working with agents and publishers, writing and marketing fiction and nonfiction, dialogue, characterization, voice, research, basic and advanced fiction writing, the business of writing, and workshops for genres. **Previous agents/speakers have included:** Malaika Adero, Stacey Barney, Sha-Shana Crichton, Jessica Faust, Dena Fischer, Mickey Freiberg, Jill Grosjean, Anne Hawkins, Jim Hornfischer, Jennifer Joel, David Hale Smith, Elisabeth Weed. Agents will be speaking and available for meetings with attendees.

Costs $220-275.

Additional Information Contests and awards programs are offered separately. Brochures/guidelines are available on request.

ASPEN SUMMER WORDS LITERARY FESTIVAL & WRITING RETREAT

Aspen Writers' Foundation, 110 E. Hallam St., #116, Aspen CO 81611. (970)925-3122. Fax (970)920-5700. E-mail: info@aspenwriters.org. Web site: www.aspenwriters.org. **Contact:** Jamie Abbot, director of programs. Estab. 1976. Annual conference held the fourth week of June. Conference duration: 5 days. Average attendance: 120 at writing retreat; 300 at literary festival. Retreat for fiction, poetry, creative nonfiction, magazine writing, travel writing, and literature. Festival includes author readings, craft talks, panel discussions with publishing industry insiders, professional consultations with editors and agents, and social gatherings. **Previous agents/ speakers have included:** Suzanne Gluck, Jonathan Pecarsky, Ken Sherman, Elizabeth Sheinkman, Jody Hotchkiss (agents); Carol Houck Smith, Jordan Pavlin, Joshua Kendall, Hilary Black (editors); Pam Houston, Colum

McCann, Ann Patchett, Mark Salzman, Larry Watson, Anita Shreve (fiction); Frank McCourt, Ted Conover, Madeleine Blais, Eric Schlosser (nonfiction); Jane Hirshfield, Mary Jo Salter, J.D. McClatchy, N. Scott Momaday, Paul Muldoon, Christopher Merrill (poetry); Gary Ferguson (personal essay); Laura Fraser (travel writing); Daniel Glick, Gary Ferguson (magazine writing). **Costs** $375/retreat; $150-195/seminar; $200/festival; $35/professional consultation. **Accommodations** $78-165/night. **Additional Information** Deadline for admission is April 3. Mss should be submitted for review by admissions committee prior to conference. Conference brochures are available for SASE or online.

AUSTIN FILM FESTIVAL & HEART OF FILM SCREENWRITERS CONFERENCE

1604 Nueces St., Austin TX 78701. (800)310-3378 or (512)478-4795. Fax: (512)478-6205. E-mail: info@austinfil mfestival.com. Web site: www.austinfilmfestival.com. **Contact:** Sharmane Johnson, office manager. Estab. 1994. Annual conference held in October. Average attendance: 1,500. The Austin Film Festival & Heart of Film Screenwriters Conference is a nonprofit organization committed to furthering the art, craft, and business of screenwriters, and recognizing their contribution to the filmmaking industry. The 4-day conference presents over 75 panels, roundtables, and workshops that address various aspects of screenwriting and filmmaking. Held at the Driskill and Stephen F. Austin Hotels, located in downtown Austin. **Agents/speakers attending include:** John August (*Charlie and the Chocolate Factory*), William Broyles Jr. (*Jarhead*), Thomas McCarthy (*The Station Agent*), Andrew Stanton (*Finding Nemo*), Lawrence Kasdar (*Raiders of the Lost Arc*), Harold Ranis (*Groundhog Day*), The Coen Brothers (*Fargo*), Bill Wittliff (*The Perfect Storm*). Agents and production companies are in attendance each year. **Costs** 2006 rate: $300 before May 16 (includes entrance to all panels, workshops, and roundtables during the 4-day conference, as well as all films during the 8-night film exhibition, the opening night party, and closing night party). Please look online for other offers. **Accommodations** Discounted rates on hotel accommodations are available to conference attendees if the reservations are made through the Austin Film Festival office. Contact Austin Film Festival for holds, rates, and more information. **Additional Information** The Austin Film Festival is considered one of the most accessible festivals, and Austin is the premiere town for networking because when industry people are here, they are relaxed and friendly. The Austin Film Festival holds annual screenplay/teleplay and film competitions, as well as a Young Filmmakers Program. Check online for competition deadlines and festival and conference information. Inquiries by e-mail and fax OK.

ⓝ THE BAY AREA WRITER'S LEAGUE SPRING FLING WRITING CONFERENCE

P.O. Box 580007, Houston TX 77058. (281)542-6867. E-mail: info@bawl.org. Web site: www.bawl.org. **Contact:** Melinda Porter, president. Annual conference held in April or May at the Houston Yacht Club. **Previous editors/ speakers have included:** Robin T. Popp (author), Leslie Kriewaldt (Barnes & Noble), Brian Kleins (*Writer's Digest*), Margie Lawson (author). **Costs** $50/members; $65/nonmembers.

FRONTIERS IN WRITING

7221 Stagecoach Trail, Amarillo TX 79124. (806)383-4351. E-mail: fiw2006@hotmail.com. Web site: www.panh andleprowriter.org. Estab. 1920. Annual conference held in June. Conference duration: 2 days. Average attendance: 125. Covers screenwriting, children's writing, nonfiction, poetry, and fiction (mystery, romance, mainstream, science fiction, fantasy). **Previous agents/speakers have included:** Devorah Cutler Rubenstein and Scott Rubenstein (editor/broker for screenplays), Andrea Brown (children's literary agent), Elsa Hurley (literary agent), Hillary Sears (editor with Kensington Books). **Costs** 2006 early bird rate was $100/members; $130/nonmembers; $150/nonmember and non early bird. Critique group costs extra. **Accommodations** Special conference room rate is available. **Additional information** Sponsors a contest. Guidelines available for SASE or online.

GLORIETA CHRISTIAN WRITERS CONFERENCE

CLASServices, Inc., 3311 Candelaria NE, Suite I, Albuquerque NM 87107-1952. (800)433-6633. Fax: (505)899-9282. E-mail: info@classervices.com. Web site: www.glorietacwc.com. **Contact:** Linda Jewell, executive director. Estab. 1997. Annual conference held October 11-15. Conference duration: Wednesday afternoon through Sunday lunch. Average attendance: 350. Includes programs for all types of writing. Conference held in the LifeWay Glorieta Conference Center. Agents, editors, and professional writers will be speaking and available for meetings with attendees.

Costs $350/early registration (1 month in advance); $390/program only. Critiques are available for an additional charge.

Accommodations Hotel rooms are available at the LifeWay Glorieta Conference Center. Sante Fe Shuttle offers service from the Albuquerque or Sante Fe airports to the conference center. Hotel rates vary. "We suggest you make airline and rental car reservations early due to other events in the area."

Additional Information Brochures available April 1. Inquiries by phone, fax, or e-mail OK. Visit Web site for updates and current information.

NATIONAL WRITERS ASSOCIATION FOUNDATION CONFERENCE

P.O. Box 4187, Parker CO 80134. (303)841-0246. Fax: (303)841-2607. E-mail: sandywrter@aol.com. Web site: www.nationalwriters.com. **Contact:** Sandy Whelchel, executive director. Estab. 1926. Annual conference held the second week of June in Denver. Conference duration: 3 days. Average attendance: 200-300. Focuses on general writing and marketing.

Costs Approximately $200.

Additional Information Awards for previous contests will be presented at the conference. Conference brochures/guidelines are available online or for SASE.

NETWO WRITERS ROUNDUP

Northeast Texas Writers Organization, P.O. Box 411, Winfield TX 75493. (903)856-6724. E-mail: netwomail@netwo.org. Web site: www.netwo.org. **Contact:** Galand Nuchols, president. Estab. 1987. Annual conference held in April. Conference duration: 2 days. Presenters include agents, writers, editors, and publishers.

Costs $60 (discount offered for early registration).

Additional Information Conference is co-sponsored by the Texas Commission on the Arts. See Web site for current updates.

THE NEW LETTERS WEEKEND WRITERS CONFERENCE

University of Missouri-Kansas City, College of Arts and Sciences Continuing Education Division, 215 4825 Troost Bldg., 5100 Rockhill Rd., Kansas City MO 64110-2499. (816)235-2736. Fax: (816)235-2611. E-mail: newletters@umkc.edu. Web site: www.newletters.org. **Contact:** Betsy Beasley, Sharon Seaton. Estab. 1970s (as The Longboat Key Writers Conference). Annual conference held in early June. Conference duration: 3 days. Average attendance: 60. The conference brings together talented writers in many genres for lectures, seminars, readings, workshops, and individual conferences. The emphasis is on craft and the creative process in poetry, fiction, screenwriting, playwriting, and journalism, but the program also deals with matters of psychology, publications, and marketing. The conference is appropriate for both advanced and beginning writers. The conference meets at the beautiful Diastole conference center of The University of Missouri-Kansas City. Two- and 3-credit hour options are available by special permission of the instructor.

Costs Participants may choose to attend as a noncredit student or they may attend for 1 hour of college credit from the University of Missouri-Kansas City. Conference registration includes continental breakfasts and Saturday and Sunday lunch.

Accommodations Registrants are responsible for their own transportation, but information on area accommodations is available.

Additional Information Those registering for college credit are required to submit a ms in advance. Ms reading and critique is included in the credit fee. Those attending the conference for noncredit also have the option of having their ms critiqued for an additional fee. Conference brochures/guidelines are available for SASE after March. Inquiries by e-mail and fax OK.

ⓝ OKLAHOMA WRITERS' FEDERATION CONFERENCE

1213 E. 9th, Sand Springs OK 74063. (918)519-6707. Fax: (918)245-0090. E-mail: conferenceinfo@owfi.org; rangerjudy@cox.net. Web site: www.owfi.org. **Contact:** Judy Miller Snavely, publicity chair. Estab. 1968. Annual conference held in May. Average attendance: 500. Features writers, editors, agents, and informative programs to help authors write well and get published. Editor/agent appointments are available. **Previous agents/speakers have included:** Daniel Lazar (Writer's House), Robyn Russell (Amy Rennert Agency), Bryan Painter (*The Oklahoman*), Mike Sanders (Alpha Books).

Costs $125 before April 15; $150 after April 15 (includes sessions, dinner/banquet). Per-day conference sessions are $60 (no dinner).

Accommodations Embassy Suites Hotel in Oklahoma City (within walking distance of the airport).

Additional Information "We have a writing contest with 27 categories that pays cash prizes."

PIKES PEAK WRITERS CONFERENCE

4164 Austin Bluffs Pkwy., #246, Colorado Springs CO 80918. (719)531-5723. E-mail: info@ppwc.net. Web site: www.ppwc.net. Estab. 1993. Annual conference held in April. Conference duration: 3 days. Average attendance:

400. Workshops, presentations, and panels focus on writing and publishing mainstream and genre fiction (romance, science fiction/fantasy, suspense/thrillers, action/adventure, mysteries, children's, young adult). Agents and editors are available for meetings with attendees on Saturday.
Costs $260-325/PPW members; $285-350/nonmembers (includes all meals).
Accommodations Wyndham Colorado Springs holds a block of rooms for conference attendees until late March at a special rate.
Additional Information Readings with critiques are available on Friday afternoon. Brochures available in January. Inquiries by e-mail OK. Registration form available online. Also offers a contest for unpublished writers; entrants need not attend conference. Deadline: November 1. See Web site for entry form and rules.

ROCKY MOUNTAIN FICTION WRITERS COLORADO GOLD
P.O. Box 260244, Denver CO 80226-0244. Web site: www.rmfw.org. Estab. 1983. Annual conference held in September. Conference duration: 3 days. Average attendance: 250. Themes include general novel-length fiction, genre fiction, contemporary romance, mystery, science fiction/fantasy, mainstream, history. **Previous agents/ speakers have included:** Terry Brooks, Dorothy Cannell, Patricia Gardner Evans, Diane Mott Davidson, Constance O'Day, Connie Willis, Clarissa Pinkola Estes, Michael Palmer, Jennifer Unter, Margaret Marr, Ashley Kraas, Andren Barzvi. Approximately 4 editors and 5 agents attend annually.
Costs $189-229, depending on when you sign up (includes conference, reception, banquet). Editor workshops cost an additional $20-30.
Accommodations Special rates will be available at the Renaissance Denver Hotel.
Additional Information Editor conducted workshops are limited to 10 participants for critique, with auditing available.

ROMANCE WRITERS OF AMERICA NATIONAL CONFERENCE
16000 Stuebner Airline Rd., Suite 140, Spring TX 77379. (832)717-5200. Fax: (832)717-5201. E-mail: info@rwanational.org. Web site: www.rwanational.org. **Contact:** Nicole Kennedy, professional relations manager. Executive Director: Allison Kelley. Estab. 1981. Annual conference held July 11-14. Average attendance: 2,000. Over 100 workshops on writing, researching, and the business side of being a working writer. Publishing professionals attend and accept appointments. Keynote speaker is a renowned romance writer. Conference will take place at the Hyatt Regency in Dallas.
Costs $340-390/members; $415-465/nonmembers (depending on when you register).
Additional Information Annual RITA awards are presented for published romance authors. Annual Golden Heart awards are presented for unpublished romance writers.

THE SCREENWRITING CONFERENCE IN SANTA FE
P.O. Box 29762. Santa Fe NM 87592. (866)424-1501. Fax: (505)424-8207. E-mail: writeon@scsfe.com. Web site: www.scsfe.com. **Contact:** Larry N. Stouffer, founder. Estab. 1999. Annual conference held the week following Memorial Day. Average attendance: 175. The conference is divided into 2 components: The Screenwriting Symposium, designed to teach the art and craft of screenwriting, and The Hollywood Connection, which speaks to the business aspects of screenwriting. Held at The Lodge in Santa Fe.
Costs $695 for The Screenwriting Symposium; $200 for The Hollywood Connection. Early discounts are available. Includes 9 hours of in-depth classroom instruction, over 2 dozen workshops, panel discussions, a screenplay competition, academy labs for advanced screenwriters, live scene readings, and social events.

SOUTHWEST WRITERS CONFERENCE MINI-CONFERENCE SERIES
3721 Morris St. NE, Suite A, Albuquerque NM 87111. (505)265-9485. Fax: (505)265-9483. E-mail: swwriters@juno.com. Web site: www.southwestwriters.org. Estab. 1983. Annual mini-conferences held throughout the year. Average attendance: 50. Speakers include writers, editors, agents, publicists, and producers. All areas of writing, including screenwriting and poetry, are represented.
Costs Fee includes conference sessions and lunch.
Accommodations Usually have official airline and hotel discount rates.
Additional Information Sponsors a contest judged by authors, editors from major publishing houses, and agents from New York, Los Angeles, etc. There are 19 categories. Deadline: May 1. Entry fee is $29/members; $44/ nonmembers. Brochures/guidelines available on Web site or for SASE. Inquiries by e-mail and fax OK. A one-on-one appointment may be set up at the conference with the editor or agent of your choice on a first-registered, first-served basis.

STEAMBOAT SPRINGS WRITERS CONFERENCE
Box 774284, Steamboat Springs CO 80477. (970)879-8079. E-mail: sswriters@cs.com. Web site: www.steamboatwriters.com. **Contact:** Harriet Freiberger, director. Estab. 1982. Annual conference held in mid-July. Conference

duration: 1 day. Average attendance: 35. Featured areas of instruction change each year. Held at the restored train depot home of the Steamboat Springs Arts Council. **Previous agents/speakers have included:** Carl Brandt, Jim Fergus, Avi, Robert Greer, Renate Wood, Connie Willis, Margaret Coel.

Costs $35 prior to June 1; $45 after June 1 (includes seminars, catered luncheon). A pre-conference dinner is also available (limited enrollment).

Additional Information Brochures available in April for SASE. Inquiries by e-mail OK.

ⓝ WOMEN WRITING THE WEST

8547 E. Araphoe Rd., Box J-541, Greenwood Village CO 80112-1436. E-mail: wwwadmin@lohseworks.com. Web site: www.womenwritingthewest.org. **Contact:** Joyce Lohse, Annual conference held the third weekend in October. Covers research, writing techniques, multiple genres, marketing/promotion, and more. Agents and editors will be speaking and available for one-on-one meetings. Conference location changes each year.

WRITERS WORKSHOP IN SCIENCE FICTION

English Department/University of Kansas, Lawrence KS 66045-2115. (785)864-3380. Fax: (785)864-1159. E-mail: jgunn@ku.edu. Web site: www.ku.edu/~sfcenter. **Contact:** James Gunn, professor. Estab. 1985. Annual conference held in late June or early July. Average attendance: 15. Conference for writing and marketing science fiction. Classes meet in university housing on the University of Kansas campus. Workshop sessions operate informally in a lounge. **Previous agents/speakers have included:** Frederik Pohl, Kij Johnson, Chris McKitterick.

Costs Tuition is $400. Housing and meals are not included.

Accommodations Housing information is available. Several airport shuttle services offer reasonable transportation from the Kansas City International Airport to Lawrence. During past conferences, students were housed in a student dormitory at $14/day (double); $28/day (single).

Additional Information Admission to the workshop is by submission of an acceptable story. Two additional stories should be submitted by the middle of June. These 3 stories are distributed to other participants for critiquing and are the basis for the first week of the workshop. One story is rewritten for the second week. Brochures/guidelines are available for SASE. This workshop is intended for writers who have just started to sell their work or need that extra bit of understanding or skill to become a published writer.

ⓝ WRITING FOR THE SOUL

Jerry B. Jenkins Christian Writers Guild, 5525 N. Union Blvd., Suite 200, Colorado Springs CO 80918. (866)495-5177. Fax: (719)495-5181. E-mail: watcheson@christianwritersguild.com. Web site: www.christianwritersguild.com. **Contact:** Wayne Atcheson, admissions manager. Annual conference held February 15-18. Workshops cover fiction, nonfiction, magazine writing, children's books, teen writing, and writing with flare. Appointments with more than 30 agents, publishers, and editors are also available. The keynote speakers are Jerry Jenkins, Tim Lahaye, Liz Curtis Higgs, and Ted Haggard.

Costs $635/members; $795/nonmembers.

Accommodations $145/night at the Broadmoor Hotel in Colorado Springs.

WEST (AZ, CA, HI, NV, UT)

ASA INTERNATIONAL SCREENWRITERS CONFERENCE

269 S. Beverly Dr., Suite 2600, Beverly Hills CA 90212-3807. (866)265-9091. E-mail: asa@goasa.com. Web site: www.goasa.com. **Contact:** John Johnson, director. Estab. 1988. Annual conference held in September in partnership with the San Diego Film Festival. Festival duration: 5 days. Average attendance: 250. "The conference focuses on writers and filmmakers who want to be better storytellers through their scripts and want to know how to successfully market their work to the industry. Attendees go to panels, small group workshops led by a faculty of Hollywood experts, private consultations with faculty members, 4-hour pitch sessions with producers and development representatives, networking parties, film premiers, and a red carpet awards evening with celebrities. **Agents/speakers attending include:** Michael Hauge, Ellen Sandler, Gary Ross, Linda Seger, Syd Field, Shane Black, Aaron Sorkin, Terry Rosio.

Costs Approximately $450 (includes conference, festival, pitch session).

Accommodations Approximately $140/single; $70/double.

Additional Information "This is the premier screenwriting conference of its kind and the longest running in the world. Go online for more information."

ⓝ BIG SUR WRITING WORKSHOPS

Henry Miller Library, Highway One, Big Sur CA 93920. Phone/Fax: (831)667-2574. E-mail: magnus@henrymiller.org. Web site: www.henrymiller.org/CWW. **Contact:** Magnus Toren, executive director. Annual workshops

held in December for children's/young adult writing and in March for adult fiction and nonfiction.
Costs $595 (includes meals, lodging, workshop, Saturday evening reception); $385 if you don't need lodging.
Accommodations Big Sur Lodge in Pfeiffer State Park.

DESERT DREAMS

P.O. Box 572, Scottsdale AZ 85252-0572. (866)267-2249. E-mail: desertdreams@desertroserwa.org. Web site: desertroserwa.org. **Contact:** Susan Lanier-Graham, conference coordinator. Estab. 1986. Conference held every other April. Conference duration: 3 days. Average attendance: 250. Covers marketing, fiction, screenwriting, and research. **Previous agents/speakers have included:** Jennifer Crusie, Debra Dixon, Lisa Gardner, Miriam Kriss, Debbie Macomber, Susan Mallery, Bob Mayer, Pattie Steele-Perkins, Paige Wheeler. Speakers change at each conference. Agents will be speaking and available for meetings with attendees.
Costs $169-225/members; $189-225/nonmembers, depending on when you sign up (includes meals, seminars, appointments with editors and agents).
Accommodations Discounted rates for conference attendees negotiated at Chaparral Suites Hotel in Scottsdale.
Additional Information Inquiries by e-mail OK. Visit Web site for updates and complete details.

N EAST OF EDEN WRITERS CONFERENCE

P.O. Box 3254, Santa Clara CA 95055. (408)247-1286. Fax: (408)927-5224. E-mail: eastofeden@southbaywriters. com. Web site: www.southbaywriters.com. **Contact:** Beth Proudfoot, director. Estab. 2000. Biannual conference held in September. Average attendance: 300. "We try to cover most genres in our writing classes and panels. We usually have about 15 literary agents, in addition to a few local publishers. See our Web site for this year's list." Conference sites include the Salinas Community Center, the National Steinbeck Center, and the Steinbeck House.
Costs Varies according to options chosen—from $180 for Saturday only, to $330 for "the works." Seminars and meals are included.
Accommodations "We have made special conference accommodations available at the Laurel Inn ($65/night in 2006). We have a list of local hotels on our Web site for those who wish to make other arrangements."
Additional Information The conference is run by writers/volunteers from the California Writers Club, South Bay Branch. Brochures available for SASE, or request information via e-mail.

N HORROR WRITERS ASSOCIATION ANNUAL CONFERENCE

P.O. Box 50577, Palo Alto CA 94303. E-mail: vp@horror.org; hwa@horror.org. Web site: www.horror.org/ conference. **Contact:** Vice President. Annual conference held in June. Activities include panel discussions, workshops, seminars, and guest speaker presentation—all geared toward horror writers.
Costs $75-100 (includes programming, banquet).
Additional Information The Bram Stoker Awards Banquet recognizes a superior novel, first novel, screenplay, anthology, short story, and more.

N ICE ESCAPE WRITERS CONFERENCE

P.O. Box 8829, Scottsdale CA 85252. (480)236-4314. E-mail: info@iceescape.com. Web site: www.iceescape.c om. **Contact:** Mary Erickson. Estab. 2004. Annual 3-day conference held in March. Average attendance: 400. Focuses on how to get published and book marketing. Held at the Hilton Phoenix East in Mesa, Arizona. Panels cover how to manage TV interviews, promotions, and how to market by both traditional and unconventional ways. **Previous agents/speakers have included:** Rick Frishman, Laura Holka, Ron Pramschuffer, Eric Kampmann, Jeffrey Bowen, Jerry Jenkins.
Costs $65-105 early bird; $130 at door (includes agent consultations, workshops, lectures, consultations with guests, contests, social activities).
Additional Information Brochures available online. Send inquiries via e-mail.

IWWG EARLY SPRING IN CALIFORNIA CONFERENCE

International Women's Writing Guild, P.O. Box 810, Gracie Station, New York NY 10028-0082. (212)737-7536. Fax: (212)737-9469. E-mail: iwwg@iwwg.org. Web site: www.iwwg.org. **Contact:** Hannelore Hahn, executive director. Estab. 1982. Annual conference held March 16-18, 2007 and March 13-15, 2008. Average attendance: 80. Conference promotes creative writing, personal growth, and voice. Site is a redwood forest mountain retreat in Santa Cruz, California.
Costs $330/members; $350/nonmembers for weekend program with room and board; $125 for weekend program without room and board.
Accommodations All at conference site.
Additional Information Conference brochures/guidelines are available for SASE. Inquiries by e-mail and fax OK, or view online.

ⓝ LA JOLLA WRITERS CONFERENCE

P.O. Box 178122, San Diego CA 92177. (858)467-1978. Fax: (858)467-1971. E-mail: jkuritz@san.rr.com. Web site: www.lajollawritersconference.com. **Contact:** Jared Kuritz, co-director. Estab. 2001. Annual 3-day conference held in October. Maximum attendance: 200. "In addition to covering nearly every genre, we also take particular pride in educating our attendees on the business aspect of the book industry by having agents, editors, publishers, publicists, and distributors teach classes. Our conference offers 2 types of classes: lectures sessions that run for 50 minutes, and workshops that run for 110 minutes. Each block period is dedicated to either workshop or lecture-style classes. During each block period, there will be 6-8 classes on various topics from which you can choose to attend. For most workshop classes, you are encouraged to bring written work for review." **Previous agents/speakers have included:** The Andrea Brown Literary Agency, The Dijkstra Agency, Full Circle Literary Group.

Costs $255 early bird; $325 regular (includes access to all classes, keynote addresses, Friday evening reception, Saturday evening reception, author book signing).

Accommodations "We arrange a discounted rate with the hotel that hosts the conference. Please refer to the Web site."

Additional Information "Our conference is completely non-commercial. Our goal is to foster a true learning environment. As such, our faculty is chosen based on their expertise and willingness to make themselves completely accessible to the attendees throughout the conference." Brochure available online. Send inquiries via fax or e-mail.

MAUI WRITERS CONFERENCE

P.O. Box 1118, Kihei HI 96753. (808)879-0061. Fax: (808)879-6233. E-mail: writers@mauiwriters.com. Web site: www.mauiwriters.com. **Contact:** Shannon Tullius. Estab. 1993. Annual conference held at the end of August (Labor Day weekend). Conference duration: 4 days. Conference held at Wailea Marriott Resort. Average attendance: 600. For fiction, nonfiction, poetry, children's, young adult, horror, mystery, romance, science fiction, journalism, and screenwriting. **Previous agents have included:** Kimberley Cameron (The Reece Halsey Agency), Susan Crawford (Crawford Literary Agency), Jillian Manus (Manus & Associates Literary Agency), Jenny Bent (Trident Media Group), Catherine Fowler (Redwood Agency), James D. Hornfischer (Hornfischer Literary Management), Debra Goldstein (The Creative Culture, Inc.). Many of these agents will be at the 2007 conference, where they will be on panels discussing the business of publishing and will be available for one-on-one consultations with aspiring authors.

Additional Information "We offer a comprehensive view of the business of publishing, with over 2,000 consultation slots with industry agents, editors, and screenwriting professionals, as well as workshops and sessions covering writing instruction. Consider attending the MWC Writers Retreat immediately preceding the conference. Write, call or visit our Web site for current updates and full details on all of our upcoming programs."

MENDOCINO COAST WRITERS CONFERENCE

1211 Del Mar Dr., Fort Bragg CA 95437. (707)962-2600, ext. 2167. E-mail: info@mcwc.org. Web site: www.mcwc.org. **Contact:** Barbara Lee, registrar. Estab. 1988. Annual conference held in August. Conference duration: 3 days. Average attendance: 90. Provides workshops for fiction, nonfiction, scriptwriting, children's, mystery, and writing for social change. Held at a small community college campus on the northern Pacific Coast. **Previous agents/speakers have included:** Jandy Nelson, Paul Levine, Sally Werner, John Lescroart, Maxine Schur. Agents will be speaking and available for meetings with attendees.

Costs $300-410 (includes panels, meals, 2 socials with guest readers, 1 public event, 1 day intensive in 1 subject and 2 days of several short sessions.)

Accommodations Information on overnight accommodations is made available. Shared rides from San Francisco Airport are available.

Additional Information Emphasis is on writers who are also good teachers. Brochures available for SASE in January or on Web site. Inquiries by e-mail OK.

MOUNT HERMON CHRISTIAN WRITERS CONFERENCE

P.O. Box 413, Mount Hermon CA 95041-0413. (831)335-4466 or (888)642-2677. Fax: (831)335-9413. E-mail: dtalbott@mhcamps.org; info@mhcamps.org. Web site: www.mounthermon.org/writers. **Contact:** David R. Talbott, director of adult ministries. Estab. 1970. Annual conference held in April. Average attendance: 450. "We are a broad-ranging conference for all areas of Christian writing, including fiction, children's, poetry, nonfiction, magazines, inspirational and devotional writing, books, educational curriculum, and radio and TV scriptwriting. This is a working, how-to conference, with many workshops within the conference involving on-site writing assignments. The conference is sponsored by and held at the 440-acre Mount Hermon Christian Conference Center near San Jose, California, in the heart of the coastal redwoods. The faculty-to-student ratio is about 1 to 6. The bulk of our more than 60 faculty are editors and publisher representatives from major

Christian publishing houses nationwide." **Previous agents/speakers have included:** Janet Kobobel Grant, Chip MacGregor, Karen Solem, T. Davis Bunn, Sally Suart, and others.

Costs $686/economy; $1,029/deluxe (includes tuition, conference sessions, resource notebook, refreshment breaks, room and board). Limited scholarships are available.

Accommodations Registrants stay in hotel-style accommodations. Meals are taken family style, with faculty joining registrants.

Additional Information "The residential nature of our conference makes this a unique setting for one-on-one interaction with faculty/staff. There is also a decided inspirational flavor to the conference, and general sessions with well-known speakers are a highlight." Registrants may submit 2 works for critique in advance of the conference, then have personal interviews with critiquers during the conference. Conference brochures/guidelines are available December 1. All conference information and registration is now online only. Inquiries by e-mail and fax OK. Tapes of past conference workshops are also available.

NO CRIME UNPUBLISHED™ MYSTERY WRITERS' CONFERENCE

Sisters in Crime—Los Angeles Chapter, 1772-J Avenida De Los Arboles, #233, Thousand Oaks CA 91362. E-mail: sistersincrimela@yahoo.com. Web site: www.sistersincrimela.com. Estab. 1995. Annual conference held in June. Conference duration: 1 day. Average attendance: 200. Conference on mystery and crime writing. Usually held in a hotel near the Los Angeles airport. Offers craft and forensic sessions, keynote speaker, luncheon speaker, agent panel, and book signings.

Accommodations Airport shuttle to hotel. Optional overnight stay available.

Additional Information Conference brochure available for SASE.

PIMA WRITERS' WORKSHOP

Pima College, 2202 W. Anklam Rd., Tucson AZ 85709. (520)206-6974. Fax: (520)206-6020. E-mail: mfiles@pima .edu. **Contact:** Meg Files, director. Estab. 1988. Annual conference held in May. Conference duration: 3 days. Average attendance: 300. Covers fiction, nonfiction, poetry, and scriptwriting for beginning or experienced writers. The workshop offers sessions on writing short stories, novels, nonfiction articles and books, children's and juvenile stories, poetry, and screenplays. Sessions are held in the Center for the Arts on Pima Community College's West Campus. **Previous agents/speakers have included:** Larry McMurtry, Barbara Kingsolver, Jerome Stern, Connie Willis, Jack Heffron, Jeff Herman, Robert Morgan. Agents will be speaking and available for meetings with attendees.

Costs $75 (can include ms critique). Participants may attend for college credit, in which case fees are $103 for Arizona residents and $164 for out-of-state residents. Meals and accommodations are not included.

Accommodations Information on local accommodations is made available. Special workshop rates are available at a specified motel close to the workshop site (about $65/night).

Additional Information The workshop atmosphere is casual, friendly, and supportive, and guest authors are very accessible. Readings and panel discussions are offered, as well as talks and manuscript sessions. Participants may have up to 20 pages critiqued by the author of their choice. Mss must be submitted 3 weeks before the workshop. Conference brochure/guidelines available for SASE. Inquiries by e-mail OK.

SAN DIEGO STATE UNIVERSITY WRITERS' CONFERENCE

SDSU College of Extended Studies, 5250 Campanile Dr., San Diego State University, San Diego CA 92182-1920. (619)594-2517. Fax: (619)594-0147. Web site: www.ces.sdsu.edu/writers/index.html. **Contact:** Becky Ryan, extension programs coordinator. Estab. 1984. Annual conference held in January. Conference duration: 2 days. Average attendance: 375. Covers fiction, nonfiction, scriptwriting, and e-books. Held at the Doubletree Hotel in Mission Valley. Each year the conference offers a variety of workshops for the beginner and the advanced writer. This conference allows the individual writer to choose which workshop best suits his/her needs. In addition to the workshops, editor/agent appointments and office hours are provided so attendees may meet with speakers, editors, and agents in small, personal groups to discuss specific questions. A reception is offered Saturday immediately following the workshops where attendees may socialize with the faculty in a relaxed atmosphere. Last year 25 agents attended, in addition to editors and screenwriting experts. Agents will be speaking and available for meetings with attendees.

Costs Approximately $355-395 (includes all conference workshops and office hours, coffee and pastries in the morning, lunch and reception Saturday evening).

Accommodations Doubletree Hotel (800)222-TREE. Attendees must make their own travel arrangements.

Additional Information Editor/agent appointments are private, one-on-one opportunities to meet with editors and agents to discuss your submission. E-mail, call, or write for more information.

N SAN FRANCISCO WRITERS CONFERENCE

1029 Jones St., San Francisco CA 94109. (415)673-0939. Fax: (415)673-0367. E-mail: sfwriterscon@aol.com. Web site: www.sfwriters.org. **Contact:** Michael Larsen, director. Estab. 2003. Annual conference held President's Day weekend in February. Average attendance: 400. Top authors, respected literary agents, and major publishing houses are at the event so attendees can make face-to-face contact with all the right people. Writers of nonfiction and fiction, poetry, and specialty writing (children's books, cookbooks, travel writing) will all benefit from the event. There are important sessions on marketing, self-publishing, and trends in the publishing industry as well. Plus, there's an optional 3-hour session called Speed Dating for Agents where attendees can meet with 20+ agents. **Previous agents/speakers have included:** Gayle Lynds, Jennifer Crusie, Alan Jones, Lalita Tademy, Daisy Maryles, Jamie Raab, Mary Roach, Bob Mayer, Firoozeh Dumas, Zilpha Keatley Snyder, Maja Thomas, Sam Horn. More than 20 agents and editors participate each year, many of which will be available for meeting with attendees.

Costs $595 with price breaks for early registration (includes all sessions, workshops and keynotes, Speed Dating with Editors, Opening Gala at the Top of the Mark, 2 continental breakfasts and 2 lunches). Optional Speed Dating for Agents is $35.

Accommodations The Intercontinental Mark Hopkins Hotel is a historic landmark at the top of Nob Hill in San Francisco. Elegant rooms and first-class service are offered to attendees at the rate of $129/night. The hotel is located so that everyone arriving at the Oakland or San Francisco airport can take BART to either the Embarcadero or Powell Street exit, then walk, or take a Cable Car or taxi directly to the hotel.

Additional Information Present yourself in a professional manner and the contact you will make will be invaluable to your writing career. Brochures and registration available on Web site.

SANTA BARBARA WRITERS CONFERENCE

P.O. Box 6627, Santa Barbara CA 93160. (805)964-0367. E-mail: info@sbwritersconference.com. Web site: www.sbwritersconference.com. **Contact:** Marcia Meier, conference director. Estab. 1973. Annual conference held in June. Average attendance: 450. Covers poetry, fiction, nonfiction, journalism, playwriting, screenplays, travel writing, children's literature, chick lit, humor, and marketing. **Previous agents/speakers have included:** Kenneth Atchity, Michael Larsen, Elizabeth Pomada, Linda Mead, Stuart Miller, Gloria Stern, Don Congdon, Mike Hamilburg, Sandra Dijkstra, Paul Fedorko, Andrea Brown, Deborah Grosvenor. Agents will appear on a panel, plus there will be an agents and editors day where writers can pitch their projects in one-on-one meetings.

Accommodations Fess Parker's Doubletree Resort.

Additional Information Individual critiques are also available. Submit 1 ms of no more than 3,000 words in advance with a SASE. Competitions with awards are sponsored as part of the conference. E-mail or call for brochure and registration forms.

SOCIETY OF CHILDREN'S BOOK WRITERS & ILLUSTRATORS ANNUAL SUMMER CONFERENCE ON WRITING AND ILLUSTRATING FOR CHILDREN

8271 Beverly Blvd., Los Angeles CA 90048-4515. (323)782-1010. Fax: (323)782-1892. E-mail: scbwi@scbwi.org. Web site: www.scbwi.org. **Contact:** Stephen Mooser, president. Estab. 1972. Annual conference held in early August. Conference duration: 4 days. Average attendance: 1,000. Held at the Century Plaza Hotel in Los Angeles. **Previous agents/speakers have included:** Andrea Brown, Steven Malk, Scott Treimel, Ashley Bryan, Bruce Coville, Karen Hesse, Harry Mazer, Lucia Monfried, Russell Freedman. Agents will be speaking and sometimes participate in ms critiques.

Costs Approximately $400 (does not include hotel room).

Accommodations Information on overnight accommodations is made available.

Additional Information Ms and illustration critiques are available. Conference brochures/guidelines are available in June with SASE.

SOUTHERN CALIFORNIA WRITERS' CONFERENCE

1010 University Ave., #54, San Diego CA 92103. (619)233-4651. Fax: (619)641-0029. E-mail: wewrite@writersconference.com. Web site: www.writersconference.com. **Contact:** Michael Steven Gregory, executive director. Estab. 1986. Annual conference held February 17-20 in San Diego and September 29-October 1 in Palm Springs. Conference also held in Los Angeles (dates to be announced). Conference duration: 3 days. Average attendance: 250. Covers fiction and nonfiction, with particular emphasis on reading and critiquing. Offers extensive reading and critiquing workshops by working writers, plus over 3 dozen daytime workshops and no time limit late-night sessions. Agents will be speaking and available for meetings with attendees.

Additional Information Late-night read and critique workshops run until 3 or 4 a.m. Brochures available for SASE or online. Inquiries by e-mail and fax OK.

⚏ SPRING INTO ROMANCE

RWA—San Diego, 12265 Scripps Poway Pkwy., Suite 112-257, Poway CA 92064. E-mail: info@springintoromance.com. Web site: www.springintoromance.com. Annual conference held in March. Features keynote speakers, workshops, and agent/editor pitch sessions. **Previous agents/speakers have included:** Barbara Collins-Rosen-

berg, Mary Sue Seymour, Pam Strickler, Cameron McClure, Bob Mayer, Julia Quinn, Jennifer Crusie, Catherine Coulter.
Costs $220 (includes meals, speakers, workshops).
Accommodations $129 at the San Diego Marriott Mission Valley.

SQUAW VALLEY WRITERS WORKSHOP

P.O. Box 1416, Nevada City CA 95959-1416. (530)470-8440. E-mail: info@squawvalleywriters.org. Web site: www.squawvalleywriters.org. **Contact:** Ms. Brett Hall Jones, executive director. Estab. 1969. Annual conference held the first full week in August. Conference duration: 1 week. Average attendance: 132. Covers fiction, nonfiction, and memoir. Held in Squaw Valley, California—the site of the 1960 Winter Olympics. The workshops are held in a ski lodge at the foot of this spectacular ski area. **Previous agents/speakers have included:** Betsy Amster, Julie Barer, Michael Carlisle, Elyse Cheney, Mary Evans, Christy Fletcher, Theresa Park, B.J. Robbins, Peter Steinberg. Agents will be speaking and available for meetings with attendees.
Costs $750 (includes tuition, dinners). Housing is extra.
Accommodations Single room: $550/week; double room: $350/week per person; multiple room: $210/week per person. Airport shuttle available for additional cost.
Additional Information Brochures available in March for SASE or online. Inquiries by e-mail OK.

N TMCC WRITERS' CONFERENCE

5270 Neil Rd., #216, Reno NV 89502. (775)829-9010. Fax: (775)829-9032. E-mail: mikedcroft@aol.com. Web site: www.tmccwriters.com. **Contact:** Michael Croft, director. Estab. 1991. Annual conference held in April. Average attendance: 125. Focuses on fiction, poetry, and memoir, plus an assortment of other forms of writing, such as screenwriting, thrillers, myseries, and nonfiction. Helt at John Ascuaga's Nugget, which is a large hotel/casino, complete with 7 restaurants, health club and spa, swimming pool, and celebrity showroom. There are always an array of speakers and presenters with impressive literary credentials including agents and editors.
Previous agents/speakers have included: Dorothy Allison, Karen Joy Fowler, James D. Houston, James N. Frey, Gary Short, Jane Hirschfield, Dorrianne Laux, Kim Addonizio. Amy Rennert, Laurie Fox.
Costs Track A ($389) includes 4 days of workshops in fiction, poetry, and memoir, plus afternoon lectures, readings, and talks on the craft of writing and the business of publishing. Track B ($139) includes 2 days of lectures and readings. All participants can attend the writers' reception and the roundtable luncheons, during which attendees can chat with agents.
Accommodations The Nugget offers a special rate and shuttle service to the Reno/Tahoe International Airport, which is less than 20 minutes away.
Additional Information The conference is open to all writers, regardless of their level of experience. Individual workshops meet for 4 mornings and are conducted by the same workshop leader throughout. Every effort is made to see that writers are placed with the appropriate workshop leader. Brochures are available online and mailed in the fall. Information requests can be made via e-mail.

UCLA EXTENSION WRITERS' PROGRAM

10995 Le Conte Ave., #440, Los Angeles CA 90024. (310)825-9415 or (800)388-UCLA. Fax: (310)206-7382. E-mail: writers@uclaextension.edu. Web site: www.uclaextension.org/writers. **Contact:** Cindy Lieberman, program manager. Estab. 1891. Courses are held quarterly as 1-day or intensive weekend workshops, or as 12-week courses. A 4-day Writers Studio is held every February. As the largest and most comprehensive continuing education writing program in the United States, the UCLA Extension Writers' Program is committed to providing the highest quality writing courses possible, on site and online, to a broad-based and culturally diverse community. ''We offer an extraordinary variety of individual courses (over 550 annually), as well as certificate programs to meet the needs of our students. We also offer a screenplay competition, master classes, and script and manuscript consultations. Adult learners study with professional screenwiters, fiction writers, playwrights, poets, nonfiction writers, and writers of children's literature who bring practical experience, theoretical knowledge, and a wide variety of teaching styles and philosophies to the classrooms. Our open admissions policy and supportive atmosphere ensure that all students, whether they seek to write only for themselves or as professionals, are inspired and guided to achieve their best work.''
Costs $95/1-day workshop; $495/full-length courses; $3,250/9-month master classes.
Accommodations Students make their own arrangements. Out-of-town students are encouraged to take online courses.
Additional Information Some advanced-level classes have ms submittal requirements; instructions are detailed in the Writers' Program Quarterly or UCLA Extension course catalog. Inquiries by e-mail and fax OK.

WRANGLING WITH WRITING

Society of Southwestern Authors, P.O. Box 30355, Tucson AZ 85751-0355. (520)546-9382. Fax: (520)296-0409. E-mail: wporter202@aol.com; barbara@clariticom.com. Web site: www.ssa-az.org. **Contact:** Penny Porter, Barbara

Stanura. Estab. 1972. Annual 2-day conference held in January. Maximum attendance: 400. Conference offers 30 workshops covering all genres of writing, plus pre-scheduled one-on-one interviews with 30 agents, editors, and publishers representing major book houses and magazines. **Previous agents/speakers have included:** William F. Nolan, Ben Bova, Lee Harris, Bruce Holland Rogers, Billy Collins, Sam Swope, Andrée Abecassis.
Costs $325/nonmembers; $250/members. Scholarships are available.
Additional Information Conference brochures/guidelines are available via e-mail.

NORTHWEST (AK, ID, MT, OR, WA, WY)

CLARION WEST WRITERS' WORKSHOP

340 15th Ave. E., Suite 350, Seattle WA 98112-5156. (206)322-9083. E-mail: info@clarionwest.org. Web site: www.clarionwest.org. **Contact:** Leslie Howle, executive director. Workshop held June 17-July 27, 2007. Workshop duration: 6 weeks. Average attendance: 18. Conference prepares students for professional careers in science fiction and fantasy writing. Held near the University of Washington. Deadline for applications: April 1. Agents will be speaking and available for meetings with attendees.
Costs Workshop: $1,700 ($100 discount if application is received by March 1). Most meals are included.
Accommodations Students stay in dormitory housing ($1,200).
Additional Information This is a critique-based workshop. Students are encouraged to write a story a week; the critique of student material produced at the workshop forms the principal activity of the workshop. Students and instructors critique mss as a group. Limited scholarships based on financial need are available. Students must submit 20-30 pages of ms to qualify for admission. Conference guidelines available for SASE. Visit Web site for updates and complete workshop details.

FLATHEAD RIVER WRITERS CONFERENCE

P.O. Box 7711, Kalispeil MT 59904-7711. E-mail: conference@authorsoftheflathead.com. **Contact:** Jake How, director. Estab. 1990. Annual conference held in early October. Conference duration: 3 days. Average attendance: 100. "We provide several small, intense 3-day workshops before the general weekend conference on a variety of subjects every year, including fiction, nonfiction, screenwriting, and working with editors and agents." Held at Grouse Mountain Lodge in Whitefish, Montana. Workshops, panel discussions, and speakers focus on novels, nonfiction, screenwriting, short stories, magazine articles, and the writing industry. **Previous agents/speakers have included:** Sam Pinkus, Randy Wayne White, Donald Maass, Ann Rule, Cricket Pechstein, Marcela Landres, Amy Rennert, Ben Mikaelsen, Esmond Harmsworth, Linda McFall, Ron Carlson. Agents will be speaking and available for meetings with attendees.
Costs $150 (includes breakfast and lunch, but does not include lodging).
Accommodations Rooms available at discounted rate of $100/night. Whitefish is a resort town, so less expensive lodging can be arranged.
Additional Information "By limiting attendance to 100 people, we assure a quality experience and informal, easy access to the presentors and other attendees." Brochures available in June. Inquiries by e-mail OK.

JACKSON HOLE WRITERS CONFERENCE

University of Wyoming, Dept. 3972, 1000 E. University Ave., Laramie WY 82071. (877)733-3618, ext. 1. Fax: (307)766-3914. E-mail: jrieman@uwyo.edu. Web site: www.jacksonholewriters.org. **Contact:** Jerimiah Rieman. Estab. 1991. Annual conference held in June. Conference duration: 4 days. Average attendance: 70. Covers fiction and creative nonfiction and offers ms critiques from authors, agents, and editors.
Costs $325-400.
Accommodation Snow King Resort in Jackson Hole, Wyoming.

NORWESCON

P.O. Box 68547, Seattle WA 98168-9986. (206)270-7850. Fax: (520)244-0142. E-mail: info@norwescon.org. Web site: www.norwescon.org. **Contact:** Programming Director. Estab. 1978. Annual conference held in April. Average attendance: 2,800. General multitrack convention focusing on science fiction and fantasy literature with wide coverage of other media. Tracks cover science, socio-cultural, literary, publishing, editing, writing, art, and other media of a science fiction/fantasy orientation. Agents will be speaking and available for meetings with attendees.
Accommodations Conference is held at the Seatac Doubletree Hotel.
Additional Information Brochures available for SASE or online. Inquiries by e-mail OK.

PACIFIC NORTHWEST WRITERS CONFERENCE

P.O. Box 2016, Edmonds WA 98020. (425)673-2665. E-mail: pnwa@pnwa.org. Web site: www.pnwa.org. Estab. 1955. Annual conference held in July. Conference duration: 4 days. Average attendance: 400. Conference focuses on fiction, nonfiction, poetry, film, drama, self-publishing, the creative process, critiques, core groups, advice from professionals, and networking. **Previous agents/speakers have included:** Sheree Bykofsky, Kimberley Cameron, Jennie Dunham, Donald Maass, Jandy Nelson.

Costs $350-400/members; $450-550/nonmembers.

Accommodations Special rate of $119/night is available at the Hilton Seattle Airport & Conference Center.

Additional Information Critiques are available in small groups. Also sponsors a literary contest in these categories: romance, adult article/essay, adult genre novel, adult mainstream novel, adult short story, juvenile/young adult, screenwriting, nonfiction book, playwriting, poetry, young writers. Deadline: February 22. Awards over $11,000 in prizes. Send SASE for guidelines.

WHIDBEY ISLAND WRITERS' CONFERENCE

P.O. Box 1289, Langley WA 98260. (360)331-6714. E-mail: writers@whidbey.com. Web site: www.writeonwhidbey.org. **Contact:** Elizabeth Guss, director. Annual conference held March 2-4, 2007. Conference duration: 3 days. Average attendance: 250. Covers fiction, nonfiction, screenwriting, writing for children, poetry, travel, and nature writing. Held at a conference hall, with break-out fireside chats held in local homes near the sea. Class sessions include ''Dialogue that Delivers'' and ''Putting the Character Back in Character.'' **Previous agents/speakers have included:** MJ Rose, Martha Bolton, Ann Tobias, and many more.

Costs $340 before December 1; $375 after December 1. Volunteer discounts are available; early registration is encouraged.

Additional Information Brochures available for SASE or online. Inquiries by e-mail OK.

WILLAMETTE WRITERS CONFERENCE

9045 SW Barbur, Suite 5-A, Portland OR 97219. (503)452-1592. Fax: (503)452-0372. E-mail: wilwrite@willamettewriters.com. Web site: www.willamettewriters.com. **Contact:** Bill Johnson. Estab. 1968. Annual conference held in August. Average attendance: 600. ''Willamette Writers is open to all writers, and we plan our conference accordingly. We offer workshops on all aspects of fiction, nonfiction, marketing, scriptwriting, the creative process, etc. Also, we invite top-notch inspirational speakers for keynote addresses. We always include at least 1 agent or editor panel and offer a variety of topics of interest to screenwriters and fiction and nonfiction writers.'' **Previous agents/speakers have included:** Donald Maass, Kim Cameron, Bob Mecoy, Angela Rinaldi, Lisa Dicker, Richard Morris, Andrew Whelchel. Agents will be speaking and available for meetings with attendees.

Costs Cost for full conference (including meals) is $375/members; $425/nonmembers.

Accomodations If necessary, arrangements can be made on an individual basis. Special rates may be available.

Additional Information Conference brochures/guidelines are available for catalog-size SASE.

CANADA

ℕ ⬇ BLOODY WORDS

12 Roundwood Ct., Toronto ON M1W 1Z2 Canada. E-mail: info@bloodywords.com. Web site: www.bloodywords.com. **Contact:** Caro Soles. Estab. 1999. Annual conference held June 9-11. Conference duration: 3 days. Average attendance: 250. The conference focuses on mystery fiction and aims to provide a showcase for Canadian mystery writers and readers, as well as provide writing information to aspiring writers. ''We will present 2 tracks of programming: Just the Facts, where everyone from coroners to toxicologists to tactical police units present how things are done in the real world; and The Book track, where authors and readers discuss their favorite themes. We also we have the Mystery Café, where 13 authors read and discuss their work.''

Costs $125-170 (Canadian).

Accommodations Special conference rate will be available at at hotel in Victoria, British Columbia.

Additional Information Registration available on Web site. Inquiries by e-mail OK.

⬇ FESTIVAL OF WORDS

217 Main St. N., Moose Jaw SK S6J 0W1 Canada. (306)691-0557. Fax: (306)693-2994. E-mail: word.festival@sasktel.net. Web site: www.festivalofwords.com. **Contact:** Gary Hyland, Christie Saas. Estab. 1997. Annual festival held in July. Festival duration: 4 days. Average attendance: 1,500. The festival celebrates the imaginative uses of language and features fiction and nonfiction writers, screenwriters, poets, children's authors, songwriters, dramatists, and filmmakers. Held at the Moose Jaw Public Library/Art Museum complex and in Crescent Park. **Previous agents/speakers have included:** Alistair MacLeod, Roch Carrier, Jane Urquhart, Rohinton Mistry, Will Ferguson, Patrick Lane, Katherine Govier, Lynn Coady, Leon Rooke, Steven Heighton, Pamela Wallin, Bonnie Burnard, Erika Ritter, Wayson Choy, Koozma Tarasoff, Lorna Crozier, Sheree Fitch, Nino Ricci, Yann Martel, Connie Kaldor, The Arrogant Worms, Brent Butt.

Accommodations A list of motels, hotels, campgrounds, and bed and breakfasts will be provided on request.
Additional Information ''Our festival is an ideal place for people who love words to mingle, promote their books, and meet their fans.'' Brochures available. Inquiries by e-mail and fax OK.

⚊ MARITIME WRITERS' WORKSHOP

UNB Art Centre, Box 4400, Fredericton NB E3B 5A3 Canada. Phone/Fax: (506)474-1144. E-mail: rhona.sawlor@ unb.ca. Web site: www.unb.ca/extend/writers. **Contact:** Rhona Sawlor, coordinator. Estab. 1976. Annual conference held in July. Average attendance: 50. Offers workshops in 4 areas: fiction, poetry, nonfiction, and writing for children. Site is the University of New Brunswick, Fredericton campus.
Costs $725/single occupancy; $705/double occupancy. Meals are included.
Additional Information Participants must submit 10-20 ms pages for workshop discussions. Brochures are available after March. No SASE necessary. Inquiries by e-mail OK.

⚊ SAGE HILL WRITING EXPERIENCE

Box 1731, Saskatoon SK S7K 2Z4 Canada. Phone/Fax: (306)652-7395. E-mail: sage.hill@sasktel.net. Web site: www.sagehillwriting.ca. **Contact:** Steven Ross Smith, executive director. Annual workshops held in August and November. Workshop duration: 10-14 days. The summer program is limited to 40 people—6 groups of 5-6 participants. The fall program is limited to 8 participants. Sage Hill Writing Experience offers a special working and learning opportunity to writers at different stages of development. Top quality instruction, low instructor-student ratio, and the beautiful Sage Hill settings offer conditions ideal for the pursuit of excellence in the art of fiction, nonfiction, poetry, and playwriting. The Sage Hill location features individual accommodations in-room writing areas lounges, meeting rooms, healthy meals, walking hills, and vistas in several directions. Classes being held (may vary from year to year) include: Introduction to Writing Fiction & Poetry, Fiction Workshop, Nonfiction Workshop, Writing Young Adult Fiction Workshop, Poetry Workshop, Poetry Colloquium, Fiction Colloquium, Novel Colloquium, Playwriting Lab, Fall Poetry Colloquium, and Fall Fiction Colloquium. **Previous agents/speakers have included:** Sue Goyette, Phil Hall, Marilyn Bowering, Nicole Brossard, Warren Cariou, Steven Galloway, Mark Anthony Jarmon, Wendy Lill, John Steffler.
Costs Summer Program: $895 (includes instruction, accommodation, meals, all facilities); Fall Poetry Colloquium: $1,175. Scholarships and bursaries are available.
Accommodations Located at Lumsden, 45 kilometers outside Regina.
Additional Information For Introduction to Creative Writing, send a 5-page sample of your writing or a statement of your interest in creative writing and a list of courses taken. For workshop and colloquium programs, send a résumé of your writing career and a 12-page sample of your work, plus 5 pages of published work. Guidelines are available for SASE. Inquiries by e-mail and fax OK.

⚊ SUNSHINE COAST FESTIVAL OF THE WRITTEN ARTS

Box 2299, Sechelt BC V0N 3A0 Canada. (800)565-9631 or (604)885-9631. Fax: (604)885-3967. E-mail: info@writ ersfestival.ca. Web site: www.writersfestival.ca. **Contact:** Gail Bull, festival producer. Estab. 1983. Annual festival held in August. Average attendance: 3,500. Held at the Rockwood Centre. The festival does not have a theme. Instead, it showcases 25 or more Canadian writers in a variety of genres each year. **Previous agents/ speakers have included:** Jane Urquhart, Sholagh Rogers, David Watmough, Zsuzsi Gartner, Gail Bowen, Charlotte Gray, Bill Richardson, P.K. Page, Richard B. Wright, Madeleine Thien, Ronald Wright, Michael Kusugak, Bob McDonald.
Costs $15/event; $275/festival pass.
Accommodations A list of hotels is available.
Additional Information The festival runs contests during the 3½ days of the event. Prizes are books donated by publishers. Brochures/guidelines are available. Visit Web site for current updates and details.

⚊ SURREY INTERNATIONAL WRITERS' CONFERENCE

10707 146th St., Surrey BC V3R 1T5 Canada. (604)589-2221. Fax: (604)588-9286. Web site: www.siwc.ca. **Contact:** Lisa Mason. Estab. 1992. Annual conference held in October. Conference duration: 3 days. Average attendance: 600. Conference for fiction, nonfiction, scriptwriting, and poetry. Conference is held at the Sheraton Guildford Hotel. **Agent/speakers attending have included:** Donald Maass (Donald Maass Literary Agency), Meredith Bernstein (Meredith Bernstein Literary Agency), Charlotte Gusay (Charlotte Gusay Literary Agency), Denise Marcil (Denise Marcil Literary Agency), Anne Sheldon and Michael Vidor (The Hardy Agency). Agents will be speaking and available for one-on-one meetings with attendees.
Costs Approximately $450.
Accommodations Attendees must make own arrangements for hotel and transportation.

❖ THE VANCOUVER INTERNATIONAL WRITERS & READERS FESTIVAL

202-1398 Cartwright St., Vancouver BC V6H 3R8 Canada. (604)681-6330. Fax: (604)681-8400. E-mail: viwf@wri tersfest.bc.ca. Web site: www.writersfest.bc.ca. **Contact:** Jane Davidson, general manager. Estab. 1988. Annual conference held in October. Average attendance: 11,000. The program of events is diverse and includes readings, panel discussions, and seminars. There are lots of opportunities to interact with the writers who attend. Held on Granville Island in the heart of Vancouver. **Previous agents/speakers have included:** Margaret Atwood, Maeve Binchy, J.K. Rowling.

Accommodations Local tourist information can be provided upon request.

Additional Information Brochures/guidelines are available for SASE after August. Inquiries by e-mail and fax OK. "Remember—this is a festival and a celebration, not a conference or workshop. See Web site for current updates and details.

❖ WINNIPEG INTERNATIONAL WRITERS FESTIVAL

624-100 Arthur St., Winnipeg MB R2B 1H3 Canada. (204)927-7323. Fax: (204)927-7320. E-mail: info@winnipeg words.com. Web site: www.winnipegwords.com. **Contact:** Charlene Diehl, artistic director. Estab. 1997. Annual festival held in September. Conference duration: 6 days. Average attendance: 10,000. Covers fiction, nonfiction, and scriptwriting. **Previous speakers/agents have included:** Michael Ondaatje, George Elliot Clarke, Esta Spalding, Margaret Atwood, Douglas Copeland, Miriam Toews.

Additional Information Brochures available online. Inquiries by e-mail and fax OK.

Ⓝ ❖ WRITE! CANADA

The Word Guild, P.O. Box 487, Markham ON L3P 3RI Canada. (905)294-6482. E-mail: events@thewordguild.c om. Web site: www.thewordguild.com/writecanada. Annual conference for writers of all types and at all stages offering 3 days of solid instruction, stimulating interaction, exciting challenge, and worshipful community.

Professional Organizations

AGENTS' ORGANIZATIONS

Association of Authors' Agents (AAA), 20 John St., London WC1N 2DR England. (44)(207)405-6774. Web site: www.agentsassoc.co.uk.

Association of Authors' Representatives (AAR), P.O. Box 237201, Ansonia Station, New York NY 10003. E-mail: info@aar-online.org. Web site: www.aar-online.org.

Association of Talent Agents (ATA), 9255 Sunset Blvd., Suite 930, Los Angeles CA 90069. (310)274-0628. E-mail: shellie@agentassociation.com. Web site: www.agentassociation .com.

WRITERS' ORGANIZATIONS

Academy of American Poets, 584 Broadway, Suite 604, New York NY 10012-5243. (212)274-0343. E-mail: academy@poets.org. Web site: www.poets.org.

American Christian Writers (ACW), P.O. Box 110390, Nashville TN 37222. (800)219-7483. E-mail: acwriters@aol.com. Web site: www.acwriters.com.

American Crime Writers League (ACWL), 18645 SW Farmington Rd., #255, Aloha OR 97007. Web site: www.acwl.org.

American Medical Writers Association (AMWA), 40 W. Gude Dr., Suite 101, Rockville MD 20850-1192. (301)294-5303. E-mail: amwa@amwa.org. Web site: www.amwa.org.

American Screenwriters Association (ASA), 269 S. Beverly Dr., Suite 2600, Beverly Hills CA 90212-3807. (866)265-9091. E-mail: asa@goasa.com. Web site: www.asascreenwriters .com.

American Translators Association (ATA), 225 Reinekers Ln., Suite 590, Alexandria VA 22314. (703)683-6100. E-mail: ata@atanet.org. Web site: www.atanet.org.

Associated Business Writers of America, 1450 S. Havana St., Suite 620, Aurora CO 88012. (303)751-7844.

Aviation/Space Writers Association (AWA), 17 S. High St., Suite 1200, Columbus OH 43215. (614)681-1900.

Education Writers Association (EWA), 2122 P St. NW, Suite 201, Washington DC 20037. (202)452-9830. E-mail: ewa@ewa.org. Web site: www.ewa.org.

Garden Writers Association of America (GWAA), 10210 Leatherleaf Ct., Manassas VA 20111. (703)257-1032. E-mail: info@gardenwriters.org. Web site: www.gardenwriters.org.

Horror Writers Association (HWA), 244 5th Ave., Suite 2767, New York NY 10001. E-mail: hwa@horror.org. Web site: www.horror.org.

The International Women's Writing Guild (IWWG), P.O. Box 810, Gracie Station, New York NY 10028-0082. (212)737-7536. E-mail: dirhahn@aol.com. Web site: www.iwwg.com.

Mystery Writers of America (MWA), 17 E. 47th St., 6th Floor, New York NY 10017. (212)888-8171. E-mail: mwa@mysterywriters.org. Web site: www.mysterywriters.org.

National Association of Science Writers (NASW), P.O. Box 890, Hedgesville WV 25427. (304)754-5077. E-mail: info@nasw.org. Web site: www.nasw.org.

National Association of Women Writers (NAWW), Box 700696, San Antonio TX 78270. (866)821-5829. E-mail: naww@onebox.com. Web site: www.naww.org.

Organization of Black Screenwriters (OBS), 1999 W. Adams Blvd., Los Angeles CA 90018. (323)735-2050. E-mail: obswriter@sbcglobal.net. Web site: www.obswriter.com.

Outdoor Writers Association of America (OWAA), 121 Hickory St., Suite 1, Missoula MT 59801. (406)728-7434. E-mail: krhoades@montana.com. Web site: www.owaa.org.

Poetry Society of America (PSA), 15 Gramercy Park, New York NY 10003. (212)254-9628. Web site: www.poetrysociety.org.

Poets & Writers, 72 Spring St., Suite 301, New York NY 10012. (212)226-3586. Web site: www.pw.org.

Romance Writers of America (RWA), 16000 Stuebner Airline Rd., Suite 140, Spring TX 77379. (832)717-5200. E-mail: info@rwanational.org. Web site: www.rwanational.com.

Science Fiction and Fantasy Writers of America (SFWA), P.O. Box 877, Chestertown MD 21620. E-mail: execdir@sfwa.org. Web site: www.sfwa.org.

Society of American Business Editors and Writers (SABEW), University of Missouri, School of Journalism, 134 Neff Annex, Columbia MO 65211. (573)882-7862. E-mail: sabew @missouri.edu. Web site: www.sabew.org.

Society of American Travel Writers (SATW), 1500 Sunday Dr., Suite 102, Raleigh NC 27607. (919)861-5586. E-mail: satw@satw.org. Web site: www.satw.org.

Society of Children's Book Writers & Illustrators (SCBWI), 8271 Beverly Blvd., Los Angeles CA 90048. (323)782-1010. E-mail: scbwi@scbwi.org. Web site: www.scbwi.org.

Washington Independent Writers (WIW), 1001 Connecticut Ave. NW, Suite 701, Washington DC 20036. (202)775-5150. E-mail: info@washwriter.org. Web site: www.washwriter.org.

Western Writers of America (WWA), 1012 Fair St., Franklin TN 37064. (615)791-1444. Web site: www.westernwriters.org.

Women Writing the West (WWW), 8547 E. Arapahoe Rd., Box J-541, Greenwood Village CO 80112-1430. E-mail: wwwadmin@lohseworks.com. Web site: www.womenwritingthe west.org.

INDUSTRY ORGANIZATIONS

American Booksellers Association (ABA), 200 White Plains Rd., Tarrytown NY 10591. (800)637-0037. E-mail: info@bookweb.org. Web site: www.bookweb.org.

American Federation of Television and Radio Artists (AFTRA), 260 Madison Ave., New York NY 10016-2401. (212)532-0800. Or, 5757 Wilshire Blvd., 9th Floor, Los Angeles CA 90036-0800. (323)634-8100. Web site: www.aftra.com.

American Guild of Variety Artists (AGVA), 184 5th Ave., 6th Floor, New York NY 10010. (212)675-1003.

American Society of Journalists & Authors (ASJA), 1501 Broadway, Suite 302, New York NY 10036. (212)997-0947. Web site: www.asja.org.

Association for Women in Communications (AWC), 3337 Duke St., Alexandria VA 22314. (703)370-7436. E-mail: info@womcom.org. Web site: www.womcom.org.

Association of American Publishers (AAP), 71 5th Ave., New York NY 10003-3004. (212)255-0200. Or, 50 F St. NW, Washington DC 20001-1530. (202)347-3375. Web site: www.publishers.org.

The Association of Writers & Writing Programs (AWP), Mail stop 1E3, George Mason University, Fairfax VA 22030. (703)993-4301. E-mail: awp@awpwriter.org. Web site: www.awpwriter.org.

The Authors Guild, Inc., 116 W. 23rd St., Suite 500, New York NY 10011. (212)563-5904. E-mail: staff@authorsguild.org. Web site: www.authorsguild.org.

Canadian Authors Association (CAA), Box 419, Campbellford ON K0L 1L0 Canada. (705)653-0323. E-mail: admin@canauthors.org. Web site: www.canauthors.org.

Christian Booksellers Association (CBA), P.O. Box 62000, Colorado Springs CO 80962-2000. (800)252-1950. E-mail: info@cbaonline.org. Web site: www.cbaonline.org.

The Dramatists Guild of America, 1501 Broadway, Suite 701, New York NY 10036. (212)398-9366. Web site: www.dramaguild.com.

National League of American Pen Women (NLAPW), 1300 17th St. NW, Washington DC 20036-1973. (202)785-1997. E-mail: nlapw1@verizon.net. Web site: www.americanpenwomen.org.

National Writers Association (NWA), 10940 S. Parker Rd., #508, Parker CO 80134. (303)841-0246. E-mail: info@nationalwriters.com. Web site: www.nationalwriters.com.

National Writers Union (NWU), 113 University Place, 6th Floor, New York NY 10003. (212)254-0279. E-mail: nwu@nwu.org. Web site: www.nwu.org.

PEN American Center, 588 Broadway, Suite 303, New York NY 10012. (212)334-1660. E-mail: pen@pen.org. Web site: www.pen.org.

Playwrights Guild of Canada (PGC), 54 Wolseley St., 2nd Floor, Toronto ON M5T 1A5 Canada. (416)703-0201. E-mail: info@playwrightsguild.ca. Web site: www.playwrightsguild.com.

Volunteer Lawyers for the Arts (VLA), The Paley Building, 1 E. 53rd St., 6th Floor, New York NY 10022. (212)319-2787. Web site: www.vlany.org.

Women in Film (WIF), 8857 W. Olympic Blvd., Suite 201, Beverly Hills CA 90211. (310)657-5144. E-mail: info@wif.org. Web site: www.wif.org.

Women in the Arts Foundation (WIA), 1175 York Ave., #2G, New York NY 10021. E-mail: wiainc@aol.com. Web site: www.anny.org/2/orgs/womeninarts.

Women's Media Group (WMG), Box 2119, Grand Central Station, New York NY 10163-2119. (212)592-0961. E-mail: info@womensmediagroup.org. Web site: www.womensmediagroup.org.

Women's National Book Association (WNBA), 2166 Broadway, #9-E, New York NY 10024. (212)208-4629. Web site: www.wnba-books.org.

Writers Guild of Alberta (WGA), 11759 Groat Rd., Edmonton AB T5M 3K6 Canada. (780)422-8174. E-mail: mail@writersguild.ab.ca. Web site: writersguild.ab.ca.

Writers Guild of America-East (WGA), 555 W. 57th St., Suite 1230, New York NY 10019. (212)767-7800. Web site: www.wgaeast.org.

Writers Guild of America-West (WGA), 7000 W. Third St., Los Angeles CA 90048. (323)951-4000. Web site: www.wga.org.

Writers Union of Canada (TWUC), 90 Richmond St. E., Suite 200, Toronto ON M5C 1P1 Canada. (416)703-8982. E-mail: info@writersunion.ca. Web site: www.writersunion.ca.

Resources

Online Tools

AGENTS

Agent Research & Evaluation (www.agentresearch.com)
This is the Web site of AR&E, a company that specializes in keeping tabs on literary agents. For a fee you can order their varied services to learn more about a specific agent.

Association of Authors' Representatives (www.aar-online.org)
This site offers a searchable database of more than 300 literary agents who abide by the AAR canon of ethics.

Preditors & Editors (www.anotherealm.com/prededitors)
This site—updated weekly—offers publishing information for writers, composers, game designers and artists, and includes warnings of scams by agents and publishers.

Writer Beware (www.sfwa.org/beware)
The Science Fiction and Fantasy Writers of America posts warnings about agents and subsidy publishers on this site.

Writer's Market (www.writersmarket.com)
This searchable, subscription-based database is the online counterpart of *Writer's Market*. It includes contact information and submission guidelines for agents, publishers, magazines, newspapers, production companies and more.

WritersNet (www.writers.net)
This is an Internet directory of writers, editors, publishers and agents. It also includes a bulletin board where writers can discuss their experiences with agents.

WRITING

AbsoluteWrite.com (www.absolutewrite.com)
This Web site contains articles, columns, interviews, message boards, classifieds, announcements, writing markets and contests. Writers can also sign up for a free electronic newsletter.

Author Network (www.author-network.com)
This is an international community for writers that includes articles, columns, a newsletter and a message board.

FictionAddiction.net (www.fictionaddiction.net)
This site features articles and listings of publishers, agents, workshops and contests for fiction writers.

FictionFactor.com (www.fictionfactor.com)
Online magazine featuring tips on how to write better fiction, plus articles on how to get published and market your book.

FreelanceWriting.com (www.freelancewriting.com)
Web site containing industry news, editorial content and networking and job opportunities for writers.

Funds for Writers (www.fundsforwriters.com)
This site provides links to job markets, contests and grants for writers. It also offers advice on how to get paid for your writing, as well as the opportunity to subscribe to free updates on the funds available for writers.

JournalismJobs.com (www.journalismjobs.com)
Use this database to search for jobs by position, location or industry.

MediaBistro.com (www.mediabistro.com)
Search for jobs, showcase your work in the Freelance Marketplace, participate in forums and read in-depth articles and interviews with media professionals.

OnceWritten.com (www.oncewritten.com)
From original book reviews and contests to writing prompts and advice, this site is a great resource for new writers.

The Writer Gazette (www.writergazette.com)
This site offers a free weekly newsletter filled with articles, job postings, resources and tips.

Writer's Digest (www.writersdigest.com)
This online counterpart to *Writer's Digest* magazine includes daily market updates, writer's guidelines, articles and advice.

The Writer's Life (www.thewriterslife.homestead.com)
Here you can access articles and interviews, get involved with online forums, look through a list of paying markets and more.

WritersBreak.com (www.writersbreak.com)
This site provides articles on fiction writing, nonfiction writing, conducting interviews and book marketing. Also included are writing resources and book recommendations.

WritersWeekly.com (www.writersweekly.com)
Freelance writing e-zine that includes articles, expert advice, agent and publisher warnings and job postings.

Writing.com (www.writing.com)
This online community is for writers and readers of all interests and skill levels.

Writing-World.com (www.writing-world.com)
This site offers a free biweekly newsletter for writers, as well as instructional articles.

YouCanWrite.com (www.youcanwrite.com)
This is a place for nonfiction writers to get information on query letters, book proposals, agents and more.

SCREENWRITING

Daily Variety (www.variety.com)
> This site archives the top stories from *Daily Variety*. Check here for the latest scoop on the movie and TV business.

Done Deal (www.scriptsales.com)
> Useful features of this screenwriting site include descriptions of recently sold scripts and lists of script agents and production companies.

Hollywood Creative Directory (www.hcdonline.com)
> By joining this Web site, you'll have access to listings of legitimate players in the film, television and new media industry.

The Hollywood Reporter (www.hollywoodreporter.com)
> Get the buzz on the movie business with the online version of *The Hollywood Reporter*.

Hollywood Scriptwriter (www.hollywoodscriptwriter.com)
> This online version of the trade magazine features articles and interviews with producers, directors and screenwriters.

HollywoodLitSales.com (www.hollywoodlitsales.com)
> Find out what your fellow scribes are writing by reading their loglines on this Web site sponsored by two major Hollywood production companies.

IMDB (www.imdb.com)
> Locate movie quotes, trivia and news on this site. You can also submit questions to professional screenwriters, directors and cinematographers.

MovieBytes (www.moviebytes.com)
> Subscribe to ''Who's Buying What'' for listings of the latest screenplay sales. Free access to one of the most comprehensive lists of screenplay contests is also offered on this site.

Scryptic Studios (www.scrypticstudios.com)
> Pertinent news, discussions and resources for TV, radio and film scriptwriters are posted on this site.

Wordplay (www.wordplayer.com)
> This site includes message boards and columns and essays written by industry professionals working in Hollywood.

MARKETING AND PUBLICITY

Authorlink (www.authorlink.com)
> This marketing community for editors, literary agents and writers showcases manuscripts of experienced and beginning writers.

Book Marketing Update (http://bookmarket.com)
> This Web site by John Kremer, author of *1001 Ways to Market Your Book*, offers helpful tips for marketing books and many useful links to publishing Web sites. It also offers an e-newsletter so writers may share their marketing success stories.

BookTalk (www.booktalk.com)
> This site offers authors an opportunity to announce and market new releases to viewers across the globe.

BookWire (www.bookwire.com)
This comprehensive site includes industry news, features, reviews, fiction, events, interviews and links to other book sites.

Guerrilla Marketing (www.gmarketing.com)
On this Web page, the writers of *Guerrilla Marketing for Writers* provide many helpful resources for successfully marketing your book.

Publishers Lunch (www.publisherslunch.com)
This site has a free newsletter that offers daily updates on what's going on in the world of publishing.

Publishers Weekly (www.publishersweekly.com)
Read the latest book publishing news and reviews on this electronic version of the popular print magazine.

MISCELLANEOUS

Bartleby.com (www.bartleby.com)
This reference site for literature offers thesauri, dictionaries and quotations.

Common Errors in English (www.wsu.edu/~brians/errors/index.html)
Solve grammar questions quickly with this alphabetical list of misused words.

Creative Writing Prompts (www.creativewritingprompts.com)
Visit this site for more than 200 quick and easy writing prompts.

LiteraryLawGuide.com (www.literarylawguide.com/resources.htm)
Keep up to date on legal issues for writers by viewing the free articles and podcasts on this site, or sign up for the e-mail newsletter.

The Quotations Page (www.quotationspage.com)
Search by author or subject for the perfect quote—from more than 24,000.

RefDesk.com (www.refdesk.com)
Visit this site if you're on deadline and need to check a fact on anything from the weather to gas prices.

U.S. Copyright Office (www.copyright.gov)
This site provides an application form to register your work and answers questions on how long copyright lasts, what it protects, how to use someone else's work, etc.

Glossary

#10 Envelope. A standard, business-size envelope.

Acquisitions Editor. The person responsible for originating and/or acquiring new publishing projects.

Adaptation. The process of rewriting a composition (novel, story, film, article, play) into a form suitable for some other medium, such as TV or the stage.

Advance. Money a publisher pays a writer prior to book publication, usually paid in installments, such as one-half upon signing the contract and one-half upon delivery of the complete, satisfactory manuscript. An advance is paid against the royalty money to be earned by the book. Agents take their percentage off the top of the advance as well as from the royalties earned.

Adventure. A genre of fiction in which action is the key element, overshadowing characters, theme and setting.

Auction. Publishers sometimes bid for the acquisition of a book manuscript with excellent sales prospects. The bids are for the amount of the author's advance, guaranteed dollar amounts, advertising and promotional expenses, royalty percentage, etc. Auctions are conducted by agents.

Author's Copies. An author usually receives about 10 free copies of his hardcover book from the publisher; more from a paperback firm. He can obtain additional copies at a price that has been reduced by an author's discount (usually 40 percent of the retail price).

Autobiography. A book-length account of a person's entire life written by the subject himself.

Backlist. A publisher's list of books that were not published during the current season, but that are still in print.

Backstory. The history of what has happened before the action in your script takes place, affecting a character's current behavior.

Bible. The collected background information on all characters and story lines of all existing episodes, as well as projections of future plots.

Bio. A sentence or brief paragraph about the writer; includes work and educational experience.

Blurb. The copy on paperback book covers or hardcover book dust jackets, either promoting the book and the author or featuring testimonials from book reviewers or well-known people in the book's field. Also called flap copy or jacket copy.

Boilerplate. A standardized publishing contract. Most authors and agents make many changes on the boilerplate before accepting the contract.

Book Doctor. A freelance editor hired by a writer, agent or book editor who analyzes problems that exist in a book manuscript or proposal and offers solutions to those problems.

Resources

Book Packager. Someone who draws elements of a book together—from the initial concept to writing and marketing strategies—and then sells the book package to a book publisher and/or movie producer. Also known as book producer or book developer.

Bound Galleys. A prepublication—often paperbound—edition of a book, usually prepared from photocopies of the final galley proofs. Designed for promotional purposes, bound galleys serve as the first set of review copies to be mailed out. Also called bound proofs.

Category Fiction. A term used to include all types of fiction. See *genre*.

Clips. Samples, usually from newspapers or magazines, of your published work. Also called tearsheets.

Commercial Fiction. Novels designed to appeal to a broad audience. These are often broken down into categories such as western, mystery and romance. See *genre*.

Concept. A statement that summarizes a screenplay or teleplay—before the outline or treatment is written.

Confession. A first-person story in which the narrator is involved in an emotional situation that encourages sympathetic reader identification, concluding with the affirmation of a morally acceptable theme.

Contributor's Copies. Copies of the book sent to the author. The number of contributor's copies is often negotiated in the publishing contract.

Co-Publishing. Arrangement where author and publisher share publication costs and profits of a book. Also called co-operative publishing.

Copyediting. Editing of a manuscript for writing style, grammar, punctuation and factual accuracy.

Copyright. A means to protect an author's work.

Cover Letter. A brief letter that accompanies the manuscript being sent to an agent or publisher.

Coverage. A brief synopsis and analysis of a script provided by a reader to a buyer considering purchasing the work.

Creative Nonfiction. Type of writing where true stories are told by employing the techniques usually reserved for novelists and poets, such as scenes, dialogue and detailed descriptions. Also called literary journalism.

Critiquing Service. An editing service offered by some agents in which writers pay a fee for comments on the salability or other qualities of the manuscript. Sometimes the critique includes suggestions on how to improve the work. Fees vary, as does the quality of the critique.

Curriculum Vitae (CV). Short account of one's career or qualifications.

D Person. Development person; includes readers, story editors and creative executives who work in development and acquisition of properties for TV and film.

Deal Memo. The memorandum of agreement between a publisher and author that precedes the actual contract and includes important issues such as royalty, advance, rights, distribution and option clauses.

Development. The process in which writers present ideas to producers who oversee the developing script through various stages to finished product.

Division. An unincorporated branch of a company.

Docudrama. A fictional film rendition of recent news-making events or people.

Electronic Rights. Secondary or subsidiary rights dealing with electronic/multimedia formats (the Internet, CD-ROMs, electronic magazines).

Elements. Actors, directors and producers attached to a project to make an attractive package.

El-Hi. Elementary to high school. A term used to indicate reading or interest level.

Episodic Drama. An hour-long, continuing TV show, often shown at 10 p.m.

Erotica. A form of literature or film dealing with the sexual aspects of love. Erotic content ranges from subtle sexual innuendo to explicit descriptions of sexual acts.

Ethnic. Stories and novels whose central characters are African American, Native American, Italian-American, Jewish, Appalachian or members of some other specific cultural group. Ethnic fiction usually deals with a protagonist caught between two conflicting ways of life: mainstream American culture and his ethnic heritage.

Evaluation Fees. Fees an agent may charge to evaluate material. The extent and quality of this evaluation varies, but comments usually concern the salability of the manuscript.

Exclusive. Offering a manuscript, usually for a set period of time, to just one agent and guaranteeing that agent is the only one looking at the manuscript.

Experimental. Type of fiction that focuses on style, structure, narrative technique, setting and strong characterization rather than plot. This form depends largely on the revelation of a character's inner being, which elicits an emotional response from the reader.

Family Saga. A story that chronicles the lives of a family or a number of related or interconnected families over a period of time.

Fantasy. Stories set in fanciful, invented worlds or in a legendary, mythic past that rely on outright invention or magic for conflict and setting.

Film Rights. May be sold or optioned by the agent/author to a person in the film industry, enabling the book to be made into a movie.

Floor Bid. If a publisher is very interested in a manuscript he may offer to enter a floor bid when the book goes to auction. The publisher sits out of the auction, but agrees to take the book by topping the highest bid by an agreed-upon percentage (usually 10 percent).

Foreign Rights. Translation or reprint rights to be sold abroad.

Foreign Rights Agent. An agent who handles selling the rights to a country other than that of the first book agent. Usually an additional percentage (about 5 percent) will be added on to the first book agent's commission to cover the foreign rights agent.

Genre. Refers to either a general classification of writing, such as a novel, poem or short story, or to the categories within those classifications, such as problem novels or sonnets. Genre fiction is a term that covers various types of commercial novels, such as mystery, romance, western, science fiction and horror.

Ghostwriting. A writer puts into literary form the words, ideas, or knowledge of another person under that person's name. Some agents offer this service; others pair ghostwriters with celebrities or experts.

Gothic. Novels characterized by historical settings and featuring young, beautiful women who win the favor of handsome, brooding heroes while simultaneously dealing with some life-threatening menace—either natural or supernatural.

Graphic Novel. Contains comic-like drawings and captions, but deals more with everyday events and issues than with superheroes.

High Concept. A story idea easily expressed in a quick, one-line description.

Hi-Lo. A type of fiction that offers a high level of interest for readers at a low reading level.

Historical. A story set in a recognizable period of history. In addition to telling the stories of ordinary people's lives, historical fiction may involve political or social events of the time.

Hook. Aspect of the work that sets it apart from others and draws in the reader/viewer.

Horror. A story that aims to evoke some combination of fear, fascination and revulsion in its readers—either through supernatural or psychological circumstances.

How-To. A book that offers the reader a description of how something can be accomplished. It includes both information and advice.

Imprint. The name applied to a publisher's specific line of books.

Independent Producers. Self-employed entrepreneurs who assemble scripts, actors, directors and financing for their film concepts.

IRC. International Reply Coupon. Buy at a post office to enclose with material sent outside the country to cover the cost of return postage. The recipient turns them in for stamps in their own country.

Joint Contract. A legal agreement between a publisher and two or more authors that establishes provisions for the division of royalties the book generates.

Juvenile. Category of children's writing that can be broken down into easy-to-read books (ages 7-9), which run 2,000-10,000 words, and middle-grade books (ages 8-12), which run 20,000-40,000 words.

Literary. A book where style and technique are often as important as subject matter. Also called serious fiction.

Logline. A one-line description of a plot as it might appear in *TV Guide*.

Mainstream Fiction. Fiction on subjects or trends that transcend popular novel categories like mystery or romance. Using conventional methods, this kind of fiction tells stories about people and their conflicts.

Marketing Fee. Fee charged by some agents to cover marketing expenses. It may be used to cover postage, telephone calls, faxes, photocopying or any other expense incurred in marketing a manuscript.

Mass Market Paperbacks. Softcover book, usually 4×7, on a popular subject directed at a general audience and sold in groceries, drugstores and bookstores.

Memoir. An author's commentary on the personalities and events that have significantly influenced one phase of his life.

MFTS. Made for TV series.

Midlist. Those titles on a publisher's list expected to have limited sales. Midlist books are mainstream, not literary, scholarly or genre, and are usually written by new or relatively unknown writers.

Miniseries. A limited dramatic series written for television, often based on a popular novel.

MOW. Movie of the week. A movie script written especially for television, usually seven acts with time for commercial breaks. Topics are often contemporary, sometimes controversial, fictional accounts. Also called a made-for-TV-movie.

Multiple Contract. Book contract with an agreement for a future book(s).

Mystery. A form of narration in which one or more elements remain unknown or unexplained until the end of the story. Subgenres include: amateur sleuth, caper, cozy, heist, malice domestic, police procedural, etc.

Net Receipts. One method of royalty payment based on the amount of money a book publisher receives on the sale of the book after the booksellers' discounts, special sales discounts and returned copies.

Novelization. A novel created from the script of a popular movie and published in paperback. Also called a movie tie-in.

Novella. A short novel or long short story, usually 25,000-50,000 words. Also called a novelette.

Occult. Supernatural phenomena, including ghosts, ESP, astrology, demoniac possession and witchcraft.

One-Time Rights. This right allows a short story or portions of a fiction or nonfiction book to be published again without violating the contract.

Option. Instead of buying a movie script outright, a producer buys the right to a script for a short period of time (usually six months to one year) for a small down payment. If the movie has not begun production and the producer does not wish to purchase the script at the end of the agreed time period, the rights revert back to the scriptwriter. Also called a script option.

Option Clause. A contract clause giving a publisher the right to publish an author's next book.

Outline. A summary of a book's content (up to 15 double-spaced pages); often in the form of chapter headings with a descriptive sentence or two under each one to show the scope of the book. A script's outline is a scene-by-scene narrative description of the story (10-15 pages for a ½-hour teleplay; 15-25 pages for 1 hour; 25-40 pages for 90 minutes; 40-60 pages for a 2-hour feature film or teleplay).

Picture Book. A type of book aimed at ages 2-9 that tells the story partially or entirely with artwork, with up to 1,000 words. Agents interested in selling to publishers of these books often handle both artists and writers.

Pitch. The process where a writer meets with a producer and briefly outlines ideas that could be developed if the writer is hired to write a script for the project.

Platform. A writer's speaking experience, interview skills, Web site and other abilities which help form a following of potential buyers for his book.

Proofreading. Close reading and correction of a manuscript's typographical errors.

Property. Books or scripts forming the basis for a movie or TV project.

Proposal. An offer to an editor or publisher to write a specific work, usually a package consisting of an outline and sample chapters.

Prospectus. A preliminary written description of a book, usually one page in length.

Psychic/Supernatural. Fiction exploiting—or requiring as plot devices or themes—some contradictions of the commonplace natural world and materialist assumptions about it (including the traditional ghost story).

Query. A letter written to an agent or a potential market to elicit interest in a writer's work.

Reader. A person employed by an agent or buyer to go through the slush pile of manuscripts and scripts and select those worth considering.

Regional. A book faithful to a particular geographic region and its people, including behavior, customs, speech and history.

Release. A statement that your idea is original, has never been sold to anyone else, and that you are selling negotiated rights to the idea upon payment.

Remainders. Leftover copies of an out-of-print or slow-selling book purchased from the publisher at a reduced rate. Depending on the contract, a reduced royalty or no royalty is paid on remaindered books.

Reprint Rights. The right to republish a book after its initial printing.

Romance. A type of category fiction in which the love relationship between a man and a woman pervades the plot. The story is told from the viewpoint of the heroine, who meets a man (the hero), falls in love with him, encounters a conflict that hinders their relationship, and then resolves the conflict with a happy ending.

Royalties. A percentage of the retail price paid to the author for each copy of the book that is sold. Agents take their percentage from the royalties earned and from the advance.

SASE. Self-addressed, stamped envelope. It should be included with all correspondence.

Scholarly Books. Books written for an academic or research audience. These are usually heavily researched, technical, and often contain terms used only within a specific field.

Science Fiction. Literature involving elements of science and technology as a basis for conflict, or as the setting for a story.

Screenplay. Script for a film intended to be shown in theaters.

Script. Broad term covering teleplay, screenplay or stage play. Sometimes used as a shortened version of the word manuscript when referring to books.

Serial Rights. The right for a newspaper or magazine to publish sections of a manuscript.

Simultaneous Submission. Sending the same manuscript to several agents or publishers at the same time.

Sitcom. Situation comedy. Episodic comedy script for a television series. The term comes from the characters dealing with various situations with humorous results.

Slice of Life. A type of short story, novel, play or film that takes a strong thematic approach, depending less on plot than on vivid detail in describing the setting and/or environment, and the environment's effect on characters involved in it.

Slush Pile. A stack of unsolicited submissions in the office of an editor, agent or publisher.

Spec Script. A script written on speculation without confirmation of a sale.

Standard Commission. The commission an agent earns on the sale of a manuscript or script. For literary agents, the commission (usually 10-20 percent) is taken from the advance and royalties paid to the writer. For script agents, the commission (usually 15-20 percent) is taken from script sales. If handling plays, agents take a percentage from the box office proceeds.

Subagent. An agent handling certain subsidiary rights, usually working in conjunction with the agent who handled the book rights. The percentage paid the book agent is increased to pay the subagent.

Subsidiary. An incorporated branch of a company or conglomerate (e.g., Knopf Publishing Group is a subsidiary of Random House, Inc.).

Subsidiary Rights. All rights other than book publishing rights included in a book publishing contract, such as paperback rights, book club rights and movie rights. Part of an agent's job is to negotiate those rights and advise the author on which to sell and which to keep.

Syndication Rights. The right for a station to rerun a sitcom or drama, even if the show originally appeared on a different network.

Synopsis. A brief summary of a story, novel or play. As a part of a book proposal, it is a comprehensive summary condensed in a page or page and a half, single-spaced. See *outline*.

Teleplay. Script for television.

Terms. Financial provisions agreed upon in a contract.

Textbook. Book used in a classroom at the elementary, high school or college level.

Thriller. A story intended to arouse feelings of excitement or suspense. Works in this genre are highly sensational, usually focusing on illegal activities, international espionage, sex and violence.

TOC. Table of Contents. A listing at the beginning of a book indicating chapter titles and their corresponding page numbers. It can also include brief chapter descriptions.

Trade Book. Either a hardcover or softcover book sold mainly in bookstores. The subject matter frequently concerns a special interest for a general audience.

Trade Paperback. A soft-bound volume, usually 5×8, published and designed for the general public; available mainly in bookstores.

Translation Rights. Rights sold to a foreign agent or foreign publisher.

Treatment. Synopsis of a television or film script (40-60 pages for a two-hour feature film or teleplay).

Unsolicited Manuscript. An unrequested manuscript sent to an editor, agent or publisher.

Westerns/Frontier. Stories set in the American West, almost always in the 19th century, generally between the antebellum period and the turn of the century.

Young Adult (YA). The general classification of books for ages 12-17. They run 50,000-60,000 words and include category novels—adventure, sports, career, mysteries, romance, etc.

Literary Agents Specialties Index

This index is divided into fiction and nonfiction subject categories. To find an agent interested in the type of manuscript you've written, see the appropriate sections under the subject headings that best describe your work.

FICTION

Action/Adventure

Comic Books/Cartoon

Erotica

Ethnic

Specialties Index

Literary

Mainstream/ Contemporary

Military/War

Multicultural

Multimedia

Mystery/Suspense

Acacia House Publishing Services, Ltd. 87
Ahearn Agency, Inc., The 88
Alive Communications, Inc. 89
Ampersand Agency, The 89
Amster Literary Enterprises, Betsy 90
Appleseeds Management 91
August Agency LLC, The 92
Authentic Creations Literary Agency 93
Axelrod Agency, The 93
Barrett Books, Inc., Loretta 94
Bernstein Literary Agency, Meredith 94
Bleecker Street Associates, Inc. 96
Blumer Literary Agency, Inc., The 96
BookEnds, LLC 97
Bova Literary Agency, The Barbara 98
Brandt & Hochman Literary Agents, Inc. 99
Brown, Ltd., Curtis 101
Brown Literary Agency, Inc., Andrea 101
Browne & Miller Literary Associates 101
Browne, Ltd., Pema 102
Bykofsky Associates, Inc., Sheree 102
Carvainis Agency, Inc., Maria 104
Castiglia Literary Agency 105
Chelius Literary Agency, Jane 105
Choate Agency, LLC, The 105
Congdon Associates Inc., Don 107
Cornerstone Literary, Inc. 108
Crichton, Sha-Shana 109
D4EO Literary Agency 110
Dawson Associates, Liza 110
DeChiara Literary Agency, The Jennifer 111
DeFiore & Co. 111
Delbourgo Associates, Inc., Joëlle 112
DHS Literary, Inc. 113
Dijkstra Literary Agency, Sandra 113
Dupree/Miller and Associates Inc. Literary 115

Dystel & Goderich Literary Management 116
Ellenberg Literary Agency, Ethan 117
English Literary Agency, The Elaine P. 118
Farber Literary Agency, Inc. 119
Farris Literary Agency, Inc. 119
Folio Literary Management, LLC 122
Gelfman, Schneider, Literary Agents, Inc. 125
Gislason Agency, The 125
Goodman Literary Agency, Irene 127
Grayson Literary Agency, Ashley 127
Greenburger Associates, Inc., Sanford J. 127
Grosjean Literary Agency, Jill 128
Grosvenor Literary Agency, The 128
Halsey North, Reece 129
Hamilburg Agency, The Mitchell J. 129
Harris Literary Agency, Inc., The Joy 129
Hartline Literary Agency 130
Harwood Limited, Antony 130
Hawkins & Associates, Inc., John 131
Henshaw Group, Richard 131
Imprint Agency, Inc. 133
J de S Associates, Inc. 134
Jellinek & Murray Literary Agency 135
JetReid Literary Agency 136
Kidd Agency, Inc., Virginia 137
Klinger, Inc., Harvey 138
Koster Literary Agency, LLC, Elaine 139
KT Public Relations & Literary Services 140
Lampack Agency, Inc., Peter 141
Langlie, Literary Agent, Laura 141
Larsen/Elizabeth Pomada, Literary Agents, Michael 142
Lazear Agency, Inc. 143
Lecker Agency, Robert 144
Lescher & Lescher, Ltd. 144

Levine Greenberg Literary Agency, Inc. 144
Levine Literary Agency, Paul S. 144
Lipkind Agency, Wendy 146
Literary & Media Representation 148
Literary Group, The 147
Lord Literary Management, Julia 148
Love Literary Agency, Nancy 148
Lowenstein-Yost Associates 148
Maass Literary Agency, Donald 149
Maccoby Literary Agency, Gina 150
Manus & Associates Literary Agency, Inc. 151
Marshall Agency, The Evan 152
McBride Literary Agency, Margret 153
McCarthy Agency, LLC, The 153
McGrath, Helen 153
Mendel Media Group LLC 154
Millard Literary Agency, Martha 155
Mura Literary, Dee 157
Muse Literary Management 157
Naggar Literary Agency, Inc., Jean V. 158
New Brand Agency Group, LLC 159
Oscard Agency, Inc., Fifi 159
Picard, Literary Agent, Alison J. 161
Pistek Literary Agency, LLC, Alicka 162
Popkin, Julie 163
Prospect Agency LLC 163
Quicksilver Books—Literary Agents 164
Raines & Raines 165
Rees Literary Agency, Helen 165
Regal Literary Agency 165
Rhodes Literary Agency, Jodie 167
Rights Unlimited, Inc. 167
RLR Associates, Ltd. 168
Robbins Literary Agency, B.J. 169

Short Story Collections

Spiritual

Sports

Thriller

Translation

Westerns/Frontier

Specialties Index

Child Guidance/ Parenting

Computers/Electronic

Cooking/Foods/ Nutrition

Crafts/Hobbies

Creative Nonfiction

Current Affairs

Specialties Index

Gardening

Gay/Lesbian Issues

Government/Politics/Law

How-To

Humor/Satire

Interior Design/ Decorating

Juvenile Nonfiction

Language/Literature/ Criticism

Multicultural

Music/Dance

Psychology

Recreation

Regional

Religious/Inspirational

Specialties Index

Science/Technology

Picard, Literary Agent, Alison J. 161
Pistek Literary Agency, LLC, Alicka 162
Prospect Agency LLC 163
Quicksilver Books—Literary Agents 164
Rabiner, Literary Agent, Inc., Susan 164
Regal Literary Agency 165
Rein Books, Inc., Jody 166
Rhodes Literary Agency, Jodie 167
RLR Associates, Ltd. 168
Rosenkranz Literary Agency, Rita 170
Ross Literary Agency, The Gail 170
Rubie Literary Agency, The Peter 172
Russell & Volkening 172
Sagalyn Agency, The 173
Schiavone Literary Agency, Inc. 173
Seligman, Literary Agent, Lynn 175
Serendipity Literary Agency, LLC 176
Snell Literary Agency, Michael 179
Susijn Agency, The 183
Swetky Agency, The 183
Talcott Notch Literary 184
United Tribes Media, Inc. 187
Venture Literary 188
Ware Literary Agency, John A. 191
Watkins Loomis Agency, Inc. 191
Weingel-Fidel Agency, The 192
Weinstein Literary Management, Ted 192
Writers House 194
Zachary Shuster Harmsworth 196
Zeckendorf Assoc., Inc., Susan 196

Self-Help/Personal Improvement
Agents Ink! 87
Ahearn Agency, Inc., The 88
Alive Communications, Inc. 89
Artists and Artisans Inc. 91

August Agency LLC, The 92
Authentic Creations Literary Agency 93
Barrett Books, Inc., Loretta 94
Bial Agency, Daniel 95
Bijur Literary Agency, Vicky 95
Bleecker Street Associates, Inc. 96
Blumer Literary Agency, Inc., The 96
BookEnds, LLC 97
Books & Such 97
Bova Literary Agency, The Barbara 98
Brands-to-Books, Inc. 98
Broadhead & Associates Literary Agency, Rick 99
Brown, Ltd., Curtis 101
Browne & Miller Literary Associates 101
Browne, Ltd., Pema 102
Bykofsky Associates, Inc., Sheree 102
Castiglia Literary Agency 105
Collins Literary Agency 106
Connor Literary Agency 107
Creative Culture, Inc., The 108
D4EO Literary Agency 110
DeChiara Literary Agency, The Jennifer 111
DeFiore & Co. 111
Delbourgo Associates, Inc., Joëlle 112
Dijkstra Literary Agency, Sandra 113
Doyen Literary Services, Inc. 114
Dupree/Miller and Associates Inc. Literary 115
Farris Literary Agency, Inc. 119
Finch Literary Agency, Diana 120
Flaming Star Literary Enterprises 120
Folio Literary Management, LLC 122
Franklin Associates, Ltd., Lynn C. 122
Fredericks Literary Agency, Inc., Jeanne 123
Freymann Literary Agency, Sarah Jane 123
Full Circle Literary, LLC 124

Gartenberg Literary Agency, Max 125
Grayson Literary Agency, Ashley 127
Greenburger Associates, Inc., Sanford J. 127
Grosvenor Literary Agency, The 128
Hamilburg Agency, The Mitchell J. 129
Hartline Literary Agency 130
Harwood Limited, Antony 130
Hawkins & Associates, Inc., John 131
Henshaw Group, Richard 131
Herman Agency, LLC, The Jeff 131
Hornfischer Literary Management, Inc. 133
J de S Associates, Inc. 134
James Peter Associates, Inc. 134
Jellinek & Murray Literary Agency 135
Kern Literary Agency, Natasha 136
Klinger, Inc., Harvey 138
Konner Literary Agency, Linda 139
Koster Literary Agency, LLC, Elaine 139
KT Public Relations & Literary Services 140
Larsen/Elizabeth Pomada, Literary Agents, Michael 142
Lazear Agency, Inc. 143
Levine Greenberg Literary Agency, Inc. 144
Levine Literary Agency, Paul S. 144
Lippincott Massie McQuilkin 146
Literary Group, The 147
Love Literary Agency, Nancy 148
Lowenstein-Yost Associates 148
Mann Agency, Carol 150
Manus & Associates Literary Agency, Inc. 151
Martin Literary Management 152
McBride Literary Agency, Margret 153
McGrath, Helen 153
Mendel Media Group LLC 154

Sex

Sociology

Women's Issues/ Studies

Young Adult

Script Agents Specialties Index

This index is divided into script subject categories. To find an agent interested in the type of screenplay you've written, see the appropriate sections under the subject headings that best describe your work.

Script Agents
Format Index

This index organizes agents according to the script types they consider. To find an agent interested in your script, see the heading that best describes your work.

Openness to Submissions Index

This index lists literary and script agencies and publicists according to how receptive they are to new clients. Check this index to find an agent or publicist who is appropriate for your level of experience.

🔄 AGENCIES SEEKING MOSTLY ESTABLISHED WRITERS THROUGH REFERRALS

Script Agents

Publicists

Geographic Index

This index lists agencies and publicists by state. They are also separated according to the sections in which they appear in the book (Literary Agents, Script Agents or Publicists).

Valcourt Agency, Inc., The
Richard R. 188
Vesel Literary Agency, Beth
189
Vicinanza, Ltd., Ralph 189
Wald Associates, Inc., Mary
Jack 190
Ware Literary Agency, John A.
191
Wasserman Literary Agency,
Harriet 191
Watkins Loomis Agency, Inc.
191
Waxman Literary Agency, Inc.
191
Weil Agency, Inc., The Wendy
192
Weingel-Fidel Agency, The
192
Wieser & Elwell, Inc. 193
Writers House 194
Writers' Representatives, Inc.
195
Zachary Shuster Harmsworth
196
Zeckendorf Assoc., Inc., Susan
196

Script Agents
Abrams Artists Agency 199
Amato Agency, Michael 199
Beacon Artists Agency Inc. 200
Freedman Dramatic Agency,
Inc., Robert A. 204
French, Inc., Samuel 204
Gersh Agency, The 205
Graham Agency 205
Gurman Agency, LLC, The Su-
san 205
Ketay Agency, The Joyce 206
Lantz Office, The 206
Marton Agency, Inc., The 207
Palmer, Dorothy 208
Subias Agency, Mark Christian
210
Whittlesey Agency, Peregrine
211

Publicists
Cerand, Lauren 217
Greater Talent Network, Inc.
219
⌐lsberg Marketing and Management, Michele 220
⌐aab Associates 223

Rosen Publicity LLC, Sherri
223
Royce Carlton, Inc. 224
Zegarek Public Relations, Inc.,
Meryl 229

NORTH CAROLINA
Literary Agents
Adams Literary 87
McMillan & Associates, Inc.,
Sally Hill 154

OREGON
Literary Agents
Tolls Literary Agency, Lynda
186

PENNSYLVANIA
Literary Agents
Bigscore Productions, Inc. 95
Collin, Literary Agent, Frances
106
Fox Chase Agency, Inc. 122
Gartenberg Literary Agency,
Max 125
Hartline Literary Agency 130
Kidd Agency, Inc., Virginia
137
KT Public Relations & Literary
Services 140
Triada U.S. Literary Agency,
Inc. 187

Publicists
Rocks-Dehart Public Relations
223

TEXAS
Literary Agents
DHS Literary, Inc. 113
Dupree/Miller and Associates
Inc. Literary 115
Farris Literary Agency, Inc.
119
Fogelman Literary Agency 121
Hornfischer Literary Manage-
ment, Inc. 133
Kraas Literary Agency 139

Publicists
Adventures in Media, Inc. 214

UTAH
Literary Agents
Swetky Agency, The 183

VIRGINIA
Literary Agents
Goldfarb & Associates 126
Paraview, Inc. 160

Script Agents
Filmwriters Literary Agency
203

WASHINGTON
Literary Agents
Kern Literary Agency, Natasha
136
Wales Literary Agency, Inc.
190

Script Agents
Cedar Grove Agency Enter-
tainment 201

Publicists
Acheson-Greub, Inc. 214

WISCONSIN
Literary Agents
Lazear Agency, Inc. 143
Scribe Agency, LLC 175
Sternig & Byrne Literary
Agency 181
3 Seas Literary Agency 185

AUSTRALIA/NEW
ZEALAND
Literary Agents
Bryson Agency Australia 102
Golvan Arts Management 126
Richards Literary Agency 167
TFS Literary Agency, The 185

CANADA
Literary Agents
Acacia House Publishing Ser-
vices, Ltd. 87
Broadhead & Associates Liter-
ary Agency, Rick 99
Cooke Agency, The 107
Lecker Agency, Robert 144
Slopen Literary Agency, Bev-
erly 178

Script Agents
Characters Talent Agency, The
201

Agents Index

This index lists all of the agents in this book, along with the agency for which they work. Find the name of the agent you're looking for, and then check the agency's listing.

General Index

This index lists every literary agency, script agency, publicist and conference appearing in the book. Markets that appeared in the 2006 edition, but don't appear in this book, are identified by a code explaining why the market was omitted: (**ED**)—Editorial Decision, (**NS**)—Not Accepting Submissions, (**NR**)—No or Late Response to Listing Request, (**OB**)—Out of Business, (**RR**)—Removed at Market's Request, (**UC**)—Unable to Contact.

General Index

More great resources
from Writer's Digest Books!

The Writer's Little Helper: Everything You Need to Know to Write Better and Get Published—This book gives you everything you need to create great characters, maintain a compelling pace, craft believable dialogue, attract the attention of agents and editors, and much more. With big ideas, time-saving tips and revision-made-easy charts, author James V. Smith, Jr. offers effective guidance with short checklists, Q&As and practical tools. Plus, the unique format allows you to read from start to finish or to focus only on the areas in which your fiction needs work.
ISBN-13: 978-1-58297-422-4
ISBN-10: 1-58297-422-5, hardcover, 256 pages, $19.99, #11038

I'm an English Major—Now What?: How English Majors Can Find Happiness, Success, and a Real Job—English majors are unconventional, so why offer them a standard career guide? In this candid, humorous book, author Timothy Lemire debunks the myth that English grads have to be teachers, editors or writers. He provides information on exciting career paths, strategies for showcasing skills to prospective employers and details on how an English background can be very marketable.
ISBN-13: 978-1-58297-362-3
ISBN-10: 1-58297-362-8, paperback, 256 pages, $14.99, #10992

The Gilded Tongue: Overly Eloquent Words for Everyday Things—For word lovers everywhere, author Rod Evans' book is a treasure trove of esoteric synonyms for everyday words. Not only does this book provide definitions, etymologies, pronunciation and illustrative sentences for 500 weird words, but it also shares esoteric terms for common items and includes a reverse dictionary for looking up words.
ISBN-13: 978-1-58297-382-1
ISBN-10: 1-58297-382-2, hardcover, 224 pages, $16.99, #11006

Take Joy: A Writer's Guide to Loving the Craft—Author Jane Yolen combats the perception that writing is a strenuous, solitary craft in this sweet, insightful book. She reveals the silver lining of the writing life through 15 easy-to-digest essays on plot, beginnings and endings, voice, point of view, writing poetry, and more. This optimistic guide urges writers to re-experience the joy of doing what matters most to them.
ISBN-13: 978-1-58297-385-2
ISBN-10: 1-58297-385-7, paperback, 208 pages, $14.99, #11008

These and other fine Writer's Digest Books are available at your local bookstore or online supplier.